Only the Clothes on Her Back

Only the Clothes on Her Back

Clothing and the Hidden History of Power in the Nineteenth-Century United States

LAURA F. EDWARDS

OXFORD
UNIVERSITY PRESS

Oxford University Press is a department of the University of Oxford. It furthers
the University's objective of excellence in research, scholarship, and education
by publishing worldwide. Oxford is a registered trade mark of Oxford University
Press in the UK and certain other countries.

Published in the United States of America by Oxford University Press
198 Madison Avenue, New York, NY 10016, United States of America.

© Oxford University Press 2022

All rights reserved. No part of this publication may be reproduced, stored in
a retrieval system, or transmitted, in any form or by any means, without the
prior permission in writing of Oxford University Press, or as expressly permitted
by law, by license, or under terms agreed with the appropriate reproduction
rights organization. Inquiries concerning reproduction outside the scope of the
above should be sent to the Rights Department, Oxford University Press, at the
address above.

You must not circulate this work in any other form
and you must impose this same condition on any acquirer.

CIP data is on file at the Library of Congress
ISBN 978-0-19-756857-6

DOI: 10.1093/oso/9780197568576.001.0001

The manufacturer's authorised representative in the EU for product safety is
Oxford University Press España S.A. of El Parque Empresarial San Fernando
de Henares, Avenida de Castilla, 2 – 28830 Madrid (www.oup.es/en or
product.safety@oup.com). OUP España S.A. also acts as importer into Spain
of products made by the manufacturer.

To four people who mattered more than they know
Susan Spencer
John Shedd
Carl Smith
Jacquelyn Hall

To the memory of Jan Reiff

And to Liz Kobesky and the women at Mulberry Silks

Contents

Acknowledgments	ix
Abbreviations	xv

Introduction Elizabeth's and Caty's Failed Escapes: The Materials of Legal Meaning	1

PART I OLD CLOTHES IN A NEW COUNTRY

1. Polly's Yarn: Legal Principles	21
2. Roger Taney's Long Underwear: Federalism	39
3. Mr. Robinson's Fabrics: Merchants	58
4. Rebecca Coles's Factory: Manufacturers	78

PART II PROTECTIVE COVERINGS IN A HOSTILE WORLD

5. The Prison Society's Problem: Currency	107
6. Jane Cooley's Loom: Capital	130
7. Margaret Ten Eyck's Accounts: Credit	152
8. Eliza Cauchois's Shift: Exchange	173

PART III RAGS

9. Sarah Allingham's Sheet: Enforcement	195
10. Catherine Brennan's Haul: Criminality	212
11. Charles Lohman's Dresses: Suppression	233
12. Mrs. Harris's Marriage: Erasure	256
Conclusion Mrs. Lincoln's Old Clothes: Just Material	279

Notes 301
Bibliography 385
Index 417

Acknowledgments

I began writing this book before I knew I was writing it. Textiles have always distracted me. Even when researching other topics, I took notes on all matters relating to cloth, clothing, and related accessories, sometimes wondering why and sometimes not noticing at all. They accumulated and ultimately came together in the outlines of this book, one that I never set out to do, but one that found me. It has been a joy to write, because of what textiles reveal about the history of the long nineteenth century: beauty, joy, wisdom, humor, and the creativity and resilience of people who clung to fine filaments of hope at a difficult juncture in our nation's past.

This book would not have been possible without the generous financial support of institutions dedicated to the support of the humanities and the social sciences. I began researching this project as an actual book with a grant from John Simon Guggenheim Foundation, which provided me a year's leave from teaching. A grant from the Library Company of Philadelphia and the Historical Society of Pennsylvania supported research at a crucial, early stage of the project. I began putting that research together during another year's leave, as the Visiting Neukom Fellows Chair in Diversity and Law at the American Bar Foundation in Chicago. After that, fellowships from the Newberry Library in Chicago and the American Council of Learned Societies gave me the time to write. I am grateful to Duke University for providing the support that allowed me to take these fellowships. I owe a particular debt to Kevin Moore, vice dean for faculty affairs, who went out of his way to make sure I could take full advantage of the opportunities offered to me. Thank you, Kevin, for all you do for the faculty at Duke. I am grateful to members of the History Department at Princeton University, who saw the potential of this project and provided a warm welcome as I was finishing it.

This book is the product of years of research in archives all over the country. I could not have done it without the assistance of archivists who went out of their way to guide me through the sources. In particular I wish to thank Jennifer McDaid and Greg Crawford at the Library of Virginia, Kimberly Nusco at the John Carter Brown Library, Sally Reeves at the Office of the Clerk of Civil District Court for the Parish of Orleans, Kelly Kerney and Kristen Stewart at the Valentine, Elizabeth Bouvier at the Massachusetts Supreme Judicial Court, Kimberly Reynolds at the Boston Public Library, Kenneth Cobb at the New York Municipal Archives, Linda Purnell and Elizabeth Dunn at Duke University, and Brianne Barrett at the American Antiquarian Society. I also wish to thank Melissa Murphy at the Baker Library, Harvard Business School, for helping me secure permission to use material from the R. G. Dun & Co. credit report volumes.

Karen Clancy, master weaver, spinner, and dyer at the Colonial Williamsburg Foundation, spent an entire morning showing me the basics of spinning and weaving. Janea Whitacre, mistress milliner and mantua maker at Williamsburg took out several hours to explain sewing and tailoring in the eighteenth and early nineteenth centuries. Those visits were incredibly important to the analysis in the following pages. Linda Baumgarten, then at Williamsburg, patiently answered questions in not one but two visits. Wayne Phillips, curator of costumes, textiles, and carnival collections, toured me through the vast collection at the Louisiana State Museum. Natasha Thoreson, assistant curator at the Helen Louise Allen Textile Collection, University of Wisconsin, Madison, spent an afternoon introducing me to the collections there and sharing her knowledge about them. Sara Hume, associate professor and curator, did the same at the Kent State University Museum. I thank both Natasha and Sara, in particular, for helping me make connections between the scholarly literature and the material qualities of cloth and clothing that I had not seen before.

I could not have completed the research for this book without the help of Jenette Wood-Crowley, Emily Margolis, Meggan Cashwell, Mandy Cooper, and Siobhan Barco. Jenny sampled reels and reels of microfilmed wills from the Library of Virginia. Emily did all kinds of work, including photographing crucial sources at the New York Historical Society for me. Meggan was instrumental in obtaining the microfilmed records of the New York Municipal Court through Interlibrary Loan and beginning the arduous task of finding and copying cases involving textiles. Mandy finished that job, which took several years. Far more was involved than just duplicating cases; to do that, Meggan and Mandy mastered the intricacies of the legal issues that framed these cases. I benefitted enormously from Meggan's own work with these materials, which resulted in an incredible dissertation. While this research was further afield from Mandy's scholarship, she provided key insights that have been crucial to the analysis. In the last stages of research, Siobhan did a stunningly thorough job of gathering up statutes and appellate cases involving textiles and searching the proceedings of women's rights conventions for textile references.

This book bears the marks of many generous readers and patient friends: Siobhan Barco, Juliana Barr, Susanna Blumenthal, Molly Brady, Meggan Cashwell, Emily Clark, Jo Cohen, Mandy Cooper, Chris Desan, Sally Gordon, Mike Grossberg, Dirk Hartog, Bob Korstad, Bruce Mann, Ajay Mehrotra, Jolie Olcott, Yvonne Pitts, Seth Rockman, Chris Schmidt, Karen Tani, Allison Tirres, Chris Tomlins, Felicity Turner, Mike Vorenberg, Priscilla Wald, John Wallis, and Barbara Welke. Dylan Penningroth saved me from a crisis about footnotes that actually involved much larger conceptual issues. Beth Lew-Williams identified exactly what was wrong with chapter 8. Deborah Cohen helped me make chapter 4 work. Beth Schweiger generously shared her knowledge about the Cooley family. Kate Masur and Susan Pearson sorted through early chapters and provided much needed direction. Kate then circled back and gave feedback on later chapters. Cindy Hahamovitch put me up and listened to me rattle on about the book while I was visiting at Williamsburg. The suggestions of Martha Jones, who read the entire manuscript with her characteristic insight and wisdom, have made for a much stronger book. So did the readings of four other anonymous readers.

Grey Osterud then took the manuscript in hand, found solutions to the readers' points, and uncovered numerous other weaknesses that had escaped their notice. I am in awe of Grey's ability to ferret out the problems that I tried to bury in a mountain of words, and I am continually amazed at the depth and breadth of her knowledge. I also appreciate her fine sense of humor. I hope to be as good a historian as she is someday. Until then, I am grateful for the opportunity to work with her.

Nick Abbott, Margaret Abruzzo, Felice Batlan, Molly Brady, Emily Clark, Nina Dayton, Alex Finley, Van Gosse, Anne and Jack Heinz, Scott Nelson, Gautham Rao, Seth Rockman, Joshua Rothman, Nora Slonimsky, Felicity Turner, Mike Vorenberg, and Jon White all generously shared material from their own research with me. The book is better for the insights of participants at the Fellows' Seminar at the Newberry Library; the American Studies seminar at Princeton University; the American Bar Foundation's Legal History Roundtable; the Legal History Seminar at the University of Minnesota Law School; the Legal History Seminar at the University of Virginia Law School; the Tobin Project's Workshops on American Democracy; the conference on Emancipations, Reconstructions, and Revolutions at CUNY and the University of Pennsylvania; the History Seminar at Dartmouth College; the

Legal History Seminar at Vanderbilt University; the Symposium on Clothing and Fashion in Southern History at the University of Mississippi; and the History Department seminar at Tulane University.

Conversations with the scholars involved in the book project *Deciphering American Democracy*, sponsored by the Tobin Foundation, have been particularly important in shaping the book. I am particularly grateful for the insights of Maggie Blackhawk and Naomi Lamoreaux, my collaborators on that project.

I don't know where I would be without the support of my writing group, Jacquelyn Hall, Nancy MacLean, and Lisa Levenstein. They read and reread pieces of this project, guiding its progress from its earliest stages as proposals and talks to the final manuscript. In addition to providing keen writing advice, they held me up in other ways as well. I am the last of the group to produce a book. If it is half as successful as the others, I will consider myself fortunate.

Susan Ferber understood the book right away. She took it under her wing, guiding it through the review process and providing expert editing suggestions while letting me be me and helping me turn it into the kind of book I wanted it to be. Thank you. I am also in debt to Jeremy Toynbee, who shepherded the book expertly through the production process.

I let this book go with reluctance, because of the place it has occupied in my life. It has been an oasis, which took on added significance when the pandemic hit. The book gave me somewhere to go when there was nowhere to go. It also provided much-needed stability in a time of upheaval, as we closed down our beloved home mid-pandemic in Carrboro, North Carolina, to move to Princeton, New Jersey. Not knowing the outcome, I held on tight to this book.

Letting go, however, gives me the opportunity to acknowledge a few people who may not be aware of how important they have been. Susan Spencer, my oboe teacher in junior high school, gave me emotional shelter, taught me to believe in myself, and encouraged me to dream big dreams. I ended up in history, not in music, but the musical world to which she introduced me opened up a future far wider and much richer than the one that I had envisioned before I met her. John Shedd, my history teacher when I was a senior in high school, got me through a particularly difficult year, when my dreams seemed to be moving beyond my reach. Carl Smith, who ran the American Culture program at Northwestern, picked me up, got me back on track, pointed me toward graduate school, and made sure I got there. Jacquelyn Hall was there to meet me when I arrived and has been an inspiration ever since. When I returned to North Carolina to teach at Duke, she and Bob Korstad folded me into their world and made me feel like I belonged. I have always wanted to write history like Jacquelyn did. With her encouragement, I finally realized that to do that, I had to write history in my own way. The book is dedicated to these four people and also to the memory of Jan Reiff, whose sudden passing knocked the wind out of me just as I was finishing the final edits of this book. I am grateful that I had the foresight to tell her how much she meant before it was too late, although it was not nearly enough, given all that she had done for me. I feel her absence in my bones.

Then there are the women at Mulberry Silks, the fabric store in Carrboro, North Carolina, run by Liz Kobesky and her daughter Susan. I have been going to sewing class there for the better part of two decades. I started with Liz. I knew I had a friend after my second class, when she told me I could stay afterward to keep sewing if I wanted. I did. A few years later, I moved to the longstanding Tuesday class, run by the amazing Maggie Simmons. Liz took over the class a few years ago, when Maggie retired. I have spent Tuesdays with Peggy Abrams, Diana Parrish, Jan Williams, Pam Justice, and Nancy Quaintance since 2008 or thereabouts. Nancy Turner, Elizabeth Buak, and Jane Murray are more recent, welcome additions. These women's companionship, humor, and support have been mixed with material advice, literally, involving color, style, and fit. I hope that they see a bit of themselves in these pages, because they are all there.

And, finally, there is John, my love, my joy, and my adventurer in life for over forty years. Here's to many, many more.

Abbreviations

AP	The Avalon Project: Documents in Law, History, and Diplomacy, https://avalon.law.yale.edu
BL	Baker Library, Harvard Business School, Cambridge, Massachusetts
BPL	Boston Public Library, Massachusetts
CHM	Chicago History Museum, Illinois
CSL	Connecticut State Library, Hartford
DU	Special Collections, Duke University, North Carolina
HSP	Historical Society of Pennsylvania, Philadelphia
JCBL	John Carter Brown Library, Brown University, Providence, Rhode Island
LC	Library of Congress, Washington, DC
LCP	Library Company of Philadelphia, Pennsylvania
LV	Library of Virginia, Richmond
MHS	Massachusetts Historical Society, Boston
MSA	Massachusetts State Archives, Boston
NA	Notarial Archives, New Orleans, Louisiana
NARA-NY	U.S. Circuit Court of Southern District of New York, RG 21, National Archives and Records Administration, New York
NCSA	North Carolina State Archives, Raleigh
NYMA	Indictment Papers, New York Municipal Archives, New York
NYHS	New York Historical Society, New York
NYPL	Manuscript and Archives Division, New York Public Library, Astor, Lenox, and Tilden Foundations, New York
RLCW	Special Collections, Rockefeller Library, Colonial Williamsburg, Virginia
RU	Special Collections, Rutgers University, New Jersey
SCDAH	South Carolina Department of Archives and History, Columbia
SCL	South Caroliniana Library, University of South Carolina, Columbia
SCHS	South Carolina Historical Society, records now located at the College of Charleston, South Carolina
SHC	Southern Historical Collection, University of North Carolina, Chapel Hill
UV	Special Collections, University of Virginia, Charlottesville
UW	Special Collections, University of Wisconsin, Madison
VM	Valentine Museum, Richmond
VMHC	Virginia Museum of History and Culture, Richmond
WM	Special Collections, Swem Library, College of William and Mary, Williamsburg, Virginia

Only the Clothes on Her Back

Introduction
Elizabeth's and Caty's Failed Escapes
The Materials of Legal Meaning

In 1795, Elizabeth Billings had had enough of her dreary life as a servant on a remote South Carolina farm. During a drinking binge, fortified with copious amounts of gin, she decided to flee. Even inebriated, Elizabeth knew that just leaving her employer was not enough. That was why she also took the building blocks for a new life, in the form of her mistress's wardrobe, including a gown, petticoats, and "a pair of Ladies florentine shoes," which were generally high heeled and covered in flowered silk. And so we have the image of Elizabeth Billings, tottering boozily down a country road, with her mistress's clothing and every hope of escape. She might have worn some of the garments. She might have stowed them in a pack, slung over her shoulder, with a bit of the gown fluttering behind her like banner. However it went down, Elizabeth never made it. Someone saw her with the clothes, knew they were not hers, and turned her over to a magistrate in nearby Camden, where she was charged with theft.[1]

What was Elizabeth thinking? Actually, the problem with the plan lay in its execution, not in its conception. All that gin. Those shoes. (One hopes that she put them in her pack and donned footwear more appropriate for travel.) Still, what she did made a certain amount of sense, given the legal principles attached to textiles and the legal practices that upheld those principles. In the decades following the Revolution, the law connected clothing to the person who wore it. That relationship was so strong that it extended to accessories, such as Florentine shoes, cloth that had not yet been made into clothing, and even bed linens. All were handled similarly in law, which is why they are grouped together under the term "textiles" in this book. Even married women and enslaved people could make legal claims to textiles, although marriage and slavery limited their rights to other property. Claims to textiles did not erase other restrictions: they were not recognized as property rights, nor did they lead to the recognition of other rights. Even so, people of marginal status assumed distinct legal forms when draped in textiles: they could own this form of property; they could trade it; and they could expect courts to uphold their claims to it. It was the property that most Americans had, if they could claim anything of value at all, because the law made possession possible.[2]

While largely forgotten today, the legal principles associated with textiles were widely understood and closely followed in the nineteenth-century United States. Deeply rooted in the colonial period, they flourished in the decades following the American Revolution. Caty, an enslaved woman in New York City, articulated their importance with stunning clarity in 1805. Like Elizabeth, Caty ran away from her master and took a parcel of clothing with her. Her escape, too, was unsuccessful. Unlike Elizabeth, however, Caty was charged with absconding as well as theft because of her legal status as a slave. In court, she admitted to running away. But when it came to theft, she insisted that she was taking what was hers, because she had been given the garments by her master and had worn them while working in his house. The defense speaks volumes: she could make legal claims to her clothing, but not to the body that wore them.[3]

Those legal principles also explain Elizabeth's plan. Like Caty, escaped servants and enslaved people generally took their own clothing, assuming those garments were theirs. But some, like Elizabeth, appropriated their masters' and mistresses' clothing, which was generally nicer and more valuable than their own. The sale of good clothing could fund the journey to a new location, with enough left over for a tidy nest egg. Quality garments held out the possibility of a new life in another way as well, if the thief could manage to inhabit them and, by extension, the social status they represented.[4] While that kind of transformation might seem like a longshot, the law evened the chances of success. The simple act of wearing clothing carried weight as evidence of possession, establishing a visible, verifiable relationship between a person and the garments in question. The legal power of that connection, however, cut two ways. It worked only if others had not created prior claims of their own in a similar fashion. Going about in clothing known to belong to someone else constituted definitive evidence of theft, not ownership. Those legal principles determined the outcome of Elizabeth's scheme. To pull it off, she needed to distance herself not only from her mistress but also from the entire community where she, her mistress, and their wardrobes were well known. Unfortunately for Elizabeth, she never got that far.[5]

Elizabeth and Caty failed in their escapes. But plenty of others like them—people with weak claims to rights, property, or both—used textiles to launch new lives, particularly in the first decades following the Revolution, when it was easier to act on the legal principles associated with textiles. Paying close attention to the physical qualities of these goods, this book shifts attention from written texts to objects that also constitute and express meaning, considering how material culture shaped individual circumstances as well as broader social, cultural, and economic dynamics in the period between the Revolution and the Civil War. Textiles were—and still are—particularly evocative objects, functioning as an outer skin that mediates between their wearers and the world around them. The work lavished on making fine cloth and clothing underscores the importance of these goods: beauty mattered, as did the sound of rustling silk or the feel of soft, warm wool. People went out of their way to obtain particular colors, textures, and patterns, not only to mark their status or fulfill external standards of fashion but also as a means of self-expression and personal fulfillment. The garments that have survived bear silent witness to the intimacy of their relationship to their owners, whose sweat, oils, and movement left an imprint on the fabric, making it possible even now to see the outlines of their long-gone bodies.[6]

The particular legal principles that attached to textiles distinguished them from other material goods. People did not accumulate these things just because they were necessary and desirable, although both considerations were important. They also did so because law made textiles into an economic rarity for those on the margins: a secure form of property. Legal practice recognized similar claims to other kinds of property, particularly food and tools. But neither worked well as a means of exchange or a way to store value: food went bad, and the market for tools was limited, what with people wanting only so many axes, awls, and hammers. By contrast, textiles were relatively durable and very much in demand. The material qualities of textiles combined with the legal principles attached to them to enable their use as currency, credit, and capital, all crucial components of the developing economy that were otherwise extremely difficult for the majority of the population to access.

It is easy to overlook the importance of textiles as economic instruments, backed by law, because they simultaneously functioned as consumer goods. People's savings lay side by side with goods that they used; they could even be one and the same. Shirts, shifts, handkerchiefs, and hose that people could wear went into trunks and cupboards along with yards of unused cloth and garments that they had no intention of ever putting on. Women had vests and trousers. Men had fabric suitable only for gowns. People without tables, let alone houses to put them in, had table linens. They acquired and stored them all, awaiting the right moment to leverage their value.[7]

Textiles situate the new republic within broader patterns of global trade, highlighting elements of law and the economy that were neither new nor specific to the republic.[8] Focusing on these goods means pulling back and taking a longer view, revealing continuities that carried over from the colonial period and following their course as they intermingled with the legal and economic changes of the Revolutionary era. The result is a re-periodization of the new republic's founding decades. The legal system set up after the Revolution gave people on the legal margins the institutional space to use and even expand on the legal principles and practices associated with textiles. They made use of those opportunities not just to acquire and control property but also to enforce longstanding rules of exchange. At the same time, however, the legal system was moving in directions that began undermining the principles on which so many people relied. At the very moment when the extension of rights seemed to be opening up the legal system and other governing institutions to broader segments of the population, the deterioration of the legal principles associated with textiles was closing off other means of access. As textiles show, the everyday actions of ordinary people had profound legal implications in the decades between the Revolution and Civil War. Their insistence on inclusion shaped the substance of law and its practice. To the extent that people with weak claims to rights had access to the legal system, it was because they expected it and insisted on it.

The legal principles associated with textiles are inseparable from the long history of trade in these goods. Silks and cottons from India, China, and the Middle East had been circulating in the trading world of the Indian Ocean since at least the eleventh century. From there, they moved through Indonesia and Africa, spreading in the early modern period to continental Europe and the British Isles, where the contrast between these fabrics and the dull, scratchy linen and wool cloth that predominated there is hard to overstate. The visuals were arresting. Emerald, crimson, azure, vermillion: even the names sounded like something you wanted to see. Indian manufacturers had developed techniques to form brilliant, intricate designs that twined and bloomed across entire lengths of cotton. With silk, colors acquired such luminosity that they almost glowed. The feel of these fabrics also kept people coming back for more. Cloth made of silk was so lightweight that it seemed to float, even when it was woven densely. Soft to the touch, cotton cloth could be made thick and sturdy or sheer to the point of transparency, and it was easy to work with and washable to boot.[9]

Europeans' obsession with these fabrics and the profits they promised powered trade, first with Asia and then elsewhere. The Portuguese led the way, using their maritime might to control the water route around Africa. Textile producers in India, China, and the Middle East were not only trading directly with Portugal by the early seventeenth century but also producing textiles specifically designed for the Portuguese, adapting traditional patterns and color palettes to suit the tastes of customers halfway around the world. All these fabrics soon found their way into other parts of Europe as well.[10]

Profiteers and their royal patrons from Britain and Europe then folded the Americas into the textile trade, even as they searched for other ways to wring profits from these continents. Those who came to exploit the North Atlantic's fisheries soon realized that furs offered far more return. By the mid-seventeenth century, people in Britain and continental Europe were sporting beaver hats, while Native people were wearing imported cloth, which constituted over 60 percent of the goods shipped to the Americas through the fur trade.[11]

Textiles underwrote the slave trade. Europeans used brightly colored Indian cottons, commonly called calicos, which had long been staples in African markets, to pay for captive people whose forced labor enabled the exploitation of resources in other parts of the Americas. The plantations, mines, and farms in the Americas then produced more demand for imported textiles, which European merchants with long experience in the trade were well positioned to supply. Between 1785 and 1789, Spain exported 4,704,948 yards of domestically produced calicos to the Americas—yardage that would stretch from present-day New York City to San Francisco.[12]

European nations did what they could to control the movement of textiles, because the trade was so lucrative. Monarchs granted monopolies, giving huge companies authority over trade abroad and carving out spheres of influence that merged commerce with national power. The British East India Company, whose tea was unceremoniously dumped in Boston Harbor just before the Revolution, was one among many such national monopolies. Even as Europeans cultivated trade with far-flung parts of the globe, they kept a close eye on their rivals closer to home, barring the importation of goods manufactured in other European countries or imported from elsewhere by merchants based in other European countries. It was difficult to get

French-made silks in the British colonies, just as it was difficult to get British-made wool in the French colonies.[13]

Trade policies, however, could only do so much. In fact, they acknowledged a well-established reality: a highly competitive global market, characterized by mass production, using hand labor, that made imported cloth more profitable than many domestically produced varieties. Merchants could offer quality imports at a price that domestic producers—in the colonies, Britain, or continental Europe—never could have matched.[14] The fate of restrictions on the importation of Indian calicos suggests the difficulty of controlling the global market in textiles. These colorful cottons were so popular and so threatening to the domestic wool and linen industry in Britain that officials there not only banned their importation but also made it a crime to wear them. Spain and France enacted similar policies for the same reasons. But none of these laws were particularly effective in tamping down the enthusiasm for calicos, which continued to make their way into people's wardrobes.[15]

It was not just calicos. All kinds of textiles from all over the world found their way onto people's backs and into their trunks and cupboards in North America. The people who lived there had wound textiles and their legal principles into their lives long before European colonists ever contemplated a Revolution. Declarations of political independence from Britain did nothing to change that situation: textiles remained the form of property that most Americans owned after the Revolution, just as they had before. Centuries of practice had made textiles unlike other commodities in which merchants and manufacturers trafficked and unlike other consumer goods that people regularly bought. Economics and culture alone do not explain those differences.

More important was law. Many works on material culture explore the social meanings and far-flung exchange of textiles. So do studies of capitalism, one strand of which deals with the flow of commodities and credit across national borders and another strand of which focuses on the economic strategies of marginalized people. *Only the Clothes on Her Back*, by contrast, reveals the place of law in all those dynamics: the social and economic value of textiles derived from the legal principles attached to them, which were enforceable in the new republic's courts. Unlike rights, those legal principles were not limited to the privileged few—the white male merchants, manufacturers, and political leaders thought to dominate the new republic's economy and governing institutions or even the white men who could claim the rights to property ownership and political participation. The legal principles of textiles extended to *all* the people who produced them, traded them, and wore them. Even those without rights could use these principles to make claims to property within the new republic's governing institutions.[16]

Following these legal principles and their enforcement, *Only the Clothes on Her Back* uncovers the efforts of ordinary people—particularly people without strong claims to rights—to engage in the economy on their own terms. The results broaden our view of the economic landscape to include practices typically characterized as marginal, even illicit: pawn shops, public auctions, secondhand stores, peddling, ad hoc markets, and exchanges among friends and relatives. None of that was possible without law. It all depended on well-established rules, linked to the legal principles associated with textiles.

Attention to textiles changes perspectives on early American law as well. Courts in the new republic recognized and enforced the principles associated with textiles. In disputes involving the ownership and exchange of textiles, people regularly marched down to local courts with the expectation that officials there would uphold their claims and resolve their conflicts. Their confidence was well founded, as evidenced by the thousands of court cases involving textiles in both urban and rural areas. It is remarkable that people without property rights felt confident in pursuing cases that looked an awful lot like assertions of property rights. Equally remarkable is the response of local officials, who dutifully sorted through the evidence involving sheets, shifts, shirts, handkerchiefs, and shoes to figure out what property was whose.

The connections between textiles and law can be difficult to ferret out. One problem lies in the nature of the evidence: the people who relied on textiles' legal principles worked hard to cover their tracks. Making claims to cloth, clothing, and related accessories required considerable subterfuge as well as determined effort. While well established, the principles of textiles vied with other bodies of law that denied people the rights necessary to claim property and to access the new republic's governing institutions. People like Caty and Elizabeth were constrained within status relationships of domestic dependency—slavery, servitude, marriage, and childhood. That body of law not only denied rights to the people legally positioned as slaves, servants, wives, and children but also gave the men legally defined as masters, husbands, and fathers rights to any property their dependents had, made, or acquired. Given those rules, it was wise for married women, minors, menial servants, and enslaved people to keep their textiles away from unsympathetic household heads and their creditors, who could make legal claims to them. The tentacles of status relationships also ensnared nominally free people, including free Blacks, unmarried women, and the working poor, justifying restrictions based on race, gender, and class. All these people could claim textiles, using the legal principles associated with them. Still, they regularly found themselves defending their possessions, particularly textiles thought to be above their station and out of their reach. As a result, they were careful about revealing what was theirs. Those who needed to know did; others did not. In all likelihood, Elizabeth's escape failed because she displayed her haul too conspicuously.

When people did go public, the legal principles on which they relied do not seem particularly "legal" now, in the twenty-first century, given current presumptions about what constitutes law. What mattered with textiles were the material qualities of the goods and their relationships to particular people. Those making claims brought their clothing, household linens, and fabrics to court to prove a direct, physical connection. They lined up witnesses to confirm those relationships, with testimony about the making, using, wearing, and exchanging those goods. All that clashed with the evidentiary standards of civil suits in the area of private law, which specialized in the adjudication of property disputes then and is assumed to have a monopoly on such matters now. By the late eighteenth century, civil suits increasingly relied on the kind of written documentation that has become commonplace in establishing ownership and tracking exchange: receipts, invoices, bills of sale, contracts, and account books. Given those standards, it is hard to see the dresses, bonnets, vests, and coats that people hauled into court or the ramblings of friends and neighbors as legal evidence. It seems more like the stuff of daily life, to which we—mistakenly—no longer ascribe legal meaning.

The courts' handling of textiles further distanced cases involving these goods from the kinds of cases seen nowadays as legal disputes over property, namely, those civil suits that appealed to facts memorialized in writing. Yet the underlying issues in cases involving textiles were often similar to those in civil suits. Say, hypothetically, that Elizabeth Billings made off with her mistress's clothing because she had not been paid the wages that had been promised to her. That actually happened all the time. If both the laborer and the employer could claim rights, the resulting conflict could become a civil action: a contract dispute. But legal officials could not adjudicate that kind of conflict between Elizabeth Billings and her mistress as a civil suit, even if they had wanted to, because her mistress was a married woman, without the rights to own property and, by extension, to make contracts. They faced a legal impossibility: there was no way to confirm the property rights of an individual who had no rights. Unable to untangle that knot, legal officials set it aside and moved such claims to the area of public law, which dealt with crimes and other matters affecting the social order. In that body of law, officials could ignore the whole question of rights. Instead, they could turn property disputes into criminal offenses, usually theft, against the public—the state, the commonwealth, or the people.

That legal framing creates the appearance of difference where there was none. It makes property conflicts that would have been handled as civil suits if they involved white men look like something else when they involved people with weak claims to rights. When a married woman claimed ownership of property that happened to include silk dresses and Florentine shoes, the whole thing became theft. Maybe it was. Maybe it wasn't. In Elizabeth Billings's case, as in so many others, there is no way to know what was really going on. The surviving documents in other cases only occasionally offer clues about the underlying issues. In most, what was once clear, but nonetheless disputed, has been lost in the past, leaving only silence.

That silence has allowed other interpretations to take over. At the time, contemporary commentators dismissed the production of cloth and clothing within households as an extension of domestic labor that only women did, treating it as if it were of nominal economic value. They pooh-poohed the trade in textiles in patronizing tones as the silly attempts of women to earn a bit of pin money; the tragic efforts of those on the economic margins to eke out a living; the outmoded forms of barter in which only the most ignorant would engage. Even sympathetic historians tend to duplicate those biases. This part of the economy is still presented as "informal" or "underground," as either tattered remnants of past practices or defiantly illicit ones that took place outside the law.[17]

But this dimension of the textile market did not exist outside the law. The legal principles associated with textiles supported a highly regulated market that was anything but informal or underground. It was out in the open for all to see, despite the misrepresentations within the legal system and elsewhere. It also operated under widely observed rules that the new republic's courts continued to enforce, without open acknowledgment.

The multiple, overlapping jurisdictions within the new republic's governing order provided spaces for those legal principles to flourish. That governing order, often referred to as federalism, contained many moving parts at the federal, state, and local levels. After the Revolution, the legal principles associated with textiles remained firmly fixed in areas that have not received much attention until recently: local jurisdictions, such as municipal and county courts, and thoroughly ordinary cases at all levels of the legal system that dealt with everyday disputes among merchants and manufacturers about broken contracts, overdue bills, and unpaid customs duties. Following those principles, *Only the Clothes on Her Back* joins recent efforts to excavate the various layers of the federal system and explore their significance to the development of law and the practice of governance.[18] The book also builds on recent work that has shown how people of marginal status used parts of law and the governing order once thought closed to them.[19]

Textiles reveal new elements to the developing federal system, by shifting the focus away from the legal status of persons, particularly the rights that they did or did not have in state and federal law. The emphasis on persons sorts everyone out according to the rights they enjoyed and the restrictions placed on them, putting enslaved people, free Blacks, Native people, poor white men, and free women (married and unmarried) into different categories from white men and from one another, as if their bundles of rights—big, small, or nonexistent—described the entirety of their relationship to the governing order. In fact, many of the terms that we apply to people actually derive from their legal status. Masters, husbands, servants, slaves, wives, free Blacks, free people of color, children—those are all legal terms that were and are now used more generally to refer to actual people, suggesting the profound ways that rights inflect social relationships and even individual identities.[20] Because all these people suffered so many restrictions, the emphasis lies there, on what people of marginal legal status could *not* do, to the point that marginalized people's creative uses of the law seem surprising, even impossible. This entrenched view reinforces a particular narrative arc, which proceeds from a point of departure defined by exclusion or the denial of rights and then moves toward inclusion with the extension of rights. Underlying that narrative is the erroneous assumption that rights provided the only means of accessing the new republic's economy and governing institutions and that the real story lies in efforts to obtain them.[21]

Textiles show that this conceptual frame is incomplete. The legal principles that attached to property also figured into the new republic's governing order. In law, textiles, in particular, did not function as inert goods that people could claim, exchange, and squabble over, depending on their legal status. The principles associated with these goods carried over to the people who possessed them, altering their relationship to the governing order. Yet those principles remained firmly attached to the form of property, not to the people who relied on them; those people's legal status remained unchanged, even as they made use of the legal principles attached to textiles. That is why this book includes an array of people whose legal statuses were fundamentally different from one another and who are usually treated separately: women as well as men, including those whose legal status was compromised by race, class, or ethnicity. In their legal status as persons, Caty and Elizabeth Billings did not have that much in common. But they had a great deal in common when it came to their uses of the legal principles attached to textiles.

Textiles also reveal the lasting legal importance of relationships—for good and for ill—in the new republic's governing order. When the emphasis is on the rights of persons, relationships seem problematic, and for good reason. The relationships of domestic dependency—marriage, servitude, and slavery—restricted rights of dependents in law, with implications that reached well beyond those relationships. All those people who were not domestic dependents but could be—in other words, all women, men of color, and the working poor—had more limited rights. In this context, relationships seem like as the legal problem that rights eventually solved. What everyone needed were rights as individuals, just like white men.[22]

It was not that easy. To extend rights to those enmeshed within the status relationships of domestic dependency, without altering the power dynamics associated with them, created a contradiction that undermined the intended results. Those relationships did not just deny rights to the people who experienced subordination within them; they redistributed power to maintain structural inequalities of gender, race, and class more broadly within the social order. To complicate matters, those inequalities became linked to rights during the nineteenth century in ways that obscured those underlying dynamics. By mid-century, the power of individual household heads was no longer conceived of as a grant of authority exercised in the interests of the public order but as rights that individual men claimed in their dependents' property, labor, and bodies. Other elements of household heads' authority also took the form of individual rights that all white men could claim: rights to dominate all those who could be or once had been domestic dependents, even if they no longer were. Those elements of status relationships remained in place when rights began to be extended, in piecemeal fashion, through measures that secured married women's property rights and, more dramatically, abolished slavery and protected African American men's civil and political rights. As the inequalities created by relationships of domestic dependency lingered on, they continued to reinforce structural inequalities that the extension of specific rights did not address. The effects then undermined the ability of the people who remained subordinate to use what rights they did have.

Whereas relationships of domestic dependency blocked marginalized people's claims to property and their access to governing institutions, the legal principles associated with textiles created property claims and provided entrée. Those principles also derived their power from relationships: the ties of people to their textiles and to other people who could validate those connections. These relationships could be mobilized to assert legal claims to valuable textiles. They could move someone from abject poverty to relative prosperity, from grinding despair to hope. They also gave whole groups of people a route into the economy and the governing order, where their presence and importance have not been fully appreciated.

The tragedy is that the relationships that supported people's claims to textiles only had so much legal power. Legal recognition of them did not extend as broadly through the federal system as rights or the restrictions that resulted from relations of domestic dependency. By the time of the Civil War, the legal principles of textiles had begun to move out of the realm of law, as it was defined at that time, and into the realm of culture. As legal changes in the handling of textiles suggest, however, linear narratives that follow a trajectory from exclusion to inclusion or inclusion to exclusion miss the mark. At stake were the terms of inclusion, which changed dramatically over time, often with unintended results.

Ultimately, Elizabeth's and Caty's failed escapes foretold where others would find themselves later in the century: without either rights or textiles to navigate a governing order of which they had always been a part. Textiles mattered in the decades following the Revolution because so many Americans were so vulnerable. But their legal powers were fragile, dependent on a specific context at a fleeting moment in time. By the end of Reconstruction, most Americans had only the clothes on their backs. The legal principles that attached to this form of property could no longer protect them from a governing order that remained rigidly hierarchical, despite the extension of rights to a broader segment of the population.

Yet even as the book charts the declining legal power of textiles, it highlights the creativity and persistence of the people who wielded the legal principles associated with this form of property and the forgotten implications of their efforts. They could imagine a world where they might claim their labor, possess property, define their own destinies, and aspire to beauty and meaning. To be sure, historians have documented such claims, sometimes puzzling over their origins, sometimes explaining them in terms of the particular political cultures among enslaved people or middle-class white women or laborers or immigrants. But these political cultures cut across and through these different groups of people, suggesting they had common roots. They did, in a lost legal world that textiles reveal.

Only the Clothes on Her Back ranges widely over the territory within the jurisdiction of the United States in the period between the Revolution and the Civil War. It simultaneously pans out beyond the new republic's borders and then zooms in on localities, rather than states and the federal government. That geographical frame follows the legal principles associated with textiles and the legal practices that supported them, none of which observed the jurisdictional bounds of states and nations. Textiles and their associated legalities moved over those imaginary lines and settled into local communities, where people wove them into their lives and governing institutions.

The book is divided into three parts, which trace the legal principles of textiles, the people who used them, and the governing institutions that dealt with them. The first part, "Old Clothes for a New County," begins with the goods themselves, focusing on the legal principles attached to them, the legal system that supported them, and the implications for the trade and production of textiles. As this section shows, the Revolution did little to alter observance of the legal principles associated with textiles, which persisted within the new republic's federal system. That legal context, in turn, created space for economic practices with deep roots in the global textile market to persist into the nineteenth century, blurring the sharp line so often drawn between the commercial economy of white male merchants and manufacturers and the non-commercial world of everyone else, at least for the decades following the Revolution. People on the legal margins were more engaged in commercial exchange than previously thought, but economic exchange did not conform to the impersonal dynamics associated with the commercial market and presumed to be ascendant in this period. Married women, enslaved people, and others on the legal margins acted as merchants and manufacturers, while white men who were engaged in trade and production acted a lot like the subordinated people who made and traded textiles.

The second part, "Protective Garments in a Hostile World," turns to the creative ways that people claimed and used textiles within the legal order of the new republic. The legal principles associated with textiles and enforced in courts provided the foundations of a vast market in which this form of property functioned as the means as well as the object of exchange. A piece of cloth was not just something to turn into clothing or household linens. It could also be dollars and cents—literally. In fact, a handkerchief was better than a dollar bill, given legal restrictions that kept so many early Americans from using currency and the instability of banknotes, the printed value of which rarely expressed their actual value. Not only was the value of handkerchiefs more stable than a banknote, but claims to them were also more secure. As a result, some textiles circulated without ever fulfilling the material uses for which they were created. When people had items that they could spare, they traded them, pawned them, lent them, or saved them to fund future ventures.

The final section, "Rags," follows the legal principles of textiles through the institutional layers of the federal system. That system, as constituted in the first decades of the nineteenth century, enabled people without strong claims to rights to use and enforce those principles. The means of enforcement, however, eventually undercut their ability to do so. Changes in the decades leading up to the Civil War eroded the place of textiles in the legal system, as authority began to shift toward those areas of law that emphasized the rubric of rights and their restrictions based in relations of domestic dependency. This framework, which focused on the legal status of individuals, stripped away all the relationships necessary to establish claims to textiles: the relationships between people and their clothes, as well as the relationships to other people who witnessed their production, trade, and use. Either an individual had the rights necessary to own property or they did not—and most Americans did not. Rights belonged only to the minority who were not encumbered by the inequalities of status relationships, that is, white men with property.

Some restrictions began to loosen as strong movements challenging slavery and the constraints based on race and gender gained ground and culminated in the policy changes of the Civil War and Reconstruction. But those changes explicitly excluded women. Where men could claim rights, if only in theory, women were left with only the clothes on their backs, which by then had become pretty flimsy legal coverings. Only in the twentieth century would women obtain equal access to the same rights as men. A common narrative of US history follows the extension of rights first to African American men and then to women of all races. But it misses what textiles reveal: the extension of rights cannot be told as a straightforward narrative of inclusion and progress. After all, many men, particularly African American men, also had little more than the clothes on their backs in the post–Civil War era, because so many were denied access to rights.

The book's title, *Only the Clothes on Her Back*, gestures toward this retelling of the new republic's history by positioning women as the representative legal actors. Women are often treated as a deviation from a norm, defined as the possession of the full range of rights. Particularly in the first half of the nineteenth century, that condition applied to only a minority of the population, which did not include all white men, let alone all men. They too lived lives of compromised rights, enmeshed within relationships—domestic and otherwise—with powerful legal meanings. They too relied on the legal principles associated with textiles and the relationships that supported them. They too paid the price as the rights of individuals were elevated over those principles, without addressing the inequalities that made them so important.

As *Only the Clothes on Her Back* shows, law was central to all these people's lives long before they acquired rights. They knew the rules of law that regulated economic exchange and demanded that governing institutions apply those rules to their dealings. Their efforts provide the necessary context for understanding hard-fought and protracted battles for equality. Those on society's margins expected to be part of the new nation and insisted on it from the outset, at a time often portrayed as merely a prelude to later, more consequential movements. Their successes were meaningful but ephemeral, resulting in a trajectory of change that was anything but linear. The importance of this piece of the past has faded over time, as subsequent events made it difficult to imagine that it ever existed at all. *Only the Clothes on Her Back* restores color, texture, and pattern to that time.

PART I

OLD CLOTHES IN A NEW COUNTRY

The people of colonial North America wore the world on their backs. Long-term trends in the global textile market had been increasing the supply of textiles, bringing down prices, and putting more goods from more places in the hands of more people since the seventeenth century, if not before. British trade policies only magnified the underlying economics that made imports cheaper and better than the goods colonists could produce themselves. While the term "imports" conjures up images of glossy silks, colorful calicos, fine linens, and rich wools, those were not the only kinds of cloth that North Americans imported. Most of the fabric brought into the colonies was basic cloth used for the work clothes, bed linens, and blankets that even the poorest took for granted. Even if colonists had wanted to, they could not possibly have made enough cloth to supply all their needs.[1]

The presence of far-flung parts of the globe in the everyday lives of North Americans was difficult to ignore because all that imported cloth bore the names of its place of production: Norwich stuffes, Kersey, Worsted, Spitalfields silk, Irish linen, Holland cloth, Marseilles cloth, German buckram, Silesia linen, Russia duck, Bengal taffety, Bombay stuffes, Madras, Canton cloth, China silk, Kashmir, Cambay cloth (in Gujarat), Calicos (Calcutta), and Nankeen (Nanjing), just to name a few. When domestic weavers ramped up production in the mid-eighteenth century, different kinds of cloth with North American place names were added to the list. Other fabrics retained names in the languages of the places they were produced. The ones from India were melodically evocative, at least to the ears of English speakers: alliballies, carridarries, doofooties, gorgorons, humhums, izzarees, and mulmuls.[2]

All these fabrics arrived at North American ports jumbled together in crates, chests, and boxes. Once unpacked and separated out, they were cut up into shorter lengths and made into shirts, shifts, coats, gowns, and bed linens. In that form, cloth from around the world would become linked to the particular individuals who possessed it. Nonetheless, those fabrics retained their own names and their connections to the people who produced them, no matter how far they traveled and how closely they became associated with individuals in their new homes. In short, textiles linked far-flung places together through fabrics associated with the places where they were made, even though they were destined for people elsewhere.[3]

That cloth came with a lot of baggage. Just as textiles moved across the borders of nation-states, so too did the economic dynamics that enabled their trade. The demand for more, cheaper textiles in the early modern period undermined the position of people engaged in their production all across the globe: from the agricultural workers who produced raw wool, flax, cotton, and silk to the artisans who fashioned those fibers into cloth and finished garments. When colonial merchants pried open crates of fabrics, they also unleashed those economic dynamics where they lived. And so the changes that made it possible to produce inexpensive humhums and mulmuls for the export market spilled out into North America and then rippled back to India. North American women who took up weaving in the mid-eighteenth century were responding not just to British trade policies but also to the reorganization of production in the world market that had been pushing skilled, male weavers out of the trade for over a century. In the early nineteenth century when white planters in southern states grew cotton using the forced labor of enslaved people, they marked out an economic strategy that others elsewhere in the world would follow.[4]

Textiles also came with legal baggage. The booming global textile market rested on the close association between people and their clothing. That one simple link allowed a wider array of people to buy and control this form of property. It also turned textiles into a means to store and exchange value. Those practices then became legal principles when officials recognized and enforced them. Even as textiles traveled across the boundaries of nation-states, the legal principles associated with them took specific form within the legal systems where they landed. In early modern Latin America, continental Europe, and Great Britain, for instance, officials enacted sumptuary laws to limit the kinds of cloth and accessories that all non-elite people could wear, despite the limited effectiveness of such dictates. While similar kinds of laws remained on the books in the United States, they were rarely used in local courts as a means of punishing people or separating them from their clothing. The new republic's legal system dealt with those issues differently, on a case-by-case basis entirely in keeping with the structures of law there.[5]

The American Revolution did nothing to change either the economics or the legalities of textiles. In fact, unmediated access to the global textile market was one of the goals of the revolt. Colonial merchants resented British efforts to reserve the lucrative textile trade to themselves, although they managed to tap into it through a combination of compliance and evasion. That fragile equilibrium fell apart in the 1760s, with stepped-up enforcement of existing trade restrictions and the imposition of additional taxes. The fact that chests of tea, not bundles of cloth, ended up in Boston Harbor may say something about the value of textiles; even a mob of angry colonists would not have countenanced such waste. The value of textiles certainly explains why so many Revolutionary leaders were merchants who dealt in imported cloth. It also explains why the promotion of homespun and the rejection of British textile imports acquired such political resonance during the war.[6]

When the focus is fixed on the borders of the United States at the state and federal level, the power of the men who led the Revolution and profited from textiles is thrown into sharp relief. The Revolution's outcome opened up new opportunities in the textile trade for these men, just as they had hoped. Textiles also continued to provide a leg up for white men on the make.[7] Benjamin Franklin's journey from rags to riches was literal as well as metaphorical: he amassed his fortune by making paper from rags that he bought from housewives and the working poor in Philadelphia. And Franklin was just one of many prominent white men who used textiles to launch careers in trade, industry, and politics in the period between the Revolution and the Civil War.[8]

Focusing elsewhere, on the production and circulation textiles in people's lives and the legal venues that regulated their exchange, exposes dynamics over which the new nation's leaders had far less control. Textiles provided opportunities for a wide range of people, because the governing institutions of the new republic did nothing to eliminate the economic practices and the legal principles associated with them. Those legal principles had made their way into the formal written texts by the time of the Revolution. But if anything, their reach was far more robust than those texts would suggest. It was simply assumed that everyone could make legal claims to textiles, not just to their own clothing but also to clothes they were not wearing, lengths of fabric, household linens, and related accessories, such as ribbons, hats, and shoes. Those legal claims then begat other economic practices that also became legal principles. Unlike individual property rights, moreover, claims to textiles were handled as part of the public order: the legal principles associated with textiles involved foundational cultural values and social customs that defined the good order of society more generally and, by extension, were available to everyone. As such, they allowed marginalized people entry into commerce and government in ways that were at odds with coverture, slavery, and all the other laws restricting people's rights in the new republic. Despite all the changes ushered in by the Revolution, textiles continued to embed people within a wider a global market, the legal principles and practices of which remained widely accessible.

North Americans still wore the world on their backs after the colonies became the United States. To be sure, by the nineteenth century the names of textiles no longer referred to their place of production. Nankeens could be yellow cottons produced in Nanjing, China, or cloth of a similar style produced elsewhere. Similarly, calicos could be produced in England, Spain, France, or the United States, not just India. But even after fabrics were no longer produced exclusively in the places for which they were named, the place names still signaled style and quality in a dynamic market characterized by the volume and diversity of its goods. In the 1790s, Rebecca Coles, a Virginia textile manufacturer, was weaving nankeens that she and her customers knew full well were knock-offs of Chinese goods. But Coles still needed to call her fabric nankeens, because that was how that kind of fabric had always been identified. Coles ran her own business and kept the proceeds from what she produced, even though she was a married woman, because that was what the law allowed when it came to textiles. The country might be new, but the economics that clothed its people were not. And those clothes came with a whole legal universe of their own that continued to operate within the new republic.[9]

1

Polly's Yarn

Legal Principles

Polly knew the law, knowledge that she asserted in no uncertain terms when claiming several hanks of handspun yarn, stolen from her yard in South Carolina's upcountry in 1842. Because Polly was enslaved, the case wound up in the Magistrates and Freeholders Court, the legal venue in her state that dealt with issues relating to men and women legally classified as enslaved and free people of color. Given her legal status, she could not prosecute the case in her own name. Instead, it was the man who claimed her as property whom the magistrate named as the complainant. Aaron Vandiver, he wrote, "missed from his negro houses two hanks of spun cotton, one of a blue colour & the other white." Then, after filling in the necessary blanks of the form as required by state law, the magistrate promptly turned to the evidence presented by the enslaved people who were actually involved. Polly started off, asserting her claims through the legal qualities of textiles, not property rights. The "spun cotton belonged to her." The wording says it all: *she* could not own the spun cotton; but *it* still belonged to her. The court agreed. In this case, as in so many others, local officials determined that the public interest was served by returning textiles to their rightful owners, even if their property rights were restricted or, as with Polly, nonexistent.[1]

People without strong claims to the rights necessary to claim property clustered in the textile trades for a reason. Customary practice had cohered into legal principles that meant even enslaved people and married women could make claims to these kinds of goods in law, something they could not do with other forms of property. Law was what made textiles valuable, turning them into a secure form of property for those whose legal status made such claims tenuous, without actually altering their legal status.

Americans conducted their lives with the presumption that everyone could make legal claims to textiles. That mattered to people, like Polly, whose economic and legal status made it difficult for them to buy or keep property. It also mattered to wealthy white male merchants and manufacturers who built their businesses selling property to people without strong claims to property, the rights necessary to own it, or both. Those legal practices went largely unremarked at the time, precisely because they were so common and hence unremarkable. That silence has carried over into the present, making it seem as if the constant circulation of textiles among people without property rights was unrelated to law.[2]

The law's written record compounds the problem. The books that lined the shelves of post-Revolutionary lawyers were devoted to the bodies of law—and there were many—that dealt with rules governing the exchange of property among people with rights, not those without rights. These bodies of law placed restrictions on people who could not claim rights, which underscored, and even accentuated, existing inequalities. The rules not only denied or limited property rights to all those defined as domestic dependents (wives, children, slaves, and servants, the legal term for menial wage workers) but also gave rights in dependents' property to the heads of the households in which they lived and labored. Those same rules underlay a wide range of other restrictions imposed on people associated with domestic dependency: people of color, all women, and the poor. Without property rights there was no need for the civil or political rights necessary to defend then. Without that wider array of rights, all these people were vulnerable to other limitations. Because they possessed so few rights to violate, states and municipalities were free to "regulate" all aspects of their lives.

To be sure, animating ideas of the Revolution provided a powerful critique of existing inequalities, laying the groundwork for reform efforts to end slavery, to improve the legal positions of women and people of color, and to open political participation to a broader array of "the people." But even among the new republic's most radical political leaders, the commitment to broad-based change was uneven, at best. Not only did existing inequalities remain in place, but they were also followed by new, rigid rules that further restricted the economic, legal, and political possibilities of many Americans.[3]

Where married women were concerned, published legal texts in the new republic adopted increasingly restrictive readings of coverture, based on Sir William Blackstone's influential *Commentaries on the Laws of England*. In general terms, coverture subsumed wives' legal identities within those of their husbands and limited their ability to act legally in their own names. But its specifics changed over time and differed from place to place, sometimes tightening, sometimes loosening. Blackstone erased those variations, fashioning a new synthesis by selecting from among conflicting common law principles and making it seem as if married women had never been able to control property legally or to act in their own names in law at all. In his memorable words, coverture entailed the suspension of "the very being or legal existence of the woman . . . during the marriage." This definition of coverture accentuated married women's subordination by forcing them to work through their husbands in all economic and legal matters, thereby elevating the marital tie over the other relationships in their lives. It not only undercut wives' connections outside their households but also characterized husbands' authority as an unconditional right they held as individuals, rather than a privilege exercised for the public good. Over the course of the nineteenth century, the Blackstonian view made its way into treatises, statutes, case law, and even magistrates' handbooks.[4]

As went marriage, so went other domestic relationships: parent and child, master and slave, and master and servant, which served as the basis for the legal relationship between wage workers and employers. Published legal texts in the United States duplicated Blackstonian logic in these domestic relationships as well, rendering the authority of husbands, fathers, masters, and employers more absolute and the subordination of dependents more complete. By the 1830s, these interpretations of domestic dependency had moved from published texts into legal practice, particularly in bodies of law that dealt with property and in all areas of law at the state and federal levels, although they seeped into public law in local venues as well.[5]

Enslaved people were forced to the extreme end of this spectrum of inequality. After a brief flirtation with abolition, southern states doubled down on the institution of slavery in its most draconian form, as a perpetual, inheritable condition that reduced the enslaved to chattel, without the rights necessary to participate in the economy or to defend their interests in their states' legal institutions. The global textile market's new, insatiable demand for cotton was partly to blame. Cotton enhanced slavery's economic viability in the first decades of the nineteenth century, at just the point when Revolutionary fervor and support for abolition were waning. The promise of fat profits from its cultivation combined with white supremacy to overwhelm whatever remaining doubts white southerners had about slavery. Then, in the decades leading up to the Civil War, slave states piled even more prohibitions on those who were enslaved, regulating everything from movement to literacy and worship.[6]

The same currents swept up all people of color, even those who were free. Free Blacks pushed back hard, working to establish their place as citizens of the new republic with the same legal status as other free Americans. But it was an ongoing battle, as state and local governments in the North, South, and Midwest passed a host of restrictions limiting where free Blacks could live, what work they could do, what property they could own, and how they could participate in the legal system. In places along the east coast where Native people had been dispossessed and no longer lived on tribal lands, they were legally lumped together with free Blacks. They too became "free people of color" in law, terminology that reflected the conflation of slavery and race in the new republic's governing institutions: the laws assumed that all people of color were enslaved unless otherwise indicated. In the Northwest Territory and the Old Southwest, Native nations lost their grip on both their lands and their sovereignty as American settlers poured into those areas and government at all levels elevated their claims over those of native peoples.[7]

Not all white Americans enjoyed the full range of rights and privileges either. As the legal status of married white women deteriorated, that of propertyless white men seemed to improve. Appearances were deceiving. Even as states extended suffrage to most white men, those without property still found themselves legally disadvantaged in all kinds of situations. White male wage workers were like property-owning white men in the sense that they owned their own labor, could sell it at will, and could enjoy whatever they earned in doing so. But in practice, they were legally subordinated to their employers, whose property rights gave them extensive authority over their factories, workshops, and farms. In law, employers and their employees were contractual equals, even though they were clearly unequal in practice. As property owners, moreover, employers could do whatever they wanted with their property, which meant they could dictate the terms of labor to their employees, who had no recourse.[8]

There is no doubt that all the restrictions enacted by municipalities, states, and the federal government played an outsized role in the lives of the vast majority of Americans. They circumscribed, even destroyed lives. There is also no doubt of the importance of all the hard-fought efforts to change that situation. Nonetheless, these restrictions did not define the entirety of people's relationship to law and government, which included practices and principles from the colonial past that, among other things, recognized the legal qualities of textiles.

The legal principles associated with textiles were so well established that they even made their way into written texts that otherwise passed over them. Even Blackstone affirmed longstanding Anglo-American practice that gave married women control of "paraphernalia," which referred to wearing apparel and jewelry. Tellingly, however, he placed that principle in volume 4, which dealt with the "rights of things." It did not appear in the chapter "Husbands and Wives" in volume 1, which covered the "rights of persons." In other words, wives could claim paraphernalia because of the qualities of the goods themselves, not because of any rights that they held as persons. That same legal principle was equally well established in continental Europe. Anglo-American and continental law also gave married women the ability to trade for necessities, including clothing, without their husbands' permission. Similarly, customary practice allowed free servants to maintain possession of their clothing, including items given to them by their masters and mistresses.[9]

In the early modern period, those legal principles had allowed women, even married women, a degree of economic leeway that Blackstone and those who followed his interpretation later denied. Continental law gave married women the ability to pursue their own business interests apart from their husbands. In France and the Netherlands, for instance, married women could simply declare themselves free traders and conduct business in their own names. New York textile merchant Mary Alexander provides a particularly compelling example. Born in 1693, she learned the business from her Dutch grandmother, the wife of a merchant and a successful merchant herself. Like her grandmother, Alexander traded in her own name throughout her life: during her first marriage, while she was widowed, and after she remarried. Her business was extensive and highly capitalized, focused on costly, high-end fabrics. Otherwise, her circumstances were hardly unusual. Under Dutch rule in New York, married as well as single and widowed women regularly worked as merchants and traders.[10]

Elements of British common law were more restrictive. Married women, for instance, were required to apply to local authorities for permission to trade in their own names. But in the early modern period, such restrictions lay alongside other conflicting practices and principles. The city of London specifically allowed married women to establish themselves as traders through social practice, simply by keeping their businesses separate from their husbands' financial dealings. What London made explicit was followed informally in parts of British North America, where married women operated their own businesses both before and after the Revolution, despite other common law restrictions. That situation opened space for continental legal traditions to persist, long after colonies fell under British control. Married women in New York continued to work as merchants and traders when the colony passed from the Dutch to the British. In fact, the British guaranteed those prerogatives, which women of all backgrounds and ethnicities continued to use. While plying her trade in the mid-1700s, Mary Alexander was also teaching her niece the business. Given all the crosscutting legal principles and practices at play in colonial British North America, it was possible for married women's businesses to acquire legal legitimacy over time, through their continued operation.[11]

The legalities of textiles facilitated those enterprises by solidifying married women's legal claims to this form of property. In colonial British North America, married women regularly produced and sold textiles without attention to the legal niceties of whether or not they were registered as free traders. Some women operated on a grand scale, like Mary Alexander, as merchants, just like their white male counterparts. Some oversaw what were then called manufactories: businesses that produced large quantities of cloth, generally by putting out raw materials to spinners and weavers who worked in their homes and then were paid by the piece for their labor. Many married women operated on a smaller scale. They made cloth themselves, sometimes with family labor, or they ran stores out of their homes, selling textiles along with groceries and liquor in the neighborhood. Even more, like Polly, traded what they spun, wove, or sewed with each other, neighbors, and merchants, keeping the proceeds for their own or their family's use.[12]

The legal principles that connected people to textiles and allowed married women to trade in these goods remained embedded in the new republic's legal order after the Revolution, although their appearance in written sources was uneven at best. Wives' ability to trade for necessities "suitable to [their husbands'] degree, estate, or circumstances" were well elaborated in treatises.[13] References to wives' claims to paraphernalia, which included clothing, jewelry, and sometimes bedding, were more sporadic. In the 1795 edition of his influential treatise on domestic relations, *Law of Baron and Femme; of Parent and Child; of Guardian and Ward; of Master and Servant; and of the Powers of Court of Chancery*, Tapping Reeve affirmed wives' claims to paraphernalia, although he divided such property into two categories. Wives had absolute claim to bedding and wearing apparel, but not to "ornaments," including jewelry and laces, which could be seized by husbands' creditors to cover debts. Reeve did not explain why he departed from established precedent in excluding "ornaments" from the category of paraphernalia. The omission of jewelry is particularly mysterious, since the value of run-of-the-mill textiles frequently outstripped that of ordinary jewelry. The reclassification of laces, however, suspiciously coincides with the reorganization of the industry, which had deep roots in Connecticut, where Reeve lived. Not only did lacemaking expand in the late eighteenth century, but control over it also moved out of the hands of women and into the hands of male merchants, who took over both production and marketing. Leaving lace legally in the hands of the married women who made it would undercut the property rights of the men who employed them. Blowing past his obvious revision of history, Reeve insisted that the principles he outlined were well established in English law and had been "universally adopted in the United States." By 1862, the revised version of Reeve's treatise indicated that wives' claims to paraphernalia, as he defined it, had been affirmed by statute in Massachusetts, Pennsylvania, and Vermont.[14]

Other treatise writers handled paraphernalia differently. In his 1803 adaptation of *Blackstone's Commentaries*, Virginian St. George Tucker accepted that writer's rigid conception of coverture in the chapter "Husband and Wife" and then raised him in a footnote, declaring that "a woman's personal property, by marriage, becomes absolutely her husband's." Personal property, in any form, was not the *right* of wives, as persons. But, like Blackstone, Tucker allowed for the principle of paraphernalia in a separate volume on the "rights of things," where he duplicated Blackstone's paragraph on wives' claims to items in this category—with the implication that it included jewelry and other ornaments, unlike Reeve's definition of the term. As the placement of paraphernalia in the work indicates, those claims lay in the legal qualities that attached to the textiles, not the married women themselves. Paraphernalia, however, did not appear at all in either James Kent's *Commentaries on American Law* or Zephaniah Swift's *A System of Laws of the State of Connecticut*, which was odd, since both closely followed Blackstone's text. Perhaps Kent and Swift thought the practice so universal that nothing needed to be said. Then again, the omission may have been a purposeful denial of custom. Similarly, the 1851 revision of Swift's treatise indicated that wearing apparel purchased during marriage did not belong to the wife, which fit the larger trend of increasingly restrictive readings of coverture.[15]

Magistrates' manuals further muddied the waters. References in them to wives' ability to trade for necessities were common, just as they were in the treatises. Not so much with wives' claims to paraphernalia. That situation owed, in part, to the continued influence of two English standards on which many magistrates' manuals in the new republic were based: Michael Dalton's *The Countrey Justice* (1618) and Richard Burn's *The Justice of the Peace and Parish Officer* (1755). Neither mentioned married women's relationship to property at all. Magistrates' manuals in the early republic then duplicated that silence. In the early nineteenth century, more manuals began incorporating Blackstone and his statements on married women's property. In Virginia, for instance, the first edition of William Waller Hening's guide did not mention wives' claims to paraphernalia; the second edition, which incorporated Blackstone, did. Generally, references to women's claims to paraphernalia were few and far between in magistrates' guides. Like the treatises, these manuals contained broad statements about wives' inability to own property, while omitting their ability to own a particular kind of property, textiles.[16]

The issue flitted through statutes and appellate decisions as well. Wives' claims to paraphernalia were clearly stated in Louisiana, which followed French and Spanish law. In other states, stay laws, which shielded some household property from seizure by creditors, acknowledged the fact that textiles did not necessarily belong to the male household head who incurred the debts. Pennsylvania's 1828 statute, for instance, excluded the family's clothing and linens, cloth manufactured in the household, and the materials necessary to make it, along with a basic store of food and the household head's tools. As Reeve suggested, Massachusetts, Pennsylvania, and Vermont put wives' claims to paraphernalia in writing. James Kent noted that Pennsylvania and South Carolina followed the custom of the city of London, which allowed women the ability to trade in their own names if they kept their dealings apart from those of their husbands.[17]

State laws were even less forthcoming on enslaved people's claims to clothing. Although statutes and appellate decisions in states that recognized slavery made it abundantly clear that enslaved people did not have property rights, scattered opinions did recognize their possession of "small perquisites." Those rulings and those statutes, moreover, never dealt specifically with clothing. Given the fact that legal practice acknowledged wearing apparel as a unique form of property for other people with restricted rights, the resulting silence effectively made enslaved people's relationship to those items analogous to that of wives and servants and thus stronger than they might otherwise have been.[18]

The legal qualities of textiles derived primarily from the realm of practice, not the pages of the statutes, appellate opinions, or treatises. Telling in this regard are the bits of fabric attached to the files of infants left at London's Foundling Hospital in the eighteenth century. These "threads of feeling," as historian John Styles calls them, were the tokens left by mothers to establish connections to their children. Should a mother ever return, she could identify her child by these bits of cloth: lengths of ribbon, scraps of embroidery, pieces cut from their own garments or those that they dressed their children in before leaving them, all carefully chosen and assembled as expressions of affection, potentially a mother's last. The economic, cultural, and legal elements of these tokens are difficult to tease apart. They reveal the increasing availability of textiles, even to mothers too poor to keep their children, as well as the personal meanings attached to them. But the tokens left at the London Foundling Hospital did much more. They also established a connection with legal force should she come to reclaim her child.[19]

The power of cloth to establish a legal relationship between mother and child continued in the post-Revolutionary United States, where items of clothing often featured as the most definitive pieces of evidence in infanticide cases. Juries carefully inspected the garments of dead infants, looking for clues to the mother's identity and intent. In an 1826 North Carolina case, the apron that served as a shroud connected the dead infant to its mother and established her guilt. A child found dressed carefully indicated that the birth was expected and death was natural, while improvised coverings, such as an apron, suggested otherwise. The article in an 1859 Chicago newspaper, which indicated that the child "was wrapped in a piece of cotton batting, around which was a child's skirt," might seem unremarkable but was exactly the kind of evidence that had determined the outcome of infanticide cases for decades.[20]

Such legal connections were why people without strong claims to property rights felt comfortable openly trading for textiles. When women purchased or sold textiles, merchants generally did not bother to make inquiries about what the husband might think, despite laws that prohibited wives from trading without their husbands' permission beyond what was required for their basic maintenance. Instead, merchants assumed the husband's permission based on the fact of the wife's presence in the store. Of course, many shopkeepers knew their female customers well enough to gauge how much

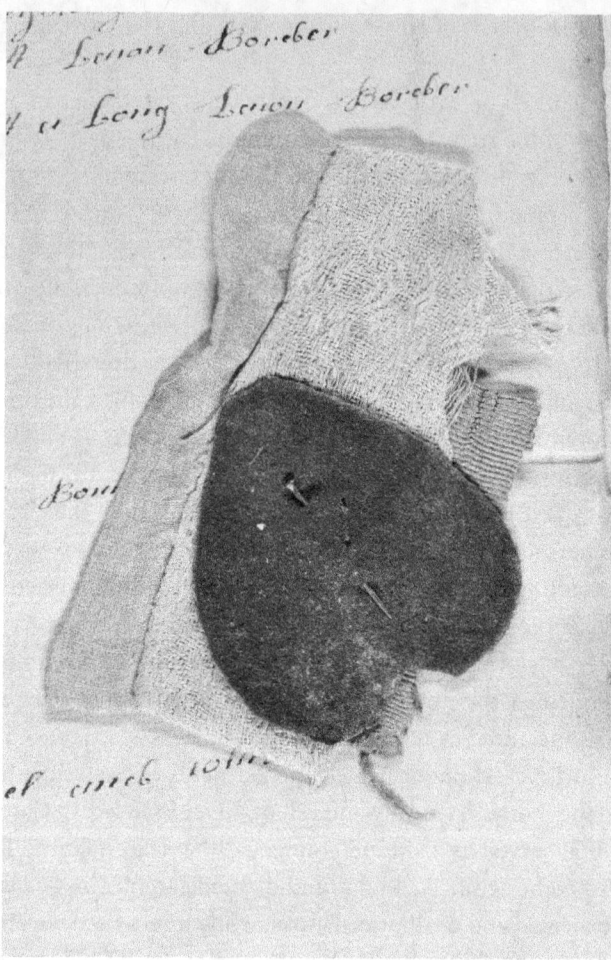

Figure 1.1 Token left by a mother in the mid-eighteenth century to identify the child she left at the London Foundling Hospital, which continues as the children's charity Coram, (http://www.coram.org.uk): "The Bit of Red Cloth Enclosed was pined to the Child's Cap: a heart cut from red woollen cloth, a ribbon of blue paduasoy silk, and a piece of linen diaper" (a type of cloth used for all kinds of linens, not just babies' diapers), Foundling 10563, a girl admitted November 22, 1758. Permission to use the image by the Thomas Coram Foundation for Children (Coram).

leeway to allow.[21] Such was the case with Jane Cooley, who lived and worked in southwest Virginia in the first half of the nineteenth century. Cooley, who will return in later chapters, drew on the legal customs that allowed married women to establish businesses in their own names through social practice.

Not only did she oversee a thriving spinning, weaving, and tailoring business during her marriage, but she also controlled the proceeds of what she made. Cooley regularly went "a trading" in town, where she negotiated with merchants over the price of her goods and the price of theirs. While she did not leave accounts of her own, her daughters' diaries suggest that she was paid in store credit, which she used at her discretion to buy goods for herself, her daughters, and the household. Local merchants had no reason to question Jane Cooley's ability to trade when she walked into their stores. It was just the way it was: they accepted her dealings as a matter of course.[22]

Others regularly sold to women they did not know, employing what can only be called an extremely generous definition of "necessities." Such was the experience of one North Carolina woman on an out-of-state shopping expedition. "Three days in Paris," she gushed, "is not to be mentioned in the same breath with the three days we spent in Baltimore." She describes the final day as they were packing up their bags as "a scene for Hogarth," with "all the milliners girls & shoemakers' boys waiting ... with their bills, not a thing packed up." She and her friends purchased all manner of personal apparel on their own, with the storeowners' knowledge that they were from out of town and with the expectation that they would pay before they left. In fact, what this woman described was regular practice, with storeowners selling women textiles and then dispatching clerks to collect payment. Tellingly, merchants were concerned with payment, not with the legal implications if husbands or fathers protested. The sale was what mattered. New England newspapers were filled with advertisements placed by husbands who charged wives with abusing their credit and warned storekeepers that they would no longer be responsible for wives' debts, which usually involved purchases of cloth and clothing. The ads created the impression of profligate women unable to control their spending. But the fault lay with the merchants, whose businesses depended on married women's legal ability to trade in textiles.[23]

In cities, even southern cities, retailers regularly sold cloth and wearing apparel to enslaved people, despite statutes and ordinances that prohibited such trade. So did storekeepers in the rural South, where some merchants even specialized in it, specifically stocking items known to be popular with enslaved people, such as handkerchiefs, shawls, and ready-made waistcoats.[24] The trade rested on the assent of the people legally positioned as owners, who tended to treat clothing as property over which the enslaved maintained control. Enslaved people also expected to keep items they procured or made themselves. These expectations were honored, which explains the cases in which owners filed theft charges on

Figure 1.2 The young woman from North Carolina was making fun of herself in the reference to William Hogarth, an English eighteenth-century engraver and painter, whose satirical style was so well known that it came to be called Hogarthian. *The Inspection* is the third in a six-image series, *Marriage A-la-Mode*, a sendup of upper-class marriages based on money, not love. The six paintings feature a wealthy merchant who essentially sells his daughter to a spendthrift nobleman in need of cash. The superficiality of the whole exercise is represented in the conflation of individual character with material goods. William Hogarth (1697–1794), National Gallery, London/Art Resource, NY.

behalf of the people they enslaved, as was the case with Polly. Enslaved people also took their clothing with them when they were sold or, if they had been hired out, when they moved to another position. In fact, some sales agreements specifically allowed for an enslaved person to collect their clothing before relocating. Slaveowners had a vested interest in enslaved people's clothing: well-dressed slaves were worth more. Perhaps the most chilling illustration is found in the account book of Hector Davis and Company, one of the largest slave dealers in Richmond, Virginia. Running through the ledger are regular payments to seamstresses for new clothes so that those being sold would fetch a higher price at auction.[25]

People without strong claims to rights acquired clothing because they had confidence in their ability to keep it. Enslaved people notably possessed wearing apparel beyond the coarse uniform clothing provided by their enslavers. Many could afford only small items: a bright bandana, a piece of lace, an apron, or a shawl. But others purchased more substantial items as well, such as cloth for a gown, a ready-made coat, or a whole outfit. Minute descriptions of clothing appeared in the advertisements for runaway slaves and servants, local court cases, and merchants' account books. Even the ridicule heaped on enslaved people for their fashion choices is revealing. As a contributor to Georgia's *Southern Cultivator* complained, "The *town* negroes of this State are the b'hoys of the South, sporting their fine Havanas and twirling their fancy canes on the side walks." For readers in the 1850s, even those in in the South, the reference to the flamboyantly attired Bowery boys of New York City would have conjured up additional sartorial imagery beyond canes and wide-brimmed hats: colored pants; long, elaborately draped neckerchiefs; patterned silk vests; and short, tight-fitting jackets that cinched in at the waist.[26]

Confidence in textile ownership was well grounded. Consider the impressive collection of cloth, worth the enormous sum of twenty dollars, claimed by Rosenah Gray, an enslaved woman in New York City. Included were striped satins of black and bright blue, gray silk, and dark calico. These luxury fabrics might seem like an unwise investment for someone who was African American, even if she were free, because they would be so likely to draw suspicion and, perhaps, disciplinary action. But in many circumstances, the legal qualities of textiles could silence such doubts. Gray kept her cloth, even though she was charged with theft. So did Amy Hazard, a free Black woman who was accused of stealing a gown made of tamboured muslin, fabric that was even more freighted with meaning than Gray's silks and satins. Plain muslin was associated with the elite, not just because it had the diaphanous quality essential to the fashionable styles of the time (and so well known to devotees of Jane Austen costume dramas) but also because it was difficult to keep clean. Tambouring, an all-over design accomplished by a technique similar to embroidery, added to the fabric's value. Yet Hazard, who lived in a rented room in the Bowery, managed to convince the New York City Mayor's Court that the dress was hers.[27]

In cities, local officials regularly took complaints of stolen textiles from African Americans without bothering with their legal status, even though it should have made all the difference. According to state laws, enslaved people could not prosecute a case in their own names, while people legally classified as "free blacks" could. But on the ground, legal status could be murky. In New York, the terms of gradual emancipation put African Americans in an ambiguous position somewhere between slavery and freedom through the first decades of the nineteenth century. Some nominally free people lived as slaves, subject to those who kept them in bondage. Some people who were still enslaved or indentured lived as free people because they had been released from service or allowed to live on their own in exchange for a portion of their wages. Still others had escaped bondage in other states. Who was enslaved? It could be difficult, even impossible to tell.[28]

Faced with this situation, New York City officials elevated the principles associated with textiles over the legal restrictions of slavery. Such cases occurred regularly because clothing was the property Black New Yorkers were most likely to possess and most likely to have stolen from them. Such was the experience of Silvan, an enslaved man who filed charges in 1802 when his three shirts, four handkerchiefs, and one waistcoat were taken. In his case, as in so many others, New York City officials named the enslaved person as the complainant and property owner. Given the laws relating to slavery, that made no sense. But it was the best available option, given circumstances on the ground and the legal principles associated with textiles.[29]

The Mayor's Court in Richmond did the same in the 1830s. Although slavery was still in full force in Virginia, there were parallels to the situation in New York. Richmond had a mixed population of African Americans: free Blacks, people enslaved to white residents in the city, and people enslaved to white people who lived elsewhere but had been hired out. The practice of hiring out, in particular, confused questions of legal status. By the 1830s, it had become embedded in the economy of the upper South, where white people invested in enslaved people not to labor directly for them but to produce a steady income by hiring them out to others. While laws prevented white masters from allowing enslaved people to hire their own time, enforcement was lax. Hirers did not always bother to keep tabs on their workers as long as they showed up. As a result, many enslaved African Americans in the upper South lived as nominally free people, particularly in cities like Richmond. The implications are evident in the Mayor's Court, where officials clearly struggled to determine the legal status of the African Americans who appeared before them. Sometimes they listed masters who lived in outlying counties. Sometimes they supplied the name of the hirer. Sometimes the only information they recorded for either master or employer was a place of residence. But those relationships did not shape the handling of African Americans' complaints. Even though officials attempted to identify masters, they did not bother to name them as complainants or attribute the stolen property to them. They simply cut to the chase. The entry noting a complaint by Rosetta, "a slave of Nathanial Crenshaw," against Bob, an enslaved man whose master was unnamed, "for breaking into her house & stealing a pr. of shoes," was typical. Like officials in New York, those in Richmond upheld legal claims to textiles.[30]

Those legal principles shaped married women's relationship to law as well. While Tapping Reeve's affirmation of married women's claims to clothing was not backed up by other treatise writers, legal officials scrupulously followed them nonetheless. In the new republic, it was assumed married women simply kept such items, no questions asked. In states that followed British common law, inventories of married men's estates rarely included their widows' clothing. The practices of continental law offered more commentary, providing insight into the underlying logic. Such was the case with a New Orleans notary responsible for inventorying the estate of Pierre St. Pé. The notary went through the deceased's house room by room, methodically writing down every piece of property that was part of his estate. Most of the property was, since there had been no marriage contract that kept specific items in the widow's name. But the notary stopped short in his perusal of one particular armoire, indicating that "the other effects" were "the wearing apparel of the widow." So he closed the armoire door and moved on.[31]

Although Tapping Reeve included bedding along with clothing in the category of paraphernalia, that was more ambiguous in practice. The term "bedding" was so expansive as to be meaningless. It could include the mattress, pillows, sheets, blankets, and quilts, as well as bed curtains for one bed or for all the beds in the house. Those items were usually the costliest goods in estate inventories, outstripping the value of furniture, china, and even silver. The stakes were high. Could married women claim *all* the household's bedding? If so, that gave them claims to the most valuable moveable property in the estate. Or was it just the textiles associated with the marital bed? Or just the textiles they had brought into the marriage and made afterward?[32]

Sheets, blankets, and other bedding were more liable to slip out of the hands of free married women and enslaved people, because their connection to particular people was less strong than wearing apparel. The treatise literature captured those ambiguities. Where Tapping Reeve included bedding among the property that married women could control, other writers limited them to just clothing and jewelry. The fact that bed linens, blankets, and quilts made their way into estate inventories at all underscores the problem: while they were associated with wives, legal officials still attributed these items to husbands. It is likely that some of the household's bedding remained in the widows' hands and therefore never made it into estate inventories. But it is impossible to know. In estate sales, widows also purchased bedding at rock-bottom prices, suggesting that executors' categorization of it as the husbands' property did not negate other legal practices that attached them to wives. But, again, it is impossible to know.[33] Similarly, in divorce cases local officials sometimes granted domestic property to wives, including bedding and other items they had brought into the marriage as part of their trousseaus. But that was not always the case. Perhaps there was no mention because there was no need: women just assumed possession. That was certainly the case in some separations adjudicated in church courts, where women took property they considered their own despite their husbands' protestations. Still, some women had to bargain to maintain control. Peggy Long charged her husband with domestic violence, which was part of an effort to leave her husband. The magistrate who issued the warrant for Long's husband offered him a deal: if he "would give [Polly] up some bed[ding] & other furniture which she claimed, then he would abandon the warrant and consider the matter settled."[34]

The legal qualities of textiles carried over to the tools required to produce them. Those legalities were evident in Orange County, North Carolina, a region of relatively small, diversified farms, which ramped up textile production in the late eighteenth century. In the estates inventoried between the 1780s and 1840s, only a few households did not have equipment to produce cloth, such spinning wheels, looms, cards (to process wool and cotton), hackles (for process flax for linen), and reels (on which spun thread was wound). Even when such items were listed as the husband's property, widows maintained possession. Cards, spinning wheels, reels, and looms ended up back in their hands at estate sales, often at reduced prices, just like bedding. Either no one else bid or the goods were never auctioned off: everyone knew the widow needed those means of support.[35] These presumptions explain the appearance of cards, spinning wheels, and looms in the inventory of Jane Cooley's husband, a farmer and watchmaker. No matter what the legal form said, the property was hers, and everyone knew it. Cooley kept up her business, employing those tools long after her husband's death. The smaller but not necessarily inexpensive tools for clothing production, such as needles, and pins, usually did not make it into the inventories at all. Widows simply kept them.[36]

Law made all the difference in securing property. The lack of rights did not keep enslaved people or others of nominal legal standing from amassing property other than textiles. Some married women possessed silver and china, pots and pans, furniture, tools, livestock, houses, and even land. So did enslaved people, although their holdings were smaller and less varied. But when claims to those forms of property were contested, neither married women nor enslaved people could depend on the law to support them. Possession of other property was questionable, even for women who were not married and African Americans who were not enslaved. When a woman presented a bank note at a local store, she might be suspected of passing counterfeit bills. When people who were poor or Black wore a gold watch or locket, they might be charged with theft. But textiles were different. Their legal qualities solidified a relationship that secured ownership in law—if, of course, it could be proved.[37]

That relationship explains the outcome of a convoluted South Carolina case involving a free Black man, Wyatt Harris, accused of stealing an expensive overcoat from a white man. Harris was able to prove a lengthy chain of custody through witnesses: he bought the overcoat from Daniel, an enslaved man, who bought it from Douglas, also enslaved, who got it from the man who enslaved him. Daniel paid for the coat with a fiddle; Harris paid for it with pantaloons and a pair of shoes. Then Harris sold it to another man for ten dollars, in a public transaction with witnesses. It was wise of Harris to conduct the sale in public, given that the amount was the equivalent of over two hundred dollars today. Thomas Woodruff, the white man who accused Harris of theft, had no chance. Not only was he a well-known wastrel, but he also faced a wealth of evidence against him, based on the assumption that everyone could own and trade clothing. Harris was acquitted.[38]

At the same time, the testimony in Harris's case exposed inconsistencies in Daniel's claims to the coat, which resulted in a theft case against him. Daniel was ultimately convicted, not because he possessed such a fine coat but because he kept waffling as to how it came into his possession. Daniel testified that he had purchased the coat from Douglas. But he initially said that he had obtained it from his own master. Telling in this regard is an exchange between Daniel and a white man who had encountered him with the coat before it was sold to Harris. Daniel's possession of it gave this man pause, but only because "it was a strange coat to him." So he asked Daniel "who he stoled the coat from." The question carried double meanings, depending on the tone and context in which it was asked. If this interchange had been between equals, he could have been asking how Daniel came by this coat with the kind of dry humor still common in the South. But this was a white man challenging and interrogating an enslaved man. So Daniel responded with yet another origin story: "He got it from Sam," who "got it from his master Robin." That response satisfied the questioner, who let it go at the time. The whole matter would have ended there had Daniel not been caught out while testifying for Wyatt Harris. Even so, Daniel's conviction did nothing to change the acquittal of Harris, who kept his coat.[39]

How did that happen? How could the legalities of textiles override the laws of coverture and slavery, as expressed in other laws spelled out in treatises, passed by state legislatures, and also upheld in local, state, and federal courts? While that situation seems impossible today, it made complete sense in the economic and legal context of new republic. Political independence from Britain did nothing to alter North Americans' dependence on the economy of textiles and the deeply rooted legal principles and practices that accompanied it. Those elements of life in North America persisted through the upheaval of war and political reorganization. Transferred to the colonies, the legal principles associated with textiles persisted within the new United States, because of the structures of federalism, as the next chapter shows. The overlapping jurisdictions of the federal system not only honored the longstanding personal connection between people and their textiles but also legally embedded that relationship within the public order.

2

Roger Taney's Long Underwear

Federalism

To be clear: the long underwear in question did not actually belong to Chief Justice Roger Taney, although like most men in the 1840s he probably had a pair or two, what with heating being what it was. This long underwear came to the attention of Taney in his position as judge of the US Circuit Court of the Southern District of New York in a case that hinged on whether a packet of imported undergarments should be categorized as ready-to-wear or hosiery. The collector of customs in New York City insisted that they were ready-to-wear, which carried a duty of 50 percent. The importer disagreed, claiming that long underwear had always been made and traded as hosiery, which had a duty of 25 percent.[1]

The issues required careful attention to detail. "Samples of the said shirts and drawers" were produced, exhibited, and carefully scrutinized. Unfortunately, the material evidence refused to yield a definitive answer. While the items "were finished and completed and ready for wearing," they had been produced on the kind of knitting frame also used to produce hosiery. So Taney called for further witnesses: local retailers, wholesalers, and importers as well as customs officials, who opined on the handling of long underwear in the markets, and hence in law. The evidence was again inconclusive, despite the custom collector's lengthy disquisition on the legal treatment of long underwear in federal law and the particularly difficult case of "Guernsey Frocks," "which were imported as they came from the loom." That statement that might seem unrelated to law, but the collector's point was entirely legal: the comptroller of the treasury had rated even Guernsey frocks as ready-made clothing and charged the 50 percent duty accordingly. Taney, however, refused to take the collector's side. Instead, he reverted to the merchants' treatment of long underwear. As he instructed the jury members, if they found that "commercial men, dealers, and traders therein" used "the name and denomination of Hosiery" for long underwear, then it did not matter how customs officials had interpreted federal law. They should find that long underwear was hosiery. And they did.[2]

We find Roger Taney puzzling over the legal classification of long underwear because the justices of the US Supreme Court spent much of their time serving as judges in the federal district courts in the first half of the nineteenth century. Unlike the lofty matters involving rights and citizenship heard in the US Supreme Court, the business of the district courts involved matters of a more material nature. The incompatibility is such that a casual observer would be forgiven for missing the fact that the judge in the long underwear case was the same Roger Taney known for his decisions in *Dred Scott v. Sandford* (which denied US citizenship to all people of African descent) and *In re Merryman* (in which Taney defended individual rights against President Abraham Lincoln's assertion of war powers). In fact, Taney spent a great deal of his career listening to the retailers, wholesalers, and importers of lower Manhattan talk about customs, in both senses of the term: the duties that the federal government imposed and formed its primary income stream and also the social practices that guided the trade of goods, particularly textiles, which ranked among the country's chief imports.[3]

In New York, Taney's work bore a striking resemblance to that of the South Carolina magistrate who decided the case involving Polly, the enslaved woman whose handspun thread had been stolen. Both officials accounted for the legal principles of textiles that were connected to social practice in particular communities. They also acknowledged the power of those legal principles to override other bodies of law generated at the state and federal levels. If anything, the legal principles associated with textiles moved across national borders more easily than the material goods themselves, which were encumbered by duties and trade restrictions. But even as these legal principles traveled widely, they took specific form in the different experiences of people's daily lives. Once landed, they tended to dig in and stay put, outlasting the fabrics to which they were attached. By the time of the Revolution, those legal principles had become the customs that made up the public order that legal officials were supposed to protect. Given their position in the legal landscape, the new republic's officials had no choice but to deal with them, even when they conflicted with other bodies of law.

This chapter is not so much about the legal principles of textiles as it is about the legal institutions in which they lodged and flourished. Following textiles, rather than the development of new institutions at the state and federal level, it reveals a layered federal system with many moving parts. New governing institutions at the state and federal level were built atop existing practices and principles that persisted from the colonial era and continued to shape law and governance after the Revolution. Legal authority remained widely dispersed among distinct institutional jurisdictions, with the federal government, states, counties, and municipalities all tending to their domains, sometimes in coordination, but usually not. Different bodies of law moved across those jurisdictions, where they operated simultaneously in different parts of the federal system and occasionally merged. In this context, law was not confined to statehouses and courthouses. Nor was it the exclusive province of elected officials and legal professionals. It also rested in the social practices of ordinary people, be they jobbers in lower Manhattan or enslaved people in the South Carolina upcountry, who all expected to have a say in translating their customs into law. The resulting practices sustained the legal principles attached to textiles and their place within the public order in a federal system that was not neatly ordered or easily controlled by its elite leaders.[4]

The legal principles associated with textiles settled into North America long before the founding of the new republic, following paths that predated the emergence of modern states. The notion that states could claim sovereignty within certain geographic bounds developed slowly over time. Early modern states exercised more power in some places than others. They also defined it more in terms of water than land, with state power centered in ports and extending along waterways inland. The further away from the water that carried representatives of state authority in and out, the lighter the presence of the state. Corporations—which included business enterprises, municipalities, and voluntary organizations—retained considerable autonomy from the states in which they were located. As a result, the territorial borders of early modern states did not correspond with strong jurisdictional boundaries. Instead, overlapping legal regimes connected to different governing authorities operated alongside one another in the same place.[5]

Similar dynamics existed within nation-states as well. The legal order of early modern England, for instance, consisted of a patchwork of jurisdictions associated with different governing bodies, all operating simultaneously and handling similar issues: estates, municipalities, corporations, the military, Parliament, the church, and the king. Authority was dispersed rather than centralized. The governing bodies in these venues did not coordinate their efforts to create an integrated system of justice in the modern sense. They determined which disputes they would adjudicate on a case-by-case basis, using bodies of law developed within their own jurisdictions. People picked their legal venues based on their calculations of which official would be most sympathetic and which body of law would be most beneficial to their causes.[6]

The North American colonies were no different. As historian Stanley Katz has described it, the legal system in early America was "a complex, pluralistic, asymmetrical, gendered, and multicultural set of systems—messy systems, if indeed the term 'system' can be applied . . . at all." One of the most dramatic examples is South Carolina, where the slaveholding elite in the low country saw the colonial government as a body that addressed its own needs and interests, not those of the colony generally. Colonial government, in other words, was more like local government. These planters apportioned representation to the colonial legislature so as to exclude other parts of the colony and located the colonial court in Charleston, which was convenient for them but inaccessible to everyone else. The colonial government belonged to the community of low-country slaveholders, who felt no obligation to share it with others just because they happened to live within the same colony. They could get their own government, if they wanted one.[7]

All that messiness—to continue with Katz's term—persisted after the Revolution and became a defining feature of the new republic's federal system and people's expectations of how that governing system should work. The Articles of Confederation created "the United States of America" but located sovereignty within the states, which retained "the sole and exclusive Regulation and Government of its internal police." That term, "internal police," referred to an open-ended grant of authority, which covered virtually any issue that touched on the public order, including most criminal offenses, the provision of poor relief and other forms of social welfare, and the regulation of public health, markets, and morals. Those powers had long been rooted at the local level, so their removal to the states marked an important innovation. But even as Revolutionary-era state constitutions and the US Constitution affirmed states' authority over the internal police on paper, local control continued in practice. Conceptions of police power remained exceptionally broad as well as decidedly local, empowering authorities at both the county and municipal levels. States generally kept that system in place for most of the period before the Civil War. While the US Constitution did elevate the federal government as a sovereign authority in certain arenas, it did not alter the situation otherwise. On paper, the division of authority was clear, with the federal government handling certain issues, the states holding authority over matters relating to the public welfare, and local governments administering state policies. In practice, however, this system operated just like the overlapping jurisdictions of the colonial era: a less distant, although considerably weakened central government, states that theoretically had more powers over the public good than the colonies they replaced, and local governments that still exercised expansive authority, particularly in matters involving public order.[8]

In this context, states and even the federal government shared legal authority with each other and with counties and municipalities. At the same time, they also dealt with principles created through customs that had become part of the public order. Given their basis in custom, those principles were inseparable from the people involved, which explains both Roger Taney's long underwear case and the case of Polly's thread. Taney interpolated the customary, local handling of textiles into his reading of federal law, giving more weight to the practices of merchants than to the legal arguments of federal customs officials. Similarly, the South Carolina magistrate who tried Polly's case followed both state law and the legal principles attached to textiles as articulated by enslaved people. When he filled out the forms, he listed the man legally identified as Polly's master as the complainant and attributed the stolen thread to him, following state law that denied enslaved people the rights to own property or to pursue cases in their own names. But he then tried the case as theft, an offense against the public order, in which the legal qualities of textiles and the experiences of the enslaved people determined the outcome. Ultimately, he returned the thread to Polly, overriding state law that denied her property rights.[9]

A similar orientation toward law shaped other matters as well. People approached governing venues with the expectation that they would have a direct voice in the formulation of law and policy, particularly on matters involving the public order. Paying little heed to the jurisdictional differences between localities, states, and the federal government, they insisted that government, at all levels, should deal with their problems. Judge John Faucheraud Grimké, the father of the famed abolitionists and women's rights activists Sarah and Angelina, followed the same logic as Roger Taney and Polly's magistrate in his charge to a Charleston grand jury in 1789. After going over grand jurors' various duties, which included careful attention to the actual evidence and the need to set aside the partisan divides, Grimké encouraged jury members to review and revise the 1740 statute on slavery,

Figure 2.1 This 1840s street scene depicts New York's Custom House, where trials in the US Circuit Court of the Southern District of New York were held, suggesting the extent to which even federal courts were rooted in specific localities, particularly when it came to textiles. Chief Justice Roger Taney listened to testimony from those who worked outside the doors of the courthouse where he worked. The building, with its austere façade, separates those legal proceedings from the people whose work and experiences were central in making the legal principles associated with textiles and in participating in the practices that upheld them. But they were just outside, and often inside as well. *Views in New York* by Robert Kerr, architect. No. 1, *The Custom House, Wall Street viewed from Broad Street*, 1845. Library of Congress Prints and Photographs Division, Washington, DC.

which he clearly thought too harsh. "Give it an attentive perusal," he directed, and alter "any defects in the policy of it." Grimké presided over a legal order where it was possible for a judge to tell a local grand jury to ignore or revise a statute if they saw fit.[10]

Grimké's charge directed jurors to a particular issue, namely, slavery, which they might have bypassed otherwise. The rest of his invitation was entirely in keeping with accepted practice: grand jurors in South Carolina did not shy away from expressing themselves, as their presentments (statements about problems that required attention) to the legislature throughout the period between the Revolution and the Civil War suggest. Skipping across jurisdictional boundaries, jurors mingled statements on international affairs and national issues with updates on assaults, bastardy, and apprenticeship in their own backyards. As they saw it, all these issues lay within their purview because they mattered to the people in the places that grand juries represented. Even as jurors laid these matters at the feet of their state's government, as if its powers were such that it could alter the course of foreign wars, their appeals did not necessarily imply that the state's authority was superior to that of other jurisdictions. Rather, these jury presentments reflected widely held assumptions that government at all levels should be an active presence in people's lives and would involve itself in maintaining the public order. People expected whatever level of government could do something to act.[11]

That vision was embedded within many states' Revolutionary-era constitutions. Perhaps the most radical institutional innovation in state constitutions of this era lay in the attribution of sovereignty and authority over the internal police to "the people" generally, not just those who could claim the vote, rights, or even citizenship. Not all states went this route. Neither South Carolina's first Revolutionary-era constitution nor subsequent revisions made mention of the people, their rights, or their relationship to government. That was no oversight. Lawmakers saw the state government in the same limited terms as the colonial government. Apart from moments of crisis, state government dealt with the concerns of those white men with property and the full array of rights who lived near Charleston—a point they made abundantly clear by setting property requirements for suffrage so high that only about 10 percent of the white male population qualified. New York's constitution staked out a middle ground, basing sovereignty in the people but providing no ongoing role for them in the governing process. Some states went further, establishing a direct relationship between the people and the practice of governance. Pennsylvania's Revolutionary-era constitution gave "the people ... the sole, exclusive and inherent right of governing and regulating the internal police." So did Maryland, North Carolina, and Vermont.[12]

Accessibility did not extend in equal measure to all areas of government. People's constitutional authority over the internal police assumed a governing order composed of multiple layers. While access to some of the state and federal layers required the vote, the possession of other rights, or the ability to travel, access to others at the county and municipal levels did not. In fact, the restrictions at the state and federal levels explain why so many people in the new republic resisted efforts to remove governing authority from local jurisdictions. The operation of federalism placed considerable discretion over such matters with counties and municipalities, particularly local courts, which were more accessible to a wider range of people than government at the state or federal levels.[13]

State constitutions' emphasis on rights also presumed a layered governing order. Many Revolutionary-era constitutions began with direct references to the Declaration of Independence. The Pennsylvania state constitution, for example, declared that "all men are born equally free and independent, and have certain natural, inherent, and inalienable rights, amongst which are, the enjoying and defending life and liberty, acquiring, possessing, and protecting property, and pursuing and obtaining happiness and safety." State constitutions also established an array of individual rights, including freedom of religion, speech, and the press. In some cases, they even made state government responsible to a broader segment of the population through an expansion of suffrage. For example, the Massachusetts Supreme Judicial Court found slavery incompatible with the rights enshrined in its state's constitution in a series of cases in the 1780s. But none of these constitutions addressed the obvious fact that the vast majority of the population was constrained within status relationships—as a wife, a child, a servant, or a slave—which limited their access to rights and property, the issues with which state governments were primarily concerned. More than that, the responsibility for regulating relationships of domestic dependency did not lie with states. Although state legislatures passed laws that affected such relationships, household heads held extensive authority and local courts exercised oversight, to the extent that oversight was exercised at all.[14]

Even so, expectations of government's responsibility to the people were such that most state constitutions as well as the US Constitution provided access through routes other than civil and political rights, namely, through the petitioning process. Petitioning was a longstanding, formalized practice that gave people without rights or the vote access parts of government that were otherwise inaccessible. State legislatures and the US Congress had set procedures for responding to petitions, which obligated lawmakers to act on such claims, even if they did nothing more than acknowledge receipt. But people petitioned because petitioning got results. Individuals obtained redress for specific wrongs and shaped political debate on a wide range of issues. Petitions even resulted in substantive change, including policies involving the rights of free Blacks and women.[15]

These layered structures of authority persisted, even as Revolutionary idealism faded and states that had rooted police powers in "the people" began to dial back that commitment. Over time, references to "the people" said less about their actual role in governance and more about their sovereignty as an abstract principle. The preamble of Pennsylvania's revised constitution of 1790, for instance, still based governing authority in the people: "We, the people of the commonwealth of Pennsylvania, ordain and establish this constitution for its government." But the constitution jettisoned the language that gave the people "the right of governing and regulating the internal police." In Pennsylvania and other states, lawmakers also worked to subordinate local jurisdictions to state government. In practice, however, considerable governing authority was still held by venues to which access was not determined by individual rights or the vote, although that began to change in the 1830s. In fact, the idea that state laws over which they had little control would take precedence over local jurisdictions struck many Americans as problematic, if not downright wrong. In North Carolina, one group of petitioners gently reminded their governor of the state's limited authority in their request for the pardon of a man convicted of trading with slaves. "In this section of the state," they wrote, "there seems not to exist the same necessity for enforcing the rigid execution of this act of Assembly as in other parts." They did things differently where they lived. Surely the governor would acknowledge that.[16]

While it is tempting to dismiss these petitioners as bunch of ignorant bumpkins, they articulated deeply rooted assumptions about the relationship between people and law as well as the legal valence of social practice in all areas of government. The merchants whose customs disputes took up so much of the federal judiciary's time assumed that local practice carried legal authority in the realm of federal law. Deeply in debt at the end of the Revolution, the federal government depended on the revenue from customs duties, collected at every major port in the country. Merchants were willing to recognize the new government's authority and pay the duties it imposed, just as they had under British control and in the other countries where they bought and sold goods. In return, they expected the federal government to recognize longstanding practices associated with the collection of customs, which predated the new republic. Creative interpretations had been crafted, exceptions had been made, and eyes had been averted so often that the results had acquired legal standing, which customs collectors violated at their peril. Given that context, the new republic's officials had little incentive to follow a strict reading of customs law. Knowing the impossibility of enforcement at far-flung ports, they settled for some revenue rather than none at all. While customs law had become more standardized by 1840, when Taney heard the long underwear case, federal officials still deferred to local practice as laid out by merchants and manufactures who plied the textile trade in lower Manhattan. What looked like a uniform set of federal standards captured neither the law's content nor its operation.[17]

That same situation held true for state law. In the decades following the Revolution, it was entirely possible that a statute—even one worded in universal terms—was intended to apply only in a specific place or to specific individuals. The idea that the primary business of state legislatures was to pass laws that applied to *all* the state's residents was not institutionalized until the 1830s and 1840s. Until then, private bills, which responded to the requests of particular counties, groups, or individuals, far outweighed general legislation, even that related to property. When state legislatures passed general laws relating to the public interest, local jurisdictions retained considerable discretion over their interpretation. State legislatures in the Midwest, for instance, passed statutes restricting these people's movement and imposing registration requirements. But enforcement was left to localities, which meant that some free blacks struggled under the laws' weight, while others lived without much sense of them at all.[18]

Messiness applied to the content of the law as well as its institutional structure, as the lack of uniformity in state and federal law suggests. The new republic's governing bodies accommodated various bodies of law inherited from the colonial past. Military authorities maintained their own legal jurisdictions, and the remnants of church law held on despite disestablishment—which meant that no denomination had a place within the government, as the Church of England once had in some colonies. Many states set up separate courts to deal with common law and equity, which dealt with similar kinds of issues using entirely different principles and procedures. Within common law, all states observed the distinction between private (civil) and public (criminal) matters. Private law dealt primarily with property, including disputes over it and its sale and exchange through wills, contracts, notes, and other negotiable instruments. Commercial and mercantile law overlapped with private law, although dealing with the particular issues facing merchants who worked across the jurisdictional lines of states and nations. Unlike private matters, which were decided in terms of the rights of those involved, public matters involved the interests of the entire community, even people who were not directly implicated in the dispute. This area of law was closely aligned with internal police powers and included crimes as well as a broad, open-ended range of issues that affected the public order.[19]

While some bodies of law stayed put within specific jurisdictions, others appeared in a variety of venues. Military law, for instance, applied within military courts. But private and public law moved across jurisdictions. Property matters, the stuff of private law, were tried in local, state, and federal courts, as were public matters, although the specific depended on the jurisdiction. While states and the federal government worked from the same body of principles, they generated their own specific rules. In public law in particular, the discretion exercised by localities resulted in wide variations in practice. All that mattered when it came to textiles.

The legal qualities of textiles lodged themselves in both private and public law. But people without the full range of rights struggled with civil suits in private law, which dealt with disputes over all kinds of property, including textiles. States and the federal government policed the boundaries of private law, generating page after page of written rules that kept people without rights on the outside. Of course, rules still required interpretation, no matter how numerous. Married women with shops and other businesses did sue in civil court to recover debts in the port cities of Charleston, South Carolina, and Newport, Rhode Island. But their cases went forward under their husbands' names. Similarly, local officials in Mississippi and Louisiana took considerable license in civil suits, even accepting cases from enslaved people, who lacked the necessary legal status to own property or prosecute a case. But those moments were always exceptions. People without strong claims to rights could never count on private law to protect their property claims in their own names. In theory, free black men and unmarried free women of all races could operate in this area of law. In practice, however, the other social, economic, and legal inequalities that circumscribed these people's lives often made it impossible for them to claim and use rights that were theoretically their due. By contrast, the merchants who appeared as witnesses in the long underwear case could more easily bend private law to advance property claims based in the legal principles of textiles.[20]

The implications are evident in the experience of John Capus and his wife, who ran up a bill for lodging in Richmond, Virginia, in the 1780s. Although they were married, their landlord kept separate accounts for the work that they did in payment of their bill, a common practice in this period. He submitted both in a debt dispute: one with John's name, which indicates he may have been an itinerant painter, and one for Mrs. John Capus, with credits for washing, mending, and sewing, labor associated with the maintenance and production of textiles. The conventions of debt filings in civil law, however, erased the distinction that was so clear in the documentation and, doubtless, in the lives of Capuses and their landlord. Following the rules of coverture, Mrs. Capus's property was lumped together with that of her husband, who was the named defendant, which also positioned him as the property owner in civil law. Even the legal qualities of textiles could not override the dictates of coverture in this context.[21]

The emphasis on rights added to private law's rigidity. In the area of private law at this time, rights referred to a narrow band of claims: the rights that enabled the ownership and exchange of property and the rights—often referred to as procedural rights—necessary to access the courts in order to defend those property rights. This area of law did not involve the concerns of the individuals who brought their problems for adjudication, let alone larger matters involving the public order. The point was to uphold the abstract principles that rights represented, not a just outcome as established by the facts of the case or as envisioned by others affected by the conflict.[22]

Public law was far more accommodating for people without rights, which made it easier for them to bring claims to textiles. In this body of law, the point was the maintenance of the public order, not the rights of individuals. In the terminology of the time, public law kept "the peace"—a well-established concept in Anglo-American law that expressed the ideal order of the metaphorical public body, subordinating everyone within a hierarchical system and elevating its collective interests over those of any given individual. It was supposed to keep everyone and everything in their appropriate places, as defined by the rigid inequalities of the early nineteenth century. As such, keeping the peace necessarily involved liberal applications of police power, with the intent of punishing those who challenged the existing order. Yet this body of law necessarily incorporated those without rights into its basic workings because they were part of the public order: even as it maintained the subordination of free white women, enslaved people, free people of color, immigrants, and the poor, it also

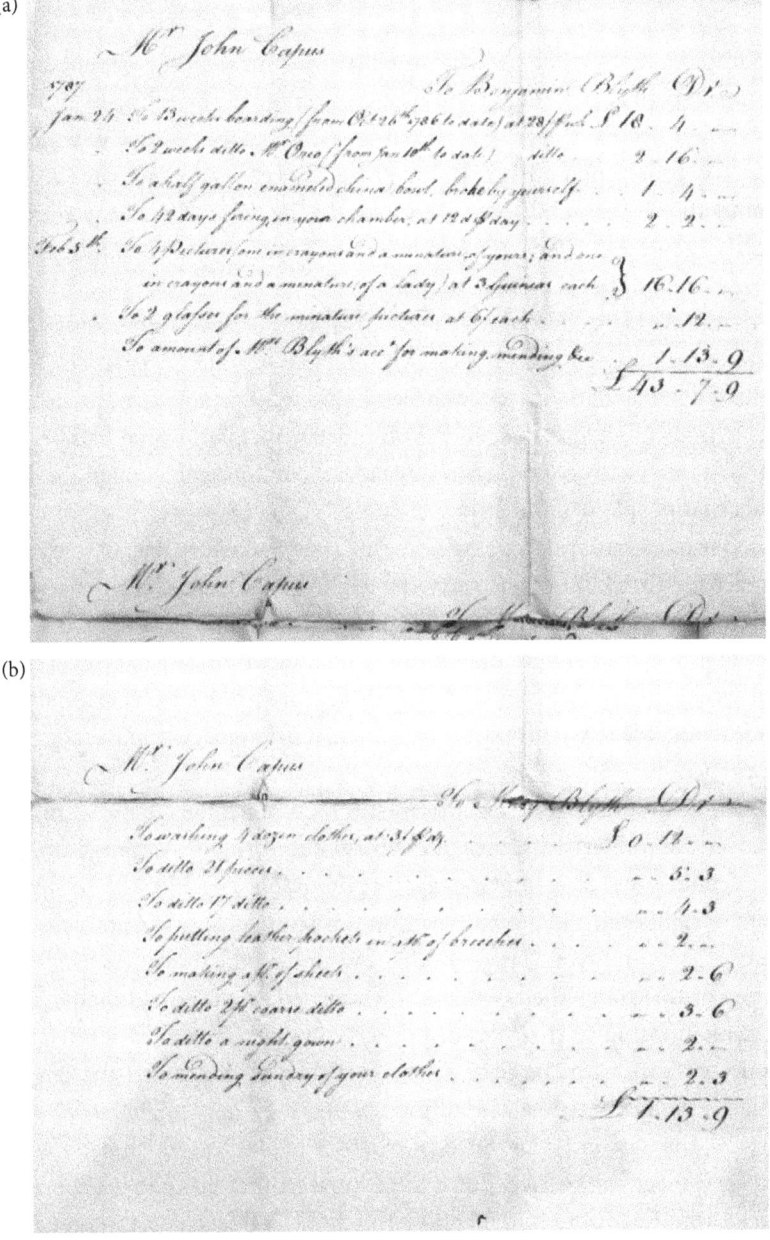

Figure 2.2 In *Blythe v. Capus*, one side of the disputed bill shows what was owed to Mr. John Capus and the other side shows what was owed to Mrs. John Capus, who kept her accounts in their joint business separately from those of her husband, as was common at the time. While private law turned her labor and what she produced into the property of her husband, customary practice gave married women more scope to claim certain kinds of labor and property as her own. Richmond City, Hustings Court, Suit Papers, Ended Causes, folder May 1787 no. 3, box 8, May 1787, Library of Virginia.

accommodated—in fact, relied on—the information they supplied about community disorder. Public law also allowed for the handling of situations that might not have had legal standing in other areas of law. Officials, for instance, prosecuted husbands, fathers, and masters for excessive violence against their wives, children, and slaves. In the logic of public law, the authority granted to heads of household was not absolute but contingent on the maintenance of the social order.[23]

That same logic allowed for the recognition of claims to textiles by those without property rights. Public law protected established practices, which generally included the practices based in the legal principles of textiles. The textile trade at all levels depended on those principles, which had been integrated into local economies in ways that were impossible to ignore. It was a fact that people without strong claims to rights or property not only possessed textiles but also exchanged them. They had every reason to demand respect for that kind of property ownership, and local officials had every reason to grant it. To do so, officials simply labeled the matter as theft and moved it into the realm of public law, which was supposed to protect things that were entirely ordinary and part of accepted practice. That legal form made it possible to put property back where it belonged, without recognizing property rights.[24]

Even this more flexible legal form still required some creative stretching to cover the property disputes of people without rights. Although criminal cases could proceed as offenses against the public, people without the full range of rights still had difficulty within this realm of law. The problem lay in the overlap with private law—another example of the messiness of the legal system at this time. Theft, while always treated as a criminal matter, had a close relationship to the rules of property in civil law, which limited ownership to those with the necessary rights. How could married women or enslaved people initiate a case of theft, when they were unable to own property?[25] The answer lay in the legal qualities of textiles, which had been established through practice. But it took some maneuvering to get there. The official who heard the initial complaint about Polly's stolen thread considered the situation serious enough to constitute a threat to the public order. But he had to have a complainant and an offense. So he leaned on the man legally positioned as Polly's master, listing him as the complainant and identifying the property as his. Once he did that, establishing the offense as a public matter, the state of South Carolina figured as the wronged party, a framing evident in the titling of the case: *State v. Brummer*.[26]

Similarly, another South Carolina slaveholder made a complaint on behalf of "his Negro man James," whose "chest was broke open ... and the following articles taken out, one pear of velvet pantaloons, one pear of suspenders, one pear of store socks and shavenbox." Once the complaint and offense were recorded, the case became *State v. Cain, Meshack, and Charles*. While the names of the men legally identified as James's and Polly's masters were needed for the proceedings to move forward as thefts of enslaved people's property, the involvement of these men often ended there. Not all masters named as complainants s appeared as witnesses and some may not even have been present at the proceedings. Once the complaint was accepted, it became an offense against the public order, not one against the master or even the enslaved person whose property had been taken. Magistrates then set about putting lost property back where it belonged.[27]

While public law subordinated the enslaved people's interests to the public interest, it made their problems legally visible and actionable by removing them from their bodies (which lacked the rights necessary for legal action) and making them part of the public body (which had the legal authority to act). In civil matters, the question of whether someone could own property had to be answered before going forward. Criminal law could dispense with that question and determine which person could claim the property and why. That was what these South Carolina magistrates did, treating the property as the possession of the enslaved people, not of the men legally positioned as masters. The forum to which local officials directed these cases underscored the point. They were tried in the Court of Magistrates and Freeholders, the court that the state set up to handle offenses involving enslaved people and free people of color, rather than courts that handled matters involving white people. Ultimately, the magistrate awarded the thread to Polly not because he recognized her property rights but because he determined that the thread belonged with her. Similarly, James's pants, which had been recovered, went back to him because that was where they belonged. The public interest was best served with these outcomes, according to the South Carolina magistrates who tried these particular cases.[28]

Court officials applied the same logic to married women's claims to textiles. Typical is the case filed by Sarah Allingham to reclaim her sheet in the New York City Mayor's Court. Officials followed the rules of coverture as practiced in both civil and criminal law throughout the state at the time, identifying the complainant as the woman's husband rather than Sarah Allingham, who actually made the complaint; attributing ownership of the sheet to him even though she was the one claiming it; and noting the marital status of the women involved, despite the fact that it did not really matter in how the case was handled. After checking the obligatory boxes, officials then set the rules of coverture aside to deal directly with the married women and their disputed sheet within the framework of public law, where the conflict could be handled as an offense against the social order. There is no evidence that husbands were ever anywhere near the court. All that was required was their names, inserted into the appropriate places in the form. The real point was to put the textiles back where they belonged, which theft charges allowed. In so doing, court officials neither suspended nor challenged the rules of coverture. Married women's property rights were not in question, since they had none. Officials simply acknowledged what was in front of them: married women who could possess linens, despite their lack of rights. All that was entirely ordinary and part of accepted practice, which could be protected and adjudicated within the realm of public law.[29]

Social practice regularly entered into private law as well, as the long underwear case indicates. But in that body of law, the customary handling of textiles competed with reams of written rules laid out in statutes, appellate decisions, and treatises. In this sense, the close association of public law with localities was less about the physical places where the cases were tried and more about the bodies of law that determined their outcome. Public law at all levels relied as much on the social practices in particular places and lived experience there as on the written rules memorialized in texts. In fact, local officials handled most of the caseload in public law *and* private law. The vast majority of cases in both bodies of law ended there, with rural magistrates and city officials or in county and municipal courts. Some moved up in the next level of the system, in circuit courts with judges and juries. But they went there only if they met the necessary requirements set by state legislatures: if the debt in civil cases was over a certain amount or if crimes were deemed serious enough to warrant such a trial. Even then, the venue was the same for both civil and criminal cases: court officials simply exchanged their public law hats for their private law hats. The difference was in the legal authority conferred by those hats and the bodies of law they represented. Public law hats allowed local officials more discretion than private law hats, which were festooned with all kinds of written rules. In this area of law, their job was to follow the principles formulated elsewhere in the system. In public law, by contrast, the rules emerged from everyday practices deemed part of the public order.[30]

When it came to textiles, the absence of written documentation did not necessarily mean the absence of law, particularly in the period between the Revolution and the Civil War, when law and the written word were not as tightly tied together as they later became. Colonial legislatures had not bothered to record or archive their work, which meant that no state entered the post-Revolutionary period with a complete collection of its statutes. State legislatures did not exactly strain themselves to rectify that situation. So individuals stepped in to collect statutes and privately publish compilations, which did not actually have official sanction as a record of state law, even though they often passed as such. Written documentation of appellate law was not much better, although that reflected the institutional layers that persisted under federalism. Not all appellate courts were designated as courts of record, with precedent-setting authority over state law. Some heard appeals, gave advice, and then sent the cases back to circuit courts to be retried. Even after appellate courts acquired more power, judges did not always write out their opinions. When they did, states did not always publish them in full. Individuals stepped in here as well, publishing compilations of appellate decisions, sometimes reconstructed after the fact from notes, memory, or inference. But like the privately published statute compilations, these volumes did not constitute an official expression of state law.[31]

The incomplete nature of the documentary record left by states explains the attention given to published legal treatises, such as Blackstone's *Commentaries*. Blackstone wrote beautifully, providing clear, quotable summaries of legal concepts that seem like authoritative expressions of the law. Yet Blackstone, like other treatise writers, sought to give a more definitive shape to the amorphous, conflicting principles that actually defined the legal world at the time. To do that, they mobilized a fictional past to recreate the law as they thought it should be in the present and future, nudging—sometimes shoving—it in particular directions, just as compilers of statutes and appellate decisions did.[32]

Even when legislatures began publishing their statutes and appellate decisions, the written record reflects the areas of law in which state lawmakers and appellate courts tended to concern themselves, namely, private matters involving property. Those texts gave the inaccurate impression that the ownership and exchange of property—particularly real estate, slaves, and other forms of capital and labor—dominated law and the business of the legal system. Actually, they dominated the published record far more than they did all aspects of the law or the workings of the legal system. There was a reason for that. The rules for property law applied in commerce and trade, where such standardization facilitated trade in different places, over long distances.[33]

These published texts also make it seem like the legal restrictions imposed on the vast majority of Americans resulted in their exclusion from the legal system. That view, however, misconstrues the context in which law operated. Not only did the law vary widely over geographic space in the new republic, but it also moved through overlapping jurisdictions and was defined by different bodies of law, the rules of which were not always captured in writing. The legal meanings associated with textiles flourished in these institutional interstices, where a wide range of people used them to build and maintain a different relationship to law and the legal system than the one posited in published sources. In fact, all those people with tenuous claims to rights were marginalized in published texts, not in law.

Textiles had resonance within public law that other forms of property did not. To be sure, the logic of public law allowed people without the full range of rights to make claims to other forms of property: to food, including butter, eggs, poultry, and even livestock; to tools; and to jewelry. Like textiles, all these items had special qualities. Food was necessary for life; tools were necessary for economic support; and jewelry was akin to textiles, closely associated with people and usually classed as paraphernalia. Textiles were not only associated with a person's identity but also necessary for warmth and propriety. Going around naked was frowned upon, so much so that it was liable to end in arrest for disorderly conduct. It was not in the public interest to separate people from these forms of property, even if they did not have rights to it. Necessity acquired legal force, to the point where claims to these kinds of property became part of the public order—at least in some times and places. Textiles, however, were more valuable, more liquid, and more widely circulated than the other forms of property that those without property rights could claim.

That effort was always fraught. Public law was part of a larger federal system that was never about the interests of subordinated people. It favored the interests of men like the retailers, wholesalers, and importers in Roger Taney's long underwear case. Even as South Carolina magistrates acted on the claims of enslaved people like Polly and James, they were actually more concerned with defusing neighborhood conflicts and upholding property rights. Ultimately, the claims of people like Polly resulted in the recognition of their interests and their subordination within the public order as magistrates defined it. Still, the operation of public law was especially useful for those who experienced structural inequality because of their race, gender, economic position, or a combination thereof. This area of law had obvious attraction for those without rights. It also was attractive to those who could claim rights in theory but had difficulty exercising them in practice, given the vast inequalities in American society between the Revolution and the Civil War. For some people, government intervention within the realm of public law was more consistent and reliable than its backing of rights. In public law, it was possible for those on the margins to have an ally in the form of government authority, if only for a fleeting moment.

No wonder those who suffered inequalities leaned so heavily on the legal principles associated with textiles, despite the dangers. Polly's testimony, which affirmed the attachment of textiles to the person who possessed them, was one of many strategies that people used to tap into the legal potential of textiles and obtain recognition of their property with remarkable success. In the decades between the Revolution and the Civil War, people without strong claims to property rights stretched legal principles associated with an individual's clothes to cover a variety of other practices and uses. This legal backdrop opens a wider perspective on the new republic's economy, expanding the stage to include actors who were not elite white male merchants and manufacturers.

3

Mr. Robinson's Fabrics

Merchants

Mr. Robinson, a dry goods merchant in Philadelphia, left little about himself other than a letterbook of outgoing correspondence, dated 1810–25. Mr. Robinson's first name is unknown, and the volume is unattributed, although it contains a small slip of paper, obviously inserted later, identifying it as the "Robinson Letterbook," with no explanation. Perhaps he was not Mr. Robinson at all? What is certain is that the man who kept this letterbook struggled in business, at least when it came to textiles. He imported wools from England, cottons from India, and silks from China. But he had trouble selling those goods, because he could never seem to direct the right cloth to the right places. After receiving shipments at his Philadelphia warehouse, he divided them up and sent them to mercantile firms for sale in various locations, including Rio de Janeiro, Saint Thomas, Savannah, Augusta, and Cincinnati. (Family ties within a far-flung Quaker network explain what might otherwise seem like a completely random assortment of places.) Each packet was accompanied with the hope that the contents would "suit your market." They rarely did. Subsequent correspondence detailed the loss he was willing to sustain to offload unwanted goods or provided instructions to pass them along to another market where someone might buy them. By 1825, the man identified as Robinson admitted defeat and dropped textiles to specialize in tea.[1]

In nineteenth-century America white men like Mr. Robinson occupied the most lucrative and visible occupations in the textile trade as exporters, importers, wholesalers, and retailers, all of which are now grouped under the category "merchant." But the focus on these men also rests on unexamined assumptions about the importance of law, particularly rights: that rights were what allowed individuals to control their property legally and, therefore, to participate in the economy. With primacy placed on rights, it seems like it would have been impossible to buy or keep property, let alone set up a business without them. Only white men had them, so only white men could be merchants. As such, the ventures of people with a smaller bundle of rights—or no rights at all—seem fundamentally different: marginal, underground, informal, and definitely apart from the "real" economy.

The trade in textiles, however, also depended on legal principles that even people without rights could use to make property claims. Those principles had become so central to the public order of the new republic that officials would step in to protect them, even when they conflicted with rights-based laws. But they derived from different sources than property rights. What mattered, when it came to textiles, were the material qualities of the goods—the colors, textures, and designs. These elements created the personal attachments that, in turn, established legally enforceable claims. Legal security then opened up other economic options, allowing people without rights to trade in ways associated with merchants. People bought textiles not just to use, but also to employ as currency, capital, and the basis of credit, which added value to the goods and blurred the lines between merchants and their customers.

The legal principles associated with textiles placed more power in the hands of customers and allowed those without rights to act as merchants, doing the buying and selling themselves. More than that, merchants like Mr. Robinson depended on the legal principles associated with textiles, because they allowed a wider range of people to buy these goods. White male merchants regularly acknowledged that situation in the meanings they gave to the term "the market." There was the global market configured as an abstract set of dynamics that existed nowhere in particular and everywhere in general. In that market, rights were a prerequisite for participation and textiles were traded in bulk, as if their individual qualities did not matter. Then there were local markets composed of real people and located in real places, where individuals bought specific items, based on very definite ideas about what they liked and why, with the assumption that those qualities created attachments with legal meanings. While the market-as-an-abstraction was in the process of replacing the market-as-a-physical-space even before the nineteenth century, these two aspects of economic exchange comingled when it came to finished textiles, which meant that the Mr. Robinsons of the new republic were never completely in control. Their fortunes were bound to the legal principles associated with textiles, the people who used them, and the markets that governed by them.

North Americans went through a lot of cloth. It was not just used for clothing. Stacks upon stacks of it were needed for the sails on ships, the bagging and packing used to transport and store goods, and the towels and rags used by all kinds of tradespeople in their work. The accounts of John Tayloe, who owned numerous plantations and business ventures in early nineteenth-century Virginia, are suggestive. In the fall, a time when planters purchased supplies for the coming year, Tayloe placed orders for textiles every few weeks, each for several hundred yards of basic linens, cottons, and wools. That was thousands of yards of cloth in just one season of one year, for just the business operations of one planter. Admittedly, Tayloe had unusually large holdings and nearly a thousand enslaved people to clothe. But that was the point: people went through a lot of cloth.[2]

Throughout the colonial period and into the nineteenth century, most of that cloth was imported. Dependence owed, in part, to British policies that actively discouraged textile production in the colonies to maintain the market for British-made goods. Officials kept close tabs on the situation. The 1732 report of the Board of Trade and Plantations expressed concern that New England, New York, Connecticut, Rhode Island, Pennsylvania, and Maryland "have fallen into the manufacture of woolen cloth and linen cloth," although production was "for the use of their own families only." The "greatest part of the woolen and linen clothing" in Massachusetts, however, "was imported from Great Britain, and sometimes from Ireland." Despite worrying signs of domestic production, imported cloth predominated in other colonies as well, largely because the shortage of labor made it impossible "to manufacture their linen cloth at less than 20 per cent more than the rate in England, or woolen cloth at less than 50 per cent dearer than that which is exported from hence for sale." In the world of imperial officialdom, all was well: the North American colonies provided markets for British textiles, not competition to them.[3]

By the middle of the eighteenth century, stores throughout North America stocked a startling variety of imported textiles, priced so that even the working poor and the enslaved could afford a bit of finery. A yard or less could be made up into a handkerchief, a neck or head scarf, a vest or waistcoat, the lining in a coat, or an apron, all of which could turn everyday clothing into something more distinctive. Aprons, which people today use to protect their good clothes from kitchen splatter, also served the opposite purpose in the eighteenth century: they dressed up work clothes, which most women wore most of the time. When visitors stopped by during the day, women whose status allowed them control over their time would set aside their tasks and don their good aprons, carefully decorated with hand embroidery or imported lace, if the owner were fortunate enough to afford it. What might seem like utterly impractical garments, with their frills and furbelows, served an important purpose, signaling the transition from work to sociability. For men, the addition of a silk neck scarf or a fanciful waistcoat accomplished much the same thing.[4]

Ads for runaway servants and slaves in British North America indicate that they possessed garments notable for their quality and style. While some of these items had been stolen, others had been carefully acquired and were obviously treasured. Consider the advertisement for an Irish servant, who left dressed in "a grey homespun cloth coat, almost new, lin'd with blue shalloon in the forepart, and with brown cloth in the back," and "a Leather Fawn skin vest . . . lined with scarlet shalloon." The coat and vest were of dull, serviceable materials, domestically produced. But they were partially lined with brightly colored shalloons, a finely woven, expensive woolen import. Those touches were exactly the kind of additions that brought color and distinction to otherwise unremarkable garments. That was why the blue shalloon was placed in the "forepart" of the coat, where it would be seen. Enslaved people, too, embellished what the people who enslaved them supplied, as best they could. Some merchants stocked goods, including Indian cottons that had long been popular in African markets, specifically for sale to people of African descent in the Americas.[5]

Native people throughout the Americas also bought imported cloth, which dominated trade and even figured into peace treaties. Those imports dramatically transformed the dress of Native people involved in the fur trade. Men wore shirts as outer garments, with ties around their waists, sometimes with the addition of a top coat or strowd (two or three yards of fabric made into a drape or shawl). Women also wore shirts and strowds over skirts and leggings, all made of imported cloth. Not just any kind of cloth would do. Native people "were difficult and demanding customers who refused to trade when cloth was poorly made or an undesirable color," according to historian Susan Sleeper-Smith. They wanted quality fabrics in particular colors and designs, and they got them. English traders fell all over themselves to copy French goods when they were entering the trade. After British cloth became more popular, the French were the ones in a bind. "Escarlatines from England are an indispensable necessity for the beaver trade in Canada," wrote frustrated officials in New France, who were unable to obtain these popular red wool blankets from England because of the Seven Years War. These officials had appealed to French manufacturers, who tried and failed to imitate the coveted escarlatines. So they resorted to a roundabout method of importation, buying the blankets in England, shipping them to Holland, and then reloading them onto neutral boats to take them from Holland to France.[6]

All these fabrics flowed into the North American colonies through tight business networks, often based in family ties. In Virginia, mercantile firms in England or Scotland would typically send a family member or trusted servant to set up shop in a port city, such as Alexandria or Williamsburg. While running that business, the agent would scout out the next location. If it suited, the firm would send another emissary to oversee that new store. And so the process continued, as stores associated with the mercantile house slowly fanned out across the colony—that is, if the business partners did not overextend, misjudge their customers, or encounter a disaster beyond their control. Dutch merchants and Spanish textile producers operated similarly, with family members and their retainers spreading across the Americas to anchor trade. So did the fur trade, which also depended on close familial ties.[7]

Merchants in colonial British North America had to establish and maintain ties with their counterparts in England or Scotland to obtain credit and goods. While intermediary importers sold to retail merchants, it was impossible to obtain the best goods without direct ties to sources in Britain. Those ties explain the success of New York textile merchant Mary Alexander. Born into a family of Dutch merchants, she relied on her extended family network in England, which included the Barclays, powerful Quaker bankers and merchants. Those connections meant access that other merchants did not have, even if they were men. Elizabeth Murray, a shopkeeper in Boston, was more typical of colonial merchants, male and female. A relative set her up with suppliers in London, but she had such difficulty wringing goods and credit from them that she ended up making buying trips to London herself. Regardless of their size or familial connections, all these shops relied on British suppliers, who in turn were connected to global trade networks that had been moving textiles across land and sea for centuries.[8]

Imported textiles poured in after the Revolution, despite the increase in domestic production in the late eighteenth and early nineteenth centuries. To be sure, British policies in the 1760s, which raised taxes and cracked down on colonial merchants who defied trade restrictions, disrupted imports. So did the Revolutionary War. But none of that altered the direction of overall patterns, which snapped back into place at the end of the Revolution. The flow of textiles over the new republic's borders resumed, although now through merchants based in America with ties abroad. Opportunities narrowed with President Thomas Jefferson's embargo in 1800 and the end of the Napoleonic Wars in 1815. American merchants had to deal with British policies when trading in that nation's spheres of influence, particularly India and China. But they exploited the available openings, establishing direct trade with Asia as well as parts of Europe and South America that had been closed to them during the colonial era. According to the Treasury Department's annual report in 1821, imports of textiles dwarfed the value of other imported goods. Woolen cloth was divided into three categories, indicating the scale of the trade: cloths and cassimeres, worsteds and stuff-goods, and blankets and rugs. The total came to about seven million dollars. Cottons, which were broken out into categories of printed and colored, white, and nankeens, came to about the same amount. Silks and linens had a combined total value that was almost that of wools, even though the value of linens was on a downward slide at this point. The only import of comparable dollar value was, tellingly, gold and silver coin, which came in at about eight million dollars. In 1821, the value of wools, cottons, silks, and linens, which totaled $21,530,663, surpassed the export value of raw cotton, at $20,157,484. Although domestic producers were churning out significant amounts of cloth by that point, exports were so insignificant that they did not appear in that year's report. By 1840, the United States was exporting about three million dollars of cotton cloth. But the country was still importing far more than it was exporting: about twelve million dollars each in cotton goods and wools.[9]

In the decades following the Revolution, the business strategies of US merchants mirrored those of their British counterparts in the colonial era, although with an eye toward acquiring as well as selling textiles. Like Mr. Robinson, they sent out family members and trusted retainers to various points around the world to study the market, make contacts, and facilitate business. In the absence of relatives and employees, merchants cultivated ties with commission merchants and intermediaries who could navigate foreign markets. Such contacts were particularly important in India and China, where the language, customs, and laws made it impossible for Americans to deal directly with manufacturers. But merchants also had similar contacts in distant cities within the new republic. Brown and Ives, a firm based in Providence that later moved into textile production corresponded with their representatives in Charleston, Alexandria, and Fayetteville, just as they did with those in China and India. The fact that some of those places were in the United States did not necessarily make them any more knowable or accessible.[10]

By the early nineteenth century, domestic production prompted some adaptations in this business model, although those changes were more elaborations of existing practices than departures from them. The line between wholesale and retail grew brighter, and some manufacturers gave up on selling goods themselves and hired outside firms to do their distribution. Such was the case with Cocheco Manufacturing, which produced printed cottons. Located in Dover, New Hampshire, Cocheco had started out as Dover Manufacturing, which began spinning cotton yarn in 1815, expanded into weaving in 1816, and then added a print works in 1827. By 1830, the operation was one of the largest textile firms in the country. But instead of marketing cloth themselves, Cocheco hired Mason and Lawrence, a commission firm that sold textiles throughout the United States. That arrangement made sense, given the scale of the operation. Individual manufacturers simply did not have the wherewithal to supply individual merchants in cities and small towns all over the country. Mason and Lawrence did, with well-placed wholesale operatives who sold to retailers.[11]

Merchants kept a steady supply of textiles flowing in the decades following the Revolution, despite conflicts abroad and political upheaval at home. The clothing of people who escaped servitude and slavery tells the tale. When Peter fled enslavement in Baltimore in 1806, he had a blue cloth coat, a brown coatee, a dove colored twilled nankeen coatee, several Marseilles vests, some shirts of fine white Irish linen, pantaloons of India nankeen, and a beaver hat. The clothing of Ned, another enslaved man, was more typical, but still notable. When he left the Eastern Shore of Maryland in 1806, he was wearing a short jacket made of fustian (a common, heavy, twill fabric, usually of dark color, made of cotton or linen), a white waistcoat (of unspecified cloth, indicating that there was nothing remarkable about it), and a black hat (not beaver, like Peter's). But Ned also had a pair of velveteen pantaloons, which were a particular luxury: velveteen was made from fine silk or cotton thread, tightly woven, then trimmed and brushed so that it had a soft pile that was unsuitable for work because it did not wear well and needed special cleaning. The ad also warned that Ned was likely to change clothes because he took other garments with him, including a long frock coat and several pairs of nankeen pantaloons. There was no indication that Ned or Peter had stolen any of these items from the men legally identified as their masters.[12]

All those textiles meant lots of potential profits. But the devil was in the details, a fact that was as true in the nineteenth century as it had been in the colonial era. The value of finished textiles depended on their unique characteristics, which made them unlike other trade goods, whether luxury items such as china, tea, spices, and wine or commodities like sugar, cotton, or grains, all of which were easier to buy and sell in large, undifferentiated lots. While cloth had been mass-produced since at least the fifteenth century, mass production did not result in standardization. Finished textiles still came in a dizzying array of patterns, colors, and textures in the nineteenth century. All those elements became even more important when textiles hit local markets. While the textile market was global in reach, there was no agreement on style and no uniform fashion standard within it. What sold in one place would not sell in another. Merchants did their best to figure it all out. But the underlying logic remained elusive, largely because the dynamics of fashion were more arbitrary than logical.[13]

To be sure, the particularities of local markets characterized other goods as well. People were picky about china patterns. They liked some teas, spices, and wines, but not others. But the variation among finished textiles was truly mindboggling. That situation owed, in part, to the fact that fabrics were defined by the characteristics their makers gave to them, and those variations could be endless. In 1738, a Northamptonshire manufacturer listed thirty-five different kinds of woolen fabric being made in his English county.[14] Similar kinds of fabrics had different names in different languages. The French, fussed one merchant in the new republic, "were not only ignorant of the Taste in patterns, and the quality of the Goods that suits our Countrymen, but all the Dictionaries in the World could not translate the names of the goods ordered." "Order a French Merchant to ship a piece of Book Muslin, and he would endeavor to find a piece of Mouseline de Livre," although European manufacturers outside France would be unable to supply it because they called that kind of fabric by another name. Then the French merchant would write that it could not be found, "unless some American were to tell him that a piece of Goods called ourgandi answers . . . except in the folding it."[15] Merchants persisted nonetheless, because of the potential payoff: the variations that rendered finished textiles completely worthless in some places might make them worth a small fortune in others. In this sense, merchants in the colonial period and those in the nineteenth century were in the same boat, despite all the changes in production and transport. Hence Mr. Robinson's constant search for the markets that suited his goods.

These challenges were on full display in the orders from the colonial era, which included fabric swatches, copious notes, and firm instructions about what "the market" wanted. Europeans involved in the fur trade chased after specific kinds of cloth, knowing full well that if they did not stock the right goods, Native people would take their furs to a trader who did. People in colonial towns and cities were equally discerning. Bright colors and floral patterns, all in fabrics intended for dresses, dominated many a merchant's orders to London in the 1700s. Like others in the textile trade, Mary Alexander included swatches to provide examples of styles, colors, and textures and then added notes surrounding each fabric sample. She used some swatches to communicate color, pointing out that she wanted different elements in the patterns or the quality of the cloth, and used others to provide a sense of the patterns she wanted, but then specified different colors and weaves.[16] Those details mattered—a lot. As Philip Livingston explained through obviously gritted teeth to his London supplier in 1739, he wanted calico with large flowers in flowing patterns this time, not "small single flowers as you sent me last year which I can't sell."[17]

Ophelia Cary, who lived a hundred years later in western Virginia, would have sympathized with the women who turned up their noses at Livingston's calico. When her hunt for dress silk failed with local merchants, she enlisted the aid of her husband, who was making a trip to Richmond. That was not unusual. At the time, elite white men regularly shopped for their female relatives when they visited urban centers. His shopping experience was not unusual either. After scouring Richmond's stores, Cary's husband sent her samples of fabric that he thought satisfactory but which produced a flurry of admonitions about the shade ("jet black, not the blue black, which will fade more and spot") and the price ("do try and get it at $1.25 per [yard]"). He tried to reassure her. The fabrics in Richmond, he wrote, were better than the samples she had sent from merchants near their home. Nonetheless, she had doubts. So her husband tried a different tack, offering to "get some lady to select" it for her—which, conveniently, would also shift the blame to someone else if the cloth did not satisfy his wife. Mollified, Cary agreed to take the

Figure 3.1 For the sample marked "J," Mary Alexander wanted "a broad strip, not a flower between," but of "these colors." Samples 11–14 were "only to show the colors and cloathe." For samples 15–19, she wanted "the goodness of the cloathe," but "different colors and smaller patterns." Swatches of fabric used by Mary Alexander, December 1726. Alexander Papers, New York Historical Society Library, 26276b.

plunge, as long as he got "a tailor or some lady to pick it" and was "sure to get the jet black." It was not that Cary's husband was a complete dolt when it came to the selection of textiles. On a previous trip, he had a new overcoat made all on his own. She never offered advice on that particular purchase, and for good reason. Both husband and wife had strong opinions about what they wanted in their own clothes.[18]

Strong opinions extended to basic cloth as well, even though it might seem that price differences would be negligible and variations in quality would be less noticeable and less important. On an 1820 voyage to Calcutta, an agent for the firm of Brown and Ives bought Indian cotton piece goods (a catch-all name for mass-produced cotton cloth) in white for sale in America, but not blue, which sold only in Africa. The color made all the difference. As the agent reported, it was unwise to purchase cottons for the African market at all, because the closure of the slave trade meant that prices there were in free fall.[19] Another errand that Ophelia Cary entrusted to her husband was to buy cotton sheeting at a particular factory in Richmond, even though that kind of cloth was available at all the stores in her own town.[20] As the records of Mason and Lawrence suggest, factory names began to replace geographic place names as the means of defining a fabric's characteristics, with customers insisting on goods from particular factories based on experience and reputation. In what evolved into branding, clients ordered Salmon Falls drills, Cocheco prints, and Lebanon sheetings, all named for the factories where they were produced.[21]

The white male merchants who sold to Ophelia Cary and her husband operated in the two senses of the market simultaneously. There was the global market, which they used as a guide to determine value when buying and selling goods to each other. Even wholesalers and commission merchants in minor trading towns deep in the interior of the United States had information about prices for various kinds of fabrics in major port cities around the world. Then there were particular, local markets: not just in regions, cities, and towns but also in the streets and buildings that were designated locations for trade. The conditions of those markets rested on a variety of local factors, ranging from the weather, the number of ships in port, and the local harvest. They also depended on the buyers—the actual people—who made up those markets: the women in New York City who favored large flowers in flowing patterns and the individual women all over the country on the hunt for the exact kind of black silk that suited their particular needs.

The new republic's merchants moved seamlessly from one sense of the market to the other, because the distinction was so obvious to them. They passed along information about the prices of goods in particular cities, as if impersonal market forces set them. Then, in the same letter, they would attribute prices to the unique circumstances of that specific local market. "We have the Calcutta goods" (brightly printed Indian cottons), wrote the firm of Talcott and Bowers in New Orleans to Brown and Ives in 1817, "but no prospect of sales at present, this market is glutted." The global market brought Calcutta goods to New Orleans, New York, Philadelphia, Baltimore, Boston, and elsewhere in the Caribbean and South America. But the New Orleans market was glutted because too many merchants had landed those particular goods there. Elsewhere, the situation was different. In fact, Brown and Ives's Calcutta goods had ended up in New Orleans because ports in South America, where there were markets for these goods, had been closed to American ships.[22]

Tobacco was tobacco, cotton was cotton, sugar was sugar, and wheat was wheat, no matter where you sold it. Finished textiles? That was another matter entirely. Goods that sold in London did not necessarily sell in New York. Goods that sold in New York did not necessarily sell in Philadelphia. Goods that sold in Philadelphia did not necessarily sell in New Orleans. And goods that sold in New Orleans did not necessarily sell anywhere else. The small flowers that the women in colonial New York rejected would fly off the shelves in another time and place. One of those times and places was the port city of Veracruz, Mexico, in 1847, then occupied by the US army. The New Orleans firm of DeForest and Company begged its supplier for printed cottons with designs of "small to medium size." "The Mexicans are tired of large patterns," DeForest's agent wrote, as if that statement explained the situation.[23] More common was the utterly opaque comments of a commission agent in La Quira, Venezuela to a Philadelphia merchant: "I am sorry that I have not the pleasure of communicating to you somthing more favourable respecting your goods," but "I expect I shall have great difficulty to Dispose of them as they do not Answer to the market." He did elaborate on the problem with the ribbons that had been sent for sale, although the explanation was so circuitous that it did not really answer the question as to what made the them so unsuitable: "If [they] had have been narrow they would have don extremely well But in consiquence of them being so wide they do not know what use to appropriate them to as the Females in this Country do not make any use of them." But all was not lost. The agent promised to "Smuggel" the offending ribbons on board an outbound ship to return them to Philadelphia—a statement that speaks volumes about mercantile priorities in the period between the Revolution and the Civil War. It was worth defying the laws of the United States to get ribbons to markets where they would sell.[24]

When it came to the local sense of the market, colonial merchants like Mary Alexander and Phillip Livingston had it easy. They knew their customers well because they moved in the same social circles in a particular city. By contrast, the merchants involved in the long-distance trade catered to people whose preferences were unfamiliar and far more difficult to understand, given the cultural divide that separated them from their customers. Calcutta goods, for instance, were known to be popular in the "southern market," which included the Caribbean and South America as well as parts of the southern United States, largely because of the perception that people of African descent favored them over printed cottons produced elsewhere. That may have been the case. But given that these people were enslaved, with few buying options, they had little choice in the matter anyway. Dictating to markets was not always so easy. Those kinds of challenges multiplied by the time of the Revolution and metastasized in the decades afterward, as the market for textiles expanded, with more goods going to more people in more places.

"The goods do not answer to the market": textile merchants in the new republic repeated the phrase over and over. Were the flowers too large or too small? Were the ribbons too narrow or too wide? There were so many ways to get it wrong because there were so many kinds of fabrics. Mechanization did nothing to remedy the problem. While reducing the variety of some kinds of fabric, mechanization increased it for others, particularly cotton prints. Mason and Lawrence, which distributed the printed cottons produced by Cocheco Manufacturing, struggled to get the right kinds of designs to the right people. No one bought prints sight unseen, so the firm sent its agents sample cards with swatches of all the designs that it produced. The agents then took orders from local merchants, who selected the specific patterns they wanted, often buying in small amounts to hedge their bets in case they misjudged their customers. Once they sold out of particular patterns, they would order more, but only as needed.[25]

The resulting challenges run through the business records of merchants. Brown and Ives was among many mercantile firms in the new republic that traded with China and India during the 1790s and early 1800s. Initially, the firm contracted directly with ship captains, who oversaw both the voyage and the purchase of goods. But a ship captain's navigational abilities did not necessarily lend themselves to the selection of desirable cloth. After a series of bad experiences with cargos of unsaleable goods that sat moldering in warehouses, the firm began hiring a separate person called a supercargo to purchase goods, including cloth. The contracts of many supercargos encouraged their expertise as buyers by giving them a stake in the voyages, allowing them space on the vessel to carry privately owned goods intended for sale or for which they traded.[26]

Moldering was a real problem. Cloth deteriorated rapidly, given the conditions in which it was shipped and stored. Some fabric was packed in bales—stacks of similar kinds of fabric, tightly bound together and wrapped in thick cloth, like today's burlap. Some was packed in cases or crates that were hastily made and often insubstantial. The bales, cases, and crates were then put into the holds of ships, which were never climate controlled, not reliably watertight, and always home to all manner of vermin. Some fabric arrived in port already damaged beyond repair by salt water, mold, scaly insects, or furry mammals. What arrived undamaged was best sold as quickly as possible. Otherwise, it was consigned to warehouses and stores, which had many of the same problems as ships, especially those perched on piers that were built out over the water and subject to damaging storms. The dangers are evident in Eliza Lucas Pinckney's account of procuring plain cloth in Charleston during the Revolutionary War. Pinckney had pioneered in the culture of indigo, the plant that produced the dye necessary to turn plain white fabric a rich, beautiful blue, and was not one to give up easily. After rooting around in the front part of the store, she finally found what she was looking for in a back room, where there was also some cheese. "The Rats had [begun] upon it," she explained in a letter to her daughter, but then clarified. The rats had been eating the cloth, not the cheese—which, apparently, was far less tasty. "I have now tyed it [meaning the cloth, not the cheese] up to the ceiling," which she hoped would protect it.[27]

Pinckney's solution would not have worked if the fabric in question had been wool, a favorite of moths. Mr. Robinson begged his agent in Augusta, Georgia, to have the wool cloth he consigned there to be "beaten and brushed from time to time." "Otherwise the Moths will much injure" it before it could find a buyer when the weather turned cold again. (The fact that he had shipped fine woolens to Augusta, Georgia, in the spring suggests the lack of foresight that ultimately led him to drop textiles for tea.) He knew whereof he spoke: another shipment to Savannah had been infested by moths and all but destroyed.[28]

Textiles could not be stored indefinitely. But what would sell? The inability to predict frustrated Mason and Lawrence as well as the Cocheco Printing Company. It was not cost-effective to stock large quantities of all the prints offered because no one had a good idea what would be popular and where. But filling orders as they came in meant that agents lost buyers who wanted fabrics in a timely fashion. So Mason and Lawrence's agents made educated guesses. In January 1850, the agent in Philadelphia asked for "chocolate and purple" patterns, which he thought would sell, even though he did not have orders in hand. In March, he wanted "styles 516, 518, 485, 486 ... particularly 516 and 518." But agents could not always sell what was sent, which meant that Cocheco ran the risk of making plain cloth unsaleable by printing it with the wrong kind of design.[29]

Markets closer to home could be equally impenetrable, which was why merchants from Boston, New York, Philadelphia, Baltimore, and New

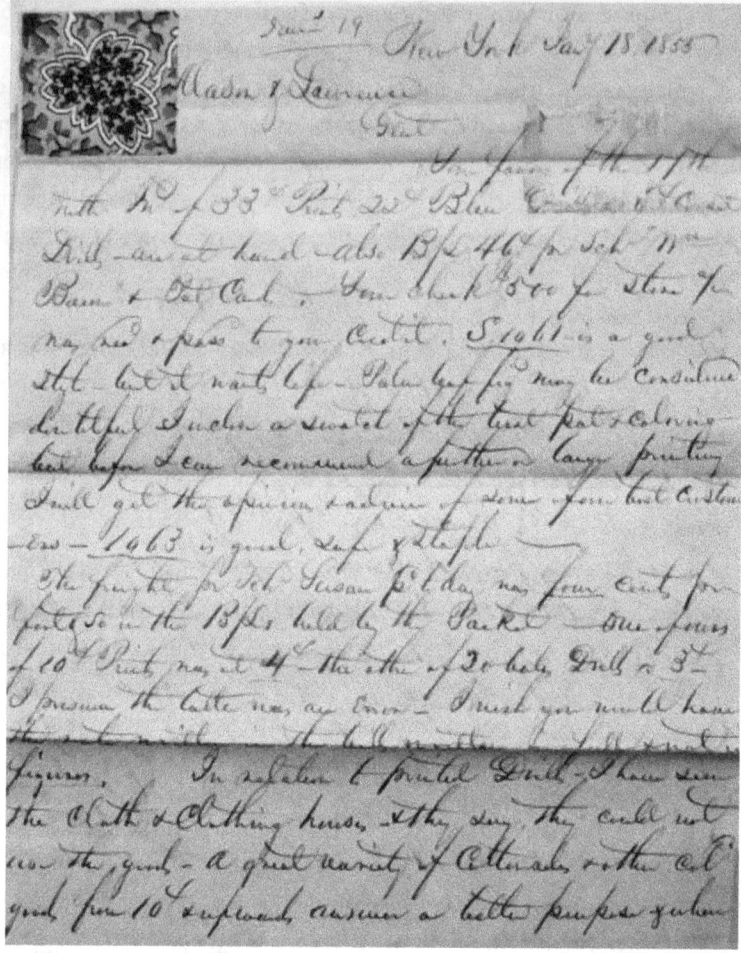

Figure 3.2 Letters from agents to Mason and Lawrence often included fabric samples, to ensure that they received prints of the right colors and patterns. L. Bacon, in 1855, wrote that print #1961 "is a good style, but wants life. Palm leaf fig[ure] may be considered doubtful," although the colors of the sample he enclosed seemed better. He was going to consult with customers before ordering more. By contrast, #1963 was "good, safe, and staple." L. B. Bacon to Mason and Lawrence, January 18, 1855, Lawrence & Company records, Baker Library, Harvard Business School.

Orleans cultivated contacts in smaller cities in the South, Midwest, and West, all of which had their own maddeningly unique markets. The fact that many of those markets were now part of one country did nothing to eliminate the local conditions that differentiated them. When Mr. Robinson sent shipments of goods to Augusta and Nashville to test the markets there, he included silk that would not sell in Philadelphia, not because he was trying to offload unwanted goods on the provinces (although that was a consideration) but because he was certain that the markets in those cities were different. The Philadelphia firm that failed to supply the right kind of ribbons to Venezuelan women had a standing relationship with a New York firm so that they could exchange goods between the two cities.[30]

Success depended on knowledge of the varieties of cloth and the local markets in which they were sold. Supercargoes studied the places where they landed closely, trying to figure out which goods would answer to which markets and why. In 1800, on a voyage to Canton by way of South America, Samuel Brown took careful notes about everything everyone was wearing and buying. In Valparaiso, "the European fashions are now introduced & the *Bell Peticoat* so generally worn a short time since is now entirely laid aside, at least among the People of fashion." In Lima, he managed to get hold of the invoice for a Spanish ship's cargo and copied it out carefully, word for word, knowing how valuable the information was: the Spanish knew the market in Valparaiso far better than the Americans. He also summarized what he learned from observation, personifying the market as an entity with desires and volition. English silk stockings would sell, but "white ribbed are preferred to others," although some colored "would answer." "English cotton velvets of a good quality, principally black & blue, with a few pieces of other colours are . . . *a very saleable article.*" So were white tamboured muslins, although only if they were a half yard wide. Dimities, muslin handkerchiefs, and English cotton plaid pocket handkerchiefs would sell, as would calicos and chintzes, although they had to be of "lively colours" and "*mostly low priced.*" There was demand for "camblets for Ladies Petticoats," but black and cinnamon were "the only colours that will answer." As was the case with so many merchants, "the market" always took precedence over US trade policies. "If a cargo is intended to be smuggled on the coast of Peru," he concluded, "it ought to consist of articles of *little bulk and great value*, a larger proportion in fine muslins & dimities, and English patent silk stockings."[31]

Supercargoes filled orders for particular merchants and individuals, just as colonial merchants had done. The logbook of Charles Frederick Bradford, who worked as a supercargo for a Boston firm on voyages to South America and China in the 1820s and 1830s, was filled with orders from women in his home city, complete with descriptions and fabric samples. The entry for Mrs. Channing suggests the specific characteristics of cloth that buyers like Bradford were expected to obtain. He was to find her "4 or 5 pieces, of 20 yards each of Satin, 3 to be dark, 2 light colored such as will answer for evening clothes." In addition, she wanted "15 Yards of Silver Gray," but only if he could "match that of last year; otherwise not any." And that was only one among many individual orders he had to fill, in addition to selecting cloth for merchants and for sale on commission in Boston and other markets.³²

Agents, who either worked on commission or were salaried employees for a mercantile firm, performed functions similar to those of supercargoes. The agent of DeForest and Company later attached himself to the US army during the Mexican-American War so as to keep his foot in the door there. While tagging along with the army and dodging bullets, he kept his employers apprised of what people were wearing. The ladies in Veracruz, he wrote in one missive, were wearing "Shell Lawn Dresses," "satin Slippers," and white stockings, although he regretted that he "did not get near enough to examine

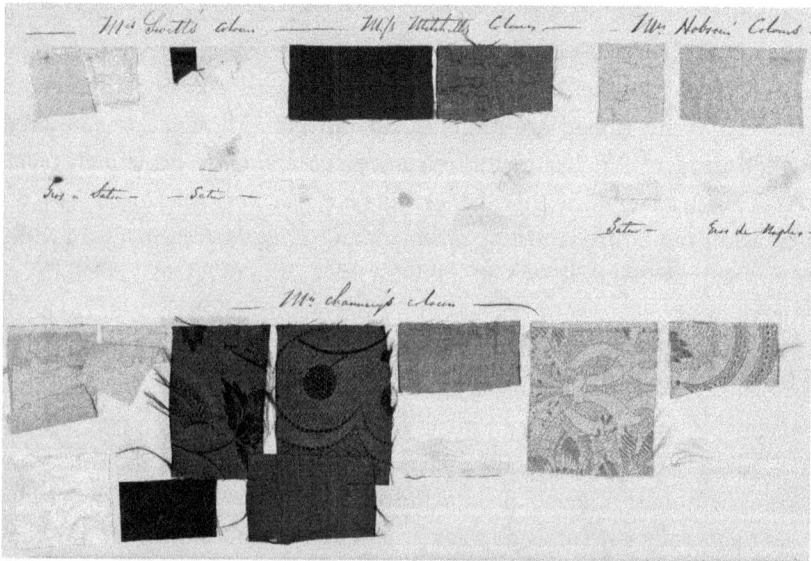

Figure 3.3 Charles Frederick Bradford included fabric samples as well as detailed notes for individual customers, mostly women, he bought for on his trips to China. Supercargoes, such as Bradford, were allowed to buy for their own customers in addition to the buying that they did for the firms that hired them. Memo Book, Charles Frederick Bradford, box 1, Edward Hickling Bradford Family Papers, 1825–1920. Collection of the Massachusetts Historical Society.

the material" of the dresses so that he could determine the grade of cloth and where it was manufactured. This textile agent used an international military conflict to get close enough to women's dresses to figure out what they were made of so that he could sell more of them. It is difficult to imagine a better example of textile merchants' dependence on the people who made up the market and on the federal government—whose policies they routinely disregarded—to protect access to these places.[33]

The risks of misjudging all these highly localized markets led to the downfall of many an aspiring merchant and manufacturer. In fact, failure was far more common than success in the decades following the Revolution. Like so many others, Mr. Robinson lost the war. Given the risky conditions of the time, he was remarkably successful at procuring goods. Like other American merchants, he had to maneuver around the trade policies of European powers and his own country, which sometimes led to long delays and the seizure of goods at foreign ports. He faced threats on the open seas from pirates and vessels that ignored American ships' neutral status. But Robinson navigated all that, only to stumble when it came to marketing. His decision to specialize in something more reliable than textiles was not uncommon. By the 1820s, commission merchants who once sold a range of imported goods—textiles as well as tea, spices, china, and wine—began focusing on particular products. Talcott and Bowers, a New Orleans general commission house that sold textiles for Brown and Ives, dissolved in 1821, and Davis Talcott set up his own firm, which specialized in wine. Like Robinson, Talcott left the sale of textiles to those who thought they could predict what would sell.[34]

The merchants and manufacturers who continued to deal in finished textiles cycled rapidly through credit reports, which began appearing in the 1840s. R. G. Dun and Company, which started compiling information about the creditworthiness of businesses all over the country, would enter the appearance of a new firm in its records and then try to suss out its sources of capital and drill down on its business practices. More often than not, the firm would disappear after a year or two, sometimes with an explanation for its failure, sometimes not. When a reason was supplied, it was often simply "failed," "dissolved," "insolvent," or "sold at auction." There was no need to elaborate further, because the peculiar difficulties of the textile trade that made failure so common were well known. To be sure, regular cycles of boom and bust made business ventures of all kinds a challenging proposition in the late eighteenth and early nineteenth centuries. But merchants and manufacturers who were involved in finished textiles faced another wild card that other businesses did not: the variety in both the goods they sold and the people who made up their market. It was the merchants and manufacturers who had to answer to the market. That was true even for those who wrung riches from the collection of marketplaces, composed of real buyers, many of them without the range of rights necessary to own any other kind of property.[35]

When Americans separated from Great Britain, they remained within a textile market that was simultaneously global and local. The federal government of the new republic figured less prominently. To be sure, its policies provided access to foreign markets, its laws could hinder or facilitate trade, and its customs' duties determined profits. Merchants did their best to shape those policies and harness the power of the federal government to ease access to markets. When they failed, they worked around federal policies, as merchants' open discussion of smuggling suggests. But when it came to the sale of finished textiles, the difference between New York City and Philadelphia, or any other locality in the United States for that matter, was akin to the difference between New York City and London or Philadelphia and Amsterdam. Given that geographic orientation, merchants like Mr. Robinson had more contacts in far-flung localities throughout the world than they did nearer to home. That was particularly true in the first two or three decades following the Revolution, when merchants continued trading practices oriented toward Britain, the Caribbean, South America, Europe, Africa, and Asia.

By the 1820s, textile merchants and manufacturers were eyeing the new markets opening up within their own country. Brown and Ives, for instance, sent agents to explore the interior of Ohio, Kentucky, Tennessee, and North Carolina, even as they sent ships off to Canton, Calcutta, St. Petersburg, and Madeira. If anything, though, the places in North America's interior seemed more foreign. As agents made their way into the continent, their news of economic swings, cultural preferences, and contagious diseases read as attempts to fathom the unknown and to bring order to chaos. Assessing economic prospects as he made his way up the Red River, away from New Orleans, toward Shreveport, one New York merchant recoiled. "The manners of the people here are harsh and rough," he wrote. "I could not therefore advise our

Mother and sisters to remove to it at present."³⁶ In this sense, the addition of new markets within the United States was an extension of existing dynamics within the global textile market that had been incorporating new localities for centuries. As the next chapter shows, the persistence of established dynamics applied to the production of textiles as well.

4

Rebecca Coles's Factory

Manufacturers

Rebecca Coles operated a textile business at Enniscorthy, her family's plantation in Virginia, right down the road from the Madisons and the Jeffersons. The Coles family and the people they enslaved were no different than other Americans in their need for cloth. No sooner was it purchased than it had to be replaced, not because of wastefulness or extravagance but because it flat wore out. For most of the eighteenth century, much of that cloth would have been imported. By the time of the Revolution, however, Rebecca Coles had started coordinating production herself, relying on the labor of enslaved women (who spun and wove on the plantation) and free women (who worked from their own households) to make fabric for sale as well as for use.[1] Coles built her business at the same time that the white male merchants who signed the Declaration of Independence were exploiting new opportunities in the textile trade at home and abroad. But even though both men and women organized enterprises similar to that of Rebecca Coles during and after the Revolution, it is the elite white men who are remembered as manufacturers today. Coles, however, was a textile manufacturer too.

Before and immediately after the Revolution, the term "manufacturing" referred to all kinds of textile production, be it small or large scale, based within or outside households, including work done by Rebecca Coles and the free and enslaved artisans who worked for her. Even so, commentators in the new republic became increasingly fixated on textile production organized by men, particularly when done by machines and centralized in factories. That, in their minds, was the future of manufacturing, and it certainly was the prevailing trend in Britain, their primary point of reference. Those commentators were not wrong. It was just that the future took far longer to arrive than its proponents anticipated. Until then, the production of textiles in massive quantities for the global market continued as it had before: by hand, in households, often with women's labor. Supplying markets was a matter of scaling up, using existing methods with more, lower-paid workers.

That was what many manufacturers in the new republic did, combining time-honored methods of production with new technologies as they became available. Fascination with the future, however, overwhelmed facts on the ground. When it came to textiles, the terms "manufacturing" and "mass production" came to be associated with machines and factories owned by men long before that kind of production actually described the manufacture of textiles. The connection has solidified to the point that it is now difficult to imagine what Coles was doing as manufacturing.[2]

Given the devaluation of women's labor generally, it is not surprising that the economic value of their labor in textile production was dismissed at the time and misunderstood later. A tight constellation of gendered assumptions has persisted over time and across cultures, rendering women both inferior and subordinate to men. Everything they did was considered less valuable than what men did. What they produced, moreover, was never entirely their own. The nature of textile production further muddied the waters, because the work tended to merge seamlessly with the other, uncompensated domestic chores that were expected of women as part of their duty to husbands, fathers, and masters, particularly when they did that labor within their households. The association with domestic labor then followed them outside their households, justifying lower pay than men. Economic changes associated with the intensification of capitalist economic relations magnified those trends. By the early nineteenth century, all women's labor was characterized as disconnected from the commercial world and, as such, fundamentally different from that of men.[3]

Textiles were the exception. When it came to these goods, economic value did not depend solely on where they were produced or who produced them. Before mechanization, the work of textile production was done by hand, within households, regardless of whether women or men did it or whether the goods were intended for commercial dissemination or household use. The value of all those textiles was determined by skill, which was a matter of dexterity, experience, and aesthetics, not gender or the location of production. Good cloth was worth more than bad cloth; well-made garments were worth more than shoddy ones. The importance of skill, combined with the persistence of hand labor, opened up economic opportunities for all those on the margins in the decades following the Revolution. That is why this chapter focuses on the work involved in making textiles: those processes reveal the spaces where people without strong claims to rights and, therefore, access to credit or capital could set themselves up as manufacturers.[4]

If it is difficult to imagine the work of Rebecca Coles as manufacturing, it is even more difficult to imagine her or the women who worked for her as manufacturers. That difficulty owes to the dominance of rights-based legal frameworks in the minds of contemporary commentators and later scholars. In that legal universe, people without the full range of rights—even free wage laborers—could not control the value of their economic output. How could Rebecca Coles be a manufacturer, when she had no legal claim to the textiles she produced? Her husband, who had legal claims on her labor, would be the manufacturer, not her. Enter the legal principles of textiles, which hover in the background of this chapter, although they are not its subject. Those principles made it possible for people with tenuous claims to rights to control what they produced—or, at least, to make a stab at it. They also made it possible to turn these goods into economic instruments, further blurring the line between the commercial and the domestic. A towel could be currency and a product for domestic use, both at the same time. As such, the legal principles of textiles added value, beyond the prices affixed to shirts and shifts, coats and dresses, sheets and pillowcases. No wonder so many of the people on the legal margins entered the textile trades in the decades following the Revolution. The legal context made those trades far more attractive than the other bad alternatives available, despite the grueling working conditions and low pay.[5]

Accounts of textile production that do not acknowledge the importance of skill or textiles' legal principles miss a lot. Even as the production of cotton cloth was mechanized and located in factories, skilled weavers—women and men—continued to make wool, linen, and silk fabrics by hand, in their households. Yet that long period of transition has disappeared from view, replaced by the assumption that the mechanization of wool, linen, and silk followed a trajectory similar to that of cotton, although the arc was longer and the pace of change slower. The end point is the same: machines located in factories replaced handwoven fabric that had been made by skilled male artisans, who exited the scene, leaving hand weaving to industrious housewives who knew how to pinch a penny. Even as the manufacture of clothing and other wearing apparel was consolidated in the putting-out system, in which materials were handed out to women who worked in their households and were paid by the piece, skilled dressmakers and tailors continued to make and repair garments by hand. Yet accounts of clothing production follow a similar story line as that of cloth production, although without mechanization and factories. Mass-produced clothing for the commercial market put skilled male tailors out of work, replacing them with unskilled female pieceworkers.[6]

Cloth, clothing, and thread could be made for sale or use, depending on household needs and market prices. This mingling of the domestic and the commercial, which had marked textile production for centuries, persisted in the nineteenth-century United States. Some people produced goods for sale or trade sporadically, folding it into their daily routines when they could steal a moment to themselves. Others worked regularly on a small scale to produce a steady income stream. Still others, like Rebecca Coles, expanded further, coordinating production by putting out materials necessary for spinning and weaving to other women who labored in their households. Women did this work alongside the other labor they performed as wives and daughters. But so did many men who were engaged in textile production. Was it domestic labor when women did it but commercial when men did it? Did production become commercial only if the goods were sold to someone else? Did it matter if they were sold to a merchant or to a neighbor? Were goods that were sold more valuable than those that were not? Those questions are impossible to answer, suggesting that the categories underlying them, particularly the gendered distinction between domestic and commercial labor, obscure more than they reveal. What is missing is a consideration of skill, which determined the economic value of textiles.

"Homespun" captures the importance of skill. In colonial British North America, the term referred to bad cloth and linked that bad cloth to women, who were only beginning to enter the weaving trade. To describe cloth as home*spun* was akin to saying it was not really cloth at all. Spinning produced thread, not cloth, and was the domain of women. Within the artisanal hierarchy of the time, it occupied a place below weaving, a trade dominated and controlled by men until the mid-eighteenth century. So homespun referred to cloth made by weavers who lacked the skills to make good cloth and who should have stuck to spinning—in other words, women. The fact that it was *home*spun was a further dig at the women who made it, indicating that they could not even spin that well. Thread produced for the commercial market was spun within households, just as most cloth was. As such the "home" part of homespun, referred to where the cloth used, not where it was made. Homespun stayed at home, where it could be foisted off on family members who had no choice but to grin and bear its itchy awfulness.[7]

The term homespun acquired additional layers of meaning in the hands of nineteenth-century historians who wrote about the Revolution. The "myth of homespun," as historian Laurel Thatcher Ulrich calls it, wedded Revolutionary-era political conflicts to a false portrayal of both textile production and women's labor. The myth's basic outlines should be familiar to anyone who attended grade school in the United States, even if they were not paying much attention: Patriots turned their backs on imported cloth in favor of homespun, the workaday fabric produced by women who were as dedicated to the Revolutionary cause as they were to their domestic duties. Imported textiles, by implication, were the kind of luxuries that practical Patriots could do without, unlike the degenerate aristocracy against whom they were rebelling. It was a snap for hardworking Patriot women to replace these politically dodgy imports. All they had to do was step up production of homespun, which they had always made as part of their domestic work. Men tolerated the uncomfortable, unfashionable results produced by their well-meaning womenfolk because it was politically important to do so. But, in fact, weaving was not a household chore like sweeping, mopping, and washing. It also required skills that were not an attribute of gender. Men could and did make bad cloth, just as women could and did make good cloth. The imports that Revolutionaries shunned, moreover, included all kinds of cloth, which were all produced by hand in households and depended, in large part, on women's skilled labor. Quality was what distinguished commercial goods, not the location of its manufacture or the gender of its manufacturer.[8]

Government reports, on which historians have long relied in their work on the new republic's political economy, picked up where the myth of homespun left off, erasing the importance of hand labor, skill, and women in textile manufacturing. That so much textile manufacturing continued to be done within households in the early republic facilitated the erasure. In their *Report on Manufactures* (1791), Alexander Hamilton and Tench Coxe marveled at the "vast scene of household manufacturing," as if they had discovered something brand new. "Great quantities" of cloth were produced by "family manufacturing," as they also termed it: "coarse cloths, coatings, serges, and flannels, linsey woolseys, hosiery of wool, cotton, and thread, coarse fustians, jeans, and muslins, checked and striped cotton and linen goods, bed ticks, coverlets and counterpanes, tow linens, coarse shirtings, sheetings, toweling, and table linen, and various mixtures of wool and cotton, and of cotton and flax." Output was "not only sufficient for the supply of the families in which they are made, but for sale and, even, in some cases, exportation," they exclaimed. Production rivaled that of the "regular trades," which included pretty much everything else.[9]

Given that colonists had been so dependent on British imports, Hamilton and Coxe's tone of puzzled amazement had to refer to the scale of production, not its location. Both men knew that commercial cloth production took place within households. Coxe had been involved in a scheme in Philadelphia to promote the manufacture of cloth that relied in part on the putting-out system, which doled out materials to people who worked in their own households. Even so, the two men classified textiles as "household manufacturing," distinct from the "regular trades." In fact, household manufacturing and textile production are synonymous in the *Report on Manufactures*: textiles are the only goods listed in that category. They did not appear among the "regular trades," with the exception of specialized work controlled by men: men's hats, women's silk shoes, cables, sail cloth, cordage, twine, and packet thread. Most of those trades also required spacious workshops clearly separated from the dwellings where workers lived that, consequently, accentuated their distance from "household manufacturing," at least in Hamilton and Coxe's reckoning. All this exclamation about textiles produced within households hid the point that the commercial production of textiles had always taken place in households and still did so in the 1790s. There really was no difference between textiles and the regular trades, except that household production usually included women.[10]

The commercial production of textiles continued to be conducted in households even after the advent of mechanization, although that tight connection did begin to loosen. The 1810 census nodded to those changes by distinguishing between textiles produced within households and by manufacturing establishments. The figures, however, underscored the continued importance of households: families made about 112 times as much cotton as manufacturing establishments, approximately 16.5 million yards, compared to only about 147,000; families made about 134 times as much woolen cloth, approximately 9.5 million yards compared to only 71,000; and they made all the linen cloth, approximately twenty-one million yards, because all linen was still produced within households.[11]

In his summary of those statistics, Tench Coxe downplayed the importance of household production, situating it within a narrative in which it would be inevitably eclipsed by machines, housed in workshops and factories, overseen by men. On the very first page of his report, he acknowledged the continued importance of household manufacturing but characterized it as a transitory stage in the settlement process, one that "facilitate[s] the first struggles of American settlers." He laid out the evidence for that argument with statistics from several counties on Pennsylvania's far western border, although even here he affixed an asterisk. One of the counties with a particularly high number of looms, he noted, did not really fit the pattern, because they were "worked by *male weavers regularly in the trade*." For Coxe, the location of production, the identity of the producer, and the producer's control of the finished goods determined its commercial value. When men controlled production, it was a "regular trade," even if they made textiles and worked in their own households. Household production referred to goods made with the labor of dependents, particularly wives and children, who might also be able to retain legal control over those goods, particularly if they were textiles.[12]

Coxe then launched into an enthusiastic discussion of labor-saving machinery that would transform the production process of all kinds of goods, although his emphasis was on textiles. He foresaw those changes applying both outside and within households, suggesting the extent to which household production still figured into his conceptual universe. He also worked with a generous definition of "mechanization," which included minor improvements to hand-powered spinning wheels and looms as well as machines that replaced hand labor. But the implication was that household manufacturing in textiles would become secondary, as machines located in workshops and factories made goods faster, cheaper, and better. More to the point, mechanization would move control over production out of the hands of household dependents.[13]

Later censuses followed Coxe's narrative that textile production done within households was not really part of the commercial economy and had no measurable economic value, particularly when done by wives and other household dependents. To be sure, mechanization was poised to take the production of cotton cloth out of households in 1810. But wool, linen, and silk would linger behind for some time, although that was utterly unclear from the census reporting. The digest of the 1820 manufacturing census, for instance, dropped the distinction between households and manufacturing establishments in its records of textile production, while providing information about the kinds of tools involved and the number of workers—men, women, and children—employed, county by county in every state. As a result, it seemed like all textile production took place outside of households, in workshops or factories, staffed by employees. Yet the list of tools included wheels and hand looms, particularly for wool cloth, as well as carding machines, spindles, and power looms, making it clear that a good deal of production still done by hand, within households. Notably, there were counties with carding machines but no cloth production. What happened to all that carded cotton and wool? Most glaring was the general omission of linen, which rarely appeared in the county-by-county list of manufactures, even though it continued to be produced by women within their households. Given the county-by-county tallies, it was if all of the approximately twenty-one million yards of linen and most of the 9.5 million yards of woolens reported in that year had appeared out of thin air.[14]

The surge of textile production recorded in US reports actually conformed to longstanding patterns in the global textile trade, in which traditional methods of skilled hand labor were scaled up. Historian Jan DeVries has termed those dynamics the "industrious revolution," whereby people produced more of what they had always made for their own use in order to sell it. All that industriousness fueled the expansion of textile production in Great Britain and Europe in the early modern period. In the colonial period, however, the boom had fizzled on the shores of North America, because domestic textile production could not compete with imports. Recall the relief of England's Board of Trade and Plantations on finding that colonists were importing far more textiles than they were producing in the 1730s. Colonists, who were as industrious as their European counterparts, did make cloth, as that report acknowledged. But they produced basic cloth, intended for use close to where it was produced, not for trade within the colonies, let alone outside them, all of which was restricted by British trade policies. The results were highly variable and often poor in quantity and quality. Even so, the global textile trade still shaped production. For those with the time to devote to the work and the necessary skills and tools to do it, the textiles they produced themselves saved them from buying imports.[15]

While North Americans produced on a smaller scale than their counterparts across the Atlantic, the work took the same forms. The initial stages depended on the labor of women, who had been barred—by law and custom—from the higher-paid levels of textile production for centuries. The output of male weavers was limited by the quantity of thread, the spinning of which was considered women's work: one male weaver required several female spinners working constantly. Given that division of labor, the textile industry needed far more women to turn wool, flax, and cotton into thread than it did men to weave, which was why so much effort was expended on the mechanization of carding and spinning. Even as images of women at their wheels symbolized a kind of domesticity far removed from the economic calculus of the global textile market, actual women in the early modern period were spinning because that market gave their work value. Some worked in a putting-out system, in which they received raw fibers and were paid by the piece. Some worked within artisanal families, in which male household heads were identified as the primary workers but relied on their wives and daughters to spin and often to assist in weaving as well. Even women who spun as part of their domestic chores realized value from their work, by selling what they produced or having cloth made from it. Either way, they saved on the cost of fabric that they and their families needed.[16]

While portrayed as an expression of women's domestic nature, the work of getting raw fibers to the point where they could be made into cloth actually required skill, born of knowledge, dexterity, and experience. The wool sheared from sheep needed to be picked clean of debris and then washed and washed again to remove dirt and excess oils that matted the fibers together. Cleaned wool was then carded to smooth out the tangles, a process that involved combing the fibers between two wooden paddles, studded with sharp metal bristles, which might be best described as the evil relatives of a hair brush. Cotton also needed special handling before it could be carded. The plant's delicate pink flowers turned into seed pods, called bolls, which burst into fluffy, white puffs. After they were extracted from their pods, those puffs needed to be separated from their seeds, which really preferred to stay where they were and clung insistently to the fibers that protected them. The labor involved was why cotton cloth was an expensive import, less commonly used in basic clothing than wool or linen before the invention of cotton gins in the late eighteenth and early nineteenth centuries. Flax, with its long, fine fibers, posed different difficulties than wool or cotton. It came from the stalks of plants with delicate, sky-blue flowers that hated to get their roots too wet, wore out the soil in just a year or two, and needed to be harvested in bare feet so as not to damage its valuable fibers. Once harvested, the plants were soaked in water to loosen the outer coverings, which were then dried and separated with hackles, a piece of wood impaled with long, iron spikes. There is a reason why the phrase "raising one's hackles" is associated with a rising temper: hackles made wool and cotton cards look dainty by comparison. Women slung handfuls of stalks through the hackles, catching them on the spikes and pulling them through, and then doing the same thing again and again, until the outer coverings fell off. Raw wool, cotton, and flax was then

Figure 4.1 Otto Bacher, an American painter and illustrator, erased the economic value of spinning and its necessary connection of women's work to the mass production of cloth in his 1884 image, *A Wheel of Three Generations*. The image, like so many others depicting women and spinning wheels, was more about the virtues of domesticity. Generations of women spun for the market. In 1884, they were still spinning, just as their mothers and grandmothers had done, but in factories for a wage. Otto Henry Bacher, *At the Spinning Wheel*, ca. 1884, Reba and Dave Williams Collection, Gift of Reba and Dave Williams, National Gallery of Art, Washington, DC.

Figure 4.2 With mechanization, the work that women had done by hand moved from households to factories. The setting and the contrast to idealized conceptions of women's labor, such as Bacher's *The Wheel of Three Generations*, made the work seem like more of a departure than it was. In fact, spinning had been low-paid work before mechanization, even though it required considerable skill. Winslow Homer, *The Bobbin Girl*, Mill Girls in Nineteenth-Century Print, American Antiquarian Society.

spun into long strands, the fineness and uniformity of which determined their value. While lots of women spun, not all of that thread was suitable for fine cloth. Some of it was definitely destined for homespun.[17]

The thread that women spun then went to weavers, a trade dominated by men until the late eighteenth century. Weavers fled declining conditions in early modern Europe only to find that the dynamics of the global textile market had followed them across the Atlantic. Some abandoned their trade without ever looking back, thankful for new opportunities. Others continued, often in less than optimal conditions, given the competition from imports and all the restrictions placed on domestic production. Like many male weavers, George Taylor of New Jersey combined the trade with farming. The entries for weaving in his account book from the 1760s to the 1790s are scattered haphazardly among those for planting, mowing, reaping, and slaughtering hogs, making it clear that weaving alone would not have supported him. Other male weavers traveled from place to place, doing the work for one community and then moving on to the next. Such was the life of Benjamin Davies, a weaver who worked in eighteenth-century Virginia. He carried a pocket-sized notebook with weaving patterns, pricing, and fabric samples as well as home remedies for various ailments—all of which would have been handy for an aging man constantly on the move, trying to keep body and soul together.[18]

Weavers faced a double bind in colonial British North America. They were simultaneously underemployed and utterly unable to satisfy the needs of their markets. Taylor, Davies, and their fellow weavers could never have supplied enough basic cloth for their local communities, let alone all of North America. Nor could most North American weavers provide quality cloth at a price to compete with imports. Some weavers possessed the skills to produce high-end wool or linen fabric that was indistinguishable from what was woven elsewhere for the export market, which was presumably what they had been doing back in Europe. But that was not usually what they were asked to do in the colonies. George Taylor did have entries for worsted (a smooth, fine wool) and broadcloth (wool that was woven 50–75 percent wider than other cloth and then processed to shrink it down so that it acquired a density that made the threads of the warp and weft almost disappear). But most of what he did was basic cloth used for work clothes and everyday linens: tow and hemp (both for bags), ticking (for mattresses), dimity (for bed linens and curtains), huckabuck (for towels), diaper (for table linens as well as actual baby diapers), blankets, and carpets. The samples in Davies' notebook were for rough linens, wools, and linsey-woolsey (a linen-wool mix), in simple patterns of stripes and checks, for work clothes and everyday linens.[19]

By the mid-eighteenth century, the incentives that had favored imports for so long began to change, which explains the timing of Rebecca Coles's textile business. From the Seven Years War through the War of 1812, a series of trade disruptions made imports more expensive and less plentiful, so North Americans began producing more cloth themselves. In New England, women moved into weaving before the Revolution, taking over another labor-intensive part of textile production that had been in decline for some time and was being abandoned by men for other, better opportunities. In that section and elsewhere, women expanded their work afterward, as suggested by the record of wheels, looms, and other equipment in North Carolina estates and the impressive output recorded in the 1810 census. But it was not just women who ramped up textile production. Men also expanded their output, although their efforts have been described differently, as manufacturing and skilled labor. Down the road from Coles, near the Chesapeake Bay, John Tayloe organized textile production for his many plantations in the same way, at the same time, and for the same reasons that Coles did. Production also increased in the mid-Atlantic, where many weavers had settled and the trade remained in the hands of men who either expanded their artisanal workshops or managed to retain control of their labor by producing high-end products.[20]

While mechanization coincided with North Americans' entry into the mass production of textiles, hand labor remained central. In fact, mechanization generated the need for more hand labor, even as it undermined the working conditions and pay for those who did it, many of whom were women. In the early nineteenth century, machines could not match the quality of handmade goods, a fact painfully evident in the desperate efforts of cotton manufacturers to find engineers who could coax passable products from unreliable equipment. They were clunky. They did some tasks better than others. And they were often on the fritz and failed to work at all. Even in those areas where they excelled, such as the spinning and weaving of cotton, the results were far from ideal at first. At their best, they could only do basic cloth: plains, in the descriptive terminology of the time. Given that situation, handwork remained necessary, particularly when it came to wool, silk, and linen, which resisted mechanization. Success rested on the same elements required in the mass production of cloth for centuries: the skill necessary to produce high-quality cloth quickly and efficiently. Mechanization accentuated the need for those qualities by reducing the cost of all cloth. The implications forced hand laborers to work faster and better, even when they were not in direct competition with machines. At the same time, mechanization accelerated elements of mass production that generated the need for more hand labor. The deluge of cloth, for instance, also required more people with the skills to turn it into clothing.[21]

The first technological innovations shifted the work of hand labor from one area of textile production to another, work that was often done by women. Carding machines, for instance, eliminated a major bottleneck, making it possible for women to spin more wool and cotton than was possible when they were limited by what could be carded by hand. They also took over work that no one really wanted to do. Powered by water and easily added to mills that ground grain, carding machines appeared all over the new republic, catering to local populations that had turned their attention to textile production. Some entrepreneurs used them to scale up production, contracting with local women to spin the carded wool and cotton and then selling the spun thread to be made up into cloth.[22]

Mechanization jumped quickly from carding to spinning and weaving, although unevenly and most successfully with cotton, which was more consistent in texture and easier to work with than wool, flax, or silk. Men generally worked the early versions of spinning machines; the hand-powered jenny and the mule required considerable skill and strength to operate and maintain. In their tightly organized trade, male spinners retained control over the handling and repair of their machines, passed their skills on to young men raised up in the trade, and hired workers or enlisted family members to assist them. Some textile centers, notably Philadelphia, still relied on male mule spinners operating the machines well into the nineteenth century.[23]

By the late eighteenth century, however, water-powered machines made it possible for women and children to replace male spinners. In 1790, Samuel Slater set up the first mechanized cotton-spinning factory in Pawtucket, Rhode Island. The work of weaving was mechanized shortly thereafter. In 1814, the Boston Manufacturing Company established the first US factory that integrated all aspects of the production process—carding, spinning, and weaving—under one roof. The firm later built Lowell, an entire factory town, named after one its founders, Francis Cabot Lowell, who had made his fortune as a merchant. These factories relied on the labor of women and children, moving the location of work they had traditionally performed in with their households. That situation also reflected the fact that the gendered division of labor had never been as strictly defined in cotton as it was in wool, linen, and silk, largely because the production of cotton cloth was relatively new to Britain and continental Europe. As mechanization moved skills from people to machines, this model of the division of labor collapsed altogether.

Lowell and other New England factories replaced native-born women with immigrant workers, male and female, after a series of strikes in the 1830s. While women still monopolized the ranks of spinners and were paid less than weavers, male and female weavers worked together and received the same low wages. By the 1830s, most cotton cloth was machine loomed, although more complicated varieties still had to be woven by hand. Even with mechanization, however, it would be a mistake to describe factory operatives as unskilled. Tending the machines that spun and wove cloth still required skill, even when women did it.[24]

Mechanization took different forms with silk and wool than it did with cotton but still devalued hand labor, while not replacing it completely. Silk cloth was an expensive luxury for good reason: it was extremely difficult to make. Its fibers were harvested from the cocoons of silk worms, which were carefully unwound onto spools. The thread was so fine and so strong that it was used for sewing as well as silk cloth. But weaving with these strands took time and patience. Not only did it take pass after pass of the shuttle to creep forward on the loom, but the textures and designs woven into the fabric required skill and experience, both of which silk weavers jealously guarded. The Jacquard loom, invented in early nineteenth century, transformed all that by mechanizing the skill required to produce the patterns that made silk fabric so valuable. In fact, the Jacquard loom was not really a loom at all. It was a device that attached to a loom and replaced the skill that weavers brought to the process, by preprogramming all the steps necessary to create patterns in colors and textures. This mechanism would be used on a variety of looms, including those used for wool and, ultimately, power looms. Silk weaving was not mechanized until later in the nineteenth century. Even so, the Jacquard mechanism made it possible for more people with less skill to weave quality silk faster, exposing the artisans who had monopolized the industry to more competition.[25]

While the conditions of male silk weavers deteriorated, the demand for silk thread increased. Women in the new republic stepped up, turning over rooms in their houses to the fussy little worms whose cocoons were the source of silk fibers. The worms would only eat mulberry leaves. Even then, only certain mulberry leaves would do. They not only liked to have their own space, but they also had definite opinions as to temperature, humidity, and airflow. As Deborah Logan, a well-known silk producer in Philadelphia, explained, "They require to be kept very clean . . . in an open airy room free from damp or wet, and to be regularly fed with the white mulberry leaves." Her worms were particularly fond of the succulent leaves from younger shoots. Should any of those conditions fall short of the worms' exacting standards, then they would up and leave or just give up and die. Logan was among the elite women who experimented with the cultivation of silk worms in the late eighteenth century, when the British slapped additional taxes on imports. In the 1830s, she was advising a friend of her niece, who was only one among many women revisiting silk production at that time. That made sense for these elite women, because it involved hand labor and little capital: they could devote space in their houses to the worms, unwind the cocoons, and sell the thread either for use as sewing silk or for cloth making. Women's hand labor was crucial, even when silk was produced on a larger scale. In a letter to Amos A. Lawrence, one of the founding investors in Lowell Mills, Massachusetts, the silk producer J. H. Cobb noted that the included samples were "wound from cocoons here today by my little daughter."[26]

Wool was finicky too, which meant that mass production required hand labor for the first half of the nineteenth century, just as it always had. By then, however, more of those handworkers were women than had been the case earlier. While wool could be carded mechanically, unlike flax, the consistency of the fibers varied and required a degree of dexterity that only experienced hands could provide. Wool's quality also depended on the finishing process, done at fulling mills, where woven cloth was shrunk, treated, and combed to create a tighter texture and finer appearance. Wool manufactories adopted machinery slowly, grafting it onto existing processes, overseen by small-scale producers who coordinated production and distribution, using the labor of local spinners and weavers. The industry's development in the Delaware River Valley near Philadelphia was typical. Manufacturers there replaced the hand labor of female spinners with machines in the 1830s but put out the spun thread to weavers who worked in their own households rather than in centralized factories. By that time, women as well as men were weaving. Manufacturers then finished the cloth at fulling mills and sold it. When weaving was mechanized in the 1840s, factory owners consolidated all those stages of the production process under one roof.[27]

The production of wool cloth was not entirely mechanized until the late nineteenth century, which kept the industry more focused on small manufactories and independent artisans than was the case with cotton. Everyone knew that the best wool was spun and woven by hand, and discerning customers sought out skilled artisans, known by reputation. That was true even when the cloth was mass-produced and sold to distant markets. The

Irvine family, which had a large wool manufacturing business in western Pennsylvania, shipped all over the United States, particularly to southern states. Their customers still requested particular weavers by name. Machines also failed when it came to some kinds of basic wool cloth, such as blankets or carpets, which were so bulky that they were more easily produced by hand. As a result, merchants were still buying handmade thread and cloth into the 1840s and 1850s, long after the spinning and weaving of some fibers had been mechanized.[28]

Linen proved the most resistant to mechanization and continued to be made by hand in households, usually by women, well into the twentieth century. Turning flax's long, inflexible fibers into thread and then weaving them into cloth required fine adjustments that clunky nineteenth-century machinery simply could not handle. That was one reason why cotton replaced linen as the go-to basic cloth for everyday use: machine-made cotton was cheaper than hand-made linen, no matter how little workers were paid. Changes in the term "linens" capture cotton's ascendance. Linens for personal use and the household, such as sheets and towels, earned their name because they had been made of linen. By the first decade of the nineteenth century, however, linens were as likely to be made of cotton. Despite cotton's popularity, linen was used widely for a variety of purposes, particularly for work clothing, because it was far more durable than cotton. While much of it was still imported in the early republic, linen also was produced by women who made cloth for their own use and for sale, if they had the skill necessary to make quality cloth.[29]

Women could turn their labor into goods with value to which they had legal claim through the many small businesses specializing in the hand production of thread, cloth, and clothing that flourished alongside mechanized and centralized factories. The evidence of their output is everywhere in merchants' accounts. It also runs through women's personal records. Mary Palmer Tyler's manufactory in Brattleboro, Vermont, looked a lot like that of Rebecca Coles, although it did not depend on the labor of enslaved women. Tyler had begun like so many other women in the new republic, first spinning thread and then giving it to a neighbor to weave. Eventually she acquired a loom and expanded the business, relying on the labor of daughters, other female relatives, and hired workers. Later she got into silk production. Women continued to produce for decades after machine-made thread and cloth were widely available. In the 1830s, Elizabeth Bagby, a Virginia plantation mistress, wove up to a thousand yards of cloth each year. The women in the Cooley family were still working their wheels and looms in the 1850s. Women like them could be found all over rural America.[30]

The same dynamics extended to clothing production. The Cooley women not only spun and wove but also did tailoring work for the men and women in their community. Their business reflected the fundamental connection between the mass production of cloth and clothing: the more cloth, the more clothing. Turning two-dimensional pieces of fabric into three-dimensional garments made to fit irregular bodies was a complicated process, requiring copious applications of hand labor. In Britain, the ready-made clothing industry emerged in the sixteenth century, because not everyone had the skills required to produce garments. Basic sewing of the kind acquired by most women was all that was needed for simple work clothes and undergarments, which had few pieces and did not require much in the way of fit. Even then, many people paid to have such garments made for them. After all, not everyone lived in a household with a woman who was willing or able to provide the necessary labor. Production of outer garments definitely required professionals, who could oversee all the steps: the cutting of the fabric into the necessary pieces, the multiple adjustments required to put all those pieces together to fit individual bodies, and the final sewing. Cutting and fitting, in particular, required skill and experience. Cutters did not just slap down preformed paper patterns on a piece of cloth and have at it with a pair of scissors. They had to draft the various pieces of the garment in just the right sizes and then arrange them so as to use every valuable square inch of cloth. Fitting usually required several sessions and multiple adjustments, in extremely close quarters with touchy clients. By the time the garments had been fit, the pieces had already been basted together—that is, put together with large stitches that could be quickly put in and pulled out, so as to make the necessary adjustments. The last step was going over the basting with smaller stitches that would hold up under the wear and tear of daily life. Tailors and dressmakers usually handed that task over to apprentices or sometimes even the clients themselves.[31]

Given all those complications, mass production initially targeted the kinds of garments that were more two-dimensional and where the most complicated finish was a few buttons or a drawstring. As with the mass production of cloth, the manufacture of ready-made clothing was about scale, not technological innovation: large, consolidated firms, which coordinated production and marketing, replaced the male-controlled guild system. Manufacturers bought cloth in volume, cut out the pieces, and then put them out to female seamstresses whom they could pay less than male tailors. Some manufacturers gathered their seamstresses together in factories, which were actually large workrooms. But most seamstresses labored at home, which saved manufacturers even more. The ready-made industry specialized in the shirts and pants that men wore for work and the shifts and petticoats that women wore under their outer garments. Slops, ready-made, utilitarian clothing for sailors, perfectly described the construction and design of what the industry produced. At the same time, ready-made manufacturers produced fashionable quilted petticoats made of silk with elaborate designs wrought all over them in tiny stitches. While a staple for the fashionable elite, petticoats were easy to fit: a flat piece of fabric was joined at both ends to form a cylinder, with a drawstring at the top to adjust to the size of a woman's waist. The only customization required was the length.[32]

Merchants in colonial British North America had adopted a system similar to that used by their counterparts across the Atlantic, although on a much smaller scale. Women sewed the cut pieces together or, in the case of petticoats, did the delicate needlework required for quilting. Like spinners, seamstresses worked for less than men and at home, often in a putting-out system. Merchants who sold cloth contracted with local women to make it up into shirts, shifts, work clothes, and other basic garments. As cities in the new republic grew, so did the volume of ready-made clothing. Over time, ready-made expanded into more complicated clothing, particularly for men, such as jackets and coats.[33]

The industry was most visible in New York City, where needlewomen's low pay and poor working conditions became notorious. But women were doing similar work everywhere in the new republic, although their geographic isolation hid their plight and inhibited collective action. When Elizabeth and Amanda Cooley started keeping their diaries as teenagers in the 1840s, the sisters had begun to sew for neighbors, making up simple garments, such as men's shirts, vests, and pants, which were easy to cut and fit. In urban areas, even market towns, these items would have been available as ready-to-wear, sewn by seamstresses who did piecework. In the rural South, it was easier and cheaper to purchase items directly from local seamstresses, who were basically doing the same thing as New York's needlewomen, for the same measly pay. The Cooleys worked on their own. But merchants in rural stores had seamstresses on call, just as merchant tailors did in the cities. Customers came in to buy cloth, and then the merchant arranged with the seamstresses to have items made up. Even in rural areas, such work was usually for basic garments for men, exactly the kinds of garments that were mass-produced and sold ready-made. Geography clearly did not determine the possession of basic sewing skills. People who lived in the country were as likely to be all thumbs as those in the city and as a result needed dressmakers and tailors just as much as their urban counterparts.[34]

The greater availability of cloth fueled demand for the kind of garments that could not be stamped out in the same manner as ready-made goods and required skilled hand labor: dresses, coats, and other kinds of outerwear that were made of finer fabrics, had more pieces, and required more time, attention, and skill to put together. People, even working people, began acquiring more clothing of better quality during the eighteenth century. Peter and Ned, enslaved men from the previous chapter, fled with several items that required skilled tailoring, including dress shirts, overcoats, and coatees (short jackets that were worn like sport coats are today). Like other people of marginal means, they likely acquired such finery secondhand. If they had the resources, they would have had it altered to fit. If not, they made do.

The demand for overcoats, jackets, shirts, and dresses was so strong that it loosened the grip of men on the tailoring trades. In the new republic, the movement of women into types of clothing production once controlled by men was particularly noticeable in the late eighteenth century. In towns and cities, dressmakers cut out new clothes, tailored them, and refurbished used garments. Every rural community had women like the Cooleys, who assisted other women with their wardrobes. Near neighbors came to the Cooleys for a variety of services. Some just needed to have garments cut out. Others needed help with tailoring and sewing. For those who needed more, the sisters made extended visits, staying with customers for a week or two until all the sewing and tailoring for the season was finished. The Cooleys also made men's coats, although they did so reluctantly at first. Coats were different than dresses, in both their cut and construction. Mistakes resulted in the destruction of expensive fabric, unflattering garments, and angry customers unwilling to pay, all of which were best to avoid. After a few tentative forays into this area, they received instruction on pattern making and fitting from an itinerant male tailor who seemed inexplicably unconcerned about the competition his advice was creating. Thereafter, the Cooleys took orders for coats regularly, doing a brisk business right before militia musters, where all the local men wanted to look smart in properly cut and decorated attire, made from appropriately bright fabrics, with contrasting piping, braid, and epaulettes. The fashion demands of muster were probably why the Cooleys were under pressure to make coats even before they knew how.[35]

The Cooleys' experience suggests the difficulties for women and, for that matter, many men who made clothing. The key to moving up was to combine production with the sale of the cloth and accessories to make it. Being located in a city or market town was essential. Beyond that, success depended on copious amounts of credit, which was not available to most people, particularly women. Credit furnished the means to purchase quality goods as well as the social networks to access those goods and the cultural information to anticipate customers' needs. Some women managed to navigate these tricky shoals. In eighteenth-century France, women set themselves up as fashion merchants, an organized trade that specialized in hats, head coverings, scarves, and decorations for dresses. Fashion merchants did not just select goods, although the ability to do so often made the difference between success and failure. They also engaged in production, putting materials together in original ways to create unique looks. Those operating at the pinnacle of the trade exercised outsized cultural influence as arbiters of fashion. In England and British North America, milliners operated similarly to fashion merchants. While associated with the decoration and sale of hats, milliners also supplied fashion advice along with cloth and all manner of accessories, such as shawls, gloves, handkerchiefs, and ribbons. Some dressmakers had shops where they sold the cloth that they then turned into dresses, coats, and other garments. Both men and women continued to operate these kinds of businesses in the nineteenth century. In fact, the sale of textiles and the production of clothing were the businesses that women were most likely to be in, judging from the credit reports of R. G. Dun and Company in the 1840s and 1850s.[36]

Male tailors and female dressmakers operated at a distinct remove from the seamstresses who stitched ready-made garments because they retained control of the value of their skills. By the late eighteenth century, however, they were on the verge of falling into the ranks of low-paid pieceworkers. Credit became even less accessible to all those without the full range of rights. Mass production kept eating into their businesses, moving from slops and undergarments to men's dress shirts, vests, jackets, and coats and then to women's wear as well. Mechanization did nothing to help matters. Sewing machines, invented in the 1840s, were widely available to seamstresses by the 1850s. Their marketers promised that the machines would put high-quality clothing production within reach of every woman by eliminating its drudgery and difficulty. But that was only partially true. Manual sewing machines were awkward, unwieldy, and painful to operate for any length of time. These machines were to the tailoring trades what manual typewriters were to secretaries: they replaced one kind of drudgery with another, which was then offloaded to women, as if the work required no knowledge or skill at all.

Sewing machines, moreover, did not really mechanize clothing production, which was never just about sewing. Even as the machines supported the expectation that all women could and should sew, they did nothing to simplify the most difficult part: the design, drafting, and fitting that had to be done before sewing was ever started. Standardized sizes and pattern-drafting systems addressed those issues, mechanizing the skill of tailors and dressmakers, much like the Jacquard loom mechanized the skill of weavers. The process takes key measurements, such as the neck circumference and the sleeve length, and uses them to calculate the dimensions of the rest of the garment. Standardized sizes sort of fit everyone, because they really fit no one. Mass production was impossible without them. In theory, standardized sizes also made it possible for women with sewing machines to make complicated garments that once required the skill of tailors and dressmakers. The problem was that standardized sizes worked better for men than they did for women, which was why the ready-made industry produced a wide variety of garments for men, including relatively complicated outer garments, but confined itself to basics when it came to women. Through much of the nineteenth century, women wore a single garment, a dress, which multiplied the difficulty of creating standardized sizes. A single, theoretical size had to account for the dimensions of both the upper and lower body, which did not reliably correspond to each other. Men's garments solved that problem by dividing the body in half: pants could be one size, while shirts and coats could be another. So, despite the promises of mechanization, women's clothing still required hand labor long after men's wear had been standardized and available as ready-to-wear. Even men's garments continued to require hand sewing (and still do) if they were to be fitted properly.[37]

In the new republic, the men and women who plied their skills in the textile trades worked in an economically uncertain environment in which mass production was opening up more work while undermining the conditions of that labor even before the advent of mechanization. That was why men had been leaving the textile trades and ceding the work to women. Molly

Current, who wove for Rebecca Coles, struggled to piece together a living just as the weaver Benjamin Davies had done before her. The circumstances of Ruth Bangs in Higham, Massachusetts, were not unlike that of George Taylor. She wove for her neighbors in order to support herself and her six children after her husband died in 1770. The difference was that she did not have a farm to supplement her income or yield a subsistence. Hannah, an enslaved weaver on Robert Carter's plantation in Virginia, asked that she be allowed to purchase her loom when she was emancipated so that she could continue her trade. How else would she support herself?[38] None of these women were going to make a fortune weaving, any more than the men before them had. Still, the production of cloth and clothing provided economic opportunities that were otherwise unavailable to them in the decades between the Revolution and the Civil War. Much of that work masquerades as domestic labor, distinct from the commercial world, because so much of it was done by hand within households. But it was actually an extension of the global textile market, where mass production had always been done by hand in households. Like the legal principles that attached to textiles, the textile economy of the new republic was not really all that new: its roots reached back in time and beyond the new country's borders.

Machines did not transform mass production as much as they intensified processes long associated with it. Suggestive in this regard is the correspondence of Mason and Lawrence, the wholesale textile distribution firm based in Boston that set up shop in the 1830s. Mechanization meant that one of the firm's clients, Salmon Falls Manufacturing, could turn out yards and yards of various kinds of basic cotton cloth: plains, sheeting, shirting, and drills (named, appropriately, for its use in pants and jackets for soldiers, sailors, and enslaved and working-class men). Competition from cheap, machine-made cottons like the ones produced at Salmon Falls decimated the Asian cotton industry as well as the linen industry in continental Europe and Britain, which relied on many poorly paid workers who did the labor by hand, instead of fewer poorly paid workers who tended machines. By the 1850s, Mason and Lawrence was filling orders to send to India and China, which had once supplied cloth to North America. Mechanization altered the patterns of production and trade, but it did not initiate mass production, which was already a fact of the global textile market. Salmon Falls produced exactly the kinds of cloth that had been mass-produced and ordered in bulk in the colonial era, although usually handwoven linen or Indian cotton, not machine-made cotton produced in the United States.[39]

The conditions of textile production were already harsh by the late eighteenth century, and they deteriorated from then on. Textile workers in the new republic traveled a well-marked, well-worn path, trod by countless men and women at other times and in other places within the global textile market. The way became far more treacherous in the nineteenth century, as mechanization accentuated dynamics that had been busily grinding down artisans and turning them into low-paid workers. But the legal principles associated with textiles carried over into the new republic just as the dynamics of textile production did. Even as global economic currents took away control over the production process from textile workers, the goods themselves gave those on the margins the legal means to reclaim the value of their labor. Those legal principles did not negate the uncertain future that textile workers faced. They were not always even within reach. Still, they had the potential to turn low-paid labor into meaningful toeholds in the commercial economy at a time when such openings were few and far between. That is exactly what people did. Their efforts are the subject of the next section.

PART II
PROTECTIVE COVERINGS IN A HOSTILE WORLD

The commonplace book that Elizabeth Bagby kept in the 1820s and 1830s might not seem like an important legal artifact, but it is. Bagby, a white married woman who lived on a modest Virginia plantation, began the book with a remarkable inscription. In the family account, she wrote, "Charge yourself for every article bot [sic] for, and used . . . whether to eat, drink, wear, furniture for the House or Kitchen . . . Doctors Fees &c &c." But "such things as you pay for, in weaving, in butter, cloth or any thing made entirely within yourself, it may be as well to take no acct of, except in way of memorandum." What followed was page after page of memoranda, listing the cloth that she wove each year, the people to whom she sold it, and the amounts that they paid for it. That Elizabeth labeled those transactions as memoranda and not accounts had profound legal significance, and she knew it: accounts tallied up property that lay within the legal purview of her husband, while memoranda kept track of property that belonged to her. More than that, memoranda represented the legal separation of her property from that of her husband by creating evidence of her connection to it.[1]

Like the majority of Americans in the period between the Revolution and the Civil War, Elizabeth Bagby lived in a legal world structured by practices and principles that established the status of textiles as well as laws that limited her own status. For married women like Elizabeth, those restrictions had a specific term: coverture, French for protective covering. In theory, coverture protected wives by subsuming their legal identities within those of their husbands and restricting their ability to act legally in their own names. In practice, it left them exposed, precisely because it was so difficult for them to act legally in their own names. The same logic applied to other status relationships as well: parent and child, master and servant, master and slave. Although these domestic dependents, as they were called, experienced different degrees of subordination, all were positioned within the private domain of the household, under the authority of the household head, from which there was no public appeal. They too were covered in law—to the point of smothering to death. Bagby's reminder to record everything she bought on the family account underscores the presence of such restrictions in the ordinary dealings of everyday life. All the things on that account were the responsibility of her husband. As her husband's agent, Elizabeth needed to keep careful written records, so that he would not be vulnerable to his creditors.

The second part of Elizabeth's inscription, however, captures a very different manifestation of coverture, one that also shaped the lives of those covered by legal restrictions that limited their control of property and their ability to act as their own legal agents. This part—the one about goods made entirely "within" herself—referred to the protective coverings that Bagby and others made in a material as well as a legal sense. Not only did Elizabeth weave cloth that covered the bodies of wearers, but she also tapped into the legal meanings associated with textiles and made them part of the legal order. While longstanding principles recognized the attachment of clothing to the person who wore it, they did not exist as things that people could simply pick up and use whenever they felt like it. Nor did they come to life magically as raw fibers were twisted into thread, cloth emerged on a loom, or seams pulled a garment together. Like all laws, they had to be legitimized through regular use, constant maintenance, and savvy updating. Turning the theoretical principles attached to textiles into legal practice required work, just as the process of turning raw wool, linen, and cotton into cloth did. The memoranda in Elizabeth's commonplace book were one of many strategies that people used to tap into the legal potential of textiles and obtain recognition of them. They did so with remarkable success. In the decades between the Revolution and the Civil War, people without strong claims to property rights stretched the legal principles associated with an individual's own clothes to cover textiles that were clearly produced and traded as part of business enterprises. Courts, particularly local courts, regularly recognized claims to these forms of property.

It was a struggle, given the powerful pull of countervailing currents, both economic and legal. The same dynamics that left so many eighteenth-century textile workers impoverished had reached into all areas of the trade by the early nineteenth century. In case the economics were insufficiently menacing, the principles of private law hovered just above, like dark clouds threatening to coalesce into a storm. When it struck, the logic of civil law could move the textiles of those legally classified as dependents to their household heads' side of the ledger, forever out of their reach. Those same principles extended to free people—men and women—who lacked sufficient property to support themselves and worked for wages instead. Although they were not domestic dependents, wage workers labored under the authority of employers, whose control over the workplace was legally analogous to that exercised by husbands, fathers, and masters over their households. The expansiveness of that legal paradigm kept many people from maintaining control of their textiles and tapping into their legal meanings. Not everyone even tried. For some, particularly at the lowest rungs of the social ladder, the effort seemed pointless, given the forces arrayed against them. For others, particularly wealthy white women, it seemed unnecessary, either because the status relationships that encased them seemed to be working in their favor or because they found it too difficult to imagine alternatives.

Still, the production and circulation of textiles provided legal options that did not exist otherwise. In the first few decades following the Revolution, the ranks of those who availed themselves of those opportunities—or tried to do so—included people who lacked strong claims to rights, property, or both. They ranged across the social spectrum, from elite white women to the enslaved and everyone in between. White women, particularly those of families with some means, were best positioned to make use of the leverage provided by textiles, because of their racial and class privilege. While those privileges never translated into the same range of economic opportunities and legal protections that they did for white men, they did provide white women a wider range of possibilities when it came to textiles—which is why they feature so prominently in the following pages. Poor women, women of color, and enslaved women faced greater restrictions and fewer opportunities than either wealthier white women or men of their same status, even in regard to textiles, saddled as they were with racial and class constraints. But the circumstances of factory operatives, pieceworkers, and even the prison inmates who were forced to make their own clothes were similar to those of wives and daughters, like Elizabeth Bagby, as well as servants and the enslaved in one key respect: they all made attempts to convert time and labor that was not their own in some areas of law into a form—cloth and clothing—that could belong to them in other areas of the legal order. While textiles could not extinguish the structural inequalities in their lives, they offered a means to reshape them.

Those legally resonant coverings that Elizabeth and so many other Americans created existed in close relationship to the laws that distanced them from the governing institutions in the new nation. Yet histories have tended to define the legal order primarily in terms of the restrictive laws, as captured in statutes, appellate cases, and treatises. Views of economic change follow suit, positioning textiles as inert material goods that were made, bought, and sold either within those laws or outside them, in an underground economy, unregulated by law at all. This part of the book argues that the material world had consequences for the legal order as profound as the dominant conceptions of law. The dual aspects of coverture—as legal restrictions imposed by others and as legal coverings that people fashioned themselves—figured in Elizabeth Bagby's life, just as textiles and legal restrictions shaped the lives of so many Americans. Like the warp and weft of Elizabeth's loom, these visibly separate threads came together in a single piece of cloth. The laws that restricted most Americans' legal status formed the warp, the strong threads strung vertically that formed the fabric's basic framework. The weft—the threads that ran horizontally through the warp—consisted of the textiles that people made legally meaningful, by working their shuttles back and forth, making, buying, saving, and selling them, documenting their claims to them, and insisting on recognition of those claims. In so doing, people with only nominal legal standing participated in the construction of the legal fabric that defined governance in the new nation.

5

The Prison Society's Problem

Currency

The Pennsylvania Prison Society had a problem. Between 1789 and 1820, it regularly lamented the poor state of the prisoners' clothing at Philadelphia's Walnut Street Jail. But, as it explained in its 1789 report, the society was struggling because "clothing distributed by the Society to the apparently destitute has in many instances been quickly exchanged for rum." Prisoners not only sold their own clothing but also "forcibly stripp[ed] others on the first admission in Gaol, which though a custom of long standing by the name of Garnish is often productive of great subsequent sufferings." To combat the problem, the society advised the adoption of uniforms that inmates would not be able to sell because no one on the outside would want them. It is unclear whether anyone followed up on that suggestion, because the problems continued. In 1809, the warden advised that clothing given to vagrants be collected when they left the prison. As he explained, some stayed only a short time, accepted clothing, and then sold it "to obtain liquor, [the] injurious effect of which soon brought them back again."[1]

The intractability of the Pennsylvania Prison Society's dilemma was rooted in the fact that clothes were not just necessities or desirable consumer goods. They also circulated as currency. That was particularly true for those whose economic and legal status made it difficult for them to acquire property or credit. Wages often took the form of cloth and clothing. The exchange of textiles for food and liquor was so common that taverns doubled as used-clothing stores, and other businesses accepted cloth and clothing as payment for goods and services. Taverns were inundated mainly because their stock in trade was so popular, as the situation of those housed in the Walnut Street Jail suggests. The connection makes sense of an 1824 complaint to Baltimore's mayor that one city street had become a "mere harbor for drunk and disorderly persons" since vendors of used clothing had moved in.[2]

State and federal policies encouraged the use of textiles as currency, although that was not their intention. Decentralization of the new republic's governing structure extended to regulation of the currency. After the establishment of the First Bank of the United States in 1791, US dollars replaced the units of account in use before the Revolution, when individual colonies set their own standards, often denominated in pounds and tied to the British pound. But that transition took place slowly, as individuals continued to use pounds instead of dollars as the unit of account. Neither the introduction of dollars nor the issuance of coins and banknotes in increments of dollars, moreover, resulted in centralized control of the currency by the federal government, a situation unlike that in European nation-states, particularly Britain. If anything, the financial system became more decentralized with President Andrew Jackson's closure of the Second Bank of the United States in 1836, which gave state banks greater leeway in issuing currency. As a result, currency of the federal government and that of state banks all circulated together and varied wildly in value. Not even US currency was legal tender before the Civil War, which meant that it could be refused as payment—just as notes issued by state banks with questionable records often were. And there was never enough currency to go around anyway, particularly in the decades following the Revolution. The supply of banknotes increased in the 1830s, but those notes added more volatility to system, because their actual value was so unstable. At the same time, legal restrictions on the vast majority of the population created demand for secure, reliable mediums of exchange that ordinary Americans could actually use.[3]

The combination of lax financial regulation and zealous social regulation opened up alternative economic spaces. Yet those spaces remained firmly tethered to the existing legal order. Textiles circulated just like mediums of exchange that bore the imprimatur of states and the federal government. Notably, their value was pegged to the units of account set by those governing institutions. Courts tacitly acknowledged that situation when dealing with disputes over textiles. In this instance, courts were affirming long-standing practice, which appropriated widely known, widely used rules of exchange and applied them to textiles. Through use, people turned textiles into banknotes—which is where textiles eventually ended up anyway, since banknotes were made of rags. Spinners, weavers, seamstresses, dressmakers, tailors, and even washerwomen were all, essentially, printing money.[4]

If anything, the people who used textiles as currency improved on the systems of exchange overseen by states and the federal government. Textiles stored value reliably. There was considerable consensus as to their value. They were extremely liquid. And they were protected by a clutch of law and culture so tight that they had become fused. Clothing was attached by law to its wearer, because it was thought to be deeply expressive of individual character. But the dynamic worked the other way around as well: proper clothing was thought to be the necessary precondition for the achievement, maintenance, and display of inner virtue. It was widely assumed that people needed decent clothing to be decent. By extension, the pursuit of that goal was morally uplifting and socially beneficial. The Pennsylvania Prison Society ran headlong into the implications when it put inmates to work making cloth and clothing. The women spun, sewed, and knitted. The men chipped in as well; as it turned out, there were quite a few tailors in the jail, especially during periods of seasonal unemployment. The hope was that busy hands and better attire would elevate them all. But the results were mixed. While the inmates dutifully attended to their work, the clothes they made were just as likely to be spent as worn. It was difficult to stop that practice inside the Walnut Street Jail. It was hopeless on the outside.

Textiles mediated the relationship between the individuals and the world through which they moved. Garments were so closely connected to the individual who wore them that they literally defined the essence of that person, a connection that made for a distinctive way of seeing people and understanding who they were. In the Renaissance, portrait painters lavished far more time and attention on their subjects' clothing than on their physical features. Viewers looked to the clothing—the colors, the fabrics, the trimmings, and the construction—for information about who the subjects were and why they were being memorialized.[5]

Elements of that visual culture were still current in the eighteenth and early nineteenth centuries and on full display in advertisements for runaway servants and slaves. Ads did include descriptions of the runaways' physical attributes, particularly race and height, as well as features that would distinguish them from other people. But it was clothing that received the most sustained attention, because that was what people focused on when they looked at someone else. For example, in the complaints of criminal activity that the residents of one Philadelphia ward made to their alderman in the 1840s and 1850s, the bodies and clothing of offenders were so intertwined that it was difficult to tell where one ended and the other began. One aggrieved constituent described "defendants unknown" who had "conspired to cheat and defraud him": "one a short man with red Whiskers dress, a blue tight body coat, black hat, another a slim man rather tall dark frock coat and cap, and Whiskers another tall man stoope shoulder dark frock coat." To be fair, the blurred boundaries between bodies and clothing owed, in part, to the harried alderman's haphazard punctuation and omission of conjunctions. The passage nonetheless highlights what the complainant saw and remembered of the men who tried to defraud him: general physical shapes, short and tall, with and without facial hair. But he saw very particular kinds of garments: a blue coat cut to fit closely; dark frock coats, long and loose; and two different kinds of headgear, a cap and a hat.[6]

The bond between people and their clothing was why favored items were saved and passed them down through families: more than anything else, clothes evoked the person who had worn them. That was also why people in the post-Revolutionary United States would drop what they were doing to chase down someone wearing the clothing of a friend or neighbor. They were retrieving a piece of someone they knew, along with a piece of their property, while also restoring the public order that guarded those connections. John McFadden, an Irish laborer in New York City, must have breathed a sigh of relief when he nicked a hat from the house of Timothy Youle and made it halfway down the street with his prize in hand. At that point, though, the thief was nabbed by a neighbor, who marched him back to Youle's house to return the hat to its rightful owner. Intervening could be risky business. In Charleston, Ole Christian made a valiant effort to stop the theft of his boarder's clothing, only to suffer an assault and an attempt "to Gouge him." Even so, people kept a watchful eye on other people's clothes. When Caty Bloomfield complained of a missing dimity petticoat, muslin shift, two pairs of cotton stockings, and one black silk handkerchief at the New York City Municipal Court, she knew exactly where they were and who had taken them: they were at the grocery store of Laurence Rooney, on "the corner of Orange and Criss Streets," where Mary Barnes had pawned them for liquor. Bloomfield did not witness the transaction. Rooney, who profited from it, certainly did not tell her. Someone else who knew Bloomfield had been there, recognized her clothing, and informed her.[7]

Those close, personal connections made theft particularly risky in rural areas, where everyone knew everyone else and it was difficult to disappear into a crowd. Recall Elizabeth Billings's failed escape. Rural people proved surprisingly well versed in their neighbors' wardrobes. In rural Anderson County, South Carolina, Colwin Glasby accused an enslaved man named Henry of taking a "certain frock" from her house, "which has since been recognized and restored to me." James, an enslaved man, who was introduced in the first part of the book and who lived in the same county, recovered his striped velvet pantaloons because they were recognized in the hands of someone else. When Henry Braswell had several items of clothing stolen from his house, including a waistcoat and hat, he could line up witnesses to identify the property, which had been found, presumably by a third party, in the trunk of the supposed thief. Witnesses took their job seriously. As one stated, he was "certain" that "the wescoat" belonged to Braswell, "but cannot testify positively as to the Hat." Confronted with a particularly tricky theft case, officials in rural Granville County, North Carolina, called in a skilled needle woman to identify the provenance of a stolen shawl by its decorative trim. A witness in another North Carolina county swore that a stocking belonged to the man accused of stealing it because "she assisted his wife Jerusha in footing it & put some stitches with a needle near the heel & therefore thinks she knows it to be the same piece."[8]

To succeed, it was necessary to disguise the goods by either remaking them or moving them as far away as possible, as fast as possible. The testimony in a case involving several enslaved people in South Carolina is suggestive. By the time charges were filed, most of the goods had disappeared, and tracing the rest proved nearly impossible. Judy claimed that she got a length of cloth and a handkerchief, alleged to have been stolen, from Sally and Jane. Sally said she got the cloth from Frank. Frank said he got it from Lim. While Lim's connection to that length of cloth fizzled out, he claimed to have gotten another piece of cloth in question from "the Cherokee Ford." That cloth seems to have been a "pants pattern"—that is, precut fabric ready to be made into pants. Jourdan, who was found with it, claimed to have gotten it from "Wiley and that Wiley said he got them from McKees store. Cato says that he saw Wiley have the pants pattern. Primus says that he heard Wiley bargain the pants pattern to [Jourdan] and that he saw him let prisoner have them. Frank says that Wiley offered to sell him a pair of pants pattern such as produced on trial and that Wiley said that he got them at the Springs." It was a complete fog. While the records suggest that at least six enslaved people were charged, they do not reveal whether any of them were convicted.[9]

People noticed clothing because it was thought to provide valuable insight into who that person was. The judgments involved more than class, although elements of early modern law and culture would suggest otherwise. Sumptuary laws pegged dress to social station, limiting what all those outside the elite could wear. Commentators at the time reinforced those connections with constant complaints about the propensity of the working poor to dress above their station, but the volume and velocity of those complaints suggest the extent to which sumptuary laws were losing their power. Poor English women owned and wore prized but prohibited calicos in the eighteenth century. The same was true in Spain and the Spanish empire. It was not just the expense of the materials, moreover, that mattered. The condition of garments, their cut, and the overall aesthetics said even more about who a person was, regardless of social station.

References to clothing served as shorthand for both individual character and broader social issues into the nineteenth century. Clean, well-tended clothes were the universal sign of good order: of diligence, capability, and trustworthiness. Dirty and ragged clothing signaled disorder: an inner state so chaotic that the person could be dangerous to others. In novels, writers introduced their protagonists through descriptions of their clothing. In visual imagery, the clothes of a person supplied insights not just into the individuals but also into the whole situation being portrayed. When people were well dressed, all was well. A person in dirty rags indicated something amiss. In newspaper articles, clothing served as metaphor for pretty much everything, with old clothes signaling the circulation of immorality, disease, and undesirable people. A New York storekeeper ran up against those presumptions when he accused a customer of stealing an expensive cloak. Not only had the storekeeper helped the customer try it on, but he had also let him take it home on approval. Court officials were dubious, given the appearance of the defendant, who clearly did not present well. "Was this man poorly dressed when he came into your store?" the storekeeper was asked. "He was dressed the same as he is now," he admitted sheepishly, "but looked rather cleaner." The storekeeper only had himself to blame if he sold on credit to such an unkempt customer.[10]

Neatness mattered. As explained in 1795 by one advice writer, whose name, Mrs. M. Peddle, sounded as though she were destined for this particular genre: "Resolve to be always neat, or you can never be well-dressed;—a dirty ruffle, a torn apron, &c. are sufficient to disgrace the most splendid apparel." Those admonitions still had currency more than fifty years later. In an advertisement for his New Orleans shop, one tailor touted his "large and elegant assortment of cloths, cassimere, satin, silks, &c." and his competence in making them up "in a style of neatness and fashion not to be surpassed." The achievement of neatness required not just economic resources but also control over mind and matter. One of the insults that wives hurled at their husbands in divorce cases was that they were "without the necessary means to purchase a decent suit of clothes." The implication was clear: any able-bodied man should be able to do that much, unless there was something really wrong with him.[11]

Unsavory characters of all kinds paraded in filthy rags throughout popular culture between the Revolution and the Civil War, not because those people actually dressed that way but because that depiction was used to signal danger and social inversion of all kinds. Rags were not just about poverty; they were about impoverished people who posed a threat or who had been unjustly treated or exploited. They also marked sexual immorality, particularly in women. The term was "ragged" or, for those who favored a bit of embellishment, "raggedy." Raggedy people might also be described as "naked," although that was not technically the case. Naked indicated that what they were wearing was so indecent that it did not rise to the level of real clothing. Typical was the symbolic quality of clothing in the popular tale of a wealthy miser, reprinted widely in early nineteenth-century newspapers. "At one time he afforded himself two shirts annually" but then cut back to just one, which he bought at "an old clothes shop" even though he did not need to. Worse, he wore it "without washing or mending." Enough said. Today, the first title of Horatio Alger's bestselling series, *Ragged Dick; or, Street Life in New York with the Boot Blacks*, might prompt confusion or snickers. But to readers in the 1860s, the term "ragged" made the meaning crystal clear. The series was about a boy who was forced to make his way on his own. If he had parents who could care for him, he would have had clean, mended clothing.[12]

This visual imagery needed no captions. By the late eighteenth century it followed a conventional formula. Ragged clothes had shading and crosshatches to depict dirt and edges so frayed and torn that they would have fallen off a real person. They conveyed serious character flaws, as with a caricature of the miserly woman, published sometime between 1840 and 1880. The caption read: "Vain, hoarding miser, worst of all thy kind." Her love of money leaves no room in her heart for anyone else, particularly a husband: "Let filthy lucre be thy Valentine." The verse was hardly necessary. Her pile of coins and ragged attire told the tale.

The obsession with neatness reached beyond the moralizing middle class. Mrs. Peddle managed to load that bit of truth with heavy condescension: "Neatness is always within our power, and will always render you respectable in whatever rank of life you are placed; but finery, without it, is nothing more than a ridiculous glare, which is never seen but with disgust." Even poor

Figure 5.1 Comic Valentine Collection, Library Company of Philadelphia.

people aspired to neatness, which was about the quality of the garments' construction and the overall aesthetics of the ensemble. Clothing of inexpensive materials could pass the test, just as that of expensive materials could fail. Working people went to great lengths to acquire and maintain clothes whose quality was regarded as above their station by their social betters. The effort mattered—a lot. For the poor, whether free and enslaved, doing laundry could be an ordeal. They had few, if any, changes of clothing, which complicated matters. Then they had to find the time to wash and dry the clothes as well as soap and clean water, or the money to pay someone else to do it for them. Clothes that were in frequent use also required regular attention, which was why worn but neatly patched garments were different from ragged clothes in need of mending. If anything, neatness mattered more to those with few resources because they had to sacrifice so much to accomplish it.[13]

Judgments based on clothing had real consequences and profound implications. Clothing as ragged as Dick's signaled parents' dereliction of their duties, compromising their legal claims to their children. Attention to dress meant better employment, better marriage options, and better treatment more generally. That was particularly true in the lives of those who faced the most restrictions and the fewest opportunities. Toby, an enslaved man in New York City, tried to tap into the magic of clothing when he fled his master. The first thing he did was purchase a new suit of clothes, which he obtained from a tailor on credit by representing himself as a servant of the wealthy, well-known Van Rensselaer family. He lied because he knew it would be impossible to obtain employment without suitable clothes, and it was impossible to obtain those clothes without credit, which he did not have. Ultimately, the whole scheme came crashing down when the tailor demanded payment and Toby had yet to procure a job. Unable to come up with the funds or return worn clothing, he was convicted of theft.[14]

Moralists had been agonizing about the increasing availability of textiles—and, more accurately, their cultural and legal powers—for at least a century by the time of new republic's founding. The calico craze of the early eighteenth century had prompted handwringing all across Europe. All those colorful Indian cottons blurred the lines of status, not only by dissolving the visual distinctions that separated rich and poor but also by encouraging the poor to imagine different lives for themselves. In England, one author argued that a ban on this kind of fabric would "be an inducement to Virtue and Good Manners, and Servants will not think themselves above their proper Imployment." If anyone could dress well, then how could you tell those of real status from those who were striving to achieve it or, worse, merely pretending to occupy it? How could you tell who anyone was at all? More gravely, such fluidity would undermine the entire social structure. By the nineteenth century, declining prices and the greater availability of all kinds of textiles had further scrambled those visual cues. Those concerns led to a cultural obsession with confidence men and painted women in the early republic—people who should have been clad in rags but were instead dressed as upstanding members of society.[15]

Best for those on society's margins to temper their concern with clothing. Clean, well-tended clothing was one thing. But, as moralists warned, too much interest not only led to depravity, poverty, and (inevitably) rags but also defined a weak, inferior constitution. As the inimitable Mrs. Peddle put it: "A fanatical and expensive turn in dress, is the certain mark of a little mind." She was speaking to elite white women in the late eighteenth century, a time when republican values cautioned against luxury and excess. But similar advice was directed at all women, domestic servants, common laborers, the enslaved, and people of color throughout the period between the Revolution and the Civil War. Even if they could afford fine clothes, they should temper their desires lest they be seen as silly and shallow or, worse, end up on the primrose path to ruin.[16]

Here again, visual imagery gave those cultural conceptions concrete form. Print culture put white women, African Americans, and working-class men in outlandish getups. Edward W. Clay's infamous series of cartoons, *Life in Philadelphia*, featured vicious caricatures of free Blacks trying to follow fashion but missing the mark. The woman's bonnet was grotesque, and the point was abundantly clear: even if free Blacks could buy quality clothing, they could never wear it well, just as they could never occupy the same status as white Americans. Just in case anyone missed the point, Clay added dialogue. "What you tink of my new poke bonnet, Fredrick Augustus?" asked the woman. He replied, "I don't like him, no how. Cause dey hide you lobly face, so you cant tell one she nigger from another." The punch line plays on whites' racist notions that Black faces were not distinguishable. They all bore the marks of little minds.

White women's fondness for fashion was also a target of criticism. Images of them in spectacularly bad attire were so common by the early nineteenth century that it seemed as if the pursuit of fashion was a uniquely feminine weakness—although that was hardly the case, as the unpaid accounts of tailors specializing in men's wear suggest. Artist James Gillray managed to skewer both wealthy and poor white women at the same time in one particularly brutal cartoon. On the left side was a thin, elite woman, looking absolutely terrible in a high-waisted Regency-style dress, with the label "a soul without body." On the other side was an overweight, working-class woman looking equally terrible in the same dress, with the label "a body without soul." It was clear that neither had much sense. Gillray and Clay were working in different times and places: Gillray in England in the 1790s and Clay in the United States in the 1820s and 1830s. But the similarities in their work are striking, suggesting how widespread the visual conventions had become.[17]

Ridicule recognized the very thing that it sought to constrain, namely, the value of clothing, which took economic forms that were well known by the late eighteenth century. People in the new republic had enough familiarity with textiles and clothing that they could spot fine linen, silk, and wool at ten paces and assess trimmings, such as ribbon and braid, just as accurately. At closer range, they might be able to determine where the items had been produced or even who had produced them. And everyone knew the difference between

Figure 5.2 Edward Williams Clay, *Life in Philadelphia*, plate 14, Philadelphia 1830. Library of Congress Prints and Photographs Division, Alfred Bendiner Memorial Collection, Washington, DC.

well-made garments and poorly constructed ones. When Caty Bloomfield made her complaint in the New York City Mayor's Court, for instance, she was deliberate with the details. It was not just a petticoat; it was a petticoat made of dimity, a sheer cotton fabric, often woven with stripes or checks, which was still something of a luxury in 1817. Similarly, it was a *muslin* shift, *cotton* stockings and a *black silk* handkerchief. Those designations were meaningful as well. Cotton stockings, generally machine-loomed and store-bought, were

Figure 5.3 James Gillray, Following the Fashion, London, 1794. Library of Congress Prints and Photographs Division, British Cartoon Prints Collection, Washington, DC.

a splurge for most people. So was a handkerchief made of black silk, which added a bit of flourish to an ensemble. Muslin, a plain cotton, was more ordinary, although its ordinariness was duly noted and recorded.[18]

All the details included in an advertisement for Peter, the fugitive from slavery in part I, take on new meanings in this light. He had:

1. A blue cloth coat, a term that usually referred to a heavy overcoat.
2. A brown coatee, which was a tight-fitting jacket, modeled after military uniforms, waist length in the front, with short tails, worn under an overcoat and over a shirt and vest.
3. A dove colored twilled nankeen coatee that had either been purchased used or was an older garment that he had grown out of, because it was faded from washing and had sleeves that had been let out.

4. Several Marseilles vests, so called for the fabric, which had raised designs woven into it so that it resembled quilting.
5. Some shirts of fine white Irish linen, a description that indicated high-quality shirts.
6. Pantaloons of India nankeen, a designation—like the reference to Irish linen—that indicated quality fabric and a fitting choice for pantaloons, which were more current than breeches, with their outdated cut that stopped at the knee instead of falling to the ankle.
7. A beaver hat, which was still a mark of distinction, although widely available by the early nineteenth century.

The man legally positioned as Peter's master assumed that everyone would know the difference between a coat and a coatee or an old, altered garment and a new one made to fit. Similarly, he expected that everyone could distinguish Marseilles fabric, Irish linen, and India nankeen from lesser-quality goods and a beaver skin hat from one made of felt or straw.[19]

He was right. People not only noticed all those details but quickly translated them into standard units of account, just like states, banks, and private individuals did when they evaluated notes and other bills of exchange. Those conventions were on prominent display in theft cases across the United States, since textiles ranked high among stolen items. Parties to these cases could rattle off information about fiber content, colors, and patterns that most people today would never notice, let alone remember. Then they attached value to them expressed in standard units of account, with which people had surprising facility. Susan Munro, for instance, bought three gowns from a vendor on the street in New York City for five dollars. But she paid in dollars and shillings.[20]

In fact, the value given to articles did not indicate the medium in which value was satisfied. Rosenah Gray, who appeared in part I, sold a piece of gray silk from her collection of cloth to a neighbor woman for six shillings, which was paid in a "silk quilt & dimity petticoat." Margaret Cooney, who had a store in her New York City house, agreed to pay a peddler seven shillings and six pence a yard for a length of silk. "Accordingly," she gave him "twenty four Dollars and what liquor he Drank & Crackers & Cheeses he & the other man had eaten" while they were there. Of course. The calculations of Margaret Guignon, who took in boarders, were equally circuitous. One man, "not having any money" to pay for his board, sewing, and mending, gave her three pairs of silk stockings and two shawls, which Guignon valued at nine dollars and put toward his bill. Then she turned around and sold one pair of the stockings for ten shillings. Try to figure that one out.[21]

Those exchanges took place in New York City in the first two decades of the nineteenth century, but the patterns were similar all over the United States in the years between the Revolution and the Civil War. In Kershaw County, South Carolina, John Godwin accepted spun thread and handwoven cloth as payment for goods in his store. In one notation, he indicated that "5 yds homespun = 3 yds muslin," which was valued in dollars and cents. Wyatt Harris, the free Black man who lived in rural South Carolina and was embroiled in a court case over an overcoat, bought his coat for five dollars and paid for it with a pair of shoes and a pair of pants. Amos, an enslaved man who did a tidy business selling goods to other enslaved people in the adjacent county at about the same time, had to deal with such calculations on a regular basis. In one exchange, he offered three pairs of shoes for seventy-five cents each in cash or a dollar each on credit, with the higher price covering the longer time before payment was due. His customer agreed to the cash price, and paid in "40 watermellons at 10 & 5 cents," an oven (a covered pot) worth a dollar, and a debt owed him by another enslaved man that he transferred to Amos. The whole thing ended up in a fist fight when the customer failed to deliver the promised watermelons in a timely fashion and Amos demanded payment at the higher price he charged for credit.[22]

Not only were textiles easily valued, but they also came in a variety of forms, which gave them considerable flexibility as a medium of exchange. It was possible to store value in textiles and exchange them for a loaf of bread or a tanker of ale, all without much haggling. Outer garments—coats, dresses, shawls, and long lengths of cloth—could cost hundreds, even thousands of dollars, if they were made of high-quality fabrics, such as silk, wool, or chintz (elaborately painted cottons, with a shiny finish that would be ruined if washed, which made them utterly impractical for most people). But such highly valued items were cumbersome for small transactions. It was like bringing a hundred-dollar bill to buy a stick of gum: the mechanics of making change made the whole thing impossible. So it was fortunate that there were other options. Outer garments were less expensive if they were made of more common materials, such as cotton or linen. Even pricey lengths of cloth could be cut up into small pieces or made into less costly items, such as vests or the short jackets that women wore over skirts and dresses. Petticoats, shirts, and shifts were not only worn under outer garments but also tended to fall below them in value, although that varied depending on the fabric's quality. At the lower end were items like handkerchiefs and neckerchiefs—the lengths of fabric that men secured around their necks to keep their shirt collars clean and that women draped around their shoulders, with the ends tucked into their bodices, for modesty and warmth. Basic linen or cotton handkerchiefs served much like dollar bills today, which was why handkerchiefs were a favored mark for Fagin in Charles Dickens's *Oliver Twist*. Value always depended on the condition of the textiles and the garments made of them, with wear and tear functioning as a discount. When people specified the details of cloth and clothing, they were offering information that established its value as surely as the numbers on a banknote.[23]

Textiles filled the need in the new republic for a flexible, reliable, accessible medium of exchange, which was particularly acute for those who could not access the dominant medium of exchange, namely, credit—the practice of extending payment for goods over time. In the period between the Revolution and the Civil War, merchants ran credit accounts in the name of a family's male head of household. Other members of the household bought goods, charging them to that account, and paid for them over time in goods, labor, cash, and the transfer of other goods or debts. The relationships that these accounts created were as important as the value they represented, which was why they were settled at irregular intervals. Some merchants settled up at the end of each year, although in those cases it was more likely that a balance due would be carried over than paid up. Most accounts stayed open and active, without a full settlement, until something disrupted the relationship: a death, which forced a reckoning of the estate, or an event that resulted in the financial collapse of either the merchant or the customer. While backed by law, these credit practices also rested on direct, personal knowledge. It was about confidence, born of experience. Without it, merchants would not willingly extend credit. Yet even longtime customers could be too slow to pay off their accumulated arrears. In fact, merchants did not have much choice but to extend credit to those who came in their stores if they were going to do business at all. The trick was to keep all the balls in the air, getting enough from their customers to satisfy their own suppliers. But that was not always possible. While some merchants were loath to pursue the resulting debts through civil suits for fear of alienating customers and losing their accounts, they often had no choice. Neither did artisans and tradespeople who operated closer to the margins. They needed to be paid, as the voluminous case files in local courts suggest.[24]

The inherent instability of the system was why it depended on law—actually, private law. Accounts were in the names of white men, because the law offered a number of options to collect on their debts if it became necessary. Not only did white men have the full range of rights, which made it possible for them to enter into contracts in their own names and to be sued if they failed to meet their obligations, but they also acquired responsibility for the debts of their dependents—wives, children, slaves, and even hired servants. Those dependents could not contract in their own names, which made it impossible to mount a civil action in private law to collect the debts they had incurred. The implications were clear in the credit reports of R. G. Dun and Company. Mrs. M. B. Harris, a Virginia milliner, had "conducted bus[iness] for yrs in an honest & efficient manner, paying for all she buys & no doubt will continue to do so." But she was married and had "no ppty in her own right," which made it impossible to collect on her debts. The property that she had belonged to her husband in civil law. Similarly, another milliner "stands well & regarded good for her purchases" and was doing "a very good little bus[iness]," but was "not legally respons[ible] or reliable," a judgment that referred not to her business acumen but to her marital status.[25]

The legal underpinnings of credit made it difficult for the vast majority of the population to buy goods and services, even if they had the legal status to contract. A Dun report on a Connecticut milliner from the 1880s captures the general problem. The agent considered her "an honest Girl" who would "pay all bills she might contract for." But, he added, "at the same time I do not know of any way to collect a debt of hir [sic] as she has no property" apart from her earnings. In short, those without property could not always obtain credit, even if they had what seemed like sufficient incomes from their work and the necessary legal standing to claim property and access to private law.[26]

Actually, dealers in textiles could and did extend credit to all sorts of people, outside the framework of private law. Within it, however, the availability of credit was limited, given the legal rules. In private law, the debts of domestic dependents were not actionable because they were not their own, which was why existing laws limited wives to the purchase of necessaries and prohibited merchants from selling to enslaved people. The debts of poor people were not really actionable because they had no way to cover them.

Even banknotes and coins did not eliminate the kinds of personal assessments and legal barriers that characterized credit. In theory, they did: with them, payment was made at the point of purchase, eliminating the risk to merchants as well as the biases that kept so many people out of commercial exchange. Practice was altogether different, however, because banknotes and coins were not always what they purported to be. Popular culture brimmed with warnings about women passing counterfeit bills. In these tales, white women whose dress would have passed muster with Mrs. Peddle posed the greatest threat: their propriety gave them free access to stores and protected them from scrutiny inside, allowing them to breeze in and out, drop counterfeit bills with impunity, and leave flustered clerks powerless to act. Those stories may have had some basis in fact. But they also served to undercut all women's credibility as traders, making their possession of banknotes and coins suspect in all circumstances. One thief in Charleston used those cultural biases to silence the young daughter of his victim, who found him with cash that he had stolen from her mother's trunk. "If you say any thing of what you have seen," he threatened, "your mother will be sent to the work house as an imposter, for having so much money about her, & you and your Brothers will be bound out." Even though he was the thief, he was betting that his claims to this form of property would be far more believable than that of his victim simply because he was a white man.[27]

Class as well as gender figured into the thief's calculations. His victim was a working woman who lived alone with her two children in a rented room. The fact that she had "bank notes amounting to 50 dollars" and "one hundred silver dollars commonly called Spanish milled dollars" did not square with her circumstances, suggesting that she had come by them through nefarious means. That was why those on the economic margins used these mediums of exchange with caution. Marking bills and coins was one way to trace ownership. Even then, marks did not always work, as two enslaved people in the South Carolina upcountry found out. One witness testified that Jemima had changed four quarters of a dollar with Doctor, who had marked each with a cross to identify them. In this instance, changing literally meant cutting up the dollar, which was likely a Spanish dollar, not a banknote issued in the United States. According to another witness, the quarters were then passed them along to Scipio, who testified that the pieces were all marked. From there, they went to Boatswan, who claimed to have received "4 quarters from Scipio and marked them for the purpose of a Raffle." He "returned them to Scipio . . . that same quantity . . . all marked." Other testimony muddled that chain of custody. What was clear was that the markings served to legitimize the currency's circulation through the hands of enslaved people whose possession was bound to be suspicious. The evidence was sufficient to convince the court that only one of the slaves was guilty—although the records do not indicate who.[28]

These enslaved people used marks for good reason. Like many southern states, South Carolina limited their use of banknotes. Furious at finding an enslaved person buying goods at a local store in Camden, South Carolina, with a banknote, a white customer who worked as an overseer insisted that the transaction was prohibited. State law, he maintained correctly, forbids a merchant from accepting banknotes from a slave. What then unfolded seems so choreographed that it had to have been played out many times before. The merchant solemnly agreed with the irate overseer. The enslaved man took that as his cue and gave the banknote to a free Black man standing nearby, who gave it to the merchant. The merchant then handed the goods over to the enslaved man. The jury apparently agreed with this rendering of the law; it acquitted the merchant of trading with a slave. This outcome, however, was not guaranteed, which is another reason why the use of textiles as currency was so widespread.[29]

Textiles not only accomplished what banknotes and coins promised, but they actually did the job better. If anything, textiles represented and held value far more reliably than banknotes. Textiles did deteriorate over time. But the same thing happened with banknotes, given financial policy in the United States, a fact lampooned in a widely circulated pamphlet, *The History of a Little Frenchman and His Bank Notes: Rags, Rags, Rags*. The Frenchman in question came to the United States from Cuba with eight thousand dollars in gold. On his arrival in Savannah, he deposited the gold in a bank there, thinking that it would be secure. But when he tried to take it out, he was told that they did not pay specie and that he had to accept banknotes. He did, thinking that banknotes were worth their face value wherever he went. But as he traveled north, he found out that the notes declined in value the further away he moved from Savannah. When he presented these notes—which he calls rags—to merchants and innkeepers, they discounted them and gave him different, locally issued notes in exchange, which were discounted in turn, although not always at the same rate. Confused, he poured out his tale of woe to a fellow traveler. Why, he asked, would the "legislature of your country" allow a monetary system that meant surrendering sovereign power? "Is the privilege of coining money, one of the highest attributes of sovereignty, permitted thus to be exercised by bankrupts, and tavern-keepers, whose notes will either not pass at all, or pass under a depreciation, which increases in a ratio with the distance you are from the place of emission?" Had he known that banknotes also were prone to decline in value over time as well as geographic space, his diatribe would have been much longer. (He probably did. The Frenchman's facility with the English language casts doubt on his purported nationality and his naiveté in regards to the US financial system.) By the time working people in Baltimore received their pay at week's end, for example, the banknotes they received were worth far less than what they had been promised at the beginning of the week, when they were hired.[30]

The Frenchman was right: the figures on a banknote were rarely what they claimed to be. To add to the complications, there were all kinds of them: notes issued by the federal government; notes issued by states and state-chartered private banks; notes issued by individuals, often called notes of hand or promissory notes. They were all, literally, notes: a promise to pay, reduced to writing on a piece of paper, sometimes no more impressive than a Post-it, although without the sticky part. Notes issued by states and banks, which had the backing of known institutions, had advantages over notes issued by individuals. But who knew if the bank would keep its promises? Who knew if it even existed? There were so many banks, and it was impossible to keep track or check them out, particularly if they were far away. Even states were not all entirely reliable. That is where James Allison, a merchant in Hillsborough, North Carolina, ran into trouble. In the formal language of the indictment, he "did Expose for Sale, sundry Goods, Wares and merchandize . . . to be paid in Gold or Silver Only, and then and there with force and arms did absolutely and utterly refuse to receive in payment . . . the paper currency of the said State, emitted by the Legislative authority and by Law made a tender in all payments whatever." It was 1783. Allison might be excused for having doubts about the creditworthiness of his newly created state.[31]

The characteristics of textiles, by contrast, were out in the open, and everyone knew what they meant. Silk was worth more than cotton; well-made clothes were worth more than badly made ones; new garments were worth more than used ones. In the 1830s, a basic linen or cotton handkerchief in good condition hovered at about a dollar, depending on quality, size, and wear. Good silk handkerchiefs went for about two dollars, again depending on quality, size, and wear. It was possible to find someone who would give a fair price for a handkerchief, because there was consensus as to what a fair price was. That was not the case with banknotes, which could even lose all value without any warning. The weaknesses of cloth and clothing were more predictable. They got dirty. But they could be rehabilitated with a good scrub. They got worn. But a good dressmaker or tailor could restore their value by

Figure 5.4 A parody of worthless banknotes, or "shinplasters." This one appeared during the Panic of 1837, which many blamed on the policies of President Andrew Jackson and his successor, Martin Van Buren. Note the giant bug marring the figures that establish the note's value. New York, H. R. Robinson, 1837. Prints and Photographs Division, Library of Congress, Washington, DC.

taking them apart and turning them inside out or otherwise mending and refreshing them. It was clear when textiles were reaching the end of their life, making it possible to get value out of them before they actually turned to rags. The Frenchman and others using banknotes were just stuck. You could stare at a banknote all day and never be able to reckon its true value. Nor could you do anything about it. All the washing and mending in the world would not make those "rags"—to use the Frenchmen's term—any more valuable.

People approached other goods more warily for good reason. When George Mayhew was offered what looked like a good deal on a gold watch, he was sorely tempted. The watch looked expensive. But he hesitated, because he had so little familiarity with fine watches. Was it really gold? Was it all flash, with the inner workings just junk? After hemming and hawing, he insisted on taking it to a jeweler for appraisal. It was only after being reassured that the watch was, in fact, worth between forty to forty-five dollars that he agreed to pay the purchase price of twenty dollars: fifteen dollars to the seller and five dollars to another man to cover a debt owed by the seller. But the difference between the appraised value and purchase price should have raised alarm bells. The watch had been stolen. But the seller also took a risk if he accepted banknotes from Mayhew. Theft cases involving banknotes regularly list their printed value and their actual value, because they were not always the same. An 1850 case, for instance, included a ten dollar bill of no value from the Bank of Lower Canada. Even coins could be confusing. Not only did they come from different countries, but they were commonly cut into pieces so as to eliminate the necessity of making change. In 1805, one theft case included a half Johannes, ten pistareens, ten shillings, twenty-five cents, ten six-penny pieces, silver dollars, and silver half dollars. An 1839 case listed values that suggested a similar jumble of coins: one piece of silver coin worth one dollar, one silver coin worth ninety-three cents, ten other pieces of silver coin worth thirty cents each, and eight other pieces silver coin worth twenty-five cents each. The legal terminology of "pieces" in this and other cases could mean, literally, pieces of coins. To complicate matters, coins were often shaved, meaning that someone filed off the edges, reducing their value.[32]

That situation made textiles more liquid than banknotes. "Being without money," as one New York City woman explained in 1804, she took one of her husband's shirts and "sold it to Mary Fogerty for five shillings." The shirt was as good as money. Actually, it was the same thing as money, or about as close as you could get to it. In rural areas, women regularly paid for store goods with spinning or weaving. Apprentices usually received a suit of clothing—a freedom suit—at the end of their service, a longstanding tradition that was written into their contracts. In Philadelphia, one alderman would substitute cash "in lieu of clothing," because these grants of clothing were not just tokens. The payments, in the range of thirty and forty dollars, were substantial. Whatever form they took, freedom suits not only allowed apprentices to occupy their new status of free people but also provided a tidy nest egg that they could use to get themselves started. The fine line between textiles and currency collapsed completely in the case against James Millander of Charleston. Millander was accused of stealing "two promissory notes," actually "Bank Bills by which the President Directors & Co. of the Bank of the United States promised to pay or demand . . . the respective sums of twenty dollars and fifty dollars and one waistcoat and one pair of overalls of the value of sixteen pounds twelve shillings sterling." (Overalls were pants that fit over shoes or boots, not the work clothes that we associate with the term today.) Even banks treated textiles as currency.[33]

Liquidity was why local courts across the country adjudicated a steady stream of cases involving stolen handkerchiefs, hats, shirts, shoes, coats, and dresses. Textiles were likely targets for theft because they could be used to buy pretty much anything, anywhere, at any time. In 1820, Mary Menix admitted that she took a counterpane (a bedspread) off a wash line in New York City, where it was drying, and "took it immediately down to the market & there sold it to Mr. Cornell for twelve shillings." In Richmond, a free Black man was convicted of stealing a five dollar banknote and ordered to return the property, which he grudgingly handed over in the form of a pair of shoes and $1.92. That presented no problem whatsoever for the original owner, since shoes could be spent just as easily as $3.08 in banknotes or coins. Textiles circulated freely in rural areas, as evidenced in the experience of Robert Haskins, who was robbed of a watch, six pairs of stockings, knee buckles, a black cravat, and a purse containing about four pounds while staying at a rural inn outside Charlottesville, Virginia. The thief was apprehended the next morning. By that time, he had managed to sell the cravat and five pairs of the stockings. The other items proved harder to dispose of. The Frenchman would have understood.[34]

The prevalence of theft underscored the importance of law in constituting textiles as currency. People flaunted the law to obtain textiles because the law made textiles so easy to spend. Paradoxically, it was the law's recognition of the deeply personal nature of clothing that made it possible for people to turn them into currency. Textiles existed simultaneously as a unique form of property so personal that it could not be separated from its wearers and a ubiquitous form of property so liquid that it could be sold without a second thought. People performed that transformation through practice, a constant whirl of exchange in which textiles passed from hand to hand, allowing those with few economic options a means to buy necessary goods and services as well as other textiles. Even as textiles took the place of other mediums of exchange that were beyond the reach of most Americans, their movement followed the same paths, established and overseen by Britian and, then, by states and the federal government of the United States. The circulation of textiles was a product of the existing legal order. The laws generated it; they also regulated it.

When rural women spun and wove, what they were doing was no different than what their husbands were doing when they worked in the fields: they were producing goods of value, whether used or sold. More than that, they were creating economic instruments that could be exchanged, just like their husbands did when they traded their crops. The same could be said for spinners, washerwomen, seamstresses, dressmakers, tailors, and the inmates at the Walnut Street jail—really anyone in the textile trades. People with few economic options and weak claims to property rights then leveraged the value of those instruments, not only circulating them but also accumulating them as capital, as the next chapter shows.

6

Jane Cooley's Loom

Capital

Jane Cooley lived deep in the Blue Ridge Mountains with her husband, son, three daughters, and a loom. Her husband was old and frail. Her son was something of a wastrel. Her daughters were far more reliable. With them, she ran a textile business, which allowed her to cover a significant part of the household budget, including food and clothing for the family as well as linens, cooking utensils, and decorative items for their home. Jane's textile business also allowed her to amass capital in the goods that she produced. The results shaped her experience of coverture, the legal doctrine that subordinated wives to their husbands, as well as the expectations of her daughters, Elizabeth and Amanda, who wrote about their lives and dreams in their diaries. Both mixed updates about work and family with musings about transporting themselves out of their lives as dependent daughters and into futures that looked a good deal like their mother's life.[1]

The full value of the goods made by the Cooley women and other textile producers like them have been hidden amid presumptions that wives, daughters, the enslaved, and even wage workers could not legally control the goods they produced. From this perspective, the economic dealings of all those people appear fundamentally different from those of white men whose possession of rights allowed them to move freely within the commercial economy. More than that, it appears as if those restrictions represented a legal world of the past, one that emphasized social ties, not the impersonal dynamics of contract and the cash nexus. Those enmeshed in that world still engaged in barter, exchanged gifts and favors, and labored for reasons other than monetary compensation, because their legal status made it impossible to engage in the commercial economy.[2]

The focus on restrictions, however, obscures the legal qualities of textiles, which gave these items value beyond what they fetched at the store. Like the inmates of the Walnut Street Jail, the Cooley women were producing goods to which they had powerful claims and that they could leverage in a variety of ways. Cloth and clothing could not only be turned into currency; they could also be made into capital that people without strong claims to rights could control and use to support themselves and their loved ones. They amassed capital in the same way that they spun, wove, tailored, sewed, mended, and laundered: through the creative application of their labor in circumstances not of their own choosing.

The same legal texts and government reports that hid the extent of household production also separated those involved, particularly women, from the value of their work. Amplified by popular culture, this toxic miasma enveloped everyone associated with domestic dependence. Their labor appeared as something different from real work. The skill involved was negligible, as was its value. What little value was there, moreover, belonged to someone else.

The ideology of white supremacy that whites used to legitimate slavery spilled over onto all people of African descent, characterizing them all as incapable of anything other than menial tasks closely supervised by whites. That false narrative was self-perpetuating, limiting free Blacks' opportunities while erasing the value of the actual work that all people of African descent did. Many municipalities and states barred from free Blacks participating in skilled trades. The men and women legally positioned as masters and mistresses not only appropriated the labor of enslaved people, even skilled artisans, but also attributed it to themselves. Promoters of white supremacy went to so far as to argue that the burdens of slavery lay more heavily on the people defined as masters and mistresses in law than on the people they enslaved. While enslaved people lazed around shirking their duties, their masters and mistresses labored round the clock, working their fingers to the bone, just to support their ungrateful charges.[3]

The value of women's labor slowly evaporated within the scripts of nineteenth-century culture as well. During the first decades following the Revolution, the rhetoric of male independence associated all white women, even unmarried women, with a domestic realm characterized by altruism and sentiment. Later, the ideology of separate spheres further distanced women's productive labor from commercial exchange, by construing it as a component of women's nature, more an expression of love than actual work. Those stereotypes divided women along the lines of race and class, excluding those who were enslaved or too poor to maintain the requisite domestic standards in their own households. Of course, those middle-class standards required domestic servants, whose labor was also devalued. The overall effect was to obliterate the value of all women's work. Even as these cultural narratives blithely dismissed the grinding work that poor and enslaved women performed for their families, they also turned domestic labor into a social obligation and then attributed its value to male household heads, be they husbands, fathers, masters, or employers. In fact, women's labor was rarely portrayed as their own in the late eighteenth and early nineteenth centuries—which was why Rebecca Coles's textile manufactory was attributed to her husband.[4]

Alexander Hamilton and Tench Coxe, who exclaimed about the volume of textiles produced domestically in their *Report on Manufactures* (1791), also revealed the importance of household dependents' labor, particularly that of women, and then separated them from it. One correspondent from Ipswich, Massachusetts, sent a detailed report on lacemaking, which included samples as well as yardage; the area produced about 41,979 yards of lace between August 1789 and August 1790. All that lace, according to this correspondent, involved the labor of over six hundred women—about 25 percent of the total female population in Ipswich. Correspondents elsewhere supplied similar reports, which was how Hamilton and Coxe were able to construct that "vast scene of household manufacturing."[5] Yet even as Hamilton and Coxe acknowledged this fact, they erased the labor of everyone but the male household heads, separating "household manufacturing" from the "regular trades," a distinction that simultaneously acknowledged and subsumed the labor of all those households' domestic dependents, particularly that of women. It was dependents' labor that distinguished "household" or "family" manufacturing from the "regular trades." But their labor was not their own. It belonged to the household head.[6]

Later reports blotted out "household manufacturing" altogether. The category lingered on in Coxe's 1810 summary, although with the assumption that it would be replaced by centralized factories using machine rather than hand labor and overseen by men. Still, the 1810 census counted cards, spinning wheels, and looms along with other kinds of tools and machinery. It also broke out textile production in terms of goods produced by "families" (which would have included Rebecca Coles's manufactory) and those produced in "manufacturing establishments" (which were unlike Coles's manufactory).[7] The figures for family production—which implied the presence of wives, daughters, and other domestic dependents within the household—dwarfed those of manufacturing establishments, suggesting the importance of this form of production in textile production. Even so, direct references to domestic dependents as laborers were few and far between. Women appear once in the opening index, under F, as "females, now much employed in manufactures," as if they had not been before. On two of those pages, Coxe gushed about the possibilities of using the labor not just of adult women but also of children and the elderly, impoverished, and infirm, both free and enslaved, in textile production. Only on the third page did he mention the presence of women in weaving, "a good knowledge" of which, he noted, "may be obtained in a few weeks." Even women could do it! In his comments, Coxe managed to bury the presence of women and the importance of their skills in textile production.[8]

How could anyone trace the connection between household dependents and the work they did when there was no way to track them by name? Until 1850, they all appeared as unnamed appendages of their household heads in the population censuses. In 1840, Jane Cooley figures only as a check mark in the column marked "free white persons, females, 50 thru 59." In that year, the census form lists six people in the Cooley household, with two employed in agriculture and one in manufacture or trade. While it is possible that the census taker was referring to Jane, it is unlikely. Jane's husband followed a trade, watchmaking, in addition to his work on the farm. Had the census taker seen Jane's work as an actual occupation, he would have counted Jane and her daughters in that category. Innovation in the census forms did not alter the habits of recording of women's work. While the 1850 forms contained spaces to write in the names and occupations of free household members, it still excluded the names of enslaved people. Census takers dutifully filled in the new spaces for names. But, as per their instructions, they only asked free males fifteen and older for their trade, occupation, or profession. So, in 1850, the census taker listed the names of Jane and her daughters, Amanda and Juliann, who were unmarried and still living with her. He left the spaces for their occupations blank. Following standard practice, he did not position Jane as the head of her household, although her husband had died a few years earlier and left control of the family farm to her. Instead, she appeared as the dependent of her son, who headed up the list of family members and was the only one with a recorded occupation.[9]

In the US census, it was as if Jane and her daughters were just living with their kin. A census of free Black residents of Philadelphia, taken in 1847 by a committee of Quakers, provides a telling counterpoint. Where US census takers walked through Philadelphia neighborhoods without noting the occupations of the women who lived in male-headed households, the Quakers were far more attentive. Their census contained forty-seven categories, including the occupations of all household members, women as well as men. Work mattered to the Quakers, who were trying to show that free Blacks were supporting themselves and that, given their economic conditions, women had to labor for wages. Although the census did not record the names of women who lived in male-headed households, their occupations unspooled in a long, continuous list, revealing the pervasiveness of work that so often went unrecognized. The numbers are startling. The 4,309 households surveyed included 3,358 working men and 4,249 working women—figures that included children. Textiles dominated women's work, with 1,970 employed as washerwomen, 486 as needle women, and 103 in the rag trade. The next largest category, with 786, was general labor, described as "doing a day's work," which referred to women doing daily domestic service in white households, as distinct from those who lived in. Only 290 were listed as "occupied at home," referring to keeping house—which the Quakers, unlike US authorities, recognized as work. On the Quaker census, the wife of Miles Cutcheon was "washing and sewing." On the 1850 US census, Jane Cooley appeared to be doing nothing at all.[10]

That was hardly the case. Jane Cooley's "domestic dependency" was a fiction, for her household depended on the economic value of what she produced and what she made of that value. Like so many men in the period between the Revolution and the Civil War, Jane's husband was unable to support his family through his labor alone. He plied his trade as a watchmaker and tended to the fields on his modest farm. But there were only so many watches to fix in the sparsely populated part of Virginia where the Cooley family lived, and only so many ways to get crops to market, which limited the farm's commercial potential. Enter Jane and her textile business, which included everything from raising sheep for wool through spinning and weaving it into cloth, to cutting, sewing, and fitting clothing for local men and women. Jane's daughters worked in her manufactory before they married and left home. By the time Amanda and Elizabeth began their diaries in the early 1840s, they and their younger sister Juliann were the only daughters still living at home. Elizabeth then married and set out for Missouri in the mid-1840s, leaving just Amanda and Juliann. But Jane was always on the lookout for labor. When her son married, she promptly took his wife into the business. She also relied on Jinsy, a young enslaved girl, who worked as a farm hand and, occasionally, for Jane.[11]

The economic value of the textiles that women produced altered the dynamics of their legal subordination. If anything, Jane Cooley's son was more dependent on her than she was on him. Not only did she control the family farm, house, and personal property in 1850, but she also had managed an independent business her entire adult life. Her son, by contrast, struggled, at least according to Jane's daughters. The Cooleys, like other households, relied on the significant value of domestic production. If women did not produce those goods and provide those services, then their families had to buy them. Women also monetized their domestic skills by taking in boarders and selling foodstuffs as well as washing, mending, and sewing. But within the realm of work open to women, the textile trades were particularly lucrative. To be sure, no one got rich. Washing was hard, dirty, low-paid work. If there had ever been a golden age for women who spun decent thread or sewed an adequate seam, it was so far in the past that no one could remember it by the nineteenth century. Even highly skilled artisans struggled for a livelihood, long before Lowell opened its doors and the readymade clothing industry planted itself in lower Manhattan. Those economic conditions explain why once lucrative areas of textile production opened up to women as well as men whose race, ethnicity, or lack of property foreclosed other options. Still, textile production had definite attractions that the other kinds of work open to women—and even work open to many men—did not have.[12]

Consider the term "pin money." The term was—and still is—used to brush aside the importance of women's work, particularly textile production, as something so insignificant that it could only cover minor purchases like pins. In fact, pin money constituted an essential part of the economy and a considerable source of wealth for women. In a metaphorical sense, pins referred to valuable property—textiles—that lay within women's purview. In a literal sense, they were neither inexpensive nor insignificant. In the late eighteenth and early nineteenth centuries, pins were costly imports, valued as gifts and kept in ornate boxes. They were essential tools for dressmaking, tailoring, and even basic sewing. Before the 1820s, when new forms of fastenings replaced them, pins kept women's clothes on their bodies: they fastened the fronts of outer dresses worn over shifts, petticoats, and corsets. The term pin money offers a very different perspective from that of Hamilton and Coxe. It captured actual economic practice, in which many married women in particular controlled household manufacturing and maintained some control over what was done with the income it produced.[13]

Jane and her daughters were part of a long line of free women, white and Black, who relied on the proceeds of textile production to support themselves and their families. Where the income from men's work could be sporadic and uncertain, women's textile work could provide a steady income stream that smoothed out those ups and downs, filled in the gaps, and kept families afloat. In urban areas, men who worked as day laborers and in the trades earned low wages, experienced irregular employment, and could be gone for long periods of time. Absence was a fact of life for sailors. It was also common for other men in the ranks of the working poor, as the criminal records in New York City suggest. Many of the men who landed in court came to the city from all points up and down the East Coast and abroad looking for work. More often than not, they came alone, leaving their families to fend for themselves while they were gone. Those patterns held in other port cities, which were communities of transient men and settled women, who assumed responsibility for themselves and their families while their menfolk were away. Even men who remained in place could not always bring home a wage that could support their families. The working poor scrambled to make ends meet in an economic context with few good options, a situation that often meant moving from job to job. That economic instability, coupled with discrimination against Black men, was why so many African American women in the Philadelphia census worked as washerwomen, seamstresses, dressmakers, and rag pickers.[14]

It was not just the working poor who faced uncertain economic conditions. The economic realities of the late eighteenth and early nineteenth centuries meant that volatility was a fact of life even for the well-to-do. The Ipswich lacemakers who appear in Hamilton and Coxe's *Report of Manufactures* are a case in point. Those lacemakers sustained their town's economy from the early eighteenth century well into the nineteenth century. The original migrants to Ipswich came from lacemaking areas of England and, after a brief hiatus, returned to the work when the area suffered a series of economic blows that undermined its agricultural economy. Lacemaking carried Ipswich families through the upheavals of the Revolution and nearly constant war among European powers, the effects of which spilled over into the new republic, especially in coastal towns like Ipswich. Lace had advantages that the goods produced by men did not. Not only was it light and easy to transport, but it was also in relatively constant demand. In 1760s, when a bushel of corn sold for two or three shillings, a single yard of lace brought eighteen shillings or more. One person could carry hundreds of yards of lace to market in their pockets, which was impossible with bushels of corn. From the outset, Ipswich lacemakers fed the growing demand by adopting fashionable styles and altering them so that they could be made quickly and priced reasonably. Initially they sold to merchants or agents, some of whom were women, who then resold the lace through their commercial contacts in other towns and cities. By the early nineteenth century, the industry had become organized in the same way as other kinds of textile work: as outwork, controlled by commission merchants, usually men, who handed out supplies and then paid for finished work by the yard. But the commercial importance of Ipswich lace had been well established long before men became involved.[15]

In addition to the structural instability of the economy, women had to contend with the frailties of individual men, whose abilities and conduct did not always warrant the open-ended grant of authority placed in their hands. The textile manufactory of Mary Palmer Tyler, who appeared briefly in part I, had everything to do with the incompetence of her well-connected husband, Royall Tyler, a lawyer and playwright. Blessed with all the benefits of his wealthy merchant family, Royall managed to squander them. By the time of his marriage to Mary, he had blown through most his inheritance on women and drink, pastimes in which he continued to indulge after he became Mary's husband. His debauchery was well known, which was why John and Abigail Adams breathed a sigh of relief when their daughter, Nabby, ended her courtship with him. As Abigail put it, Tyler was "rather negligent in pursueing [sic] his business . . . and dissipated two or 3 more years of his Life and too much of his fortune to reflect upon with pleasure; all of which he now laments but cannot recall." Mary Palmer, eighteen years Tyler's junior, might not have had much of a choice, marrying as she did amid a swirl of rumors that pregnancy had forced her into the union. What followed was a lifetime of making ends meet, in which textiles figured prominently.[16]

But it would be a mistake to see textile production as something forced on women because of economic destitution. It was just a fact of life for many women, even relatively wealthy women, because they expected to contribute to the household economy and to their own economic well-being. Jane Cooley had no illusions that her husband would be able to support the family through his labor alone, even though he was responsible and hardworking. But if her daughters' diaries are any indication, she also enjoyed the work and the value of what she made. Similarly, Rebecca

Coles's textile business cannot be explained by financial necessity. Married to a man far wealthier than Jane Cooley's husband and far more careful with his finances than Mary Tyler's, Coles did not have to produce cloth. But she did. So did Elizabeth Bagby, whose husband owned a store, plantation, and twenty-six slaves.[17]

One attraction of textile production was that it offered women the means to turn the value of their labor into a material form that they could keep. Those rewards were tucked into Rebecca Coles's records in an entry detailing the large order of fabric that Coles purchased herself, which included linen, calicos, muslin, lustring (either a glossy silk or polished cotton), and ribbons—all expensive imports with colors and textures that she could not manufacture. In this she was like other female textile producers, who traded what they made for other kinds of cloth, usually finer, more colorful, and more valuable than what their skills and equipment would allow. In 1772, Sarah Tisdale paid for most of her account, which included an expensive selection of imported muslin, silk gauze, and chintz, with thirty and a half yards of Virginia cloth that she made. A neighbor, Ruth Mosse, paid for six yards of red-striped Holland, a fine linen, with bags of coarse cloth that she likely wove herself. In the 1840s, Jane Cooley and her daughters were still going to town "a trading," to buy silks, wools, and printed cottons fine enough for dresses as well as ribbons, laces, and other trimmings with the wools, linens, coverlets, and carpets that they produced.[18]

Jinsy, the enslaved girl who worked in the Cooleys' household, did the same. While unable to leave the Cooleys, live on her own, or claim the value of her own labor, Jinsy was able to exercise some discretion over her time, at least as Amanda and Elizabeth described it. She spent some of it spinning, weaving, and sewing, and kept the value of some of those products for herself, just as Polly did. In July 1843, Elizabeth noted that Jinsy "has been weaving her cotton dress." The attribution of possession was meaningful. Later, Elizabeth noted that Jinsy "went to town" and "got a dress and a heap of finery." Like so many other people without strong claims to property, Jinsy plowed her resources back into textiles, a form of property that she could keep.[19] Her strategy echoes that of Hannah Gray, a free Black woman living in New York City in the first decade of the nineteenth century. On coming into possession of several banknotes in large denominations, Gray immediately exchanged them all for textiles: a hat, a long gown, a cap, a pair of stockings, a pair of shoes, a check apron, some red flannel, a short gown, a handkerchief, and a jacket. Her possession of the notes was suspicious—for

Figure 6.1 The Virginia Museum of History and Culture identifies the woman in this image as Elizabeth Ann Cooley McClure, although she is identified elsewhere by family members as Amanda Cooley. Either way, her dress is made of expensive silk, lace, and trimmings, which she likely purchased with the proceeds from the textiles she, her sisters, and her mother produced. Virginia Museum of History and Culture.

good reason, since her daughter had spirited them away from the man legally indentified as her master. The clothing was less so.[20]

The Burnham sisters, who worked on and off in the textile factories in Lowell, employed a similar strategy. While in Lowell, they took the opportunity to buy cloth in bulk, at low prices, to send home for resale. Augusta's letter to her sister Lucy Ann in June 1844 was typical. "If you are not perfectly satisfied" with all the goods "that I sent up for your dresses you had better sell them & I will get you something els [sic] that will suit you better." But "if you do like the goods & can sell it for" a good price, then "I think you had better sell it . . . & I will get you something that you will like as well, if not better." But she was full of admonitions. Augusta did not want to extend credit: "If any one wants it & cannot pay for it, immediately," "you may let them have it," but only "if you are sure of your pay in a short time." Nor did she want to divide up the cloth into smaller, less valuable segments: "Be sure & not cut the goods." They were still wheeling and dealing in 1850. "If you have not sold that table cloth you may sell it for one dollar & eighty seven cents . . . or you may sell the pair for 3.75 cts or you may compare them with the one that I bought for you, the white one I mean & if you think it will do to ask 2.00 dollars a piece or . . . four dollars for the pare [sic]," wrote one sister to another. "If you can sell that pair," she continued, "I will let you have one of those [blankets?] & sheet brown table cloth for 3.25 cts." Sales required tact and skill. "I don't want you should tell any person out of the family what I gave for those blankets and tablecloths," she wrote, clearly concerned that others might expect a discounted price given the good deals available in Lowell. The sisters knew what they were about when it came to value. In 1850, Augusta took pains to explain why she had not withdrawn her sister's money from the bank, as she had been asked. "If I should take the money out now you would not receive any interest from the first of May up . . . as the next quarter commences the first Saturday in May." The interest was a "measly one quarter" percent and would not amount to much, but "a penny saved is better than two earned." That was true, be it textiles or currency.[21]

Why buy cloth? Women were turning property that they made and controlled into more valuable forms. While the new republic's leaders sunk their fortunes into land, everyone else had cloth. As local court records suggest, all kinds of people, all over the country, had stored away surprisingly large stashes of textiles, not all of which they were going to wear or even use. Rosenah Gray, the enslaved woman whose stock of fabric included silks and calicos, was clearly investing in textiles. As she explained, she had twenty dollars and then converted it into fabric and clothing, which she bought from a peddler and intended to resell. She sold some right away and put the rest aside to sell later, which makes sense. A wardrobe made from that cloth would have been completely impractical for anyone who had to do manual labor for a living, as Gray did. One dress, yes; several, no. Similarly, it is hard to imagine that the store of cloth owned by two Charleston carpenters was meant for their own use or even that of their wives, if they had them: forty-six pieces of Canton crepes, thirteen pieces of China satin, and ten pieces of Nankeen, each piece worth five dollars each. They could have made pantaloons out of the Nankeen; their wives could have made dresses from the crepes and satin. Even then, this amount of cloth would make many more pairs of pants and dresses than two men and two women could possibly need, considering that each piece contained many yards. These fabrics were intended for other people. Worth the equivalent of seven thousand dollars today, they represented a small fortune or an investment of their earnings.[22]

It is easy to miss the use of textiles as financial instruments to store value because they also functioned as consumer goods. Rosenah Gray's and the Charleston carpenters' stashes were obviously investments because they were so large. The savings of other people lay alongside textiles that they used. They could even be one and the same. In 1786 Boston, for instance, Margaret Foxwell reported the theft of one white corded dimity vest and trousers, two shifts, two pair of thread hose, four cloth laces, and one handkerchief. It is difficult to parse this list. She might have been using the shifts, hose, and handkerchief. But what of the cloth laces, which were hand-worked lengths of lace that could be the size of handkerchiefs or larger? Perhaps she used them to decorate a dress she wore only occasionally. And what about the vest and trousers? It was unlikely that they belonged to her husband, if she had one, because they would have been identified as his property, not hers. The same would have been true for a son old enough to wear them. While all these items could have been in use, it is also possible that were being stored, until Foxwell found the right moment to leverage their value. The collection of fabric taken from Ann Lewis in Charleston had a similarly ambiguous quality. In 1814, she reported the theft of five gowns, one damask silk shawl, and nearly three yards of Russia duck, a type of heavy linen or hemp fabric that was used for sails (if thick enough) or men's work clothes (if it was of a finer weave). The articles as well as their location, locked within a trunk, suggest that they were not being used. To be sure, Lewis might have stored the gowns that she was not wearing. But people generally hung everyday wear on pegs. Besides, gowns usually referred to fancy dress, not ordinary dress. The Russia duck might have been waiting for Lewis to get around to making it up into clothing for a male relative. Yet, like Foxwell's stash, this collection of textiles was useful not just as clothing but also as a way of storing value. The practice was clear with a boarder of Ole Christian, who also lived in Charleston. In 1824, the boarder left six shirts, two coats, three pantaloons, and seven vests in Christian's care to be saved, not worn.[23]

Textiles were investments that fit within the material circumstances of people's lives. The vast majority of the population did not have a room of their own, let alone their own house, which made it difficult to store property safely even when they had clear legal claim to it. In urban areas, families with their own houses lived cheek by jowl with servants, extended family members, and boarders. Neighbors, family members, workers, and boarders flitted in and out. The absence of hallways, seen as wasted space and impossible to heat, magnified the lack of privacy. Even rented rooms were not really separate from other parts of the house, which meant that people were about all the time, on their way through to somewhere else in the building. If there was a partition, it was a flimsy wall or a door without a lock. Some rooms did not seem habitable at all: basements had no light or air; attics were freezing in the winter and scorching in the summer; and outbuildings were used for work and storage and not designed for human habitation. People nonetheless lived there, and lodgers might sublet a corner of the space or even half of the couch on which they slept to someone else. Similar circumstances were common in rural areas, where living conditions could be more crowded than in cities because the housing stock was so rudimentary. The term "dwelling house" applied loosely to buildings that housed people, not farming operations, although they were often used for such work. Their intended function was the only thing that distinguished them from outbuildings. More substantial dwellings were larger but still crowded, with several people sleeping in each room. Unless they were insulated and built to facilitate ventilation, houses soaked up the summer heat and let in winter's cold, and they were usually dark and dreary. The elite might have might have larger houses and more space to themselves, but they were still living among other people all the time.[24]

The pervasive lack of privacy helped to establish individual possession of textiles, a form of property that required witnesses to establish ownership. People could make legal claims to textiles, but they had to be seen with them to tap into their legal qualities. When ownership was questioned, litigants lined up witnesses who could testify to those physical connections: dealers who had sold them items; seamstresses, dressmakers, and tailors who had made or altered garments; and neighbors who had witnessed the transactions through which textiles were acquired as well as the items' proximity to and use by their claimants. When Rosenah Gray was charged with stealing the impressive store of cloth in her possession, she proved her innocence through neighbors who witnessed their purchase and who, in turn, bought items from her. In Charleston, Timothy Halley ran into trouble because he lacked such witnesses. The property in question consisted of household linens and clothing, which had been locked in a trunk and stored in the house of Deborah Davis, the accused thief. The clothing was nowhere to be found, although a sheet and towels did turn up in Davis's house. But a servant undercut Halley's claims to ownership, testifying that Halley had given the items to Davis in payment for storing the trunk, and they had been in use by the household since then. No one else could establish the existence of the other items Halley claimed to have been stolen, let alone his connection to them, because he had kept them secreted in his trunk. For all anyone knew, he had made them up out of whole cloth. Davis, by contrast, had a demonstrable connection through acquisition and use, observed by others. She was acquitted.[25]

While textiles needed to be seen, they could not be out in public all the time because they would deteriorate. To preserve their value, they had to be stored. Trunks served that purpose, in both practical and legal terms. Trunks were mobile storage units for those without houses or rooms of their own. But they also could establish a legal connection between the property within and person who claimed it, particularly if the property in question was textiles. While people talked about trunks as a kind of property even those without rights could own, they were really more like fences. People owned the fences surrounding their land. Apart from the land they encircled, however, fences had little value. They were just a pile of lumber, a bunch of rocks, or decorative flourishes of wrought iron. Similarly, the conception of ownership of trunks was as much about the items within as the container itself: trunks had legal value when they contained items that could be claimed by their owners, which was why they so often contained textiles. Trunks could not establish ownership of property that a person could not own. Nor could they establish ownership by themselves. But they helped in making those claims by separating the property inside the trunk from that of others: the landlord who owned the house where the trunk owner resided, or the husband, father, or master who had claims to the trunk owner's body and, hence, property. Timothy Halley's case suggests the underlying logic. His problem was not that he put his textiles into a trunk but that most of the textiles he claimed to have been in the trunk had never been seen and had not turned up in anyone else's possession. The few items that had surfaced had been in use by someone else in her own house. That particular combination of factors undercut the power that trunks ordinarily had to override the presumption that moveable property belonged to the person who owned the house where it resided.[26]

When people put textiles in trunks, closed the lid, and locked it, they legally reduced these objects to their possession. If the lid was still up, the property had yet to be claimed. Technically, the trunk was still open if the lid was closed but unlocked, because anyone could get into it. The rules were well known, which was why Catharine McPhee faced theft charges when some of her master's handkerchiefs were found in her trunk. In court, she offered a series of explanations, hoping to counteract the impression that she was trying to establish ownership by placing the items there. As she contended, she put the property in her trunk "without any intention of defrauding" her master and "intended to give it to him before she took her trunk away." To support that claim, she explained that her trunk remained unlocked while in her master's house, which meant that she did not control its contents. She was acquitted. Those practices were as closely followed in the South Carolina upcountry as they were in New York City. When Elijah Gould complained of theft, he noted that the perpetrator not only "opened his door and entered his house" but also "opened his chest that was locked." The house might not have been his; the trunk definitely was. Those details carried such weight that they often appeared on complaint forms, which contained the basic information necessary to establish the crime: names of the complainant and the suspect (if known), the date of the alleged crime, the items stolen, their value, and the location of the incident. That location was often a trunk. Those legalities also explain the search warrant issued by a local magistrate in Kershaw County, South Carolina, for a suspect's "cloths & pockets" and "his trunk." The clothes that he wore and the contents of his trunk, which likely included textiles as well, were the suspect's property.[27]

Like fences, trunks made for good neighbors. Without them, who could tell whether property not currently in use belonged to the wife or the husband, the boarder or the landlord, the enslaved person or the people legally positioned as master and mistress? With them, the boundaries were clear, which why was trunks were routinely invoked in theft cases. Consider the dilemma of a free Black sailor who boarded with Sarah Thomas in her basement room in New York City. Thomas claimed that her boarder stole goods, including men's clothing a sailor would likely have: a pair of pantaloons, two shirts, one bandana handkerchief, a fur cap, and a plaid silk handkerchief, which was a particular luxury. He claimed the goods as his own, but the court convicted him of theft largely because the clothing was in Thomas's room, which gave her stronger claims to ownership, even though it was difficult to imagine that she would ever wear the property. The sailor would have had more luck making his claim if his clothes had been stored in a locked trunk.[28]

To say that everyone had trunks is an overstatement, but only just. They were everywhere. People with more resources had larger, decorative trunks that were also valuable, in and of themselves, as pieces of furniture. It was no accident that the wife of Pierre St. Pé stored her textiles in an armoire. It was a glorified trunk. When the notary opened it and saw her things, he closed the door and moved on because he knew that the armoire was a legal container for her property as well as a piece of furniture.[29] Other trunks were smaller and portable, but still showy, with painted exteriors and lavishly lined interiors. Many more were simply serviceable, constructed of wood, metal, or heavy cardboard, battered, beaten, and nothing to look at. In a pinch, other textiles could serve the same purpose as a trunk. The standard image accompanying advertisements for runaway servants and slaves featured their belongings wrapped up in a bandana, dangling from a stick. Everyone knew what the bandana meant. John Thomas invoked those meanings in an effort to escape charges against him for stealing two coats, two pairs of pants, a shirt, a vest, and two handkerchiefs from a very unhappy shoemakers' apprentice. It was not theft, he insisted, because the items were found in a bandana that belonged to him. In this instance, it was not much of a defense, because the clothing was known to belong to the apprentice. Tying up someone else's clothing in your own bandana was like putting it in your trunk, closing the lid, and locking it. It proved that Thomas had tried to reduce the apprentice's clothing to his own possession.[30]

At a time when houses were not private spaces, the kind of legal separation provided by trunks was essential even for homeowners. The complaint of Ann Lewis, the Charleston woman who claimed that her five gowns, shawl, and Russia duck had been stolen, indicated that the items had been stolen from her house. But she was identified elsewhere in the documents as Mrs. Ann Lewis, so it might have been the house where she lived as a renter, not a house that she owned. Even if the house were hers, there were an awful lot of people coming and going: not only the thief, who seemed to have wandered in without much difficulty, but also a female witness whose relationship to Lewis was unclear. Her presence was fortunate because she could provide the details necessary to establish Lewis's claims to the property. As she testified, she saw the thief break open Lewis's trunk and take the items from it. If there were any doubt as to Lewis's ownership of the property, the testimony put that to rest. For those without a steady place of residence, trunks allowed them to carry their property with them and keep it secure. The property of Ole Christian's boarder was in a trunk—in a sense the boarder was really the trunk, not its owner, who had left the trunk in Christian's care while he was

Figure 6.2 The standard image that accompanied advertisements for servants and slaves included a bandana with the runaway's clothes. Courtesy of Freedom on the Move, https://freedomonthemove.org/.

away from town. The thief failed to break it open, foiled by the twenty iron padlocks that secured it. So he stole the entire trunk instead.[31]

Even enslaved people had trunks, which allowed them to cordon off the kinds of property to which they could make legal claims, particularly textiles. In one complaint a Kershaw County magistrate was careful to distinguish between the property of the white man who made the complaint and the property of the people he enslaved. The "negro dwelling house" from which the property was stolen was "the property of this deponent," the man legally positioned as a master. But the clothing was stolen from "a large chest & one trunk," which made them the property of the people who lived in the house. The logic was clearly stated in another case. The complaint identified a suspect who "has been guilty of the crime of committing an outrage at the farm of Elijah Wyatts . . . by breaking into some locked chests . . . and plundering them of their contents and carry[ing] off certain articles by violence belonging to a servant belonging to said E. Wyatt." That "servant" was an enslaved man named Charles. The formal complaint emphasized the salient legal points: while the location of the crime was a house belonging to Elijah Watts, the property belonged to an enslaved man because it was taken out of a locked trunk. In this instance, however, the formalities concealed a more complicated dispute between Charles and the suspect, who was also enslaved. According to one witness, the trunk belonged to Charles, but some of the textiles inside belonged to the suspect, who had purchased them from Charles but had apparently been unable to take possession of them. They remained within the trunk, a situation that undercut the suspect's claims to them and obviously enraged him, as was evident in the nature of the crime. The suspect not only broke open the trunk but also cut a bed tick to pieces, spewing feathers everywhere. Ultimately, it was the means by which the suspect tried to repossess his property, not the fact of ownership, that was in question—hence the charge of outrage, a catchall category used when no other charge quite worked, including theft.[32]

While textiles accumulated in trunks, they did not stay there. For many women in particular, textiles and the skills to make and trade them constituted their legacy to their female relatives, an inheritance they distributed during their lifetimes. The Cooley daughters routinely made purchases with resources from Jane's manufactory, amassing a trousseau of linens, clothing, and cloth, which they took with them when they married. Trousseaus required the cooperation of fathers, in the sense that they came from the collective household budget. In many instances, however, it was mothers who covered the actual expenses, which gave them authority over how much and what kind of goods their daughters received. That is what Jane Cooley did. The frequency with which her daughters bought goods and the quality of their purchases suggest her generosity. In effect, Jane was distributing the profits of her business to her daughters, instead of keeping them for herself or putting them back into the household, where the value would transfer to her husband. Other women also directed the value of their labor and that of their daughters back to their daughters. Elizabeth Foster Sutton, an Ipswich lacemaker who was married to a leather dresser, managed to earn enough to provide each of her five daughters a silk dress before marriage—a particularly pricey luxury in the late eighteenth century and one that might seem well above the social station of a leather dresser's daughters. But what might seem like unnecessary finery actually constituted a valuable bequest to daughters who likely entered married life with little or no other property to their names.[33]

The presence of silk dresses in young women's trousseaus was common enough by the late eighteenth century to draw the ire of critics, who characterized the practice as yet another example of feminine weakness, dangerous to the nation's future. In a letter to the *American Museum* in 1787, "a farmer" explained that he had started out with little and prospered by working hard. He expected the same for his children but realized that the ground was shifting beneath him as his daughters married. He told the first daughter "to take the best wool and flax and spin herself gowns, coats, stockings, and shifts." He even "suffered" her to buy cotton to make into sheets—cotton being an expensive replacement for linen at that time. Two years later, when the second daughter married, his wife insisted that she be better "fitted out" and insisted that he give her money to do so. Then she went to town and purchased "a callico gown, a calamanco petticoat, a set of stone teacups, and half-dozen pewter teaspoons and teakettle." Those things, he huffed, "had never been seen in my house before." Three years after that, with the third daughter, his wife "came again for the purse" and bought even more: "a silk gown, silk for a cloak, a looking-glass, china, tea-geer [sic], and a hundred other things." As the farmer claimed, the expenditures of his wife on behalf of his daughters had led him down the proverbial road to ruin, paved with pointless consumer goods.[34]

The farmer's story was an utterly formulaic diatribe on the dangers of purchasing consumer goods, not an accurate description of actual property arrangements within households, let alone the meaning of textiles to women. To the extent that the tale was true, the farmer took credit for generosity that was not his. That fact is still visible, although just barely. The way he described his household—whether real or fictional—suggests one in which textile production lay within his wife's purview. Not only did he identify himself as a farmer, not a weaver, but his description of spinning raw fibers into finished garments also indicates a certain fuzziness on the specifics of the production process. When daughters knew how to weave as well as spin and sew, they usually acquired those skills from mothers. The materials that his first daughter received would have come from her mother, as would the permission to use her labor for her own benefit. If the farmer's wife was like Rebecca Coles or Jane Cooley, as the extent of textile production in the household suggests, she would have exchanged textiles she made—all those gowns, coats, stockings, and shifts that she and her daughters "spun"—for the goods in her second and third daughters' trousseaus. She would not have had to ask for her husband's purse, because she would have had her own.[35]

Not all the goods in this farmer's daughters' trousseaus had the same legal status. The calico, calamanco, and silk represented the most value, which they had in two distinct economic registers. They cost the most and could be easily traded, pawned, or otherwise leveraged. But for married women, textiles also had value above and beyond their stated price, because they did not pass into their husbands' hands. To be sure, women had a chance of maintaining the claim to the other household goods they had brought into the marriage, including the teacups, kettle, spoons, looking glasses, and china that filled out the farmer's daughters' trousseaus. But those claims were never certain. Estate inventories in North Carolina, for instance, identified china, silver, pots, pans, tea kettles, and other cooking implements and domestic tools, including the tools for making textiles, as the property of husbands. If widows wanted them, they had to buy them back with whatever resources were left to them from the estate. That was true even with household linens, particularly bedding, including mattresses, curtains, blankets, coverlets, sheets, pillows, and pillowcases—despite Tapping Reeve's insistence that bedding was included within the legal definition of paraphernalia. Those items were part of women's trousseaus, and women remained responsible for making and procuring them during their marriages. Even so, these textiles were often moved over to the husband's side of the accounts. Clothing and cloth that could be made into clothing rarely made it into inventoried estates, however, because it was assumed to be the possession of widows. As such, gowns of calico, calamanco, or silk were not one-off gifts to be worn a few times and forgotten but a legacy that could mean all the difference in hard times.[36]

The dual value of wearing apparel—valuable goods that also remained securely connected to their purported owners, regardless of their legal status—is why such items had been common in wills from an earlier period. Garments still appeared occasionally in the wills of both women and men during the period between the Revolution and the Civil War. In her 1785 will, Sarah Winston Syme Henry divided her "wearing apparel" among her daughters. Jeremiah Neale willed his clothing and a gold watch to his son. When Henrietta Perry freed Mary Washington, the woman she had claimed as a slave, she also gave her "my wearing apparel, one yarn coverlid, two quilts, one pair of blankets, and one pair of sheets." But if a sampling of wills in Alexandria, Virginia, is any indication, clothing and linens were only rarely passed on this way. Instead, women distributed their wealth through textiles during their lifetimes. Like Jane Cooley and the farmer's wife in the *American Museum*, they not only filled their daughters' trousseaus with clothing, linens, and fine fabrics but also passed along the skills necessary to make textiles.[37]

Those bequests acknowledged the economic instability of married women's lives. Unlike most fathers, mothers gave daughters forms of property over which they could maintain legal control. The farmer from the *American Museum* set his daughters up by giving their husbands land, moving their inheritance out of their hands forever. By contrast, his daughters could keep the clothing and, perhaps, even the linens that they and their mother made. Similarly, Jane Cooley's husband provided each daughter with $250 at the time of her marriage, a substantial sum, in addition to their store of textiles, which acknowledged the value she had added to the parental household. That part of their dowries, however, moved over to their husbands' side of the ledger immediately upon marriage. Such was sister Nancy's fate. She and her husband hoped for new opportunities in Missouri, but it did not turn out that way. As Nancy put it in a letter home, her husband could not make a "sufficaint farm." Her brother, who lived nearby, filled in the details: Nancy's husband was "not Rite well pleased with this Country for he has found out that going to the Missouri is not all that has to be done to get along." In all likelihood, the dowry from Nancy's father was long gone by then, eaten up by the first, failed venture at farming. "I have been weaveing sewing and such like," Nancy wrote. "I can make as good a coat as any woman in the Missouri and butiful two." After the inheritance she received from her father had disappeared, Nancy still had her mother's legacy of skills to sustain her.[38]

In a particularly elegant article, "Hannah Barnard's Cupboard," historian Laurel Thatcher Ulrich traces the ways in which women maintained a maternal lineage in a patriarchal world by passing on property—particularly textiles and the cupboards in which they were kept—through the female family line. It was law that secured such transfers. Jane Cooley amassed property and then distributed it to her daughters in a form that they could keep. In the process, she modeled a kind of marriage in which coverture did not mean complete subordination to her husband or the submersion of her identity into her role as a wife. Her daughters took note. Jane's daughter Nancy could have been embarrassed that she did not marry a man who was able to provide for her. Instead, she acknowledged that reality and took pride in the work that she did weaving and sewing. Even more striking were the aspirations of Amanda and Elizabeth. Following conventions of the time, both were critical of debt and dependency. "I would sacrifice most anything," wrote Elizabeth, "to gain my own livlihood by my own work and to know that I lived altogether on my own exertions. It would be a satisfaction beyond description." Amanda despaired, unable to see a way forward: "Neither do I know what I am to do in future years . . . for alas I have no plan that I can think will answer my purpose. Do what I will it all tends to the same point. I will still be here dependent on my parents for everything."[39] Elizabeth's concern was that if she remained unmarried, she would be a dependent daughter in her parents' household. The choice they faced was not between abject dependency or fully realized self-possession. The Cooley daughters were distinguishing between kinds of dependency. They both aspired to marriage, seeing that as a way out of a dependency that they found particularly oppressive, not a path that ended in an even greater subjection. Both ultimately married, following in their mother's footsteps, confident that they could carve out a space for themselves within that relationship.[40]

Textiles made the Cooley daughters see marriage differently than later historians, making it possible for them to imagine a measure of independence within it. Of course, husbands, fathers, and masters could still make claims on women's textiles. So could their creditors. Had Jane Cooley's husband run up a debt at the store, she might have found herself at the merchant's mercy. The new republic's legal order recognized the legal qualities of textiles as well as the laws that upheld the authority of fathers, husbands, and masters. Context determined which body of law prevailed. Not every daughter, wife, servant, or slave was able to control the value of the textiles she made or acquired. Maintaining their possession was always iffy for enslaved people. And wage laborers could claim only a wage, rather than the full value their labor added to the raw materials. Existing laws not only protected the authority of individual white men; they also provided the foundation for all kinds of economic relations in areas of law, particularly private law, from which those without the full array of rights were excluded. Although the unevenness of the resulting patterns might seem like an affirmation of patriarchal control, they actually highlight the importance of ordinary people in shaping the application of the widely acknowledged legal qualities associated with textiles. As the next chapter shows, people had to document and use those legal qualities to claim them. They did that in the same ways they turned textiles into capital: through the creative application of their labor in constrained circumstances.

7

Margaret Ten Eyck's Accounts

Credit

Margaret Ten Eyck made her living by her needle in North Branch, New Jersey, just about halfway between New York City and Allentown, Pennsylvania. Her accounts, which she kept from 1834 to her death in 1844, took the form of a running, annotated list, laid out in a loosely bound volume, detailing not only her sewing but also what she owed and was owed to her. Margaret worked for nearly half of each year in the homes of clients, who paid in board, meals, credit, and cash. Otherwise, she lived with family members, primarily a brother, to whom she paid room and board, a bill she satisfied by sewing for his family and through interest that he paid her on a loan. Actually, the loan was a bond, a common arrangement among family members at this time: her brother acquired use of her capital in exchange for a small but steady income stream for Margaret, in the form of interest, paid annually until her death, when the capital reverted back to him. If her accounts are any indication, nothing Margaret did was solely out of the goodness of her heart, even when it involved her family. Her notations suggested that she always expected to be compensated. In fact, Margaret's records make it nearly impossible to distinguish paid labor from work done for her family. She translated all her obligations into monetary units, both dollars and shillings, only occasionally noting what the values represented, which further obscured the distinction between family members and clients. In 1840, for instance, toward the end of Margaret's diary (her dating is irregular, to say the least), she "let Isable [sic] and Mary Ann have each one dollar when Gideon died for to git vailes [veils]." The phrasing might bring to mind a doting aunt presenting treasured nieces an extravagant gift. Perhaps Margaret had finally admitted an emotional connection in her accounts, making sure that Isabel and Mary were appropriately attired for a family funeral? Not so. The verb "let" usually referred to a loan or sale. As Margaret ended that entry, "It goes on my Board."[1]

Margaret's accounting methods were like those of other literate women who kept their accounts in journals, diaries, and commonplace books as well as correspondence, when they bothered with writing all. While recorded in ink on paper, these records did not derive their authority from the written word. The running tallies and thick descriptions documented accounts that were maintained in practice, through relationships with other people. They also connected women to the textiles they claimed.[2]

At first glance, this form of accounting might seem fundamentally different from that found in ledgers. These books, made to accommodate what had become a standard form of record keeping well before the new republic's founding, generally had an alphabetical index in the opening pages, which listed individuals who were legally responsible for all the transactions associated with their name and the page numbers on which their accounts appeared. Each account consisted of two facing pages or two columns. The page on the left recorded debits, with descriptions of items purchased and their cost, which was added to the previous running total. The one on the right had credits, with descriptions of the form of payment and its value, all added up over time as well. At designated intervals, often the end of the year, credits were entered into the debit side, showing payments that reduced the overall amount owed. Those who could not afford the preprinted ledgers used blank books or notebooks.[3]

The differences, however, can be overstated. Like merchants' ledgers, the accounts of people like Margaret tracked what was made, to whom it went, and what was owed as a result. The formulaic order that characterized merchants' accounts, moreover, was imposed after the fact. All those neat columns were transcribed from often messy lists of transactions in day books that could look a lot like Margaret's records. Even as the ledgers focused on the monetary value of goods, they could not erase the importance of the social relations that made those transactions possible. As the ledgers revealed, accounts were rarely resolved, meaning that the merchant and his customers were involved in an ongoing relationship created through the exchange of goods, just like Margaret. In one sense, form was inconsequential. These were all financial accounts.

In another sense, however, the differences in record keeping mattered. Ledgers distanced exchange from social context, although not completely. The methods used by people like Margaret did not take that step. They established property claims directly through relationships to people and the material goods, purposefully blurring the boundaries between textiles and persons. The production and distribution of textiles created not just economic value but also credit, with the power to blunt the legal restrictions that weighed so heavily on all women and so many men. Credit came in the form of relationships to the textiles as well as with the people who could establish and support possession of them. To say that claims to textiles moved those without the full range of rights from a legal status of abject dependency to that of a fully realized, possessive individual would be to mistake the underlying logic of the legal order. At best, textiles modified the implications of other legal restrictions. Still, the credit networks created through the production and distribution of textiles had power, as women's shifts back and forth between "we" and "I" in their accounts suggests. Jane Cooley's daughters routinely confused the two, saying in one breath that "we" had made or sold this or that and then abruptly shifting to say that "I" made a purchase. But the conflation of the singular and the plural made legal as well as social sense. For those without strong claims to rights or property, "I" was only possible in the context of "we"—a community fashioned, in part, through the production and distribution of textiles. The relationships that constituted "we" were essential for everyone who was unable to fit within legal paradigms that assumed an individual "I" for the possession of rights; "we" made it possible for individuals on the legal margins to make legal claims to property.[4]

Ledgers took the form that they did because of the law. Although they seem like strictly economic records, they were never intended to record all business transactions and were woefully insufficient to enable business owners to track profits and losses, assess the viability of past projects, or plan for future ones. These books were legal records. Their value lay in their power within private law, which governed property disputes in civil suits, where they figured as authoritative documentation of property exchanges. Ledgers tracked the dealings of those individuals with rights necessary for standing in this body of law and thus could be held legally liable for their debts in civil suits: adult men, usually white, with some property to their names. They omitted the transactions of everyone else or subsumed them under the name of their household head. It made no sense to waste space in expensive account books on people who could not be sued in civil court. Even poor people with the legal standing to be sued were often left out of account books, particularly in urban areas where accounts were less likely to be paid in labor: the whole project was pointless when there was nothing to wring from them in a civil suit anyway. So why bother with the formalities?[5]

When merchants brought out their ledgers to demonstrate what was owed, they invoked the legal principles of private law, even if the matter never involved lawyers or entered a courtroom. The uniformity of the books, as physical objects, underscored their legal authority. Oversized, usually oblong, and leather-bound, with gold lettering on their covers, they were instantly recognizable without even consulting their contents. The theft of an account book was different from the theft of other goods, because it was unlike other objects. Its form signaled the value that lay within, recorded in each individual account and protected by an entire body of law. Similarly, receipts, invoices, bills of lading, and other written instruments of commercial exchange took particular physical forms that contributed to their legal authority.[6]

The legal underpinnings of ledgers meant that they represented only certain parts of their owners' business, particularly when it came to textiles. When dealing in that form of property, merchants regularly traded with people who had no standing in civil matters, including women who were married, enslaved, or otherwise subsumed within male-headed households. They even extended credit to such people, although generally with the expectation that family ties or social censure, not private law, would ensure repayment. In some merchants' accounts, married women or enslaved people might merit their own page if their business was significant enough, although that was more a convenience than a legal statement. Other merchants listed married women, enslaved people, and other dependents by name, but then linked them to the free white men who headed the households where they lived, which was a legal statement. But the records relating to all these people were more likely to be ephemeral. If committed to writing at all, they would go into notebooks or on scraps of paper, which were apt to get tossed when matters were settled.[7]

The legal principles that shaped ledgers also explain why the accounts of people with weak claims to rights so often took different forms. To modern eyes, these other methods of accounting do not look like accounts at all. Perhaps the most famous example is the Maine midwife Martha Ballard's diary, the terse entries of which historian Laurel Thatcher Ulrich used to reconstruct this woman's life and her expansive economic dealings. Women who kept written records of their accounts followed the same practice, using volumes that bore no physical resemblance to account books and that are now labeled variously in archives as diaries, commonplace books, receipts (recipe books), memoranda, or household accounts. In them, they buried

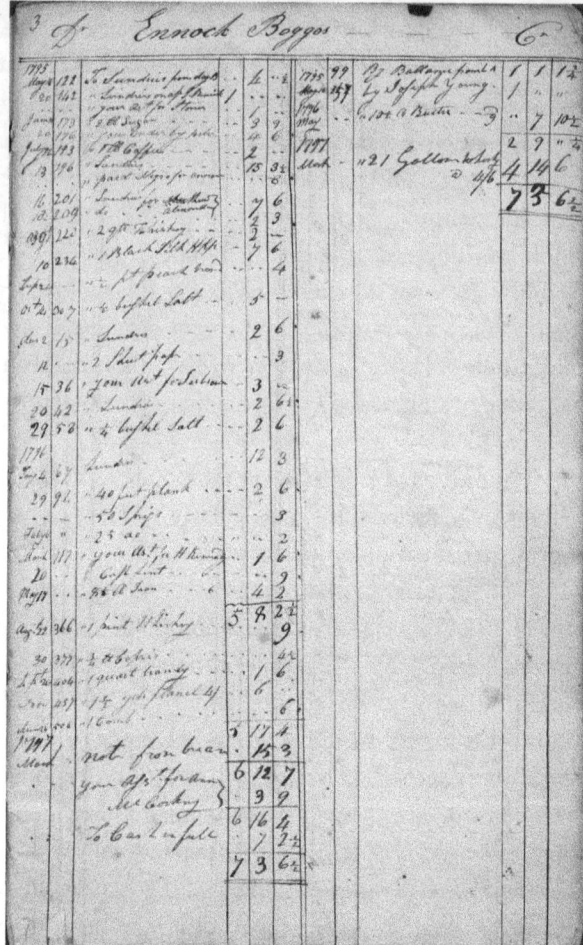

Figure 7.1 The accounts of Enoch Boggos, from the account book of Virginia merchant James Campbell, who followed standard recording procedure. The right side of the page is devoted to debits—purchases. The far left column lists the date of the purchase; the second column likely indicates the page on which the transaction was listed in the day book; the third column is devoted to a description of the goods; the last column is for the purchase price and is divided into three sub-columns for pounds, shillings, and pence. The right side of the page is devoted to credits—payments on the account. Boggos had three entries: a debt owed him and paid off to the store by Joseph Young; butter, likely made by Boggos's wife; and twenty-one gallons of whiskey. Like so many customers, Boggos lived on credit, with his purchases far outstripping what he could pay. James Campbell Account Books, 1793–1799, vol. 12, Mss. MsV Ame11-13, James Campbell Account Books, Special Collections Research Center, William and Mary Libraries.

notations about the textiles they produced, what they spent, and what was owed amid shopping lists, recipes, household tips, and notes on their work, health, visits, and the weather. Such records provide a partial, uneven reckoning of women's lives. Each woman had different standards of what mattered and what required accounting. In general, however, they usually left out routine chores and lingered on seasonal or otherwise notable labor that resulted in items of value, whether intended for use or sale.[8]

Written accounts took various forms, because the writing itself did not carry the same legal weight that it did in account books. In account books, the written tallies of goods and prices constituted the accounts: the notations on the page *were* the accounts. The form and its meaning had been standardized through centuries of legal practice. Writing had different meanings in the accounts of women like Martha Ballard. Elizabeth Bagby put it perfectly when she called them memoranda, a reminder of transactions rather than an actual representation of them. As such, the written form in this method of accounting was not standardized. Some records tracked monetary value; others did not. Some took the form of lists; others did not. Some were ordered by date; others were not. Some provided full names; others did not. One woman—inexplicably—alphabetized everything: lemons (which seemed like a splurge) came under "L," pork under "P," and sheets and shirtings under "S". The neater the records, the more they seemed to suggest the recordkeeper's familiarity with the conventions of accounting as well as their legal meanings. Elizabeth Bagby's well-ordered lists are relatively easy to identify as records of her business accounts, even though they were not kept in the two-columned debit and credit form. Yet Elizabeth also knew that, no matter how neat, her lists did not carry the same legal meanings as the household accounts kept in her husband's name. Recall her admonition. In the family account, she wrote, "charge yourself for every article bot [sic] for, and used . . . whether to eat, drink, wear, furniture for the House or Kitchen . . . Doctors Fees &c &c." But "such things as you pay for, in weaving, in butter, cloth or any thing made entirely within yourself, it may be as well to take no acct of, except in way of memorandum."[9]

The form of such records reflected the principles of a different area of law. Ledgers were about the property claims based in the rights of individuals. Their entries contained detailed lists of goods, as if they materialized out of nowhere. Presto: nails, hammers, and barrels; whiskey, salt, and nutmeg; calico, linen, and sewing thread; hats, shoes, and suspenders. All appeared magically, fully formed and ready to use. Those goods were inseparable from their prices, creating a relationship between goods and their value, represented in a fixed amount, which was enforceable in law. Legal responsibility for those purchases belonged to a single individual, who existed as a name floating at the top of the page, completely abstracted from context. By contrast, Elizabeth Bagby's memoranda recorded the work that she did and the social context in which it was done: how much cloth she wove, what it sold for, and who bought it. At the same time, she also revealed the social web that supported her business, turning those people into witnesses to the facts on the ground that she had created. She made cloth for particular people, whom she named; she sold it them and they paid her; then she kept what they gave her. In the process, she implicated all her customers in her claims to the value of what she made.[10]

Other recordkeepers did the same, including notes about their textile production in descriptions of notable activities and blending it all together so thoroughly that the memoranda can be difficult to separate out. A cursory reading of Anne Kagey Wayland's diary, for instance, yields the impression of a particularly industrious Virginia farm wife in the 1850s. It only becomes clear that much of Wayland's work was done for neighbors, for pay, if the reader carefully tracks her textile production and then makes notes of the names. What looked like an account of her life was also a business record, because business was integral to her daily life. Martha Frink, a young woman who lived with her parents in New Berlin, New York, in a remote rural area between Albany and Binghamton, carefully recorded all the work that she and her mother did spinning, knitting, and sewing as well as what they spent on various textiles. But Martha never differentiated her commercial work from her domestic chores or, for that matter, from any of the other events in her life. The diaries of Amanda and Elizabeth Cooley, discussed in the previous chapter, followed the same pattern, with records of textile production so embedded within accounts of the rest of their lives that it is difficult parse the commercial from the personal.[11]

That was the point. The commercial elements of textile production were inseparable from the other elements of these women's lives, which is why their records so often ignored the line between domestic and market-oriented production. Particularly revealing in this regard is the diary of Rebecca Cate, who lived on the outskirts of Boston in the 1850s with her husband and their two children as well as Mary, who seems to be Rebecca's unmarried sister, and Sarah, a hired servant who may have been a relative as well. Rebecca followed a strict schedule that underscored how much time she spent on the production and maintenance of textiles: she washed on Mondays, although the work sometimes ran into Tuesdays; she ironed on Tuesdays, although that often ran into Wednesdays; and she cooked on Fridays and Saturdays. Other days found her sewing at home, sometimes with Mary, when Mary was not working out as a seamstress in her client's homes. When Rebecca sewed, she usually did so for her family: shirts for her husband, clothes for her two children, and dresses for herself. It might seem as if the work of Rebecca and Mary were different: Rebecca was a wife who did uncompensated domestic labor; Mary was a worker who earned a wage. But that was not how Rebecca recorded it. She described the work that she and Mary did in similar terms. They both washed, ironed, and sewed.[12]

Accounting appears in two forms in Rebecca's diary. The last pages definitely look like the accounts of a middle-class housewife, who had limited economic responsibilities within a larger household budget that her husband oversaw and for which he was legally liable. On those pages, Rebecca listed the amounts spent for clothing on each of the household's members: her husband, her children, herself, Mary, and Sarah. The grouping reflects the members' place within the household and the lines of economic responsibility within it. Rebecca recorded the purchases for herself, the children, and Mary together, giving the dates and amounts but no description of the items, suggesting a single budget for them all. Given the practices in other households, it is likely that her husband may have provided the funds—probably in the form of credit—and Rebecca took responsibility for their allocation. It is also possible that Rebecca provided the funds for her own and her children's clothing, as other women—including the Cooley women—did. Either way, these were records of specific expenditures that she would not have to justify to anyone but herself, even though the general sum lay within the larger household budget. By contrast, she separated out the purchases made for her husband on a different page, where she described each item, in addition to providing dates and amounts. The implication was that he would settle up for those items, even though she had overseen their purchase. She did the same for Sarah, the hired hand. So much for accounts in the conventional form. The rest of the volume looks like a diary, describing what Rebecca did, where she went, who she saw, the state of her family's health, and what the weather was like.[13]

That would be a misreading of Rebecca Cate's diary. The diary's descriptive entries also recorded accounts, although of a different kind. In them, Rebecca detailed the work that she and Mary did, when, and for whom.

Mary occupied dual roles in Cate household: while she lived with Rebecca and was grouped with the other household dependents, she also made her living as seamstress, which meant that she did not always labor for Rebecca. The nature of that arrangement becomes clear in Rebecca's diary entries, which note the days Mary stayed at home and the days that she worked out of the house, so as to track control of Mary's labor. Mary claimed what she earned when she was away. But when she worked at home, she handed its value over to Rebecca as payment for room and board. In February, Rebecca noted, "Mary has gone to the city to work to day." She had spent the previous week with Rebecca: "I have done my washing, Mary is here to help me this week," Rebecca wrote. That week Mary also "fitted my dress." The term "help" obscured the fact that Mary was expected to wash, iron, and sew to cover her keep. Rebecca sometimes made those expectations clear. As she noted in July, "Mary is here and has been to work for me today we have been to work on the children's cloths." Rebecca also differentiated between the work that Mary did for her and for herself when Mary was staying with her: "Mary has been washing for herself, and she has washed some for me." In fact, Mary's situation bore a remarkable resemblance to that of Margaret Ten Eyck. Both women made their living with their needles. Both women paid their relatives to cover their living expenses. But there was one difference: Rebecca never attached a specific value to the work that she or Mary did.[14]

What good were accounts without values attached? The reasons for Rebecca's accounting were different than that of merchants with their account books or even Margaret Ten Eyck with her messy notebook. Records of work and relationships captured facts on the ground that were absolutely essential for those without rights to make property claims to textiles. As a single woman, Margaret had property rights. As a married woman, Rebecca Cate did not. So Rebecca, like others in compromised legal positions, documented her work, connecting herself to the textiles that she produced, tended, and traded—property that she could control if she could establish a connection to it. The importance of those connections is evident in other entries she made in her diary. "I bought me a pair of gloves," noted Rebecca after she and Mary had gone to town. She used the same phrasing in early March: "I bought me a Black silk dress," meaning the purchase of fabric for a dress.[15] The "I" and "me" said it all: she bought these things for herself. She could do that because of the work accounted for in the rest of the diary: the washing, ironing, and sewing that she did, making her labor and its value visible. Even though she did not give it a monetary value, her accounts gave her the leverage to spend on gloves, dresses, and other items, as if the money were her own. She put that work into the first person, even when she had company, skipping easily from the first person singular to the first person plural and sometimes combining them: "I have been sewing all day"; "Mary and I have been sewing all day"; "[W]e have been ironing this forenoon and I have been sewing this afternoon." But for Rebecca, it was always first person, regardless of who was working. Her diary tracked the value of work that belonged to her, even when it had been done by Mary, Sarah, or other servants hired by the day. The point was to establish those claims, not to calculate their monetary value.[16]

As adult unmarried women, Elizabeth and Amanda Cooley held a legal position that was more like that of Mary, in that they had property rights. In practice, however, they were shadowed by dependency and its legal restrictions. As they lived in their father's household and unable to support themselves on their own, their claims to property depended on each other and their mother, Jane. When the family went "a trading," Jane was the one who took the cloth around to merchants and decided whether the price they offered was acceptable. If not, she took it home to wait until the market improved. When she found quality goods that she or her daughters needed or wanted, she bought them. What Amanda and Elizabeth were recording in their diaries was the work that they did for their mother, who had secured a connection to its value. Just as Rebecca Cate controlled the value of Mary's labor that was performed within her household, so Jane Cooley controlled the value of what her daughters made, although Jane shared the proceeds with them. In July 1846, for instance, Amanda wrote, "We all went to Hillsville a trading," but "we could not sell our cloth and did not get many things." "We" had two meanings: the group of family members who went to town that day and the people within that group who had claims to the cloth. The constitution of that second "we" was revealed in an entry later than month, when Amanda wrote that she had sold her mother's brown jeans and flax dimity at good prices and that she had purchased a bonnet, a bolt of cloth, and a few other things for herself. In that same entry, she also noted her mother had purchased a red silk handkerchief and an alpaca fabric for her sister Juliann.[17]

Martha Frink, a young woman living with her parents in central New York state, also mixed the first-person singular with the first-person plural, without bothering to explain. "A pedlar to dinner here to day," she wrote in January 1858. "We got a pocket handkerchief for 2 p, a pair of gloves for

1/6. I got some sleeve elastics for 6 pense, he was owing us 3 shillings before." (Frink was still using shillings and pence to express the value of her purchases in 1858, long after dollars had been established as the unit of account, which was not uncommon because that means of measurement was so familiar; she was expressing the value of the goods, not actually handing over shillings and pence.) In February she wrote, "There has been a pedlar here to day, I got a pocket handkerchief for 2/3 and a yard of indigo blue cord for 2 cents, we gave him his dinner." (In this instance, Martha expressed the value of the handkerchief in shillings and pence but priced in the indigo blue cord at two cents, suggesting that she might have used coins to pay for that.) The "I" obviously referred to Martha, who was making her own purchases out of her own funds, probably obtained from the textile production that she did. As the context suggests, "we" referred to Martha and her mother, who was making textile purchases for the family and paid in cash, goods, and services, including dinner and lodging. Martha's mother provided the services as well as goods and some cash obtained from textile production, although Martha helped—hence the "we." By contrast, "we" never included Martha's father and brother, whom she always named separately. Even when the peddler was paid in items that probably had been produced by the Frink men, such as the "2 bushels of oats and a bushel and a half of beans" that helped pay for one particularly large purchase of cloth, the "we" was still Martha and her mother, who felt confident in appropriating the value of other goods because of their own contributions to the overall budget.[18]

Even women and men who could claim property rights found security in relationships. The records of Margaret Ten Eyck, like those of Elizabeth Bagby and other women encumbered by the various legal restrictions of domestic dependency, track property through relationships. The material quality of the records distanced them further from account books, with Margaret's undisciplined handwriting sprawling all over the pages. The effect is one of informality, if not utter chaos. Where merchants copied information into their accounts after the fact, Margaret and other women recorded events in real time. The book also captures the uncertainty of someone who was expected to be responsible for herself but without the full array of economic and legal tools necessary to do so. The situation deteriorated over time, in both Margaret's records and her life, as her energy lagged and her eyesight obviously failed. Ruth and Nabby Bangs, weavers in Massachusetts, also recorded accounts as annotated lists that tracked their textile production through relationships. But if anything, their handwriting was worse, which made their volume look even more like a hot mess than a business record. But, as with Margaret Ten Eyck, their accounts suggest the difficulties of their lives. Ruth and Nabby Bangs's names appear nowhere in the book, erasing their connection to the business within. The volume is now described as the "Orderly book kept by Nathaniel Bangs.... Also included are the accounts of the Bangs family for cloth weaving from 1777 to 1846." But Nathaniel Bangs died in 1770, the same year that his wife Ruth gave birth to daughter Nabby. At the time the records were kept, the "Bangs family" was headed by Ruth and, after her death, by Nabby.[19]

Written records are the tip of this accounting iceberg, preserving practices that usually did not make their way onto paper at all. Most people without the full range of rights relied instead on their memories and those of witnesses, both of people and of the textiles they claimed. When Susan Munro, the free African American woman who was charged with stealing three gowns in chapter 5, testified in her own defense, she lined up all the facts relating to the purchase so as to establish a connection between herself and the gowns that would legitimate ownership. As she explained, she was walking down New York City's Chatham Street, a working-class commercial district, when she saw a "woman shewing some gowns to a white

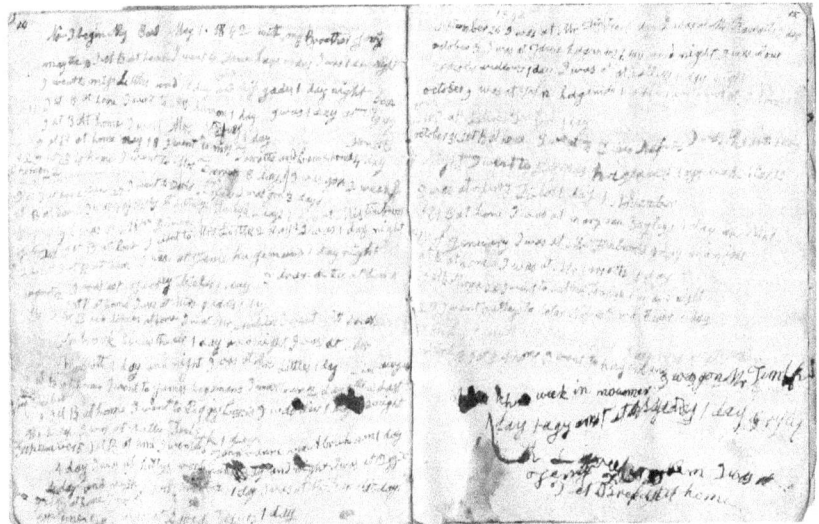

Figure 7.2 A page from Margaret Ten Eyck's accounts. Margaret Ten Eyck Diary, 1834–1844, Ten Eyck Family Papers, Special Collections and University Archives, Rutgers University Libraries.

woman on a stoop." The vendor "offered to sell all the articles" to that customer, who ultimately decided against it. Munro then asked the seller to "see her things." Satisfied with all the goods, she "bargained . . . for [the] three gowns" and "agreed to pay . . . five dollars for them." After the two came to an agreement, they went to Susan's "lodgings," where she "paid two dollars" on the gowns. The trip was necessary so that the vendor would know where to return to collect the remaining installments. "Afterwards," the vendor came back twice. On the first of those visits, Susan paid her "her four shillings." The other time she paid "a dollar and four shillings which made up the sum of money she agreed to pay." Whereas literate white women wrote those details down in their diaries, poor women like Susan Munro committed them to memory and embedded them within the physical geography of their lives. She was acquitted.[20]

Rosenah Gray, who also has appeared in previous chapters, did the same. Gray, an enslaved woman in New York City, had acquired an impressive store of textiles from a peddler and then was accused of stealing some of those items. In her defense, she reeled off a wealth of detail about the purchases: not only the date and place, but also the specifics about what she bought. For example, she bought "the piece of Striped Black Sattin wound on a stick, one end of which has a cut in with a saw, also the piece of lead coloured silk wound on the same stick also another piece of striped Black Sattin" from a peddler "last Friday evening." She paid "seven shillings a yard for the last piece of striped Sattin and six shillings a yard for the first above mentioned piece of sattin and also six shillings a yard for the lead colour'd silk." At the same time, she also bought "fourteen yards of Mazarine Blue striped sattin for a dollar per yard." "Also one piece of striped cotton for three shillings & six pence per yard, also two check muslin handkerchiefs for four shillings and six pence, also about half a piece of linen for which she paid about three shillings and four pence a yard, one full piece of Dark Callico for three shillings and six pence per yard, 14 yards of Red Callico for three shillings and six pence per yard." She paid for it all "in Dollars," twenty dollars "of her own money" and also "four or five dollars of her husband's money." Then, as she explained, on "Satturday afternoon last she exchanged eight yards of the Lead Coloured Silk before mentioned with a young woman by the name of Sally who lives . . . in the House of a Mr. Carpenter." All those details mattered. In Gray's case, they showed that she had bought and sold her cloth before the merchant's goods went missing from his store. But in some ways the sheer volume of detail was more significant. All those points figured as entries in a verbal account book, establishing a connection between Rosenah Gray and the textiles so as to prove that a transaction had actually taken place.[21]

Witnesses helped, be they the textiles themselves or others who could testify as to their possession and use. Susan Munro had no witnesses to her purchase of her gowns, and the vendor from whom she bought them was long gone. But she offered other witnesses: the gowns, to prove that they were in her possession, and a neighbor who had seen them with her. Rosenah Gray found herself in similar bind. Admitting that "there was nobody but just herself in her house when she bought" her textiles, she fell back on a neighbor, who not only testified that she had purchased some of the goods in question from Gray but also brought them with her so the court could see them. At first glance, such evidence may not seem particularly compelling. Witnesses could lie. And why bring in the items alleged to have been stolen? Neither the possession of textiles nor witnesses to possession proved that the goods had not been stolen in the first place. But, like the details that people rolled out about purchases, this kind of evidence was a means of accounting. It proved that the textiles in question had in fact moved to the claimant's side of the ledger.[22]

Some witnesses lacked credibility. When John Summerville, in rural South Carolina, accused several members of the Marshall family of stealing cloth and clothing from his house, the entire Marshall clan tumbled all over each other to lay out the kind of evidence that Susan Munro and Rosenah Gray had presented. "Mr. Marshall got the Flannel in Camden . . . two or three years ago," and it was used for a waistcoat for Mr. Marshall as well as a coat for Mrs. Marshall. One of the sons got the material cut to make "4 pair pantaloons" some time ago, and the other wore one of them, once they had been made up, when he "went over the River"—referring to a past trip of which everyone, apparently, was aware. A Marshall daughter had been wearing the "green pair of Morocco Slippers" in question for some time, and another daughter had cut the red flannel dress she was wearing from the "hind part of her coat"—meaning the coat that her mother claimed to have made, which indicated that the cloth had been in the family's possession long enough for it to have been first a coat and then a dress. But where such evidence worked in other cases, it failed the Marshalls. While voluminous, it was neither consistent nor believable, coming as it did from family members with every reason for collusion. A skeptical court found Mrs. Marshall and one of her daughters guilty of theft. The court's ability to lay blame on those two suggests a familiarity with the family and the situation that the records do not convey. Even so, the problem lay in the quality of the evidence, not in the basic conception of the defense.[23]

Who would guess that all these lists—written, oral, and material, in the form of stacks of cloth and items of clothing—were accounts? It was almost as if these people did not really want anyone to see what they were doing as accounting. In fact, that is an apt description of what was going on, because certain kinds of written records had such legal power. If kept in the form favored in private law, accounts held real danger for all those legally categorized as domestic dependents, as Elizabeth Bagby's differentiation between accounts and memoranda suggests. Elizabeth clearly knew that coverture positioned her as the legal agent of her husband. If she included the records of her textile production with the household accounts or even kept them in the same form, her property was liable to be merged with the economic dealings of her husband. That was why she kept memoranda, which recorded accounts fixed in practice. That was why other women embedded running tallies of debits and credits in volumes that bore no resemblance to account books. And that was why so many people committed nothing at all to writing. Even receipts held risks, documenting a property transfer in a written form with legal meaning that moved the goods in question out of the hands of the married women, children, or enslaved people who purchased them and into the hands of the men who held legal authority over them as husbands, fathers, or masters.[24]

People knew what they were doing. The experience of Harriet Ann Ames—whose memoir Elithe Hamilton Kirkland used as the basis for her flamboyantly titled, bestselling 1959 novel, *Love Is a Wild Assault*—served as a cautionary tale. Having "learned the sad lesson" that she "could neither look to" her husband "for help" nor "consider him in my plans for making a living," she set up a store in her house in New Orleans. Then her husband reappeared and asked her to go to Texas with him. The offer was enticing. "He said that I could get a piece of land if I went; that the [Mexican] Government would give it to me, and, best of all, promised he would go to work." More than that, he would let her keep her "little store." So she packed everything up and went off with him to Brazoria, located south of present-day Houston near the Gulf of Mexico. It did not go well. Her husband gambled away the property she had accumulated before he ever got to Brazoria and then disappeared. Fortunately, her family came to her aid. Her brother "managed to get back all of my things except the groceries," although Ames does not say what means he employed to do so. At that point, Brazoria was still part of Mexico, which allowed married women to keep property in their own names if they had a marriage contract or, while more difficult to prove, if they acted as free traders. (That also was why the Mexican government was handing out land to wives.) But even as Ames and her brother were enforcing longstanding practices that established legal possession, it is likely that formal legal processes were less helpful than other forms of persuasion. Ames's success in this instance did not erase the larger lesson: the presumption was that wives' property belonged to husbands. If it were recorded in receipts or household accounts, those documents eliminated any remaining slivers of doubt on that point.[25]

Even written records that did not take the forms that carried specific meanings in civil matters could be dangerous. Race, class, and slave status increased those risks. The lists that Elizabeth Bagby kept could be devastating for enslaved people, who always faced more challenges in claiming property, even textiles, than white women. In a context where property could be seized, a written list jeopardized ownership by revealing too much to people who did not need to know and might use that information against the owners. Written receipts were even more dangerous. That written form documented exactly what those without strong claims to rights hoped to keep to themselves, namely, property ownership and thriving businesses. Written records could even backfire on white married women by revealing property to which their husband's creditors could lay claim. It was safer to keep track of textiles in diaries and journals or, better yet, by wearing them, using them, or just displaying them for others to see, all of which created a different sort of evidence.[26]

Those methods of documentation turned the stuff of daily life into practice, which had legal meaning, particularly in the area of public law. The records of all these people in this chapter functioned similarly, taking stray pieces of this and that, making them into fulsome lists, and then situating those lists within a densely populated world full of witnesses. With pen to paper, page after page, women detailed their efforts to embed the textiles that they made, bought, and sold in the public order. Oral and material documentation functioned similarly, although only indistinct shadows of it now survive. At the time, witnesses—in the form of textiles as well as other people's testimony—could be louder and harder to ignore than written records. There were good reasons why Rosenah Gray brought in her neighbors to testify for her and Susan Munro offered to bring in her dress as evidence. Those aural and visual elements gave substance and permanence to events that would have otherwise disappeared without a trace.[27]

These practices existed within relationships to the material goods as well as the people by and for whom they were made. Those relationships were so important that documentation of them often took precedence over evidence of the goods' monetary value. Martha Frink recorded what kind of sewing she did and for whom, but not how much she was paid, or even if she was paid, although in some cases it becomes clear that she was. On February 12, 1858, for instance, Martha noted, "Ma has been spinning for Mrs. Cole to day," meaning that she would be compensated by Mrs. Cole. The previous entry, on January 30, said that her mother "finished Pa's pants," indicating that the sewn article was intended for use rather than for sale. At the same time, Martha made that work visible, ensuring that its value would remain connected to her mother.[28] Amanda and Elizabeth Cooley tended to identify family members by their first names unless they were referring to their mother or father. They reserved last names for those outside the immediate family. "For the last week," wrote Elizabeth on May 1, 1842, "I have been putting in some dresses & weaving some. I have three yeards wove. I have been making Matilda Banks a dress—it is not done yet." Unlike the dress for Matilda Banks, the cloth was not for a particular person, which meant that it was likely destined for sale in town. But it needed to be accounted for in order to connect its value to Elizabeth. "We have been busy today," Elizabeth wrote a few weeks later; "we begun to spin wool and cut out James [her brother] a jacket and Ma a frock Sunday." The spun yarn was like the cloth. While it was not done for a specific person, it was done by specific people, namely, Elizabeth, her sister, and perhaps her mother as well. The jacket and dress, while for family members, made the value of the sisters' and mother's labor visible within the household economy, just as Martha made her own and her mother's labor visible.[29]

People tended those relationships carefully. The way Jane Cooley took her daughter-in-law into her business is suggestive. Soon after the death of her husband, her youngest son married a young woman eighteen years his junior. Amanda, who still lived at home, thought it precipitous and profoundly irresponsible, concerns driven by fears that she, her mother, and her younger sister Juliann would be marginalized with the installation of her brother's bride. While Amanda fretted, her mother got to work, teaching the new bride to spin, weave, and sew. Not only did Jane acquire another pair of needed hands, but she also solidified her own position as matriarch within the household, despite how the census categorized her.[30]

Textile production brought other people into Jane's house on a regular basis. People dropped off spun thread to be woven into cloth and fabric to be made into dresses or coats. They stayed longer for fittings, for advice and assistance in making their own garments, or to borrow time on Jane's looms. When neighbors were not at the Cooleys' house, the Cooley women were often at the neighbors' houses. In November 1843, Elizabeth noted a busy but not unusual week, although she was out of sorts enough to voice her annoyance with her neighbors in her diary. She and Amanda "went to Aunt Mary's to a sewing" on a Tuesday, where she was "truly disgusted at the crafty meaness" of the people. She "wove on Polly Ward's counterpane" and "put in a piece of table cloth for Jestin" on Wednesday, which she noted without comment, probably because it was done in the quiet of her own household. She and Juliann "went to Delia Hankses to a quilting" on Thursday, where there was a "gang of ignorant fools." The Cooley women regularly went to neighbors' homes to work on their wardrobes and linens, just as Mary, Rebecca Cate's sister, did. Such work was common. Typical was the 1839 announcement in the *New Orleans Daily Picayune*: "Wanted: A situation as Seamstress and Dress Maker, in a private family, by one that can come well recommended." While those seeking seamstresses could peruse classified ads, they also went to registry offices that specialized in matching up workers and employers. As the experiences of the Cooley daughters and Mary suggest, employment was also obtained through word of mouth, in situations where the social distance between the employer and worker would not have been as great as it was in positions with more affluent families who could hire fulltime workers.[31]

Men as well as women with tenuous claims to rights relied on relationships to secure their property claims. Like women, men brought witnesses— people and textiles—to substantiate their claims to textiles. Men who labored under legal restrictions also kept records of accounts that looked more like those of women. But the importance of these relationships was most visible in women's lives, largely because legal restrictions applied to them all—even to literate women in families where men could claim rights. As their records reveal, women moved in and out of their own and others' homes as they made and remade textiles, embedding themselves in networks that reached outside their households and altered their relationships to the people who held legal power over them—fathers and husbands as well as masters and mistresses. All those people were witnesses to the creation and transfer of property.

They knew who made the goods and the circumstances of production, which shaped the producers' claims to value. They also knew for whom the goods had been made and that person's claims on them. Quiltings, sewing circles, and dress fittings were as much about creating property claims as they were about sociability, charity, or the pooling of labor necessary to create specific garments, linens, or quilts. When a group of women descended and settled in, the household head's authority became a little less absolute, which may be why they complained about these gatherings so much.

That was true of poor women, white and black, and enslaved women as well. The need to buy and make clothing put women in working-class neighborhoods in each others' homes all the time, as the New York City court records suggest. Poor women in urban areas hired seamstresses and dressmakers to remake used clothes or to make up the fabric they bought on the street, at auction, or from each other. In cities, everyone was dependent on the services of washerwomen, who made the round of households in their neighborhood collecting dirty clothes. Enslaved people also depended on relationships to establish claims to textiles. All those who witnessed the production and exchange of these goods were the ones who appeared to testify when ownership was questioned. Where the legal restrictions placed on all these people stripped them of property rights, the networks sustained through the textile trade created and maintained them.

The experiences of two well-known enslaved women are suggestive. Elizabeth Keckly, who became Mary Todd Lincoln's dressmaker, bought her way out of slavery with the assistance of the elite white women she sewed for in St. Louis. Once free, she moved to Washington, DC, where her skills made her one of the most sought-after dressmakers among the wives of the nation's political elite. Like Keckly, Mary Walker was a talented seamstress. Unlike Keckly, however, she did not have the option of buying her way to freedom. Instead, she lived as a fugitive, always on the run, always in fear, and always dependent on sympathetic allies—black and white—to keep her secret. Still, her skills with a needle enabled her escape. As a seamstress, she accompanied her master's daughters on their extended stays in Philadelphia. While there, she established ties within the city's free black community, which made her initial escape possible. From there, she continued to rely on her needle as well as the discretion and support of the women for whom she worked. For Walker, like Keckly, textile production was a means of support in more ways than one.[32]

What textiles offered came at a higher price for all those on the margins. Claims to textiles, as well as the interracial and cross-class relationships that sustained Keckly and Walker, were always fraught because of the structural inequalities they faced. As a seamstress, Walker worked closely with her master's daughters and traveled with them, a situation that brought her into regular contact with a cruel, volatile master who beat her and ultimately threatened her life. Although concerned, her young mistresses could not shield her from their father's violence. More to the point, they did not question her enslavement. In that sense, Walker's work as a seamstress magnified the horrors of slavery even as it enabled her escape. Nor could her work make her fully independent, once she was out of the orbit of the household of the man who claimed her as property. It took the Thirteenth Amendment, which abolished slavery, to do that. Keckly, while free, found it impossible to extract herself from Mary Todd Lincoln's financial difficulties following Abraham Lincoln's assassination, which contributed to the loss of her once-thriving business. The relationships created by her needle ultimately overwhelmed her.[33]

Although Margaret Ten Eyck's sloppy records and the other methods of accounting used by those without strong claims to rights existed alongside ledgers recording the transactions of free men, operating in conversation with them, they did not leave much trace—by design. The absence of many people with nominal legal standing from the ledgers of retailers and the scarcity of written documentation of their trade constitutes an accommodation to property law, not their exclusion from law, let alone from trade. In fact, the legal principles and practices associated with textiles confounded merchants and manufacturers, who resisted elements of this part of the textile market even though they depended on the business of people with tenuous claims to property and rights. Merchants and manufacturers wanted to sell textiles to people without property rights because they wanted those people to be consumers, not competitors. Consumers bought new textiles and paid for them at the point of purchase with cash or through book credit, carefully laid out in written accounts, which enabled prosecution should the debt go into arrears. Consumers then took their textiles home, where they (ideally) wore them out so they would come back and buy more. They were not supposed to strike out on their own and turn the items into economic and legal power: currency, collateral, savings, and the means of mobilizing the courts as active members of the public order.[34] But that is exactly what they did. The result was a vast market that extended well beyond the stores, warehouses, and factories dominated by the elite white men, as the next chapter shows.

8

Eliza Cauchois's Shift

Exchange

In 1803, Sarah Bliss accused her New York City neighbor, Eliza Cauchois, of stealing a shift—a women's undergarment, like a slip, made of finely woven linen or cotton. Cauchois insisted on her innocence. "Sarah Bliss loaned her the said shift," she explained, "and therefore she did not steal it." Right. She *borrowed* it. Court officials accepted Cauchois's explanation and acquitted her. Why? The defense was both plausible and persuasive in a context where textiles were valuable, liquid, and could be put to many uses, which could be utterly noncommercial, absolutely commercial, or a combination thereof, depending on context. People like Sarah Bliss and Eliza Cauchois did not just wear clothes or even buy other things with them. They also sold them at a profit; they loaned them, often with the expectation that their value plus interest would be returned at a later date; and they used them as collateral to obtain credit and access to opportunities and resources otherwise beyond their reach. Regardless of the terms, everyone knew that loans were different from theft, which is why the New York City Mayor's Court acquitted Eliza Cauchois.[1]

The part of the textile market that facilitated these exchanges was composed of real people who met to buy and sell textiles. These markets were everywhere and nowhere in particular, operating openly on the margins in cities and rural crossroads, just outside the purview of retailers, governing officials, masters, husbands, fathers, and their creditors. They were called the "street trade" in Britain and continental Europe. Commentators in the nineteenth-century United States used the same terminology, referring to street sellers, street vendors, and street markets. What distinguished this part of the market, however, was not its location on streets but the transitory nature of the trade. These markets were the most visible when run by designated sellers, who worked in identifiable if not always permanent locations: pawnshops that took clothing and household linens as collateral for loans of cash; taverns, inns, storefronts, and market stalls that accepted and sold secondhand clothes and lengths of cloth; public auctions that offloaded confiscated, damaged, and excess goods to the highest bidder; and even peddlers with their carts and packs of goods. These markets could also materialize out of thin air and then disappear just as quickly. People sold out of their homes. They hawked goods on city streets. They bought and sold after church. In fact, they might exchange textiles whenever and wherever they got together. The participants were all those people whose legal standing or economic status made it difficult for them to use other economic instruments to accumulate, store, and leverage value. They did not just buy in this part of the market; they also sold, often selling what they made. More accurately, they often made and bought to sell. Women figured prominently among the small-time dealers, even though they were depicted primarily as consumers in popular culture. Enslaved, free Black, and immigrant men were deeply involved as well. Famed abolitionist David Walker, for instance, began as a used clothing dealer in Boston, where many other free Blacks also were in the trade. Jews, who had more mobility than free Blacks, took to the road as peddlers. But this part of the textile market extended beyond those who made their living as traders because it was as much about accumulating capital and circulating credit as it was about the distribution and consumption of goods.[2]

The street trade was tolerated, but only just, because it altered the rules governing exchange elsewhere in the legal order. This kind of grudging acceptance has led this part of the market to be dubbed "underground," "informal," or even "extralegal."[3] It was anything but. Not only did it take place out in the open, but it also followed set rules that mirrored those in civil law, the area of the legal system that governed property exchange and from which those without rights and resources were excluded. Such business has been characterized as fundamentally different from that of the new republic's business elite: as part of a "moral economy," dependent on the exchange of goods and more about the maintenance of social relationships than the creation of economic value. How could it be otherwise, since all these people were excluded from the areas of law that regulated economic exchange and therefore are presumed to have been ignorant of the rules?[4] Although this part of the market existed in the physical spaces of everyday life, it still depended on a deep familiarity with economic abstractions that, as they developed, tended to generate bodies of law around them: conceptions of value, supply, and demand; practices that were more like capital formation than simple accumulation; and expectations that the terms of the resulting exchanges would follow certain forms. The transactions within this part of the textile market only *seem* different, because the participants' legal and economic standing meant that they used shirts, shifts, and handkerchiefs, not notes and bills of exchange.

Until recently, the part of the textile market in which Eliza Cauchois and Sarah Bliss were engaged has been overlooked, even though they generated economic wealth alongside the part of market controlled by merchants like Mr. Robinson. Gradually the focus has shifted from white male merchants and the trade they controlled to reveal the central place of others, particularly women and the working poor, in the commercial life of the late eighteenth and early nineteenth centuries.[5]

Among the working poor and the enslaved in new republic, the pawning of household items was not a cry for help, as portrayed in popular literature of the time and by later historians. The working poor used pawnshops as banks, depositing goods as collateral to obtain loans and then regularly paying off the interest. In the new republic's cities, pawnshops anchored a world of exchange that operated just beyond the thoroughfares with fashionable retail shops. Those narrow and crowded streets featured stores, open air markets, and carts that offered an array of inexpensive goods, both new and used. Contemporary accounts lingered on the jumble of goods and people in the neighborhoods where these establishments clustered, often with a tone that suggested economic dislocation and impending social collapse. But the crowds were thick because there was so much business to be done. As the records indicate, the volume of business in this part of the trade was staggering: between August 1838 and February 1839, for instance, John Simpson's New York City pawnshop listed over twenty-seven thousand entries.[6]

The ranks of merchants included white, free Black, and enslaved women as well as free Black, enslaved, and poor white men, who did their trading beyond the wholesale and retail establishments owned by the Mr. Robinsons of the world. Textiles feature prominently in this domain. When people without strong claims to rights set themselves up as traders, they often dealt in textiles. Harriet Ann Ames, whose husband gambled away her property in chapter 7, explained how it was done. Living in New Orleans in the 1830s, she "rented a house," "bought some dressed planks," "borrowed a hammer and saw," and "put my shelves and counter up with my own hands." "That done I went down to Chartres St. where the principal wholesale houses were and bought such things as were necessary to stock my little shop and had them taken up to my house." "That was on the Sixth of Jan. On the Eighth I moved my little family and all that I had to my home and opened the store." The various vendors who catered to the working class not only bought and sold textiles but also accepted them in payment for other goods. According to historian Wendy Woloson, women comprised at least 35 percent and as much as 70 percent of pawnbroker John Simpson's customers. Most of what they pawned was textiles. When enslaved people could purchase goods, they tended to buy textiles. In fact, the trade in textiles extended well beyond traders who operated out of designated, physical spaces—whether freestanding buildings, storefronts, stalls, or carts.[7]

Municipalities and counties tried to contain trade within particular spaces through licensing and zoning that turned buildings into stores, streets into markets, and neighborhoods into commercial districts. The thicket of regulation also served to limit the ranks of traders. Licenses—basically a fee paid to the government for the right to trade—favored businesses located in permanent structures with a large volume of business. Zoning, which designated areas where certain kinds of goods could be sold, pushed up rents in those areas and closed out traders who worked on the margins. So did municipal ordinances regulating the location of "nuisances." The fees imposed on small-time traders, such as peddlers and street vendors, were intended to push them out of business so as to cut down on competition with merchants who operated in fixed locations. In some areas, peddlers were placed within the ranks of criminals. South Carolina's open-ended 1786 vagrancy statute, which was liberally applied in the decades before the Civil War, included unlicensed peddlers among a long list of undesirables: fortune tellers, thespians, sturdy beggars, those who harbored horse thieves, those who were able but unwilling to work, landowners who failed to cultivate their property appropriately, and everyone who led "disorderly lives." Other regulations were applied selectively as well. Most municipalities kept a close eye on pawnshops out of longstanding concerns that they dealt in stolen goods. Local ordinances limited trade to particular days and times, which made it difficult for those who dabbled on the side to do business. The Richmond Mayor's Court was always busy, working through complaints of exchange that crossed over the line into illicit trade on Saturdays as well as Sundays, when all trade was prohibited.[8]

The very fact that the Richmond Mayor's Court was always busy with such cases suggests the limits of local regulations. Licensing and other requirements were meant to make that kind of trade illicit and push it to the margins. But it could be difficult to apply those regulations to the textile trade because its forms were ephemeral and so often masqueraded as something else. Margaret Cooney, last seen purchasing a length of silk for seven shillings and six pence a yard from a peddler in chapter 5, provides a good example. She ran a store. But it was never listed in a city directory, not did it have its own building or a name. She sold from her New York City kitchen, which was not even her kitchen, because she was married and the house where she lived belonged to her husband—at least according to the rules of coverture in private law. When she was charged with theft, the court officials clearly had difficulty sorting all that out and alternated in identifying Cooney and her husband as the owners of the store. Technically, both designations were accurate. While her husband owned the house, she owned the "store," which consisted of the goods she stored and sold there: liquor, groceries, and textiles. When people came for a pint or some eggs, they stayed for a chat and perused her fabrics, when she had them. Other traders like Cooney bought small lots at auctions, from peddlers or acquaintances and friends, and then sold them in even smaller lots to customers in their neighborhood. But Cooney's "store" was difficult to get your arms around: it was there sometimes and sometimes not. The Mayor's Court did not even bother to look into the question of an unlicensed business, which seemed like a more clear-cut violation than the theft charges that they took so seriously.[9]

Margaret Cooney's kitchen was one of many places to trade textiles. The impression left by the New York City Mayor's Court is that it was difficult to walk down the street without running into someone hawking cloth or clothing. The extent of the trade is evident in the explanation offered by so many people charged with possession of stolen goods: they had purchased the items from an unknown person they met by chance during the course of daily business. What might seem like a dodgy defense was actually a plausible description of a common transaction. Susan Munro, introduced in earlier chapters, bought her three gowns from a woman selling from a stoop on a sidewalk. New York City's streets were particularly busy, but typical of commercial centers. Itinerant vendors were a fixture in the new republic's towns and cities as well as rural areas. Peddlers moved goods from place to place, facilitating their circulation through overlapping social networks. Rural

Figure 8.1 Peddler's wagon, Charles Breen Bush, *Harper's Weekly*, June 20, 1868. The large building in the background is a church, and the structures near the peddler are the stalls where churchgoers kept their horses and wages while at services. Library of Congress Prints and Photographs Division, Washington, DC.

people traded whenever they got together, including the time after church services on Sunday—a day closed to trade by municipal ordinances in most towns and cities, at least in theory.[10]

People like Susan Munro preferred to buy on the streets or from peddlers because the retail establishments run by white men could be hostile territory. That was true for ordinary country stores as well as slick city establishments, for wealthier white women as well as the working poor and people of color. Goods in these stores were kept locked up in display cases and stacked behind imposing counters out of the reach of customers, who needed assistance from the merchant or a clerk to look at them. Those men were not always accommodating, because it placed them in the position of serving the very people who—in their minds—should be serving them. The dynamics also made customers feel like they ought to purchase goods that they might not really want because the merchant or his clerk had gone to so much trouble to help them.[11]

These contradictions found expression in popular culture, where elite white women figured as the bane of merchants' existence. Treating shopping

Figure 8.2 Country stores still kept goods behind counters well into the twentieth century, as was common practice all over the United States in the first half of the nineteenth century. McAllister General Store, Gravette, Arkansas, 1920. The store was owned by the family of the author's husband. Courtesy of J. W. McAllister, Memphis, Tennessee.

as pleasure rather than business, they sashayed into shops, demanded to put their hands on all the goods, and then left without buying anything, keeping clerks and merchants from their work—although, of course, tending to these customers was their work. Who else was going to be buying all those colored silks and flowered calicos? That was the portrayal of female customers in Asa Green's famous sendup of the wholesale and retail end of textile trade, *The Perils of Pearl Street, Including a Taste of the Dangers of Wall Street*. One of Green's first employers, Mr. Smoothly, had "an extensive and fashionable dry goods establishment, which was much resorted to by the ladies." But Mr. Smoothly had two faults. "He had acquired the reputation of selling cheap, which is usually of great consequence with females, because they pride themselves on buying bargains." (How dare they search for a good deal, instead of accepting whatever price was offered.) Second, Smoothly "did not, like some other shopkeepers, grudge the labor of exhibiting his goods to the inspection of bright eyes, and submitting them to the examination of fair hands, even though he was perfectly assured that he should not derive any advantage from such exceeding complaisance." (How dare they want to examine goods before they bought them.) As a result, his store was "thronged with the beauty and fashion of the city. It was the great shopping mart—or, perhaps I should say, the great shopping theatre—for the goods were rather exhibited than sold." All that made for rough going. Mr. Smoothly went out of business.[12]

The kind of discipline that Green's account advised was practiced elsewhere, as Eleanor Spence discovered. In 1816, she entered a store in New York City and "enquired the price of several pieces of cloth." As Spence told the story, the storekeeper showed her one piece and offered it for $6.75 a yard. She countered at six dollars, which he refused. Then, before they had settled on a price, the storekeeper cut off a length of the cloth and insisted that she pay for it. Spence walked out. But he followed her and tried to force her back into the store to complete the transaction, which she found totally unacceptable. The storekeeper told the story differently. As he insisted, Spence had behaved like a frivolous female shopper: she had agreed to buy the goods, but then changed her mind about the color at the last moment and refused to pay. Spence fought back, filing charges for assault. Ultimately, she was awarded damages in the amount of forty dollars, but only because the merchant used excessive physical force to obtain her compliance. Touching a lady was out of the question; denying her access to the goods she wished to buy and refusing to bargain with her was not. Even her own lawyer drew on the trope of a thoughtless woman out for some entertaining distraction, playing on a poor storekeeper's last nerve.[13]

The gauntlet was far more daunting for those of lesser status. If anything, the young white men who were hired as clerks had bigger chips on their shoulders than the merchants for whom they worked. That was why Asa Green wanted a job in wholesale, rather than retail. He did not want to be in the position of serving women—even white women with money to burn. Catering to enslaved people, free Blacks, or working-class whites was that much more demeaning for the young, white men on the make who filled the ranks of clerks. No wonder cartoonist Edward W. Clay mocked both free Blacks and the white clerks who served them. The point of the foreign, effeminate clerk in one caricature was clear: serving African Americans made one not only less than white but also less of a man. Actually, the whole scene was utterly upside down. If free Blacks managed to talk merchants into bringing out the goods they wanted to see, they still had to bargain for a decent price and persuade them to accept whatever form of payment they had—which was not a given, what with the difficulties of credit and all the uncertainties attached to banknotes. Working-class whites experienced similar difficulties. But enslaved people faced the worst treatment. The white supremacy expressed in Clay's portrayal of free Blacks in the North took on harsher tones when it came to enslaved people in southern states. Not only did merchants refuse to serve enslaved people, but laws there also restricted such trade. Although merchants regularly ignored them, legal prohibitions created a situation in which every purchase was fraught and always a favor.[14]

Figure 8.3 Edward Williams Clay, *Life in Philadelphia* (Philadelphia: 1829), plate 11. Library of Congress Prints and Photographs Division, Washington, DC.

Secondhand stores, auction houses, pawnshops, and cheap shops in working-class commercial districts proved more accommodating. These businesses were more like Margaret Cooney's store, in the sense that the shopping experience was less restrictive. The goods tended to be piled on counters and tables, where it was possible for customers to sort through them without assistance. Proprietors were less concerned about the economic or legal status of their customers, and they would take payment in a variety of forms, including textiles.

Nonetheless, the experience could be difficult. Owners kept a close eye on customers, so those handling goods a little too much could find themselves accused of theft. Hugh McManamy got in trouble when he took a piece of blue broadcloth across the street to show a friend. While that would be obvious evidence of theft today, it was more of a gray area at the time. The court documents identify the place where he was shopping as both an auction house and a stand, designations that capture the fact that the store was about the goods as much as the location where they were kept: stores were often in buildings, but where any store began and ended was not entirely clear. Some buildings, like stalls, did not have four walls. Those that did were dark, hot in the summer, cold in the winter, and always crowded with merchandise. In short, they were less than ideal places to display goods. So stores spilled out onto streets, which were themselves commercial zones. Merchants often put their wares outside. If goods were inside, customers would take goods to the front windows or just outside the door so that they could see what they were buying before they committed to the purchase. Hence the terminology in complaints, which indicated that goods had been taken "from the door," meaning that they had been taken away from the building, not just outside it. McManamy might have been stealing. But he might have unintentionally moved beyond some unseen perimeter when he stepped away from the auction stall to show goods to his friend. It was hard to tell. Another man who ran into trouble at an auction stall clearly stepped over the line. Spotting a hat that he admired, he took it from the door without paying. When found out, he admitted not only to stealing but also to violating the basic rules of shopping. "It was wrong to touch any . . . goods," he confessed. As the wording suggests, customers needed permission to try items on, particularly hats, given the prevalence of lice. Even at auction houses where the goods were arrayed in the open, handling them without the assent of the proprietor was problematic.[15]

The experience was different with small-time dealers. For them, the store was the goods, as it was for Margaret Cooney. In this shopping experience, the goods were placed where customers could see them and handle them. Bargaining occurred on a more even playing field. Consider Susan Munro's purchase of three gowns. She spied the goods as the vendor was showing them to another customer. They haggled but did not come to an agreement, and the customer was able to walk away without being accosted. Munro then asked the woman to see the gowns and was able to handle them before making a decision. Satisfied, she agreed to pay five dollars for them, which was the same price offered to the first customer. But the price was not the only issue over which to negotiate. Munro also had to establish the terms of payment. Vendors like the woman from whom she bought would extend credit, which constituted the most important difference between small-time vendors and retail establishments run by white men or even businesses like secondhand clothing stores and auction houses. Without credit, Munro never would have been able to afford three gowns, worth somewhere in the neighborhood of one hundred dollars today. After the two women reached an agreement, they went to Munro's lodgings, so that Munro could pay the first installment and the vendor would know where to return to collect the remaining ones. That kind of flexibility continued to draw women to the small stores operated by other women.[16]

People bought cloth and clothing to leverage their value. Rosenah Gray immediately set about selling the cloth that she had purchased. So did Margaret Cooney. Others loaned the textiles for which they traded. Susan Munro did not plan to wear all three of the expensive dresses she bought; she wore one, loaned the second, and saved the third. People put borrowed items to use as well, pawning them, loaning them, or even selling them, with the expectation of replacing either the item or its value plus interest. The economics were clear to those involved, as one New York City woman explained in no uncertain terms. When she heard that Sally Armstrong had stolen some clothing from a neighbor, she immediately headed "to where the auctions are kept in Chatham Street." Why? Because she knew that "Sally Armstrong frequently speculated at the different auctions about the city." Auctions took place in designated stores or stalls, where people brought new and used goods to be sold to the highest bidder. Armstrong was taking a chance that someone would pay more for cloth and clothing in the heat of a moment than what she had paid for them. It was a definite possibility. Auctioneers shouted above the din, taking bids and finalizing sales as people milled about amidst the goods. One man thought he had bought a pair of pants from the auctioneer, a "stout man who stood on a table ... crying out things for sale." Actually, he had, but he paid the wrong person. The "young man on the stoop of the auction room" to whom he gave his five shillings and six pence was a poser, unconnected to the business.[17]

Rural areas did not have auction houses, but the trade worked the same way at auctions that were held in public places at specific times. Recall the case of Wyatt Harris, who escaped charges of stealing a coat with the help of a chain of witnesses who established ownership in part 1. Those witnesses were involved in the same kind of exchanges that auctions facilitated in cities and that easily shaded into speculation. Daniel, an enslaved man, had obtained the overcoat through dubious means, which meant that he was willing to sell low in order to move it along, out of his possession. The circumstances meant that Harris was able to buy it for a pair of pantaloons and a pair of shoes, the equivalent of five dollars. He obviously knew it was a steal, because he immediately turned around and sold it to another man for double what he had paid for it. The initial price was so low that it must have occurred to Harris that the coat might have been stolen. Still, the potential profit made it worth the risk. Those calculations were based on shrewd assessments in a market characterized by widespread agreement as to the value of textiles as well as a high velocity of circulation. It was easy to spot a deal, and it was easy to sell goods of uncertain provenance quickly. Those dynamics encouraged theft, because illicit goods could be made licit so easily through a process that resembled nothing so much as money laundering. In cities, everyone knew where to go to sell textiles quickly, no questions asked. By the time anyone noticed them missing, they were long gone. It was more difficult in rural areas, where everyone knew everyone and you had to travel a considerable distance to escape those networks. But it could be done. While Daniel's bet did not pay off, Harris's did. Since none of the evidence suggested that he knew the coat to be stolen, he was acquitted of theft. Nor was he charged with trafficking in stolen goods.[18]

Buying textiles was often about selling them: people traded with an eye toward profit. Those practices were so common that some people found it difficult to resist the opportunity to speculate, which they distinguished from theft but which trod just shy of its border. They "borrowed" textiles from the shelves of stores they frequented and the storerooms of the houses in which they lived, hoping to leverage their value and return them before they were missed. That may well have been what Sally Armstrong thought she was doing: borrowing, rather than stealing, from her neighbor, with the hope that she would somehow be able to replace the items or their value before she was found out. When unauthorized borrowers were caught, their explanations hinged on the distinction between taking and stealing: they admitted to taking the goods but insisted that they did not steal them because they intended to replace them. Accused of stealing a coat, Benjamin Chamberlain admitted that "he did take the . . . Coat." But he did not steal it, because he "pledged" (pawned) it. That made all the difference—at least in some circles. A pawned item could be reclaimed at any point and returned, which was different from selling something or otherwise reducing its value to his possession. Considered in those terms, he had not stolen the coat.[19] The distinction Chamberlain made between taking and stealing rested on expectations that textiles were property that had financial value beyond their immediate, material uses. A shirt could be worn; if not, it could create more value. So why leave something of value just lying around?

People leveraged textiles in a variety of ways, besides selling them at a profit. If they wanted the items back, they pawned them, essentially using textiles as collateral for a loan. That was why pawning was so often trotted out as a justification in theft cases. Where selling meant a permanent transfer of the property to someone else, pawning did not. Not only could pawned goods be reclaimed, but it was also assumed that they would be reclaimed. Everyone knew the goods were safe and sound at the pawnshop, making it impossible for the owners to loan the items again or sell them. In that sense, pawnshops were akin to banks, which did not make loans to women, particularly married women, working people, or the enslaved. Pawnshops also preyed on the economically marginal, undervaluing objects and charging high rates of interest for the money they loaned. Still, it was the best and only option for many people, who deposited textiles there and drew on their value while keeping them safe. It was customary for those in the clothing trades to pawn goods that belonged to their customers before they had to be returned. Washerwomen did it, wringing a little more value out of the textiles that they were rehabilitating. Tailors and dressmakers pawned cloth that their clients gave them before they made them up into garments. The people in these trades added value to textiles through their labor. Pawning provided a way to reclaim a bit more of what they added without charging their clients more. The practice was not considered theft, as long as the articles were returned to their owners within a reasonable time and the owners did not complain.[20]

Loaning was different than pawning. Sometimes loans were more like outright gifts, with no expectation that they would ever be returned. Sometimes they were short-term grants of use, given with the understanding that items would be returned in a timely manner and in good order. But sometimes loans were about leveraging the value of the item. The lender expected to get the value of the items back, with interest of some kind, instead of the items themselves. When Susan Munro loaned one of her dresses, the borrower immediately cut it up to remake it, either for her own use or for resale. But Munro did not mind, because she expected repayment in another form. This example conformed to widely accepted practices, whereby loans of specific textiles could be repaid with goods or services of comparable value, with interest, as agreed to at the time of the exchange. Why insist on the return of the borrowed item, when its value would be diminished by the time it was returned? Did anyone really want a used handkerchief back? Those practices explain the dismay of Aurelia Thompson, who admitted to taking two pairs of stockings from a neighbor, but not to stealing them. To the contrary, she had offered her accuser "a shawl & petticoat" to settle the debt. Thompson was convicted. In this case, the problem was the fact that Thompson failed to secure the consent of the stockings' owner as to the value of the items and the terms of repayment. Thompson thought the debt could be settled with a shawl and a petticoat, but the lender did not. Similarly, the case against the speculator, Sally Armstrong, may have been a loan gone awry. While she was charged with theft, the circumstances could have been characterized as borrowing had Armstrong not been using the garments in a risky economic venture without securing their owner's permission. Her neighbors thought the risk unwarranted—perhaps because they were familiar enough with Armstrong to know that her business acumen did not match her ambitions.[21]

Municipal law made these practices illicit but did not move them outside the law's reach. They all had analogs in the market governed by civil law. Merchants like Mr. Robinson also needed to prove possession, although it was increasingly done through written documentation, not witnesses, trunks, and bandanas. Similarly, the exchanges made by the men usually identified as merchants needed witnesses. While the form of documentation was receipts, not neighbors' testimony, the practices were the same. Written documentation fixed a moment of time on paper, whereas witnesses committed it to memory. Textiles and pawn tickets that represented their value passed from hand to hand, just like notes and other written instruments of exchange that facilitated the circulation of credit within the realm of civil law. They served as collateral, just like real estate and other kinds of property, allowing their owners to leverage their value. The value of textiles could be increased, just like other forms of capital, through proper care and attention to the market. In fact, many of the practices associated with the exchange of textiles were deeply rooted in civil law. Courts in the seventeenth and eighteenth centuries began mediation in debt disputes in private law with written records, but then delved into the kind of oral evidence that proved so decisive in matters involving textiles. In that area of law—the one that white, male merchants used to govern their economic dealings—those practices were being replaced by more formal, impersonal modes of settlement by the late eighteenth century. But they continued to structure economic exchange in the textile market.[22]

Consider the case of Amos, the enslaved man who ran a business trading textiles, groceries, and other goods to other enslaved people in his upcountry South Carolina county. He was charged with stealing shoes from a merchant's storehouse. But as the proceedings unfolded, the magistrates who gathered to hear the case ended up sorting through evidence involving a conflict between Amos and one of his customers over an unpaid debt—which might seem unrelated to the theft charges but was not. Amos presented the evidence of this debt dispute to prove that he was not a thief but a legitimate trader. The first enslaved witness affirmed that Amos was selling shoes, but claimed that they were far inferior to those he was accused of stealing. This witness knew, because he was looking for higher-quality footwear and had passed over Amos's merchandise for that reason. He also knew that the indebted customer had purchased two pairs of those inferior shoes from Amos for a price that included two loads of watermelons. The problem was that it took far longer to haul the watermelons to town than expected at the time of the deal. Given the delay, Amos thought that the customer should pay the higher price he charged for credit purchases. The customer disagreed. As a slave, he argued, he had to accommodate his master's schedule, which made it impossible for him to get the watermelons to town sooner. An intermediary, who was also enslaved, had arbitrated, doing his figuring with a stick in the dirt in front of a group of witnesses. But mediation had not settled the dispute, which ended in a fight. That fight had not drawn the attention of the court until it was disclosed at trial, and its admission raised the possibility of criminal charges for all those involved, in addition to the theft charges already pending against Amos.[23]

Why admit to all those details? Because they resulted in Amos's acquittal. The legal qualities of textiles—which, in this case and others, extended to shoes—go a long way in explaining the rather stunning fact that the magistrates were not inclined to punish Amos, even though he had admitted to trading regularly and openly with other enslaved people. Law also framed the relationship between Amos and his indebted customer. The magistrates and white male jurors who heard the case knew that, although they never openly recognized it. But the context is clear in the evidence that Amos provided. Just like other merchants, he charged higher prices for purchases made on credit than for those paid in cash. Even in the retail trade, cash sales often involved goods or the transfer of debt through oral promises or notes of hand (written promises of payment), just as they did for Amos and others trading on the secondary market. For merchants, as for Amos, "cash" could refer as much to the timing of payment (immediate, at the point of purchase) as to its form (coins or banknotes). Amos also produced witnesses to the transaction, testimony that also would have carried some legal weight had he been a free person trying to collect on a debt. Similarly, the customer's explanation for the delay in payment had direct referents in debt cases. In the seventeenth and eighteenth centuries, disputed debts were as much about social relationships as they were about economics. Illness, injury, or other misfortunes beyond a debtor's control—in this case, the demands of a master on a slave—mattered in determining intent and arriving at a settlement. While those legal practices had been attenuated, they had not been completely eradicated or forgotten. The white magistrates in this rural county would have been familiar with them. So were Amos, his customer, the enslaved arbitrator, and the other enslaved men who witnessed the purchase and subsequent mediation and who lined up to tell what they knew in order to prove that Amos was a trader, not a thief. Although the court officials did not openly acknowledge that fact, they ultimately agreed.[24]

Transactions like those between Amos and his customer happened everywhere, all the time. In this part of the textile market, the distinction between buyers and sellers was not particularly clear, because buyers were not just consumers. None of this was what merchants and manufacturers wanted. Established practice nonetheless mattered. It had the power to legitimate people's claims to property in the realm of public law where the protection of the existing order was the point, as the next chapter shows. Of course, there were no guarantees. People nonetheless persevered, insisting on enforcement and dragging local officials along with them. In the decades following the Revolution, local courts enforced the legal principles that structured this part of the textile market, albeit hesitantly and unevenly. They did so without recognizing the cases as disputes involving trade or the people involved as traders. In most instances, local courts did not even recognize the participants as legal actors. What distinguished this part of the textile market was the marginal relationship of its participants to the new republic's governing institutions, not its marginalization from law.

PART III
RAGS

Textiles had supported Jane Cooley. But they failed her daughters, Elizabeth and Amanda. Elizabeth longed for adventure outside her Blue Ridge Mountain community. For her, that meant the West, with its open skies and endless possibilities, although it never seemed to have occurred to her that reality might not be as rosy as all that. At least she knew enough to realize that she could not make her way by herself. So she found a young man with ambitions that matched her own, married, and set off for Texas. But the war with Mexico, in 1848, diverted them back to Missouri, where Elizabeth found herself in the same situation that she had left: living in the household of relatives. That winter, she fell ill in a typhus epidemic and died. Brokenhearted, her sister Amanda carried on in southwestern Virginia, spinning, weaving, sewing, and teaching, while hoping to do something more with her life. Instead, she barely managed to keep body and soul together in circumstances that grew all the more difficult when her troublesome brother took over management of the farm after her father's death. When she finally married, the match seemed like an act of desperation. Still, her diary entries were full of plans for a future she thought would be her own. Like Elizabeth, she never saw the fulfillment of her worldly dreams. She died of tuberculosis just a few days after her wedding. Her younger sister Juliann wrote the final entry in her diary: "The writer of this journal is now no more.... She died in full hope of inheriting a crown of Glory. God grant her hopes may be realized and I believe they will."[1]

Of course, textiles cannot be held responsible for the ravages of typhus and tuberculosis. But the Cooley daughters' untimely deaths provide an apt metaphor for the declining power of textiles. Like all the people in parts I and II, the Cooley women had produced and traded textiles amid profound economic and legal changes. The new republic allowed people without property rights to claim possession of textiles and use them to leverage their way into the commercial economy. Yet these changes were built on the foundations of the past, which gave textiles an aura of stability and even permanence. Looking forward from the perspective of what had been, the legal principles and practices that gave these goods added economic value seemed substantial and dependable, not flimsy and fleeting. That was how Elizabeth and Amanda saw the situation when they came of age in the 1840s. While certainly aware of the constraints placed on them in some areas of law, they saw their world through the possibilities textiles offered, not the restrictions that other laws imposed. That situation explains their remarkably outsized expectations: both women wanted meaningful lives on their own terms. It might seem odd for women who lived in the middle of nowhere at this time in the United States to have such dreams, let alone hold on to them so tightly. Yet the legal order that made those expectations possible also led to their demise.

The current condition of the local case records from which this book is built illustrates the eventual fate of textiles within that judicial order. In some places, records were never kept or, if they were, did not survive. The New York City Mayor's Court records have been preserved on microfilm. The journals from Boston, Richmond, and Philadelphia have withstood the rigors of time fairly well, because of the quality of the paper and the durability of their bindings. The loose records with statements and other descriptive material are hit and miss. At the time they were produced, it was customary to gather together the documents for each case, fold them in thirds, and tie them up with a ribbon. Some of the archives where these materials ended up had the resources to open each bundle, steam the papers flat, and file them in acid-free folders. Even so, neglect had already taken its toll. Not only do these records bear the marks of damage from water, insects, rodents, and other elements (the exact nature of which are probably best left unexamined), but the cheap, acidic paper on which they were written is also slowly dissolving. Some now resemble the intricately wrought lace doilies that once graced the backs of upholstered sofas and chairs in the living rooms of great aunts. In other archives, the records remain in their unopened original state, folded and tied in thirds, sometimes stacked upright in long, thin boxes made for that purpose and sometimes pitched into cartons in no particular order. Reading them inevitably entails their destruction. They crumble as the ribbons are undone and the creases are gently flattened out, leaving trails of paper particles on hands, clothes, desks, and the floor. Wearing white or light colors is ill-advised: the past does not wash off easily, although it vanishes with alarming ease.[2]

The bottom line: these records exude must and mold, not legal authority. That outcome is the result of slow-moving changes that pushed textiles to the margins of the new republic's legal institutions. That trajectory, however, was anything but obvious at the time, which is why the first chapter in this part of the book does not move the narrative forward. It begins with the decades following the Revolution, not those preceding the Civil War, and circles back to consider the legal contradictions generated by people's use of the legal principles governing textiles. Those ideas and practices appeared to be a dependable fixture within the legal order. They also had experienced a makeover in the new republic's federal system, whose overlapping jurisdictions enabled people to use them and, more importantly, to enforce them. What could go wrong?

Everything. Federalism continued to evolve in ways that left the legal principles and practices of textiles behind. The principles existed in the layers of the federal system that could recognize the very material practices that supported them, practices that not only assumed a meaningful connection between persons and the goods they were claiming but also required the participation of other people, at least as witnesses. They tended to lodge in the realm of public law at the local level, which was more open to the people who relied on the legal principles of textiles and offered them an arena to make visible the practices necessary to establish them. But in the decades leading up to the Civil War, legal authority began shifting toward those layers of the federal system that focused on what was called "general laws," based in purportedly universal principles. Those laws were memorialized in written texts, not unwritten practices. Their universality derived from the emphasis on the rights of individuals, unencumbered by relationships and removed from social context, not the material world that made individuals legally visible through their relationships to goods and other people. Those general laws were not all that general, despite their rhetorical packaging. The rights that they upheld did not extend to people who were enmeshed in status relationships or the racial, gender, and class-based restrictions imposed on subordinates. They belonged only to free white men. More than that, the rights of those men depended on their denial to others. Husbands, masters, and fathers acquired rights to exercise authority over the property and bodies of the people legally positioned as their slaves, servants, children, and wives. The rights of household heads were then generalized outward, granting all white men authority on the basis of gender, race, age, and class.

While the legal principles of textiles were everywhere in the federal system during the decades between the Revolution and the Civil War, they could not do what rights did. Only certain people without the legal status necessary to secure property through rights depended on the property *claims* that they created. Rights-based property claims had definite advantages over those that derived from textiles. They traveled freely through the system, whereas claims to textiles emerged and stayed in particular contexts. If individuals had rights, they could own all kinds of property, across all the messy jurisdictional lines—from state to state, from states to territories, and within states.

Portability made rights the legal lingua franca in a governing system that badly needed a common language. Of course, portability had mattered long before the nineteenth century. Mobility and trade characterized the colonial era as well: that was how textiles and the legal principles and practices associated with them got to North America. What made rights so much more important in the United States was the federal system set up in the Revolution's aftermath. Even as its overlapping layers generated new legal possibilities, it also created profound inequality, unsettling indeterminacy, and uneven outcomes that seemed more like injustice than justice. In this institutional context, rights acquired a particular currency, as the only relative constant across jurisdictional lines. No wonder, then, that the elimination of restrictions on rights, particularly the property rights of women and African Americans became key political issues in the decades leading up to the Civil War. These groups sought access to that particular legal language, which was recognized everywhere.

As rights occupied more space, people found it increasingly difficult to enforce the legal principles associated with textiles. The problem was that rights could not replace those principles for most Americans. Rights remained problematic because they did not—and could not—eliminate inequalities related to status relationships, which kept all women, African Americans, and even poor white men in positions of subordination. Relationships unconnected to rights—legally recognized relationships to textiles and each other—gave all these people cover in a hostile legal world. Without them, they were vulnerable. They could only watch as the legal principles on which they had depended turned to rags.

9

Sarah Allingham's Sheet

Enforcement

In October 1804, five women gathered in the New York City Mayor's Court to argue over a homespun linen sheet. The case was initiated by Sarah Allingham, who filed charges against Judith Friel, a washerwoman, for stealing it. But the case was actually about an overdue debt, not theft, and Friel was an innocent bystander, not the real culprit. It was another woman, Sally Riley, who was the scofflaw. Having borrowed a sheet from Allingham, Riley had turned around and sold it to Rosanna Marara, who bought it for six shillings. The fact that Riley borrowed a sheet and sold it was beside the point. The real problem seems to have been that the debt remained unpaid nine months later, which clearly infuriated Allingham, who decided to reclaim what she considered to be her property. When she spied Friel on her rounds collecting dirty laundry, she seized the opportunity. Betting that the sheet might be in her possession, she waylaid the unfortunate washerwoman, grabbed her bundles, and rummaged through them. On finding what she insisted was her sheet, Allingham marched off to file charges.[1]

Enforcement was essential if textiles were to fulfill all the economic capacities for which people used them. When Sarah Allingham made her loan, she did so with the expectation that the transaction would follow certain rules. She first tried to enforce them herself. That failing, she went to the New York City Mayor's Court, determined to be heard. Her complaint involved five other women as well as Friel, each with her own opinions about their neighbors, the sheet, and what the law should do about it. These women, most of whom were working class, Irish, and married, were not unusual witnesses in trials concerning textiles. Local courts across the new republic in both rural and urban areas dealt with similar kinds of people in such cases: married women and minor children, who had limited or no rights to own property or to act in their own names in law; enslaved people, who had no rights at all; free Black men and single adult women, who did, at least in principle; and recent immigrants, impoverished men, and unmarried women, all of whom had property rights but faced considerable barriers to legal action. It is remarkable that all these people insisted that the law recognize their possession of property. Even more remarkable is the response of local officials, who dutifully went along.[2]

Those officials did not respond as they did because they wanted to recognize these people's claims. They were dragged along by a configuration of forces that took particularly powerful form in the decades following the Revolution: the legal principles of textiles, the expectations of those who relied on them, and a decentralized governing order in which those principles could be enforced. Remedies through civil suits remained out of reach for all those without the property rights that private law upheld. But they could bring claims, even to property, as criminal complaints in the area of public law, which looked after the interests of the social order. The point in this area of law was to right egregious wrongs, to put things back where they belonged, and to tamp down on excessive uses of violence, all with the goal of keeping individual conflicts from escalating into general disorder. The locations of this area of law were as accessible as its logic. After the Revolution, states either explicitly delegated discretion to local venues like the New York City Mayor's Court or just left it there by doing nothing to change established practice. People made a range of complaints in these local venues that were not possible elsewhere in the system, including claims to property in textiles.

So it was that local officials up and down the Eastern Seaboard found themselves in the presence of angry, opinionated people like Sarah Allingham demanding that they recognize claims to cloth, clothing, and accessories. These claims were rooted in legal practices that extended across the ocean and back in time, predating the municipal ordinances, state laws, or federal statutes usually assumed to define the law. Local officials responded, often grudgingly and always unevenly, based on the specific circumstances of each conflict. In theory, they could use public law to recognize property claims—even the claims of those with tenuous claims to rights, property, or both—as an element of the public order, which they were bound to protect. But they did not have to. After all, state and federal law, local ordinances, and the reference works used by magistrates and other local officials did not spell out the principles or processes by which those without rights could claim property in this area of law. When officials took action, they acknowledged the strong legal resonance of practices attached to textiles, which provided a counterpoint to the absence of written documentation. These practices and the principles they supported gave visibility to conflicts that otherwise would never have made it into the system and buttressed people's claims to this form of property. To retain the limited power that they had, however, the legal qualities associated with textiles had to be asserted and reiterated openly and repeatedly. That is exactly what people like Sarah Allingham did. They insisted that the legal principles of textiles be recognized as part of the public order. In the process they made their property claims enforceable in law, perpetuating conceptions of ownership and exchange based in relationships, not rights. It was never ideal. But for many it was their only recourse.

Americans' efforts to enforce legal claims to textiles often masqueraded as something else. That peculiar form of legal impersonation was evident in Sarah Allingham's case. The New York City Mayor's Court, which handled both criminal and civil matters, tried her complaint as the criminal charge of theft in the body of public law, not through one of the civil actions used to recover property, such as replevin, to restore seized goods to their owner pending the outcome of an action; debt, to recover a sum of money; detinue, to recover a specific item of property; trover, to recover the value of personal property that had been wrongfully disposed of by another person; or trespass, to recover the value of damages done when another person unlawfully entered property, an action that was liberally interpreted to encompass other forms of property besides real estate, including assaults on people's bodies. That determination owed to Allingham's legal status; as a wife, she did not possess the rights necessary to own property or prosecute a case in her own name according to New York law—and the law of every other state—at that time.[3]

Those principles did not describe the entire legal order, let alone social practice, which had special force in the realm of public law. People knew that: not just working-class white women like Sarah Allingham but all kinds of people without strong claims to rights. The business of local courts reflects that situation. Two kinds of cases predominated in these venues: violence and petty theft. Cases of violence far outstripped theft in rural areas, where people kept close tabs on everyone else's personal property, particularly their linens, clothes, and accessories. The cases that did end up in court were outliers, the result of ongoing conflicts or disputes that individuals had tried and failed to resolve. In 1832, for instance, Thomas Vickery claimed that "his Loom with a Web of Cloath . . . was set on fire" and accused an enslaved man named Drury, who was ultimately acquitted. There had to have been more involved than the complaint suggests. Similarly, a neighbor's charges against James Campbell and his wife for trading homespun cloth likely concealed a longstanding conflict. The neighbor, who lived within sight of the Campbell house, professed surprise that she had happened upon Mrs. Campbell measuring out cloth for an enslaved man one day. But she had clearly been lying in wait and knew exactly what she was looking for. When Edward Calvit went in search of a parcel of clothing and some banknotes stolen from his family, the confrontation took a violent turn. Calvit marched into the house of his neighbors, the Millses, and "feeling the pocket of William Mills found . . . the Dollar that he lost." While he was doing that, Susannah Mills "pulled a Linen Handkerchief of[f] her neck" and "threw it in the fire, which was immediately burnt." But that was not the end of it. According to Calvit, Burwell Mills had the stolen breeches on "under his overalls." He knew, because "he saw the waistband and veryly believes that they were his Breeches." When he demanded "to search him," Burwell "swore he would kill him." It was only after this botched recovery attempt that Calvit filed charges.[4]

By contrast, a significant portion of court business in more urban areas involved claims to textiles made by people with tenuous claims to rights and to property. Between mid-December of 1826 and mid-February of 1827 in New York City, there were fifty cases of assault and seventy-two cases of theft, forty-six of which involved textiles of some kind, including shoes and hats. From early April to early June in 1832, the figures were much the same, with fifty-six cases of violence and fifty-one cases of theft. Thirty-one of those thefts involved textiles. Court dockets in Richmond, Charleston, and Boston were also filled with cases involving the theft of textiles.[5]

High theft rates have been attributed to poverty when it comes to cloth and clothing. Only the truly down and out, it is assumed, would bother to steal a handkerchief, shirt, shift, or sheet. But that is only partly true. Textiles were attractive targets because of their value as well as their ability to change people's economic situation. These cases were not just about economics; they were also about the legal principles attached to textiles and the legal practices that uphold them, all of which were inseparable from the goods' economic significance. Textiles appeared so often in local courts because their legal qualities enhanced their usefulness for those of marginal standing. A handkerchief was more than something to blow your nose with; it was also a dollar bill, an investment, and a business venture. All those people, moreover, had a strong sense of legal entitlement, despite their marginality: they expected local courts to protect one of the few forms of property that they could claim, because of the longstanding legal principles associated with them.[6]

The legal forms used to adjudicate these conflicts have obscured what was really going on. While the mere mention of legal forms has been known to cause everyone but the most dedicated legal scholars to run fleeing from the room, they are crucial in recovering the economics of the textile trade. Too often, the legal forms assigned to offenses have been treated as if they accurately described the conflicts themselves. Nothing could be farther from the truth. The form did not always have much to do with what was really going on; it was merely legal packaging. When local officials decided to act on any complaint about anything, they had to put it into the proper *legal* form that would allow them to proceed through the legal system.[7]

Details mattered. While large municipalities had preprinted documents for common violations, most officials in the first decades following the Revolution copied out the proper language by hand, relying on books that provided examples. The fact that most forms were handwritten did not make them any less formulaic. Regardless of the size of the paper, the legibility of the handwriting, or even the location where they were written, forms had certain details in common. They named the offense in the appropriate legal language: criminal charges, such as assault or theft; civil actions, such as debt, detinue, trover, or trespass. They also provided basic information about the offense: a description of what went wrong; who and what was involved, including the value and owner of the property, if property was at issue; the date and place of the offense; and the names of the complainant and the defendant. All those details mattered. A crime had to occur somewhere at a certain time and be perpetrated by someone, even if by persons unknown; otherwise it was not a crime. A debt had to involve a specific sum of money agreed to on a specific date by specific people; otherwise it was not a debt. Be it civil or criminal, the offense had to take place within the geographic area over which the court had jurisdiction; otherwise officials could not act.[8]

The real challenge was choosing the right form for the offense. That could be tricky, because people's problems did not always match up with the categories laid out in law. In practice, people of all legal statuses—free and enslaved, married and unmarried, Black and white—entered into all kinds of agreements whereby they exchanged property. When those transactions went awry, people used the terms "theft" and "debt" loosely and interchangeably to describe what had happened: an unpaid debt might be termed theft. Those terms, however, had specific meanings in different bodies law. In public law, theft was a criminal charge, which could apply to a range of circumstances in which property had been illegitimately taken, including instances of unpaid loans. By contrast, the civil action of debt in private law was so narrow that it applied only to debts in which money was owed, not other forms of property—although, of course, local officials did not always bother with such legal niceties. To complicate matters, the available forms in civil and criminal law did not describe the entire range of legal practice, let alone social practice. Neither debt nor any other action in private law could cover the loans contracted by those who lacked the necessary legal standing, even when the details of their disputes fit within that legal form. If a white man came in to complain about a bundle of clothes that had been taken from him, those claims could be translated into a civil action. Not so for a married woman with a sheet, because it was impossible for wives to recover anything in this area of law, nor could anything be recovered from them.[9]

The docket for Charleston's Magistrate's Court is typical of the sorting that took place as a result of these complications. In what seems to be a debt case, there is a note that the defendant's wife was a "a sole trader and not liable under the Law." That was not the case with most other wives, whose identities were joined with those of their husbands, if they appeared at all. A trover case, *C. Kingman and wife vs. L. Jones*, ended with a decree for the plaintiff and a note that the disputed clothes had been returned. One suspects that those clothes may have been Mrs. Kingman's, but it is impossible to know, because she could not act legally in her own name. In fact, her full name never appeared in this civil suit.[10]

Given all that, the best option for the local official who took Sarah Allingham's complaint was the criminal charge of theft, which was how local courts throughout the new republic handled all kinds of disputes involving those of nominal legal standing and textiles. All these cases proceeded on the presumption that even those with weak claims to property and rights could make claims to textiles. The point was to figure out who had best claim to them. No one ever questioned whether Sarah Allingham or Rosanna Marara could own a sheet, even though both were married women. Officials dutifully sorted through the evidence and awarded the sheet to Marara, not her husband. It was the same in the case of James, the enslaved man in South Carolina in chapter 2, whose "pear of velvet pantaloons" was returned because someone recognized them, although they had passed through several hands by the time they were found. To identify the thief, the local officials heard the testimony of all those involved to determine who had done the stealing. The fact that James and these other enslaved men had purchased velvet pantaloons never came up. Nor did the documentation ever suggest that they might be the property of James's master, even though he was the one listed as the complainant.[11]

Local officials took claims to textiles seriously. When Alice Jansen, a white woman, descended on a local official in Charleston complaining of a stolen bandana worth one cent, he did not show her the door, as might have been expected. Instead, he filled out the necessary forms to proceed with the case. (It was not even a genuine bandana, as Jansen herself ultimately admitted; it was an imitation, an admission that caused the official to knock its value down to a half cent.)[12] Local officials listened to evidence, despite ingrained cultural preconceptions that associated people of color and the poor with criminality. Take the cases of two African American women, both from New York, who have appeared in previous chapters: Rosenah Gray, the enslaved woman with an impressive stash of cloth, and Susan Munro, the free Black woman with three expensive gowns. We know about their textiles because both were charged with theft. Gray explained in great detail how she came by her cloth in defending herself against the complaint of a white merchant, who insisted that some of it belonged to him. Despite that evidence, the outcome of this case might seem like a foregone conclusion. An enslaved woman accused of theft by a white man, a prosperous merchant no less? But at no point did anyone, even the merchant, question her ability to purchase and possess textiles. In the end, she maintained ownership. So did Susan Munro. She was accused of theft by a physician, who claimed that one of those gowns had been stolen from his house. (The physician, not his wife, took the lead in this matter, making the complaint and also testifying, although the gowns clearly belonged to his wife or daughters. But he chose his words carefully and never claimed ownership: the gowns "were stolen from his house"; they were not his gowns.) It might seem like Susan Munro was doomed, given the status disparity between accuser and accused. But the court acquitted her.[13]

Outcomes like those depended on evidence—lots of it, all carefully compiled and methodically presented. To say that local officials were not inclined to believe the enslaved, free Black, immigrant, and working-class people who appeared before them would be an understatement. For that matter, they were not all that favorably inclined toward white women, even those who belonged to respectable families. Still, many local officials were willing to set aside their prejudices if the litigants who appeared before them had compelling evidence. Local court officials would have preferred that evidence to take the form of account books, receipts, bills of exchange, or notes—the kinds of written documentation that appeared so often in civil cases in the nineteenth century. They rarely got it because of the risk those records carried for people without strong claims to rights or property.[14]

The practices of civil law nonetheless seeped into criminal matters. People of nominal legal standing not only tried to supply evidence that they thought would be the most persuasive to local officials, but they also relied on the same basic concepts of ownership and exchange in their own dealings. Litigants routinely offered up the same information that would have been in written documents, just in other forms. In Sarah Allingham's case, Rosanna Marara brought two witnesses, who recalled the date of her purchase (it was the previous winter because there was snow on the ground), the qualities of the property (it was a coarse linen and homespun sheet), and its value (priced at six shillings). The testimony conveyed all the details that would have been on a receipt. Allingham had only bluff and bluster. How was anyone to know whether she ever even owned the sheet? Not surprisingly, officials awarded it to Marara. In the absence of witnesses, litigants provided details to anchor transactions in time and place just as receipts, notes, or bills of exchange would have done. That was what Rosenah Gray and Susan Munro did when they offered detail after detail about the purchase of their disputed textiles, including the date of purchase, the particulars of the sale, and an inventory of the goods.[15]

It was wise to trade in public, so as to acquire witnesses. Even without witnesses, however, public knowledge had legal weight. What it documented was not unlike the entries in account books, which also made transactions public. Where account books fixed exchanges on the page, witnesses committed them to memory. But both forms of recording had value because of the assumption that transactions done in public were less likely to be illicit; only those who had something to hide traded in the shadows. Publicity served the enslaved men who bought James's pantaloons. The fact that they purchased the pants openly indicated that they did not know they had been stolen. Although they could have been charged with trafficking in stolen goods, they were not. Only the man accused of actually taking the pants from James's trunk was convicted of a crime. Susan Munro had no witnesses to her purchase, but she was careful to explain that she had bought the gowns openly on the street and could show the court where they now were: she was wearing one, another was at home, and the last had been loaned to a woman who could be called as a witness. Everything took place in public, indicating that she had nothing to conceal. No one saw Rosenah Gray buy her textiles. But she had a witness who could testify to the fact that she had purchased a length of cloth from Rosenah's stash and could bring it in for inspection. Such evidence seems dubious, at best. The enslaved men who traded for James's pantaloons could have known, or at least suspected, that they were purchasing stolen goods. Susan Munro and Rosenah Gray could have stolen the goods in question and then turned around and loaned or sold them. But evidence of this kind appeared over and over in theft cases. When claims to textiles were questioned, litigants related not just the details of their purchase but also the particulars of subsequent trades, because that sort of evidence carried weight at the time. The ability to trace the movement of goods as well as the willingness to do so gave transactions an aura of legitimacy, undercutting suspicions that those involved were getting rid of stolen goods quickly and anonymously.[16]

Oral testimony could be better than a receipt, at least when it came to textiles. A receipt, after all, was meaningful only if the person who had it could make legal claims to the property in question through the possession of rights. They were of more limited value for people without strong claims to property rights. In fact, they could be downright dangerous: within the rules of civil law, receipts established ownership for the male household head with property rights, not for the wife, child, or slave without them. Receipts were so unusual in this part of the textile trade that their presence could be suspicious. When Cornelius Dougherty produced a receipt for a carpet that he was accused of stealing, he also had to come up with a witness to prove his receipt—so to speak—of this receipt, because the whole thing was so unbelievable. The witness did not exactly clear things up. He did testify to seeing Dougherty buy the carpet and obtain a receipt. But when asked whether the piece of paper in evidence was that receipt, he admitted that he could not be sure, because he could not "read writing" (meaning that he could only read printing, not handwritten script). Nor could he explain where the seller "got ink to write the receipt with," since the transaction was done outside, on a bench "in Chatham Street, opposite the porter House of Mr. Harrison," where such accoutrements were generally in short supply. Court officials had clearly encountered fake receipts before.[17]

Unlike receipts, witnesses also could speak to context, the key element of ownership for this kind of property. Timothy Halley, who had charged his landlady with stealing items from his trunk in a previous chapter, ran afoul of just such a witness. While the charge was theft, the issue seems to have been more complicated, perhaps a disputed loan or bill. While he claimed that the items had been taken from his trunk without his consent, a servant of his landlady testified that she had been present when Halley gave her some of those items, specifically a pair of sheets and a blanket, to pay his lodging bill. The servant, moreover, was certain that "he has never had them in possession since." Not only did the servant witness the exchange, but she could also testify to what happened next. After accepting the property, the landlady reduced it to her possession by using it, with the apparent assent of Halley, who knew where the property was but made no attempt to reclaim it. Context legitimized an act that Halley regarded as theft. The landlady was acquitted.[18]

If the point of exchange was too far distant to be documented, litigants regularly offered evidence of possession and use to create legitimacy. One way to establish a meaningful connection to textiles was to mark them with initials or other distinguishing signs. There were good, practical reasons, besides a desire for embellishment, for embroidering initials onto handkerchiefs. Handkerchiefs then were as common as dollar bills today. Not only did they circulate constantly, but they all looked a lot alike. Given that, it was best to mark your property as your own, lest it move into the hands of someone else. Yet even here, writing could not overcome the evidence of use. Cloth and clothing changed hands so frequently that initials did not always correspond to those of the person who claimed them. It was sufficient to know what the markings were. That was the basis of Fanny Reeder's claims to a sheet marked with the initials JR. Actually, the complaint identified the item as the property of her husband, William Reeder, although the rest of the case suggested that the items really belonged to her. Still, the initials on the sheet were not those of her or her husband. No matter. She knew how the sheet had been marked, so it had to be hers.[19]

Local officials recognized the connections that trunks created between people and the textiles within them. But trunks also posed an evidentiary dilemma because they established possession by hiding their contents. If no one had seen the property stored in a trunk, then it was possible that it had never existed at all. That was what undid the case of the unfortunate Timothy Halley, who claimed that many things had been stolen from his trunk, although just a few items had turned up in his landlady's house. The only person who saw what was in his trunk was the servant who coyly refused to confirm that the property he claimed was in it. She accounted for what had been found, which included the pair of sheets and a blanket that supposedly covered the bill with her employer and a towel that she claimed had been given to her. As in all things regarding textiles, it was wise to publicize a trunk's contents. When James's master filed his complaint, he made it clear that James's pantaloons, suspenders, store-bought socks, and shaving box had been taken from his trunk. That fact established theft; taking textiles out of a locked trunk was akin to breaking and entering a house. It established James's possession of the property in question. It also established possession as part of practice, in the form of the knowledge and assent of the man legally positioned as his master. The magistrate had no reason to question the fact that all that property had been in James's trunk, which was why it appeared on the complaint form. In other cases, local officials listened to testimony as to the contents of trunks and weighed the credibility of those involved. Then they delved into evidence of whether the trunk had been open, closed, or broken into, so as to determine whether items had been stolen from it.[20]

While initials and trunks were helpful, evidence of use was more persuasive because it established an actual connection, not just a theoretical one. More than that, use constituted a public acknowledgment of possession. Timothy Halley's linens had been stored in his trunk and marked with his initials. But he was up against evidence of use, offered by the servant who claimed he had given her a towel. That towel had been in use in the landlady's household, supporting the servant's story that he had given it to her. If someone else was using it, then how could it be his? That was why the Marshall clan, who appeared in the chapter 8, went to such lengths to explain not just how long they had been in possession of the cloth and clothing that they had been accused of stealing but also how they had used it. In his testimony, Mr. Marshall piously pointed out that he was wearing a waistcoat made of the red flannel in question right there at the hearing. The point was so clear that he did not need to state it: he would never have worn something made of the very cloth he was charged with stealing. That claim was based in use, which demonstrated that the cloth was his. While Mr. Marshall's attire may have had nothing to do with the court's determination in the case, he was acquitted. It was his wife and daughter who were convicted.[21]

Use established a physical relationship with legal weight. The legal meaning of that connection explains why Matilda Brownlee brought in a piece of the carpet that she claimed to have been stolen from her and that was found in Cornelius Dougherty's hands. That small corner, cut from the larger piece, was valuable evidence. Brownlee knew the rules: proving possession of something no longer in her possession would be a challenge. So she had clipped this piece from her carpet and kept it separate and safe, just in case she ever needed it. As it turned out, she did. While Dougherty had a receipt, she had evidence of an actual connection to the carpet.[22]

The underlying issues in all these theft cases can be difficult to see. The records are like hostile witnesses. Their whole point was to conceal, which they did admirably, transforming complicated conflicts over property into a legal form of convenience and then providing only the bare minimum of information. Officials and litigants collaborated in the ruse, although they often worked at cross-purposes. Officials grudgingly shoved property disputes through the system as criminal matters, often without bothering to keep records, while litigants massaged the facts to make their causes more believable in a context where they were unlikely to be believed. In the process, all kinds of property exchanges—sales, loans, unpaid bills, disputed ownership—were repackaged as theft.

Some litigants threw up their hands in frustration. Eliza Cauchois drew a clear distinction between theft and an outstanding loan. As she stated, her accuser had loaned her the shift in question, and "therefore she did not steal it." Elizabeth Cornell used virtually the same words: her accuser had loaned her a disputed shift, so "she did not steal it." John Miers waved away his brother-in-law's accusation of theft with the same justification. He admitted that "he took a great coat . . . some time ago." But it was now "safe," an explanation he considered sufficient, because his brother-in-law "loaned him the said coat." One woman carefully differentiated between the property she had stolen and the property she had borrowed. She admitted to stealing a black silk gown but insisted that a bed spread she was charged with taking had been loaned to her. Unpaid loans might be a problem, but they were not theft. All these people had a point: in law, unpaid debts were not the same thing as theft. But theft was an easier charge to prosecute against people of nominal legal standing.[23]

In most cases, the conflict comes filtered through the existing legal form, with all the attendant distortions. Take Sarah Allingham's case. Allingham filed charges in October 1804, although the sheet was stolen about nine months earlier. Why? The record provides an indirect, entirely opaque explanation: it was in October that Allingham saw her long-lost sheet "in the possession of Mrs. Friel who the Deponent believes either stole the same herself or knows who did steal" it. Somehow Allingham found out that the sheet was in Judith Friel's possession, which meant that she could produce two of the elements necessary for a theft charge: the goods and a culprit. But the case was never really about Friel. In her statement, Allingham implicated another woman, Sally Riley, whom she thought "aided and assisted the said Mrs. Friel in taking the said articles." In her testimony, Riley neither admitted nor denied taking the sheet. As she explained, she boarded with the Allinghams during the winter of 1804, but "never took any thing but her own clothes out of the Allingham House and has not even taken the whole of them." The testimony of Judith Friel, Rosanna Marara, and two other witnesses suggested otherwise. Friel insisted that the sheet was among the things she picked up from Marara and flatly denied having stolen anything with Riley or having received anything from her "either by way of purchase or any other way." She was backed up by Marara, who claimed the sheet as her own, having purchased it from Riley during the time she was living with Allingham. Marara then produced two witnesses to confirm that transaction. So Riley did have a sheet that could have belonged to Allingham. But how did she come by it? Theft, or some other means? When the court called Riley back to explain, she maintained her story, denying possession of the sheet and, hence, its sale.[24]

This case was about theft only in the most general sense. Neither Sally Riley nor Judith Friel snatched Sarah Allingham's sheet while no one was looking. In fact, no one ever pretended that was what happened. Theft served as a proxy for some other kind of property dispute that was assumed but never named. The witnesses danced around it, dropping the occasional clue. In addition to the sheet, the case involved other missing bedding, a broken pitcher, and simmering conflicts among neighbors who probably lived closer to each other than they would have liked. The key to making sense of it all was the nine months between when the property was alleged to have been stolen and when the complaint was filed, a situation that usually indicated a case of borrowing gone awry. If Riley had stolen the sheet in January when she was living with Sarah Allingham and Allingham knew it was stolen, as she testified, then why wait so long to file charges? It made no sense that Allingham overlooked the sheet's absence in January but was so outraged by October that she needed to make a public scene and file charges. A loan explains that lapse in time.

A loan also makes sense of other elements of the case, particularly the relationship between Allingham and Riley. Riley stated that she did not take all her clothes with her when she left Sarah Allingham's to board elsewhere. Why leave some of her clothes behind, when those were her only possessions in the world? Why underscore that point in testimony about a sheet? Allingham might have agreed to store Riley's clothes, although that seems like a stretch given the obvious bad blood between the two. It is more likely that Riley "left" them there—perhaps less than voluntarily—because she owed on her bill. Landlords were known to seize their tenants' clothing for past due rent, just as tenants pawned their landlords' bedding as a way of making ends meet. In fact, this smattering of facts suggests that Sally Riley may have owed Allingham for more than board: she also may have owed her for the sheet, which she took and sold while boarding there. Perhaps Riley took the sheet without Allingham's assent, with the intention of returning it before it was found missing. But, according to Allingham, Riley took the sheet along with other bedding, none of which had surfaced since it disappeared from Allingham's house. Surely, the absence of all those items would have been difficult to conceal. And if the point was to take these items and then return them, then why not pawn the sheet instead of selling it? If Sally Riley took the sheet—and presumably the other bedding—without asking, how did Allingham know when the sheet was stolen? The fact that Allingham was so certain as to the exact date when the items went missing suggests that she had loaned them to Riley with the understanding that she would receive their value back. It was after her relationship to Riley soured that Allingham decided that she needed to repossess whatever property she could locate. That would be the sheet, which she asserted that she had found in the washtub of Judith Friel. When Friel refused to hand it over, Allingham took the whole matter to the Mayor's Court. The records do not reveal what she told the official there. All we know is that the official turned whatever she said into the only legal form that provided a way to resolve this convoluted conflict: theft.[25]

What distinguished civil actions from criminal cases like that of Sarah Allingham was the legal status of the participants, not the nature of the conflicts. Both civil actions and theft cases involved small claims to property of some kind. In both, the point of legal proceedings was to distinguish illegitimate claims from legitimate ones. Suggestive in this regard is an 1805 case from Richmond, Virginia, in which Thomas Sterne charged Isaac Allen with taking his clothing. Had Sterne and Allen not been white men, the official who heard his complaint would have had no choice but to call it theft. But they were. So the official chose to convert the complaint into the civil action of trover: the recovery of the value of personal property that had been wrongfully disposed of by another person. Trover actually described Sarah Allingham's case as well. She too claimed property that—at least in her interpretation—had been taken from her and wrongfully disposed of. She too wanted the value back. But, given her legal status, that civil action was impossible.[26]

In Sterne's case, theft might have been a better choice, because the official clearly struggled to contain Sterne's story within the legal form of trover. Sterne, he wrote, had been "possessed of one bag of clothes containing several articles of wearing apparel," which he "casually lost" and then inexplicably found "in the hands and possession" of Allen. How does anyone casually lose a bag of clothing? How did it go from being casually lost to being formally found? While the losing and the finding remained murky at best, what happened next fit more clearly into the legal action of trover. Not only did Allen refuse to give back the clothes, but he also sold them, knowing "them to be the goods and chattels of [Sterne], and to [Sterne] of right to belong and appertain, and contriving and fraudulently intending . . . craftily and subtlelly to deceive and deny the said bag of clothes . . . altho of law required." Still, just as Allen refused to give back Sterne's clothes, so the elements of this case refused to stay within the confines of the legal form selected by the local official. How did Sterne know that Allen had them and then sold them? How did Allen know they were Sterne's clothes, if he just happened upon them? The confusing mash of detail suggests that this case involved a transaction that went awry, not "lost" clothing. Whatever it was, the local official labeled it trover, thereby artificially separating these men's property disputes from those of people like Sarah Allingham.[27] In fact, they were much the same thing.

Yet they were not the same in law, because of the differing legal forms given to them. The case of Polly's missing thread, from the first chapter, provides a particularly compelling example. In this case, the legal form identified the crime as theft, the complainant as a man legally positioned as Polly's master, and the accused as an enslaved man named Brummer. But the testimony centered on a complicated property dispute involving Polly, Brummer, and Polly's husband, who was also enslaved. As Polly testified, the cotton thread in question belonged to her. She had spun it and dyed the hanks, which were hanging outside to dry, when Brummer came by and admired them. "This is mighty pretty cotton," he told her. The comment had an edge, because both she and her husband were indebted to Brummer. She owed him "twenty five cents for a Basket she bought of him last fall," although that debt was not in dispute. She had agreed to pay him in a form other than the cotton thread. It was the debt that her husband owed to Brummer that was the problem. Her husband met up with Brummer to come to a settlement and then went off "to get his pay." She did not know how her husband settled the matter. But when she got home, her hanks of cotton thread were gone. Other witnesses, both enslaved and free, testified to seeing Brummer with white and blue cotton that matched the description of Polly's thread. Using the legal charge of theft, the court affirmed Polly's claims. She got her thread back.[28]

That outcome came at a cost. What that legal form gave with one hand it took away with the other by making an ordinary property transaction into something illicit. One litigant always became a criminal. Yet this case actually involved the kinds of issues that characterized civil suits. There were the claims of Polly, who was married, to textiles that she produced on her own. There were the claims to that same property by her husband, who used the thread that she had made to cover a debt he had incurred. And there were the claims of a creditor to debts owed him by both Polly and her husband. In awarding Polly her thread, court officials admitted that it was possible for enslaved people to own textiles. By implication, however, the property claims of enslaved people were different than those of free people who could claim rights. Brummer, who was trying to collect a debt owed him for baskets that he made and traded, was convicted of theft for taking the property of his debtor's wife. Had he been free and white, the decision might well have gone in his favor, not just because court officials treated white people more favorably but also because the whole conflict would have gone through the system as a civil action that favored the property rights of men, not a criminal one that acknowledged wives' property claims through the legal qualities of textiles. But, as a criminal, Brummer was sentenced to ten lashes. That outcome spilled over onto Polly, whose victory came at the expense of undermining the general principles of property ownership without rights. It might seem like one litigant won and the other lost. Really, they both lost in the long run.[29]

While cases that affirmed claims to textiles could have substantial financial benefits for some of the people involved, they did not challenge the basic structure of the social order. That was not the point of criminal law, the body of law in which these cases were handled. This same body of law inflicted horrific punishments on those, particularly enslaved African Americans, who did not comply with their subordination. In fact, everyone who stepped out of their place fared badly in this legal arena. To the extent that anyone with a subordinate status had credibility, it was through the social ties that defined their subordination. The wives and daughters of respectable white men had standing, as did women known for attention to their families and their neighbors. Poor white, free Black, and enslaved women could maneuver in this area of law, but they needed stellar reputations and, better yet, connections to powerful people—which often meant conforming to the rigid hierarchies of the time. The outcomes then affirmed those hierarchies. Some people were allowed to keep textiles as their own property because local officials chose to recognize the legal principles associated with these goods. But those people did not acquire the property rights that made such cases unnecessary. Even as textiles allowed some people more options, they did nothing to change the basic logic of inequality that placed white men with property in positions of authority over others. Still, criminal charges were the only recourse available to people without strong claims to rights and property.

10

Catherine Brennan's Haul

Criminality

In 1844, Catherine Brennan, a recent Irish immigrant, found herself in circumstances all too familiar to many domestic servants. She and a friend, Ann Allison, also Irish, stood in the New York City Mayor's Court accused of stealing from Brennan's employer, the Taggarts. The property in question included three shawls, a pillowcase, a handkerchief, a morning gown, a piece of lace, a frock, six chemises, eight shirts, twelve towels, and twenty-four napkins. While the charge was theft, neither Brennan nor Allison used that term. They each described the situation as borrowing, despite knowing that it was problematic in this particular instance. Catherine Brennan insisted that it was Ann Allison who proposed the scheme. She asked Brennan "to let her have some articles belonging to Mrs. Taggart to raise money on." The phrasing said it all: Allison was asking to tap into Brennan's credit, in the form of access to her employer's property. It was not really stealing, as Allison purportedly explained to Brennan, because "Mrs. Taggart was not in the habit of wearing the articles" and "would not be likely to miss them before they would be returned." All that made sense in terms of the logic of the textile trade, the conflicts of which were adjudicated within the legal form of theft, generously and flexibly defined. But it made no sense within a narrower, more rigid definition of theft, focused only on the criminal taking of property, which probably explains Brennan's pious insistence that she had refused Allison's entreaties to "borrow" the property. Ann Allison's version of events was remarkably similar, although she dumped responsibility onto Catherine Brennan. As she told it, it was Brennan who had done borrowing in order to pay a debt she owed to Allison. It was Brennan who had directed Allison "to pledge them for money," which Allison had dutifully done. And it was Brennan who claimed that "she would be able to redeem the articles and return them before they would be missed." But, unlike Brennan, Ann Allison did not bother to deny her participation when it came to pawning the borrowed goods. So what? Brennan owed her.[1]

By the 1830s, theft cases had a different feel than they previously did. That situation owed, in part, to economics. Cheap and readily available textiles were everywhere, owned by ordinary people in greater quantities. People experienced their proliferation as a combustible mix of boom and bust. As consumers, they could buy more. But it was an entirely different story when it came to textiles' function as currency, credit, and capital. In that capacity, textiles became unstable, which had profound implications for the legal principles and practices associated with them. Instability encouraged people to defy the legal principles governing their exchange and simply take what they could. At the same time, they relied on the legal principles they were flouting to pass off stolen goods as legitimate within the vast part of the textile market known as the street trade. While loosely regulated by local and state governments, this part of the market still depended on practices that upheld the legal principles of textiles.

Catherine Brennan's and Ann Allison's statements are suggestive in this regard. While relying superficially on the legal principles associated with textiles, they clearly disregarded them. Brennan, who lived with her employers, had ready access to their property. Allison, a visitor to the servants' quarters, did not. Yet in Catherine Brennan's version of events, Ann Allison managed to scour the house, collect a stack of clothing, linens, and accessories and then carry everything away, without anyone, including Brennan, interfering. Really? As a live-in domestic, Brennan might have been able to spirit away goods, a little at a time, without anyone's knowledge. That was usually how servants pilfered their employers' property. But according to Allison, Brennan brought all the items to her at once with instructions to pawn them. Here again, the logistics seem daunting, to say the least. How did Brennan get everything out of her employer's house in one load and lug it to Allison's lodgings without assistance? Why take the risk of discovery that came with removing such a large quantity of goods at one time? It made more sense that Allison and Brennan had been in cahoots and, when caught, turned on each other. That may also explain why the case was forfeited, meaning that either the Taggarts or, more likely, the defendants failed to show for the trial. It is easy to imagine Brennan and Allison disappearing into the city, like so many other accused thieves. Unlike earlier cases in which borrowing masqueraded as theft, the case against these two women appears to be theft masquerading as borrowing.

Who could tell? Theft left a stain that was impossible to wash away, undermining the ability of textiles to serve as currency, collateral, and capital. At best, this legal form made the property claims of people with the full range of rights visible but contingent. They were always dependent on the specifics: the form that the property took, the people involved, the circumstances, and the sufferance of legal officials. They were always limited, applicable only to the successful claimant and the property in question. And they were always punitive. The affirmation of the complainant's claims necessarily turned the unsuccessful defendant into a criminal, who then faced stiff penalties: corporal punishment and/or imprisonment, in addition to court costs and monetary restitution to the victim. The outcomes of individual cases, moreover, provide only a partial accounting of their costs, which, with interest, accumulated over time. Theft turned all property claims into crimes. Even as individuals affirmed their own claims, the process worked in the opposite direction, making the property defended in this manner seem different and, ultimately, illegitimate, clouded with suspicions of theft, fraud, or some other dodgy ploy. Those debts started coming due in the decades preceding the Civil War.

The deterioration in textiles' legal powers is inseparable from the economic context in which these goods were made and used. That context changed dramatically in the decades leading up to the Civil War. The prices of textiles continued to decline and their availability continued to increase through the second quarter of the nineteenth century. But according to studies of consumer prices, the cost of cloth, clothing, and related accessories fell far more rapidly than that of other goods in the period between 1780 and 1860. The other basics that economic historians put in the bundle of items that make up the consumer price index, including food, rent, and transportation, also declined, but not as precipitously as textiles.[2]

Cheap, machine-made cottons had inundated the market by the 1830s. Personal and household linens once made from actual linen were instead made from cotton fabrics that rolled off power looms and bore utilitarian names derived from their uses: plains, shirtings, sheetings, and drills, all basic cotton fabric, usually in white or a standard blue (think modern-day oxford cloth shirts), with no elaborate textures woven into them and no designs printed on them, although shirtings sometimes had colored stripes (just as they do now). Plains were made fancy through newly streamlined printing processes. The numbering of Cocheco Manufacturing's sample cards for printed cotton cloth suggests the variety. Beginning in 1827, its first year in business, Cocheco introduced new styles seasonally, giving each one a new number. In 1850, a commission agent in Philadelphia ordered styles 516, 518, 485, and 486, meaning that the company had gone through over five hundred styles, although only the most popular were still in production—and that was just one company. Cocheco, which remained in business until 1940, was known for selling quality cotton fabrics with a high thread count in a range of weights: sheer lawns and batistes; delaines with more heft and opacity, although still relatively lightweight; and more substantial percales, cambrics, and satines, suitable for colder weather. Cocheco was also known for its quality printing, with clear, strong colors and well-spaced designs with defined, consistent borders. The company used different techniques to produce different effects, from simple calicos with small repeating patterns in a few colors to satines and foulards with multiple colors and complicated designs with a high-gloss finish intended to resemble silk. Other firms made lower-priced goods with coarser fabric and cruder patterns, with wide or irregular spacing and dull colors that spilled over the designs' borders.[3]

Cheap cottons changed the way people interacted with all textiles, making them more like other consumer goods, rather than property in which to store and exchange value. Printed cottons had formerly been expensive imports reserved for fancy dress, but women also used them for everyday wear by mid-century. It was possible to have many dresses for each season and occasion: winter, spring, summer, and fall; work, everyday, and Sunday best; all in different weights, colors, patterns, and styles. People expected to have more of other fabrics as well, even though not all were machine made. They still relied on linen's durability for heavy cloth, such as bagging and sails. They continued to prize silk's rich colors and textures for formal wear and upholstery. And they never gave up wool for men's suits, women's winter dresses, outerwear, blankets, and work clothes.

Of all fibers other than cotton, wool remained in demand because of its versatility. It came in a variety of weights and textures, from light, airy, and soft as down to thick, heavy, and scratchy. At its finest, it draped beautifully and had the ease necessary to shape itself to the contours of three-dimensional bodies and move with them. At its heaviest, it kept its wearers warm even when it was wet. It was so essential that Thomas Jefferson linked the production high-quality wool cloth to the new republic's future prospects. As president, he risked relations with England and Spain to smuggle in merino sheep, whose export was prohibited by both countries because the breed sustained their woolen industries. The American wool industry continued to

Figure 10.1 The detail from cheap, badly printed cotton contrasts with the precision, complexity, and colors of the more expensive cotton prints. Detail from *The Valentine*, Terry Brown, photographer.

play a central role in the country's political economy. The 1828 tariff, which protected domestic manufacturers, including textile manufactures, is usually remembered for alienating cotton growers to the point that South Carolina's leaders threatened its nullification. Cotton producers, who sold on an unprotected market, had to pay higher prices for all manufactured goods, including all the textiles they went through at a rapid rate. Among the tariff's chief beneficiaries was the US woolen industry: duties for those fabrics were higher than other kinds of cloth.[4]

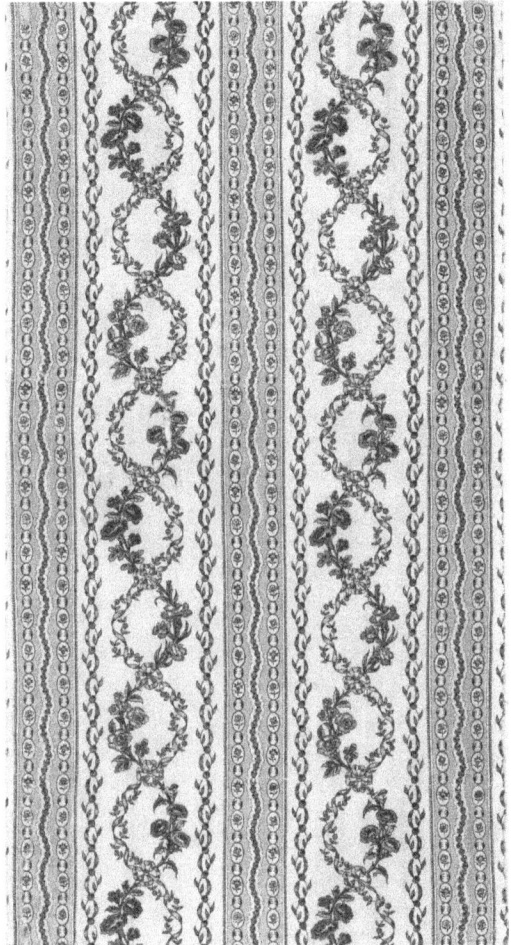

Figure 10.2 Block-printed cotton, dress fabric, ca. 1790, England, given by Miss M. H. Tattersall, Victoria and Albert Museum.

Cotton fueled the demand for wool. Even enslaved people who grew cotton dressed in clothes made of that fiber. By the 1830s, according to historian Seth Rockman, entire New England towns depended on the production of wool cloth to outfit enslaved people in the cotton South. Given the region's sweltering summers, woolen work clothes might seem like yet another instance of slaveholders' casual cruelty. But wool was (and is) more durable and comfortable than cotton in certain circumstances. Cotton soaks up sweat and then clings uncomfortably to the body, refusing to give or move. Unable to take the strain, the fabric rips immediately or slowly disintegrates.

Figure 10.3 Dress fabric of printed muslin with floral sprigs, 1820s, given by Cora Ginsburg Inc., Textiles and Fashion Collection, Victoria and Albert Museum.

To increase durability, it has to be woven tightly and thickly, like the denim jeans made by the Levi brothers for miners in the 1848 gold rush. But thickness does not remedy cotton's other deficiencies, which are well known to anyone who has worn heavy jeans on summer day. In the heat and humidity, jeans become damp as well as stiff, resisting movement until they stretch out of shape to the point where they no longer fit at all. That is the reason why denim overalls hang loose from the shoulders. Unlike cotton, wool breathes and gives. Its fluffy fibers trap the air, spiriting away sweat in the heat and keeping its wearers warm in the cold and damp. Wool also has enough flexibility to accommodate movement without losing its shape. Today, work shirts and exercise gear are made with polyester and spandex, the combination of which approximates the stretch and wicking qualities of wool. Some high-end purveyors now charge a premium for wool gear intended for use in summer as well as winter. Those qualities mattered then, just as they do as now. As Rockman also shows, enslaved people had plenty of opinions about the performance of their work clothes. Planters took note, because durability and fit had financial consequences for them. It was hard to chop cotton in shirts that tore to shreds or in britches that kept falling off.[5]

Wool also anchored working men's wardrobes in the form of ready-to-wear suits, which represented a revolution in men's fashions. These suits—with pants, vest, and jacket made of the same fabric in dull, monochromatic browns, grays, blues, and blacks—played down class differences among men by putting them all in the same uniform outfit. Before their introduction, men's wear had been mix and match, in part because garments were so expensive. Most people bought one piece at a one, putting together an entire outfit slowly: some shirts, a jacket here, an overcoat there, then pants, a vest, and a neckerchief. Only the well-to-do could afford to purchase a matching suit of clothes. Of course, fashion played into the selections as well. Men were drawn to colors, textures, and patterns just as women were. They paired yellow cotton nankeen pants with bright blue wool jackets lined in vivid colors. Vests in eye-catching hues, flowing patterns, ornate embroidery, and rich textures added dash to an ordinary outfit of browns and olives. A neckerchief in a flashy print or brilliant white (a more classic look) pulled it all together. The matching suits in John Trumbull's *The Declaration of Independence* (1819) reflect the fact that most of the founding fathers could afford to purchase an entire outfit all at once. But the uniformly drab colors convey as much about Revolutionary ideology—republican simplicity and the rejection of all things British, including imported textiles—as they do about actual sartorial practice. Jefferson's red vest, peeking out from his somber suit, is more on the mark. The actual founders, not to mention the men they represented, wore brighter colors, often in striking combinations.[6]

By the 1830s, if not before, merchant tailors all over the country stocked ready-made men's wear in a range of cuts, colors, and fabrics, so that customers could create their own distinctive style. While lucrative, the practice was also confounding because there were so many options. It is hard to miss the frustration running through the 1830s correspondence between

Figure 10.4 John Trumbull, 1756–1843. The Declaration of Independence.

F. H. Cooke, a merchant tailor who sold ready-made men's clothing in Augusta, Georgia, and James Edney, his New York supplier. Edney generally fielded Cooke's continual demands with polite detachment. But he clearly lost it when Cook informed him that a recent shipment of pants had been too old-fashioned. It was surprising, Edney noted acidly, since Cooke had "generally spoken against fashionable things." Their relationship ended badly during the Panic of 1837, with Edney begging an unresponsive Cooke to make good on his unpaid bills.[7]

Woolen suits cut down on the options. In the 1840s, merchants began offering made-to-order suits, with matching pants and jacket. Sold in volume at low prices, with quick turnaround times, made-to-order suits were not exactly ready-made. Although the designs were standardized, the suits were fitted to individuals. The underlying logic, however, was the same: to centralize and systematize the production of garments that had once been custom made. From there, merchant tailors moved on to ready-made suits, sold off the rack, in a range of sizes that could accommodate anyone, at least in theory. Customers could walk in and walk out with a suit and all the necessary accessories without the fuss of measuring, fitting, and waiting—and for far less to boot. "While marveling at prices low / They try them on, and buy and go," promised Oak Hall, Boston's famous men's wear emporium, in a promotional pamphlet, done inexplicably in rhyme. Brooks Brothers of New York City claims to have been the first to offer ready-to-wear suits in 1849. Whether or not that is true, similar stores could be found all over the country in the 1850s, selling matching suits in fashionably boring colors, generally made from wool. Ready-to-wear only worked in areas where the customer base was large enough to support the necessary inventory. Made-to-order suits continued to be available well into the twentieth century in rural areas, where merchants could not stock a sufficient selection of styles and sizes in ready-made. Manufacturers supplied rural stores with samples of fabrics and styles. Local clerks helped customers make their selections and the necessary measurements and then sent off the order. A (sort of) fitted suit arrived back in the store for pickup soon thereafter. In fact, the line between ready-made and made-to-order had collapsed by that point. "Made-to-order" suits were really ready-to-wear made when customers ordered them.[8]

Men's wear emporiums draped ready-to-wear suits in an aura of exclusivity available to all. In 1842, Oak Hall kitted itself out with rich, dark paneling that screamed privilege and old money—decor that is associated with high-end men's clothing more generally, even today. But instead of keeping people out, Oak Hall's owner invited them in. The store's advertising touted its "fearless introduction" of "large sales for the smallest possible profits... whereby the poorest of the poor may now provide themselves with excellent garments." It also encouraged passersby to come in and look, even if they did not intend to buy—behavior so contrary to customary practice that it had to be explained. "It is the wonder of the town / Come, see the cause of its renown," a fictional Oak Hall clerk told a fictional man on the street in a promotional brochure. "Do you pretend to say that I / May enter there, if I don't buy?" asked the man. "Certainly, Sir," responded the clerk. This clerk, unlike the author of *The Perils of Pearl Street*, did not see browsing shoppers as the bane of merchants' existence. The store also offered a contract system, in which customers agreed to lock in a set price in advance for the clothing that they needed over the course of an entire year. The success of these kinds of marketing campaigns are evident in mug shots from the late nineteenth and early twentieth centuries, which show suspected criminals all dressed neatly in suits. To modern eyes, they look more like respectable businessmen than possible felons. Even riffraff could afford matching wool suits.[9]

The downward slide in textile prices had profound legal implications. When it came to textiles as consumer goods, people experienced it as part of the general increase in spending power. Not only did prices for cloth,

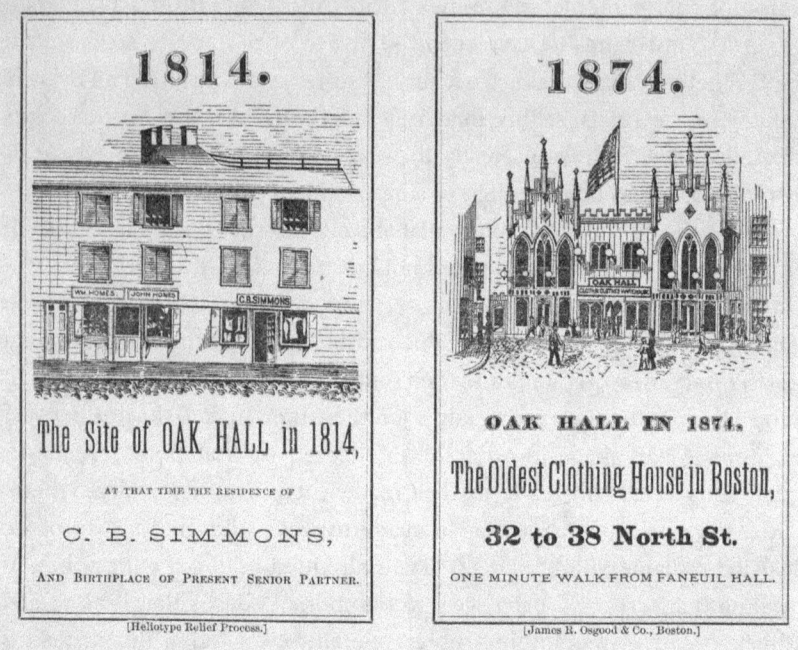

Figure 10.5 This promotional brochure contrasts the 1814 forerunner of Oak Hall with its 1874 location. It went from a store of goods located in the proprietor's house to a palace, where the building was as much a part of the attraction as the goods. Views of Oak Hall, men's and boys' one price clothing house, 32–38 North Street, Boston, MA, undated. Courtesy of Historic New England.

clothing, and accessories decline more rapidly than other consumer goods, but wages also began a slow, uneven upward climb beginning in the 1830s, putting more money in people's pockets. People could buy more attire for less—and they did. Court cases in the first decades of the nineteenth century involved a few yards of cloth, a handful of bandanas, several shirts, two or three dresses, or a single coat. By the 1830s, people were stealing more because there was more to take. Catherine Brennan and Ann Allison helped themselves to armfuls of items belonging to Brennan's mistress, hoping that she would not miss any of it because she had so much more. Even working people had a lot of textiles. In 1844, Sarah Ann Francisco's trunk was stolen from the hallway of the New York City house where she lived as a boarder. Its contents were impressive for a working woman, even though much of what she had was accessories, meant to dress up basic outfits: "two white morning

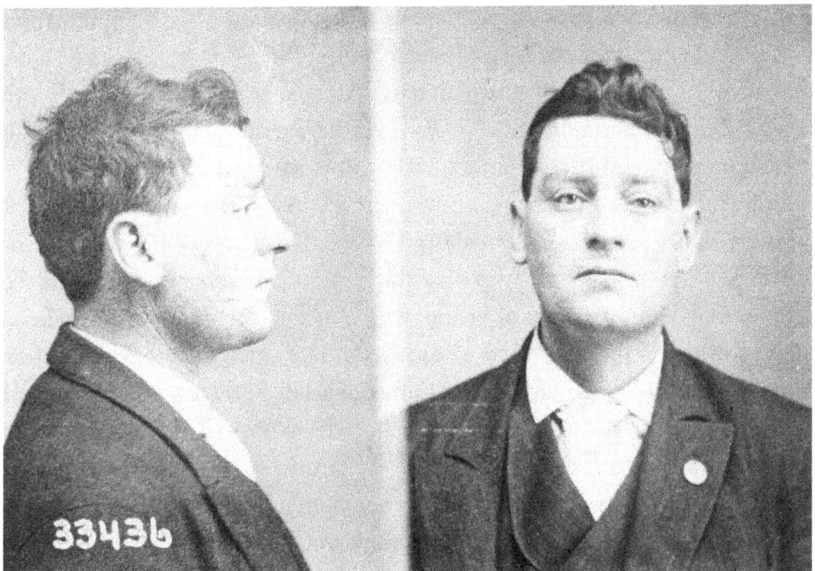

Figure 10.6 Mug-shot photographs of Duggy Hamilton, "a crook," probably taken in 1908, Chicago, Illinois. DN-0006130, *Chicago Sun-Times / Chicago Daily News* collection, Chicago History Museum.

gowns, three night Gowns, two Chemises, one olive green silk skirt, four night caps, one lace cape, one swiss cape, ruffles, two lace collars, one worked collar, one plain muslin collar, one [illegible] Handkerchief, one black Lace Veil, one Calico Apron, one Gingham Apron, one pair of stockings, one linen pocket handk[erchie]f, one remnant of silk, one silk cravat, two Fans, two paper boxes, and sundry other articles."[10]

When it came to textiles as currency, people experienced the decline in prices as inflation and instability, which made it more difficult to use textiles as currency, credit, and capital. Not only did it take more textiles to buy less, but investments in them also lost value more rapidly over time. The problem was evident in the 1850 request of a New York merchant to his Boston supplier for a reduction in his bill. Actually, his request read more like a demand, what with all the insistent underlining: "Your goods have fallen 2 per cent in value from the time of purchase & before we rec'd the goods in store." Customers might not have noticed sudden declines in wholesale prices quite as much, because retail prices tended to be more stable. But many people did not participate in the textile market only as consumers, who purchased goods in retail stores so as to use them up and buy more. They bought textiles in a wide range of venues with the expectation that they would store value. In that context, falling prices were a bane, because their property was worth less, as well as a boon, because they could buy larger quantities. Adding to the uncertainty was the wide fluctuation in prices and wages within these overall trends. Precipitous ups and downs in the short run wreaked havoc on individuals' finances, diminishing the positive effects of the general improvement in purchasing power over the long run. That context explains the draw of Oak Hall's contract program, which locked customers in to prices at the beginning of the year. Why would customers agree to such terms, when prices were trending down, not up? Only Oak Hall stood to gain. But it made sense to people in a context marked by short-term unpredictability.[11]

The economics registered in court cases. In some ways, lower prices made textiles easier targets: they were everywhere, often unattended, ready for the taking as well as the buying. At the same time, devaluation also raised the stakes. It took more goods to make theft worthwhile, which added layers of complication. Why bother with a handkerchief so cheap that it was like a modern-day facial tissue? It was hardly worth the effort to steal one when there was nothing to do with it other than blowing your nose and throwing it away. The effort and expense of having it washed, starched, and ironed was too high relative to the cost of a new one. Those calculations were evident in the bolts of cloth, stacks of ready-made clothes, and boxes of boots, gloves, and hats that regularly disappeared from merchants' stores in the decades preceding the Civil War. Typical was Lucius Eams's attempt to spirit away 124 vests, two pairs of pants, eight scarves, twenty-nine cravats, three neckties, and fifty-six handkerchiefs from Oak Hall, apparently in broad daylight. Women like Sarah Ann Francisco had their entire wardrobes evaporate into thin air thanks to bands of thieves. In 1833, William Henry Green led a group of boys who took twenty pairs of sheets, twelve tablecloths, nine blankets, fourteen pillowcases, a cloak, a counterpane, two cloaks, twenty pairs of stockings, two pairs of pantaloons, three frocks, twenty sacks, two coats, three vests, a gold ring, and a string of beads from Annis Downing's New York City house. While Downing was in the country to escape a cholera epidemic, Green and his posse slipped over the back fence, broke in, and stripped the house of its textiles.[12]

Thievery took on professional trappings. The gangs of young boys who stole from Sarah Ann Francisco and Annis Downing bring to mind the characters of *Oliver Twist*. Downing insisted that the boys resided at

New York City's House of Refuge, a more benevolent form of the workhouse where the fictional Oliver Twist was initially lodged. They did not, although their circumstances resembled Twist's. They lived on their own, sleeping outdoors and supporting themselves on what they stole, just as Twist did when he left the workhouse. But Ann Downing had a point. The boys she accused of theft would have fit right in at the House of Refuge, as the organization's case histories suggest. These profiles feature boys and girls who had been left alone or driven out onto the streets because of their parents' poverty or abuse. Struggling to survive, they fell into petty criminal activity. One boy had become "very successful in selling stolen handkerchiefs about the markets." He and his comrades took what they could, when they could, giving "curious names for different articles that they stole, so as not to be understood by honest men": shoes and boots were "crabs," handkerchiefs were "wipers," vests were "garvises," trousers were "kickers," shirts and other articles taken off clotheslines were "goodberries," and trunks were "Peter."[13] Groups of older men also relieved their targets of their clothing and other personal possessions. The gang that jumped and robbed Robert Seeley provides a particularly graphic example. While visiting New York City in 1833, he was "forcibly seized by Five or Six men, who hurried him thro an alley into a back building & there, in a room, apparently occupied by a coloured woman, dispossessed him of almost every article of clothing, money & property that he had upon him," leaving him "in nearly a state of nudity."[14]

It is tempting to characterize this kind of theft as something new. That is what the commercial press in urban areas did, conjuring up crime waves purportedly based on the general decline of community bonds and individual morals. But those reports said more about deep-seated racism and nativism than they did about crime. Heists involving significant amounts of property were nothing new. A good example is the theft case of forty-six pieces of Canton crepes, thirteen pieces of China satin, and ten pieces of Nankeen stolen in 1820 from the two Charleston carpenters who appeared in an earlier chapter. In cities, the courts had always busied themselves with what would later be called shoplifting. In 1801, a clerk at Andrew R. Miller's store described a common occurrence. "About one o'clock a man came in . . . and bought some trifles and went away." "A few minutes after," he "was told by a little girl in the Street that the man who had just come out of Mr. Miller's Store had taken some thing of the stock, upon which Deponent immediately discovered that there was a Roll of Coating missing." "Looking down the street he saw the said man going with it under his arm" and "immediately followed him and cryed stop thief upon which the said man droped the said coating and Ran off." Stores that displayed their goods were relatively easy marks. Passersby came in, waited for an opportune moment, and then made off with whatever they thought they could get away with.[15]

The links so often drawn between theft and urbanization, marked by rapid population growth and a sense of anonymity and alienation, do not hold up well. The ties among neighbors in New York City, one of the new republic's fastest growing metropolises, were close because living conditions were so tight. What happened next door did not stay next door. It inevitably creeped out to the neighbors, a situation that tended to buttress long-standing traditions of community regulation. In the decades leading up to the Civil War, bystanders in urban areas continued to involve themselves in policing, just as they and their rural counterparts had done before. Not only did they take the time to testify, but they also continued to drop what they were doing to help track down the culprits and the missing goods, particularly textiles. When George Smith's wife awoke him in the middle of the night in 1844 to tell him that she had seen someone slip in and out of the window of a neighbor's house, he knew exactly what to do. Spying an unknown man from the window, he bolted downstairs and gave chase, running up "Bayard to Christie, thence to Division St," where he tackled the man, arrested him, and took him to the "Watch House." The property at issue included a coat, two pairs of pantaloons, and a pair of gloves. Of course, Smith had no idea what had been stolen. But cloth, clothing, and accessories remained common targets as particularly meaningful and valuable forms of property.[16]

The legal principles associated with textiles continued to make these goods valuable, despite their recent devaluation. In fact, those principles were what made textiles so attractive to thieves, who depended on a market based in widely accepted rules that made it possible for stolen textiles to be traded away quickly and easily. In the decades just before the Civil War, textiles remained the most secure form of property for all those without strong claims to rights, property, or both. As such, they continued to serve as the means as well as the object of exchange in a wide range of venues, which made them easy to get rid of. They also provided a way to make illicit goods licit—in short, a way to launder money.

Thieves could and did hawk goods themselves. But it was usually best to put as much distance between themselves and the stolen property as quickly as possible, which is why they turned to pawnshops, secondhand stores, auction houses, peddlers, and sellers who kept stores of goods, not brick-and-mortar stores. Everyone knew which purveyors asked few questions. That was true not only of thieves but also of victims, who seemed to have no problem figuring out where to look for their lost possessions. The boys who took Annis Downing's property pawned everything with Walter Stevenson, who never inquired as to how a group of homeless boys acquired twenty pairs of sheets, twelve table cloths, nine blankets, fourteen pillow cases, three cloaks, a counterpane, twenty pairs of stockings, two pairs of pantaloons, three frocks, twenty sacks, two coats, three vests, a gold ring, and string of beads. The three boys who took Sarah Ann Francisco's property took it to Mary Dougherty, a pawnshop owner who had acquired a dodgy reputation, given her frequent appearance in court. Dougherty did not ask questions about the origins of goods brought to her. Nor did she seem particularly concerned with the legal niceties of what she was doing. Accused of selling stolen property, she explained that she had initially refused to buy the property when the boys offered it to her. It was only after they came back and offered it at a lower price that she finally agreed. Really, she made it sound almost like they forced her to take it. Even then, she had not put the property up for sale. When a local official came a few days later asking if she had any stolen property, she had turned these goods over to him. Was that not sufficient?[17]

The legal principles of textiles explain Dougherty's rhetorical shrug. She gave the property back, which meant that she had not yet closed the metaphorical trunk lid: she had not reduced the textiles to her possession and therefore had not really done anything wrong. It was the type of explanation that had acquired legal resonance in different kinds of cases where the principles governing the exchange of textiles were accepted and enforced. They often featured small stores of goods and even single items, as with Sarah Allingham's homespun sheet. The litigants generally knew each other, and defendants as well as complainants offered claims to the property in question that were plausible because they relied heavily on the legal principles associated with textiles. Although the parties disagreed, they generally purported to be working within the rules. Typical was the 1802 complaint filed by Keziah Darby, identified as "wife of John Darby," a merchant on Pearl Street, who claimed that John Bernard had "stolen & carried away out of her shop . . . one piece of Linnen of the value of one Dollar and Twenty five cents, which said piece of Linnen she shortly after found" in his possession. As in so many cases from this period, this wife claimed the shop and the textiles, which were probably synonymous, as her own, even though both were attributed to her husband on the legal forms. Bernard readily affirmed taking the cloth. In his telling, however, the incident was an exchange gone awry: "He was to pay for the piece of Linnen above spoken of when he should pay for a pair of shoes he had agreed to purchase of the said Keziah Darby." "He did not take the same to steal it." What seemed like shoplifting was a more complicated dispute over how payment was to be made. Darby and Bernard wound up in court, like so many others, because they understood the terms of exchange in legal terms, which they expected to be enforced.[18] People like Dougherty turned those legal principles to different ends: to excuse illicit activity that undermined the claims of people who still relied on textiles as a means of exchange and way to store value.

Catherine Brennan and Ann Allison also explained themselves in terms of the same time-honored principles associated with textiles. They had borrowed the goods, intending to return them. But their defense says more about the continued legal resonance of practices associated with textiles than their own use of them. Borrowing done without the consent of the person who owned the property had never had much legitimacy. It only worked if the property was returned before its rightful owner noticed. Even when washerwomen, dressmakers, and tailors pawned textiles owned by their clients, they did so with the tacit understanding that they would make the goods available when asked. The difference between borrowing as an excuse to cover up theft and borrowing that was really a loan is evident in the case of Eliza Cachois. Accused of stealing a shift, Cachois conformed to convention and insisted that "Sarah Bliss loaned her the said shift, and therefore she did not steal it." Cachois claimed the consent of shift's owner. Brennan and Allison did not even bother with such an explanation for the textiles taken from Brennan's employer.[19]

Nor did they bother with the kinds of explanations generally offered by workers who were embroiled in disputes with their employers. Consider the charges against Thomas Stapleton, whose ship master charged him with theft in 1810. As Stapleton explained, he and a fellow sailor cut out a piece of the ship's main sail because they had not received their wages. That they took their piece out of the middle of the sail, where it could not go undiscovered, supports the explanation: this was a statement, not subterfuge. Although both men had been involved, Stapleton, not his mate, ended up with the cloth. As he explained, they had it cut it up to make "Trowsers." But "there was not enough to make two pair," so "they cast Lotts" and he won. The case was discharged. In 1817, the employer of William Wilson and William Jones charged them with stealing two coats worn as uniforms while in his employ. Wilson and Jones maintained that they had kept the coats because their employer had refused to pay them. Ultimately they had returned the coats, based on their now-former employer's promise that he would give them their back wages. But he had failed to do so and then proceeded with the prosecution. Wilson and Jones, who also had filed suit in civil court to reclaim their wages, were acquitted of theft. In both instances, working people made plausible claims based in longstanding practices recognized in law. These laborers took textiles in lieu of wages, which were often paid in the form of textiles.[20]

Catherine Brennan and Ann Allison stole a stack of textiles worth a whopping $147.25 because they could. Like other thieves, they depended on the very legal principles that they were flouting. Their testimony speaks volumes about the ease with which this part of textile market could be turned toward the illicit, even though it rested on established rules and depended on their enforcement. The people who operated in this area of the trade acknowledged the property claims of those with a tenuous relationship to rights and property in other areas of law. While legally marginalized people managed to sustain claims to textiles, they did so within the legal form of theft, which was not really intended to mediate conflicts over the legitimate exchange of property. In fact, that form tended to erode claims by collapsing a wide range of property disputes into a single, simplistic framework that criminalized them all. The always already illicit nature of this part of the market, at least within the body of private law, made it easy to pass off illegitimate claims to textiles as legitimate ones.[21]

The power of textiles' legal principles was what undermined them. The erosion, while steady, came so slowly that it was not readily apparent at first. Desperate people had always taken textiles to cover obvious needs. That was as true in the decades following the Revolution as it was in the decades leading up to the Civil War. But what they did with those items and what those items could do for them changed. In the decades following the Revolution, people would grab a shirt, a shift, a handful of handkerchiefs, or a coat and then buy something else: food, drink, and shelter, as well as other kinds of clothing. That was also what the gangs of boys who stole from Sarah Ann Francisco and Annis Downing did. They went immediately to pawn brokers to turn textiles into cash. But while the pawnbrokers asked no questions, neither did they offer much for the goods. Mary Dougherty gave only two dollars for a large bundle of textiles. It had that sour smell of theft. There was every reason to be suspicious of a trio of young boys with a bag full of women's clothing.

But then even a woman with a bag full of women's clothing could be suspicious. Did they *really* belong to her?[22]

No wonder more poor people took textiles and put them to immediate use, instead of turning them into economic instruments. By the 1830s, courts adjudicated case after case of coats and blankets taken in an effort to keep warm during the winter months. In New York City, for instance, James Butler admitted to stealing a coat, pants, and a pair of boots in the middle of January 1833. He explained that he did so "because he had not any clothes to shield him from the inclemency of the weather and was suffering from cold." He was found under a blanket that he had purloined from someone else. Butler had taken the clothing from Daniel O'Brien, who could ill afford to lose it, living as he did in a room in a stable, which probably had no heat except that provided by the animals that were also lodged there.[23]

People like Daniel O'Brien were vulnerable to theft because their legal claims to property had always been fragile. To be sure, thieves targeted merchants because their stores had so much stuff lying around. In the 1840s, department stores and emporiums like Brooks Brothers and Oak Hall added to the temptation by taking goods from behind counters and arranging them on racks and displays where anyone could pick them up and handle them. But people with tenuous claims to property made even better marks. Unlike merchants, they had to convince court officials of their claims to the property in question, which became harder over time as the stain of illegitimacy spread and set. Perhaps court officials would think that a laborer who could only afford a room in a stable did not really own a coat, pants, and boots. They might never believe that a working woman like Sarah Ann Francisco had such an extensive wardrobe packed away in her trunk. They might dismiss the claims of Polly, the enslaved woman whose thread was taken. Who would ever think that James, an enslaved man, had a pair of striped velvet pantaloons? Surely a jury of white men would scoff at the defense mounted by Amos, the enslaved man who sold shoes to other slaves. Why not take the chance of stealing? When that happened, why take the chance of appealing to authorities?[24]

All the negative implications were evident in the growing differentiation between property disputes tried as criminal matters and those handled in other areas of law. In the decades following the Revolution, the line was not as bright as it later became. Cases were tried in the same courts by the same officials, often using the same kinds of legal principles. Even the penalties in civil and criminal matters were similar, at least for those who were white.

In both areas of law, the guilty party was required to pay the value of the goods and sometimes damages to the injured party, along with court costs, which could be considerable. In theft, the guilty party sometimes received additional punishment to satisfy the offense done to the public: corporal punishment or service in the first years after the Revolution, but usually fines or imprisonment thereafter. In practice, however, the outcomes looked much the same as those in civil cases. State lawmakers eased up on the harsh physical punishments levied on those convicted of theft, and some local jurisdictions regularly suspended the punishments that remained. Lawmakers also liberalized the handling of civil actions in the decades following the Revolution, although change unfolded more slowly in this area of law, where imprisonment remained the remedy for all those unable to meet their obligations. While most states enacted insolvency laws that allowed civil offenders to petition for their release, there was no guarantee that their requests would be granted. To be sure, debtors enjoyed better conditions than those convicted of crimes. Still, those who were convicted languished in jail, barred from working to repay their debts. A 1787 Pennsylvania statute that provided relief both to "insolvent debtors" and to "felons unable to make restitution of stolen goods" captures the similarities between criminal and civil cases at that time.[25]

By the 1830s the differences were harder to ignore. Civil offenders were no longer imprisoned by most states. The civil form became less punitive: it became a means of mediating property transactions among those legally allowed to own property, rather than a means of punishing debtors. As a result, those convicted in civil cases no longer became social outcasts. The consequences of criminal convictions tended in the opposite direction, transforming a person's legal status and turning them into a criminal. To be sure, offenders in civil law became failures and bankrupts. They were ruined or embarrassed, in the terminology of the time. But that did not keep many of them from brushing themselves off and starting new enterprises. Criminals endured imprisonment and even corporal punishment to atone for what they had done and repay their debt to society. All those connotations stuck to property disputes that went through this legal form, particularly as the rules that had governed property exchange in the textile market began to fall apart. The property claims of people who were either poor or without rights seemed potentially criminal. They were always the exception, never the rule, and always suspect. They were also risky. In criminal cases, property claims could destroy a person's life.[26]

As the legal principles and practices that structured the textile trade had begun to fray, providing their owners with less robust legal claims, textiles became less reliable as currency, credit, and capital. That situation owed in part to the specific legal form used to mediate disputes over them. When people with tenuous claims to rights managed to sustain claims to textiles, they did so within the legal category of theft, which was never intended to mediate complicated conflicts over property. While form affirmed individual claims, it eroded the principle of ownership in a general sense, collapsing a wide range of property disputes into a single, simplistic framework that criminalized them all. Disputed wages became thefts. Disputed sales became thefts. Disputed loans became thefts. All ended up looking illegitimate. The results cast a shadow on claims to the legal principles of textiles more generally, leading to one damning question: Were the goods in question stolen? The question applied to textiles possessed by anyone whose poverty or lack of rights made property ownership dubious, which then made it difficult to tell what was unlawfully obtained and what was not.

These changes also resulted from shifts in the larger legal landscape of the federal system toward those areas of law that relied on rights. That transformation made the legal principles of textiles less enforceable and moved them out of the ambit of law altogether, as the next chapter shows. The majority of the population could not make the transition to bodies of law that required the possession of rights and voice. They had no choice but to continue putting their resources into textiles, even as that became increasingly problematic.

11

Charles Lohman's Dresses

Suppression

In 1850, Charles Lohman was robbed of five silk dresses, worth the enormous sum of twenty dollars each. According to the legal principles attached to textiles, the dresses were not really his. They belonged to his wife, Ann, otherwise known as Madam Restell, the infamous New York City abortionist. Once a seamstress, Ann became involved in progressive reforms, which opened her eyes to the inequalities that circumscribed all women's lives and inspired her to begin providing contraception and abortion. She took considerable risks to do so, enduring inflammatory press coverage as well as continual harassment by local officials and professional associations. In 1850, when her dresses were stolen, she had recently returned from a stint at Blackwell's Island Prison. All that attention owed, in part, to her success. Ann turned women's reproductive health into a thriving business, which she ran in her alias out of her well-appointed brownstone on Fifth Avenue. But when the local court attributed ownership of silk dresses that she obviously wore and probably purchased with money that she earned herself, they were not hers.[1]

The legal principles of textiles did not figure prominently in this case—or so it seemed. In cases from the post-Revolutionary decades, the names of husbands and sometimes masters appeared on the legal forms as owners of the property in question and as prosecutors of the resulting cases. But the forms also made it clear that local courts actually treated disputed textiles as the property of the married women and enslaved people to whom they belonged. Masters hovered around the edges cases, probably because the property claims of the enslaved were always the most tenuous. Husbands generally kept their distance from proceedings involving their wives' textiles.

Lohman's case was different. Not only do the forms identify Charles Lohman as the owner, complainant, and prosecutor, but the recorded information also positions him front and center as the one steering the whole matter through the system. Ann Lohman is relegated to the backseat, filling the role that husbands previously did. Although she provided a statement, unlike husbands in earlier cases, her recorded words characterize the dresses as property to which she had only an incidental connection. She never claimed them as her own. The only place where the legal principles and practices associated with textiles seeped through was in the deposition of a woman who boarded in the Lohman household. She confirmed that the dresses produced in evidence at the preliminary hearing were "precisely the colour and pattern shown (per sample) by Mr. Lohman of the kind of dresses stolen from Madam Restell, otherwise Mrs. Lohman." Even then, the record pivots away from the legal principles that this woman acknowledged. It was "Mr. Lohman" who showed the fabric samples in court, although the boarder saw them as evidence connecting the dresses to "Mrs. Lohman." This case repurposed the legal principles of textiles. The kind of evidence that had established the claims of those *without* rights verified Charles Lohman's property right to dresses that he never wore.

In the decades immediately preceding the Civil War, people without strong claims to rights faced formidable barriers when it came to enforcing the legal principles of textiles. By the 1850s, when the Lohman dresses were stolen, a large cadre of influential lawyers had embraced a highly professionalized view of law that ignored those principles. This conception of law is the one with which we are all familiar today: law as a set of universal principles, often based in the rights of individuals, that resides in books and is available only to the trained few, not law as practice, based in the customs of local communities and known widely by all. This idea had reshaped broad areas of legal practice even before the Revolution, particularly in property disputes that did not involve textiles. Its logic shifted adjudication in civil suits from questions about the relationships that shaped property conflicts to questions about the rights of individuals regardless of the circumstances. From there, it was an easy jump into the parts of the new republic's governing institutions that focused on the kinds of people and economic dealings governed by those areas of law, which included all areas of law at the state and federal levels as well as private law at the local level. By the 1830s, this legal logic was insinuating itself into criminal cases in local courts. As professionally trained lawyers elbowed their way in, they imposed the general principles that they had learned, which elevated procedural rights over the principles associated with textiles.

Only some individuals could claim those rights. Not only did a process based in rights push the legal principles of textiles aside, but it also silenced people like Ann Lohman and her boarder. Nonetheless, it is possible to overstate the extent of change. New procedural dynamics obscured the continued importance of textiles' principles and the practices that upheld them, which still mattered enormously to people on the margins. Those legal elements were evident in the Lohman case, even though court officials skipped over them. Procedural change, however, carried consequences that were impossible to escape. Without the institutional backing necessary for enforcement, the legal principles and practices associated with textiles drifted out from the realm of law as defined in the new republic.

The legal principles and practices associated with textiles spread widely across the United States in the period between the Revolution and the Civil War, carried along by the distribution of the material goods to which they were attached. Roger Taney, the chief justice of the US Supreme Court, dealt with them, just as local officials in New York City and rural South Carolina did. The goods mattered, regardless of the venue. Like so many other participants in local cases, Charles Lohman brought in fabric samples to prove his relationship to these particular dresses. Merchants did the same thing in cases at the federal level. Those conflicts involved not just customs duties, as in Taney's long underwear case, but also damaged cargo, shoddy goods, and short deliveries. The material qualities of textiles figured prominently in them all. Merchants brought in scarves, socks, and gloves as well as long underwear and dresses to establish the nature of the goods and thus their legal relationship to them. Was the long underwear hosiery or ready-to-wear? Were the scarves more wool than cotton? Did the shipment of cotton gloves also contain some silk hose? It was impossible to sort through disputed contractual obligations without the goods themselves, which all had legal meanings. Samples remain attached to the records of some cases, serving as both the legal evidence and the legal argument that determined the outcome of the case.[2]

To make their rulings, federal judges heard from a range of people with direct connections to the kinds of goods in question, just as local court officials did. In the US Circuit Court of the Southern District of New York, that circle was a tight-knit community of manufacturers, jobbers, wholesalers, and retailers in lower Manhattan, all of whom had acquired a deep familiarity with these goods through daily interactions with textiles and with one another. This metropolitan community had a wider geographic reach than

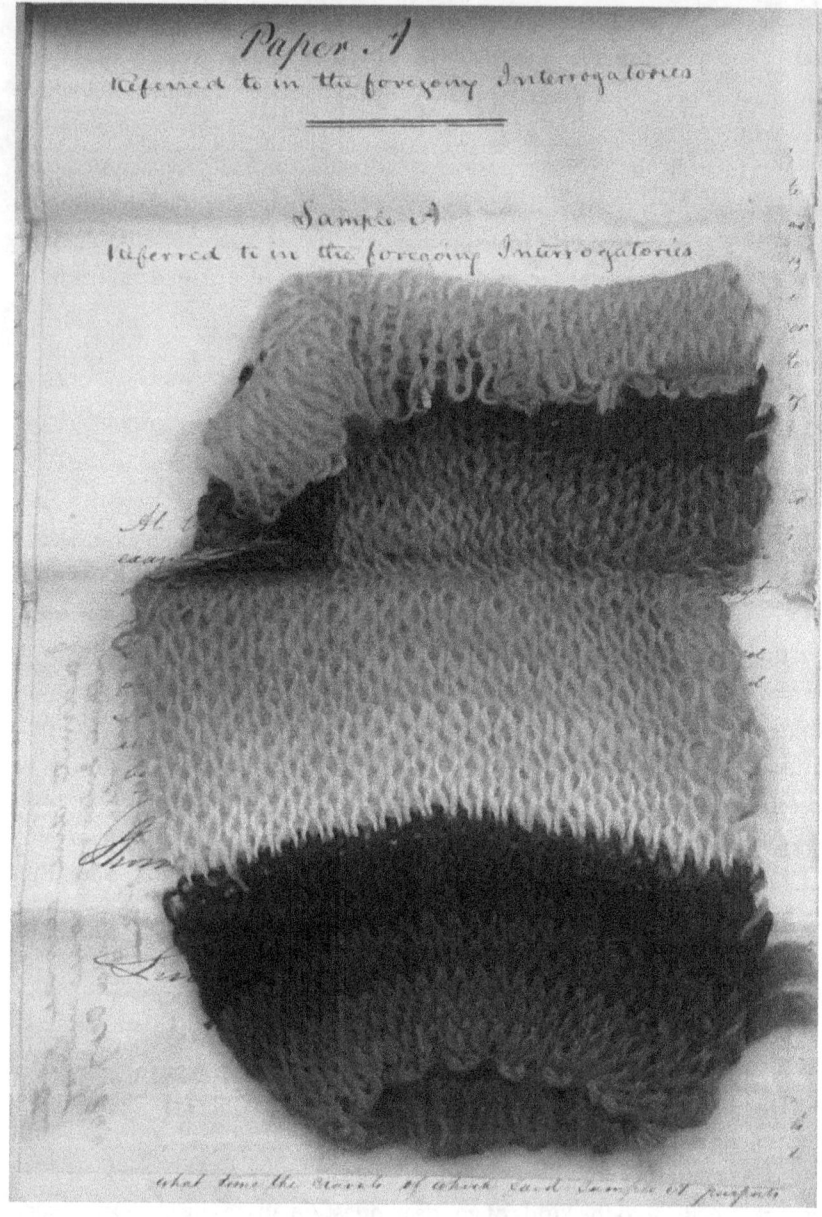

Figure 11.1 Samples featured prominently in federal customs cases, as in this one involving woolen cravats. *Thomas Paton and David Stewart v. Jesse Hoyt*, Depositions, BOX 55, Case Files in Suits Against Collectors of Customs, 1833–1903, NARA-NY.

those in rural towns and urban neighborhoods, given that its members were in the import-export business. Some case files contain depositions obtained from experts elsewhere, usually England, who spoke to the classification and handling of particular goods. Regardless of where they lived, however, these community members knew each other and the rules that bound them together.³

The legal principles of textiles were embodied in the goods themselves and their ties to the people who made, used, wore, and traded them. Those principles were fundamentally different than the ones asserted, mediated, and established in terms of rights. To decide property disputes, judges in the US Circuit Court of the Southern District of New York and the New York Municipal Court needed to know about different kinds of textiles and their relationship to the merchants who imported and sold them. The emphasis on relationships rooted the resulting property claims in place, within the communities in which they were made. Federal courts seem like places that deal in universal legal principles. But these cases involved legal principles attached to textiles that mattered to a specific group of manufacturers and merchants, whose disputes rested on the legal classification of textiles. The status of long underwear as knitwear or ready-to-wear was lodged in the practices that guided the production and distribution of these goods but did not extend far beyond that specific community. No one else cared; they just wanted the garments to keep them warm. Similarly, knowledge of Ann Lohman's connection to specific silk dresses was limited to a small group of people. Claims to them would be hard to establish outside that circle. Nor did that matter much to anyone else, who would see them as just a bunch of secondhand dresses.⁴

Yet these similarities in cases at the local and federal levels masked a larger truth. The legal principles of textiles had utterly different meanings for litigants in federal court than they did for people with weak claims to rights whose disputes were adjudicated in local courts. The men in federal court— and they were all men—did not need the legal qualities of textiles to establish the principle of property ownership. It was already assumed, because white men had the rights necessary to own any kind of property throughout the federal system. The legal principles associated with textiles worked around the edges, doing work that rights could not by resolving questions about the nature of the contractual obligations. The stakes were higher for the people who appeared with textiles in local courts. Given their legal status, they could not own property anywhere in the legal system—unless they were claiming textiles. Widely followed legal principles not only extinguished rights for wives, children, servants, and slaves but also extended the logic of domestic dependency to limit the rights of free women and men on the basis of gender, class, and race. And it was not just that rights were denied, a situation that could be resolved by extending them to those without them. The restrictions placed on some defined the prerogatives of others. Husbands, fathers, and masters gained what their wives, children, slaves, and servants lost. They acquired rights in the property, labor, and bodies of their household dependents, which included menial wage workers who were legally classified as servants. Here, too, the logic extended beyond the borders of households. White men also gained what other lost in the form of privileges over people with more tenuous claims to rights. When propertyless white men were granted the vote, new racial restrictions meant that propertied free Black men who once could vote lost that right and, more than that that, all free Black men found themselves politically subordinated to all white men. Wherever rights were conferred, restrictions and inequality for others followed. This dynamic could be found everywhere in the federal system, which was why the legal principles and practices associated with textiles mattered so much to so many people. They established property claims for those on the legal margins that the men in Taney's court took for granted.[5]

Given the pervasiveness of rights and the accompanying restrictions, the legal principles of textiles only worked to establish property claims in certain parts of the federal system. In theory, the possession of rights was necessary to initiate legal proceedings in any body of law and all legal venues. In practice, public law at the local level remained open enough and flexible enough to accommodate people with weak claims to rights, particularly in the first decades after the Revolution. The body of law mattered: public law allowed officials to proceed by substituting the "public" for complainants who lacked the right to sustain prosecution in their own names. The institutional structure of the federal system mattered: local courts had played an outsized role in matters involving the public order before the Revolution and continued to do so in the decades that followed. The nature of the jurisdiction mattered: the proximity of local courts and their strong connections to the communities in which they were situated made it possible for people without rights to bring in all the evidence required to establish their claims to the textiles in question. But it was the conception of law that guided public law in local venues that mattered most: it was broadly defined to include principles established in practice as well as those memorialized in written texts.[6]

In the decades following the Revolution, local courts operated much as they had before when it came to public law. People made their complaints directly to local officials, whose duties to the public were secondary to their other occupations. Rural magistrates were also farmers, millers, storekeepers, lawyers, and doctors, or just members of well-established families. In urban areas, initial contact with the legal system often came through "the watch": men charged with overseeing their communities. Magistrates and members of the watch resolved what disputes they could, mediating some matters without turning them into legal cases. When conflicts proved irreconcilable, they moved up in the legal system and became cases at law. At this point, members of the watch handed cases off to urban officials, such as mayors and sheriffs, who oversaw the lowest levels of the court system and filled the role of magistrates. In rural areas, magistrates simply took off their mediation hats and put on their trial hats. Most petty crime lay within these magistrates' jurisdiction, including minor instances of violence and stolen property valued below a specified amount, which meant that they oversaw a lot of cases involving textiles. They took care of everything within their jurisdiction and handed off contested cases or more serious matters to parts of the local court system that were run by full-time officials: clerks, states' attorneys, and judges, as well as the mayors and other government representatives who served as judges. Even then, the process was still relatively unprofessionalized. Many of these officials had other duties. They had close ties to the communities in which they worked. Not all had legal training, nor were they supervised by officials who did. And they applied a body of law, based in practice, that aimed to restore public order. As a result, they tended to adjudicate matters in terms of a more flexible set of principles, which included those associated with textiles.[7]

The voices of the people involved in disputes dominated the process. In rural areas, complainants made their own statements, gathered evidence, brought in witnesses, and posed questions during hearings and trials, without the aid of lawyers. While lawyers were more common in urban areas, they were much less involved in criminal matters than they were in civil suits. *New York City-Hall Recorder* identified lawyers by name in its summaries of the municipal court's "most interesting trials and decisions." By "interesting," its author, Daniel Rogers, meant the most sensational, titillating, and likely to appeal to paid subscribers. But, as Rogers's summaries also made clear, not all criminal defendants had counsel representing them at trial, particularly in cases of petty violence and theft.[8]

Defendants definitely did not have counsel before trial, during preliminary proceedings to screen complaints, or at grand jury hearings to determine whether the evidence against a defendant was sufficient to take the case to trial. The case files of the New York City Municipal Court contain all the documents leading up to trial: complaints, statements, and indictments. Conspicuously absent are the names of lawyers, including those of states' attorneys, who were more likely to be in attendance than counsel for the defendants. Attorneys for the state were appointed by the court. Defendants would have had to find legal representatives and pay them out their own pockets, although losing parties ended up paying for the fees of states' attorneys as well, since they were held liable for all the costs involved in trying the case. Like their rural counterparts, complainants and defendants in New York City brought in their own evidence and made their own statements, which were more full-blown theories of the case than terse recitals of the bare facts. Lawyers might have been present. If so, it was hard to tell, what with complainants, defendants, and witnesses nattering on about fabric colors, the cuts of coats, and who wore what when.

Many of these features of the legal system had changed by the time Ann Lohman's dresses went missing. The entire process had become more professionalized, particularly in cities. Daniel Rogers's portrayal of cases in the *New York City-Hall Recorder*, first published in 1817, anticipated those changes. Not only did lawyers figure prominently in his presentation of the cases, but his summaries followed a form that elevated legal professionals over the people involved in the disputes. Rogers named the case, presented a brief synopsis of the facts, identified the lawyers and the judge, explicated the legal arguments offered by the lawyers, and elaborated on the judge's decision. This format, which was widely used in the reporting of state and federal cases and familiar to anyone with legal training, put law in the hands of legal professionals. They were the ones who knew the most about it. They were the ones who made arguments about it. And they were the ones with the final say over it. In the pages of the *New York City-Hall Recorder*, legal professionals provided a sober contrast to their colorful clients. Rogers played it up, creating a sensational underworld that lurched from the humorously slapstick to the downright frightening. Not to worry, though: professionals stood by, ready to swoop in and keep chaos at bay with considered applications of law. That legal balm took a particular form: universal principles focused on rights and their restrictions, which in theory applied to everyone, everywhere, regardless of context or the relationships of those involved. As Rogers explained in his preface, his goal was "to illustrate and enforce, by examples deduced from a variety of cases, the genuine principles of morality; and to convey to the public, in language clear and perspicuous, legal principles, important to be understood and known by every citizen."[9]

Members of the public needed instructions from Rogers because his view of law was not theirs. He was part of an influential group of lawyers who began turning law into an esoteric science after the Revolution. Law was scientific, in that it followed general principles that were universally applicable. It was esoteric, in that those principles could only be ascertained and mastered through the sustained, rigorous study of written texts, which were available to only a few. That conception of law ran through debates over the structure of the federal system and the place of law within it. We now think that US Supreme Court Justice John Marshall resolved the role of the judiciary within the federal system when he clearly separated it from the legislative and executive branches, most notably in *Marbury v. Madison*. But the judiciary at the state level remained deeply involved in the business of legislation—that is, framing laws, not just pronouncing on their constitutionality. James Kent, who served on New York's highest courts and later explained his vision in his influential *Commentaries on American Law*, argued that judges had no choice but to get down into the fray because they could supply what legislators could not, namely, general laws that expressed universal principles. He had a point. At the time, legislatures at both the state and federal levels dealt mainly with private legislation that affected particular groups and individuals. They were in the business of suspending general laws in order to hand out favors to friends and friends of friends. Only in the 1830s did state legislatures begin to restrict themselves to the passage of general laws that applied everywhere in the state. While Kent and Marshall represented different visions of the judiciary's role, they agreed on what kind of law the judiciary should be enforcing: universal principles applied uniformly, regardless of the particular circumstances.[10]

In the first decades following the Revolution, that vision of law had far more influence in the realm of legal education than it did in actual practice, notwithstanding the aspirations of Daniel Rogers and other systematizers. Even then, change came slowly. By modern standards, legal training in the new republic seems as informal and unprofessionalized as it had been before the Revolution. Most aspiring lawyers still learned through apprenticeship, which involved observing an established practitioner and reading law books in his office. Like other lawyers, Tapping Reeve initially took apprentices, starting in 1774. He proved such a successful teacher that he turned his law office into Litchfield Law School in 1784. William and Mary Law School, chartered by Thomas Jefferson in 1779, was a similar operation, with George Wythe in charge. The University of Pennsylvania Law School emerged from lectures given by James Wilson in 1790. Yale Law School followed a similar course. Joseph Story was the leading light behind the reinvention of Harvard Law School. Law school founders tended to be men who were or had been active in the Revolutionary cause and the new republic's founding, suggesting how important this vision of law was to that whole project.[11]

Attending school in any form, however, was not required to practice law. Admission to the bar was based more on social contacts than the rigorous testing of an applicant's legal knowledge. Basically, anyone could hang out a shingle and become a lawyer, although relatively few who set up in this way made a living from their practice alone. Certain parts of legal practice were reserved to white men. Only they appeared as counsel in trials and in all matters at the state and federal level. Paid positions as clerks and judges also went to them. But then as now, legal practice extended beyond those elements of law. It included the writing of wills, contracts, deeds, and bills of exchange as well as the navigation of all kinds of disputes. A wide range of people, even women, practiced in these areas of law, in the sense of legal practice at that time: they had legal knowledge, and they used it in their own lives and to advise others. There was nothing to keep them from doing so, since knowledge of those areas of law was available and necessary to all.[12]

Daniel Rogers's *New York City-Hall Recorder* captures the currents that were transforming legal education, directing it toward law as memorialized in legal texts and away from law as constituted through practice. Of course, books had always mattered in legal education. The size of a mentor's law library distinguished a good legal education from an inadequate one. Even the terminology, "reading law," reflected the centrality of texts. Books became even more important to legal training in the new republic, as legal educators emphasized texts over practice. In so doing, they followed the lead of Sir William Blackstone, who argued that apprenticeships usually began "at the wrong end" with legal practice, not "the ... principles upon which the rule of practice is founded." Practice taught students to imitate, rather than reason. US Supreme Court justice Joseph Story agreed. Applauding the opening of Harvard Law School in 1817, he brushed aside "the common delusion, that the law may be thoroughly acquired in the immethodical, interrupted, and desultory studies of the office of a practicing counsellor." Students needed to have "the foundation in elementary principles, under the guidance of a learned and discreet lecturer." Otherwise they turned into "drudge[s], versed in the forms of conveyancing and pleading, but incapable of ascending to the principles that govern them." Those principles were all memorialized in books, which were the basis of this kind of legal education. Law students read books. They listened to lectures based in books. Lectures were published as books, closing the circle of knowledge. James Kent fashioned his *Commentaries on American Law* from the lectures he gave at Columbia Law School. Tapping Reeve's lectures formed the basis of his treatise, *Law of Baron and Femme; of Parent and Child; of Guardian and Ward; of Master and Servant; and of the Powers of Court of Chancery*, first published in 1816 and regularly updated thereafter. Joseph Story produced several treatises, including *Commentaries on the Constitution of the United States* (1833) and *Commentaries on Equity Jurisprudence* (1835–36), while he was serving as a professor of law at Harvard and on the US Supreme Court. Those treatises then found their way into law libraries all over the country, where they became the stuff of legal education for other aspiring lawyers.[13]

It was an utterly self-referential world. Reeve's lectures followed the structure and content of *Blackstone's Commentaries*. Kent's *Commentaries* considered existing legal texts, including Blackstone. Blackstone's *Commentaries*, in turn, commented on many of the same legal texts that Kent engaged. These jurists were talking to one another, rather than to litigants, legal practitioners, and local or even state judges. Law schools structured their curricula around the same topics that appeared in the same set of legal texts, which also filled the libraries of practitioners who took on apprentices. In 1851, the University of Virginia's law school advertised its three-year course of study in terms of the books assigned each year, which included "Federalist Papers"; "Blackstone's Commentaries"; "Coke on Littleton"; "Smith's Mercantile Law"; "Stephen on Pleading"; "Greenleaf's Evidence"; "Story's Equity"; "Chitty on Contracts"; "Lomax on Executors"; "Byles on Bills and Notes"; "White and Tudor's Leading Cases"; and "Smith's Leading Cases." The shortened titles and their merger with the authors' last names indicate that the attraction lay in the books' familiarity, not their novelty. They were what prospective students expected of a law school.[14]

As the University of Virginia's book list also reveals, legal education centered on particular kinds of property disputes, namely, those involving men with the full range of rights. A review of the 1905 edition of John William Smith's *Compendium of Mercantile Law* noted that "it had taken and preserved a firm hold upon the affections of the legal profession" since its first publication in 1834, although the reviewer thought it overrated and outdated, covering too many subjects too superficially. The book's chapter titles read as a greatest hits of commercial law: partners, joint stock companies, principal and agent, shipping, patents, goodwill and trademarks, bills of exchange and promissory notes, contracts with carriers, contracts of affreightment, maritime insurance, insurance upon lives, insurance against fire, bottomry and respondentia (a real page turner), contracts of hiring and service, contracts with seamen, contracts of apprenticeship, guaranties, contracts of sale, contracts of debt, stoppage in transit, and lien. Smith's *Compendium* was confined to mercantile law of a very specific variety. There was nothing in it to aid the merchants without rights who bought and sold textiles in pawn shops, at public auctions, and in open-air markets or from urban stoops and rural kitchens. But it purported to contain *all* mercantile law.[15]

Other texts were also narrowly focused. Significantly, Blackstone limited his discussion of the legal status of wives, children, and servants to the implications for the property rights of their household heads. In his influential *Commentaries*, he explained the rules that transferred dependents' property to their heads of household and those that determined the limited property claims dependents could make when separated from their household heads, be it through death or divorce in the case of wives, death or the attainment of maturity for children, or the termination of labor contracts for servants. There was a single paragraph referring to wives' claims to paraphernalia—the sum total of any reference to property claims that wives could make outside the framework of rights in all four volumes in the *Commentaries*. Tellingly, the mention of paraphernalia comes in the second volume, on the "rights of things," not the first volume on the "rights of persons." Unlike lengthy discussions of a husband's legal liability for his wife's debts or his control over property she brought into the marriage, there was little elaboration on the legal logic that supported wives' claims to clothing. It was part of the rights of things.[16]

The legal principles associated with textiles appeared nowhere in Blackstone's volume on public wrongs. It dealt only with crimes involving the kinds of property that those with rights could own, namely, land, buildings, credit, and personal property of a value or form that put it out of most people's reach. Even that discussion is short. He devoted the bulk of the volume to the process of trying accused criminals, not the acts that constituted crimes, the circumstances that surrounded them, or the evidence required to prove them. The chapters on process go on and on: indictment and bail, modes of prosecution, process upon an indictment, arraignment, plea, trial and conviction, benefit of clergy (a pleading whereby punishment could be suspended), judgment, reversal of judgment, reprieve and pardon, and execution. American treatises, such as Reeve's *Law of Baron and Femme* and Kent's *Commentaries*, duplicated the form, emphasizing these areas of law and leaving out almost everything else.[17]

The review of Smith's *Compendium of Mercantile Law*, which appeared in the 1906 edition of the *Canadian Law Times*, suggests not just how widespread the treatises' version of law became but also why it was so attractive. Smith was a barrister qualified to advise on cases in England and Wales, but his treatise on mercantile law became standard reading in the Anglo-American legal world for nearly a century. Like other treatise writers, he elaborated rights-based claims that reached across all kinds of jurisdictional borders: the borders of nations, those of states and localities within the United States, and those dividing the different bodies of law in all those places. The merchants who depended on the principles outlined in Smith's *Mercantile Law* traded across national borders and depended on portable legal principles to create stable claims to property that would be enforced wherever they bought or sold goods. The same is true of treatises that dealt with other kinds of law. Even texts that dealt with laws specific to the United States sought to distill general legal principles that should apply within all states and then to elevate them over the differences that existed between states. Authors relegated all the variations to the footnotes at the bottom of the page, where they were printed in a much smaller font than the regular text. The format visually subordinated that locally specific information to general rules that were, literally, larger. That was the point. Texts conjured up a legal world of principles that moved through various jurisdictions within the United States (federal, state, local, military) and all the various bodies of law (private, public, equity) within the United States, just as mercantile law sailed across national borders.

Advocates of this form of legal education founded the United States. By the mid-nineteenth century, its students ran the country. Aspiring lawyers from almost every state made the pilgrimage to Litchfield Law School, which had trained over a thousand lawyers by the time it closed in 1833. Its alumni include two vice presidents of the United States, Aaron Burr and John C. Calhoun; 101 members of the United States House of Representatives; twenty-eight United States senators; six United States cabinet secretaries;

three justices of the United States Supreme Court; fourteen state governors; and thirteen state supreme court chief justices. Lawyers with similar legal training filled all parts of the federal system. They applied the law, wrote endlessly about it, and trained other lawyers in their own image. Regardless of where all these lawyers lived and worked, the law in which they were trained provided a common language they all used and understood.[18]

They had far less facility in other legal idioms. So they translated, forcing unfamiliar bodies of law into the language they understood. Daniel Rogers, for instance, put criminal cases at the municipal level into a form more commonly used for recording appellate cases at the state and federal levels, making it appear as if they were resolved according to same legal principles and through the same legal processes as other cases elsewhere in the system. That was not entirely accurate. Local officials did follow the procedural rules laid out in the texts that Rogers and other lawyers studied. Those basic principles were widely known and generally followed, even for those who had not studied in law schools, which was why, for instance, local officials listed husbands as the owners of textiles that belonged to their wives. But even those officials who had legal training relied on other legal principles, which treated those dresses as the women's property. Rogers's recording methods did not exactly capture practice at the state and federal levels either, despite the efforts of treatise writers to make it so. The mingling of different bodies of law continued well into the 1840s and 1850s, allowing some space for the legal principles of textiles.[19]

Although they persisted in a wide variety of legal venues, the legal principles of textiles were never translated into the language of legal systematizers. They do not appear in written texts—treatises, statute collections, or published appellate decisions at either the state and federal level. Indexes to these volumes do not contain references to the rules that allowed people to make claims to textiles: all the rules necessary for sorting through all the evidence that turned possession into ownership. Even references to wives' claims to paraphernalia were sporadic and became increasingly more so over time. In a legal world defined through writing and publishing works that were regarded as authoritative, the legal principles of textiles no longer seemed particularly legal or even necessary. How did coats, dresses, socks, and handkerchiefs have legal authority? At best, the goods were evidence, like the bizarre tales told by litigants in the *New York City-Hall Recorder*. They did not convey legal meaning. Even if they did, why would anyone be interested in property claims created through relationships to textiles and the people who knew about them? The rights outlined in legal texts created far more reliable claims.[20]

Institutional changes muffled the legal principles that governed the ownership and trade of textiles as well. The focus is usually trained on the balance of power between states and the federal government, which exploded in armed conflict during the Civil War. But conflicts over the balance of authority within the federal system involved much more. The federal government inserted itself into matters once reserved to localities as well as states when it began taking up questions involving the status of African Americans who crossed state lines. The resulting policies and court cases, including Roger Taney's decision in *Dred Scott*, trod on the ability of states to define the legal status of those who lived within their borders. The implications also eroded the authority of localities, which had had considerable discretion in applying state laws. States were chipping away at that authority as well. Statute collections from the late eighteenth and early nineteenth centuries acknowledged local discretion in the area of public law, omitting discussion of misdemeanors and explicitly ceding a range of matters involving the public interest to localities. That changed by the mid-nineteenth century, as state legislatures took it upon themselves to write rules for localities to follow. A volume summarizing New York statutes in 1802, for instance, devoted only four pages to crimes, all serious felonies. It left everything else for local officials to figure out. The 1859 edition ran to nearly forty pages and included lengthy descriptions of forty-four different misdemeanors.[21]

As the institutional balance of federalism swayed, rights-based rules spilled over into new areas. New statutes on crime not only undercut local discretion but also made the procedural rights that dominated treatise literature more important in the area of public law that localities traditionally oversaw. Personal liberty cases at the federal level put the emphasis there as well: on the rights that African Americans could carry with them across state lines, not the property or privileges they could claim without rights. These rights-based principles left their mark as they moved through the legal system. They elevated professionals who read law over people who knew the law because they lived it. They elevated procedural issues over the substance of the conflicts and their social context. They elevated people with the legal standing necessary to claim procedural rights over those without it. And they made it harder to articulate, let alone use, the legal principles associated with textiles.

Figure 11.2 This painting of Elijah Boardman at his store in New Milford, Connecticut, captures two forms of legal authority: the silks, wools, linens, and printed cottons that were his stock in trade and the ledgers beneath his work desk. Legal texts recognized and regulated the accounts that made it into those ledgers while largely ignoring all the principles connected to the textiles that allowed for a much wider array of claims and exchanges. Painted by Ralph Earl, 1789. Courtesy of the Metropolitan Museum of Art, Bequest of Susan W. Tyler, 1979, 1979.395.

The establishment of professional police forces in urban areas buttressed the authority of lawyers. New York City replaced its watch system with a professional police force in 1844. Boston followed suit in 1848. The point of professionalization, at least in theory, was to integrate officers into a legal order based on a rigid definition of theft and the procedural rights of those involved, not on the legal principles of textiles or other forms of property. In practice, attention to procedural rights was spotty at best, producing hard-fought battles over control of nineteenth-century urban police forces. Still, professionals replaced community members in the practice of policing. It was the police who did searches, turned up evidence, and provided testimony, all within the rights-based framework set up by lawyers.[22]

Over time, the records produced by local courts began to look more like Daniel Rogers's reports in the *New York City-Hall Recorder*. The case of John Ryan, charged in 1833 with stealing a watch and a trunk of clothing in New York City, would have been typical of earlier cases if not for his lawyer. The complainant had tracked down the items in a trunk in Ryan's "lodging room," produced them at trial, and proved his connection to them. Ryan insisted that he had purchased some of the items. But his testimony was evasive, and he could provide no evidence to substantiate his claims. The whole thing ended, like so many similar cases, in Ryan's conviction. This time, however, a lawyer filed a motion for arrest of judgment on Ryan's behalf, based on defects in the indictment that violated his procedural rights: (1) "that it does not aver the part of the Dwelling [of the victim] through which the forcible entry was made"; (2) "because it does not aver the manner of the alleged Braking"; (3) "because it does not aver the means employed in the said Braking"; and (4) "that it does not designate the degree in which the traverser is guilty." Those issues had not been burning points of contention in cases of this kind before the entrance of lawyers.[23]

There is no indication that Ryan's lawyer was successful. But lawyers' fingerprints are in evidence everywhere. By the 1840s, it was their voices that dominated the proceedings in the New York Municipal Court, not those of the complainants, defendants, and their witnesses. Lawyers directed the entire examination process, posing questions, cross-examining, and keeping attention focused on the legal issues they thought important. Their questions came straight out of legal texts, which emphasized procedural rights. Did the indictment indicate the exact manner and means by which the accused had broken in? That question got to the proper framing of the charge, since breaking and entering to steal goods carried higher penalties than entering through an open or unlocked door. As a result, there was a lot more evidence about skeleton keys, chisels, axes, and other implements used to smash locks. What part of the building did the accused enter? That question also involved the framing of the charge: breaking and entering required not just breaking but also entering. As a result, there was a lot more evidence about the location of people's rooms and the means of entry to them through halls, stairways, and doors. To what degree was the accused guilty? That question, again, involved the framing of the charge. The proliferation of criminal codes generated by state legislatures created tighter definitions of various crimes and more elaborate gradations of culpability that went beyond the broad, traditional categories of petty theft, grand larceny, and burglary, which included breaking and entering a dwelling house and incurred higher penalties if done at night. In the 1850s, New York City had printed forms for larceny in the first, second, and third degrees, based on the value of the property.[24]

Those new rules squeezed out the legal principles that had so long attached to textiles and silenced the people who depended on them. None of the questions that lawyers asked were meant to elicit discussion about the actual property, who owned it, and who did not. They were all about filling out the forms properly and making sure that the procedural rights of their clients were followed. In 1844, for instance, David Kipp refused to answer questions on "advice of my counsel." That kind of legal advice proved difficult for some defendants to follow, perhaps because it was so novel. People were used to explaining themselves and engaging in the law, particularly in local courts. Why keep quiet? Kipp ultimately disregarded his lawyer's advice, apparently hoping to exonerate himself by implicating his conspirators, with the improbable names of One-Armed George and Buffalo Bill, a common moniker for men known for hunting and killing both bison and Native people, long before it became associated with the famed Buffalo Bill Cody. (To make the whole thing even more improbable, Kipp stated that he last saw Buffalo Bill going "west with a part of the property.") Increasingly, though, defendants stuck to their silence. Where they had once blurted everything out, attempting to explain themselves and justify their actions, they let their lawyers tell their tales. "I am entirely innocent," declared Mary Reed in 1844, "but under advice of Thomas Warner Esqr. my counsel I decline answering any further questions." After all, what did she know about the legal distinctions among different degrees of larceny? Best let the lawyers figure it out.[25]

These changes were not confined to urban areas, although they were more pronounced there. In rural areas, the legal principles and practices of textiles held on. But even there they lost their luster, connected as they were to women, people of color, the enslaved, and the poor. The cases involving enslaved people in the South Carolina upcountry in the 1830s, 1840s, and 1850s are instructive in this regard. Many of those cases, like the one involving Polly's claims to thread that she had spun, still centered on the legal principles of textiles. But this profoundly rural part of the United States had not managed to escape the changes remaking the legal process elsewhere. In South Carolina, legal matters involving enslaved people and free people of color were relegated to a separate court, the Court of Magistrates and Freeholders, where justice was still meted out by lay people, not legal professionals. The men who made up these courts were all white and not disposed to trust the testimony of the enslaved people who appeared before them. But they were well versed in the legal principles of textiles, as were the enslaved people who invoked them. The process that recognized them, however, also stigmatized them by locating them in racially segregated courts. The legal principles of textiles were for African Americans. Rights-based claims were for white men.[26]

The gendered implications of rights-based understandings of law were evident in the disappearance of women from the documentation of theft cases in the New York Municipal Court. Cases involving women, not just married women, constituted a smaller proportion of overall cases in each term than they had in the first decades following the Revolution. Did married women stop using local courts to enforce claims to textiles? Or did the recording just obscure their presence? While women disappeared from the court docket, their gowns, dresses, aprons, shifts, chemises, shawls, and hats did not. Neither did the sheets, pillowcases, quilts, and napkins that married women also called their own. All the property that women owned was still there, but those disputes no longer included the women who owned the property. The legal form in the case against Catherine Brennan and Ann Allison identified William H. Taggart as the owner of the stolen property. He linked the missing goods to his wife, as did Brennan and Allison. But Mrs. Taggart did not appear in the record except through the words of others. It was her husband who made the complaint and prosecuted the case, as did Charles Lohman, who relayed information about the goods and their disappearance when he had no direct connection to any of it.[27]

Some women were not named at all. In 1844, Samuel Jackson claimed that "three silk dresses," "a merino shawl, two calico dresses," "three silk and cotton shawls," and "other articles of female wearing apparel" had been stolen from him. End of story. While all of this property could have represented Jackson's own savings, these kinds of garments usually belonged to women, not men. In previous decades, those women appeared in cases involving such property, even if only around the edges. Similarly, in 1850, John Elton complained of the theft of a basket, which contained a "Ladies Dress and two Ladies' skirts," along with "numerous articles of women's underclothing and children's clothing." But there were no ladies, women, or children anywhere at all in the court records of this case. The goods were just his.[28]

The problem was not that the legal principles associated with textiles no longer mattered. It was that they were more difficult to enforce in local courts. No one thought that "female wearing apparel" belonged to men. Women still had legal claims to the clothing they wore, the household linens they used, and the textiles they made. But the legal framework in use as early as the 1830s, particularly in urban areas, tended to sideline those legal principles as well the women, particularly the married women, who depended on them. When what counted was rights, neither married women nor their claims to textiles mattered. They did not need to be named or even noticed, because they had neither the rights necessary to own property nor the procedural rights necessary to press legal charges. As went married women, so went other people with weak claims to rights, which was why so many defendants in the New York Municipal Court heeded their lawyers' advice and remained silent. Why bother trying to assert legal claims to textiles at all?

Women activists, in particular, took umbrage. References to women's claims to clothing and textiles peppered the proceedings of women's rights conventions in the 1840s and 1850s. While many of these conventions discussed women's status in law, what they meant was the law memorialized in legal texts: principles that were not new but that had acquired new force within the legal system, squeezing out other principles enshrined in practice, including those associated with textiles. In report after report, speech after speech, they railed furiously against all those legal principles, which handed out rights to men and only restrictions to women. The tone was telling, equal parts outrage and surprise. A report on common law presented at an 1851 convention in Akron informed attendees that a very Blackstonian definition of coverture now defined wives' legal status. By these rules, widely followed in all states, a wife "is incapable of making a contract; her name, her person, her property, are not her own. . . . At marriage, the entire personal property in possession of the wife, except her jewels and legal paraphernalia, become the property of the husband." Other speakers made the implied injustice explicit. "Let me call your attention to my position," thundered Clarina Nichols, "that the law which alienates the wife's right to the control of her own property, her own earnings, lies at the foundation of all her social and legal wrongs." Those laws could not have been news. The Vermont-born Nichols, for instance, was a well-educated teacher, journalist, and activist who divorced her first husband in 1843 to marry the newspaper editor with whom she had been working. Education, moreover, was not necessary to acquire familiarity with the law. Women regularly interacted with the legal system, despite—and sometimes because of—restrictions on their rights. What rankled activists was the elevation of "laws of general application" over others that had allowed them more leeway in practice. They decried those legal principles because their injustices were increasingly difficult to escape.[29]

Nichols made that point clear with set pieces to illustrate the evils of the laws of general application. In one, her target was dower, which allowed wives the use of one-third of the family estate after their husbands' death, but not ownership rights. The anecdote involved a woman who "had accumulated something, for she was capable in all the handicrafts pursued by women of her class"—in other words, the production of textiles. She ultimately "married a worthy man, poor in this world's goods," whose children were grown and gone. Given her husband's limited finances, she "applied her means, and by the persevering use of her faculties, they secured a snug home, valued at some five hundred dollars, he doing what his feeble health permitted towards the common interest"—which was, by implication, not much. So far, the story could have been about any number of women who have appeared in this book—Jane Cooley and her daughters or even Polly, although the structural dynamics of slavery meant that she never could have made enough to purchase a house, even if she or husband were permitted to own one, which they were not. The story also would have been familiar to all the women in the convention, and it likely cut close to the bone for many. But then Nichols revealed the pernicious effects of those general laws that had been elevated over other, countervailing principles and practices. When the woman's feeble husband died, "two thirds of that estate was divided among *his* grown-up children." The remaining one third went to her. But that was not all. "No, she could only have the *use* of one third, and must keep it in good repair" so that it would go to his heirs at her death. Why? "The *law* said so." The industrious widow did her best with one-third of the estate that she had amassed. But it was not enough, and she was unable to support herself. What happened then? "*They set her up at auction, and struck her off to the man who had a heart to keep her at the cheapest rate!*" The general laws robbed her first of her property, and then her human dignity.[30]

Even the property that women could once claim was no longer theirs under these general laws, which could take the clothes right off women's backs—a particularly powerful image of injustice. One of Clarina Nichols's favorite stories involved a woman whose ne'er-do-well husband "pawned the clothing which she had provided for herself and babes, sold her only bed, and drove her into the streets." The unfortunate woman went to work, but her husband "pursued her from place to place, annoying her employers, collecting her wages by process of law, and taking possession of every garment not on her own or children's persons." Nichols raised the roof at one convention when she told the tale of the "rum-drinker" who "took his wife's clothing to pay his rum bill" and the magistrate "decided that the clothing could be held, because the wife belonged to him." Over a hundred years later, in the 1960s, anti-lynching activist Jessie Daniel Ames described her political awakening to historian Jacquelyn Dowd Hall in exactly those terms. In 1905, Ames faced an obstreperous bank cashier who would not let her open a savings account in her own name without her husband's permission. Ames "hit the ceiling." "No it's my money," she said. But that situation, as she recalled, described all married women's plight at the time. "The husbands owned everything—the clothes on her back! She owned absolutely nothing." By that time, a rights-based view of law had set so firmly that it was difficult to imagine owning anything—even clothing—without rights.[31]

In 1905, Jessie Daniel Ames needed a savings account, not a trunk filled with sheets, blankets, and dresses, because textiles no longer functioned as a reliable means to store value. For women's rights activists in the antebellum period, however, textiles still mattered a great deal. The problem lay in the enforcement of the principles that gave them value, given the increasing focus on rights-based principles within the legal system. In that context, textiles failed to counter the workings of a legal system that not only denied rights but also upheld inequalities that kept a majority of Americans subordinated to white men. They seemed more like hand-me-downs, a bit frayed and definitely outdated, particularly in comparison to the new legal fashions.

No wonder activists on behalf of women and African Americans preferred rights. Even when enforced, the legal principles associated with textiles could not create legal claims to property and legal access that individuals could take with them across jurisdictional lines. They remained rooted in place, mired in a body of law that coated all property claims with a dirty film that was impossible to wash off.

12

Mrs. Harris's Marriage

Erasure

Mrs. M. B. Harris ran a millinery shop in Scottsville, Virginia, just south of Charlottesville. That this married woman ran a successful business in her own name would have remained lost in the past if not for the records of R. G. Dun and Company, a credit reporting firm established by Lewis Tappan, a well-known merchant and abolitionist in New York City, who appreciated the need for reliable information about the financial health of businesses and their owners. He also realized the potential of monetizing that information. Drawing on a national network developed through his contacts among likeminded reformers, Tappan contracted with agents across the country to find out what they could about local businesses. Many were lawyers, trained in the principles and processes outlined in the last chapter, whose bread and butter were civil suits. As a result, they were well positioned to know who was indebted to whom and for how much, and eager to make a little money on the side by selling knowledge obtained through their legal practice to Tappan. Tappan then aggregated their reports and sold the results. After he stepped down in 1849, the firm expanded rapidly and continued to grow, first under Benjamin Douglas and then in the hands of Robert Graham Dun, who renamed it after himself.[1]

Textiles explain the presence of Mrs. M. B. Harris and other married women in the records of R. G. Dun and Company. Without the legal principles and practices attached to textiles, Dun's agents might not have bothered with Harris, who did not have the legal status to sustain the kind of credit in which the company's customers trafficked: commercial or mercantile credit, extended to merchants, manufacturers, and other business owners, often in the form of goods. One of the key elements of commercial credit was the possession of capital to serve as collateral. That, in turn, presumed possession of the rights necessary to own and manage such property. Harris did not have them, living as she did in a state that did not modify coverture to allow married women to own property in their own names until 1877. Dun's interest in her business, however, was not unusual. In the 1840s, 1850s, and even the 1860s, the company's agents gathered information on the enterprises operated by married women, whether or not they lived in states with married women's property acts. Not surprisingly, many of the women who appeared in Dun's records were involved in producing or purveying textiles, most often as storeowners or dressmakers who dealt in fabric, trimmings, and other accessories. Their presence underscores the widespread acceptance of married women's legal claims to textiles—particularly those of married women who were white—even when they did not have formal arrangements that established them as free traders or otherwise separated their property from that of their husbands. The report of the agent who wrote up Dun's evaluation of Harris in 1858 makes sense in that context. Harris "does a good bus[iness] and [is] regarded very good for contracts." That would be impossible without the legal principles and practices that governed the exchange of textiles.[2]

Nonetheless, those principles and practices had limits. R. G. Dun and Company's reports reveal yet another problematic dimension within the new republic's legal system. The firm usually recommended credit only in small amounts to white female proprietors, because of the parallel legal world created by "general laws," to use the terminology of women's rights activists, that included restrictive readings of coverture. That was why Dun's agent in Virginia did not bother to record Mrs. M. B. Harris's first name. It was also why he made note of her husband, whom he judged to be "a worthy man." It was a legal as well as an economic observation: in a pinch, the husband of Mrs. Harris could cover her debts. Coverture's tentacles also ensnared white women who were unmarried, a status that Dun's agents clearly saw as suspect and usually temporary. In their minds, all adult women were supposed to be married, which is why they never recommended women for credit in the same amounts allowed to men, no matter their marital state or their business acumen. At least white women made an appearance in Dun's records. The restrictions of slavery and race were such that African American proprietors rarely made their way into the firm's records before passage of the Reconstruction amendments, which abolished slavery and eliminated the racial restrictions that kept African American men from exercising the rights necessary to qualify for commercial credit.[3]

Dun's records point to a legal order in transition. It was federalism, with its multiple jurisdictions and bodies of law, that enabled people to make such creative use of textiles. That changed as governing authority shifted toward institutional venues and bodies of law that emphasized the rights of autonomous individuals. It was not just that the legal principles of textiles were difficult to enforce, although that was true. Without frequent use, they receded from the legal system and faded from memory, leaving the possession of rights as the necessary prerequisite for participation in commerce. Dun's reporting on Harris suggests the difficulties for married women and others who could not claim them. By 1870, Harris's business required explanation. "Is married, has no p[ro]p[er]ty in her own right," the agent wrote. Then he stopped and scratched his head, trying to reconcile what, to him, seemed irreconcilable: that she also had "conducted bus[iness] for y[ea]rs in an honest & efficient manner, paying for all she buys & no doubt will continue to do so." How could she do that without rights? The question hung heavy between the lines of his report. No wonder, then, that activists—including Lewis Tappan—focused on the extension of rights, to African American men as well as to women regardless of race. While necessary, the extension of rights only went so far. Not only did they reinforce the very inequalities they were supposed to ease, but they also moved the legal principles of textiles further away from the practice of law.[4]

The R. G. Dun and Company's reports read as if they had been written by nosy local gossips, not hard-nosed men of affairs. That was because "credit" was not yet a purely economic assessment, even among white businessmen. It still rested on evaluations of a person's character as judged by family, friends, neighbors, and associates, which meant that credit was synonymous with reputation. So Dun's agents noted work habits and leisure activities, particularly drinking. They made pointed observations about household spending, the value and condition of real estate, the solvency of other family members, and whether business owners held property themselves or were acting for someone else. An agent in Charlottesville, for instance, dismissed a tailor there as "too lazy to do much bus[iness]." Jews came under particular scrutiny. "We don't know why he has been d[oin]g a g[oo]d bus[iness]," wrote an agent of a ready-made clothier in Richmond, adding "Another Jew invasion!!!" in parentheses. Agents kept an ear to the ground to figure out where, how, and from whom merchants and other business owners purchased their goods and supplies. Cash or credit? From local merchants or out-of-state suppliers? In 1853, an agent waved away Moses Hecht and Brother as "a miserable petty Jew affair, c[on]taining ab[out] a wheelbarrow full of goods." The tune changed soon thereafter, when Moses Hecht and his brother had been identified as connected with "the Hecht firm with branches in Baltimore, Abington, Virginia, and Newbern, North Carolina, plenty of means." All those observations became evaluations of subjects' character, be it good or bad, which was assumed to explain their past business history, their current economic status, and their future prospects—in short, their creditworthiness.[5]

Dun's agents did acknowledge that bad fortune could overwhelm even the most disciplined individuals. According to one agent, John Cochran came to Cincinnati, Ohio, "as a single man, steady, economical, and prudent, but has met with losses." Like many good men, he encountered misfortune for which he was not personally to blame. The Charlottesville agent who kept tabs on the lackadaisical tailor seemed genuinely dismayed when drinking destroyed the man's business and, ultimately, took his life—or as genuinely dismayed as it was possible to be in the Dun Company's terse recording style. The connection between individual character and creditworthiness, however, ran one way and one way only in Dun's logic. Good intentions alone did not constitute creditworthiness, although it was always possible for those in that category to redeem themselves if they fell on hard times. By contrast, individuals of bad character never merited credit under any circumstances. For them, the trappings of economic success became nothing more than a flimsy façade, liable to collapse at any moment. Agents urged caution.[6]

The mix of the personal and the professional in the Dun Company's reports says a great deal about the changing nature of credit in the first half of the nineteenth century. It is commonly assumed that the reliance on relationships, particularly family ties, gave way to assessments of an individual's personal habits, business dealings, and property holdings during this period. As Dun's reports suggest, however, those changes say as much if not more about evolving conceptions of credit than they do about the actual means of assessing and evaluating it on the ground. Individual character had always been a significant element in the extension of credit. People in the seventeenth and eighteenth centuries were perfectly capable of distinguishing wastrel relatives from reliable ones. Likewise, familial ties remained important throughout the nineteenth century and beyond, not only because family members distributed property and credit to each other but also because the rules of private law made husbands responsible for property their wives received from their families unless provisions were made to keep it in the women's hands. Dun's agents regularly scoped out the holdings of fathers, brothers, uncles, cousins, and, in the case of married women, husbands, with the assumption that they would bail out an overextended family member if necessary.[7]

Toward the middle of the nineteenth century, the familial model required modification so that business owners could tap into knowledge and resources outside their family circles. To extend their reach, eighteenth-century merchants and manufacturers had worked through family members and, from there, people who knew family members. The time-honored method of extending the reach of the business was to incorporate a new business partner through marriage to a current partner's daughter. Quakers improvised within this general model, working through their network of Friends, who were tied to each other through common religious affiliation forged through considerable personal sacrifice, which fostered a tight sense of community even among people who did not know each other personally. While the importance of close, personal ties continued well into the nineteenth century, they were no longer sufficient. To expand, firms had no choice but to extend goods on credit to people they did not know and could not make into family. In this context, the problem lay in access to knowledge about the relationships as well as the individual character of all the people with whom merchants and manufacturers did business. Who were all these people? How could you know them when you really knew nothing at all about them?[8]

The struggle to answer those questions, which showed up pretty much everywhere in the first half of the nineteenth century, underscored the erosion of textiles' cultural currency. Popular culture at this time fixated on confidence men and painted women: people whose outward appearance, particularly their clothing, made it seem like they were respectable and trustworthy when they were not. In fact, questions about the cultural meaning of textiles were inseparable from questions about credit. They both resulted from market forces that made textiles cheaper and more widely available. Newspapers and journals regaled their readers with cautionary tales in which the traditional means of assessing character failed. The dangers were clear; the answers, not so much. Readers were supposed to tut-tut as well-dressed men swept unsuspecting daughters and business associates off their feet, only to reveal themselves as morally and financially bankrupt. They were supposed to root for wealthy but upstanding women and men who dressed down to test the purity of their suitors' hearts or, in the case of men, their business partners' intentions. And they were supposed to dab tears from their eyes as honest women did everything that they could to maintain their honor, despite circumstances that left them with little more than rags. That both marriage and business fit within the same narrative conventions says a great deal about their continued alignment in the nineteenth century. Marriage still determined the economic prospects of husbands, wives, their progeny, and their natal families, just as business remained rooted in personal relationships and carried emotional overtones that skated on the edge of romance. At the same time, these tales also led back to the importance of individual character and its indeterminacy.[9]

These sentimental tales had a foot in the real world, even as they overstated people's loss of faith in the connection between textiles and their wearers. Textiles were increasingly accessible because businesses needed customers and customers had more money to spend. But it was really hard to tell who could pay. Courts were filled with people whom tradespeople, tavern owners, and shopkeepers had thought reliable and to whom they had extended goods and services on credit, but who failed to pay their bills. The bulk of the cases in the Richmond Hustings Court between the 1780s and 1820s were for small debts owed to tradespeople and shopkeepers for ordinary things. *Blythe v. Capus* involved an unpaid Richmond tavern bill, which all came to about forty-three pounds (probably Virginia pounds, given the 1787 date). Two years earlier, the merchant Philip MacRae sued William Harris for about two pounds outstanding on goods worth about nine pounds, including a pair of breaches, a hat, stockings, a pair of shoes, eight yards of printed linen, a handkerchief, a shirt, several yards of ribbon ("ribband"), and some cash denominated in dollars. In 1815, the firm of Crawford and Dunn sued Daniel Organ for a debt of about twenty-two dollars on an account that included textiles made of wool and linen as well as velvet. In 1822, Samuel Horner proved unable to pay his debt of fifty dollars to local merchants John Henry and George Read. So the court laid an attachment on his property, which suggests how little he had: a feather bed, a bedstead, a chair, a trunk, a chest, a lantern, scales and weights, twenty-one books, a kettle, and various pots and pans.[10]

A potent sign of economic change is the rising number of cases in which wholesalers sued local retailers in the 1830s. Before the Revolution, local stores were part of commercial networks, often based in Scotland and England, or they bought through commission merchants, who either were based in Scotland and England or worked out of major colonial ports but had transatlantic ties. Although commercial connections to Great Britain persisted after the Revolution, wholesalers were increasingly based in the United States. The term "wholesalers" actually covers a range of different suppliers: importers who sold in bulk as well as jobbers, commission merchants, factors, and brokers who put both imported and domestically produced goods into the hands of local retailers. The career of merchant James Colles illustrates the changes. He started out in the 1810s as a clerk in the New York City dry goods firm of H. K. Toler and Co., where his duties included smuggling a cargo of goods from England, through Halifax, Canada, during the embargo connected to the War of 1812. Soon thereafter, he set up his own wholesaling firm catering to what was called the "country trade," directing dry goods, particularly textiles, to the small general stores that dotted rural areas and clustered in small towns. These shopkeepers could only pay their dry goods wholesalers in country produce or, if the wholesaler did not take such goods, when the merchants to whom they sold had paid them. Toler specialized in central New York. When that business failed, he set up with another partner, shipping dry goods to New Orleans and, from there, to planters and storekeepers in the booming cotton states of Louisiana, Mississippi, and Alabama. Colles's commercial ties were with England, although wholesalers increasingly handled textiles produced within the United States as well. But the planters and storekeepers whom he supplied dealt directly with him.[11]

Wholesalers like Colles had the same problem as the local merchants to whom they sold. They too needed customers. But it was difficult to tell who could pay, given the illogic of what was generously called a system of credit. The short biography that precedes Colles's letters describes his time supplying small stores in central New York as "journeyings in the wild." It was a "painful and unprofitable" experience, in which he acquired "knowledge of how much easier it is to buy than to sell—and be paid." His partner at that time spent a good deal of time on the road, alternately begging and threatening clients to pay their bills and then grousing to Colles. These letters were from 1816, which became known as a "year without a summer," reflecting the global impact of volcanic eruptions in southeast Asia that destroyed crops in the United States and left farmers impoverished. This environmental catastrophe came at a particularly inopportune moment. The economic situation was already dire, having started on a downward slide with the conflicts that led to the War of 1812, and did not bottom out until the Panic of 1819. The dead ends that Colles's partner described in Oneida County, New York, were typical. A local merchant named Farwell had offered two securities, men who would cover his debts if he could not. Neither was good. The first was a man named Brown "to whom Farwell had sold part of the goods," but who refused to pay on the note he had signed, "although he acknowledged the debt." The second was a man named "Dewitt, who had bought [Farwell's] farm last fall, having agreed to meet at Geneva to pay the debt." But Dewitt never showed. "Farwell's brother in law came in his stead with excuses of illness and the death of a child" but with no money. Another debtor's security, a man named Hunt, could not be found. In fact, "there was no Hunts within thirty miles." Although Colles's partner had "not collected a cent," he was about to leave for Troy and Washington County. That did not turn out well either. He left "with empty pockets." Not to worry, though. "Although we have been very unfortunate this far, yet I venture to say there will be at the end of the year Houses in Pearl Street [the commercial street in New York City] *apparently* of sufficient magnitude to *swallow us at a mouthful* in a worse situation than what we shall be." Why? These firms had extended even more goods on credit than Colles and his partner had.[12]

Colles's firm tried to collect debts personally because civil suits were so fraught. It has become conventional wisdom that merchants, particularly those who acted as middlemen, shied away from civil actions. The volume of cases in local courts, however, suggests that local retailers and tradespeople regularly made use of the courts to collect on debts. It was just that they did so strategically. So did wholesalers. Court actions strained the personal ties on which their businesses rested. Given the dense webs of indebtedness, the ripple effects could extend beyond an errant individual, pulling in an entire family enterprise and from there circling back to undermine the creditor's own interests. Better to find other ways of extracting resources, as Colles and his partner did. In the nineteenth century, as the ties between wholesalers and their clients became more impersonal, out-of-state wholesalers faced other obstacles. The time and expense involved in civil cases were not always worth the bother. Local bias could make it difficult for outsiders to obtain judgments. A favorable verdict, moreover, did not ensure that there would be anything of value to collect. Local merchants accepted goods on credit and then sold on credit, which remained outstanding, just like their own obligations. A successful civil suit might yield nothing more than some used furniture, worn linens, and broken crockery. In New London, Connecticut, Simon Carew's New York supplier pursued a civil suit because he knew Carew still had property: the inventory of his store, mostly textiles, ran to forty-nine pages. A few years later, in 1842, Hamilton, King & Dow, "wholesale dealers in fancy and staple dry goods," came after two other New London merchants for unpaid accounts of several hundred dollars each. It is likely that these suppliers had reason to believe that they could wring payment out of these merchants as well.[13]

But it was impossible to get water from a rock. Particularly telling are the criminal charges of fraud that began to appear more frequently in the courts of large commercial cities. The formulaic language of the 1844 indictment against John H. Piker, of Dover, New Hampshire, suggests how easy it was to turn the inability to pay into a criminal offense. Piker, "being a person of an evil disposition and devising and intending by unlawful ways and means to obtain and get into his hands and possession the goods, merchandise, chattels and effects" of Samuel F. Phelps and James W. Kimball "on the pretense of buying the same fairly on credit" did "falsely pretend and represent to the said Phelps & Kimball that" he was "worth Three Thousand Dollars," when he was not. Specifically, Piker had said that he had a successful business manufacturing artificial flowers (used for women's hats) and employed "many young women." He also claimed to have $2,000 in capital, part of which was in a mill, valued at $2,500, for which he had paid $1,600 in cash and had taken out a mortgage on the rest. Other than the $1,600, he claimed to have no outstanding debts. Phelps and Kimball believed "the said false pretenses and representations" and "being deceived thereby were induced" to deliver $800 worth of "English goods" on credit, consisting of finished textiles, trimmings, and accessories, such as gloves, hose, shawls, tablecloths, veils, and fans. Subsequently, they delivered $200 more in another shipment of similar goods. All the while, Piker was "insolvent," without an artificial flower to his name or, for that matter, any other capital.[14]

When defined as fraud, the kind of misrepresentation that plagued James Colles and his partner became a crime. Piker accepted goods with the "intent to cheat and defraud the said Phelps and Kimball." The line between those who intended to defraud their suppliers and those who did not was blurry, to say the least. But even criminal charges could not solve the problem. Like civil suits, criminal verdicts in cases involving property included compensation to the victims as well as damages. Criminal cases also carried steeper penalties for those who were convicted, including jail time, which raised the stakes. Even so, defendants like Piker had no incentive to comply. There was no trace of him when the indictment against him was read either the first or the second time in the Boston Municipal Court. So the court ordered "that this indictment lay on file," where it could be used, should he ever be found.[15]

Similar cases appeared in New York City. In 1844, Moses Bramhall of the New York firm of Bramhall, Abernethy, and Collins complained that Gustavus Thompson, a merchant living near Annapolis, Maryland, represented himself as a property owner, with a farm all paid off. Based on that, Bramhall extended a significant order of goods on credit: 362 yards of woolen cloth, 269 yards of cotton cloth, thirty yards of worsted cloth, two pieces of diaper cloth, eight yards of plaid cloth, 694 yards of cotton cloth, ninety-four yards of unspecified cloth, twelve cloth skirts, twelve cloth comforters, eleven cloth table covers, twelve silk handkerchiefs, and eighteen yards of cloth for vesting. But Thompson was not who he appeared to be. He disappeared and never paid. Still, there was not much the court could do, other than listen, file the charges, and then mark the case not prosecuted. People whom wholesalers did not really know could easily slip away.[16]

The problem was a lack of knowledge about relationships, which still mattered in business. Wholesalers and other suppliers needed to know about people whom they might never meet. While locally available, that knowledge was not accessible to merchants based in New York, Philadelphia, Boston, or Baltimore, based as it was in social networks that were impenetrable to outsiders. While East Coast merchants had begun gathering information about their customers in the 1830s through in-house operations, their efforts were sporadic and incomplete. Tappan had personal experience with the value of such information. The silk wholesaling firm that he ran with his brother, Arthur, failed in the crash of 1837, ruined by the overextension of credit to people who seemed reliable but were not. He launched his new business after that failure, knowing that the financial panic had spread so rapidly and been so devastating because a lack of information led to a cascade of bankruptcies. Tappan's agents gathered information and sent in their reports. After being transcribed in very tiny handwriting within very large, leather-bound volumes, the information was sold. Customers came to the New York office, where they were greeted by clerks who stood behind bars and read the requested reports aloud. Customers stood at a suitable distance, scribbling down notes. While awkward, the whole arrangement underscored the fact that the information collected by R. G. Dun and Company was proprietary: customers could not consult the volumes themselves. (In fact, those rules still carry over for researchers, who can now consult the volumes themselves but must still take written notes. No photography is allowed.) Mercantile firms complied. It was worth the trouble and expense to focus on the distribution and sale of their goods and leave all the messy questions—about who drank too much, worked too little, dressed too well, spoke too smoothly, and lied too believably about their property holdings—to the professionals.[17]

Lewis Tappan's genius was to turn credit, which still existed in the context of relationships, into an individual characteristic, much like the rights on which credit was based. Then he turned it into information that could be separated from those individuals, commodified, and sold. Not only were Tappan's assessments produced in local networks, but they were also dependent on people's relationships in particular places. Once that information was aggregated, all those ties disappeared. The reports in the Dun company journals list individuals, who were either creditworthy or not. Family ties mattered, but only to the extent that they said something about the individual's access to capital. Social relationships mattered, but only if they took the form of customers who patronized the individual's business and paid on time and in full. Place mattered not at all. Although reports were listed by towns, counties, and states, that was more an artifact of the manner in which records were acquired and organized than a meaningful statement about who these individuals were. Each entry was self-contained, unrelated to the others, as if they had nothing in common. In fact, they did not, at least by the logic employed by R. G. Dun and Company. The point was to disentangle credit assessments from the messy relationships that actually gave them form so as to make them legible to mercantile firms in distant places. While individuals and their businesses stayed in local areas, assessments of their character—the basis of credit—could move across state lines to wholesalers and suppliers quickly and efficiently.[18]

Creditworthiness and the access to commercial credit that it provided were absolutely essential to local businesses. Only those from well-connected families had been able to make that kind of leap in the eighteenth and early nineteenth centuries. Recall Mary Alexander, whose familial ties to prominent New York mercantile families and the Barclay network in England enabled her to stay in business as a textile importer. Family was so important that it outweighed the disadvantages of gender: well-connected women had advantages over unconnected men. The advent of credit reporting remade that equation by giving suppliers standard measures with which to evaluate the economic potential of people they did not know. As a result, unconnected men who never would have been able to compete with Mary Alexander could establish credit on their own. Once consigned to the commercial fringes in small, local shops with little or no inventory, they could work their way up to well-stocked establishments, connected to big-city suppliers.[19]

Take Alexander Duval, a clothier in rural Virginia. As Dun's agent reported, Duvall had "bought out Naylor and Saunders, which bought out James McChambers," indicating that the business had already been consolidating and expanding before he became involved. Duvall's "character is good, he is industrious and attentive to bus[iness]." Although "he is w[o]rth nothing," he "has tolerable good credit at home"—meaning he had good credit among local merchants. Despite having little or no capital, "he intends to borrow some money to take East for goods." That was possible because of the changing nature of credit, although it did not work out for Duvall. One year later, the agent reported to have come into "certain information . . . that [Duvall] cannot or will not pay his debts." "He owes a great deal here, besides large bills in Wheeling & is buying more cloths in Wheeling because he says those he pur[chase]d in Phil[adelphia] are not suited to this" area. He bet and lost. But other merchant tailors—a designation that referred to tailors who had taken advantage of credit's availability to secure sufficient stocks of fabric, dry goods, and ready-to-wear clothing to set up large stores—succeeded. Their names graced department stores, some of which morphed into private investment banks. Brooks Brothers, Macy's, Wanamaker's, and Marshall Fields, as well as Lehman Brothers and Goldman Sachs, highlight the close connections between textiles and merchant capital more generally.[20]

Federalism posed a challenge to the portability of credit. The whole enterprise of evaluating individuals in far-flung locations and extending credit to them rested on the expectation that the legal status of those individuals was also portable, not only from locality to locality but also from state to state. Wherever they lived, the individuals granted credit had to have the legal status necessary to own property, manage it, and be held accountable for their debts. But that legal order did not exist in the United States between the Revolution and the Civil War. Only white men with property could claim the full range of rights necessary to move freely in the economy, regardless of where they lived, which was why Tappan's agents focused primarily on them. The legal status of everyone else, who comprised the vast majority of the population, varied wildly, depending on the state and even the locality where they lived. Bound up in status relationships and tied down by the implications, their credit could not move outside of the tight circles of people who knew them. As Dun's agents put it, they should "stay at home"—terminology they used for all individuals whose credit could not extend beyond their locality and hence were not of interest to out-of-state suppliers.[21]

The implications of immobility were most pronounced for people of African descent. Enslaved people could not move legally without the permission of the white people positioned as their masters. Some enslaved people moved around a lot, at their masters' discretion, as trusted servants who did business for their owners. Typical was the experience of Charles, a boat pilot who was enslaved to James Chesnut, father-in-law of the famous Civil War diarist Mary Chesnut, who lived near Camden, South Carolina. Chesnut had sent Charles and a crew of enslaved men to "town" (presumably Charleston) for supplies. On the way back, Charles docked the boat for the night in Sumter County, near the plantations of two men well known to Chesnut: Richard Singleton and Thomas Clarkson. The next morning, according to Chesnut, Charles and his crew were accused by Singleton's and Clarkson's overseers of stealing a hog and were then violently attacked by the two white men. Writing to Singleton afterward, Chesnut expressed dismay. As he explained, his boat was "commanded by a faithful fellow in whom I laid great trust." Given that and rumors of the overseers' cruelty, Chesnut saw the accusation of theft as a pretext "to gratify a savage passion." He hoped Singleton would agree and punish the overseers accordingly. Where both they and "my man Charles" were known, "I suspect Charles word would be credited" over theirs. While Chesnut's trust allowed for Charles's mobility, it did not keep him safe. Charles's credit, like that of other enslaved people, did not travel. The same dynamics applied to their property in textiles. Some enslaved people had a secure enough place in local communities, among people they knew, to own textiles or even to produce and trade them on their own behalf. But those spaces were firmly rooted in space, dependent on practices that they had created and sustained over time as well as on the people who had witnessed them and could affirm them. In a literal sense, the credit of enslaved people stayed "home."[22]

Slavery also shaped the legal status of those people defined as "free blacks," making it difficult for them to move through geographic space in the new republic. As the term suggests, the people who fell into this legal category were considered slaves who had been freed, not free people. The legal presumption in slave states was that all people of African descent were enslaved unless they proved otherwise. While that presumption was consistent, its application was not. In some states, African Americans who became free had no choice but to leave. Those who remained were subject to laws that required them to register with local courts, obtain guardians, post yearly bonds, and carry written proof of their status. These provisions allowed some people legally defined as "free blacks" to put down roots in particular areas, although their free status was always precarious and subject to whites' approval. But their credit was always rooted in place, making it nearly impossible for them to move elsewhere.

The legal status of all people of African descent was dependent on geography: in some states they were assumed to be enslaved; in others they were assumed to be free. In the 1840s and 1850s, the question was whether general laws would fix African Americans' legal status as enslaved or free. Federal laws, particularly the Fugitive Slave Act of 1850, created general rules so that the legal status of particular African Americans followed them wherever they went, which meant that those people legally defined as slaves would be slaves even in free states. Abolitionists and advocates of racial equality advocated general rules that would eliminate slavery or at least make it possible for African Americans to keep their free status and move within the United States without fear that state laws would enslave them.[23]

Figure 12.1 The cartoon depicts the 1846 arrest of George Kirk, who escaped slavery in Savannah, Georgia, and was sheltered by abolitionists in New York City. After municipal authorities instituted a search, his allies tried—unsuccessfully—to ship him upstate. The lithograph hardly does justice to Kirk, who orchestrated his own escape and successfully defended his freedom in court. *Arrest of the Slave George Kirk*, American Antiquarian Society.

Even within free states, however, mobility was fraught for Black Americans. The specific restrictions varied. Some states gave people in the legal category "free blacks" nearly the full range of civil rights and state citizenship. Others required registration, bonds, and even guardians. While those restrictions applied on the basis of race, they were rooted in poor laws, with deep Anglo-American legal roots, that made local residency crucial: each person acquired it in the municipality or county of birth, and that jurisdiction then assumed responsibility for supporting its residents when they became ill, elderly, or otherwise incapacitated. Given the logic of the system, newcomers—particularly those without economic prospects, such as propertyless men and single women—could be regarded as a problem. No local area wanted an influx of needy people whom they might have to support. In the colonial era, communities "warned out" migrants, although that was less about kicking people out of town than letting them know that they were ineligible for social support in the event they needed it. While the formal process of warning out had fallen into disuse by the nineteenth century, local communities maintained considerable discretion over who could settle in their jurisdictions and under what circumstances. Restrictions were imposed on free Blacks, whom whites presumed to be economically problematic. Passes made it difficult for these people, whether residents or not, to move through states that required such documentation. Demands for registration, guardians, and bond raised barriers to settlement and, when met, tied residents down to particular places. Uneven enforcement only added to the uncertainties. Limitations on free Blacks' other civil rights—including rights to testify, to contract, and to own property—had the effect of hobbling mobility as well, contributing to a situation in which free Blacks' legal status and their credit always depended on their connections to particular people in local areas. They could not carry either across state lines.[24]

Women, regardless of race, faced limitations as well. Actually, "woman" was not a meaningful legal category for most of the nineteenth century, because the legal status of all females depended on age, marital status, race, and status as slave or free. Enslaved women were slaves, not women, in law. Free, adult, unmarried females of all races were not so much "women" in the eyes of the law as they were free individuals, legally responsible for themselves. Although the fact of their sex did limit their political rights, they could still claim the basic civil rights necessary to own and manage property, including the rights to sustain civil actions in law: they could sue and be sued, which allowed creditors to reclaim debts. Those rights were supposed to enable freedom of movement, just as they did for free men. In theory, women who were white, and therefore free, as well as unmarried, could travel from place to place unencumbered by relations of domestic dependency, secure in the knowledge that their legal status would remain pretty much same wherever they went. Widows and women who never married could own property in their own right. Some married women maintained control over property given to them by their natal families through legal provisions, such as separate estates, which were used and recognized throughout the United States. In practice, however, the insidious logic of coverture undercut all women's claims to property, as the Dun company's reports suggest. If the subject was a man, agents had only to find out whether he had the property and the character necessary for credit. If the subject was a woman, they had to take a step back and determine whether she had the legal status to own or manage property at all.[25]

It might seem that the presence of a husband would resolve the question. But that was not always the case, because the laws relating to married women's property varied from state to state even before the passage of married women's property acts. Married women regularly ran businesses in Louisiana, which retained legal practices from the French and Spanish empires that made it easier for them to own and manage property in their own names. Even those practices were situational, dependent on whether the woman and her husband had entered into the necessary legal agreements and what those agreements contained. Dun agents did not necessarily have access to those documents, so they had to go by what they could learn through observation and practice. Mrs. Henry Lichton was married, but "always carr'd on the bus in her own name." In other words, it was true because she had always done it and no one had objected. Mrs. E. W. Rogers, a widow, bought out another woman's successful millinery shop on "long credit." Dun's agent gave her high marks for industry, energy, and economy. A merchant for whom she once clerked "says if anyone can succeed it is her." Then she married. As the agent noted, she is "now Mrs. E. W. Turner," but still "does bus in her own name." The fact that she could and did was sufficient. More confusing was Mrs. Jeffers, who was married to Mr. Peck, but "still [kept] up her old name" and continued to conduct her business as her own. An agent followed up a year later, noting that "business continues as prosperous as before." Her "husband is of no [account], but he has no connection whatever with her bus or money concerns," although the implication was that he could and might if circumstances changed.[26]

Married women's claims to property were opaque even in states that did not make it as easy for them to retain claims to property as Louisiana. Although married women were subject to coverture, some controlled property through legal workarounds, such as separate estates. Sometimes it was parents who set up these arrangement to prevent the wealth of a woman's natal family from passing into her husband's hands and out of the hands of the maternal family line forever. Sometimes it was the women themselves, who drew up agreements before remarrying. Other married women not only managed and amassed property but also acquired credit themselves, through longstanding practices that acquired legal force, as they did with M. B. Harris. Similarly, Mrs. S. E. Hayth, in the southwestern Virginia town of Fincastle, earned her own entry as "a marr[ie]d woman do[ing] bus in her own name" in the 1860s. The agent did not say how he knew or how that was possible. It just was, a silence indicating that he knew that others dealt with her on that basis. The indeterminacy of married women's relationship to property also explains the entry devoted to Mrs. M. A. Butterfield, an heiress who attracted an agent's attention. She was presumed to be "very rich," but she also was married, and he did not know the nature of her claim to the property she had acquired. "Being a marr[ie]d woman, he wondered, can she contract? on her own acc[oun]t."[27]

It was a real question in states without married women's property acts as well. In those states, presumptions about the legal powers of coverture depended on the circumstances of particular women and the priorities of the reporting agents. In 1845, an Alexandria, Virginia, agent attributed Mrs. Tatsapaugh's business to her husband, a baker, noting that he also had a clothing shop, which was "attended to by wife, who is a smart woman & understands bus." He identified the shop as his and not hers, even though it was clearly her business and she likely ran it as if it were. Five years later in the same town, an agent gave Mrs. J. H. Padgett, who sold laces, her own entry as a business owner. "Very industrious and careful," she kept a small stock of goods. A year later she was still "doing pretty well." The shop and credit were hers, because that is how it appeared to that agent. Then, the report of 1853, likely filed by someone else, shifted the business to her husband. Padgett, this correspondent wrote, "is a married woman & a material aid to her husband who is a worthy man." Mrs. Minken, of Cincinnati, Ohio, experienced a similar transformation. In 1849 and 1850, reports portrayed her as running her own successful millinery business, despite the fact that Ohio did not pass its first married woman's property act until 1861. Then, in 1851, an agent slammed that door shut. "A married woman cannot do bus in her own name, her paper would be worthless," he wrote, meaning that creditors could not sue her for her debts. Her business continued nonetheless, suggesting the power of textiles and practice as well as the limits of Dun's assessments. In 1856, however, the correspondent rewrote Mrs. Minken's history with the shop, shifting ownership from her to her husband. "This concern was started by her husband, some 8 or 10 y[ea]rs ago." Her husband "had previously been in very good circumstances, but becoming reduced, opened this little shop which was generally managed by his wife."[28]

Wholesalers were loath to extend any woman credit, because of the possibility that coverture might alter the agreement, suddenly divesting parties of legal responsibility and making it possible for them to accept credit and then forfeit it without consequences. The stakes were clear in Dun's report on Mrs. Everett, a Virginia milliner. From 1845 to 1849, she was conducting her own business and rated moderate in terms of business character. But in 1849, when faced with debts, she pleaded "*coverture* and the statute of limitations," meaning that she invoked her status as a married woman to escape prosecution by her creditors. Another Virginia milliner "stands well & regarded good for her purchases" and was doing "a very good little bus" but was "not legally respons[ible] or reliable," a judgment that referred not to her business acumen but to her marital status. Yet another milliner continued her business after her husband's bankruptcy, but Dun's reporter recommended cash transactions only, "her indebtedness being his." Coverture overwhelmed both the qualities of textiles and the character, no matter how good, that these women had established in local communities.[29]

The passage of married women's property acts, beginning in the 1830s, only complicated the situation further. States passed these acts at different times and with different provisions. Mississippi led the way in 1839, pointing to the contradictory underpinnings of such measures. The legislation was less an affirmation of women's rights than an effort to sweep up the debris left by the Panic of 1837. In theory, married women's property acts affirmed *women's* rights, allowing them to own property while also making them responsible for their debts. In practice, these acts also provided a way for male household heads to shift assets to wives' names, putting them out of creditors' reach. That was what many Mississippi legislators had in mind. The crash of 1837 had hit that state particularly hard. People there borrowed big to cash in on the cotton boom and had no way to pay their creditors when the economy bottomed out. In this context, married women's property acts functioned like homestead exemptions, which allowed debtors to keep the property necessary to sustain themselves—usually the house and surrounding property, livestock, tools, and household furniture and implements, as well as clothing and linens. But married women's property acts were better, because they offered the opportunity of blanket protections. Debtors could simply sign over all their assets to their married female relatives and evade debt collectors. Maryland followed in 1843 and Arkansas in 1846, with similar acts that allowed families to move assets into the names of married women.[30]

The acts of New York and Pennsylvania, passed in 1848, emerged from a very different set of concerns. They were part of reforms advocated by activists like Clarina Nichols who had been pushing for the extension of rights to women. While these acts resembled earlier ones, they were intended to allow married *women* to control property and to assume all the legal responsibilities that came with ownership. Nonetheless, these early acts were extremely limited. They only gave women control over property that they brought into marriage or acquired afterward through inheritance. Such measures were not new: wealthy families had accomplished the same ends through marriage settlements, separate estates, and other legal arrangements for centuries. These new laws made existing legal loopholes available to the elite into a general law for everyone. Tellingly, this first round of reform did not give married women control over their earnings or wages, which is what all the women in Dun's reports were claiming, through practice established with textiles and, in the case of Louisiana, through legal arrangements that allowed women to trade in their own names. Those rights required another round of legislation that began in the 1860s. Even then, restrictions of coverture lingered. Women acquired no rights to family property, as Clarina Nichols had advocated. And it was not until the late twentieth century that married women could establish credit in their own names.[31]

The resulting legal patchwork created headaches for businesses that traded across state lines. Commercial handbooks, which summarized relevant laws, addressed that situation, providing not just the basic variations in real estate, personal property, and contracts but also common legal forms necessary for various property transactions and suits. The legal status of married women featured prominently in these handbooks, not because there were so many women in business but because married women's property acts were inseparable from the credit of men: regardless of the motivations for their passage, they could shield the property of husbands and other male relatives from creditors. In Theophilus Parsons's *Laws of Business for All the States and Territories of the Union and the Dominion of Canada*, which was reprinted numerous times, the entire second section focused on married women, describing the different laws, state by state. Only after that did the handbook move to topics more commonly associated with commercial law. So did H. A. Gaston's *The Ready Lawyer; or, The Business Men's, Farmers', Mechanics', Miners' and Settlers' Legal Adviser*. S. R. Kneeland's *The Commercial Law Register* went state by state but was careful to detail married women's relationship to property in each state. Coverture was problematic because it shielded women from responsibility. But so were married women's property acts, which could be used to shield women's male relatives from prosecution. Dun's agents were always on the lookout for such scams. One found Mrs. A. D. Johnson in Cincinnati, Ohio, suspect. According to him, she turned over her business to her son-in-law, although her daughter still managed it, suggesting that she turned it over to her, not to him. At one point, she took control again, apparently because he was indebted and in danger of losing it all. Two years later, Dun's agent characterized the business as "carried on by Mrs. A. D. Johnson," although as "a cover for Chas. E. James," her son-in-law.[32]

The implications extended to unmarried women as well. Marriage—or its mere prospect—affected the calculations of Dun's correspondents, underscoring the difficulty that women had being recognized as rights-bearing individuals. When it came to women, the agents usually recommended credit only in small amounts, if at all, regardless of their marital status or their ability to claim property rights. Credit, moreover, took the form of "home credit," the term used by some agents for credit from local suppliers, not national ones that could provide more goods, of better quality, at lower prices. The implications are evident in the career of Eliza Berry, an unmarried woman who ran a successful, high-end dry goods store for years but never earned Dun's confidence. In 1850, her report indicated that she was about forty years old, had her establishment for at least eight years, and "attends well to bus." Even so, it recommended her only for credit in "small amounts." She continued to run her shop until 1860, a feat of longevity that eluded most male merchants. But she never acquired a credit rating that would allow her to amass capital or expand her operation. Berry's business was stuck "at home" with local credit.[33]

Merchants would have preferred uniform, general laws that applied in every state because that would have made trade easier. As S. F. Kneeland wrote in the preface of his guide, *The Commercial Law Register*, there were three "chief difficulties" in the "practical enforcement of mercantile claims." The first was "the absence of correct information as to the local laws governing rights of commerce and the time and manner of applying its remedies." The second and third involved securing legal representatives who knew the rules. His guide aimed to resolve all three by supplying the information that made legal representation less necessary and less risky.[34] Lewis Tappan would have agreed. It was no accident that he supported the elimination of restrictions in order to create the kind of legal landscape associated with general laws: both the abolition of slavery and the elimination of racially discriminatory laws that limited free Blacks' rights in so many states, before and after the Civil War.

Rights that applied generally through the United States provided the necessary foundation for Tappan's credit reports. Like rights, Tappan's construction of credit focused on the individual: a mobile body, freed from encumbering relationships of status, which could take not just its property but also its business potential wherever it went, secure in the knowledge that what was established in one place would be honored in another. Those ends were achieved, in theory, when it came to African American men. By the late nineteenth century, commercial handbooks no longer had to deal with variations in the status of African American men. The Fourteenth Amendment, passed in the aftermath of the Civil War, prohibited racially discriminatory laws—at least in theory. Of course, practice was another matter entirely. But theory was all merchants, wholesalers, and other businesses needed. Even then, they still had to contend with all the inconsistencies in the legal status of women, which continued to rest on their marital status, race, and class.[35]

That Dun's agents reported on married women at all underscores the persistence of textiles' legal principles, which enabled them to trade in their own names when dealing with cloth, clothing, and related accessories. That the reports were so uneven suggests the limits of those principles, as conceptions of credit shifted from family ties and local reputation to rights and individual character, with both rendered as abstractions so as to be portable across geographic space. By the mid-nineteenth century, the ability to trade implied access to constructions of credit linked to the possession of rights.

Like Mrs. M. B. Harris, the firm of M. W. Baird operated at the crossroads of these legal changes. According to Dun's agents in 1843 and 1845, the store was the "largest most fashionable bus" in Cincinnati, Ohio. Yet the agents fretted because it was "difficult to tell who composes the firm." There were "2 or 3 Misses Bairds," and one seemed to have been recently married to a Mr. Ferris. Not only did Dun informants suspect that Mr. Ferris might be taking over the business, but they also were unclear as to shares of ownership among all those involved: "It w[ould]d be almost imposs[ible] to tell if one were to sue them whether to name all as Defend[ants]s or which of them [to] steer clear of." The conclusions were dire. In 1845, the agent wrote: "Fail'd sev[era]l times besides turning and twisting." In 1848: "They have a v[ery] bad reputation, consid'd doubtful by many, & once fail'd and cheat'd the cr[editor]s to a very good amount." In 1850, the possessive pronouns had changed, indicating that the agent considered Mr. Ferris to have taken over the firm, although it was still referred to as M. W. Baird: "M. W. Baird does ab[ou]t his usual bus." In 1851, the situation continued to be dire: "Entirely irresponsible, our merchants have told us they would not sell them g[oo]ds unless for cash." But then the reports changed suddenly, suggesting they were filed by a different agent. In 1856, the correspondent claimed that "they are making money, leader of the fashions & in fair cr[edit]." A penciled entry at the very end affirmed that assessment, not only contradicting all the previous negative reviews but also restoring the business to one of the Baird women: "Says he knows her to have bought considerable in NY for last 5 or 6 yrs & has alwaysways paid her notes promptly."[36]

What explains these contradictions? Apparently, local agents could not fathom that Cincinnati's most successful millinery shop was run by women, despite what was right in front of their noses. Concerned about the legal status, rights, and ability of the owners to fulfill their obligations, they turned ordinary business practices into serious problems: local merchants routinely failed to pay creditors on time and renegotiated their debts instead. But what was routine, even advisable, for male-owned businesses became red flags for the women who ran M. W. Baird. The agents painted the grim picture of a store always teetering on the edge, slipping into failure and back out again, while skipping out on its bills and defrauding its creditors. But that characterization of M. W. Baird did not make much sense. If that were the case, where did the store's reputation come from? How could a firm without any access to credit manage to maintain a stock of goods known to be the most extensive and fashionable in the city? How did it stay in business for so long if no one would supply them? Local agents saw M. W. Baird through the new lens of credit, which recognized only individuals with rights. As a result, they saw women of dubious legal status and hence dodgy credit, which could not travel east. But their warnings missed the mark, because the Baird women were working through established mechanisms of credit where relationships mattered. They had their own ties to New York suppliers. Perhaps they were related to wholesalers there. Perhaps they had already established a business relation with them before they moved to Cincinnati. While the records remain silent as to the nature of their relationships, they clearly counted. Increasingly, though, those relationships no longer mattered in the world of R. G. Dun and Co and to the larger legal world occupied by so many merchants. More than that, they were no longer legible as the basis of property claims, let alone thriving businesses.

Conclusion
Mary Todd Lincoln's Old Clothes
Just Material

Mary Todd Lincoln faced a common problem after the assassination of her husband. While trying to find her way through a thick cloud of grief, she discovered that she had no money. Abraham Lincoln's estate remained tied up in probate for years, as executors tried to sort through all the claims on it. Until its settlement, his widow had little to live on and no way to support herself. She sulked as obviously as she could in rented rooms but attracted no notice. She wrote hysterical letters to everyone she knew, to no avail. She applied for a pension from Congress and was refused. As a last resort, Lincoln decided to leverage the clothing that she had worn at the White House but no longer needed in her reduced circumstances. Her extensive collection of gowns and other garments, in luxurious fabrics and furs with all the trimmings, had cost a small fortune. As her dressmaker and stylist Elizabeth Keckly later disclosed, Lincoln had outstanding bills of about $70,000 at the time of her husband's death.[1]

The plan made perfect sense. In fact, it was exactly what women in her situation had been doing for generations. Women could not always count on their husbands or fathers for support, even when those men appeared solvent to others. So they leveraged the property that they could control, namely, textiles: their clothing, accessories, household linens, blankets and quilts, carpets, uncut cloth, and any other textile-related articles they could call their own. Many men did the same, storing and exchanging value in this form of property because it was more secure, in both economic and legal terms, than other available options. Pawn shops were full of these goods. An entire segment of the economy was devoted to their trade. Legal venues recognized the rules associated with them. None of that was secret.

In 1867, Mary Todd Lincoln's efforts first to pawn and then to sell her wardrobe generated national outrage. Newspapers from coast to coast sneered at a former first lady so vulgar as to think anyone would want to buy her old clothes. Commentators skewered her wardrobe and her character.

The gowns were tacky, just like her. They were too loud and too revealing, indicating not only a lack of taste but also an unladylike desire for attention that bordered on promiscuity. The condition of her clothing was even worse. Sweat stains spread from under the armholes, making unmentionable bodily functions public. Seams had given way under the strain of someone too large to fit the garment and too vain to admit it. Their fabric was threadbare and fraying but unrepaired.

Why were Mary Todd Lincoln's efforts to turn her clothes into money so controversial? Part of the answer lies in her propensity for drama, which did not always serve her well. After working herself into a state of high panic, she enlisted agents whose handling of the sale resembled a circus sideshow more than a business transaction. Unable to round up buyers, they ultimately offered to take the whole collection on the road and sell tickets for public viewings. Although traveling exhibitions of this kind were an accepted part of popular culture at the time, the public drew the line at this display, given the circumstances of the president's recent death.

But the firestorm that Lincoln faced was not all of her own making. In the post-emancipation United States, the market for used clothing had acquired negative connotations. It already carried the taint of illegitimacy, associated as it was with the crime of theft. Legal changes that followed the Civil War only solidified those associations. Selling secondhand clothing seemed uncomfortably akin to selling the body itself, a practice over which thousands of Americans had fought and died and which the Thirteenth Amendment had outlawed. While the sale of clothes savored of slavery, the market in used textiles seemed not only outdated and unnecessary but also dirty and illicit. It had been tolerated only because it served those without strong claims to property rights. But why continue such practices when the barriers to property rights were being dismantled? As the case of Mary Todd Lincoln indicates, that form of emancipation had limits. Despite the wider distribution of rights, the real economy and much of the law remained inaccessible to the vast majority of the population.

The powers that be had only accepted the exchange of textiles by those with tenuous claims to rights and property as a matter of necessity or expediency. Negative stereotypes of secondhand clothes and pawnbrokers were everywhere in the decades following the Revolution, and used clothes were regularly linked to poverty, disorder, and disease. In 1808, for instance, *Reif's*

Philadelphia Gazette announced that "the Emperour [sic] of Russia has prohibited the introduction of old clothes into his Polish states, for fear of their causing the spread of infections [sic] diseases." Within weeks, the *New-Bedford Mercury* in Massachusetts and the *Concord Gazette* in New Hampshire reprinted the same piece of news. To be sure, the used clothing trade was already global in scope, which made far-flung events more relevant to New England than it might appear at first glance. Britain regularly offloaded ready-made military clothing in the new republic, and communicable diseases, such as smallpox, were known to travel via linens, blankets, and clothing. Still, it is hard to understand the relevance of information from the Russian Empire to American readers, other than to connect secondhand clothing with medical as well as moral peril.[2]

Anti-Semitic tales of pawnbrokers and used clothing dealers taken from London dailies appeared so often in the new republic's press that its readers might have been persuaded that a cabal of Jewish merchants had descended on the country and taken over the trade. That was hardly the case. To be sure, Jews did figure prominently as purveyors of textiles, but they were not confined to running pawnshops and dealing in secondhand clothes. In fact, their business ventures ran the gamut from the rag trade to well-appointed brick-and-mortar stores that featured high-end merchandise. All the unwelcome attention lavished on Jewish merchants says a great deal about the competition they presented to others. Unlike many of those involved in the textile trade, Jewish men enjoyed the same legal status as other white men, which allowed them freedom of movement and the rights necessary to amass capital and command credit. Those privileges enabled them to peddle goods and set up businesses in growing towns and cities on the East Coast and in the new republic's hinterland. It was women and African American men who actually controlled the part of the textile trade that catered to other people with weak claims to rights. Their presence was less threatening, because their operations were smaller and rooted in place, given the legal restrictions imposed on them.[3]

In the decades following the Revolution, negative portrayals of pawnbrokers and dealers in secondhand clothing ran alongside ads for these businesses, a juxtaposition that suggests how robust and resilient this part of the market was. While some commentators wrung their hands and foretold disaster, the targets of their criticism went about their business, buying and selling this lucrative form of property. Typical was the ad in Boston's *Columbian Centinel*: "Second-hand Clothes. Bought and sold by

James Pusy, No 16 Elm Street, such as Men's and Boy's Pantaloons and Coats, Waistcoats, Women's Great Coats, Gowns, and Bonnets, Children's wear, and second hand Hats, Boots, and Shoes. Please call and see." In New Haven, Connecticut: "Military Clothing. Just Received and Now for Sale by Samuel P. Davis. . . . Any person wishing to furnish himself with a suit, will do well by calling as they will be sold on very moderate terms, if applied for soon." In Philadelphia: "SECOND-HAND CLOTHES. The subscriber has lately arrived from Europe, and has now opened a store at No. 371, N. 2d. near Green street, for the buying and selling all kinds of Second-hand Clothes, acquaints the citizens of Philadelphia and its vicinity, that he gives the most money for the above articles." In Newbury Port, Massachusetts, "WILLIAM PIKE LUNT, Informs his friends and the public that he has opened an INTELLIGENCE OFFICE, at his house in Beck-Street, a few doors from the Rev. Mr. Dana's Meeting house," putting those seeking housing and jobs in touch with those seeking renters and laborers. In addition, he received "SECOND HAND CLOTHES" and kept them for sale. It was hard to get too wound up about secondhand clothes when they were such a central feature of the economy.[4]

By the 1830s, the discourse surrounding this part of the textile market had changed. Pawnbrokers in particular had never enjoyed a stellar reputation. Before the 1830s, however, critics acknowledged the importance of a trade that enabled people to leverage the value of their property. What they decried were the circumstances that led so many people to pawnshops and the exploitative terms to which they were subjected once there: greedy brokers who took advantage of poor people in desperate straits, lending them a pittance on their possessions and then charging excessive fees to get the goods out of hock. In the 1830s, however, the concept of pawning itself came under suspicion. As the economic uses of textiles as currency, savings, and capital fell away, their remaining quality was their close personal connection to their wearers. That connection supported legal claims to these goods. But its meanings could be volatile once textiles were conceived primarily as extensions of their wearers, not as goods that could also be used for other, economic purposes. Selling them seemed like selling pieces of oneself. Reaching that point—of having to sell your own clothes—became too embarrassing to admit, at least to women with any claim to respectability. Trading in such goods veered into the realm of moral bankruptcy.[5]

Imagery from the Civil War emphasized those personal connections, while jettisoning textiles' economic uses. That shift is evident in the use of the term "peeling," which referred to the looting of soldiers' bodies during the war, as historian Sarah Jones Weicksel explains. Peeling had dual but related meanings: to rob "a person of their possessions, or seizing goods by means of violence," and to pare "away the skin of a fruit . . . , peeling tree bark, or removing an animal's hide." The combination turned the taking of property into a physical assault, with particularly gruesome overtones. Peeling was not just the theft of valuable property, in the form of shirts, pants, and coats that their deceased owner would never use. In fact, it was not really about the economic value or potential usefulness of the property at all. It was about skinning and humiliating the enemy, leaving their bodies exposed, and taking their property as trophies. US and Confederate soldiers both did it, and both sides used it evidence of the enemy's barbarism.[6]

What some lost, others gained. Illustrators for *Harper's Weekly* leaned on the visuals of clothing to communicate the drama of the Civil War, particularly when it came to the status of slavery and those caught within it. Nowhere is the association more explicit than in an 1865 drawing of recruits in Charleston, where the transformation from slavery to freedom is portrayed with the acquisition of uniforms. African Americans on the left are less than men, dressed in rags, with stooped shoulders and eyes cast down or to the

Figure C.1 "Scenes in the War—Rebel Soldiers after Battle 'Peeling' (i.e., Stripping) the Fallen Union Soldiers.—From a Sketch by an Officer." *Frank Leslie's Illustrated Newspaper*, February 13, 1864.

side. But they are standing in the light, suggesting the impending change in their circumstances. To their right is a uniformed African American soldier holding his hand out in greeting, ready to welcome them to the other side, where other neatly uniformed African American men stand tall, their heads held high and their gazes direct and strong. The metaphor was centuries old: clothing made the man. These enslaved African Americans acquired freedom, manhood, and, presumably, the attendant rights, with a new suit of clothes. All three were bound up together: they acquired what the peeled soldiers surrendered.[7]

That the new suit of clothes was a United States Army uniform underscored the connection between textiles and the larger legal changes of which they were part. The new clothes represented the transformation of individual character. The soldiers in them had been turned into men: taller, straighter, more confident. The illustrator clad them in the Union blues, drawing on longstanding cultural and legal practices that differentiated army uniforms from other kinds of clothing. Uniforms situated their wearers within a powerful set of relationships, marking them as representatives of the government whose clothes they wore and thereby extending special legal protections and cultural privileges to them. Those who donned uniforms had to be men; but once uniformed, they ceased to be individuals and became part of a collective

Figure C.2 Negro Recruits at Charleston. *Harper's Weekly*, April 1, 1865, 205. Courtesy of Wallach Division Picture Collection, New York Public Library.

unit. Those relationships were why uniformed African Americans were so controversial and so threatening to Confederates. In those garments, African Americans represented the authority of the United States, which had altered its legal order to admit them as equals and, by extension, repudiated the entire legal apparatus of slavery. Their right to wear that uniform had been a point of contention within the United States for the same reasons. It was well into the war before the US military admitted African Americans as regular soldiers rather than as "contraband" property seized from rebels or as menial laborers. Even when African Americans wore the Union blues, not all US commanders treated them as the equals of white men in the same uniform. This particular suit of clothes symbolized all African Americans' changing relationship to the body politic.

The uniform spoke to the tenuous legal status of African Americans at this moment, whether free or enslaved, male or female. In the *Harper's* drawing, the man who ushers recruits into freedom is Black, not white, acknowledging African Americans' active participation in emancipating their people and ending slavery. But, as the uniforms suggest, all these men required the backing of the United States to attain freedom, manhood, and the rights that came with that status. A good suit of clothes, no matter the quality of its fabric or tailoring, was not sufficient; the elimination of white supremacy and the resulting inequalities required collective action and structural change. The Union blues, infused with federal authority, acknowledged that.[8]

Uniforms came at a price. While the US army agreed to put African Americans in uniform, its policies subjected them to miserable conditions, driven by racism that the growing support for abolition did not eradicate. Recruits received lower pay, inferior supplies, and dangerous assignments as well as constant condescension and outright cruelty. On top of it all, the army required African American recruits to buy their uniforms themselves, deducting three dollars a month from their pay to cover the costs, while it gave uniforms to white recruits. The uniformed soldiers in the *Harper's* drawing stood in the shadows, their break from the past apparent but their future unclear. What happened when the war was over, the uniform was put away, and the authority it represented was withdrawn? What happened when their wearers were again clad in their own clothes?

The answer was supplied with the Reconstruction amendments, which made it possible for African Americans to take up rights when they put their uniforms away. The Thirteenth Amendment abolished slavery, which not only turned all African Americans into free people but also prohibited the reinstitution of slavery anywhere in the United States. The Fourteenth Amendment established birthright citizenship, striking down Roger Taney's infamous decision in *Dred Scott*, which denied that status to all people of African descent. It also extended federal protection to all states' handling of civil rights, with the intent of securing those rights to African Americans. And then it linked civil rights to US citizenship, promising that all citizens could enjoy them. The Fifteenth Amendment, ratified in 1870, further extended federal protection to voting rights.

None of these amendments created a national standard or located authority over the definition and distribution of rights at the federal level. Doing so would have been a step too far, altering the basic structure of federalism by moving power away from states. The Thirteenth Amendment was the most radical in this respect. With it, the federal government stepped in to eliminate the laws sanctioning slavery that had been the major difference between states' legal regimes. The Fourteenth and Fifteenth amendments retreated, leaving authority over the rights of US citizens with the states, where they had always lain. In them, states still defined rights; the federal government could oversee their application, *if* its leaders had the ability and the will to do so.

What rights were included within the phrase "civil rights"? While the Fourteenth Amendment studiously avoided naming them, the Civil Rights Act of 1866 did. It was a short list, limited primarily to the rights necessary to own and exchange property as well as those required for the legal standing necessary to defend control, when contested: "to make and enforce contracts, to sue, be parties, and give evidence, to inherit, purchase, lease, sell, hold, and convey real and personal property, and to full and equal benefit of all laws and proceedings for the security of person and property, as is enjoyed by white citizens." African Americans no longer needed the legal principles and practices associated with textiles to buy, sell, save, and defend their possessions. They could put their uniforms away—in theory.[9]

In practice, African Americans still needed the protective cover of federal authority. The abolition of slavery eliminated neither the cultural edifice of white supremacy nor its sturdy legal foundation. At the onset of the Civil War, white men could claim rights not just in their property and their own labor but also in the labor and bodies of their dependents. Between the Revolution and the Civil War, conceptions of dependence, once attached to an individual's structural place within households, had become more firmly linked to an individual's race and gender. African Americans were denied rights, not just because of their legal status as slaves but because of their race, which was thought to make them innately subordinate and incapable of exercising them. By the same token, all women were denied rights, not because of their status as wives but because of their gender. All white men could exercise the full range of civil and political rights, not because they actually were household heads but because their race and gender were thought to make them innately independent and capable of household governance. More to the point, white men were constituted as freemen through their rights *over* those without rights. The logic naturalized the inequalities of domestic dependency, including slavery, as expressions of immutable qualities of race and gender. It also turned rights into a zero-sum equation. Since the rights of white men included authority over women and all people of color, the extension of rights to those people represented a loss to white men.[10]

The result was violence, as white men in the states of the former Confederacy tried to claw back the rights they thought had been taken away. It was so persistent and so pervasive that it is easy to miss the legal dynamics that generated it: violence was the only way for whites to reclaim rights once sanctioned by law. Federal authority was no match for the onslaught. To be sure, Republicans supported the extension of rights to African American men because they rejected the notion that race determined human capacity or the content of individual character. But the supporters of racial equality were in the minority. Most white people in the nation believed that race made all people of African descent innately inferior. How they acted on those ideas differed. Where conservative whites in the former Confederacy lashed out, whites elsewhere in the country thought the situation might take care of itself once formal legal restrictions were eliminated. Nothing would alter African Americans' racial destiny, not even the removal of racial distinctions in law.[11]

Such racial sentiments lay just beneath the surface of federal policies, which were framed with the assumption that the rights necessary to access the legal system and the ballot box, in and of themselves, would suffice to address the legal status of formerly enslaved people. These notions acquired legal resonance in the federal courts, where, ironically, the application of a narrow, individualized construction of rights perpetuated exactly the kinds of racial restrictions that the extension of rights was intended to rectify. That was the case even in the 1870s, when federal judges supported the Justice Department's efforts to address violations of the Fourteenth and Fifteenth Amendments. Federal prosecutors approached each violation as a case unto itself, instead of grouping them together in what would later be called class actions or applying the findings in one case to other similar cases. The framework of individual rights, which allowed for federal intervention, individualized problems that were in fact systemic. The issue was an entire population of white southerners as well as the full apparatus of state governments committed to white supremacy, not the wrong-headed acts of a few errant individuals. Moreover, ensuring compliance was difficult. The various Enforcement Acts passed by Congress allowed for federal intervention in moments of acute crisis. Federal action under those acts did successfully root out Klan violence in some areas, notably in the South Carolina upcountry in the early 1870s. But those dramatic eruptions were symptomatic of a chronic condition that afflicted most of the former Confederacy. The federal government had neither the means nor the manpower necessary to monitor, let alone cure, that infirmity. As a result, victory in one case neither altered the circumstances that produced such egregious violations of civil and political rights nor repaired the broken state systems that required continual federal intervention.[12]

The federal courts then further limited the range of rights that fell within the federal government's purview, culminating in the *Civil Rights Cases* (1883). In addition to striking down the Civil Rights Act of 1875, which defined access to jury service, public accommodations, and transportation as protected rights under the Fourteenth Amendment, the *Civil Rights Cases* announced that federal courts could only consider the letter of state law, not its results. As long as state law did not explicitly differentiate on the basis of race, there was no reason for federal intervention. In fact, aggressive federal intervention to protect African Americans' exercise of rights amounted to special treatment at odds with the legal principle that all individuals were equal in the eyes of the law. "When a man has emerged from slavery, and by the aid of beneficent legislation has shaken off the inseparable concomitants of that state," wrote Justice Bradley for the court's majority, "there must be some stage in the progress of his elevation when he takes the rank of a mere citizen, and ceases to be the special favorite of the laws, and when his rights as a citizen, or a man, are to be protected in the ordinary modes by which other men's rights are protected." The rights of the individual took precedence over obvious social inequalities that federal officials sought to address. The *Civil Rights Cases* affirmed in federal law what was already a legal reality in many states, codifying racial inequalities that had long defined the nation's legal order.

African Americans fought back. Through their efforts, they were able to claim basic property rights far more successfully than voting rights and other conceptions of rights linked to public access and the vote. As historian Dylan Penningroth shows, they made them secure in the same way that their forebearers had made legal claims to textiles: through everyday use. Even so, it was impossible to stop legal trends that were turning African American men's uniforms into rags.[13]

While men entered the post–Civil War era with rights, at least in theory, women were left with only the clothes on their backs, which by then had become flimsy legal coverings, as Mary Todd Lincoln's experience suggests. Rights remained out of reach, for all women regardless of status. Women's property rights acts gestured in that direction, but hesitantly, ignoring the full range of legal disabilities that women faced. None of the Reconstruction amendments offered any relief in this regard. The Fifteenth Amendment purposefully excluded women, resulting in a decades-long campaign to obtain voting rights for women. In the meantime, the US Supreme Court swatted down efforts to include women within the terms of the Fourteenth Amendment, with tautological reasoning so strained that it is surprising it held together at all. The Fourteenth Amendment applied to citizens, the U.S. Supreme Court declared in *Bradwell v. State of Illinois*. Women were *women*, not citizens in fullest sense of the term. "The natural and proper timidity and delicacy which belongs to the female sex evidently unfits it for many of the occupations of civil life," wrote Justice Joseph P. Bradley. "The paramount destiny and mission of women are to fulfill the noble and benign offices of wife and mother. This is the law of the Creator."[14] While that argument did not actually determine the outcome of *Bradwell*, its logic continued to frame women's relationship to civil rights well into the twentieth century.

Without rights, women still needed textiles, which was why Mary Todd Lincoln determined to sell her clothes. While Congressional leaders were haggling over the terms of the Fourteenth Amendment, she faced the remnants of her life as a widow without the full range of rights: her husband's estate tied up in probate, no property of her own, no credit with which to raise capital, no way to leverage it if she could, and no occupations open to her that would produce an income. All she had were textiles: "I have many costly things which I shall never wear, I might as well turn them into money, and thus add to my income, and make my circumstances easier." It was a practical plan, since her wardrobe was not part of her husband's estate. Nor was this scheme in any way novel or exceptional. In fact, Lincoln had acquired her wardrobe with the assumption that it would be of assistance to her once her husband was no longer president. "I expect that we will leave the White House poorer than when we came into it," she confided to Elizabeth Keckly. "Should such be the case, I will have no further need for an expensive wardrobe, and it will be policy to sell it off." Like so many women, Lincoln was saving for a rainy day. In October 1867, that time had come. It was pouring.[15]

The value of cloth, clothing, and accessories was never just a matter of economics. Textiles also anchored women within protective relationships, which Lincoln also hoped would ease her life as a widow. Unfortunately, textiles underscored the fragility of Lincoln's social network, which consisted of the men allied with the Republican Party and their wives, who no longer needed to curry favor with her to get to her husband. It was that circle of so-called friends who directed her to pawn brokers in Chicago. When that failed, they suggested selling in New York, where they thought she could command better prices, particularly if she obtained an agent. At this point, Lincoln enlisted Keckly, one of the few women she considered a friend, although she treated her more like a servant. In fact, Lincoln's request for assistance sounded more like a command, a manner of interaction that underscores not just Lincoln's racism but also how careless she had been in tending the personal relationships in her life more generally. Once in New York, Lincoln made her way to the firm of Brady and Keyes, brokers connected to the Republican Party, who lulled her into a false sense of security by holding up the promise of past relationships and arguing that their power could be activated through her clothes. According to a wary Keckly, Brady and Keyes "argued that the Republican party would never permit it to be said that the wife of Abraham Lincoln was in want." Party leaders "would make heavy advances rather than have it published to the world that Mrs. Lincoln's poverty compelled her to sell her wardrobe." If the men of the Republican Party failed her, then their wives would come to her rescue, paying handsomely for her clothes because they had belonged to her. Her clothes, which Brady and Keyes valued at around $24,000, would save her.[16]

To say that the venture failed spectacularly would be a spectacular understatement. As Lincoln wrote frantically to Keckly in October 1867, "It appears as if the fiends had been let loose, for the Republican papers are tearing me to pieces."[17] It was an apt description: what unfolded in the nation's press was a symbolic peeling. The legal principles were not in question. "Of her rights to sell her property, there can be no doubt," proclaimed *Frank Leslie's Illustrated Newspaper*. But what was legally allowed was not always advisable. With the sale, "Mrs Lincoln has succeeded in amusing a part of the public, scandalizing another part, and annoying still another portion."[18] Other newspapers were less charitable. They described her efforts to leverage the value of her clothing as dirty and disgusting, a disgrace to the nation. The only explanation was insanity.[19] Brady and Keyes leaked her correspondence, hoping that evidence of her distress would shake loose Republican support. But those letters were read as extortion. As the Springfield, Massachusetts, *Republican* put it, "She comes squarely out and says to our great Republican party, 'Buy my old clothes or I will dismember you.'"[20] Her determination to go forward with the public sale after the uproar over the letters was taken as proof of her greed. Some newspapers gleefully reprinted critical remarks from other periodicals. Quoting the Cincinnati *Commercial*, a newspaper in Maine declared Mary Todd Lincoln's conduct "mortifying."[21]

Her clothing provided the metaphor for her manifold sins. "The gaudy bad taste with which she dressed, and the constant effort to make a show of herself disgusted all observers" when she was in the White House, one journalist wrote.[22] A particularly biting critique, which recirculated widely, declared that the much-hyped merchandise was "not worth much." This writer claimed to have perused the sale, in the company of his wife, whose "head is about as level as most women's" in "the matter of dry goods." She was shocked that all the dresses were "cut low in the neck." "'Why John, I wouldn't wear one of them,' she cried, 'not if they had been worn by all the presidentesses that ever sat on chairs. I've got better party dresses at home.'" Reminded that she would be wearing "Republican party dresses" and that the purchase was for "principle's sake," his wife put down her foot: "'I don't want any relics of the relict,'" a wry pairing of the term often used to describe widows and assessments of Mary Todd Lincoln's wardrobe.[23] A correspondent for the *New Orleans Times* first damned with faint praise, judging "the shawls, jewels, laces, etc." to be "unexceptionable." But he let loose about the gowns: "The dresses give unmistakable evidence of having been very much worn, and are so stained and soiled that the ladies are quite indignant at being invited to purchase what their maids would give warning for if asked to accept." "A woman of refinement would *know* that a *true lady* would shrink, as from the touch of a leper, at the idea of wearing the dresses of another," although "shawls and jewels are different." "We are ashamed of her."[24] Even sympathetic articles had an edge. "It must be recollected," wrote the *New York Herald*, "that Mrs. Lincoln came from the West, and if her toilette was offensive to our refined Eastern judgment the custom of the country must be her excuse."[25] Those from the hinterland might be excused for their vulgarity—hardly a ringing endorsement.

The reporting merged Lincoln with her clothes, making it impossible to separate the two, even as they peeled away her clothes to reveal her true

Figure C.3 According to Elizabeth Keckly, Mary Todd Lincoln preferred low-cut bodices, which she thought flattering on her figure. This photograph also shows the emphasis on ornamentation in women's fashions. Photograph by Mathew B. Brady, 1861. Library of Congress, Prints and Photographs Division.

self. Onlookers did not just see clothes; they saw Lincoln herself, as if undressed. The press recoiled in horror at the idea of asking another "lady" to wear her clothes, portraying Lincoln's character flaws as a contagion that could be transmitted through the fabrics that laid next to her skin. "This weak-minded woman," wrote a local California paper, "exhibits herself" so as to "extract from somebody a fraction more on the cost of her camel's hair shawls, or a few cents advance on a point lace parasol cover."[26] One satirical article likened Lincoln's sale of her clothes to an auction, with none-too-subtle allusions to slave auctions, featuring both Lincoln and her clothes as government property. "Now comes a beauty—a lace flounce dress, worn on State occasions by the relict of the 'government. . . . Give us a lift on it! Have pity on the poor relict of the government . . . and I know you will bid lively." "And here, gentlemen, comes ano'her shawl, a beauty. . . . It is part of the great struggle for freedom." The article concluded with bids on Lincoln herself: "Bid lively, gentlemen, for all the relics left by the martyr, including his widow."[27] The relict and her relics were one and the same. Neither had any value.

This avalanche of misogyny was not just about Mary Todd Lincoln. It also extended to the part of the textile market that catered to those without strong claims to property or rights, which remained important to many women despite the adoption of married women's property acts. To be sure, Lincoln was a difficult person and not much liked. But her circumstances should have elicited some sympathy because they were so common. Even women from wealthy families regularly pawned and sold their clothes, as part of a larger economic strategy of storing value in textiles. Before the passage of married women's property acts, this was the one form of property to which they had secure legal claims. Unmarried women, who could in theory claim the rights necessary to manage property, also found it difficult to gain access to credit and amass capital. Textiles continued to be important because the married women's property acts were so narrowly framed and did nothing to alter the larger legal landscape that limited women's economic options. They extended rights piecemeal, focusing first on real estate and only later on wages and other property. Even then, women's claims seemed suspect because the handful of property rights grudgingly allotted to them did not eliminate the other structural inequalities they faced. Long accustomed to the legal stability provided by textiles, women continued to concentrate their economic interests in this form of property; they still produced it, stored value in it, and traded it. As one of Lincoln's biographers put it, everyone in her hometown

Figure C.4 Mrs. Lincoln's Wardrobe on Exhibition in New York, *Harper's Weekly*, October 26, 1867, 684, Library of Congress, Prints and Photographs Division.

of Springfield, Illinois, "knew at least one needy widow who survived on the periodic sales of clothes." The streets of major cities were lined with stores hawking the apparel of socialites.[28] For women, textiles remained a safe haven in a hostile world.

At the same time, the legal changes of the 1850s and 1860s made textiles less secure in legal and economic terms. In particular, the extension of rights made the means by which people made claims to textiles seem outdated, unnecessary, and illegitimate. The newspapers' coverage of Lincoln expressed that position in their takedown of her effort to leverage the value of her textiles. The attacks on Lincoln's clothing undermined that form of property more generally. Articles scoffed at the idea that used clothes could ever be worth $24,000, then an enormous sum. While likely an optimistic estimate, it was not out of realm of possibility. The reporting focused on the style and cut of the dresses, but their actual value lay in the fabrics. Even wealthy women continually remade their dresses or passed them along to others, so as to reuse expensive materials. Dresses were taken apart and turned inside out, which put the stains, fading, and other signs of wear next to the skin, hidden from view. Tears were carefully patched and otherwise disguised with decorative trim or embellishments. Frayed hems, a common affliction with long skirts that were constantly kicked as their wearers walked, were covered with matching or contrasting bands of fabric. Changing fashions focused on embellishment, ribbons and trims that could be added and then replaced. Basic silhouettes changed more slowly, and when they did, it was not so dramatic as to make alterations impossible. Those practices, which recognized and preserved the value of women's property, were utterly at odds with the consumer ideal advanced and advertised in the press: that ladies wore new clothes, purchased for a single season or even a single event and soon discarded. Descriptions made it seem like wear and tear drained a garment of all value, when that was hardly the case. They also focused on style, as if rapidly changing fashions meant that women's garments immediately lost value after the first wearing.

The labor that went into making garments disappeared as well. Such was the fate of Elizabeth Keckly. Although known as Mary Todd Lincoln's dressmaker, she had a successful business as a modiste, an artisan who designed, made, and fit one-of-a-kind, high-end gowns. After using her skills to buy her way out of slavery in St. Louis, she had established herself in Washington, DC, where she acquired renown for her innovative designs and her ability to flatter any figure. Landing Lincoln's account had been a coup, bringing in more customers, while providing access to the White House. Through textiles, Keckly extricated herself from slavery and built up an independent life. Then Lincoln put Keckly's creations up for sale, and ridicule rained down, destroying her reputation. Press reports occasionally mentioned Keckly and her role as a modiste but featured the gowns as a personal extension of Lincoln. It was as if the clothes had sprung spontaneously into being fully formed. By implication, their construction required no skill and little effort. Those who made them needed no recognition and only nominal compensation. Keckly's labor mattered not—but it did, particularly to Keckly. Who would want to hire a modiste whose creations had been publicly denounced as unfashionable, tasteless, and downright ugly? Her business never recovered.

The networks through which clothing circulated did not escape the barrage either. Lincoln claimed that many of the items were gifts, invoking the power of past relationships and emphasizing the esteem in which she

Figure C.5 Elizabeth Keckly, 1861, in a beautifully fit dress, presumably one of her own designs. Moorland-Spingarn Research Center, Howard University.

and her husband had been held. But the press accused her of defiling the public's trust, selling access to her husband, government offices, and wartime contracts in exchange for silly bits of finery. Mrs. Lincoln "admits that her influence in obtaining office was sought and given, and indirectly that was of such a character as to justify a demand for recompense, or 'return in a small way,' in money," *Frank Leslie's Illustrated* acidly remarked. "Of course, this confession will be quoted all over the world as evidence that corruption invades [the] White House . . . that place and wealth hang on a woman's favor to be secured by appealing to her sympathy, pandering to her vanity, or gratifying her averice [sic]." The furor fused two ways in which women exercised authority. In the nineteenth century, well-placed men and their wives received constant solicitations for offices, jobs, loans, and other favors, usually with obsequious promises to return the favor. To exclaim at Lincoln's participation in this practice was to willfully misrepresent how business—political and otherwise—was done, characterizing the corrupt implications of cronyism as uniquely feminine when they were anything but. The many scandals of the Lincoln and Grant administrations—and beyond—could hardly be laid at the feet of Washington wives.[29]

At the same time, the connection between graft and gifting implicated women's networks, in which clothes and accessories circulated as currency, capital, and credit. In the coverage of Lincoln, these networks appeared more as an assemblage of greedy women than a prudent form of mutual assistance, much less the powerful counterweight to women's legal marginalization that they were in practice. It was unclear why Lincoln was culpable: because she received so much for so little, or because she received so little for so much? Never mind. It was all corruption, born of a peculiarly feminine inability to navigate the ways of the world. As *Frank Leslie's Illustrated* opined: "That Mrs. Lincoln should be surprised that the favors she extended to office-seekers and sycophants are not reciprocated ... shows great simplicity of mind, and suggests a charming inexperience." "Alas, poor Lincoln!" sighed the New York *Herald*. "He little thought his loved partner would find her bitterest enemies amongst those who had professed the highest friendship for him."[30] Bottom line: women could not be trusted to manage property or wield authority. In the post–Civil War world, that meant they could not be trusted with either rights or the legal and economic leverage they wielded with textiles.

The legal principles and practices associated with textiles were never just about women. They had featured centrally in the new republic's economic and governing order and were widely used by men as well. Yet the gendered assumptions embedded within the uproar over Mary Todd Lincoln's clothes have extended across time, into the twentieth and twenty-first centuries, where clothes have been—and still are—seen primary as consumer goods associated with women. Women's concern with clothing underscored their cultural, economic, and legal differences from men. Women made them as part of their domestic chores, which were regarded as separate from the commercial economy dominated by men. By categorizing textile production as domestic labor, the presumption is that it was already devalued because it was women's work, which is then used to explain why it received so little compensation after its industrialization. It is hard to imagine that this part of women's productive labor or the selling and storing of textiles involved the law, when most women could not claim the rights necessary to control property. Consumer goods have not been granted the same kind of importance within the new republic's legal order as the forms of property associated with men. And so the legal principles and practices that *all* people on the margins used in decades between the Revolution and the Civil War have been overlooked. Instead, women, men of color, and poor people have been defined by their lack of rights and their exclusion from the economy, the legal system, and political power.

In leaving out textiles, this perspective overemphasizes the benefits of rights, which in many ways proved more fragile than textiles. They were not easily transferable. While they made people equal before the law, they could also conceal the vast inequalities that characterized people's standing outside it. Despite the changes of the Civil War era, many men fared little better than women in the emerging rights-based regime. For the vast majority of Americans, rights remained powerful in theory but disappointing in practice until the civil rights movement a century later.

The focus on textiles reveals a more complicated history, in which all people with tenuous claims to rights involved themselves in the economy, law, and governance. During the first half of the nineteenth century, people on the margins were familiar with the rules of law that regulated the exchange of textiles. They relied on legal principles associated with textiles to participate in forms of production and trade that had been presumed the exclusive province of elite white men. More than that, they insisted that the new republic's governing institutions apply those rules to their economic dealings. Rights mattered, because they provided a secure means to achieve those ends. But the legalities of textiles made it possible to imagine why rights were important and what they could do. Textiles enabled people to envision a world where even those who endured grinding inequality could define their own destinies and live their lives in color.

People's efforts to alter the terms of their lives with textiles provide necessary context for understanding how hard-fought battles for equality were—and still are. Their efforts shaped a trajectory of change that was anything but linear, where inequality was always the norm. It is the experiences of women, both white and Black, rather than those of propertied white men, that best capture the actual relationship of most Americans to law and the economy—from the nation's formative decades through to the present.

Notes

Introduction

1. *State v. Elizabeth Billings*, County and Intermediate Court, Indictments, Kershaw District, SCDAH. In a similar case from 1816, Benjamin Harwell admitted to stealing "one pair of boots, one linen ruffled shirt, a cambrick neck handkerchief, one homespun coatee, one steel mounted pistol, a pair of hose, all worth forty dollars" so that he could make his way "to Orange County North Carolina where he says he was born and raised." *State v. Benjamin Harwell*, Indictments, Court of General Sessions, Kershaw County, SCDAH.
2. These dynamics and their implications are explored in this book. They draw on ideas developed in previous publications: Laura F. Edwards, "The Material Conditions of Dependency: The Hidden History of Free Women's Control of Property in the Early Nineteenth-Century South," in *Signposts: New Directions in Southern Legal History*, ed. Sally Hadden and Patricia Minter (Athens: University of Georgia Press, 2013), 171–92; Edwards, "Textiles: Popular Culture and the Law," *Buffalo Law Review* 64 (January 2016): 193–214; Edwards, "Sarah Allingham's Sheet and Other Lessons from Legal History," *Journal of the Early Republic* 38 (Spring 2018): 121–47; Edwards, "The Legal World of Elizabeth Bagby's Commonplace Book: Federalism, Women, and Governance," *Journal of the Civil War Era* 9 (December 2019): 504–23; Edwards, "James and His Striped, Velvet Pantaloons: Textiles, Commerce, and the Law in the New Republic," *Journal of American History* 107 (September 2020): 336–61. For a similar insight in reference to a form of property similar to clothing but less widely owned, see Linda K. Kerber, "Why Diamonds Really Are a Girl's Best Friend: Another American Narrative," *Daedalus* 141 (Winter 2012): 89–100.
3. *People v. Caty*, a black, 6 August 1805, Indictment Papers, NYMA. For a similar claim brought by an enslaved woman for both her freedom and her clothing, see Petition 20884427, Supreme Court of Louisiana Collection, Book: 99, University of New Orleans, Digital Library on American Slavery, http://library.uncg.edu/slavery/details.aspx?pid=16124.
4. The experience of William and Ellen Craft provides a dramatic illustration. As they explained in *Running a Thousand Miles for Freedom; Or, The Escape of William and Ellen Craft from Slavery* (London, 1860), the entire plan depended on clothing, with the light-skinned Ellen dressed as an invalid gentleman and the darker-skinned William dressed as her attendant. For the importance of clothing in their escape, also see Kathleen Hilliard *Masters, Slaves, and Exchange: Power's Purchase in the Old South* (New York: Cambridge University Press, 2014), 170. Another example is Anna Maria Weems, who escaped slavery by dressing as a man. See Tamika Y. Nunley, *At*

the *Threshold of Liberty: Women, Slavery, and Shifting Identities in Washington, D.C.* (Chapel Hill: University of North Carolina Press, 2021), 64–66, 40–69 for the importance of clothing to runaways more generally. For that point, also see Jonathan Prude, "To Look Upon the 'Lower Sort': Runaway Ads and the Appearance of Unfree Laborers in America, 1750–1800," *Journal of American History* 78 (June 1991): 124–59; David Waldstreicher, "Reading the Runaways: Self-Fashioning, Print Culture, and Confidence in Slavery in the Eighteenth-Century Mid-Atlantic," *William and Mary Quarterly* 56 (April 1999): 243–72.

5. For particularly evocative analyses of the close connection between people and their textiles, particularly their clothing, see Ann Jones and Peter Stallybrass, *Renaissance Clothing and the Materials of Memory* (New York: Cambridge University Press, 2000); John Styles, *Threads of Feeling: The London Foundling Hospital's Textile Tokens, 1740–1770* (London: Foundling Hospital, 2013); Sasha Handley, "Objects, Emotions and an Early Modern Bed-Sheet," *History Workshop Journal* 85 (April 2018): 169–94; Tiya Miles, *All That She Carried: The Journey of Ashley's Sack, a Black Family Keepsake* (New York: Random House, 2021); Daniel Lord Smail, *Legal Plunder: Households and Debt Collection in Late Medieval Europe* (Cambridge, MA: Harvard University Press, 2016). For material culture in North America, see Zara Anishanslin, *Portrait of a Woman in Silk: Hidden Histories of the British Atlantic World* (New Haven, CT: Yale University Press, 2016); Marla Miller, *The Needle's Eye: Women and Work in the Age of Revolution* (Amherst: University of Massachusetts Press, 2006); Miller, *Betsy Ross and the Making of America* (New York: Henry Holt, 2010); Ann Smart Martin, *Buying Into the World of Goods Early Consumers in Backcountry Virginia* (Baltimore: Johns Hopkins University Press, 2008); Prude, "To Look Upon the 'Lower Sort' "; Laurel Thatcher Ulrich, *A Midwife's Tale: The Life of Martha Ballard, Based on Her Diary, 1785–1812* (New York: Knopf, 1980); Ulrich, *The Age of Homespun: Objects and Stories in the Creation of an American Myth* (New York: Knopf, 2001); Waldstreicher, "Reading the Runaways"; Sophie White, *Wild Frenchmen and Frenchified Indians: Material Culture and Race in Colonial Louisiana* (Philadelphia: University of Pennsylvania Press, 2012). Following in the footsteps of Timothy H. Breen, "'Baubles of Britain': The American and Consumer Revolutions of the Eighteenth Century," *Past and Present* 119 (May 1988): 73–104, and Breen, "An Empire of Goods: The Anglicization of Colonial America, 1690–1776," *Journal of British Studies* 25 (October 1986): 467–99, recent scholarship has explored the political resonance of material goods in general and clothing in particular: Cary Carson, "The Consumer Revolution in Colonial British America: Why Demand?" in *Of Consuming Interests: The Style of Life in the Eighteenth Century*, ed. Cary Carson, Ronald Hoffman, and Peter J. Albert (Charlottesville: University Press of Virginia, 1994), 483–697; Joanna Cohen, *Luxurious Citizens: The Politics of Consumption in Nineteenth-Century America* (Philadelphia: University of Pennsylvania Press, 2017); Kate Haulman, *The Politics of Fashion in Eighteenth Century America* (Chapel Hill: University of North Carolina Press, 2011); Sophie White, "This Gown Was Much Admired and Made Many Ladies Jealous: Fashion and the Forging of Elite Identities in French Colonial New Orleans," in *George Washington's South*, ed. T. Harvey and G. O'Brien (Gainesville: University

of Florida Press, 2004), 86–118; Michael Zakim, *Ready-Made Democracy: A History of Men's Dress in the American Republic, 1760–1860* (Chicago: University of Chicago Press, 2003).

6. See Leora Auslander, "Beyond Words," *American Historical Review* 110 (October 2005): 1015–45, for material objects, rather than written texts as historical evidence. In addition to notes 5 and 7, see also Leora Auslander, *Cultural Revolutions: The Politics of Everyday Life in Britain, North America and France* (New York: Berg, 2009); Deborah Cohen, *Household Gods: The British and Their Possessions* (New Haven, CT: Yale University Press, 2006); Clare Haru Crowston, *Credit, Fashion, Sex: Economies of Regard in Old Regime France* (Durham, NC: Duke University Press, 2013); Amanda Vickery, *Behind Closed Doors: At Home in Georgian England* (New Haven, CT: Yale University Press, 2009). Recent work integrating material culture into Civil War history suggests the turn toward objects: Joan Cashin, ed., *War Matters: Material Culture in the Civil War Era* (Chapel Hill: University of North Carolina Press, 2019); Sarah Jones Weicksel, "The Dress of the Enemy: Clothing and Disease in the Civil War Era," *Civil War History* 63, no. 2 (June 2017): 133–50; Weicksel, "'Peeled' Bodies, Pillaged Homes: Looting and Material Culture in the American Civil War Era," in *Objects of War: The Material Culture of Conflict and Displacement*, ed. Leora Auslander and Tara Zahra (Ithaca, NY: Cornell University Press, 2018), 111–38. Also see Ted Ownby and Becca Walton, *Clothing and Fashion in Southern History* (Jacksonville: University Press of Mississippi, 2020); Teresa Barnett, *Sacred Relics: Pieces of the Past in Nineteenth-Century America* (Chicago: University of Chicago Press, 2014).

7. A growing body of work has uncovered the pervasiveness of the trade, particularly its extension into the lives of those at the lower end of the economic scale, while also emphasizing the importance of material goods in people's lives: Robert S. DuPlessis, *The Material Atlantic: Clothing in the New World, 1650–1800* (Cambridge: Cambridge University Press, 2016); Hilliard, *Masters, Slaves, and Exchange*, 46–68, 94–131; Steven King and Christiana Payne, "Introduction: The Dress of the Poor," *Textile History* 33 (2002): 1–8; Beverly Lemire, *Fashion's Favourite: The Cotton Trade and the Consumer in Britain, 1660–1800* (New York: Oxford University Press, 1991); Lemire, *Dress, Culture, and Commerce: The English Clothing Trade before the Factory, 1660–1800* (London: MacMillan, 1997); Martin, *Buying Into the World of Goods*; Daniel Roche, *The Culture of Clothing: Dress and Fashion in the Ancien Regime*, trans. Jean Birrell (Cambridge: Cambridge University Press, 1994); Margaret Spufford, *The Great Reclothing of Rural England: Petty Chapmen and their Wares in the Seventeenth Century* (London: Hambledon, 1984); John Styles, *The Dress of the People* (New Haven, CT: Yale University Press, 2007); Tamara Walker, *Exquisite Slaves: Race, Clothing, and Status in Colonial Peru* (New York: Cambridge University Press, 2017).

8. Recent work has revealed how well developed and extensive global networks were in the finished textile trade. See, for instance, Susan S. Bean, *Yankee India: American Commercial and Cultural Encounters with India in the Age of Sail, 1784–1860* (Salem, MA: Peabody Essex Museum, 2001); DuPlessis, *The Material Atlantic*; David Jenkins, ed., *The Cambridge History of Western Textiles* (Cambridge: Cambridge University Press, 2003), 1:395–689; Beverly Lemire, *Global Trade and the Transformation of*

Consumer Cultures: The Material World Remade, c. 1500–1820 (New York: Cambridge University Press, 2018); Amelia Peck, ed., *Interwoven Globe: The Worldwide Textile Trade, 1500–1800* (New Haven, CT: Yale University Press for the Metropolitan Museum of Art, 2013); Virginia Postrel, *The Fabric of Civilization: How Textiles Made the World* (New York: Basic Books, 2020); Marta Vicente, *Clothing the Spanish Empire: Families and the Calico Trade in the Early Modern Atlantic World* (New York: Palgrave, 2006). The new history of capitalism is a capacious field that defies easy generalizations. For an insightful recent overview, see Christine Desan and Sven Beckert, eds., *American Capitalism: New Histories* (New York: Columbia University Press, 2018). The recent work on cotton and the slave system has been particularly influential: Edward Baptist, *The Half Has Never Been Told: Slavery and the Making of America Capitalism* (New York: Basic Books, 2014); Sven Beckert, *Empire of Cotton: A Global History* (New York: Knopf, 2014); Walter Johnson, *River of Dark Dreams: Slavery and Empire in the Cotton Kingdom* (Cambridge, MA: Harvard University Press, 2013).

9. DuPlessis, *The Material Atlantic*; Linda Eaton, *Printed Textiles: British and American Cottons and Linens, 1700–1850* (New York: Monacelli, 2014); John Guy, "One Thing Leads to Another: Indian Textiles and the Early Globalization of Style" in Peck, *Interwoven Globe*, 13–27; Jenkins, *Cambridge History of Western Textiles*, vol. 1; Lemire, *Global Trade*; Florence M. Montgomery, *Textiles in America, 1650–1870* (New York: Norton, 1984); Postrel, *The Fabric of Civilization*, 129-35, Vicente, *Clothing the Spanish Empire*; Melinda Watt, "'Whims and Fancies': Europeans Respond to Textiles from the East," in Peck, *Interwoven Globe*, 82–103.

10. Maria João Pacheco Ferreira, "Chinese Textiles for Portuguese Tastes," in Peck, *Interwoven Globe*, 44–55; Guy, "One Thing Leads to Another"; Lemire, *Global Trade*; Postrel, The Fabric of Civilization, esp. 147-78; Watt, "'Whims and Fancies.'"

11. Susan Sleeper-Smith, "Encounter and Trade in the Early Atlantic World," in *Why You Can't Teach United States History without American Indians*, ed. Susan Sleeper-Smith, Juliana Barr, Jean M. O'Brien, Nancy Shoemaker, and Scott Many Stevens (Chapel Hill: University of North Carolina Press, 2015), 26–42; as the editors argue, 35, the fur trade was really the cloth trade. For the proportion of cloth among trade goods, see Dean L. Anderson, "The Flow of European Trade Goods in the Western Great Lakes Region, 1715–1760," in *The Fur Trade Revisited*, ed. Jennifer S. H. Brown, W. J. Eccles, and Donald P. Heldman (East Lansing: Michigan State University Press, 1994), 93–117.

12. For the connections to the slave trade, see John K. Thornton, *Africa and Africans in the Making of the Atlantic World* (New York: Cambridge University Press, 1998), particularly 44–53, 110–12. For the connections later in the eighteenth century, see Joseph E. Inikori, "Slavery and the Revolution in Cotton Textile Production in England," *Social Science History* 13 (Winter 1989): 343–79. See Vicente, *Clothing the Spanish Empire*, 58, for Spanish calico exports.

13. For calicos and other Asian cottons in North America, see Bean, *Yankee India*, 27–32; Haulman, *Politics of Fashion*, 31–34; Beverly Lemire, "Fashioning Cottons: Asian Trade, Domestic Industry and Consumer Demand, 1660–1780," in

Jenkins, *Cambridge History of Western Textiles*, 1:493–512; Peck, "'India Chints' and 'China Taffaty': East Indian Company Textiles for the North American Market," in Peck, *Interwove Globe*, 102–19.

14. Peck, *Interwoven Globe*; Lemire, *Global Trade*; Jenkins, *Cambridge History of Western Textiles*, 1:395–689.

15. By the 1780s, calicos were being produced within Britain and Europe as well: Serge Chassagne, "Calico Printing in Europe before 1780," in Jenkins, *Cambridge History of Western Textiles*, 1:513–27; Inikori, "Slavery and the Revolution in Cotton Textile Production"; Lemire, *Fashion's Favourite*; Lemire, "'A Good Stock of Clothes': The Changing Market for Cotton Clothing in Britain, 1750–1800," *Textile History* 22 (January 1991): 311–28; Vicente, *Clothing the Spanish Empire*.

16. Economic exchange has been a focus in legal history since the inception of the field. For foundational work, see James Willard Hurst, *Law and the Conditions of Freedom in the Nineteenth-Century United States* (Madison: University of Wisconsin Press, 1956); Morton J. Horwitz, *The Transformation of American Law, 1780–1860* (Cambridge, MA: Harvard University Press, 1977). Recent work sees law as constitutive of these relationships. For particularly compelling examples see Christine Desan, *Making Money: Coin, Currency, and the Coming of Capitalism* (Oxford: Oxford University Press, 2015); Bruce H. Mann, *Neighbors and Strangers: Law and Community in Early Connecticut* (Chapel Hill: University of North Carolina Press, 1987); Claire Priest, *Credit Nation: Property Laws and Institutions in Early America* (Princeton, NJ: Princeton University Press, 2021); Christopher L. Tomlins, *Law, Labor, and Ideology in the Early American Republic* (New York: Cambridge University Press, 1993). Yet law has been peripheral in the established body of scholarship in early American history, associated with scholars such as Gary Nash and Alfred E. Young, that has focused on the economic lives of those on the margins. Recent work has joined these concerns to the new history of capitalism and turned to the ways those people navigated the economy. For influential examples, see Seth Rockman, *Scraping By: Wage Labor, Slavery, and Survival in Early Baltimore* (Baltimore: Johns Hopkins University Press, 2009); Wendy A. Woloson, *In Hock: Pawning in America from Independence through the Great Depression* (Chicago: University of Chicago Press, 2009). For insightful collections of work by historians in this field, see Brian P. Luskey and Wendy A. Woloson, eds., *Capitalism by Gaslight: Illuminating the Economy of Nineteenth Century America* (Philadelphia: University of Pennsylvania Press, 2015); Sven Beckert and Seth Rockman, eds., *Slavery's Capitalism: A New History of America's Economic Development* (Pennsylvania: University of Pennsylvania Press, 2016). Scholarship on early America has reframed the extent of women's economic participation in similar ways: Patricia Cleary, *Elizabeth Murray: A Woman's Pursuit of Independence in Eighteenth-Century America* (Amherst: University of Massachusetts Press, 2000); ; Sara T. Damiano, *To Her Credit: Women, Finance, and the Law in Eighteenth-Century New England Cities* (Baltimore: Johns Hopkins University Press, 2021); Sheryllynne Haggerty, *The British-Atlantic Trading Community 1760–1810: Men, Women, and the Distribution of Goods* (Leiden: Brill, 2006); Ellen Hartigan-O'Connor, *The Ties That Buy: Women and Commerce in*

Revolutionary America (Philadelphia: University of Pennsylvania Press, 2009); Susanah Shaw Romney, *New Netherland Connections: Intimate Networks and Atlantic Ties in Seventeenth-Century America* (Chapel Hill: University of North Carolina Press, 2014); Linda L. Sturtz, *Within Her Power: Propertied Women in Colonial Virginia* (New York: Routledge, 2002); Serena Zabin, *Dangerous Economies: Status and Commerce in Imperial New York* (Philadelphia: University of Pennsylvania Press, 2009). For a particularly insightful analysis that critiques work in the history of capitalism from the perspective of this recent scholarship on women and gender, see Ellen Hartigan-O'Connor, "Gender's Value in the History of Capitalism," *Journal of the Early Republic* 36 (Winter 2016): 613–53, and Hartigan-O'Connor, "The Personal is Political Economy," *Journal of the Early Republic* 36 (Summer 2016): 335–41. Also see Alexandra J. Finley, *An Intimate Economy: Enslaved Women, Work, and America's Domestic Slave Trade* (Chapel Hill: University of North Carolina Press, 2020).

17. For the portrayal of white women and textiles, see Miller, *The Needle's Eye*; Miller, *Betsy Ross*; Ulrich, *Age of Homespun*. For African Americans, see Hilliard, *Masters, Slaves, and Exchange*; Michael D. Thompson, "'Some Rascally Business': Thieving Slaves, Unscrupulous Whites, and Charleston's Illicit Waterfront Trade," in *Capitalism by Gaslight: Illuminating the Economy of Nineteenth Century America*, ed. Brian P. Luskey and Wendy A. Woloson (Philadelphia: University of Pennsylvania Press, 2015), 150–67; although Thompson deals primarily with the trade in commodities, the discourse surrounding the issue is similar. For the clothing trade in cities, Robert J. Gamble, "The Promiscuous Economy: Cultural and Commercial Geographies of Secondhand in the Antebellum City," 31–52, and Adam Mendelsohn, "The Rag Race: Jewish Secondhand Clothing Dealers in England and America," 76–92; both in Luskey and Woloson, *Capitalism by Gaslight*.

18. The term "governing order" borrows from an important strand of scholarship in legal history that views law as an arena of governance that constitutes and is constituted by social relationships, not just a useful instrument available primarily to the powerful to pursue individual interests. For foundational literature, see Robert W. Gordon, "Critical Legal Histories," *Stanford Law Review* 36 (Jan. 1984): 56–107; Michael Grossberg, *A Judgment for Solomon: The d'Hauteville Case and Legal Experience in Antebellum America* (New York: Cambridge University Press, 1996); Hendrik Hartog, "Pigs and Positivism," *Wisconsin Law Review* 4 (July 1985): 899–935. Strong currents in this field have emphasized people's familiarity with law and their access to the legal system, despite their legal disabilities. Building on that historiography, recent work reframed our understanding of the legal system itself, putting more focus on ordinary people, local venues, continuities from the colonial past, and conflicts among jurisdictions—local, state, and federal—that resulted from federalism. For an overview of recent work in the early nineteenth century, see Edwards, "Sarah Allingham's Sheet and Other Lessons from Legal History." In "Federalism Anew," *American Journal of Legal History* 56 (2016): 128–38, Karen Tani and Sarah Mayeux describe similar trends in the work on the twentieth century as "federalism in practice." Work that has broadened our view of federalism and the operation of law within it include Laura F. Edwards, *The People and Their Peace: Legal Culture and the Transformation of*

Inequality in the Post-Revolutionary South (Chapel Hill: University of North Carolina Press, 2009); Ariela J. Gross, *Double Character: Slavery and Mastery in the Antebellum Southern Courtroom* (Princeton, NJ: Princeton University Press, 2000); Martha S. Jones, *Birthright Citizens: A History of Race and Rights in Antebellum America* (New York: Cambridge University Press, 2018); Alison LaCroix, *The Ideological Origins of American Federalism* (Cambridge, MA: Harvard University Press, 2010); William J. Novak, *The People's Welfare: Law and Regulation in Nineteenth-Century America* (Chapel Hill: University of North Carolina Press, 1996); Farah Peterson, "Interpretation as Statecraft: Chancellor Kent and the Collaborative Era of American Statutory Interpretation," *Maryland Law Review* 77 (2018): 712–73; Peterson, "Constitutionalism in Unexpected Places," *Virginia Law Review* 106 (May 2020): 559–609; Karen M. Tani, *States of Dependency: Welfare, Rights, and American Governance, 1935–1972* (New York: Cambridge University Press, 2016); Tomlins, Law, Labor, and Ideology. Also see Christopher L. Tomlins and Bruce H. Mann, eds., *The Many Legalities of Early America* (Chapel Hill: University of North Carolina Press, 2001). Work outside legal history is also moving in similar directions. See, for instance, Michael A. Blaakman, "The Marketplace of American Federalism: Land Speculation across State Lines in the Early Republic," *Journal of American History* 107 (December 2020): 583–608; Andrew Shankman, "Toward a Social History of Federalism: The State and Capitalism To and From the American Revolution," *Journal of the Early American Republic* 37 (Winter 2017): 615–53.

19. Legal historians have emphasized people's engagement in law in a variety of ways, in a variety of settings, even in the absence of rights. One strand emphasizes the dynamics of a legal system in which people without rights shaped the law: Edwards, *People and Their Peace*; Alejandro de la Fuente and Ariela Gross, *Becoming Free, Becoming Black: Race, Freedom, and Law in Cuba, Virginia, and Louisiana* (Cambridge: Cambridge University Press, 2020); Gross, *Double Character*; Grossberg, *A Judgment for Solomon*; Jones, *Birthright Citizens*; Hendrik Hartog, *Man and Wife in America: A History* (Cambridge, MA: Harvard University Press, 2000); Kate Masur, *An Example for All the Land: Emancipation and the Struggle Over Equality in Washington, D.C.* (Chapel Hill: University of North Carolina Press, 2010); Dylan Penningroth, *The Claims of Kinfolk: African American Property and Community in the Nineteenth-Century South* (Chapel Hill: University of North Carolina Press, 2003); Penningroth, "Everyday Use: A History of Civil Rights in Black Churches," *Journal of American History* 107 (March 2021): 871-98; Yvonne Pitts, *Family, Law, and Inheritance in America: A Social and Legal History of Nineteenth-Century Kentucky* (Cambridge: Cambridge University Press, 2013); Honor Sachs, "'Freedom by a Judgment': The Legal History of an Afro-Indian Family," *Law and History Review* 30 (February 2012): 173–203; Felicity Turner, *Proving Pregnancy: Gender, Law, and Medical Knowledge in Nineteenth-Century America* (Chapel Hill: University of North Carolina Press, forthcoming 2022); Barbara Y. Welke, *Recasting American Liberty: Gender, Race, Law, and the Railroad Revolution, 1865–1920* (New York: Cambridge University Press, 2001). Another strand emphasizes people's access to and use of the law through existing mechanisms: Meggan Cashwell,

"Rethinking Violence, Legal Culture, and Community in New York City, 1785–1826 (Ph.D. diss., Duke University, 2019); Kelly Kennington, *In the Shadow of Dred Scott: St. Louis Freedom Suits and the Legal Culture of Slavery in Antebellum America* (Athens: University of Georgia Press, 2017); Anne Twitty, *Before Dred Scott: Slavery and Legal Culture in America's Confluence, 1787–1857* (New York: Cambridge University Press, 2016); Kimberly M. Welch, *Black Litigants in the Antebellum American South* (Chapel Hill: University of North Carolina Press, 2018).

20. The book uses the terms "slave," "free black," "wife," "servant," "husband," "master," and "mistress" when referring to legal categories that people occupied. In other places, when people's actions are less clearly connected to law or I am clearly referring to what people were doing, I use the terms "enslaved people," "free Blacks", "African Americans," "married women," "the working poor," "enslavers," and "people who occupied the legal category of . . ." although even those terms underscore the fact that personal identities and social relations are never entirely separate from the law.

21. Historical fields—women's history, the history of slavery, African American history, labor history—reflect the importance of legal restrictions in defining the identity and experience of marginalized people in the nineteenth century. The work on women's activism in the first half of the nineteenth century follows a trajectory similar to that in other fields, emphasizing the denial of rights and responses to that denial. See for instance Nancy F. Cott, *The Bonds of Womanhood: "Woman's Sphere" in New England, 1780–1835* (New Haven, CT: Yale University Press, 1977); Carol Ellen DuBois, *Feminism and Suffrage: The Emergence of Independent Women's Movement in America, 1848–1869* (Ithaca, NY: Cornell University Press, 1978); Nancy A. Hewitt, *Women's Activism and Social Change: Rochester, New York, 1822–1872* (Ithaca, NY: Cornell University Press, 1982); Linda K. Kerber, *No Constitutional Right to Be Ladies: Women and the Obligations of Citizenship* (New York: Hill & Wang, 1998); Mary P. Ryan, *Cradle of the Middle Class: The Family in Oneida County, New York, 1790–1865* (New York: Cambridge University Press, 1981); Rosemarie Zagarri, *Revolutionary Backlash: Women and Politics in the Early American Republic* (Philadelphia: University of Pennsylvania Press, 2007). For an insightful critique of activists' framing of the issues, see Lisa Tetrault, *The Myth of Seneca Falls: Memory and the Women's Suffrage Movement, 1848–1898* (Chapel Hill: University of North Carolina Press, 2014). Given that Blackstonian conceptions of coverture are often assumed to be an expression of past practices, which were challenged and ultimately undermined by the liberal principals embodied in the women's movement, assumptions about free women's legal incapacities have particular salience in the literature on the slave South, an area presumed to be behind other areas of the country in legal and political development. Assumptions about all women's exclusion from law in this region remain embedded even within recent scholarship, inspired by feminist theory, which focuses on the gendered dynamics of power in the region and folds the legal incapacity of both married women and all enslaved people into the larger framework of dependency. For the clearest statement of that link, see Elizabeth Fox-Genovese, *Within the Plantation Household: Women in the Old South* (Chapel Hill: University of North Carolina Press, 1988). The assumptions about free women's

legal incapacity and their distance from law and governing institutions still pervade the literature. I have relied on them myself: Laura F. Edwards, *Gendered Strife and Confusion: The Political Culture of Reconstruction* (Urbana: University of Illinois Press, 1997). Also see Peter Bardaglio, *Reconstructing the Household: Families, Sex, and the Law in the Nineteenth-Century South* (Chapel Hill: University of North Carolina Press, 1995); Nancy D. Bercaw, *Gendered Freedoms: Race, Rights, and the Politics of Household in the Delta, 1861–1875* (Gainesville: University Press of Florida, 2003); Victoria Bynum, *Unruly Women: The Politics of Social and Sexual Control in the Old South* (Chapel Hill: University of North Carolina Press, 1992); Stephanie McCurry, *Masters of Small Worlds: Yeoman Households, Gender Relations, and the Political Culture of the Antebellum South Carolina Low Country* (New York: Oxford University Press, 1995); McCurry, *Confederate Reckoning: Power and Politics in the Civil War South* (Cambridge, MA: Harvard University Press, 2010); Amy Dru Stanley, *From Bondage to Contract: Wage Labor, Marriage, and the Market in the Age of Slave Emancipation* (New York: Cambridge University Press, 1998).

22. This framework lies at the center of classic works and still frames historiographical debates about the difference between slave states in the South and free states in the North as well as the trajectory of change in the nineteenth-century United States more generally. See, for instance, Eugene D. Genovese, *Roll, Jordan, Roll: The World the Slaves Made* (New York: Vintage, 1976); William J. Novak, "The Legal Transformation of Citizenship in Nineteenth-Century America," in *The Democratic Experiment: New Directions in American Political History*, ed. Meg Jacobs, William J. Novak, and Julian E. Zelizer (Princeton, NJ: Princeton University Press, 2003), 85–119; Carole Pateman, *The Sexual Contract* (Stanford, CA: Stanford University Press, 1988); Rogers M. Smith, *Civic Ideals: Conflicting Visions of Citizenship in U.S. History* (New Haven, CT: Yale University Press, 1997). Work on women and gender extended the paradigm in the 1990s to focus on the analogies among all relations of domestic dependency, thereby connecting the restrictions on wives and all women to other forms of subordination experienced by men.

Part 1

1. For colonial North Americans' dependence on imported cloth, see Linda Baumgarten, "Plains, Plaid, and Cotton: Woolens for Slave Clothing," *Ars Textrina* 15 (1991): 203–22; Linda Baumgarten and Kimberly Smith Ivey, "Textiles: Trade and Fashions," *Magazine Antiques* 159 (January 2001): 226–33; Carson, "The Consumer Revolution in Colonial British America"; Arthur Harrison Cole, *The American Wool Manufacture* (Cambridge, MA: Harvard University Press, 1926), 48–55. Also see Ulrich, *The Age of Homespun*, particularly 12–40, although she argues that New England women began producing more cloth in the decades preceding the Revolution.
2. Montgomery, *Textiles in America*; Bean, *Yankee India*, esp. 31–32, 74–77.
3. Peck, *Interwoven Globe*; Postrel, *The Fabric of Civilization*.

4. Cotton and the exploitative labor systems associated with it are particularly well developed in the context of US history. See Baptist, *The Half Has Never Been Told*; Beckert, *Empire of Cotton*; Gregory P. Downs, *The Second American Revolution: The Civil War-Era Struggle over Cuba and the Rebirth of the American Republic* (Chapel Hill: University of North Carolina Press, 2019); Johnson, *River of Dark Dreams*. But work on the global textile trade situates North America within broader dynamics that reached around the globe. See DuPlessis, *The Material Atlantic*; Eaton, *Printed Textiles*; Lemire, *Global Trade*; Peck, *Interwoven Globe*; Montgomery, *Textiles in America*; Vicente, *Clothing the Spanish Empire*.

5. For sumptuary laws and their increasing ineffectiveness, see DuPlessis, *The Material Atlantic*; Walker, *Exquisite Slaves*, 20–42; Lemire, *Fashion's Favourite*; Vicente, *Clothing the Spanish Empire*, 65–83. The plethora and repeated passage of sumptuary laws also indicates that they did not solve the problem of people dressing "above their station."

6. British policy not only mandated that all exports be landed in British ports before passage to the colonies but also attempted to limit domestic textile production within the colonies. Lawmakers were particularly concerned with wool, a central pillar of the British economy. See Arthur Harrison Cole, *The American Wool Manufacture* (Cambridge, MA: Harvard University Press, 1926), 3–33; Adrienne D. Hood, *The Weaver's Craft: Cloth, Commerce, and Industry in Early Pennsylvania* (Philadelphia: University of Pennsylvania Press, 2003), 40–139. While Cole tends to characterize textile production as an extension of household production, separate from the market, Hood links it to the larger, commercial market. For the importance of goods and merchants in the American Revolution, see for instance: T. H. Breen, *The Marketplace of Revolution: How Consumer Politics Shaped American Independence* (New York: Oxford University Press, 2004); Cathy D. Matson, *Merchants and Empire: Trading in Colonial New York* (Baltimore: Johns Hopkins University Press, 1998); Edmund Morgan, *The Birth of the Republic, 1763–1789*, rev. ed. (Chicago: University of Chicago Press, 1977). The importance of cotton production and the importation of textiles as well as the manufacture of cloth and clothing runs through much of the literature on the period between the Revolution and the Civil War. For a fascinating analysis of the importance of wool production to the national interest, see Margaret Byrd Adams Rasmussen, "Waging War with Wool: Thomas Jefferson's Campaign for American Commercial Independence from England," *Material Culture* 41 (Spring 2009): 17–37. For the importance of merchants and manufacturers to the development of the US federal government in particular, see Hannah Farber, "Sailing on Paper: The Embellished Bill of Lading in the Material Atlantic, 1720–1864," *Early American Studies* 17 (Winter 2019): 37–83; Farber, "State-Building after War's End: A Government Financier Adjusts his Portfolio for Peace," *Journal of the Early Republic* 38 (Spring 2018): 67–76; Gautham Rao, *National Duties: Custom Houses and the Making of the American State* (Chicago: University of Chicago Press, 2016).

7. After the Revolution, merchants eagerly moved into areas of the globe that they had been excluded from before. As the business correspondence of the Brown Family and

the records of the various vessels in which they had interests indicate, this mercantile family traded with China and India as well as various places in the Caribbean, Europe, South America, and Africa; Brown Family Business Records, JCB. The Browns' reach was capacious because they were such a large firm, but smaller businesses also had wide-reaching global networks. Watson and Paul, of Philadelphia, had business dealings in Livorno, Genoa, Amsterdam, Antwerp, Marseilles, and Bordeaux; Watson and Paul Business Papers, LCP; the merchant identified as Robinson, who begins chapter 3, had dealings in China, England, the Caribbean, and the interior of North America. Also see Bean, *Yankee India*; James B. Hedges, *The Browns of Providence Plantations: Colonial Years* (Cambridge, MA: Harvard University Press, 1952), 240–332. As the example of the Browns suggests, merchants went into textile production and other business ventures. For other examples, see Nathan Appleton, a dry goods merchant who invested in textile manufacturing with Francis Cabot Lowell, Appleton Family Papers; Amos Adams Lawrence, who set up a commission merchant business with Robert M. Mason, Amos Adams Lawrence Papers; both in MSH. Both men had their hands in state and national politics.

8. For Franklin, see Jill Lepore, *Book of Ages: The Life and Opinions of Jane Franklin* (New York: Knopf, 2013). For the close alignment of merchants' interests and the policies of the new republic, see Farber, "State-Building After War's End." For the ways state leaders defined the public good in terms of their own economic interests, see Mandy Cooper, "Cultures of Emotion: Families, Friends, and the Making of the United States" (PhD diss., Duke University, 2018). For conflicts within and over textile mills, see Thomas Dublin: *Women at Work: The Transformation of Work and Community in Lowell, Massachusetts, 1826–1860* (New York: Columbia University Press, 1979); Gary Kulik, "Dams, Fish, and Farmers: Defense of Public Rights in Eighteenth-Century Rhode Island, in *The Countryside in the Age of Capitalist Transformation: Essays in the Social History of Rural America*, ed. Steven Hahn and Jonathan Prude (Chapel Hill: University of North Carolina Press, 1985), 25–50; Morton J. Horowitz, *The Transformation of American Law, 1780–1860* (Cambridge, MA: Harvard University Press, 1977), 40–42; Jonathan Prude, *The Coming of the Industrial Order: Town and Factory Life in Rural Massachusetts, 1810–1860* (New York: Cambridge University Press, 1983), 34–64. Historians also have charted profound conflicts over labor laws and regulation, which were linked to changes in the organization of work more broadly. See, in particular, Tomlins, *Law, Labor, and Ideology*. For the importance of cotton production in the spread of slavery into the Southwest as well as the political conflicts leading up to the Civil War, see Beckert, *Empire of Cotton*; Johnson, *River of Dark Dreams*; Adam Rothman, *Slave Country: American Expansion and the Origins of the Deep South* (Cambridge, MA: Harvard University Press, 2005). For the political debates leading up to the Nullification Crisis and secession, see Manisha Sinha, *The Counter-Revolution of Slavery: Politics and Ideology in Antebellum South Carolina* (Chapel Hill: University of North Carolina Press, 2000).

9. Account book (Rebecca Coles), 1795–1800, Samuel Smith Papers, box 1, #1729, UV.

Chapter 1

1. *State v. Brummer*, #142, Trial Papers, Court of Magistrates and Freeholders, Anderson County, SCDAH.
2. References to the ability of people without property rights to keep and trade cloth and clothing are common in the historiography: Baumgarten, "Plains, Plaid, and Cotton"; DuPlessis, *The Material Atlantic*, esp. 125–63; Hilliard, *Masters, Slaves, and Exchange*; Penelope Lane, "Work on the Margins: Poor Women and the Informal Economy of Eighteenth- and Early Nineteenth-Century Leicestershire," *Midland History* 22 (1997): 85–99; Beverly Lemire, "The Theft of Clothes and Popular Consumerism in Early Modern England," *Journal of Social History* 24 (Winter 1990): 255–76; Lynn MacKay, "Why They Stole: Women in the Old Bailey, 1779-1798," *Journal of Social History* 32 (Spring 1999): 623–39; Ulrich, *Age of Homespun*, 108–41, 191–206; Melanie Tebbutt, *Making Ends Meet: Pawnbroking and Working-Class Credit* (New York: St. Martin's, 1983), 37–67; Woloson, *In Hock*, esp. 91–94; Garthine Walker, "Women, Theft and the World of Stolen Goods," in *Women, Crime, and the Courts in Early Modern England*, ed. Jennifer Kermode and Garthine Walker (Chapel Hill: University of North Carolina Press, 1994), 81–105; Walker, *Exquisite Slaves*. While historians have explored the exchange of textiles, they have not explored the legal underpinnings that enabled all those exchanges, which appear as exceptions to the law, not manifestations of it. And so the ever-widening dissemination of cloth has been limited to the realm of economic and cultural history, separate from the legal changes that resulted from the Revolution.
3. For the Revolution and its radical potential reform as well the barriers to it, see for instance Terry Bouton, *Taming Democracy: "The People," the Founders, and the Troubled Ending of the American Revolution* (New York: Oxford University Press, 2007); Cott, *The Bonds of Womanhood*; Dublin, *Women and Work*; de la Fuente and Gross, *Becoming Free, Becoming Black*; Van E. Gosse, *The First Reconstruction: Black Politics in America, from the Revolution to the Civil War* (Chapel Hill: University of North Carolina Press, 2020); Van E. Gosse and David Waldstreicher, eds., *Revolutions and Reconstructions: Black Politics in the Long Nineteenth Century* (Philadelphia: University of Pennsylvania Press, 2020); Sarah L. H. Gronningsater, *The Arc of Abolition: The Children of Gradual Emancipation and the Origins of National Freedom* (Philadelphia: University of Pennsylvania Press, forthcoming); Gronningsater, "'Expressly Recognized by Our Election Laws': Certificates of Freedom and the Multiple Fates of Black Citizenship in the Early Republic," *William and Mary Quarterly* 75 (July 2018): 465–506; Woody Holton, *Unruly Americans and the Origins of the Constitution* (New York: Hill & Wang, 2007); Holton, *Forced Founders: Indians, Debtors, Slaves, and the Making of the American Revolution in Virginia* (Chapel Hill: University of North Carolina Press, 1999); Martha S. Jones, *All Bound Up Together: The Woman Question in African American Public Culture, 1830-1900* (Baltimore: Johns Hopkins University Press, 2007); Jones, *Birthright Citizens*; Stephen Kantrowitz, *More than Freedom: Fighting for Black Citizenship in a White Republic, 1829-1889* (New York: Penguin, 2012); Linda K. Kerber, *Women of the Republic: Intellect and*

Ideology in Revolutionary America (Chapel Hill: University of North Carolina Press, 1980); Kerber, *No Constitutional Right to be Ladies*; Kate Masur, "State Sovereignty and Migration before Reconstruction," *Journal of the Civil War Era* 9 (December 2019): 588–611; Masur, *Until Justice Be Done: America's First Civil Rights Movement, From the Revolution to Reconstruction* (New York: Norton, 2020); Gary B. Nash, *The Forgotten Fifth: African Americans in the Age of Revolution* (Cambridge, MA: Harvard University Press, 2006); Honor Sachs, *Home Rule: Households, Manhood, and National Expansion on the Eighteenth-Century Kentucky Frontier* (New Haven, CT: Yale University Press, 2015); Alfred F. Young, *The Shoemaker and the Tea Party: Memory and the American Revolution* (Boston: Beacon, 1999); Zagarri, *Revolutionary Backlash*.

4. William Blackstone, *Commentaries on the Laws of England* (1765–69; repr., Chicago: University of Chicago Press, 1979),1:430. For the point about Blackstone's recasting of coverture, see Holly Brewer, "The Transformation of Domestic Law," in *The Cambridge History of Law in America*, ed. Christopher L. Tomlins and Michael Grossberg (New York: Cambridge University Press, 2008), 1:288–323. Also see Damiano, *To Her Credit*. Treatise writers adopted Blackstone early on, especially when it came to domestic relations. In some cases, treatises accentuated the rights of husband over wife, an emphasis that became more prounounced over time, as discussed in chapters 10, 11, and 12. See, for instance, the difference between Zephaniah Swift, *A System of Laws of the State of Connecticut* (Windham, CT: 1795), 1:195–96, and Henry Dutton, *A Revision of Swift's Digest of the Laws of Connecticut: Assisted by N. A. Cowdrey* (New Haven, CT: 1851), 1:24–27. Blackstone moved into magistrates' manuals slowly, although the influence was evident by the 1830s and, in some cases, before; see Edwards, "The Material Conditions of Dependency." Mary Ritter Beard raised questions about the extent of Blackstonian conceptions of coverture in Mary Ritter Beard, *Women as Force in History: A Study of Traditions and Realities* (New York: Macmillan, 1946). Recent work also emphasizes the development of expansive notions of patriarchal authority and the privacy of the domestic space over time, particularly in the eighteenth and nineteenth centuries. See Susan Dwyer Amussen, "'Being Stirred to Much Unquietness': Violence and Domestic Violence in Early Modern England," *Journal of Women's History* 6 (Summer 1994): 70–89; Holly Brewer, *By Birth or Consent: Children, Law, and the Anglo-American Revolution in Authority* (Chapel Hill: University of North Carolina Press, 2005); Brewer, "Transformation of Domestic Law"; Edwards, *People and Their Peace*; Kerber, "Why Diamonds"; Marylynn Salmon, *Women and the Law of Property in Early America* (Chapel Hill: University of North Carolina Press, 1986); Reva B. Siegel, "'The Rule of Love': Wife Beating as Prerogative and Privacy," *Yale Law Journal* 105 (June 1996): 2117–2206. Conceptions of patriarchal power as an individual right paralleled more absolute notions of private property. See Holly Brewer, "Entailing Aristocracy in Colonial Virginia: 'Ancient Feudal Restraints' and Revolutionary Reforms," *William and Mary Quarterly* 54 (1997): 307–46; Christopher Michael Curtis, *Jefferson's Freeholders and the Politics of Ownership in the Old Dominion* (New York: Cambridge University Press, 2012); Priest, *Credit Nation*. As recent work has emphasized, married women

still controlled a range of property through legal workarounds: Cooper, "Cultures of Emotion"; Stephanie Jones-Rogers. *They Were Her Property: White Women as Slave Owners in the American South* (New Haven, CT: Yale University Press, 2019); Suzanne Lebsock, *The Free Women of Petersburg: Status and Culture in a Southern Town, 1784-1860* (New York: Norton, 1984), pp. 54-86; Marylynn Salmon, "Women and Property in South Carolina: The Evidence from Marriage Settlements, 1730–1830," *William and Mary Quarterly* 39 (October 1982): 655–85. But they did not own that property through the possession of property rights. Despite all the scholarship complicating simplistic views of coverture, historians still regularly use Blackstone's work as an accurate summary of legal practices from the beginning of colonial settlement through the early years of the new republic, particularly when it comes to coverture and married women. Joan R. Gundersen and Gwen Victor Gampel, in "Married Women's Legal Status in Eighteenth-Century New York and Virginia," *William and Mary Quarterly* 39 (January 1982): 114–34.

5. For analogies across relations of domestic dependency, see James Kent, *Commentaries on American Law* (New York: 1827), vol. 2; Tapping Reeve, *Law of Baron and Femme; of Parent and Child; of Guardian and Ward; of Master and Servant; and of the Powers of Court of Chancery* (New Haven, CT: 1816); Reeve, *Law of Baron and Femme* (Albany, NY: 1862); Swift, *A System of Laws* (1795); Swift, *A System of Laws of the State of Connecticut*, rev. ed. (New Haven, CT: 1822); St. George Tucker, ed., *Blackstone's Commentaries* (Philadelphia: 1803), vol. 1, pt. 2. For wage laborers, see Tomlins, *Law, Labor, and Ideolog*. Slavery was not included within the treatises published in free states, but the analogies obtained in invocations of paternalism. The classic statement on the legal changes in the master/slave relationship is Genovese, *Roll, Jordan, Roll*. For the ramifications, see Barbara Young Welke, *Law and the Borders of Belonging in the Long Nineteenth Century United States* (New York: Cambridge University Press, 2010).

6. For cotton and slavery, see Baptist, *The Half Has Never Been Told*; Beckert, *Empire of Cotton*; Johnson, *River of Dark Dreams*; Damian Alan Pargas, *Slavery and Forced Migration in the Antebellum South* (New York: Cambridge University Press, 2015); Rothman, *Slave Country*. For the transformation of slavery, with increasing restrictions under the guise of paternalism, see Genovese, *Roll, Jordan, Roll*; Jeffrey Robert Young, *Domesticating Slavery: The Master Class in Georgia and South Carolina, 1670–1837* (Chapel Hill: University of North Carolina Press, 1999).

7. Christopher James Bonner, *Remaking the Republic: Black Politics and the Creation of American Citizenship* (Philadelphia: University of Pennsylvania Press, 2020); John Hope Franklin, *The Free Negro in North Carolina, 1790–1860* (1943; repr., New York: Russell & Russell, 1969); de la Fuente and Gross, *Becoming Free, Becoming Black*; Gosse, "In the Woodpile: Negro Electors in the First Reconstruction," in *Revolutions and Reconstructions: Black Politics in the Long Nineteenth Century* (Philadelphia: University of Pennsylvania Press, 2020), 66–83; Gosse, *The First Reconstruction*; Gronningsater, "Practicing Formal Politics without the Vote: Black New Yorkers in the Aftermath of 1821," in *Revolutions and Reconstructions: Black Politics in the Long Nineteenth Century* (Philadelphia: University of Pennsylvania Press, 2020), 116–38;

Gross, *What Blood Won't Tell: A History of Race on Trial in America* (Cambridge, MA: Harvard University Press, 2008); Leslie M. Harris, *In the Shadow of Slavery: African Americans in New York City, 1626-1863* (Chicago: University of Chicago Press, 2003); Scott Heerman, *The Alchemy of Slavery: Human Bondage and Emancipation in the Illinois Country, 1730-1865* (Philadelphia: University of Pennsylvania Press, 2018); Jones, *Birthright Citizens*; Kantrowitz, *More than Freedom*; Ted Maris-Wolf, *Free Blacks and Re-Enslavement Law in Antebellum Virginia* (Chapel Hill: University of North Carolina Press, 2015); Masur, "State Sovereignty and Migration"; Masur, *Until Justice Be Done*; Nash, *The Forgotten Fifth*; Sachs, "Freedom by a Judgment"; Samantha Seeley, "Freedom and the Politics of Migration After the American Revolution" in *Revolutions and Reconstructions: Black Politics in the Long Nineteenth Century* (Philadelphia: University of Pennsylvania Press, 2020), 84-101; Kirt Von Daacke, *Freedom Has a Face: Race, Identity, and Community in Jefferson's Virginia* (Charlottesville: University Press of Virginia, 2012). For Native Americans, see for instance Gregory Ablavsky, "Species of Sovereignty: Native Nationhood, the United States, and International Law, 1783-1795," *Journal of American History* 106 (December 2019): 591-613; Stuart Banner, *How the Indians Lost Their Land: Law and Power on the Frontier* (Cambridge, MA: Harvard University Press, 2005); Lisa Ford, *Settler Sovereignty: Jurisdiction and Indigenous People in America and Australia, 1788-1836* (Cambridge, MA: Harvard, University Press, 2010); Deborah A. Rosen, *Border Law: The First Seminole War and American Nationhood* (Cambridge, MA: Harvard University Press, 2015); Leonard J. Sadosky, *Revolutionary Negotiations: Indians, Empires, and Diplomats in the Founding of America* (Charlottesville: University of Virginia Press, 2009).

8. Strikes and labor unrest in the decades before the Civil War are telling: Blewett, *Men, Women, and Work*; Dublin, *Women and Work*; Cynthia J. Shelton, *The Mills of Manayunk: Industrialization and Social Conflict in the Philadelphia Region, 1787-1837* (Baltimore: Johns Hopkins University Press, 1986); Sean Wilentz, *Chants Democratic: New York City and the Rise of the American Working Class, 1788-1850* (New York: Oxford University Press, 1984). For the deterioration in the legal status of workers and propertyless people, see William E. Forbath, "The Ambiguities of Free Labor: Labor and the Law in the Gilded Age," *Wisconsin Law Review* 4 (1985): 767-817; Sachs, *Home Rule*, 42-70; Amy Dru Stanley, "Beggars Can't Be Choosers: Compulsion and Contract in Postbellum America," *Journal of American History* 78 (March 1992): 1265-93; Stanley, *From Bondage to Contract*; Tomlins, *Law, Labor, and Ideology in the Early Republic*; Robert J. Steinfeld, *Coercion, Contract, and Free Labor in the Nineteenth Century* (New York: Cambridge University Press, 2001).

9. Blackstone, *Commentaries on the Laws of England*, 2:433-39; by contrast, see 1:421-33. For women's control of paraphernalia and their ability to trade for necessaries, see Clare Haru Crowston, "Family Affairs: Wives, Credit, Consumption and the Law in Old Regime France," in *Family, Gender, and Law in Early Modern France*, ed. Suzanne Desan and Jeffrey Merrick (University Park: Pennsylvania State University Press, 2009), 62-100; Crowston, *Credit, Fashion, and Sex*, 283-315; Barbara Diefendorf, "Women and Property in Ancien Régime France: Theory and Practice in Dauphiné

and Paris," in *Early Modern Conceptions of Property*, ed. John Brewer and Susan Staves (London: Routledge, 1995), 170–93; Amy Louise Erickson, *Women and Property in Early Modern England* (New York: Routledge, 1993), 26; Margot Finn, "Women, Consumption and Coverture in England, c. 1760–1860," *Historical Journal* 39 (Sept. 1996): 703–22. For servants, whose claims lay in part in the fact that they were often paid in clothing, see Lane, "Work on the Margins"; Lemire, "The Theft of Clothes"; John Styles, "Involuntary Consumers? Servants and Their Clothes in Eighteenth-Century England," *Textile History* 33, no. 1 (2002): 9–21. For an example of a servant taking her clothing, see Amanda Vickery, *The Gentleman's Daughter: Women's Lives in Georgian England* (New Haven, CT: Yale University Press, 1998), 143–44.

10. Clare Crowston argues that French law gave women opportunities to trade in textiles, given the broad leeway given to married women to buy necessaries: Crowston, "Family Affairs, Wives"; Crowston, *Credit, Fashion, and Sex*, 283–315. For Mary Alexander's business, see Mary Alexander to James Nevison, September 17, 1757; Mary Alexander to William McCollom, October 10, 1756; Mary Alexander to David Barclary and Sons, October 6, 1748; all in box 10, folder 1. David Barclay and Sons to Mary Alexander, March 14, 1758, May 31, 1758, August 8, 1758, December 9, 1758, March 24, 1759, June 22, 1759; all in box 10, folder 3. Alexander was training her niece as a trader as well; Catherine Alexander to Mary Alexander, February 26, 1749, letters received, box 10, folder 3. All in Alexander Papers, NYHS. For Alexander and women traders in New York, also see Haulman, *The Politics of Fashion*, 41–46; Eaton, *Printed Textiles*, 41–55; Jean Jordan, "Women Merchants in Colonial New York," *New York History* 58 (1977): 416–18; Serena Zabin, "Women's Trading Networks and Dangerous Economies in Eighteenth-Century New York City," *Early American Studies* 4 (Fall 2006): 291–321; Zabin, *Dangerous Economies*.

11. Catherine Alexander to Mary Alexander, February 26, 1749, letters received, box 10, folder 3, Alexander Papers, NYHS. For English recognition of Dutch law, see Oliver Rink, "Life in New Netherland," 61–86, and Ronald W. Howard, "From Proprietary Colony to Royal Province," 113–29, both in *The Empire State: A History of New York*, ed. Milton N. Klein (Ithaca, NY: Cornell University Press, 2005). The classic work on women and the law is David E. Narrett, "Dutch Customs of Inheritance, Women, and the Law in Colonial New York City," in *Authority and Resistance in Early New York*, ed. William Pencak and Conrad Wright (New York: New York Historical Society, 1988), 27–55, and Narrett, "Men's Wills and Women's Property Rights in Colonial New York," in *Women in the Age of the American Revolution*, ed. Ronald Hoffman and Peter J. Albert (Charlottesville: University of Virginia Press, 1989), 91–133. Also see Martha Dickinson Shattuck, "Women and Trade in New Netherlands," *Itinerario* 18, no. 2 (July 1994): 40–49. For the broader context, see Shaw, *New Netherland Connections*.

12. For the adoption of the customary practices in London, see Kent, *Commentaries*, 136. Swift took a dim view of such practices and saw no need for them in the US context; see esp. Zephaniah Swift, *A System of Laws of the State of Connecticut* (1795), 1:200. As Hartigan-O'Connor notes in *The Ties That Buy*, 114, the women in her study were more likely to trade in cloth because of the Anglo-American legal restrictions on other forms of property. The literature is filled with examples of women trading in textiles:

Sturtz, *Within Her Power*, 134–40; Ulrich, *Age of Homespun*; Patricia Cleary, "'She Will Be in the Shop': Women's Sphere of Trade in Eighteenth-Century Philadelphia and New York," *Pennsylvania Magazine of History and Biography* 119 (July 1995): 181–202; Cleary, *Elizabeth Murray*; Claudia Goldin, "The Economic Status of Women in the Early Republic: Quantitative Evidence," *Journal of Interdisciplinary History* 16 (1986): 375–404; Hartigan-O'Connor, *The Ties That Buy*, esp. 39–68; Zabin, "Women's Trading Networks and Dangerous Economies in Eighteenth-Century New York City," 291–321. For examples, see Lea and O'Brien Journal 1784–1786 (women traders buy from them); Margaret Moulder, Ledger, 1794–1833; John Oliver Account Book; all in HSP. John E. Howard to William M. Lapsley, February 3, 1810, folder 32, box 1, Lapsley Family Business Records, McAllister Collection, LCP, refers to trading with women involved in carpets. Meeting of the Creditors of Clara Larieux, Acts of Hugues Lavergne, vol. 11, October to December 1823, act 1798, NA is one of many references to women shopkeepers in New Orleans. The New York City Mayor's Court contains numerous references to women shopkeepers. See for example *People v. Sally Johnson*, April 8, 1802; *People v. John Bernard*, October 7, 1802; *People v. James Johnson*, April 13, 1804; *People v. Sally Armstrong*, October 9, 1806; *People v. William Jackson, James Bonne, and Samuel Van Zandt*, February 8, 1817; *People v. Samuel Snediker, Adam Walker and Isaac Keeland*, February 17, 1820; *People v. Charles Zeiss*, February 9, 1826; all in NYMA. For the advantages of trading with local shops and particularly with women, see Tebbutt, *Making Ends Meet*, 37–67.

13. Quote from Zephaniah Swift, *A System of Laws of the State of Connecticut* (1795), 1:197. While Crowston, "Family Affairs," distinguishes French law from British law, Anglo-American law also gave married wide discretion in purchasing "necessaries," including cloth and clothing. For treatises, see for example: Kent, *Commentaries*, 2:123–26; Reeve, *Law of Baron and Femme* (1816) 79–85; Reeve, *Law of Baron and Femme* $56–66; Swift, *A System of Laws* (1795), 1:197–200; Swift, *A System of Laws* (1822), 1:30–35; Tucker, *Blackstone's Commentaries*, vol. 1, pt. 2, 442. For Justices' manuals, see for example Richard Burn, *Burn's Abridgement, or The American Justice; Containing the Whole Practice, Authority and Duty of Justices of the Peace* (Dover, NH: 1792), 321–32; William Waller Hening, *The New Virginia Justice* (Richmond: 1819, 2nd ed.), 601; Henry Potter, *The Office and Duty of a Justice of the Peace* (Raleigh, NC: 1816), 19; *The South-Carolina Justice of Peace* (Philadelphia: 1788): 500–501; Benjamin Swaim, *The North Carolina Justice*, 2nd ed. (Raleigh: 1846), 314.

14. Reeve, *Law of Baron and Femme* (1816), 37–39; Reeve, *Law of Baron and Femme* (1862), 99–100; Marta Cotterell Raffel, *The Laces of Ipswich: The Art and Economics of an Early American Industry, 1750–1840* (Hanover, NH: University Press of New England, 2003).

15. There is no mention of wives' claims to paraphernalia or wearing apparel in other treatises: Kent, *Commentaries*, 2:109–57; Swift, *A System of Laws of the State of Connecticut* (1795), 1:183–203; Swift, *A System of Laws of the State of Connecticut* (1822), 1:18–40. Tucker, *Blackstone's Commentaries*, vol. 1, pt. 2, 433–45, in an unnumbered note on 445 states all married women's personal property becomes her husband's property with marriage; but on 2:435 mentions the exception of

paraphernalia. See Dutton, *A Revision of Swift's Digest of the Laws of Connecticut*, 1:27, for the point that wearing apparel purchased during marriage no longer belonged to the wife. For the larger trend of increasing restrictions within coverture, despite the changes of married women's property, see chapter 10.

16. Richard Burn, *The Justice of the Peace and Parish Officer* (London: 1755), or Michael Dalton, *The Countrey Justice* (London: 1619); both went through numerous revisions thereafter. William Waller Hening, *The New Virginia Justice* (Richmond: 1795); Hening, *The New Virginia Justice*, 2d. ed. (1819), 23. Manuals that omitted the issue were far more common: Burn, *Burn's Abridgement*; J. C. Bancroft Davis, *The Massachusetts Justice* (Worcester, MA: 1847); Samuel Freeman, *The Massachusetts Justice*, 2nd ed. (Boston: 1802); Francois Xavier Martin, *The Office and Authority of a Justice of the Peace, and of Sheriffs, Coroners, &c* (n.p.: 1791); Potter, *The Office and Duty of a Justice of the Peace*; *The South-Carolina Justice of Peace*; Swaim, *The North Carolina Justice*. Also see Edwards, "The Material Conditions of Dependency."

17. *A Digest of the Civil Laws Now in Force in the Territory of Orleans: With Alterations and Amendments Adapted to Its Present System of Government* (New Orleans: Bradford & Anderson, Printers to the Territory, 1803), 334–36. These principles were closely followed in disputes over property documented in the New Orleans notarial records, NA. For Pennsylvania's stay laws, see S. Laurence Shaimon, "The History of Imprisonment for Debt and Insolvency Laws in Pennsylvania as They Evolved from the Common Law," *American Journal of Legal History* 4 (July 1960): 220–21. For a discussion of textiles in statutes and appellate cases at the state and federal level, see chapter 11.

18. For state appellate cases dealing with enslaved people's property, see Penningroth, *The Claims of Kinfolk*, 219n182 for quote, from the case of *Waddill v. Martin*, 38 N.C. 562 (1845); also see 94–95, 214n91.

19. Styles, *Threads of Feeling*. The Foundling Hospital continues as the children's charity Coram, (http://www.coram.org.uk).

20. Many thanks to Felicity Turner for her insights on this point and for sharing the evidence with me. See: *State v. Eliza Howell*, Spring Term 1826, Northampton County Superior Court Criminal Action Papers, NCSA; 9 February 1859, *Chicago Press and Tribune*, ProQuest Historical Newspapers, Chicago Tribune (1849 – 1987), 1. Also see Turner, *From Midwives to Physicians*.

21. Merchants regularly traded with married women, although they did not usually record accounts with married women in their account books; see chapter 7. But some did record transactions with married women: Andrew Shepherd Account Book, MS1966.1; Christopher Tompkins Account Book, MS1940.3; both in RLCW. Hardy Whitford Account Book, AB.85, NCSA. Lexington Milling Co. Ledger, 1840–1846, Mss. MsV Ami T2 Oversize, WM. John Goodwin, Account Books, 2 vols., Kershaw County, SCDAH. Walter E. Stephens Daybook, 1831–1836, NYHS. Mendenhall and Cope Record Book (tailor's book), vol. 5, 1795, HSP. Tilton Family, Account Books, 2 vols.; John McBride, Account Book; both in RU. Account book, 1835–1843, Wayland Family Records, Accession 22398, Business Records Collection; Ledger, Unidentified General Store, 1828–1829, Barcode 1098762, Local Government Records Collection, Frederick County Court Records; both in LV.

22. Elizabeth Ann Cooley McClure, Diary; Amanda Jane Cooley Roberts, Diary; both in VMHC.
23. Louisa Collins to Anna Mercer Harrison, December 9, 1838, Byrd Family Papers, 1791–1867, Section 6, VHS. For similar patterns, also see Sally Dortch Baskervill Accounts, 1842–1861, Baskervill Family Papers, Section 7, VMHC. Mary Beth Sievens, "Female Consumerism and Household Authority in Early National New England," *Early American Studies* 4 (Fall 2006): 353–71. Those patterns were based in a broad interpretation of the presumption that women could shop for "necessaries."
24. For mention of merchants specializing in the trade, see *State v. James Edmunds*, Indictments, Court of General Sessions, Kershaw County, SCDAH. Peddlers also sold to enslaved people: *State v. John, Brister, Sally, and Jane*, #235, Trial Papers, Court of Magistrates and Freeholders, Anderson County, SCDAH. Also see *State v. Toby and Cresia*, #239, Trial Papers, Court of Magistrates and Freeholders, Anderson County, SCDAH for a case in which an enslaved person sold property later found to be stolen quickly and easily in Spartanburg. Merchants' accounts also indicate that they sold regularly to enslaved people, keeping separate entries for enslaved people. See, for instance, John U. Kirkland Account Books, vol. 1, #405 and Cameron Family Papers, #133, subser. 6.5.1, vol. 73, 1792–1812, SHC. John W. Harris Papers, Special Collections, DU; Green & Coleman Account Book, 1827–1864 (bulk 1827–1829), Accession 43842, Business Records Collection, LV; John Goodwin, Account Books, 2 vols., Kershaw County, SCDAH. Also see Hilliard, *Masters, Slaves, and Exchange*, 69–93; Penningroth, *Claims of Kinfolk*. For examples of New York merchants buying from and selling to African Americans who were enslaved, see *People v. Toby* (a slave) of J. Coventry, October 4, 1804; *People v. Pomp*, a slave, February 11, 1805; *People v. Harry*, a black, April 4, 1805, NYMA. In another case, a dressmaker accepted a hundred-dollar bill from a young African American woman without inquiring as to her status: *People v. Susan Bakeman*, August 6, 1805, NYMA.
25. For cases filed on behalf of enslaved people, see chapter 2. For examples of enslaved people returning to their homes to collect their clothing after sale to a new owner, see Petition 20782902, Records of the Circuit Court, Case Files, Document Number 1525, box 1–21, Kentucky Division of Libraries and Archives, Digital Library on American Slavery, http://library.uncg.edu/slavery/details.aspx?pid=6072; Petition 21682406, Ended Chancery Court Causes, Document Number 676, box: 14, Lynchburg, Library of Virginia, Digital Library on American Slavery, http://library.uncg.edu/slavery/details.aspx?pid=15540. Also see *State v. Abner Gordon*, 1830–1832, Criminal Actions Concerning Slaves and Free Persons of Color, Granville County, NCSA. Hector Davis and Company Account Books, CHM. Many thanks to Alex Finley for directing me to these records and sharing her insights about them. For the work done by enslaved women to outfit other enslaved people, see Finley, "'Cash to Corinna': Domestic Labor and Sexual Economy in the 'Fancy Trade,'" *Journal of American History* 104 (September 2017): 410–30.
26. Quote from Hilliard, *Masters, Slaves, and Exchange*, 23–24. While the scholarship tends to emphasize the cultural meanings of clothing to African Americans, it also underscores the fact that enslaved people purchased clothing and considered it to

be their own. In addition to the work in note 11 above, see Stephanie M. H. Camp, *Enslaved Women and the Geography of Everyday Resistance in the Plantation South, 1830–1865* (Chapel Hill: University of North Carolina Press, 2004), 78–87; Helen Bradley Foster, *"New Raiments of Self": African American Clothing in the Antebellum Period* (Oxford: Berg, 1997), particularly 137–223; Thavolia Glymph, *Out of the House of Bondage: The Transformation of the Plantation Household* (Cambridge: Cambridge University Press, 2008), 180–83;Tera W. Hunter, *To 'Joy My Freedom: Southern Black Women's Lives and Labors after the Civil War* (Cambridge, MA: Harvard University Press, 1997), 4–5, 182–83; Nunley, *At the Threshold of Liberty*, 40–69; Prude, "To Look Upon the 'Lower Sort'"; Barbara M. Starke, Lillian O. Holloman, and Barbara K. Nordquist, *African American Dress and Adornment: A Cultural Perspective* (Dubuque, IA: Kendall/Hunt, 1990); Waldstreicher, "Reading the Runaways."

27. *People v. Rosenah Gray*, June 3, 1802; *People v. John Pierre*, April 5, 1802; both in NYMA. Gray was later convicted of stealing another lot of fabric; *People v. Rosenah Gray*, October 8, 1802, NYMA. For a discussion of that case and examples of people, see chapter 7. For examples of people amassing stores of textiles, see chapter 6.

28. The state legislature passed its first emancipation act in 1799, freeing anyone born to an enslaved woman after July 4 of that year. But that statute kept freed people indentured to their masters until they were twenty-eight if they were male and twenty-five if they were female. It also left everyone already enslaved in bondage. The 1817 act rectified that situation, declaring that anyone enslaved before July 4, 1799, would be free by the time they were twenty-one or by July 4, 1827, whichever came first.

29. *People v. John Pierre*. For the complications of slavery and freedom in New York City, see Harris, *In the Shadow of Slavery*; Gronningsater, "Delivering Freedom"; Shane White, *Somewhat More Independent: The End of Slavery in New York City, 1770–1810* (Athens: University of Georgia Press, 1991).

30. For Rosetta, see Docket of Mayor Joseph Tate, VM, 67; also see case against Adeline, 21; case against Jacob Henry, 25; complaint of Rosetta, 67; complaint of Hugh Johnson, 69; case against Nelson, 7; complaint of Dandridge, 118; complaint of Sam Givens, 132; complaint of Milly, 209; case against Monroe, 209; complaint of David Brown, 340.

31. Inventory of Pierre St. Pe, Acts of Hugues Lavergne, vol. 11, October to December 1823, Act 1874, NA.

32. Inventories and sales for Orange County, North Carolina, every five years from 1785 to 1845 underscore the value of bedding and bed linens; see Inventories, Sales and Accounts of Estates, Orange County, vols. 2, 3, 4, 5, 7, 8, 9, 10, 11, NCSA. The same patterns obtained in New Orleans notarial records. See, for instance, Inventory of Marie Elizabeth Bore Gayarre, Acts of Hugues Lavergne, vol. 11, October to December 1823, act 1693; Inventory of Guy Noel Destrechan, Acts of Hugues Lavergne, vol. 11, October to December 1823, act 2112; Inventory of Omer Fortier, Acts of Hugues Lavergne, vol. 11, October to December 1823, act 2073; Inventory of Marie Antoinette Charest de Lauzon Thibant, Acts of Hugues Lavergne, vol. 11, October to December 1823, act 2121; Inventory of Blaise Cenas, Acts of Hugues Lavergne, vol. 11, October to December 1823, act 1670; Inventory of George M.

Ogden, Acts of Hugues Lavergne, vol. 11, October to December 1823, act 1682; Inventory of Adele Morel, Acts of Louis Feraud, vol. 9, December 1829 to December 1833, act 6; Inventory of Emanual Rivas, Acts of Louis Feraud, vol. 9, December 1829 to December 1833, act 12; Inventory of Southmayd Scotville and Sally Louisa Caldwell, Acts of Paul Bertus, vol. 2, 1840–1841, act 100; all in NA.

33. These generalizations are based on research in all the inventories and sales for Orange County, North Carolina, every five years from 1785 to 1845; see Inventories, Sales and Accounts of Estates, Orange County, vols. 2, 3, 4, 5, 7, 8, 9, 10, 11, NCSA.

34. *State v. James Long*, 1828 (box 10, containing cases not filed by date), Indictments, Court of General Sessions, Anderson County, SCDAH. For examples of women simply taking domestic property, see Abbott's Creek Primitive Baptist Church, Minutes, 1783–1879, Davidson County, NCSA. Divorce judgments indicated that wives would retain certain domestic items, presumably because there had been some contention over possession. See, for instance, *Sarah Chandler v. Thomas Chandler*, 1826, Divorce Records, Granville County, NCSA; *Lydia Hussey v. Jesse Hussey*, 1854, Divorce Records, Randolph County, NCSA. Petition 20883712, Records of the Fifth Judicial District Court, Document Number 2,283, St. Landry Parish Courthouse, Opelousas, Louisiana, Digital Library on American Slavery, http://library.uncg.edu/slavery/details.aspx?pid=7972.

35. See Inventories, Sales and Accounts of Estates, Orange County, vols. 2, 3, 4, 5, 7, 8, 9, 10, 11, NCSA. For examples of widows buying back the tools of textile production, see Inventory of the Estate of Aquila Jones, 318–21; Inventory of the Estate of Edward Green, 344–46; all in Inventories, Sales and Accounts of Estates, Orange County, C.R. 073.514, vol. 2, 1800–1808, NCSA. Inventory of the Sale of Hugh McCaddamus, 118–22; An Inventory of the Estate of William Scot, Deceased, 147–48 (the framing suggests that she kept these items, among others); A List of Persons' Purchases at the Sale of John Woody, Deceased, 180–85; An Account of Sales of Notes, and Accounts of Jonathan Jones, 197–202; in Inventories, Sales and Accounts of Estates, Orange County, C.R. 073.514, vol. 3, 1808–1810, NCSA. That pattern continued later in the nineteenth century as well: Inventory and Account of Sales of the Personal Property of John Piper, 229–36; A List of Property Sold at the Sale of James Forest, 260–66; A List of the Sale of the Property of Thomas McCracken, 273–77; Account of Sales of the Property Belonging to the Estate of Hugh Crawford, 277–80; all in vol. 11, 1835, Inventories, Sales and Accounts of Estates, Orange County, C.R. 073.514, NCSA. Ulrich, *The Age of Homespun*, 175–207, argues that women began claiming the tools of the textile trade; she notes that they carved their initials into them. Those markings had legal meanings; see chapter 9.

36. The will and inventory are appended to the end of Roberts Diary, VMHC; see 181 for the tools related to Jane Cooley's textile business.

37. For married women's control of property, see Cleary, *Elizabeth Murray*; Cooper, "Cultures of Emotion"; Damiano, *To Her Credit*; Haggerty *The British-Atlantic Trading Community*; Hartigan-O'Connor, *The Ties That Buy*; Romney, *New Netherland Connections*; Zabin, *Dangerous Economies*. While enslaved people possessed all kinds of property, most of it was claimed through customary practices, which had power;

in particular, see Penningroth, *The Claims of Kinfolk*. Popular culture brimmed with warnings about white women passing counterfeit bills. See Stephen Mihm, *A Nation of Counterfeiters: Capitalists, Con Men, and the Making of the United States* (Cambridge, MA: Harvard University Press, 2009), 209–59.

38. *State v. Wyatt Harris*, #48, Trial Papers, Court of Magistrates and Freeholders, Spartanburg County, SCDAH. *State v. Daniel*, #49, Trial Papers, Court of Magistrates and Freeholders, Spartanburg County, SCDAH. See chapters 7 and 8 for further discussion of the evidence required to prove possession in law.

39. *State v. Wyatt Harris*, #48, Trial Papers, Court of Magistrates and Freeholders, Spartanburg County, SCDAH.

Chapter 2

1. Jesse Hoyt, David Hadden, James Lefforts, and William A. Hadden, Bill of Exceptions, box 54, Case Files in Suits Against Collectors of Customs, 1833–1903, US Circuit Court of Southern District of New York, RG 21, National Archives and Records Administration, NARA-NY.

2. Jesse Hoyt, David Hadden, James Lefforts, and William A. Hadden, Bill of Exceptions, NARA-NY. Box 54 is filled with cases involving Chief Justice Roger Taney. For the legal practices associated with customs, see Rao, *National Duties*.

3. Jesse Hoyt, David Hadden, James Lefforts, and William A. Hadden, Bill of Exceptions, NARA-NY. For Taney's work as Chief Justice on the US Supreme Court, see Don E. Fehrenbacher, *The Dred Scott Case: Its Significance in American Law and Politics* (New York: Oxford University Press, 1978); Mark Graber, *Dred Scott and the Problem of Constitutional Evil* (New York: Cambridge University Press, 2006); Jonathan W. White, *Abraham Lincoln and Treason in the Civil War: The Trials of John Merryman* (Baton Rouge: Louisiana State University Press, 2011).

4. Attending to textiles shifts our perspective to elements of the new republic's governing institutions that until recently have not featured prominently in the scholarship. Much of the previous literature traces the development of what was new in the new republic, namely, governing institutions at the state and federal levels. This preoccupation is so strong that historians have tended to define the government of the United States primarily, if not solely, in terms of written records produced in those institutional arenas. An emerging body of scholarship has widened that perspective, exposing a more varied governing terrain, although the findings are only just beginning to alter conventional paradigms. For an overview, see Edwards, "Sarah Allingham's Sheet." Also see, for example, Gregory Ablavsky, "Empire States: The Coming of Dual Federalism," *Yale Law Journal* 128 (May 2019): 1792–1869; Daniel Carpenter, Democracy by Petition: Popular Politics in Transformation, 1790-1870 (Cambridge: Harvard University Press, 2021); Edwards, *People and Their Peace*; de la Fuente and Gross, *Becoming Free, Becoming Black*; Gross, *Double Character*; Gronningsater, *The Arc of Abolition*; Hartog, "Pigs and Positivism"; Jones, *Birthright*

Citizenship; LaCroix, *The Ideological Origins of American Federalism*; Naomi R. Lamoreaux and John Joseph Wallis, "Economic Crisis, General Laws, and the Mid-Nineteenth-Century Transformation of American Political Economy," *Journal of the Early Republic* 41 (Fall 2021): 403-33; Masur, "State Sovereignty"; Masur, *Until Justice Be Done*; Novak, *The People's Welfare*; Peterson, "Interpretation as Statecraft"; Peterson, "Constitutionalism in Unexpected Places"; Tani, *States of Dependency*.

5. Lauren Benton, *A Search for Sovereignty: Law and Geography in European Empires, 1400-1900* (New York: Cambridge University Press, 2011). As recent scholarship has argued, European conceptions of sovereignty as exclusive power within a given geographic area was not only hard fought but also key in solidifying colonialism: Eliga H. Gould, *Among the Powers of the Earth: The American Revolution and the Making of a New World Empire* (Cambridge, MA: Harvard University Press, 2012); Ford, *Settler Sovereignty*; Rosen, *Border Law*; Sadosky, *Revolutionary Negotiations*. That work comports with recent work in Indian history, which emphasizes the persistence of native sovereignty within the geographic boundaries of the new United States as well as European colonies in North America. For Native American history, see, for instance, Susan Sleeper-Smith, Juliana Barr, Jean M. O'Brien, Nancy Shoemaker, and Scott Manning Stevens, eds., *Why You Can't Teach United States History without American Indians* (Chapel Hill: University of North Carolina Press, 2015). For a fascinating analysis of the developing conceptions of sovereignty developed in conversation between Europeans and Native Americans, see Gregory Ablavsky, "Species of Sovereignty: Native Nationhood, the United States, and International Law, 1783-1795," *Journal of American History* 106 (December 2019): 591-613.

6. See, for instance, Holly Brewer, *By Birth or Consent*; Erickson, *Women and Property*; Cynthia B. Herrup, *The Common Peace: Participation and the Criminal Law in Seventeenth-Century England* (New York: Cambridge University Press, 1987); Laura Gowing, *Domestic Dangers: Women, Words, and Sex in Early Modern London* (Oxford: Clarendon, 1996); Tim Stretton, *Women Waging Law in Elizabethan England* (New York: Cambridge University Press, 1998); Norman L. Jones and Daniel Wolf, *Local Identities in Late Medieval and Early Modern England* (New York: Palgrave Macmillan, 2007); Keith Wrightson, "Two Concepts of Order: Justices, Constables, and Jurymen in Seventeenth-Century England," in *An Ungovernable People: The English and Their Law in the Seventeenth and Eighteenth Centuries*, ed. John Brewer and John Styles (New Brunswick, NJ: Rutgers University Press, 1980), 21-46.

7. Stanley N. Katz, "Explaining the Law in Early American History: Introduction," in "Forum Explaining the Law in Early American History—A Symposium," ed. Stanley N. Katz, special issue, *William and Mary Quarterly* 50 (January 1993): 6. Also see Mary Bilder, *The Transatlantic Constitution: Colonial Legal Culture and the Empire* (Cambridge, MA, Harvard University Press, 2004); Jack Green, *Negotiated Authorities: Essays in Colonial Political and Constitutional History* (Charlottesville: University of Virginia Press, 1994); Eliga Gould, "Zones of Law, Zones of Violence: The Legal Geography of the British Atlantic, circa 1772," *William and Mary Quarterly* 60 (July 2003): 471-510; Gould, "Entangled Histories, Entangled Worlds: The English-Speaking Atlantic as a Spanish Periphery," *American Historical*

Review 112 (June 2007): 764–68; Vicki Hseuh, *Hybrid Constitutions: Challenging Legacies of Law, Privilege, and Culture in Colonial America* (Durham, NC: Duke University Press, 2010); Daniel Hulsebosch, *Constituting Empire: New York and the Transformation of Constitutionalism in the Atlantic World, 1664–1830* (Chapel Hill: University of North Carolina Press, 2005); David Thomas Konig, "A Summary View of the Law of British America," in "Forum Explaining the Law in Early American History—A Symposium," ed. Stanley N. Katz, special issue, *William and Mary Quarterly* 50 (January 1993): 42–50; Christopher L. Tomlins, *Freedom Bound: Law, Labor, and Civic Identity in Colonizing English America, 1580–1865* (New York: Cambridge University Press, 2010); Tomlins and Mann, *The Many Legalities of Early America*. For South Carolina, see Rachel N. Klein, *Unification of a Slave State: The Rise of the Planter Class in the South Carolina Backcountry, 1760–1808* (Chapel Hill: University of North Carolina Press, 1990).

8. See, in particular, Ablavsky, "Empire States"; Edwards, "Sarah Allingham's Sheet"; Edwards, *People and Their Peace*; LaCroix, *The Ideological Origins of American Federalism*; Masur, "State Sovereignty"; Masur, *Until Justice Be Done*; Novak, *People's Welfare*; Peterson, "Interpretation as Statecraft." For police powers, also see Markus Dirk Dubber, *Police Power: Patriarchy and the Foundations of American Government* (New York: Columbia University Press, 2005); Tomlins, *Law, Labor, and Ideology*.

9. Jesse Hoyt, David Hadden, James Lefforts, and William A. Hadden, Bill of Exceptions; *State v. Brummer*, #142, Trial Papers, Court of Magistrates and Freeholders, Anderson County, SCDAH.

10. John Faucheraud Grimké, December 15, 1789, Charge to the Charleston Grand Jury, October 1789, *Pennsylvania Packet and Daily Advertiser*, John Faucheraud Grimke Papers, SCL. The notion that members of the judiciary should take an active role in framing and reviewing legislation was common in this period; see Peterson, "Interpretation as Statecraft."

11. Edwards, *People and Their Peace*, 90–98. See, for instance Kershaw County, Grand Jury, April 1805, SCL (protesting importation of slaves and the state of their jail); Presentments of the Grand Jury of Wilkes County, William Lenoir's Speeches, Writings, and Notes, October 1804, folder 242, subseries 2.2.1, Lenoir Family Papers, #426, SHC (more qualified officials to be appointed to the county court; state support for the manufacture of munitions to arm the militia; opposition to Napoleon). Also see Carpenter, *Democracy by Petition*; Larry D. Kramer, *The People Themselves: Popular Constitutionalism and Judicial Review* (New York: Oxford University Press, 2004); Peterson, "Constitutionalism in Unexpected Places"; Steven Wilf, *Law's Imagined Republic: Popular Politics and Criminal Justice in Revolutionary America* (New York: Cambridge University Press, 2010).

12. Constitutions of South Carolina (1776 and 1778); for the point about the focus on planters in the low country, see Klein, *Unification of a Slave State*. Constitution of New York (1777); Constitutions of Pennsylvania (1776), Maryland (1776), North Carolina (1776), Vermont (1777), and Virginia (1776). All in AP. Also Willi Paul Adams, *The First American Constitutions: Republican Ideology and the Making of the*

State Constitution in the Revolutionary Era (Chapel Hill: University of North Carolina Press, 1980); Kramer, *The People Themselves*.

13. For resistance to the removal of legal authority from the local level to the state level, see Edwards, *People and Their Peace*. That resistance echoed the more studied opposition to the centralization of authority at the federal level. For recent analyses, see Saul Cornell, *The Other Founders: Anti-Federalism and the Dissenting Tradition in America, 1788-1828* (Chapel Hill: University of North Carolina Press, 1999); Gerald Leonard and Saul Cornell, *The Partisan Republic: Democracy, Exclusion, and the Fall of the Founders' Constitution, 1780s-1830s* (Cambridge: Cambridge University Press, 2019); Holton, *Unruly Americans*.

14. For the quote, see Constitution of Pennsylvania (1776); Constitutions of Maryland (1776), New York (1777), North Carolina (1776), South Carolina (1776 and 1778), Vermont (1777), and Virginia (1776). The Massachusetts cases are the Mum Bett or Elizabeth Freeman case of 1781 and three related cases in 1783 known today as "the Quock Walker case"; for an account and links to the original documents, see the Massachusetts court systems online guide Massachusetts Constitution and the Abolition of Slavery, https://www.mass.gov/guides/massachusetts-constitution-and-the-abolition-of-slavery#-resources-. Also see Emily Blanck, "Seventeen Eighty-Three: The Turning Point in the Law of Slavery and Freedom in Massachusetts," *New England Quarterly* 75 (March 2002): 24-51. For women's marginalization from rights, see for instance Kerber, *No Constitutional Right to be Ladies*.

15. States also guaranteed the right to petition. There is a rich literature on petitioning in women's history. For examples, see Marcia Schmidt Blaine, "Ordinary Women: Government and Custom in the Lives of New Hampshire Women, 1690-1770" (PhD diss., University of New Hampshire, 1999); Blaine, "The Power of Petitions: Women and the New Hampshire Provincial Government, 1695-1770," *International Review of Social History* 46 (December 2001): 57-77; Julie Roy Jeffrey, *The Great Silent Army of Abolitionism: Ordinary Women and the Antislavery Movement* (Chapel Hill: University of North Carolina Press, 1998); Kerber, *Women of the Republic*. Recent work, including that of McKinley (now Blackhawk), has focused on the petitioning process as central to the institutional workings of government: Maggie McKinley, "Lobbying and the Petition Clause," *Stanford Law Review*, 68 (May 2016): 1165-1205, and McKinley, "Petitioning and the Making of the Administrative State," *Yale Law Journal* 127 (April 2018): 1538-1637. Also see Carpenter, *Democracy by Petition*; Daniel Carpenter, "Recruitment by Petition: American Antislavery, French Protestantism, English Suppression," *Perspectives on Politics* 14 (September, 2016): 700-23; Carpenter and Colin D. Moore, "When Canvassers Became Activists: Antislavery Petitioning and the Political Mobilization of American Women," *American Political Science Review* 108 (August 2014): 479-98; Carpenter and Benjamin Schneer, "Party Formation Through Petitions: The Whigs and the Bank War of 1832-1834," *Studies in American Political Development* 29 (October 2015): 213-34; Groningsater, "Practicing Formal Politics Without the Vote."

16. Pennsylvania Constitution (1790), from the Pennsylvania Constitution Web Page, Duquesne University Law School, https://www.paconstitution.org/texts-of-the-const

itution/1790-2/. Petition for the Pardon of Thomas Gallion, to James Iredell, August 3, 1828, 117–18, vol. 27, Governor's Letter Book, NCSA. For changes in state constitutions generally in this period, see Fletcher Green, *Constitutional Development in the South Atlantic States, 1776–1860* (New York: W. W. Norton, 1966); Lamoreaux and Wallis, "Economic Crisis." Also see Peterson, "Interpretation as Statecraft."

17. Rao, *National Duties*. Also see Kramer, *The People Themselves*; Peterson, "Constitutionalism in Unexpected Places." For cases in which customary practices figured prominently, see for instance *Benjamin Curtis, executor of Lewis Curtis et al v. Hiram Barney*, Defendant's Bill of Exceptions, box 29; *Jesse Hoyt ads. William B. Bond*, Certificate of Division, box 54; *Thomas Paton and David Stewart v. Jesse Hoyt*, Copy Notice of Issuing Commissions, box 54; *Thomas Paton and David Stewart v. Jesse Hoyt*, Deposition, box 54; *Thomas Paton and David Stewart v. Jesse Hoyt*, Depositions, box 55; *Charles Borsdorff v. Heman Redfield*, Testimony, box 68; all in NARA-NY. Those same dynamics were at play in the legal determination of race. As de la Fuente and Gross argue in *Becoming Free, Becoming Black*, courts slowly moved away from the recognition of customary practices to physical evidence, such as hair and skin color, in determining racial status.

18. Lamoreaux and Wallis, "Economic Crisis." Masur, *Until Justice Be Done*. Also see Edwards, *People and Their Peace*, 26–63; Novak, *The People's Welfare*; Peterson, "Interpretation as Statecraft."

19. Edwards, "Sarah Allingham's Sheet." Also see Kevin Butterfield, *The Making of Tocqueville's America: Law and Association in the Early Nineteenth Century United States* (Chicago: University of Chicago Press, 2015); Sarah Barringer Gordon, "The African Supplement: Religion, Race, and Corporate Law in Early National America," *William and Mary Quarterly* 72 (July 2015): 385–422; Gordon, "The First Disestablishment: Limits on Church Power and Property Before the Civil War," *University of Pennsylvania Law Review* 162 (January 2014): 307–72; Brian Matthew Jordan, "Benjamin F. Butler, *Ex parte Millligan*, and the Unending Civil War," in Ex Parte Milligan *Reconsidered: Race and Civil Liberties from the Lincoln Administration to the War on Terror*, ed. Stewart L. Winger and Jonathan W. White (Lawrence: University Press of Kansas), 27–51; William J. Novak, "The American Law of Association: The Legal-Political Construction of Civil Society," *Studies in American Political Development* 15 (Fall 2001): 163–88; Mark S. Schantz, "The Janus-Faced Character of Martial Law in the American Civil War, or the Strange Case of Lieutenant Alanson L. Sanborn and Dr. David M. Wright," in Winger and White, Ex Parte Milligan *Reconsidered*, 72–101; John Fabian Witt, *Lincoln's Code: The Laws of War in American History* (New York: Free Press, 2012); Jonathan W. White, "Martial Law and the Expansion of Civil Liberties during the Civil War," in Winger and White, Ex Parte Milligan *Reconsidered*, 52–72.

20. Welch, *Black Litigants*, 115–60; Hartigan-O'Connor, *The Ties That Buy*, 69–100. While recent scholarship emphasizes the efforts of free blacks, women, and the poor to use the law, it also reveals the difficulties they faced. Also see Sharon Block, *Rape and Sexual Power in Early America* (Chapel Hill: University of North Carolina Press, 2006); Bynum, *Unruly Women*; Edwards, *People and Their Peace*; Heerman, *Alchemy*

of Slavery; Jones, *Birthright Citizens*; Kennington, *In the Shadow of* Dred Scott; Maris-Wolf, *Free Blacks and Re-Enslavement*; Twitty, *Before Dred Scott*; Van Daacke, *Freedom Has a Face*. The laws relating to slavery and coverture denied married women and enslaved people the rights necessary to pursue cases in civil law; treatises, statutes, and case law in the new republic upheld those general principles.

21. *Blythe v. Capus*, Richmond City, Hustings Court, Suit Papers, Ended Causes, folder May 1787 no. 3, box 8, May 1787, LV. For the practice of keeping separate accounts, see; Sturtz, *Within Her Power*, 111–40; Vickery, *The Gentleman's Daughter*, 126–60; Amanda Vickery, "His and Hers: Gender, Consumption and Household Accounting in Eighteenth-Century England," *Past and Present* 1, supplement 1 (2006): 12–38; Ulrich, *Midwife's Tale*. Rebecca Coles, from chapter 3, also kept separate accounts: Account book (Rebecca Coles), 1795–1800, box 1; Account book, John Coles of Enniscorthy (Rebecca Coles), 1801–1809, box 1; Col. John Coles of Ennisworthy (Rebecca Coles), Account Book, 1810–1815, Samuel Smith Papers, box 2; all in Samuel Smith Papers, #1729, UV. Also see Account of Mrs. Martha Mason with John T. J. Mason, Mason Family Papers (an account with her husband, from the first half of nineteenth century); Jane Catherine Fontaine Mead Account Book, 1860–1864 ("Account of things bought for myself"); Mary E. Brown, Account Book, 1855–1885 (separate account book for eggs, chickens, cloth, and clothing); Elizabeth Lumpkin Motely Bagby Commonplace Book, 1824–1832 (separate accounts for weaving and goods "made entirely within yourself"); all in VMHC. Pearl family Account Book, 1792–1845 (Mehitable Pearl's accounts are in the middle of the book, separate from the others and are for boarders, weaving, and spinning), MHS. Petition 20680910, January, 25 1809, Records of the Inferior Court, Writs 1801–1809, microfilm, box 18/97, Page 477–78, Georgia Department of Archives and History, Digital Library on American Slavery, http://library.uncg.edu/slavery/details.aspx?pid=4845; Petition 21384360, Records of the Equity Court, Bills, box 4/1847; 27, folder 3, Microfilm: Reel SP3; Order #790, Reel D1277, SCDAH, Digital Library on American Slavery, http://library.uncg.edu/slavery/details.aspx?pid=20766. For further discussion of such accounts, see chapter 7.

22. See, for instance, Maggie Blackhawk, "Federal Indian Law as Paradigm within Public Law," *Harvard Law Review* 132 (May 2019): 1764, Gale General Onefile; Edwards, *People and Their Peace*; Laura F. Edwards, *A Legal History of the Civil War and Reconstruction: A Nation of Rights* (New York, 2015); Novak, *The People's Wefare*; Peterson, "Interpretation as Statecraft"; Felicity Turner, "Rights and the Ambiguities of Law: Infanticide in the Nineteenth-Century U.S. South," *Journal of the Civil War Era* 4 (Sept. 2014): 350–72; Turner, *Proving Pregnancy*. For a particularly compelling commentary on the rigidity of rights in this period, see Tomlins, *Law, Labor, and Ideology*.

23. Historian Serena Zabin, "Women's Trading Networks," has made the same point in relation to women's commercial activity more generally in the eighteenth century. As she argues, the evidence of that activity lies not in civil cases but in criminal matters. For the accommodating nature of public law for those without rights, see Edwards, *People and Their Peace*; Edwards, "Sarah Allingham's Sheet"; Edwards, "Legal World";

and Edwards, "James and His Striped Velvet Pantaloons." On the flexibility of police power, see Masur, *Until Justice Be Done*; Tomlins, *Law, Labor, and Ideology*. Also see Dubber, *Police Power*, although he emphasizes the ways police power, in the realm of public law, upheld patriarchal power.

24. The legal dynamics involving textiles are discussed at length in the next two sections, particularly chapters 6, 7, 8, and 9. For cases similar to Polly's, see *State v. Cain, Meshack, and Charles*, #86a, Trial Papers, Court of Magistrates and Freeholders, Anderson County; *State v. Cash (negro slave)*, Trial Papers, Court of Magistrates and Freeholders, Kershaw County; *State v. Henry*, #24, Trial Papers, Court of Magistrates and Freeholders, Spartanburg County; *State v. Sam*, #221, Trial Papers, Court of Magistrates and Freeholders, Anderson County; *State v. Jere Hendrick alias Jere Hendry*, 1823-11A, 1821-3A through 1823-46A, Bills of Indictment, Court of General Sessions, Charleston District; all in SCDAH. *State v. Jordan Hawley*, 1815–1816 (although the case involved the theft of bread); *State v. Morris and Solomon*, 1857; in Criminal Actions Concerning Slaves and Free Persons of Color, Granville County, NCSA.

25. Assault, for instance, was tried as the civil action of trespass until the early nineteenth century, the logic being that violence resulted in property damage to that person. When local courts started treating it as a criminal matter instead, they retained elements of its prior form as a civil action. Some jurisdictions merged the civil and criminal components, so that the injured party could obtain damages (the elements of a civil action of trespass), while the "state," the "commonwealth," or the "people" sought justice for the public (the criminal charge). Sometimes the merger was so complete that local officials took complaints from those without rights and then proceeded with the case as a criminal matter, with the public as the injured party. But in other instances, the merger was less complete, with the public and the injured individual both occupying the position of prosecutor. To be listed as prosecutor, the injured party had to have the rights necessary to prosecute a case in civil law. For assault, see Edwards, *People and Their Peace*, 97–98. Also see Michael Meranze, *Laboratories of Virtue: Punishment, Revolution, and Authority in Philadelphia, 1760–1835* (Chapel Hill: University of North Carolina Press, 1996); Allen Steinberg, *The Transformation of Criminal Justice: Philadelphia, 1800–1880* (Chapel Hill: University of North Carolina Press, 1989).

26. *State v. Brummer*, #142, Trial Papers, Court of Magistrates and Freeholders, Anderson County.

27. *State v. Cain, Meshack, and Charles*, #86a, Trial Papers, Court of Magistrates and Freeholders, Anderson County, SCDAH.

28. Ibid.

29. *People v. Judith Friel*, October 8, 1804, NYMA. For similar cases, see part two and chapter nine.

30. Edwards, "Legal World."

31. For the point about the written word and the law, see Mann, *Neighbors and Strangers*. For the developing importance of published texts within governing institutions in the United States, see Charles M. Cook, *The American Codification Movement: A Study*

of Antebellum Legal Reform (Westport, CT: Greenwood, 1981); Edwards, *People and Their Peace*, 26–53; Peterson, "Interpretation as Statecraft."

32. For the point about Blackstone's influence, see Perry Miller, *The Life of the Mind in America: From the Revolution to the Civil War* (New York: Harcourt, Brace & World, 1965), 117–55. Brewer, *By Birth or Consent*; Brewer, "Transformation of Domestic Law." Writing was crucial in making economic claims portable and enforceable over distance and time. See, for instance, J. M. Opal, *Avenging the People: Andrew Jackson, the Rule of Law, and the American Nation* (New York: Oxford University Press, 2017), 3–5; Beth Saler, *The Settlers' Empire: Colonialism and State Formation in America's Old Northwest* (Philadelphia: University of Pennsylvania Press, 2015), 164.
33. Edwards, *People and Their Peace*, 64–99.

Chapter 3

1. Letterbook, 1810–1825, HSP, particularly the letters from 48–65.
2. John Tayloe Account Book, October 14, 1806–December 31, 1806, Tayloe Family Papers, Section 2, VMHC.
3. David MacPherson, *Annals of Commerce, Manufactures, Fisheries, and Navigation* (London: 1805), 3:187–91; quotes from 187, 188.
4. An extensive body of work shows that even those at the lower end of the economic scale not only had access to a wide range of good quality clothing but also spent a good deal of time and money on their clothes: DuPlessis, *Material Atlantic*; Steven King, "Reclothing the English Poor, 1750–1840," *Textile History* 33, no. 1 (2002): 37–47; Lemire, "A Good Stock of Clothes"; Lemire, "The Theft of Clothes"; Lemire Beverly Lemire, "Second-Hand Beaux and 'Red-Armed Belles': Conflict and the Creation of Fashions in England, c. 1660–1800," *Continuity and Change* 15 (December 2000): 391–417; Lemire, "Consumerism in Preindustrial and Early Industrial England: The Trade in Secondhand Clothes," *Journal of British Studies* 27 (January 1988): 1–24; Christiana Payne, "'Murillo-like Rags or Clean Pinafores': Artistic and Social Preferences in the Representation of the Dress of the Rural Poor," *Textile History* 33, no. 1 (2002): 48–62; Roche, *The Culture of Clothing*; Spufford, *The Great Reclothing of Rural England*; Margaret Spufford and Susan Mee, *The Clothing of the Common Sort, 1570-1700* (New York: Oxford University Press, 2017); Sam Smiles, "Defying Comprehension: Resistance to Uniform Appearance in Depicting the Poor, 1770s to 1830s," *Textile History* 33, no. 1 (2002): 23–36; John Styles, "Involuntary Consumers?"; Styles, *Dress of the People*; Styles, *Threads of Feeling*; Walker, *Exquisite Slaves*. For accessorizing, see Cissie Fairchilds, "The Production and Marketing of Populuxe Goods in Eighteenth-Century Paris," in *Consumption and the World of Goods*, ed. John Brewer and Roy Porter (New York: Routledge, 1993), 228–60.
5. Prude, "To Look Upon the 'Lower Sort'"; quote from 124. Also see Nunley, *At the Threshold of Liberty*, 40–69; Waldstreicher, "Reading the Runaways." For the availability of goods even in remote areas, see Martin, *Buying into the World of Goods*. See

Peck, *Interwoven Globe*, 283–84, for the point about merchants stocking goods intended for people of African descent.

6. Susan Sleeper-Smith, "Encounter and Trade in the Early Atlantic World," esp. 35–40, quotes from 35 and 40. For an elaboration of these points, see Sleeper-Smith, *Indigenous Prosperity and American Conquest: Indian Women of the Ohio River Valley, 1690–1792* (Chapel Hill: University of North Carolina Press, 2018). Also see Sleeper-Smith, ed., *Rethinking the Fur Trade: Cultures of Exchange in an Atlantic World* (Lincoln: University of Nebraska Press, 2009); Arthur Ray, "Indians as Consumers in the Eighteenth Century," in *Old Trails and New Directions: Papers of the Third North American Fur Trade Conference*, ed. Carol M. Judd and Arthur J. Ray (Toronto: University of Toronto Press, 1980), 255–71; Timothy J. Shannon, "Dressing for Success on the Mohawk Frontier: Hendrick, William Johnson, and the Indian Frontier," *William and Mary Quarterly* 53 (January 1996): 13–42; White, *Wild Frenchmen and Frenchified Indians*.

7. Martin, *Buying into the World of Goods*. For the importance of family in colonial trade to the Americas, also see Bernard Bailyn, *The New England Merchants in the Seventeenth Century* (Cambridge, MA: Harvard University Press, 1955); Haggerty, *The British-Atlantic Trading Community*; Vicente, *Clothing the Spanish Empire*; Alison Games, *The Web of Empire: English Cosmopolitans in an Age of Expansion, 1560–1660* (New York: Oxford University Press, 2008); Marsha L. Hamilton, *Social and Economic Networks in Early Massachusetts: Atlantic Connections* (University Park: Pennsylvania State University Press, 2009); Matson, *Merchants and Empire*; Sarah M. S. Pearsall, *Atlantic Families: Lives and Letters in the Later Eighteenth Century* (New York: Oxford University Press, 2008); Romney, *New Netherland Connections*; Vicente, *Clothing the Spanish Empire*. For the fur trade, see Jennifer S. J. Brown, *Strangers in Blood: Fur Trade Company Families in Indian Country* (Vancouver: University of British Columbia Press, 1980); Anne F. Hyde, *Empires, Nations, and Families: A New History of the North American West, 1800–1860* (Lincoln: University of Nebraska Press, 2011); Tiya Miles, *The Dawn of Detroit: A Chronicle of Slavery and Freedom in the City of the Straits* (New York: New Press, 2017); Sleeper-Smith, *Indigenous Prosperity and American Conquest*; Sylvia Van Kirk, *Many Tender Ties: Women in Fur-Trade Society, 1670–1870* (Norman: University of Oklahoma Press, 1983). Also see Julia Adams, *The Familial State: Ruling Families and Merchant Capitalism in Early Modern Europe* (Ithaca, NY: Cornell University Press, 2005).

8. Alexander's letters underscore the reach of her commercial ties: Mary Alexander to James Nevison, September 17, 1757; Mary Alexander to William McCollom, October 10, 1756; Mary Alexander to David Barclay and Sons, October 6, 1748; all in box 10, folder 1. David Barclay and Sons to Mary Alexander, March 14, 1758, May 31, 1758, August 8, 1758, December 9, 1758, March 24, 1759, June 22, 1759; all in box 10, folder 3, Alexander Papers, NYHS. Also see Haulman, *The Politics of Fashion*, 41–46; Eaton, *Printed Textiles*, 41–55; Jordan, "Women Merchants." For Murray, see Cleary, *Elizabeth Murray*, particularly 45–81.

9. *Commerce and Navigation of the United States: Letter from the Secretary of the Treasury . . . from the Year Ending the 30th September 1821* (Washington,

DC: Department of the Treasury, 1822), 8–11, 60–63, 84–85. *Commerce and Navigation of the United States: Letter from the Secretary of the Treasury . . . for the Year Ending September 30, 1841* (Washington, DC: Department of the Treasury, 1838–1845), 254, 118 (these figures total up the various categories of imports of wools and cotton manufactures). Also see Grant D. Forsyth, "Special Interest Protectionism and the Antebellum Woolen Textile Industry: A Contemporary Issue in Historical Context," *American Journal of Economics and Sociology* 65 (November 2006): 1025–58; Hood, *The Weaver's Craft*; Rasmussen, "Waging War with Wool."

10. The correspondence between Brown and Benson (changed to Brown, Benson, and Ives in 1792 and Brown and Ives in 1796) and their commission merchants, located in various places around the world, is similar, regardless of where the contacts are: Thayer and Sturgis (Charleston, South Carolina), and Ives, Series 1, Thayer and Sturgis, Subseries YYY, Domestic Trade Correspondence, B. 327 F.6; Paris J. Tillinghast (Fayetteville, North Carolina), Series 1, Subseries DDDD, Domestic Trade Correspondence, B. 330 F.8; John G. Ladd and Co. (Alexandria, Virginia, incorrectly identified as Gladd in the guide), Subseries OO, Series 1, Domestic Trade Correspondence, B.192–B.193; Talcott and Bowers (New Orleans), Subseries WWW, B.314–B.315; John Howell and Co. (Canton, China) to Brown, Benson, and Ives, November 26, 1795; Eastern Correspondents, Foreign Trade Correspondents, Series 2, Sub-Series B, B.104 F7; Ardessur Dody to Brown, Benson, and Ives, January 27, 1799, Eastern Correspondents, Foreign Trade Correspondents, Series 2, Sub-Series B, B.104 F7; M. Bickham (Isle of France) to Brown and Ives, November 30, 1807, Eastern Correspondents, Foreign Trade Correspondents, Series 2, Sub-Series B, B.104 F7; all in Brown Family Business Records, JCB. For an overview of the Brown family business history in trade, see James B. Hedges, "The Brown Papers: The Record of a Rhode Island Business Family," *Proceedings of the American Antiquarian Society* (April 1941): 21–36; Hedges, *The Browns of Providence Plantation: The Nineteenth Century* (Providence, RI: Brown University Press, 1968), 1–158. Also see Bean, *Yankee India*, for similar patterns of trade.

11. Cocheco Letters, 1864–1865, Lawrence & Company records, BL. Richard Candee, "The 'Great Factory' at Dover, New Hampshire: The Dover Manufacturing Co. Print Works, 1825," *Old-Time New England* 66 (Summer-Fall 1975): 39–51; Joyce Storey, "Printed Cottons in Victorian America," *Textile History* 15 (Fall 1984): 246–48.

12. For Peter, see *American Commercial Daily Advertiser*, October 1, 1806, 4; For Ned, see *American Commercial Daily Advertiser*, October 1, 1806, 4; both in NewsBank/Readex, Database: America's Historical Newspapers.

13. The variety is particularly pronounced in Montgomery's *Textiles in America*, which takes 235 pages, with double columns, to list all the kinds of fabrics available in the period 1650–1870. The availability of goods, particularly textiles, has been widely noted by scholars focusing on the growing consumer economy in the Revolutionary era. See, for instance, Breen "An Empire of Goods"; Breen, "Baubles of Britain"; Richard L. Bushman, *The Refinement of America: Persons, Houses, and Cities* (New York: Knopf, 1992); Cary Carson, Ronald Hoffman, and Peter J. Albert, eds., *Of Consuming Interests: The Style of Life in the Eighteenth Century* (Charlottesville: University Press

of Virginia, 1994). Recent literature has challenged top-down conceptions of fashion, arguing instead for localized styles as well as tastes that expressed social differences within given locations: DuPlessis, *Material Atlantic*; Haulman, *The Politics of Fashion*, 1–46; Lemire, "Second-Hand Beaux and 'Red-Armed Belles'"; Styles, *Dress of the People*; Lorna Weatherill, "Consumer Behaviour, Textiles and Dress in the Late Seventeenth and Early Eighteenth Century," *Textile History* 22 (January 1991): 297–310; Walker, *Exquisite Slaves*.

14. Montgomery, *Textiles in America*, 376–77. One of the books on which Montgomery relies suggests even more variety within the larger global market: John Munn, *Observations on British Wool and the Manufacturing of it in this Kingdom* (London: 1739).
15. Hedges, *The Browns of Providence Plantations*, 253. As Clare Haru Crowston argues in *Credit, Fashion, Sex*, design could make or break the value of goods.
16. Fabric Samples, December 1726, Mary Alexander, box 10, folder 4; Fabric Samples, June 1730, Mary Alexander, box 10, folder 5; Fabric Samples, June 16, 1735, Mary Alexander, box 10, folder 6; Fabric Samples, June 7, 1737, Mary Alexander, box 10, folder 7; Fabric Samples, May 1739, Mary Alexander, box 10, folder 8; Fabric Samples, March 1741, Mary Alexander, box 10, folder 9; Fabric Samples, March 1741, Mary Alexander, box 10, folder 10; all in Alexander Papers, NYHS. For these points, also see Haulman, *Politics of Fashion*, 41–46.
17. Livingston quote from Haulman, *The Politics of Fashion*, 45.
18. Ophelia Cary to William Cary, November 24, 1839, December 12, 1839, January 15, 1840, January 23, 1840, Feamster Family Papers, LC.
19. Hartford Tingley to Brown and Ives, October 29, 1819, F9, Ship *General Hamilton*, B.545 F9, Brown Family Business Records, JCB.
20. Ophelia Cary to William Cary, November 24, 1839, Feamster Family Papers, LC.
21. For orders of Salmon Falls drills, see Tiffany Ward and Co. to Mason and Lawrence, May 10, 1850, Letters Received, 1849; Josiah Fiske to Mason and Lawrence, May 11, 1850, Letters Received, 1849; Lewis and Hanford to Mason and Lawrence, July 24, 1850, Letters Received, 1849 (Lewis and Hanford specifically state that they like the fabric from this mill the best). For orders of Cocheco prints, see Day, Owens and Co. to Mason and Lawrence, August 2, 1850, Letters Received, 1849; Hunt, Daniels & Co. to Mason and Lawrence, August 22, 1850, Letters Received, 1849; Lord, Warren, Salter & Co. to Mason and Lawrence, September 6, 1850, Letters Received, 1849. For Lebanon sheeting, see Smith, Cary, and Moseley to Mason and Lawrence, October 19, 1850, and October 23, 1850, Letters Received, 1849–1855. All in Lawrence & Company records, BL. The same patterns are evident in the De Forest & Company Letter Book, Manuscript and Archives Division, Astor, Lenox, and Tilden Foundations, NYPL, in the 1840s and 1850s.
22. Talcott and Bowers to Brown and Ives, January 20, 1817, B.314 F4, Brown Family Business Records, JCB.
23. De Forest & Co. to J. Hepburn, February 6, 1847, De Forest & Company Letter Book, Manuscript and Archives Division, Astor, Lenox, and Tilden Foundations, NYPL.

24. Richard Gray to Joseph B. Lapsley, June 26, 1809, folder 23, box 1, Lapsley Family Business Records, McAllister Collection, LCP.
25. See, for instance A. M. and W. V. Strong to Mason and Lawrence, August 13, 1850, Letters Received, 1849; Hunt, Daniels & Co. to Mason and Lawrence, August 22, 1850, Letters Received, 1849; R. H. King and Co. to Mason and Lawrence, September 24, 1850, Letters Received, 1849-1855; William E. Pratt to Mason and Lawrence, January 10, 1850, Letters Received, 1849-1855; all in Lawrence & Company records, BL. Also see Storey, "Printed Cottons in Victorian America." For the general changes in marketing, see Fred Mitchell Jones, *Middlemen in the Domestic Trade of the United States, 1800-1860* (Urbana: University of Illinois Press, 1937); Glenn Porter and Harold C. Livesay, *Merchants and Manufacturers: Studies in the Changing Structure of Nineteenth-Century Marketing* (Baltimore: Johns Hopkins University Press, 1971); Hansjorg Siegenthaler, "What Price Style? The Fabric-Advisory Function of the Drygoods Commission Merchant, 1850-1860," *Business History Review* 41, no. 1 (1967): 46-61.
26. For particularly interesting examples of the responsibilities of supercargos, see Journal of the Ship Tyre, 1800-1803, Arnold Family Business Records, JCB; Memo Book, Charles Frederick Bradford, box 1, Edward Hickling Bradford Family Papers, 1825-1920, MHS.
27. Eliza Lucas Pinckney letter to Harriott Horry, ca. 1780, 43/110, SCHS.
28. Robinson to Mr. James Fraser, July 16, 1816, Letterbook, 1810-1825, HSP.
29. William E. Pratt to Mason and Lawrence, January 18, 1850; William E. Pratt to Mason and Lawrence, March 14, 1850. Also see William E. Pratt to Mason and Lawrence, January 15, 1850, January 18, 1850, January 22, 1850, January 23, 1850, January 31, 1850, February 11 and 12, 1850, March 7, 1850, March 9, 1850, March 14, 1850, March 18, 1850, March 20, 1850, March 26, 1850, March 28, 1850, April 1, 1850, April 8, 1850, May 16, 1850, June 7, 1850, August 7, 1850 (two letters on that date), October 1, 1850, October 10, 1850, October 28, 1850, December 26, 1805. All in Letters Received, 1849-1855, Lawrence & Company records, BL. Siegenthaler, "What Price Style?"
30. Letterbook, 1810-1825, HSP, particularly the letters from 48-65. Denton, Little & Co., New York, 1807-1808, folder 19, Lapsley Family Business Records, McAllister Collection, LCP.
31. Journal of the Ship Tyre, 1800-1803, Arnold Family Business Records, JCB.
32. Memo Book, Charles Frederick Bradford and Invoices of Brig John Gilpin, 7th Voyage, Charles Frederick Bradford; both in box 1, Edward Hickling Bradford Family Papers, 1825-1920, MHS.
33. John W. Donald to A. S. Chittenden, February 28, 1848, De Forest & Company Letter Book, Astor, Lenox, and Tilden Foundations, NYPL.
34. Letterbook, 1810-1825, HSP, particularly the letters from 48-65. Talcott and Bowers, Subseries WWW, B.314-B.315, Brown Family Business Records, JCB. Recent work has begun to explore those who failed as well, including Edward J. Balleisen, *Navigating Failure: Bankruptcy and Commercial Society in Antebellum America* (Chapel Hill: University of North Carolina Press, 2001); Bruce H. Mann, *Republic of*

Debtors: Bankruptcy in the Age of American Independence (Cambridge, MA: Harvard University Press, 2002); Scott A. Sandage, *Born Losers: A History of Failure in America* (Cambridge, MA: Harvard University Press, 2005).

35. See for instance John Shephard, Virginia, vol. 2, 12 ("failed"); Broughton & Green, Virginia, vol. 2, 39 ("not solvent"); J. Cropper & Co, Virginia, vol. 2, 77 (utterly worthless); Hulbert & Snipes, Virginia, vol. 2, 87 ("sold out and about to move to Rockingham"); Rudolph Massey, Virginia, vol. 3, 203 ("has become worthless"); Jacob Roxbury, Virginia, vol. 3, 214 ("Has fallen from grace & must go by the board"); Robinson & Keyes, Virginia, vol. 3, 215 (dissolved); C. B. Golden, Virginia, vol. 3, 224 ("execution is in the sheriff's hands"); all in R. G. Dun & Co. credit report volumes, BL. Also see New York Trade Agency, Reports, 1851, NYHS. For economic volatility, see Scott Reynolds Nelson, *A Nation of Deadbeats: An Uncommon History of America's Financial Disasters* (New York: Alfred A. Knopf, 2012).

36. No name given, March 8, 1818, Colles Family Papers, vol. 1, NYPL.

Chapter 4

1. Account book (Rebecca Coles), 1795–1800, box 1; Account book, John Coles of Enniscorthy (Rebecca Coles), 1801–1809, box 1; Col. John Coles of Enniscorthy (Rebecca Coles), Account Book, 1810–1815, Samuel Smith Papers, box 2; all in Samuel Smith Papers, #1729, UV. To the archivists who cataloged the Coles family collection, however, it seems to have been inconceivable that the textile business they found documented in the family papers could belong to her. So they attributed the account books to her husband instead. We now know they belonged to Rebecca Coles because historian Linda Sturtz matched up the handwriting. For the attribution of the handwriting and information about Coles, see Sturtz, *Within Her Power*, 232n13.

2. The reorganization of textile production by white male manufacturers in the new republic has been the focus of much of the scholarship. Some of the most influential work builds on the scholarship of E. P. Thompson, *The Making of the English Working Class* (New York: Pantheon, 1964), who equates efforts to centralize manufacturing with the advent of capitalism and focuses on the broader social and cultural effects. See Christopher Clark, *The Roots of Rural Capitalism: Western Massachusetts, 1780–1860* (Ithaca, NY: Cornell University Press, 1990); Dublin, *Women at Work*; Thomas Dublin, "Women and Outwork in a Nineteenth-Century New England Town: Fitzwilliam, New Hampshire, 1830–1860," in *The Countryside in the Age of Capitalist Transformation: Essays in the Social History of Rural America*, ed. Steven Hahn and Jonathan Prude (Chapel Hill: University of North Carolina Press, 1985), 51–70; Gary Kulik, "Factory Discipline in the New Nation: Almy, Brown & Slater and the First Cotton-Mill Workers, 1790–1808," *Massachusetts Review* 28 (Spring, 1987): 164–84; Kulik, "Pawtucket Village and the Strike of 1824: The Origins of Class Conflict in Rhode Island," *Radical History Review* 1 (May 1978): 5–38; Gail Fowler Mohanty, "Experimentation in Textile Technology, 1788–1790, and Its Impact

on Handloom Weaving and Weavers in Rhode Island," *Technology and Culture* 29 (January 1988): 1–33; Prude, *The Coming of the Industrial Order*, 34–64; Philip Scranton, *Proprietary Capitalism: The Textile Manufacture at Philadelphia, 1800–1885* (New York: Cambridge University Press, 1983), 75–134; Shelton, *Mills of Manayunk*, 7–53; Barbara M. Tucker, *Samuel Slater and the Origins of American Textile Industry* (Ithaca, NY: Cornell University Press, 1984), 33–120; Caroline F. Ware, *The Early New England Cotton Manufacture: A Study in Industrial Beginnings* (Boston: Houghton Mifflin, 1931).

3. Stripping away the accretion of gendered assumptions, the work of feminist scholars has revealed the relationship between the domestic (female) world and the commercial (male) world, establishing the economic value of uncompensated domestic labor, uncovering the variety of compensated labor that women performed, and showing how the devaluation of women's labor generally structured the commercial economy. For the naturalization of domestic labor in the first half of the nineteenth century, see Jeanne Boydston, *Home and Work: Housework, Wages, and the Ideology of Labor in the Early Republic* (New York: Oxford University Press, 1990). For the implications in the labor market, see Alice Kessler-Harris, *A Woman's Wage: Historical Meanings and Social Consequences* (Lexington: University of Kentucky Press, 1990). For a recent, compelling formulation of the issues, see Hartigan-O'Connor, "Gender's Value in the History of Capitalism" and Hartigan-O'Connor, "The Personal Is Political Economy." The work of Nancy Folbre makes the same point in a modern context; see, for instance, *The Invisible Heart: Economics and Family Values* (New York: New Press, 2001), and *Valuing Children: Rethinking the Economics of the Family* (Cambridge, MA: Harvard University Press, 2008). The necessity of women's economic contributions in the nineteenth century, even in white, middle-class households, is well established: Blewett, *Men, Women, and Work*; Jeanne Boydston, "To Earn Her Daily Bread," *Radical History Review* 35 (1986): 6–25; Alice Kessler-Harris, *Out to Work: A History of Wage-Earning Women in the United States* (New York: Oxford University Press, 1982); Stansell, *City of Women*; Robert Olwell, *Masters, Slaves, and Subjects: The Culture of Power in the South Carolina Low Country, 1740–1790* (Ithaca, NY: Cornell University Press, 1998), 141–80; Rockman, *Scraping By*. But the distinction between men's and women's labor lingers in the historiography, where women still fit uncomfortably within the paradigms of labor history, which has traditionally focused on men who were full-time paid laborers and not women who worked for wages irregularly or did not work for wages at all.

4. For this point, also see Anishanslin, *Portrait of a Woman in Silk*, particularly 25–103.

5. For women's presence in the textile trades as well as their movement into areas previous controlled by men, see Mary H. Blewett, "Work, Gender, and the Artisan Tradition in New England Shoemaking, 1780–1860," *Journal of Social History* 17 (Winter 1983): 221–48; Blewett, *Men, Women, and Work*; Clare Haru Crowston, *Fabricating Women: The Seamstresses of Old Regime France, 1675–1791* (Durham, NC: Duke University Press, 2001); Crowston, *Credit, Fashion, Sex*; Wendy Gamber, "A Gendered Enterprise: Placing Nineteenth-Century Businesswomen in History," *Business History Review* 72 (Summer 1998): 188–217; Wendy Gamber, *The Female*

Economy: The Millinery and Dressmaking Trades, 1860-1930 (Urbana: University of Illinois Press, 1997); Goldin, "The Economic Status of Women"; Beverly Lemire, *Dress, Culture, and Commerce: The English Clothing Trade before the Factory, 1660-1800* (London: Macmillan, 1997), esp. 43-74, 95-120; Dorothy McCombs, "Spinning and Weaving in Montgomery County," *Journal of the Roanoke Valley Historical Society* 11, no. 1 (1980): 73-104; Miller, *The Needle's Eye*; Gail Fowler Mohanty, "Handloom Outwork and Outwork Weaving in Rural Rhode Island, 1810-1821," *American Studies* 30 (Fall 1989): 41-68; Stana Nenadic, "The Social Shaping of Business Behaviour in the Nineteenth-Century Women's Garment Trades," *Journal of Social History* 31 (Spring 1998): 625-45; Elizabeth Sanderson, "The Edinburgh Milliners, 1720-1820," *Costume* 20 (1986): 18-28; Shelton, *Mills of Manayunk*; Laurel Thatcher Ulrich, "Wheels, Looms, and the Gender Division of Labor in Eighteenth Century New England," *William and Mary Quarterly* 55 (January 1998): 3-38; Vicente, *Clothing the Spanish Empire*.

6. As William M. Reddy argues in *The Rise of Market Culture: The Textile Trade and French Society, 1750-1900* (New York: Cambridge University Press, 1984), cotton textile workers came to represent the degradation of industrial labor generally in France. That same pattern also seems to apply, loosely, in the historiography of the United States, where mechanization in the manufacture of cheap cotton cloth has become the model for understanding all cloth production. See the discussion below for the deep roots of a narrative focused on mechanization and the displacement of hand labor. For its effects, see William R. Bagnall, *The Textile Industries of the United States* (Cambridge, MA: Riverside, 1893); Cole, *American Wool Manufacture*; Ware, *Early New England Cotton Manufacture*. Where the older literature tended to put other fibers into the same narrative as cotton, more recent work tends to focus on cotton, particularly in its connection to slavery, with the implication that this fiber, not others, defined the textile trade: Beckert, *Empire of Cotton*; Johnson, *River of Dark Dreams*; Baptist, *The Half Has Never Been Told*. For the continuation of hand labor, the labor of men, and artisanal traditions in textiles production, see Mary H. Blewett, "Manhood and the Market: The Politics of Gender and Class among the Textile Workers of Fall River, Massachusetts, 1870-1880," in *Work Engendered: Toward of New History of American Labor*, ed. Ava Baton (Ithaca, NY: Cornell University Press, 1991), 92-113; Adrienne D. Hood, "The Gender Division of Labor in the Production of Textiles in Eighteenth-Century, Rural Pennsylvania (Rethinking the New England Model)," *Journal of Social History* 27 (Spring 1994): 537-61; Hood, *The Weaver's Craft*; Wilbur S. Johnson, *Weaving a Common Thread: A History of the Woolen Industry in the Top of the Shenandoah Valley* (Winchester, VA: Winchester-Frederick County Historical Society, 1990); Mohanty, "Experimentation in Textile Technology"; Gail Fowler Mohanty, "Putting up with Putting-Out: Power-Loom Diffusion and Outwork for Rhode Island Mills, 1821-1829," *Journal of the Early Republic* 9 (Summer 1989) 191-216; Mohanty, "Handloom Outwork"; Seth Rockman, "Negro Cloth: Mastering the Market for Slave Clothing in Antebellum America," in *American Capitalism: New Histories*, ed. Christine Desan and Sven Beckert (New York: Columbia University Press, 2018), 170-194; Seth Rockman, "Plantation Goods and the National Economy

of Slavery" (unpublished manuscript); Scranton, *Proprietary Capitalism*; Cynthia J. Shelton, "The Role of Labor in Early Industrialization: Philadelphia, 1787–1837," *Journal of the Early Republic* 4 (Winter 1984): 365–94; Shelton, *Mills of Manayunk*.
7. As Ulrich argues in *Age of Homespun*, the term acquired positive political meanings during and after the Revolution. But it was also pejorative, indicating low-quality cloth. Spinning has been understudied, in part, because of its association with women; see John Styles, The Spinning Project, http://spinning-wheel.org/.
8. Ulrich, *Age of Homespun*, particularly 12–40.
9. US Treasury Department, *Alexander Hamilton's Report on the Subject of Manufactures*, 6th ed. (Philadelphia: 1827), 41–42, accessed via *Sabin Americana*, Gale, Cengage Learning.
10. US Treasury Department, *Alexander Hamilton's Report*, 41–42. For Coxe's participation in the Pennsylvania Society for the Encouragement of Manufactures and the Useful Arts, see Tench Coxe, *An Address to an Assembly of the Friends of American Manufacturers* (Philadelphia: 1787). Also see Shelton, "Role of Labor in Early Industrialization," 366–67.
11. US Department of the Treasury, *Statement of the Arts and Manufactures of the United States of America for the Year 1810* (Philadelphia: 1814), 2–4.
12. US Department of the Treasury, *Statement of the Arts and Manufactures . . . for the Year 1810*, opening table and xiv, l, lvii.
13. US Department of the Treasury, *Statement of the Arts and Manufactures . . . for the Year 1810*, quotes on i, vii; see i–lxi for the focus on mechanization.
14. *Digest of Accounts of Manufacturing Establishments in the United States, and of Their Manufactures* (Washington, DC: 1823). In addition to the scholarship in note 5, see the following in *The Cambridge History of Western Textiles*, ed. David Jenkins (Cambridge: Cambridge University Press, 2003): David Jenkins, "The Western Wool Textile Industry in the Nineteenth Century," 2:761–89; Natalie Rothstein, "Silk: The Industrial Revolution and After," 2:790–808; Peter Solar, "The Linen Industry in the Nineteenth Century," 2:809–23.
15. Jan de Vries, "The Industrial Revolution and the Industrious Revolution," *Journal of Economic History* 54, no. 2 (June 1994): 249–70. Hood, *The Weaver's Craft*, argues that cloth production in the colonies and the early republic was always tied to larger patterns of global trade and that handwork took place alongside mechanized production. In addition to Hood, also see the following for the continuation of household production or women's domestic work: Mohanty, "Experimentation in Textile Technology"; Mohanty, "Putting up with Putting-Out"; Mohanty, "Handloom Outwork"; Rockman, "Negro Cloth"; Rockman, "Plantation Goods and the National Economy of Slavery"; Shelton, "The Role of Labor in Early Industrialization"; Ulrich, "Wheels, Looms, and the Gender Division of Labor."
16. Styles, "The Spinning Project." Also see Gay Gullickson, *Spinners and Weavers of Auffay: Rural Industry and the Sexual Division of Labor in a French Village, 1750–1850* (New York: Cambridge University Press, 1986); Hood, *The Weaver's Craft*, esp. 67–84; Luc Martin, "The Rise of the New Draperies in Norwich, 1550–1622," in *The New Draperies in the Low Countries and England, 1300–1800*, ed. N. B. Harte

(New York: Oxford University Press, 1997), 245-74; Mohanty, "Experimentation in Textile Technology"; Carole Shammas, "The Decline of Textile Prices in England and British America Prior to Industrialization," *Economic History Review* 47 (August 1994): 483-507; Ulrich, "Wheels, Looms, and the Gender Division of Labor"; Ulrich, *Age of Homespun*, 172-207. The association of women with spinning, however, did not mean that the work was only done by women or that women did not engage in other aspects of textile production. Young men did hand spinning with basic wheels, and men operated mechanized spinning jennies and mules, which were powered by hand. Mule spinning was a skilled position that male artisans guarded and from which they excluded women. Women replaced male spinners when the jennies and mules were powered by water and steam. Women were often more involved in other parts of the production process as well. See, for instance, Martha Howell, "Women's Work in the New and Light Draperies of the Low Countries," in *The New Draperies in the Low Countries and England, 1300-1800*, ed. N. B. Harte (New York: Oxford University Press, 1997), 197-216; McCombs, "Spinning and Weaving in Montgomery County."

17. For the inability of colonial producers to supply the local market, see Hood, *The Weaver's Craft*, 112-39. For the process of turning flax into linen, see Leslie Clarkson, "The Linen Industry in Early Modern Europe," in Jenkins, *The Cambridge History of Western Textiles*, 1:473-92.

18. George Taylor, Ledger, Special Collections, Rutgers University RU. For a similar notebook, see Weaver's draft notebook/account book, MS1989.22, RLCW. For Davis, see Weaver's draft notebook, MS1989.6, Special Collections, RLCW. For weaving, see Hood, *The Weaver's Craft*; Ulrich, "Wheels, Looms, and the Gender Division of Labor"; Ulrich, *Age of Homespun*, 75-107.

19. George Taylor, Ledger, Special Collections, RU. Weaver's draft notebook, MS1989.6, RLCW.

20. For women and weaving, see McCombs, "Spinning and Weaving in Montgomery County"; Mohanty, "Experimentation in Textile Technology"; Ulrich, "Wheels, Looms, and the Gender Division of Labor"; Ulrich, *Age of Homespun*, particularly 75-107, 174-207, 277-305, 306-39. Yet, as Adrienne D. Hood argues in *The Weaver's Craft*, the movement of women into weaving varied and depended on the ethnic background and artisanal traditions of the region. Also see Blewett, "Manhood and the Market"; Adrienne D. Hood, "Flax Seed, Fibre and Cloth: Pennsylvania's Domestic Linen Manufacture and Its Irish Connection, 1700-1830," in *European Linen Industry in Historical Perspective*, ed. Brenda Collens and Philip Ollerenshaw (New York: Oxford University Press, 2003), 139-58; Scanton, *Proprietary Capitalism*; Shelton, "Role of Labor in Early Industrialization"; Shelton, *The Mills of Manayunk*. For a fascinating perspective on ethnic identity and textiles, seeMary H. Blewett, *The Yankee Yorkshireman: Migration Lived and Imagined* (Urbana: University of Illinois Press, 2009). The 1810 census commended North Carolina, among other states, for its textile production: *Statement of the Arts and Manufactures of the United States of America for the Year 1810*, viii, lvii. Estate Inventories in Orange County, North Carolina, 1780-1830, suggest the extent of textile production there. Most

inventories for Orange County have equipment for textile production between 1800 and 1835: Inventories, Sales and Accounts of Estates, Orange County, vols. 2, 3, 4, 5, 7, 8, 9, 10, 11, NCSA. For John Tayloe's cloth manufactory, see John Tayloe Account Books for 1805–1807, 1806, April 7, 1806, to September 7, 1806, January 29, 1816, to February 16, 1816, 1817–1819; all in Tayloe Family Papers, Section 2. John Tayloe Account Book, 1810–1814; Minute Book Concerning Spinning at Mount Airy, 1806–1807; John Tayloe Minute Book, 1811–1812; John Tayloe, Minute Book, 1814; Tayloe Family Papers, 1740–1860. John Tayloe Account Book, 1776–1786, Section 4, Tayloe Family Papers. All in VMHC.

21. For machinery, its uneven quality, and need for skilled oversight see for instance: John Baytop Scott Agreement, 18 May 1812, VMHC; White and Robinson Ledger, 1851–1852, Barcode 1102539, Local Government Records Collection, Botetourt County Court Records, LV; Daniel Hack Letter, 1833, Accession 22958, Personal Papers Collection, LV; William Blackburn to Brown and Ives, 15 January 1814, Series 12, Subseries D: 1811-1815, Chronological Correspondence, B. 386 F7, Brown Family Business Records, JCB; Ray Clarke to Brown and Ives, Cyrus Butler, and Samuel G. Arnold and Co, 21 September 1816, B.63 F3 Brown Family Business Records, JCB; Aaron Mitchell to Amos A. Lawrence, 6 July 1839, Box 3, Amos Adams Lawrence Papers, 1803-1887, MHS.

22. For carding mills, see Account book, 1818–1821, and Account book, 1835–1843, Wayland Family Records, Accession 22398, Business Records Collection; Jacob W. Bowman, Journal, 1847–1857, Accession 28075, Business Records Collection; Samuel Pursel, Ledgers, 1843–1860, 28585 Miscellaneous reel 515, Business Records Collection; Ledger, 1831–1832, Barcode 1102312, Local Government Records Collection, Cumberland County Court Records; White and Robinson Ledger, 1851–1852, Barcode 1102539, Local Government Records Collection, Botetourt County Court Records; John Rogers Letters, 1816–1841, 1851, Accession 37385, Personal Papers Collection; all in LV. Watson Carter Accounts, 1837–1850; Carter Watson Account Book, 1822–1859; Minor Winn, Account Book, 1797–1815; all in VMHC. Hosea Treat, Ledger; RU. Also see Johnson, *Weaving a Common Thread*.

23. For the persistence of male mule spinners, see Blewett, "Manhood and the Market"; Shelton, "The Role of Labor in Early Industrialization"; Shelton, *The Mills of Manayunk*. For a similar dynamic in France, with the persistence of hand-powered spinning machines, operated by men, see Reddy, *Rise of Market Culture*.

24. For the experience of women in early factories and then their replacement, see Dublin, *Women at Work*; Mohanty, "Experimentation in Textile Technology"; Prude, *The Coming of the Industrial Order*, 34–99; Shelton, *The Mills of Manayunk*.

25. Natalie Rothstein, "Silk in the Early Modern Period, c. 1500–1780," in Jenkins, *The Cambridge History of Western Textiles*, 1:528–61, and Rothstein, "Silk: The Industrial Revolution and After." Also see Anishanslin, *Portrait of a Woman in Silk*.

26. Quote from Deborah Logan to Deborah Norris Woodson, June 13, 1831, Papers of the Wallace Family, #2869, UV. For references to Logan's silk production in the late eighteenth century, see John F. Watson, Annals of Philadelphia, Yi2 1069.F, 230, Print Department, LCP; see 71 for references to silk production more generally.

J. H. Cobb to Amos A. Lawrence, August 20, 1838, box 1, Amos Adams Lawrence Papers, 1803–1887, MHS. For the renewed interest in silk production in the nineteenth century and the importance of women's labor, see Ben Marsh, "The Republic's New Clothes: Making Silk in the Antebellum United States," *Agricultural History* 86 (Fall 2012): 206–34. Silk production also became tied up with more radical reform movements of the antebellum period; see Christopher Clark, *The Communitarian Moment: The Radical Challenge of the Northampton Association* (Ithaca, NY: Cornell University Press, 1995). Also see Watt, "Whims and Fancies."

27. Hey Family Papers, folder 105, box 1, HSP, chart the development of the Hey family's wool mill, one of many in the area. Also see Samuel Pursel, Ledgers, 1843–1860, 28585 Miscellaneous reel 515, Business Records Collection; Wayland Family Papers, 1769–1889, Accession 22665, Personal Papers Collection; both in LV. For the Shenandoah Valley generally; see Johnson, *Weaving a Common Thread*. For an overview, see Jenkins, "The Western Wool Textile Industry in the Nineteenth Century."

28. For handloomed wool fabric, see Irvine-Newbold Family Papers, boxes 40, 41, 42, and 44, vols. 108, 109, 110, 111, 112, HSP. For women who wove wool at home see Elizabeth Ann Cooley McClure, Diary; Amanda Jane Cooley Roberts, Diary; both in VMHC. The accounts of fulling mills also suggest the persistence of handloomed wool. See for instance Tilton Family, Account Books, vol. 2, RU; Shadrach Gill and Thomas Fawcett Account Book, 1832–1842, Mss. Acc. 2011.301, WM. For the persistence of handloomed wool, either by workers in the putting-out system or by independent producers, see Prude, *Coming of the Industrial Order*, 34–99; Rockman, "Negro Cloth"; Rockman, "Plantation Goods and the National Economy of Slavery"; Scranton, *Proprietary Capitalism*; Ulrich, *Age of Homespun*, 306–39.

29. Solar, "Linen Industry in the Nineteenth Century." As Leslie Clarkson points out in "The Linen Industry in Early Modern Europe," much of linen production is not well documented, because it was done so widely and sold locally; the same was true in the nineteenth century. For a description of the work involved in linen production, see Ulrich, *Age of Homespun*, 277–305.

30. Frederick Tupper and Helen Tyler Brown, eds., *Grandmother Tyler's Book: The Recollections of Mary Palmer Tyler (Mrs. Royall Tyler), 1775–1866* (New York, 1925); also see Kathleen M. Brown, *Foul Bodies: Cleanliness in Early America* (New Haven, CT: Yale University Press, 2009), 224–25. For Tyler's foray into silk, see Marsh, "The Republic's New Clothes," 221. Elizabeth Lumpkin Motely Bagby Commonplace Book, 1824–1832; McClure Diary; Roberts Diary; all in VMHC. Also see, for example Journal of Anna Kagey Wayland, 1847–1865, Accession 24649b, Personal Papers Collection, LV; Martha Frink, Diary, 1858, Cairns Collection, UW; Pearl Family Account Book, 1792–1845, MHS; Weaving Accounts, Nathaniel Bangs Orderly Book, 1742–1846, MHS. Ulrich, "Wheels, Looms, and the Gender Division of Labor," and Ulrich, *Age of Homespun*, particularly 75–107, 174–207, 277–305, 306–39.

31. Crowston, *Fabricating Women*; Miller, *The Needle's Eye*. Even in the early modern period most people paid to have their clothing made: Anne Buck, "Buying Clothes in Bedfordshire: Customers and Tradesmen, 1700–1800," *Textile History* 22 (January 1991): 211–37; Lemire, "Consumerism"; Spufford and Mee, *Clothing of the Common*

Sort; John Styles, "Clothing the North: The Supply of Non-Elite Clothing in the Eighteenth-Century North of England," *Textile History* 25 (January 1994): 139–66.
32. For the ready-made industry, see Spufford and Mee, *The Clothing of the Common Sort*; Lemire, *Dress, Culture, and Commerce*, particularly chapters 1 and 2.
33. M. Miller, *The Needle's Eye*.
34. McClure, Diary; Roberts, Diary; both in VMHC. The Cooley women's work in sewing and tailoring fit those described by Miller, *The Needle's Eye*, for the rural Northeast. Rural merchants sold fabric to customers without the skill or inclination to make it into clothing and then set those customers up with a good seamstress. Some contracted directly with seamstresses for sewing and millinery work requested by their customers. Others served as economic intermediaries, transferring store credit from clients to the women who did work for them. See, for instance, Thomas C. Scott Records, 1817–1823, Accession 27933, vol 1., 11 (Mrs. Barnes paid her account with breaches), vol. 1, 16 (Mrs. William Stringfellow paid her account with a mohair hat and a bonnet); Easley, Holt and Company (Halifax County, Va.), Records, 1817–1857, Accession 27608, December 1837 (Maria Owens orders fabric for a client), box 3, 26 January 1838 (Owens orders fabric for a different client); Campbell, Wilson, & Co. Journals, 1833–1848, Accession 364, 365, 30 (pays Ann Mansfield for making a cloak); all in LV.
35. McClure, Diary; Roberts, Diary; both in VMHC. As historian Clare Crowston has shown, women started making inroads in late seventeenth-century France and eventually established their own seamstress guild, which oversaw dressmaking. Women elsewhere set themselves up in dressmaking and then other areas of tailoring that had been the province of men. Crowston, *Fabricating Women*; Miller, *The Needle's Eye*. For the new republic, see Marla R. Miller, "The Last Mantuamaker: Craft Tradition and Commercial Change in Boston, 1760–1840," *Early American Studies* 4 (Fall 2006): 372–424; Gamber, *Female Economy*; Anne Preston, "'To Learn Me the Whole of the Trade': Conflict between a Female Apprentice and a Merchant Tailor in Ante-Bellum New England," *Labor History* 24 (Spring 1983): 259–73.
36. Crowston, *Credit, Fashion, Sex*; Gamber, *Female Economy*; Miller, "Last Mantuamaker."
37. Drafting schemes for pattern making were widely circulated in the 1850s: D. B. Briggs, *Madame Briggs' Improved Diagram for Cutting Ladies' & Children's Dresses, Basques, Boys' Coats, &c.* (Albany, NY: [1857?]); *The Ladies' Self Instructor in Millinery and Mantua Making, Embroidery and Applique, Canvas-Work, Knitting, Netting, and Crochet-Work* (Philadelphia: 1855). Wendy Gamber, "'Reduced to Science': Gender, Technology, and Power in the American Dressmaking Trade, 1860–1910," *Technology and Culture* 36, no. 3 (July 1995): 455–82; Claudia B. Kidwell, *Cutting a Fashionable Fit: Dressmakers' Drafting Systems in the United States* (Washington, DC: Smithsonian Institution Press, 1979).
38. Account book (Rebecca Coles), 1795–1800, Samuel Smith Papers, box 1, #1729, UV. Weaving Accounts, Nathaniel Bangs Orderly Book, MHS. Hannah the weaver's note, April 5, 1792, CHM.

39. See, for instance, William Stewart to Mason and Lawrence, May 13, 1850, May 15, 1850, May 16, 1850, and May 17, 1850; G. S. Robbins & Son to Mason and Lawrence, May 20, 1850; all in Letters Received, 1849, Lawrence & Company records, BL. Also see Bean, *Yankee India*, particularly 211–23.

Part II

1. Bagby Commonplace Book. For a similar inscription, see Jane Catherine Fontaine Mead Account Book, 1860–1864; Mead described it as an "Account of things bought for myself." Both in VMHC.

Chapter 5

1. "Representation to the Supreme Executive Council," Minutes, vol. 1; January 12, 1789; February 20, 1809, Minutes of the Acting Committee, vol. 6; both in Pennsylvania Prison Society Records, HSP. Many thanks to Margaret Abruzzo for drawing my attention to these records. Such issues were not uncommon among charitable organizations. See Gamble, "The Promiscuous Economy," 35; Simon P. Newman, *Embodied History: The Lives of the Poor in Early Philadelphia* (Philadelphia: University of Pennsylvania Press, 2003), 16–39.
2. Quote from Gamble, "The Promiscuous Economy," 42. For the point about taverns taking clothing as payment and doubling as used clothing stores, see Zabin, *Dangerous Economies*, 69; Beverly Lemire, "Peddling Fashion: Salesmen, Pawnbrokers, Taylors, Thieves and the Second-Hand Clothes Trade in England c. 1700–1800." *Textile History* 22 (1991): 67–82; Styles, "Clothing the North"; Walker, "Women, Theft and the World of Stolen Goods." For the creative ways that people have made money and currency themselves, see Viviana A. Zelizer, *Social Meaning of Money* (Princeton, NJ: Princeton University Press, 1997).
3. The analysis in this paragraph and the chapter more generally is informed by Desan, *Making Money*, particularly her focus on the ways law shaped conceptions of money, its production, and its exchange. Also see Clarie Priest, "Currency Policies and Legal Development in Colonial New England," *Yale Law Journal* 110 (2001): 1303–1405. For currency in the United States, see A. Barton Hepburn, *A History of the Currency of the United States with a Brief Description of the Currency Systems of all Commercial Nations* (New York: Macmillan, 1915). For the colonial period, see John J. McCusker, *Money and Exchange in Europe and America, 1600–1775* (Chapel Hill: University of North Carolina Press, 1978). The shift from pounds to dollars as the standard unit of account is evident in the account books of both individuals and merchants, who slowly moved from one to the other between the 1810s and 1820s. Although the First and Second Banks of the United States worked with dollars as the standard unit of account, Americans did not shift to dollars until after the War of 1812. Figuring value

across different standard units of account was a fact of daily life, as suggested by tables in almanacs: Asa Houghton, *The Gentlemen's and Ladies' Diary: Or an Almanack for . . . 1797* (Worcester, MA: 1796); *North-American Calendar, or an Almanack for the Year of our Lord 1797* (Providence, RI: 1796); *Town and Country Almanack for the Year of Our Lord, 1797* (Norwich, CT: 1796); Nathan Daboll, *The New-England Almanac, and Gentlemen and Ladies' Diary, for the Year of our Lord Christ, 1797* (New London, CT: 1796). That was true even in daily pocketbooks designed exclusively for women: *The American Ladies Pocket Book for 1797* (Philadelphia,1796); *The American Ladies' Pocket-Book; or Useful Register of Business and Amusement for the Year 1803* (Philadelphia: 1802); *The American Ladies' Pocket-Book for the Year 1810* (Philadelphia: 1809).

4. The circulation of textiles as currency is well established in the literature. See: Hartigan O'Connor, *The Ties That Buy*, 114; Beverly Lemire, "Shifting Currency: The Culture and Economy of the Second Hand Trade in England, c. 1600–1850," in *Old Clothes, New Looks*, ed. Alexandra Palmer and Hazel Clark (New York: Bloomsbury Academic, 2005), 29–48; MacKay, "Why They Stole"; Mendelsohn, "Rag Race"; Tebbutt, *Making Ends Meet*; Woloson, *In Hock*; Zabin, *Dangerous Economies*, 57–80. Textiles had also served as currency in the global trade; Lemire, *Global Trade*, 32–36.

5. Jones and Stallybrass, *Renaissance Clothing*. Also see Styles, *Dress of the People*.

6. Prude, "To Look Upon the 'Lower Sort'"; *County of Penn vs. Defendants Not Known*, May 21, 1845, Martin Lutz Legal Case Book, HSP.

7. *People v. John McFadden*, January 4, 1805, NYMA. *State v. Henry Adams*, 1825-20A, 1825-17A through 1829-16A, Bills of Indictment, Court of General Sessions, Charleston District, SCDAH. *People v. Mary Barnes*, June 9, 1817, April to July 1817, NYMA.

8. *State v. Henry*, #63; *State v. Cain, Meshack, and Charles*, #86a; *State v. Cain*, #88; all in Trial Papers, Court of Magistrates and Freeholders, Anderson County, SCDAH. *State v. Elizabeth Smith*, 1800–1808, Criminal Actions Concerning Slaves and Free Persons of Color, Granville County; *State v. Jacob*, 1815, Criminal Actions Concerning Slaves and Free Persons of Color, Craven County; both in NCSA. Also see *State v. Mary*, #119, Trial Papers, Court of Magistrates and Freeholders, Spartanburg County, SCDAH.

9. *State v. Harriet, Perry, Wiley, Judy, Jordan, and Jim*, #85, Trial Papers, Court of Magistrates and Freeholders, Spartanburg County, SCDAH.

10. *People v. Napoleon Devisse*, December 10, 1839, NYMA.

11. M. Peddle, *Rudiments of Taste, in a Series of Letters from a Mother to her Daughters* (Philadelphia: 1795), 57. *Jeffersonian Republican*, June 5, 1845, America's Historical Newspapers. Petition 21386043, Records of the Equity Court, Bills, Document Number 1860-303, box 7, Microfilm: Order #27, Reel D1267, SCDAH, Digital Library on American Slavery, http://library.uncg.edu/slavery/details.aspx?pid=13241. For neatness, see Brown, *Foul Bodies*; C. M. Jackson-Houlston, "'The Burial-Place of the Fashions': The Representation of the Dress of the Poor in Illustrated Serial Prose by Dickens and Hardy," *Textile History* 33, no. 1 (2002): 98–111; Payne, "Murillo-like Rags or Clean Pinafores"; Smiles, "Defying Comprehension"; Styles, *Dress of the People*, 71–83.

12. *Frankfort (KY) Guardian of Freedom*, April 9, 1802, 4. Also in *Baltimore Telegraph and Daily Advertiser*, May 29, 1804, 2; *Stockbridge (MA) Western Star*, June 9, 1804, 2; *Portsmouth (NH) Oracle*, July 7, 1804, 1. All in NewsBank/Readex, Database: America's Historical Newspapers. Horatio Alger, *Ragged Dick; or, Street Life in New York with the Boot Blacks* (New York: A. K. Loring, 1868).

13. Peddle, *Rudiments of Taste*, 57. *Rudiments of Taste* was first published in England and then reprinted in the United States. On the importance of neatness to the poor, see note 12.

14. *People v. Toby (a slave) of J. Coventry*, October 4, 1804, NYMA. One of the most famous examples of the importance of clothing in marking free status is Craft, *Running a Thousand Miles for Freedom*, 30, 67; also see Hilliard, *Masters, Slaves, and Exchange*, 170.

15. Quoted in Beverly Lemire, "Second-Hand Beaux," 398. Karen Haltunnen, *Confidence Men and Painted Women: A Study of Middle-Class Culture in America, 1830–1870* (New Haven, CT: Yale University Press, 1986). For concerns about calicos, also see Lemire, *Fashion's Favourite*; Vicente, *Clothing the Spanish Empire*, 9–11, 65–83.

16. Peddle, *Rudiments of Taste*, 57. For a discussion of the literature on spendthrift wives, see Sievens, "Female Consumerism and Household Authority." Those concerns continued in the late nineteenth and early twentieth centuries. See Nan Enstad, *Ladies of Labor, Girls of Adventure: Working Women, Popular Culture, and Labor Politics at the Turn of the Twentieth Century* (New York: Columbia University Press, 1999); Kathy Peiss, *Cheap Amusements: Working Women and Leisure in Turn-of-the-Century New York* (Philadelphia: Temple University Press, 1985).

17. According to the Library Company of Philadelphia's digitized versions of Edward W. Clay's *Life in Philadelphia* series, he began drawing the caricatures in 1828, after seeing George and Robert Cruikshank's *Life in London* drawings while on a trip there. Published in Philadelphia between 1828 and 1830, the caricatures feature "the hyper-elegant urban black" who "would soon become one of the two essential stereotypes of the minstrel stage." For the images and description, see Anti-Abolitionist Images, Digital Collections, LCP, http://utc.iath.virginia.edu/abolitn/gallclayf.html.

18. *People v. Mary Barnes*, June 9, 1817, NYMA. For cases with similar specificity, see for example: *People v. Rebecca Tarleton*, August 7, 1807; *People v. Frank*, December 2, 1807; *People v. Joseph Deis*, March 31, 1808; *People v. Sine Marshall*, June 11, 1808; *People v. Mary Grant*, May 4, 1826; *People v. Jane Seely (2)*, April 4, 1826; *People v. Catherine Brennan and Ann Allison*, May 15, 1844; *People v. Mary Dougherty*, June 7, 1844. For the mechanisms that explain the dissemination of information about value, see Ellen Hartigan-O'Connor, "Public Sales and Public Values in Eighteenth-Century North America," *Early American Studies* 13 (Fall 2015): 749–73.

19. The availability of textiles among servants, the enslaved, and free Blacks is evident in runaway advertisements; see Nunley, *At the Threshold of Liberty*, 40–69; Prude, "To Look Upon the 'Lower Sort' "; Waldstreicher, "Reading the Runaways." Peter's master had good reason to believe that readers would know what he was talking about, given the wide distribution of cloth and clothing in the previous century.

20. *People v. Susan Munro*, June 4, 1807. It is commonplace in British history that cloth and clothing were among the most common, if not the most common, stolen goods. See, for instance, Lemire, "The Theft of Clothes"; Walker, "Women, Theft and the World of Stolen Goods." In the United States, the courts that tried cases of petty theft did not all keep records; the records of those courts that did have not all survived. But records from Connecticut, Massachusetts, New York, South Carolina, and Virginia indicate that textiles were popular targets, if not the most popular targets, of theft between the Revolution and the Civil War as well. See New London County, County Court, Records of Trials; New London County, County Court, Files; Litchfield County, County Court, Records; all in CSL. Case Files, Justices of the Peace, Adlow Collection, BPL. Municipal Court and Police Court, Boston, Judicial Archives, Massachusetts State Archives, Boston, Massachusetts. Attorney General Indictment Papers, NYMA. Indictments, County and Intermediate Court, Kershaw County; Indictments, Court of General Sessions, Kershaw County; Trial Papers, Court of Magistrates and Freeholders, Kershaw County; Bills of Indictment, Court of General Sessions, Charleston District; Trial Papers, Court of Magistrates and Freeholders, Spartanburg County; Trial Papers, Court of Magistrates and Freeholders, Fairfield County; Trial Papers, Court of Magistrates and Freeholders, Pendleton District; Trial Papers, Court of Magistrates and Freeholders, Anderson County; all in SCDAH. Richmond City, Hustings Court, Suit Papers, Ended Causes; Criminal Records, County Court, Albemarle County; LV. Docket of Mayor Joseph Tate, VM.
21. *People v. Rosenah Gray*; *People v. Thomas Cooney and others*, April 7, 1804; *People v. Joseph Guignon*, September 5, 1817, July to October 1817; all in NYMA.
22. John Goodwin, Account Books, Kershaw County, SCDAH, vol. 1, account of John N. Carpenter. *State v. Wyatt Harris*, #48, Trial Papers, Court of Magistrates and Freeholders, Spartanburg County; *State v. Amos*, #245, Trial Papers, Court of Magistrates and Freeholders, Anderson County; both in SCDAH.
23. Charles Dickens, *Oliver Twist* (London: 1839).
24. For these practices, see Margot Finn, *The Character of Credit: Personal Debt in English Culture, 1740–1914* (New York: Cambridge University Press, 2003); Mann, *Neighbors and Strangers*; Martin, *Buying Into the World of Goods*; Craig Muldrew, *The Economy of Obligation: The Culture of Credit and Social Relations in Early Modern England* (New York: St. Martin's, 1998); Priest, "Currency Policies and Legal Development"; Priest, *Credit Nation*.
25. Virginia, vol. 2, 140; Virginia, vol. 2, 135; both in R. G. Dun & Co., BL.
26. Connecticut, vol. 45, A3, R. G. Dun & Co., BL.
27. *State v. Stephen B. Daniel*, 1823-54A, 1823-47A through 1825-16A, Bills of Indictment, Court of General Sessions, Charleston District, SCDAH. For literature on women passing counterfeit bills, see Mihm, *A Nation of Counterfeiters*, 209–59; Haltunnen, *Confidence Men and Painted Women*.
28. *State v. Stephen B. Daniel*. *State v. Doctor and Jemima*, 1822, # 3, reel 2916, Trial Papers, Court of Magistrate and Freeholders, Anderson/Pendleton District, SCDAH. Although the index indicates a verdict of not guilty, there are actually two outcomes attached to the records, one indicating a guilty verdict and another indicating an

acquittal, suggesting a split decision in which only one of the defendants was found guilty. Unfortunately, the verdicts do not give the enslaved people's names. For slaves marking and otherwise keeping track of money, see Penningroth, *Claims of Kinfolk*, 97–98. For the practice of marking money more generally, see Zelizer, *Social Meaning of Money*.

29. *State v. William C. Workman*, Indictments, Court of General Sessions, Kershaw County, SCDAH. For the broad prohibitions on buying from or selling to enslaved people, see Thomas Cooper and David James McCord, *The Statutes at Large of South Carolina* (Columbia, SC: 1836–41), 7: 468–69. An Act to Amend the Laws in Relation to Slaves and Free Persons of Color (1834) prohibited enslaved people from working as clerks and expanded the prohibitions of selling to an enslaved person without a ticket from the master to cover all goods. By contrast, earlier statutes had emphasized commodities, such as indigo, rice, and cotton: An Act More Effectually to Prevent Shop-Keepers, Traders, and Others from Dealing with Slaves Having No Tickets from Their Masters; and for Other Purposes Therein Mentioned (1796), 454–55, An Act to Increase the Penalties Which Are Now by Law Inflicted on Persons Who Deal or Trade with Negro Slaves, without a License of Ticket from their Master or Owner, or the Person Having Charge of Them (1817), both in *Statutes at Large*, vol. 7. For interpretations, see John Belton O'Neall, *The Negro Law of Slavery* (Columbia, SC: 1848), 46–47. In fact, enslaved people frequently traded with each other, free people, and established merchants.

30. *The History of a Little Frenchman and His Bank Notes: Rags, Rags, Rags* (Philadelphia: 1815), quotes from 5. Rockman, *Scraping By*, 174.

31. *State v. John Allison*, folder 1783, Criminal Action Records, Orange County, NCSA. For a contemporary critique, see Benjamin Davies, *The Bank Torpedo; or, Bank Notes Proved to Be a Robbery on the Public, and the Real Cause of the Distresses of the Poor* (New York: 1810). On the difficulties banknotes posed to working people, also see Joshua R. Greenberg, *Advocating the Man: Masculinity, Organized Labor, and the Household in New York, 1800–1840* (New York: Columbia University Press, 2008), chapter 3.

32. *People v. William McCready*, February 23, 1850; *People v. George Williams*, May 13, 1850; *People v. Cuff Ivers*, November 5, 1805; *People v. Gulielmo Michelle*, September 14, 1839; all in NYMA.

33. *People v. Sally McDonald*, August 9, 1804, NYMA. For accounts paid in spinning and weaving, see James Campbell Account Books, 1793–1799, vols. 11–13, Mss. MsV Ame11–13, WM; Anah Clark, Account Book, MS1994.5, RLCW; Christopher Tompkins Account Book, MS1940.3, RLCW. Some merchants were running cottage industries, although workers were still paid in goods: Samuel and Bethel Morris Account Book, 1819–1835, Mss. Acc. 2009.142, (Fairfield County, Connecticut); Shadrach Gill and Thomas Fawcett Account Book, 1832–1842, Mss. Acc. 2011.301 (Montgomery County, Maryland); both in WM. For freedom suits and apprentices, see Martin Lutz Legal Case Book, HSP. *State v. Daniel Milander*, 1806 8A, 1786 1A though 1808-27A, Bills of Indictment, Court of General Sessions, Charleston District, SCDAH.

34. *People v. Mary Menix* (2), January 11, 1820, NYMA. Docket of Mayor Joseph Tate, October 1, 1836, 67. *Commonwealth v. Christopher Meyers alias William Lewis*, May 1790, Commonwealth Causes, reel 235, 1749-1794, Court Records, Albemarle County, LV.

Chapter 6

1. The outlines of Jane Cooley's business come through the diaries of two of her daughters: Elizabeth Ann Cooley McClure Diary; Amanda Jane Cooley Roberts Diary; both in VHS. She actually had nine children, but the others had either died or left home by the time Elizabeth and Amanda were keeping their diaries. The Cooley women and Jinsy, a young woman they enslaved, feature in Beth Barton Schweiger, *A Literate South: Reading before Emancipation* (New Haven, CT: Yale University Press, 2019). Although the emphasis is on literacy, Schweiger also details the women's textile work.
2. For powerful critiques of these historiographical tendencies that place women outside the craft tradition, see Anishanslin, *Portrait of a Woman in Silk*; Crowston, *Fabricating Women*; Miller, *The Needle's Eye*; Miller, *Betsy Ross*. For textile workers, see Blewett, "Manhood and the Market"; Dublin, *Women and Work*; Gamber, *The Female Economy*; Prude, *Coming of the Industrial Order*; Rockman, "Plantation Goods"; Shelton, *Mills of Manayunk*; Christine Stansell, "The Origins of the Sweatshop: Women and Early Industrialization in New York City," in *Working-Class America: Essays on Labor, Community, and American Society*, ed. Michael H. Frisch and Daniel J. Walkowitz (Urbana: University of Illinois Press, 1983), 78-103; Michael Zakim, "Seamstresses and Whores: Working Women, Women's Work, and the Rise of the American Middle Class, 1820-1860," *Historia: Journal of the Historical Society of Israel* 15 (2005): 73-101. For the subsumption of women's work within the domestic economy, see chapter 4.
3. These attitudes are captured in Ulrich Bonnell Phillips's classic *American Negro Slavery: A Survey of the Supply, Employment, and Control of Negro Labor as Determined by the Plantation Regime* (New York: D. Appleton, 1918). For foundational analyses, see George M. Frederickson, *Black Image in the White Mind: The Debate on Afro-American Character and Desiny, 1817-1914* (New York: Harper, 1971); Winthrop D. Jordan, *White Over Black: American Attitudes toward the Negro, 1550-1812* (Chapel Hill: University of North Carolina Press, 1968).
4. Boydston, *Home and Work*; Boydston, "The Woman Who Wasn't There: Women's Market Labor and the Transition to Capitalism in the United States," *Journal of the Early Republic* 16 (Summer 1996): 183-206; Ruth H. Bloch, "American Female Ideals in Transition: The Rise of the Moral Mother," *Signs* 4 (Winter 1978): 237-52; Cott, *Bonds of Womanhood*.
5. US Treasury Department, *Alexander Hamilton's Report*.
6. US Treasury Department, *Alexander Hamilton's Report*, 41-42. See also Raffel, *Laces of Ipswich*.

7. US Department of the Treasury, *Statement of the Arts and Manufactures . . . for the Year 1810*, 2–4.
8. US Department of the Treasury, *Statement of the Arts and Manufactures . . . for the Year 1810*, opening table and xiv, l, lvii.
9. *1840 United States Federal Census*, Grayson, VA, roll 555, Family History Library Film 0029685; *1850 United States Federal Census*, Carroll, VA; roll M432_939, page: 361A, image: 280; both from Ancestry.com. . The will and inventory are appended to Roberts's diary. For women and nineteenth-century censuses, see Edward Higgs, "Women, Occupations, and Work in the Nineteenth Century Censuses," *History Workshop Journal* 23 (1987): 59–63. For the US census more generally see Margo J. Anderson, *The American Census: A Social History* (New Haven, CT: Yale University Press, 1988).
10. *A Statistical Inquiry into the Condition of the People of Colour of the City and Districts of Philadelphia* (Philadelphia: 1849), 17–18. The raw information has been digitized, "Philadelphia African-American Census," Friends Historical Library of Swarthmore College, available at https://repository.upenn.edu/mead/32/. For Miles and Margaret Cutcheon, see *1850 United States Federal Census*, Philadelphia New Market Ward, Philadelphia, PA, roll M432_817, page 367A, image 327, Ancestry.com. They appear as household 135 on the "Philadelphia African-American Census." In Washington, DC, Black women also clustered in the textile trades. Nunley, *At the Threshold of Liberty*, 132–34.
11. McClure Diary; Roberts Diary; both in VMHC.
12. See Roberts diary, VMHC, entries from 1847 on; for the will that gave Jane Cooley lifetime control of the family property see the very end of the volume, 177–81. Boydston, *Home and Work*.
13. Raffel, *Laces of Ipswich*, 29–30. Legal treatises in the nineteenth century defined "pin money" as items given to a wife by her husband either as gifts (akin to paraphernalia) or as part of the household budget, a definition that comported with conceptions of coverture that put all family property in the husband's name. In practice, "pin money" referred to property that wives controlled, including property they made or acquired themselves.
14. O'Connor, *Ties That Buy*. Also see Damiano, *To Her Credit*; Rockman, *Scraping By*; Romney, *New Netherland Connections*; Christine Stansell, *City of Women: Sex and Class in New York, 1789–1860* (Urbana: University of Illinois Press, 1987); Zabin, *Dangerous Economies*.
15. Raffel, *Laces of Ipswich*, 1–26, 90–112; see 20 for the value of lace relative to corn.
16. L. H. Butterfield, Marc Friedlaender and Mary-Jo Kline, eds., *The Book of Abigail and John: Selected Letters of the Adams Family, 1762–1784* (Cambridge, MA: Harvard University Press, 1975), 334. Adams Papers Digital Edition, MSH, vol. 5, xxiv–xxv, xxxviii–xxxix; vol. 6, xxii–xxiii, http://www.masshist.org/publications/adams-papers/.
17. McClure Diary; Roberts Diary; both in VMHC. Account book (Rebecca Coles), 1795–1800, box 1; Account book, John Coles of Enniscorthy (Rebecca Coles), 1801–1809, box 1; Col. John Coles of Ennisworthy (Rebecca Coles), Account Book, 1810–1815; all in UV. Bagby Commonplace Book, VMHC.

18. The accounts are noted in Martin, *Buying Into the World of Goods*, 54–55; they are from the John Hook Mercantile Ledger, 1773–1775, the John Hook Daybook, Falling River, 1772–1773, and the John Hook Petty Ledger, 1771–1776, Hook Papers, DU. Also see Laurel Thatcher Ulrich, "Martha Ballard and Her Girls: Women's Work in Eighteenth-Century Maine," in *Work and Labor in Early America*, ed. Stephen Innes (Chapel Hill: University of North Carolina Press, 1988), 70–105. Account book (Rebecca Coles), 1795–1800, UV, on the page marked 1798.
19. July 9, 1843, March 31, 1844, McClure Diary, VMHC.
20. *People v. Mary and Hannah Gray*, February 7, 1806, NYMA.
21. Augusta A. Burnham to Lucy Ann, June 20, 1844; Unsigned to sister, February 8, 1850; Augusta Burnham to sister, February 8, 1850 (a separate letter); both in Augusta and Elethine Burnham Correspondence, DU.
22. *People v. Rosenah Gray*, June 3, 1802, NYMA. *State v. Thomas Doyles*, 1820-8A through 1823-46A, Bills of Indictment, Court of General Sessions, Charleston District, SCDAH. Dollar values from MeasuringWorth.com, https://www.measuringworth.com/dollarvaluetoday.
23. *People v. Rosenah Gray*, June 3, 1802. *Commonwealth v. James Ray*, 1786, Jurors' Findings, Adlow Collection, BPL. *State v. Lavinia Taylor, alias Harriet*, 1814-48A, 1814-23A through 1815-29A, and *State v. Henry Adams*, 1825-20A, 1825-17A through 1829-16A; both in Bills of Indictment, Court of General Sessions, Charleston District, SCDAH.
24. Historian Ellen Hartigan-O'Connor, *The Ties That Buy*, 13–38, has characterized living conditions in the late eighteenth and early nineteenth centuries as "housefuls," not households, a term that suggests a clearly demarcated space inhabited by a single family. Also suggestive is Damiano, *To Her Credit*; Lisa Goff, *Shantytown, USA: Forgotten Landscapes of the Working Poor* (Cambridge, MA: Harvard University Press, 2016). For rural areas, see David Steven Cohen, *The Dutch-American Farm* (New York: New York University Press, 1992); Sally McMurry, *Families and Farmhouses in Nineteenth-Century America: Vernacular Design and Social Change* (New York: Oxford University Press, 1988); John Michael Vlach, *Back of the Big House: The Architecture of Plantation Slavery* (Chapel Hill: University of North Carolina Press, 1993). By contrast, much of the literature relies on the concept of "households," which actually refers to the legal configuration of domestic authority, with a male household head and his dependents, not the material circumstances of everyday life. See, for instance, Fox-Genovese, *Within the Plantation Household*. For urban living conditions, see Cashwell, "To Restore Peace and Tranquility"; Maurie D. Innes, *The Politics of Taste in Antebellum Charleston* (Chapel Hill: University of North Carolina Press, 2005); Vickery, *Behind Closed Door*, 25–48.
25. *People v. Rosenah Gray*, June 3, 1802, NYMA. *State v. Deborah Davis*, 1816-74A, 1816-59A through 1818-20A, Bills of Indictment, Court of General Sessions, Charleston District, SCDAH. Historian Dylan Penningroth, *Claims of Kinfolk*, has made a similar observation in regard to all property claimed by enslaved people, who lacked the rights that protected ownership. Instead, they used display to create facts on the ground, linking their property to themselves in the eyes of others. With

textiles, those connections had legal power that was generally lacking for other forms of property.

26. For the importance of boxes and trunks around the same time in England, see Vickery, *Behind Closed Doors*, 38–41. Laurel Thatcher Ulrich also notes the importance of cupboards for New England women in demarcating their property in "Hannah Barnard's Cupboard: Female Property and Identity in Eighteenth Century New England," in *Through a Glass Darkly: Reflections on Personal Identity in Early America*, ed. Ronald Hoffman, Mechal Sobel, and Federicka Teute (Chapel Hill: University of North Carolina Press, 1997), 238–73; Ulrich, *Age of Homespun*, 108–41.

27. *People v. Catherine McPhee*, April 4, 1810, NYMA. *State v. Zack*, #8, Trial Papers, Court of Magistrates and Freeholders, Pendleton District, SCDAH. *State v. John Campbell*, Indictments, Court of General Sessions, Kershaw County, SCDAH. References to trunks are ubiquitous in petty theft cases across the United States, and they even supported enslaved people's legal claims to the contents. See, for instance, *State v. Cain, Meshack, and Charles*, #86a, Trial Papers, Court of Magistrates and Freeholders, Anderson County, SCDAH, in which the fact that an enslaved man's pantaloons were stolen from his trunk was a crucial detail establishing ownership. Also see, for example, *People v. Lucinda Stroud*, February 4, 1800; *People v. George Logan*, November 14, 1801; *People v. Sarah Grant*, November 12, 1801; *People v. John Lane*, December 16, 1802; *People v. Thomas Brunson*, August 8, 1804; *People v. Dorothy Johnson*, February 8, 1805; *People v. Arthur Orr*, December 10, 1804; *People v. John Christian*, June 5, 1805; *People v. Betsy Ryers*, April 24, 1806; *People v. William Hart*, February 6, 1807; *People v. John Brown, Hannah Gray, and Ann Hamilton*, August 3, 1814; *People v. Mary Ann McIntosh*, January 14, 1815; *People v. Ann Lolly*, June 4, 1817; *People v. William Young and William Scott*, May 3, 1820; *People v. Mary Rand*, February 8, 1826; *People v. James Jeffers (2)*, April 4, 1826; *People v. Mary Dougherty*, June 7, 1844; all in NYMA. The basic outlines of these legal principles conform to those in housebreaking; see Vickery, *Behind Closed Doors*, 34–38.

28. *People v. David Smith*, December 16, 1802, NYMA.

29. Inventory of Pierre St. Pe, NA.

30. *People v. John Thomas*, May 2, 1820, NYMA. Also see *People v. John Tidd, Jr.*, February 5, 1807, NYMA.

31. *State v. Lavinia Taylor, alias Harriet*, 1814-48A, 1814-23A through 1815-29A, and *State v. Henry Adams*, 1825-20A, 1825-17A through 1829-16A; both in Bills of Indictment, Court of General Sessions, Charleston District, SCDAH.

32. *State v. Cash* (negro slave), Trial Papers, Court of Magistrates and Freeholders, Kershaw County; *State v. Sam*, #221, Trial Papers, Court of Magistrates and Freeholders, Anderson County; both in SCDAH.

33. McClure Diary; Roberts Diary; both in VMHC. Raffel, *The Laces of Ipswich*, 95–96. For women buying trousseaus with their earnings, see Dublin, "Women and Outwork"; Lucy Simler, "She Came to Work: The Female Labor Force in Chester County, 1750–1820," *Early American Studies* 5 (Fall 2007): 427–53; Ulrich, "Wheels, Looms, and the Gender Division of Labor."

34. *American Museum* 1 (January 1787): 11–13, quotes from 11 and 12. For a retelling of this story that takes the narrative of moral decay at face value, see Rolla Milton Tryon, *Household Manufactures in the United States, 1640–1860: A Study in Industrial History* (Chicago: University of Chicago Press, 1917), 126.
35. *American Museum* 1 (January 1787): 11–13. For concerns regarding women and consumption in the post-Revolutionary era, see Ruth Bloch, *Gender and Morality in Anglo-American Culture, 1650–1800* (Berkeley: University of California Press, 2003), 120–66; Haulman, *Politics of Fashion*; Kerber, *Women of the Republic*. Also see Crowston, *Credit, Fashion, Sex*; Jennifer Jones, *Sexing La Mode: Gender, Fashion and Commercial Culture in Old Regime France* (New York: Berg, 2004); Elizabeth Kowaleski-Wallace, *Consuming Subjects: Women, Shopping, and Business in the Eighteenth Century* (New York: Columbia University Press, 1997.
36. Inventories, Sales and Accounts of Estates, Orange County, vols. 2, 3, 4, 5, 7, 8, 9, 10, 11, NCSA.
37. Sarah Winston Syme Henry, Will, March 12, 1785, Accession 28785, Personal Papers Collection; Will of Jeremiah A. Neale, 1812, Will Book No. 2, 75, Will Book no. 2, 1815–1821, Alexandria City, reel 39; Will of Henrietta Perry, 1840, Will Book no. 4, 1831–1846, 254, Alexandria City, reel 40; all in LV. Sampling from Alexandria City, Wills, LV, reels 38 (Will Book A, 1800–1804; Will Book B, 1804–1807; Will Book C, 1807–1810); 39 (Will Book 1, 1810–1815; Will Book 2, 1815–1821; Will Book 3, 1821–1831); and 40 (Will Book 4, 1831–1846; Will Book 5, 1847–1851; Will Book 6, 1851–1855).
38. Hezekiah Smith and Nancy Cooley Smith to Benjamin and Rebecca Cooley, October 10, 1844; William D. Cooley to Benjamin and Rebecca Cooley and daughters, August 22, 1841; both in Cooley Family Papers, VMHC.
39. McClure Diary, November 20, 1842; Roberts Diary, July 2, 1843; both in VMHC.
40. Ulrich, "Hannah Barnard's Cupboard."

Chapter 7

1. Margaret Ten Eyck Diary, 1834–1844, Ten Eyck Family Papers, RU.
2. Nancy Grey Osterud, "The Valuation of Women's Work: Gender and the Market in A Dairy Farming Community during the Late Nineteenth Century," *Frontiers* 10, no. 2 (1988): 18–24; Osterud, *The Bonds of Community: The Lives of Farm Women in Nineteenth-Century New York* (Ithaca, NY: Cornell University Press, 1991), 202–27.
3. Cohen, *The Dutch-American Farm*, 146–47. For Dutch economic practices and married women, also see Romney, *New Netherland Connections*; Zabin, *Dangerous Economies*. For alternative methods of accounting and record keeping, also see Kimberly Welch, "Arteries of Capital: William Johnson and the Practice of Black Moneylending in the Antebellum U.S. South," *Slavery and Abolition* (June 2019): 1–23, and Welch, "William Johnson's Hypothesis: A Free Black Man and the Problem of Legal Knowledge in the Antebellum United States South," *Law and History*

Review 37 (February 2019): 89–124. Suggestive in this regard are the records of gifts described by Amanda E. Herbert, *Female Alliances: Gender, Identity, and Friendship in Early Modern Britain* (New Haven, CT: Yale University Press, 2014), chap. 2. Vickery, *Behind Closed Doors*, 106–28, argues that women's household accounts in England were about household property, over which women exercised varying degrees of discretion depending on the terms of their marriages. Other historians have underscored the extensive property holdings that married women in the United States controlled through legal workarounds or because of their legal status as women who were widowed, divorced, or never married. See, for instance, Jones-Rogers, *They Were Her Property*; Kirsten E. Wood, *Masterful Women: Slaveholding Widows from the American Revolution through the Civil War* (Chapel Hill: University of North Carolina Press, 2004); Karin Wulf, *Not All Wives: Women of Colonial Philadelphia* (Ithaca, NY: Cornell University Press, 2000). The accounts discussed in this chapter are of a different nature, clearly delineating property women could claim as their own, regardless of their legal status.

4. In, *The Ties That Buy*, 69–100, Hartigan-O'Connor also makes the point that women's accounts were not that different from men's accounts and argues that women used these new forms within the context of older practices, in which credit was about social ties, particularly family ties. This chapter shifts the emphasis to the manner of record keeping and the legal implications, focusing on the difference between women and merchants, not women and men, many of whose economic dealings still took place within the context of social ties, but who were often represented differently in the context of merchants' accounts because of their legal status. For the intellectual and economic importance of accounting and the various meanings captured in the practice, see Bruce G. Carruthers and Wendy Nelson Espeland, "Accounting for Rationality: Double-Entry Bookkeeping and the Rhetoric of Economic Rationality," *American Journal of Sociology* 97 (1991): 31–69; Naomi Lamoreaux, "Rethinking the Transition to Capitalism in the Early American Northeast," *Journal of American History* 90 (September 2003): 437–61; Mary Poovey, *History of the Modern Fact: Problems of Knowledge in the Sciences of Wealth and Society* (Chicago: University of Chicago Press, 1998), esp. 29–91; Caitlin Rosenthal, "Storybook-Keepers: Narratives and Numbers in Nineteenth Century America," *Common-place* 12 (2012), http://commonplace.online/article/rosenthal/; Michael Zakim, "Bookkeeping as Ideology: Capitalist Knowledge in Nineteenth-Century America," *Common-place* 6 (2006), http://commonplace.online/article/bookkeeping-as-ideology/. For different kinds of accounting and their meaning, particularly for women, see Jacqueline Wernimont, *Numbered Lives: Life and Death in Quantum Media* (Cambridge, MA: MIT Press, 2018), esp. 107–10. Also see Dan Bouk, *How Our Days Became Numbered: Risk and the Rise of the Statistical Individual* (Chicago: University of Chicago Press, 2015). For numeracy more generally, see Patricia Cline Cohen, *A Calculating People: The Spread of Numeracy in Early America* (Chicago: University of Chicago Press, 1982).

5. For the point about account books as legal documents, see Mann, *Neighbors and Strangers*; Muldrew, *The Economy of Obligation*; Poovey, *A History of the Modern Fact*, 66–91. The transactions of people without rights or property do not always appear

in the other parts of this accounting scheme, such as day books (which recorded transactions, day by day, as they were made), because those books were connected to account books. Merchants kept daily records so they could be transferred into their account books.

6. Martin, *Buying Into the World of Goods*, 67–85, notes that the physical characteristics of account books marked them as legal artifacts, different from other books; she also notes the distinctive treatment of their theft. Those in business did not regularly use accounts to assess the health of their ventures; see Lamoreaux, "Rethinking the Transition to Capitalism." For the legal power of other written documents, see Farber, "Sailing on Paper."
7. For the methods of accounting, see Poovey, *A History of the Modern Fact*, 33–65. Also see Mann, *Neighbors and Strangers*.
8. Osterud, "The Valuation of Women's Work"; Osterud, *The Bonds of Community*, 202–27. Some women who were openly running their own business kept formal accounts. See, for instance, Sally Ann Lucy Smith Davis Account Book, 1852–1858, VMHC; Mary Murray and Co. Invoice Book, 1771–1775, MHS; Mary Ann Wheeler, Account Book, 1848–1854, NYHS. But even Rebecca Coles, whose accounts were attributed to her husband, kept records as running tallies: Account Book (Rebecca Coles), 1795–1800, box 1; Account Book, John Coles of Enniscorthy (Rebecca Coles), 1801–1809, box 1; Col. John Coles of Enniscorthy (Rebecca Coles), Account Book, 1810–1815; all in UV. Ulrich, *A Midwife's Tale*.
9. Bagby Commonplace Book, VMHC. For alphabetization, see Eliza Jones Memorandum Book, 1831–1843, WM.
10. Bagby Commonplace Book, VMHC.
11. Journal of Anna Kagey Wayland, 1847–1865, Accession 24649b, Personal Papers Collection, LV. Martha Frink, Diary, 1858, Cairns Collection, UW. McClure Diary; Roberts Diary; both in VMHC.
12. Rebecca Cate Diary, 1853–1854, Cairns Collection, UW.
13. Ibid.
14. Ibid.
15. January 22, 1853, March 4, 1853, Rebecca Cate Diary, UW.
16. See for example, January 14, 27, and 28, 1853; February 2, 3, and 18, 1853; March 1 and 5, 1853, Rebecca Cate Diary, UW.
17. July 16 and 26, 1846, Roberts Diary, VMHC.
18. Martha Frink, Diary, 1858, UW; quotes from January 14, 1858, February 15, 1858.
19. Bagby Commonplace Book, VMHC. Ten Eyck Diary, RU. Weaving Accounts, Nathaniel Bangs Orderly Book, 1742–1846, MHS. In addition to these accounts and those discussed below, also see Lucy Lilly Robinson Temple, Account Books, 1837–1850; Mary E. Brown, Account Book, 1855–1885; Elizabeth Coles Diary, 1829; Jane Catherine Fontaine Mead Account Book, 1860–1864; all in VMHC. Diary of Elizabeth Edmonia Churchill Berkeley Cooke, 1855–1858, #1197-a; Note and cash book owned by Martha Jefferson Randolph, 1824–1826, #5385-g; both in UV. Sallie Leftwich, French Exercise Book, 1854, Leftwich-Shepherd-Bowles Family Papers, 1854–1893, Accession 27988, LV. Sarah Jane Duncan, Private Account Book,

1835–1836, vol. 221, Irvine-Newbold Family Papers, HSP. Sarah Staats Bayles, Diary, 1835–1851, RU. Charlotte A. Sharpless, Diary, 1857, UW. Pearl family Account Book, 1792–1845, MHS. Receipt Book, Financial Records, Margaret Hall Moffett Adger Papers, 1825–1911, 1312.00, SCHS. Sarah Gibbs kept the form when she took over management of her family's plantation after her husband's death: Sarah Reeve Gibbs Account Book, 1807–1866, 34/585, SCHS. These methods of accounting were not confined only to women; men used them as well, although they had very different legal implications for women, particularly married women. See for example William Watson Diary, HSP; John and Hannah Edwards Receipt Book, 1841–1861, HSP; John McBride, Account Book, RU. Also see Mann, *Neighbors and Strangers*. These diaries echoed the patterns of household accounting of English mistresses in the Georgian period, described by Amanda Vickery, where they kept careful track of expenditures, servants' behavior and wages, visits, and other matters relating to their households; see *The Gentleman's Daughter*, 126–60; also see Vickery, "His and Hers." But they were also about tracking labor and property, separating goods and labor belonging to the household from that of wives. Sarah Lawrence, for instance, kept her own activities separate from household duties and expenditures: Sarah Elizabeth Lawrence Diary, April 1843–May 1861, boxes 4 and 5; Sarah Elizabeth Lawrence Account Book, 1842–1853, folder 7, box 5; Sarah Elizabeth Lawrence Account Book, 1843, folder 9, box 5; Sarah Elizabeth Lawrence Account Book, 1844, folder 10, box 5; all in Amos A. Lawrence Diaries and Account Books, 1816–1886, MHS.
20. *People v. Susan Munro*, June 4, 1807, NYMA.
21. *People v. Rosenah Gray*, June 3, 1802, NYMA.
22. *People v. Susan Munro*, June 4, 1807 and *People v. Rosenah Gray*, July 3, 1802, NYMA
23. *State v. John Marshall, Sr., Agnes Marshall, and John Marshall*, Indictments, Court of General Sessions, Kershaw County, SCDAH.
24. Bagby Commonplace Book, VMHC.
25. Harriet Ann (Moore Page Potter) Ames Memoir, 1–3, LC. Elithe Hamilton Kirkland, *Love Is a Wild Assault* (Garden City, NY: Doubleday, 1959). For background on Ames, see Gerald E. McLeod, "Harriet Ann Moore Page Potter Ames Is Known as the Bravest Woman in Texas," *Austin Chronicle*, August 6, 2010, https://www.austinchronicle.com/columns/2010-08-06/1065998/.
26. Edwards, "Sarah Allingham's Sheet," "Legal World," and "James and His Striped Velvet Pantaloons." Also see Penningroth, *The Claims of Kinfolk*, 94–97, 99–100, 126–27.
27. Bagby Commonplace Book, VMHC. *People v. Susan Munro*, June 4, 1807 and *People v. Rosenah Gray*, July 3, 1802, NYMA. For the operation of public law, see chapter 2.
28. January 30, 1858, and February 12, 1858, Martha Frink, Diary, UW.
29. May 1, 1842, and June 14, 1842, McClure Diary, VMHC.
30. November 10, 1850–May 20, 1854, Roberts, Diary, VMHC.
31. Quotes from November 5, 1843, McClure Diary, VMHC. Amanda's recollections of the work of that week were similar, although they omitted the colorful commentary; November 5, 1843, Roberts Diary, VMHC. Rebecca Cate Diary, UW. *The Daily Picayune*, December 31, 1839, 3, America's Historical Newspapers. Such

advertisements were common in nineteenth-century newspapers. Miller, *The Needle's Eye*. Also see Ulrich, *Age of Homespun*.
32. Elizabeth Hobbs Keckly spelled her name with a "y" and not an "ey," although it was often misspelled, including in her memoir. Elizabeth Hobbs Keckley, *Behind the Scenes: Or Thirty Years a Slave, and Four Years in the White House* (Hillsborough, NC: Eno, 2016); Sydney Nathans, *To Free a Family: The Journey of Mary Walker* (Cambridge, MA: Harvard University Press, 2012), esp. 9–77.
33. Keckley, *Behind the Scenes*, esp. 75–156; Nathans, *To Free a Family*.
34. Storekeepers' pursuit of theft is telling in this regard. Retailers waged a constant battle against petty pilfering, and the effort expended seems way out of proportion to the property's value: *People v. John Martin*, February 8, 1808; *People v. Theophilus Simmons*, March 16, 1826; NYMA. As Elaine S. Abelson has argued in *When Ladies Go A-Thieving: Middle-Class Shoplifters in the Victorian Department Store* (New York: Oxford University Press, 1990), both white middle-class women and working-class people pilfered goods, but legal officials singled out the poor for theft charges and carved out the new, lesser offense of shoplifting for white middle-class women. Prosecution was about enforcing a property regime that conflicted with the practices that governed the possession and exchange of textiles in the secondhand market. For a discussion of this issue, see chapter 11.

Chapter 8

1. *People v. Eliza Cauchois*, December 8, 1803, NYMA.
2. For trade in Britain and Europe, see Danielle van den Heuvel, "New Products, New Sellers? Changes in the Dutch Textile Trades, c. 1650–1750," in *Selling Textiles in the Long Eighteenth Century: Comparative Perspectives from Western Europe*, ed. Jon Stobart and Bruno Blondé (New York: Palgrave Macmillan, 2014), 118–37; Olwen H. Hufton, *The Poor of Eighteenth-Century France, 1750–1789* (Oxford: Clarendon, 1974); Sheilagh Ogilvie, *A Bitter Living: Women, Markets, and Social Capital in Early Modern Germany* (Oxford: Oxford University Press, 2003); Deborah Simonton and Anne Montenach, eds., *Female Agency in the Urban Economy: Gender in European Towns, 1640–1830* (New York: Routledge, 2013). Many thanks to David Waldstreicher and Van Gosse, who drew my attention to the fact that David Walker and other prominent African American activists worked in the secondhand clothing trade. See Peter P. Hinks, *To Awaken My Afflicted Brethren: David Walker and the Problem of Antebellum Slave Resistance* (University Park: Pennsylvania State University Press, 1997), 66–68; Gosse, *The First Reconstruction*, chap. 5. Many of the court cases already cited involved transactions that occurred on the street, in rural gathering places, such as churchyards, or in "stores" (which were really stores of goods) in people's houses: *People v. Susan Munro*, June 4, 1807; *People v. Rosenah Gray*, October 8, 1802; both in NYMA. *State v. Cain, Meshack, and Charles*; *State v. Amos*, #245, Trial Papers, Court of Magistrates and Freeholders, Anderson County, SCDAH. For the

importance of auctions, see Hartigan-O'Connor, "Public Sales and Public Values." Court records in urban areas refer regularly to auction houses in cities; note 18 in this chapter refers to people selling there, although they also bought there. Newspapers advertised ad hoc auctions: *Salem Gazette*, May 28, 1793, 3; *Gazette of the United States, and Daily Advertiser*, July 21, 1801, 4; *Newburyport Herald*, February 28, 1806, 1; *Balance, & New-York State Journal*, March, 13, 1810, 3; all in NewsBank/Readex, Database: America's Historical Newspapers. In rural areas, estate sales offered similar opportunities: Inventories, Sales and Accounts of Estates, Orange County, North Carolina, vols. 2–11, 1800–1835, NCSA. For peddlers, particularly Jewish peddlers, see Hasia R. Diner, *Roads Taken: The Great Jewish Migration to the New World and the Peddlers Who Forged the Way* (New Haven, CT: Yale University Press, 2015); Hilliard, *Masters, Slaves, and Exchange*, 15–45; Philip Kahn, Jr., *A Stitch in Time: The Four Seasons of Baltimore's Needle Trades* (Baltimore: Maryland Historical Society, 1989); Martin, *Buying Into the World of Goods*, 45–46; Mendelsohn, *The Rag Race*; Mendelsohn, "The Rag Race." Two firms based in Pittsfield, Massachusetts, listed in Fisher, Blashfield and Company Records, reference book (credit ratings), volume 14, NYPL, sold goods through peddlers. For references to peddlers in the diaries of women in rural areas, see Journal of Anna Kagey Wayland, LV; Martha Frink, Diary, UW. For peddling in court cases, see for instance, *People v. Rosenah Gray*, June 3, 1802; *People v. Thomas Cooney and others*, April 7, 1804; *People v. Amy Hazard*, June 8, 1805; *People v. Michael McFadden*, February 6, 1806; all in NYMA. *State v. Daniel (negro slave)*, Trial Papers, Court of Magistrates and Freeholders, Kershaw County; *State v. Reuben*, #55, Trial Papers, Court of Magistrates and Freeholders, Anderson County; *State v. John, Brister, Sally, and Jane*, #235, Trial Papers, Court of Magistrates and Freeholders, Anderson County; all in SCDAH. *David N. Prentice v. Gilbert Gardner*, folder 12, case 163, New London County, County Court, Files, box 403, June 1842 to November 1842, CSL.

3. See, for instance Hilliard, *Masters, Slaves, and Exchange*; Lane, "Work on the Margins"; Lemire, "Consumerism in Preindustrial and Early Industrial England"; Lemire, *Global Trade*; Mendelsohn, "The Rage Race"; Zabin, *Dangerous Economies*. All are attentive to the dynamics but tend to create an artificial dichotomy based in the categories of civil law: the formal economy, which included white male merchants with the full range of rights, and the informal economy, which included those with weak claims to property and rights. Reflecting the terms of law, the dichotomy characterizes all trade among those on the margins as something different: not only informal, with the implication that it was not regulated by legal rules, but also underground or illicit, lumping all trade by those on the margins together with the traffic in stolen goods.

4. The concept of a moral economy is perhaps most closely associated with E. P. Thompson; see, in particular, *Whigs and Hunters: The Origin of the Black Act* (London: Allen Lane, 1975), and *Customs in Common* (London: Merlin, 1991). The literature in women's history, African American history, and labor—all of which came out of the newly invigorated field of social history that Thompson pioneered—has absorbed elements of this framework in its emphasis on communal approaches to property and political action, particularly through the work of Herbert G. Gutman, especially *Work, Culture, and Society in Industrializing America: Essays in American*

Working-Class and Social History (New York: Knopf, 1976). See, for instance, Barbara Jeanne Fields, *Slavery and Freedom on the Middle Ground: Maryland during the Nineteenth Century* (New Haven, CT: Yale University Press, 1985); Julie Saville, *The Work of Reconstruction: From Slave to Wage Laborer in South Carolina, 1860–1870* (New York: Cambridge University Press, 1994); Leslie A. Schwalm, *A Hard Fight for We: Women's Transition from Slavery to Freedom in South Carolina* (Urbana: University of Illinois Press, 1997); Stansell, *City of Women*; Ulrich, *A Midwife's Tale*; Wilentz, *Chants Democratic*.

5. For women involved in trade, in both North America and Europe, see Cleary, *Elizabeth Murray*; Crowston, *Credit, Fashion, Sex*; Haggerty, *British-Atlantic Trading Community 1760–1810*; Hartigan-O'Connor, *The Ties That Buy*; Lemire, *Dress, Culture, and Commerce*; Miles, *Dawn of Detroit*; Miller, "The Last Mantuamaker"; Kristi Rutz-Robbins, "'Divers Debts': Women's Participation in the Local Economy, Albemarle, North Carolina, 1663–1729," *Early American Studies* 4 (Fall 2006): 425–41; Romney, *New Netherland Connections*; Sanderson, "The Edinburgh Milliners"; Sleeper-Smith, *Indigenous Prosperity and American Conquest*; Kirk, *Many Tender Tie*; Vicente, *Clothing the Spanish Empire*; Zabin, *Dangerous Economies*. There is an established body of scholarship in early American history, associated with scholars such as Gary B. Nash and Alfred F. Young, that has focused on the lives of those on the margins. See, for instance, Nash, *The Urban Crucible: Social Change, Political Consciousness, and the Origins of the American Revolution* (Cambridge, MA: Harvard University Press, 1979); Young, ed., *The American Revolution* (DeKalb: Northern Illinois University Press, 1976). Recent work has joined these concerns to the new history of capitalism and turned to the ways those people navigated the economy: Finley, *An Intimate Economy*; Greenberg, *Advocating the Man*; Katie M. Hemphill, *Bawdy City: Commercial Sex and Regulation in Baltimore, 1790–1915* (New York: Cambridge University Press, 2020); Brian P. Luskey, *On the Make: Clerks and the Quest for Capital in Nineteenth-Century America* (New York: New York University Press, 2016); Luskey and Woloson, eds., *Capitalism by Gaslight*; Mendelsohn, *Rag Race*; Newman, *Embodied History*; Rockman, *Scraping By*; Woloson, *In Hock*. For the slave South, see Hilliard, *Masters, Slaves, and Exchange*; Michael D. Thompson, *Working on the Dock of the Bay: Labor and Enterprise in an Antebellum Southern Port* (Columbia: University of South Carolina Press, 2015).

6. Tebbutt, *Making Ends Meet*; Woloson, *In Hock*; for statistics on John Simpson's pawnshop, see 86, 91, 93–94. For the records, see John Simpson, Record Book, 1838–1839, NYHS. For similar dynamics with pawning in England, see Tebbutt, *Making Ends Meet*, 37–67; Lemire, "Peddling Fashion." For a case that suggests the ubiquity and frequency of pawning, see *People v. James Jeffers*, April 4, 1826, NYMA. Also see note 20 in this chapter. For a vivid description of city shopping districts, see Gamble, "The Promiscuous Economy." Those dynamics are also evident in descriptions of cities in Timothy J. Gilfoyle, *City of Eros: New York City, Prostitution, and the Commercialization of Sex, 1820–1920* (New York: Norton, 1992); Hemphill, *Bawdy City*; Jones, *Birthright Citizens*; Adam Malka, *The Men of Mobtown: Policing Baltimore in the Age of Slavery and Emancipation* (Chapel Hill: University of North Carolina Press, 2019); Rockman, *Scraping By*; Stansell, *City of Women*.

7. Harriet Ann (Moore Page Potter) Ames Memoir, 1, LC. Woloson, *In Hock*, 86, 91, 93–94. John Simpson, Record Book, 1838–1839, NYHS. John Simpson's accounts are also unusual in the fact that they survived. The records of pawnshops did not make it into the archives, unlike the accounts and correspondence of the men whom the historiography identifies as merchants, which are everywhere. For examples of the dispersion of the trade, see note 2 in this chapter. Also see Lemire, *Dress, Culture, and Commerce*; Lemire, *Global Trade*; Styles, "Clothing the North"; Styles, *Dress of the People*, 135–78.

8. McCord, ed., *Statues at Large for the State of South Carolina*, "An Act for the Promotion of Industry, and for the Suppression of Vagrants and other Idle and Disorderly Persons," (1787), 5:41–44. For examples of ordinances from New York, see *Laws and Ordinance* (New York: 1812), 69–75, 92–96, 120–21, 149, 154–62. *Laws and Ordinances* (New York: 1817), 47, 51–56, 124–27, 128–36, *Laws and Ordinances Made and Established by the Aldermen & Commonalty of the City of New York* (New York: 1827), 19–21, 98, 99–116, 119–23, 168, 171. For a discussion of such ordinances, see Gamble, "The Promiscuous Economy"; Olwell, *Masters, Slaves, and Subjects*, 141–80; Woloson, *In Hock*, 54–85. For such local regulation, more generally, see Novak, *The People's Welfare*. For examples of prosecutions after busy Saturdays and on Sundays, see Docket of Mayor Joseph Tate, VM, 27–28, 51, 61, 147, 184, 191, 193, 312.

9. *People v. Thomas Cooney and others*, April 7, 1804, NYMA. For other examples of stores, as stores of goods, see *People v. Catharine Tillman and Eliza Tillman*, October 8, 1800; *People v. Rosenah Gray*, June 3, 1802; *People v. Benjamin Brown*, April 6, 1804; *People v. Jesse Honeywell and Jane his wife*, December 4, 1805; *People v. Philip Moses*, February 4, 1807; *People v. Ann Robertson and Mary McLaughlin*, June 5, 1810; *People v. Catherine Williams*, October 6, 1814; *People v. Charles Zeiss*, February 9, 1826; all in NYMA. *State v. Arthur Miles, James Franklin and Elizabeth Franklin*, 1810-14A, 1801-28A through 1811-13A, Bills of Indictment, Court of General Sessions, Charleston District, SCDAH.

10. *People v. Susan Munro*, June 4, 1807, NYMA. For just some examples of people buying and selling on streets and in homes, see *People v. Abigail Leonard*, April 9, 1801; *People v. Sally Wilson*, April 8, 1801; *People v. John Carter*, June 5, 1801; *People v. Rosenah Gray*, October 8, 1802; *People v. Polly Rogers*, April 5, 1804; *People v. James Pitney*, June 6, 1804; *People v. Henry Smith*, December 6, 1804; *People v. Judith Friel*, October 8, 1804; *People v. Margaret Stanley*, February 9, 1805; *People v. Mingus Bowler and John Primrose*, January 10, 1805; *People v. George Thompson*, November 5, 1805; *People v. John Peter*, December 4, 1805; *People v. John Bennett*, February 6, 1806; *People v. James Schuyler*, May 7, 1807; *People v. John Lewis*, March 31, 1808; *People v. Joseph Deis*, March 31, 1808; *People v. Ann Jones*, August 8, 1814; *People v. Mary Gray*, February 9, 1815; *People v. Jacob Johnson*, March 10, 1817; *People v. Samuel Browning*, January 4, 1826; *People v. Henry Dusenberry*, March 7, 1826; *People v. Patrick McGlone and William Seymour*, April 6, 1826; *People v. William Prince Ware*, December 6, 1832. *State v. James Campbell*, Indictments, Court of General Sessions, Kershaw County, SCDAH.

11. See in particular, Kowaleski-Wallace, *Consuming Subjects*. For changes in shopping, also see Richard L. Bushman, "Shopping and Advertising in Colonial America," in

Of Consuming Interests: The Style of Life in the Eighteenth Century, ed. Cary Carson, Ronald Hoffman, and Peter J. Albert (Charlottesville: University Press of Virginia, 1994), 233–51; Gamble, "The Promiscuous Economy."

12. Asa Greene, *The Perils of Pearl Street, Including a Taste of the Dangers of Wall Street* (New York: 1834), 25–26. Kowaleski-Wallace, *Consuming Subjects*. For negative portrayals of women as consumers, also see chapter 6 and chapter 6, note 43.

13. Daniel Rogers, ed., *The New-York City Hall Recorder* (New York: 1817), 1:39–40. Many thanks to Meggan Cashwell for drawing my attention to this case. For the fraught gender dynamics of shopping, see Kowaleski-Wallace, *Consuming Subjects*. Also see Abelson, *When Ladies Go A-Thieving*; Ted Ownby, *American Dreams in Mississippi: Consumers, Poverty, and Culture, 1830–1998* (Chapel Hill: University of North Carolina Press, 1999), esp., chaps. 1–3.

14. Greene, *Perils of Pearl Street*, 23–24. Slave states all had various limitations on trading with slaves, usually forbidding it without express permission from the master; see chapter 6. The difficulties African Americans faced in stores and restaurants were central to the Civil Rights Movement. For those racial dynamics in the nineteenth century South, see Ownby, *American Dreams in Mississippi*, esp. chaps. 1–3.

15. *People v. Hugh McManamy*, November 6, 1805; *People v. James Russell*, August 8, 1804; both in NYMA. For examples of stealing "from the door": *People v. George Dougherty*, April 9, 1801; *People v. William Young*, February 5, 1801; *People v. Charles Wood*, June 11, 1803; *People v. Sarah Fuller*, February 8, 1804; *People v. Peter Overholt*, February 8, 1804; *People v. Peter Bryan*, July 12, 1817; NYMA. For examples of cases where either shopping practices were contested or the line between the store and the outside was unclear, see *People v. Maria Hudger*, February 3, 1802; *People v. Aurillia Thompson*, June 3, 1802; *People v. Isaac Harman*, February 3, 1802; *People v. Vincent Chapley*, February 3, 1802; *People v. John Bernard*, October 7, 1802; *People v. Jack Moore, a slave to Mr. Bayard*, December 8, 1802; *People v. Sally Johnson*, April 8, 1802; *People v. Jeremiah Wallace and John Burns*, June 8, 1803; *People v. William Hayselop*, August 8, 1804; *People v. John Kipp*, August 8, 1804; *People v. Henry Edwards*, June 6, 1804; *People v. Frederick Creater*, December 8, 1804; *People v. Michael Lynch*, August 10, 1804; *People v. Christopher Donlevy*, February 5, 1805; *People v. Martin Grady*, December 10, 1805; *People v. John Tidd, Jr.*, February 5, 1807; *People v. Samuel Johnson*, February 5, 1808; *People v. Lucy Ferguson*, April 11, 1815; *People v. John Anderson*, June 1817, all in NYMA. *State v. John Evans*, Indictments, Court of General Sessions, Kershaw County, SCDAH. Also see Gamber, "Promiscuous Economy."

16. *People v. Susan Munro*, June 4, 1807; *People v. Rosenah Gray*, June 3, 1802; both NYMA. As historian Melanie Tebbutt shows, working-class English women in the early twentieth century still preferred to shop at small, neighborhood stores run by women they knew, even though the prices were higher than those at larger chains; see *Making Ends Meet*, caption for two images of woman-run stores on unnumbered photos pages.

17. *People v. Sally Armstrong*, October 9, 1806; *People v. David Conkling*, December 7, 1803, NYMA. For examples of people selling at auctions, see *People v. Bauke Pytters*, August 3, 1803; *People v. Thomas Cooney and others*, April 7, 1804; *People v. John*

Anderson, June 8, 1804; *People v. Patrick Coody alias Patrick Astaken*, October 8, 1804; *People v. Gitty Hamilton*, February 7, 1806; *People v. John Barginot*, June 5, 1810; NYMA. *State v. John Thomas*, 1811-39, 1811-14A through 1814-22A, Bills of Indictment, Court of General Sessions, Charleston District, SCDAH. Margot Finn, "Debt and Credit in Bath's Court of Requests, 1829–1839," *Urban History* 21 (1994): 211–36, makes a similar point about people buying textiles and then leveraging them, often by pawning them. For leveraging such property, also see Lemire, *Dress, Culture, and Commerce*, esp. 95–146; Lemire, "The Theft of Clothes"; Styles, "Involuntary Consumers?"; Styles, "Clothing the North."

18. *State v. Wyatt Harris (a free negro)*, #48, Trial Papers, Court of Magistrates and Freeholders, Spartanburg County, SCDAH. *State v. Daniel*, #49, Trial Papers, Court of Magistrates and Freeholders, Spartanburg County, SCDAH. Cases in rural areas suggest a lively market for cloth and clothing. See *Commonwealth v. Christopher Meyers alias William Lewis*, May 1790, Commonwealth Causes, reel 235, 1749–1794, Court Records, Albemarle County, Local Government Records Collection; *Commonwealth v. Mathew Casey*, 1831, Commonwealth Causes, reel 255, 1830–1831, Court Records, Albemarle County, Local Government Records Collection; both in LV. *State v. John Gilkeyson*, Indictments, Court of General Sessions, Kershaw County; *State v. Benjamin Harwell*, Indictments, Court of General Sessions, Kershaw County; *State v. Daniel Holley, Zachariah Holley, and Margaret Holley*, Indictments, Court of General Sessions, Kershaw County; *State v. John B. Matthews*, Indictments, Court of General Sessions, Kershaw County; *State v. Daniel (negro slave)*, Trial Papers, Court of Magistrates and Freeholders, Kershaw County; *State v. Dorcas (negro slave) and Jack (negro slave)*, Trial Papers, Court of Magistrates and Freeholders, Kershaw County; *State v. Job and Adney*, #50, Trial Papers, Court of Magistrates and Freeholders, Spartanburg County; *State v. Douglas and Jerry*, #51, Trial Papers, Court of Magistrates and Freeholders, Spartanburg County; *State v. Nelson*, #59A, Trial Papers, Court of Magistrates and Freeholders, Spartanburg County; *State v. Pat*, #172, Trial Papers, Court of Magistrates and Freeholders, Anderson County; *State v. Stephen*, #173, Trial Papers, Court of Magistrates and Freeholders, Anderson County; *State v. John, Brister, Sally, and Jane*, #235, Trial Papers, Court of Magistrates and Freeholders, Anderson County; all in SCDAH.

19. *People v. John Benton*, April 7, 1800, NYMA. For examples where pawning did not necessarily imply theft, see *People v. Abigail Devers*, November 14, 1801; *People v. Jane Frazier*, June 3, 1802; *People v. Lewis Valet*, June 22, 1804; *People v. Elizabeth Davis and Elizabeth Riddle* and *People v. Daniel Reynolds, Elizabeth Davis and Elizabeth Riddle*, January 15, 1806; *People v. Elizabeth Friday*, August 5, 1806; *People v. William Baker*, October 12, 1807; *People v. Peter Anthony*, June 7, 1808; *People v. Betsy Lewis*, February 6, 1817; *People v. John Bonds*, June 7, 1817; *People v. James Ruth*, September 9, 1817; *People v. Samuel Hart*, April 11, 1826; *People v. Catherine Brennan and Ann Allison*, May 15, 1844. *Commonwealth v. William Darley*, Hustings Court, Suit Papers, Ended Causes, box 113, Bar Code 1011180, LV. Those explanations were not always believable, and pawning could also serve as evidence of theft, depending on the context. For more discussion, see chapter 9.

20. For pawnshops as essentially banks, see Tebbutt, *Making Ends Meet*, esp. 11–36; Woloson, *In Hock*, esp. 86–121. For the tradition of washerwomen pawning their clients' laundry, see Tebbutt, *Making Ends Meet*, 22; for dressmakers, see 72. See MacKay, "Why They Stole," for the relationship of such borrowing networks to theft.
21. *People v. Susan Munro*, June 4, 1807; *People v. Aurillia Thompson*, June 3, 1802; *People v. Sally Armstrong*, October 9, 1806; all in NYMA. Evidence of loaning and borrowing can be difficult to see in the cases, because they were prosecuted as theft; see chapter 9. For examples, see *People v. Abigail Devers*, November 14, 1801; *People v. Margaret Eisenburgh and Winneford Barritt*, June 13, 1803; *People v. Nancy Brave*, December 4, 1804; *People v. John Miers alia Joseph Grate*, January 8, 1805; *People v. Mingus Bowler and John Primrose*, January 10, 1805; *People v. Margaret Dwire*, August 5, 1806; *People v. Christiana Armstrong*, December 3, 1806; *People v. Susan White*, January 7, 1807; *People v. Nancy Kip*, February 5, 1807; *People v. Elizabeth Chew*, April 13, 1807; *People v. Alpheus Lovell*, June 11, 1808; *People v. Silas Beadle*, February 8, 1817; *People v. Margaret Davis*, June 14, 1820; *People v. Catherine Brennan and Ann Allison*, May 15, 1844. *State v. Deborah Davis*, 1816-74A, 1816-59A through 1818-20A, Bills of Indictment, Court of General Sessions, Charleston District, SCDAH. Borrowing in these cases follows patterns outlined for poor women in England, see Lane, "Work on the Margins"; MacKay, "Why They Stole." Similar to borrowing was the shopping that wealthier women did for each other, in the sense that the procurement of cloth and clothing had value, in social terms, beyond the cost of the goods: Hartigan-O'Connor, "Abigail's Accounts: Economy and Affection in the Early Republic," *Journal of Women's History* 17 (Fall 2005): 35–58.
22. Mann, *Neighbors and Strangers*. For the increasing preference for written instruments, also see chapter 7. For the social basis of credit and its continuation, despite changes in the law that routinized such practices and fixed them in writing, see Finn, *The Character of Credit*; Naomi Lamoreaux, *Insider Lending: Banks, Personal Connections, and Economic Development in Industrial New England* (Cambridge: Cambridge University Press, 1994). Also interesting in this regard is Penningroth, *Claims of Kinfolk*, which traces federal officials' desire for written proof of ownership and their willingness to consider other evidence in its absence for African American claimants in the post-emancipation South.
23. *State v. Amos*, #245, Trial Papers, Court of Magistrates and Freeholders, Anderson County, SCDAH.
24. *State v. Amos*. For such mediations in the context of civil law, see Finn, *Character of Credit*; Mann, *Neighbors and Strangers*; Muldrew, *Economy of Obligation*.

Part III

1. McClure Diary; Roberts Diary, 176, for Juliann's description; both in VMHC.
2. For descriptions of the state of local records, see Gross, *Double Character*, 159–66; Jones, *Birthright Citizens*; Welch, *Black Litigants*, 6–10 Also see Edwards, *People and Their Peace*, 22–25.

Chapter 9

1. *People v. Judith Friel*, October 8, 1804, NYMA.
2. Recent work has underscored the access that people without rights had to legal venues; see note 21 in the introduction. But these cases are surprising, even in the context of that literature, because of the lengths to which officials went to accommodate property claims outside the context of property rights. Also see Edwards, "Sarah Allingham's Sheet," "Legal World," and "James and His Striped Velvet Pantaloons."
3. *People v. Judith Friel*, October 8, 1804, NYMA. Zabin, "Women Trading Networks," makes a similar point, although in relationship to women's economic activity. For discussion of civil actions involving personal property, see, for instance, Kent, *Commentaries*, 2:255–508; Swift, *System of Laws* (1822), 1:522–87; Tucker, *Blackstone's Commentaries*, 4:144–66. Civil suits constituted the bulk of most courts' dockets as well as the business of most lawyers. Its importance is apparent in lawyers' practices, which are composed largely of property matters. See DeSaussure and Ford Day Book, 1790–92, Timothy Ford Papers, 1776–1830 (1027.03.01); Abstract of Cases Determined in the Constitutional Courts at Charleston & Columbia, 1795–1805, William Loughton Smith Papers, 1774–1834 (1119.00); Oliver M. Smith, Docket Book, 1834–39 (34/305); all in SCHS. John Wrought Mitchell, Receipt Book, 1817–1835; Henry William DeSaussure and Timothy Ford, Record Book, 1786–92; both in SCL. Letter Book, William Gaston Papers, #272, box 7; the business-related correspondence in subser. 1.2, boxes 4–28, Cameron Family Papers, #133; both in SHC. For the preponderance of such cases, see Edward L. Ayers, *Vengeance and Justice: Crime and Punishment in the Nineteenth-Century American South* (New York: Oxford University Press, 1984), 32; Gross, *Double Character*, 23; James P. Whittenburg, "Planters, Merchants, and Lawyers: Social Change and the Origins of the North Carolina Regulation," *William and Mary Quarterly* 34 (April 1977): 215–38.
4. *State v. Drury*, #59, Trial Papers, Court of Magistrates and Freeholders, Anderson County; *State v. James Campbell*, 1826, Indictments, Court of General Sessions, Kershaw County; Susannah Mills, Burwell Mills, and William Mills, Indictments, County and Intermediate Court, 1791–1799; all in SCDAH. Also see, for instance, *State v. Jesse Hewey* (a free man of color), #44; *State v. Annica*, #175, Trial Papers; both in Trial Papers, Court of Magistrates and Freeholders, Spartanburg County, SCDAH.
5. District Attorney Indictment Records, December 14, 1826–February 15, 1827, Reel 110; District Attorney Indictment Records, April 5, 1832–June 6, 1832, Reel 143; both in NYMA. Many thanks to Mandy Cooper for compiling statistics for these and other years. Also see Docket of Mayor Joseph Tate; Bills of Indictment, Court of General Sessions, Charleston District, SCDAH; Boston Municipal Court, vol. 18 (January 1830 to December 1830), vol. 22 (January 1834 to June 1834), vol. 32, part 5 (November 1844), vol. 32, part 6 (December 1844), vol. 42, part 1 (January 1854 to March 1854).

6. Even scholarship that acknowledges the value of textiles still tends to link their theft to the lack of economic options among the working poor, see Hilliard, *Masters, Slaves, and Exchange*; Lane, "Work on the Margins"; Lemire, *Dress, Culture, and Commerce*, esp. 121–46; Lemire, "The Theft of Clothes"; MacKay, "Why They Stole"; Tebbutt, *Making Ends Meet*, esp. 69–100; Styles, *Dress of the People*, esp. 135–78; Walker, "Women, Theft and the World of Stolen Goods."
7. For a fascinating discussion of such forms, see Matthew P. Brown, "Blanks: Data, Method, and the British American Print Shop," *American Literary History* 29 (Summer 2017): 228–47.
8. The rules were clearly laid out in common law and statutory offenses. For examples of discussion in the treatise literature, see Swift, *A System of Laws* (1822), 1:588–788; Zephaniah Swift, *A Digest of the Law of Evidence, in Civil and Criminal Cases: and a Treatise on Bills of Exchange, and Promissory Notes* (Hartford, CT: 1810); Tucker, *Blackstone's Commentaries*, 4:279-92–385. Also see Commissioners on Practice and Pleadings, *Code of Civil Procedure of the State of New-York* (Albany: 1850); Meinrad Grenier, *Code of Practice of the State of Louisiana* (New Orleans: 1844); Conway Robinson, *Forms Adapted to the Practice in Virginia, Volume One* (Richmond: 1841); Joshua Waterman, *Michigan Justice's Guide* (n.p.: 1848); Joshua Waterman, *The Wisconsin and Iowa Justice* (New York: 1853); P. B. Wilcox, *Practical Forms in Action . . . Now in Common Use in the State of Ohio* (Columbus: 1848). Failure to follow them provided the basis for appeals, which were made on points of law, not fact.
9. For the restrictions on wives suing or being sued see Dutton, *A Revision of Swift's Digest*, 1:27; Kent, *Commentaries*, vol. 2, 109–57; Reeve, *Law of Baron and Femme* (1816), 1–226; Reeve, *Law of Baron and Femme* (1862), 49–343; Swift, *A System of Laws* (1795), 1:183–203; Swift, *A System of Laws* (1822), 1:18–40; Tucker, *Blackstone's Commentaries*, 2:433–45.
10. Criminal Docket, 1829–1831, Magistrates Court, Charleston County, SCDAH (there are no page numbers).
11. *People v. Judith Friel*, October 8, 1804, NYMA; *State v. Cain, Meshack, and Charles*, #86a, Trial Papers, Court of Magistrates and Freeholders, Anderson County, SCDAH.
12. *State v. Horatio Ashenwall*, 1823-1A, 1821-3A through 1823-46A, Bills of Indictment, Court of General Sessions, Charleston District, SCDAH. Many cases involved single items or everyday items, which were obviously worn. For examples, see *People v. John Kennedy*, October 7, 1801 (a single bandana worth fifty cents); *People v. Sarah Grant*, November 11, 1801 (two yards of calico worth fifty-six cents, one bedspread worth fifty cents, three papers of pins worth twelve cents each, one pair of silk gloves worth one dollar); *People v. Incognita Obstinata*, August 8, 1801 (one linen shirt worth one dollar, one linen shirt worth one dollar and fifty cents, eight neck handkerchiefs worth twelve cents, one short gown worth thirty-seven cents); *People v. John Meyers*, February 3, 1802 (one drab-colored greatcoat worth four dollars); *People v. Eliza Stores*, April 7, 1804 (one pair of stockings worth one dollar, one stocking worth fifty cents, one muslin shift worth one dollar and twenty five cents, one Madras handkerchief worth seventy cents, one pair of high-heeled shoes worth fifty cents, one stuff

petticoat worth one dollar and fifty cents); NYMA. *State v. Herman Husk* (a handkerchief worth six pence), folder 1793, Criminal Action Records, Orange County; *State v. Elisha Cate* (a piece of homespun cloth worth ten pence), 1810; both in Criminal Action Records, Orange County, NCSA. *State v. John Henderson* (a handkerchief and pair of pants worth ten shillings), 1806-6A, 1786-1A though 1808-27A, Bills of Indictment, Court of General Sessions, Charleston District, SCDAH

13. *People v. Rosenah Gray*, June 3, 1802; *People v. Susan Munro*, June 4, 1807; both in NYMA. In "To Restore Peace and Tranquility," Meggan Cashwell makes a similar point about the seriousness with which New York City officials took the evidence, although they were hardly impartial. The cases where enslaved people, free Blacks, and white laborers (men and women) were acquitted are numerous. For a few examples, involving matters where it seems like the case might have gone the other direction, see *State v. Jack*, #21, Trial Papers, Court of Magistrates and Freeholders, Spartanburg County; *State v. Jesse Hewey (a free man of color)*, #44, Trial Papers, Court of Magistrates and Freeholders, Spartanburg County; *State v. Wyatt Harris (a free negro)*, #48, Trial Papers, Court of Magistrates and Freeholders, Spartanburg County; *State v. Drury*, #59, Trial Papers, Court of Magistrates and Freeholders, Anderson County; *State v. Jess*, #74, Trial Papers, Court of Magistrates and Freeholders, Anderson County; *State v. Pat*, #172, Trial Papers, Court of Magistrates and Freeholders, Anderson County; all in SCDAH. The New York City cases are numerous; for examples between 1800 and 1805, see *People v. Lucinda Stroud*, February 4, 1800; *People v. John (a black)*, October 8, 1801; *People v. Eliza Cauchois*, December 8, 1803; *People v. Sarah Fuller*, February 8, 1804; *People v. Thomas Cooney and others*, April 7, 1804; *People v. Margaret Donaldson*, April 5, 1804; *People v. Polly Rogers*, April 5, 1804; *People v. John Hays*, April 18, 1804; *People v. Elizabeth Brakey*, June 5, 1804; *People v. Sally McDonald*, August 9, 1804; *People v. Alice O'Connor*, October 5, 1804; *People v. Andrew Powlis*, August 8, 1805; *People v. Dorothy Johnson*, February 8, 1805; *People v. John Christian*, June 5, 1805; *People v. Amy Hazard*, June 8, 1805; *People v. Peter a slave of Anthony Marshall*, June 8, 1805; *People v. Catharine Evans, Jane Harper, and Joseph Harper*, August 8, 1805; *People v. Joseph Schenck*, December 9, 1805; all in NYMA.

14. The cases bear an uncanny resemblance to claims made by African Americans in the Southern Claims Commission after the Civil War, which have been ably described and analyzed by Dylan Penningroth, *Claims of Kinfolk*, esp. 126–27. Commission officials wanted written documentation, but they made do without it. For an insightful analysis of the biases of officials in the New York Municipal Court, see Cashwell, "To Restore Peace and Tranquility." Also see Kennington, *In the Shadow of* Dred Scott; Twitty, *Before* Dred Scott; Von Daacke, *Freedom Has a Face*; Welch, *Black Litigants*.

15. *People v. Judith Friel*, October 8, 1804; *People v. Rosenah Gray*, June 3, 1802; *People v. Susan Munro*, June 4, 1807; all in NYMA. The practice of supplying oral information in lieu of a receipt was routine; for other examples in NYMA, see *People v. Abigail Leonard*, April 9, 1801; *People v. Andrew Gatty*, April 5, 1802; *People v. Margaret Eisenburgh and Winneford Barritt*, June 13, 1803; *People v. Charlotte Fairfax*, December 7, 1803; *People v. Amy Hazard*, June 8, 1805; *People v. Joseph Cole*, April

4, 1826; *People v. Patrick McGlone and William Seymour*, April 6, 1826; *People v. John Church*, April 7, 1826; *People v. Cornelius Dougherty*, June 7, 1844 (he had a receipt but it was suspect, given the nature of the transaction). Recent work has emphasized the broad dissemination of legal knowledge through subordinate communities. See, for instance, Daminao, *To Her Credit*; Edwards, *People and Their Peace*; Edwards, "Legal World"; Edwards, "James and His Striped Velvet Pantaloons"; de la Fuente and Gross, *Becoming Free, Becoming Black*; Jones, *Birthright Citizens*; Penningroth, "Everyday Use"; Sachs, "Freedom By A Judgment"; Welch, *Black Litigants*; Welch, "William Johnson's Hypothesis."

16. *State v. Cain, Meshack, and Charles*, #86a, Trial Papers, Court of Magistrates and Freeholders, Anderson County, SCDAH. *People v. Susan Munro*, June 4, 1807, and *People v. Rosenah Gray*, June 3, 1802, NYMA. The regular emphasis on buying and selling on the street or other public places, including auctions, is telling. For examples of cases where publicity was important, see *Maria Barker v. Margaret Cassady*, April 11, 1800, and *People v. Robert Bennet, Nancy Jeffreys, Martin Cassady, and Margaret Cassady*, June 4, 1800 (witnesses made much of the fact of showing people the goods in question); *People v. Abigail Leonard*, April 9, 1801 (Leonard emphasized that she bought and sold the goods in public); *People v. Charlotte Fairfax*, December 7, 1803 (witnesses to the purchase); *People v. John Casey*, June 27, 1804 (purchase made on the street, with witnesses present); *People v. Michael Lynch*, August 10, 1804 (the extent to which neighbors were involved in policing property); *People v. John Bennett*, February 6, 1806 (buying and selling in public); *People v. Elisha Williams*, March 31, 1808 (makes the point of purchasing the goods in public, although in this instance he is still convicted); *People v. Nicholas Ledwith*, April 9, 1807 (the problem was that no one was present that he knew to witness a purchase at the public auction); all in NYMA. Trading in public was important for enslaved people because it produced witnesses: *State v. Pat*, #172, Trial Papers, Court of Magistrates and Freeholders, Anderson County; *State v. Amos*, #245, Trial Papers, Court of Magistrates and Freeholders, Anderson County; SCDAH. Also see *State v. Job and Adney*, #50, Trial Papers, Court of Magistrates and Freeholders, Spartanburg County, SCDAH (the issue here was whether stolen goods would be worn publicly, which increased the danger that they could be traced). For the importance of publicity in creating claims to property, see Penningroth, *Claims of Kinfolk*, 127–30. For auctions and the importance of publicity in disseminating commercial knowledge, see Hartigan-O'Connor, "Public Sales and Public Values."
17. *People v. Cornelius Dougherty*, June 7, 1844, NYMA.
18. *State v. Deborah Davis*, 1816-74A, 1816-59A through 1818-20A, Bills of Indictment, Court of General Sessions, Charleston District, SCDAH.
19. *People v. Polly Rogers*, April 5, 1804, NYMA. For other examples of marking and initials, see *Maria Barker v. Margaret Cassady*, April 11, 1800, and *People v. Robert Bennet, Nancy Jeffreys, Martin Cassady, and Margaret Cassady*, June 4, 1800; *People v. Abraham*, February 7, 1800; *People v. Christiana Forbes*, November 13, 1801; *People v. John Lane*, December 16, 1802; *People v. James Dawson and others*, August 6, 1802 (in this case, the initials were cut out); *People v. Polly Rogers*, April 5, 1804; *People*

v. *Thomas Callipy*, November 8, 1805; *People v. Sarah Ray, Frank, and John Bradley*, December 2, 1807; *People v. James Brown*, June 9, 1808; *People v. Mary Dougherty*, June 7, 1844; all in NYMA. For marking, also see Penningroth, *Claims of Kinfolk*, 94.
20. *State v. Deborah Davis*, 1816-74A, 1816-59A through 1818-20A, Bills of Indictment, Court of General Sessions, Charleston District, SCDAH. *State v. Cain, Meshack, and Charles*, #86a, Trial Papers, Court of Magistrates and Freeholders, Anderson County, SCDAH. For other cases involving trunks, see chapter 6.
21. *State v. John Marshall, Sr., Agnes Marshall, and John Marshall*, Indictments, Court of General Sessions, Kershaw County, SCDAH.
22. *People v. Cornelius Dougherty*, June 7, 1844, NYMA
23. *People v. Eliza Cauchois*, December 8, 1803; *People v. Elizabeth Cornell*, April 10, 1815; *People v. John Miers alias Joseph Grate*, January 8, 1805; all NYMA. For other examples, see chapter 8, note 22.
24. *People v. Judith Friel*, October 8, 1804, NYMA.
25. *People v. Judith Friel*, October 8, 1804, NYMA. For cases of tenants pawning linens and other articles, see for instance *People v. Samuel Hart*, April 11, 1826; *People v. Eliza Ross*, May 8, 1826; *People v. Peter Anthony*, June 7, 1808; NYMA. For items seized in lieu of rent, see *People v. Peter James and Elizabeth Jackson*, April 5, 1815, NYMA.
26. *Sterne v. Allen, Richmond City*, Hustings Court, Suit Papers, Ended Causes, Dismissed in 1805, Bar Code 1130426, LV. *People v. Judith Friel*, October 8, 1804, NYMA.
27. *Sterne v. Allen, Richmond City*, Hustings Court, Suit Papers, Ended Causes, Dismissed in 1805, Bar Code 1130426, LV.
28. *State v. Brummer*, #142, Trial Papers, Court of Magistrates and Freeholders, Anderson County, SCDAH.
29. Ibid.

Chapter 10

1. *People v. Catherine Brennan and Ann Allison*, May 15, 1844, NYMA.
2. Paul A. David and Peter Solar, "A Bicentenary Contribution to the History of the Cost of Living in America," *Research in Economic History* 2 (1977): 1–80; see, in particular, figures from 46. For the decline in costs of textiles, also see Shammas, "The Decline of Textile Prices."
3. William E. Pratt to Mason and Lawrence, March 14, 1850, Letters Received, 1849–1855, Lawrence & Company records, BL. For Cocheco, see Richard Candee, "The 'Great Factory' at Dover"; Storey, "Printed Cottons in Victorian America." For calico printing, see Chassagne, "Calico Printing in Europe before 1780"; Eaton, *Printed Textiles*, esp. 81–125.
4. Rasmussen, "Waging War with Wool"; Forsyth, "Special Interest Protectionism." The wool industry depended on protection throughout the nineteenth century, see Cole, *American Wool Manufacture*; Chester W. Wright, *Wool-Growing and the Tariff: A Study in the Economic History of the United States* (Boston: Houghton Mifflin, 1910). For a general overview, see Jenkins, "The Western Wool Textile Industry."

5. Rockman, "Negro Cloth"; Rockman, "Plantation Goods." Also see Baumgarten, "Plains, Plaid, and Cotton."
6. For ready-made suits, see Egal Feldman, *Fit for Men* (Washington, DC: Public Affairs Press, 1960); Zakim, *Ready-Made Democracy*. For the argument about the uneven acceptance of republican simplicity, see Haulman, *The Politics of Fashion*. Karin Calvert, "The Function of Fashion in Eighteenth-Century America," in *Of Consuming Interests: The Style of Life in the Eighteenth Century*, ed. Cary Carson, Ronald Hoffman, and Peter J. Albert (Charlottesville: University Press of Virginia, 1994), 252–83, argues that the emphasis moved from color and flourish to fit and fabric, particularly garments of matching fabric. Also see Linda Baumgarten, *What Clothes Reveal: The Language of Clothing in Colonial and Federal America: The Williamsburg Collection* (Williamsburg, VA: Colonial Williamsburg Foundation, 2003); Kimberly Chrisman-Campbell, *Fashion Victims: Dress at the Court of Louis XVI and Marie-Antoinette* (New Haven, CT: Yale University Press, 2015); Aileen Ribeiro, *The Art of Dress: Fashion in England and France 1750 to 1820* (New Haven, CT: Yale University, 1995).
7. James Edney to F. H. Cooke, June 26, 1835, James Edney Papers, RU. Ready-made men's clothing appears frequently in other sources as well. Carey and Bradley Ledger, 1842–1843, Barcode 1107475, Local Government Records Collection, Charlotte County Court Records; Richard Taylor Daybook, 1818–1819, Barcode 1097500, Local Government Records Collection, Lynchburg Court Records; both in LV. For other references, see Allen to Nevins & Co., April 28, 1846, Nevins & Company Papers; Jeremiah Toole to Abner Lord Ely, February 7, 1849, Abner Lord Ely Papers, box 1 (about setting up a ready-made clothing store in Petersburg, VA); De Forest & Company Letter Book (which contains numerous references); all in NYPL. New York Trade Agency, Reports, 1851, NYHS are filled with references to merchants who specialized in ready-made clothing. For the extent of the ready-made trade in men's clothing in the United States, see Feldman, *Fit for Men*; Zakim, *Ready-Made Democracy*. Also see Lemire, *Global Trade*, 114–35.
8. *Oak Hall, or the Glory of Boston: A Poem* (Boston: 1846), 5, in the collections of the LCP. Also see Feldman, *Fit for Men*; Zakim, "A Ready-Made Business: The Birth of the Clothing Industry in America," *Business History Review* 73 (Spring 1999): 61–90; Zakim, "Customizing the Industrial Revolution: The Reinvention of Tailoring in the Nineteenth Century," *Winterthur Portfolio* 33, no. 1 (Spring 1998), 41–58; Zakim, *Ready-Made Democracy*.
9. *Oak Hall, or the Glory of Boston*, quotes from prologue and 9. Also see Oak Hall Clothing Company, National Museum of American History, Smithsonian Institution, http://americanhistory.si.edu/collections/search/object/nmah_1329962. For examples of mug shots, see *Chicago Sun-Times/Chicago Daily News* collection, Chicago History Museum; Thomas Byrnes, *1886 Professional Criminals of America* (New York: Chelsea House, 1969).
10. *People v. Mary Dougherty*, June 7, 1844, NYMA. For prices and wages, see David and Solar, "Bicentenary Contribution."
11. George W. Powers to Mason and Lawrence, September 4, 1850, Letters Received, 1849, Case 16, Lawrence & Company records, BL. *Oak Hall, or the Glory of Boston*,

LCP. Complaints about economic volatility are constant in merchants' correspondence. The sources were multiple: the insolvency of inept or unfortunate individuals; market slumps due to oversupply or other circumstances in particular areas; broader downturns that affected entire regions or the whole country. For a sense of the constant ups and downs, see W. I. Ingersoll to James Colles, February 10, 1816; W. I. Ingersoll to James Colles, February 16, 1816; W. I. Ingersoll to James Colles, December 29, 1816; W. I. Ingersoll to James Colles, April 26, 1817; David I. Rogers to James Colles, August 7, 1819; David I. Rogers to James Colles, August 5, 1822; James Colles to H. K. Toler, April 5, 1823; Robert Jaffray to James Colles, February 4, 1824; Robert Jaffray to James Colles, June 1, 1824; Addison Colles to James Colles, September 24, 1825; Addison Colles to James Colles, October 22, 1825; Addison Colles to James Colles, November 23, 1825; Robert Jaffray to James Colles, October 1, 1827; John W. Taylor to James Colles, July 9, 1828; Robert Jaffray to James Colles, August 16, 1828; Addison Colles to James Colles, September 6, 1828; Robert Jaffray to James Colles, February 7, 1829; Joseph Lovell to James Colles, October 16, 1830; Joseph Lovell to James Colles, October 16, 1830; A. Hayward to James Colles, January 14, 1832; Thomas Barron to James Colles, March 13, 1833; Thomas Barron to James Colles, February 17, 1834; A. Hayward to James Colles, February 28, 1834; Colles Family Papers, vol. 1, NYPL. Also see Balleisen, *Navigating Failure*; Mann, *Republic of Debtors*; Sandage, *Born Losers*.

12. *State v. Lucius Eams*, November term, 1844, Boston Municipal Court, vol. 32, part 5, 2204–6. *People v. Mary Dougherty*, June 7, 1844; *People v. William Henry Green, Isaac Austin, John Barnes, Robert Barnes, and Henry Tryon*, January 10, 1833; both in NYMA.

13. *Documents Relative to the House of Refuge, Instituted by The Society for the Reformation of Juvenile Delinquency in the City of New-York in 1824* (New York: 1832), 28–36, 261–70, quotes from 262. Many thanks to Seth Rockman for sharing this source with me.

14. *People v. Francis Kennedy*, January 9, 1833, NYMA.

15. *State v. Thomas Doyles*, 1820-8A through 1823-46A, Bills of Indictment, Court of General Sessions, Charleston District, SCDAH. *People v. Joseph Marshan*, 1801, NYMA. For the development of shoplifting, see Abelson, *When Ladies Go A-Thieving*.

16. *People v. John Williams*, September 4, 1844, NYMA. Cashwell, "To Restore Peace." Cashwell points out that Daniel Rogers, editor of the *New-York City-Hall Recorder*, was already sensationalizing cases in the 1810s and 1820s to create the impression of criminality on the part of the working poor and particularly African Americans. Newspapers and the penny press accentuated those trends over time. For living conditions and community regulations in working-class urban neighborhoods, see Pamela Haag, "The 'Ill-Use of a Wife': Patterns of Working-Class Violence in Domestic and Public New York City, 1860–1880," *Journal of Social History* 25 (Spring 1992): 447–77; Stansell, *City of Women*. For community regulation in rural areas, see Edwards, *The People and Their Peace*.

17. *People v. William Henry Green, Isaac Austin, John Barnes, Robert Barnes, and Henry Tryon*, January 10, 1833; *People v. Mary Dougherty*, June 7, 1844; *People v. Robert White, Robert Bowles, and George Hocum*, June 7, 1844; all in NYMA. For another

case involving Mary Dougherty that same month, see *People v. Cornelius Dougherty*, June 7, 1844, NYMA.
18. *People v. John Bernard*, October 7, 1802, NYMA. For similar kinds of cases, see chapter 9.
19. *People v. Catherine Brennan and Ann Allison*, May 15, 1844; *People v. Eliza Cauchois*, December 8, 1803; both in NYMA
20. *People v. Thomas Stapleton*, April 16, 1810; *People v. William Wilson and William Jones*, February 6, 1817; both in NYMA.
21. *People v. Mary Dougherty*, June 7, 1844; *People v. Robert White, Robert Bowles, and George Hocum*, June 7, 1844; both in NYMA For the close relationship between this area of the textile market and illicit trade, see Hilliard, *Masters, Slaves, and Exchange*; Lane, "Work on the Margins"; Lemire, *Dress, Culture, and Commerce*, esp. 121–46; Lemire, "The Theft of Clothes"; MacKay, "Why They Stole"; Tebbutt, *Making Ends Meet*, esp. 69–100; Styles, *Dress of the People*, esp. 135–78; Walker, "Women, Theft and the World of Stolen Goods"; Zabin, "Women's Trading Networks"; Zabin, *Dangerous Economies*, 57–80.
22. *People v. William Henry Green, Isaac Austin, John Barnes, Robert Barnes, and Henry Tryon*, January 10, 1833; *People v. Mary Dougherty*, June 7, 1844; *People v. Robert White, Robert Bowles, and George Hocum*, June 7, 1844; all in NYMA.
23. *People v. James Butler*, January 10, 1833, NYMA.
24. For the temptations of goods on open counters, see Abelson, *When Ladies Went A-Thieving*.
25. "The History of Imprisonment for Debt and Insolvency Laws"; reference to the statute, 217n6. For the punitive nature of debtors' prison, see Finn, *The Character of Credit*, 109–93.
26. For the transformation in the legal handling of debt, see Mann, *Republic of Debtors*. Also see Balleisen, *Navigating Failure*; Sandage, *Born Losers*.

Chapter 11

1. *People v. George Harris et al.*, May 21, 1850, NYMA. For Lohman, see Janet Farrell Brodie, *Contraception and Abortion in 19th Century America* (Ithaca, NY: Cornell University Press, 1994), 229–31; A. Cheree Carlson, *The Crimes of Womanhood: Defining Femininity in a Court of Law* (Urbana: University of Illinois Press, 2009), 111–35; Leslie J. Reagan, *When Abortion Was a Crime: Women, Medicine, and the Law in the United States, 1867–1973* (Berkeley: University of California Press, 1997), particularly 10–11. Titles of the pamphlet literature suggest the nature of the coverage surrounding Madame Restell. See for example *Trial of Madame Restell, Alias Ann Lohman: For Abortion and Causing the Death of Mrs. Purdy* (New York: 1841); Charles Henry Webb, *The Wickedest Woman in New York* (New York: 1868); *Madame Restell!: Her Secret Life-History from Her Birth to her Suicide: Full Details: Showing How She Became Rich: Who Her Victims Were, and How She Held Them in Her*

Power: Her Tricks and Devices: What She Did and How She Did: All About Her: "The Most Terrible Being Ever Born" ([New York?]: [1890?]).

2. For the long underwear case, see Jesse Hoyt, David Hadden, James Lefforts, and William A. Hadden, Bill of Exceptions, NARA-NY. Also see *Lewis Curtis et al v. Hiram Barney*, Box 29; *Benjamin Curtis, executor of Lewis Curtis et al v. Hiram Barney*, Defendant's Bill of Exceptions, Box 29; *Henry Al Hurlbut and Charles G. Landon, surviving executors of Benjamin H. Hutton, surviving partner of Benkard & Hutton v. Hiram Barney*, Defendant's Bill of Exceptions, Box 33; *Jesse Hoyt ads. William B. Bond*, Brief, Box 54; *Jesse Hoyt ads. William B. Bond*, Certificate of Division, Box 54; *Thomas Armstrong v. Jesse Hoyt*, Box 54; Jesse Hoyt ads. Edward Hardy, Certificate of Division, Box 54; *Thomas Paton and David Stewart v. Jesse Hoyt*, Copy Notice of Issuing Commissions, Box 54; *Thomas Paton and David Stewart v. Jesse Hoyt*, Deposition, Box 54; *Thomas Paton and David Stewart v. Jesse Hoyt*, Depositions, Box 55; *Charles Borsdorff v. Heman Redfield*, Testimony, Box 68; *Carl Bockhacker and Hugo Troost v. Heman Redfield*, Case, Box 68; *Frederick Butterfield, Richard Butterfield, John Butterfield, William Butterfield, and Henry Butterfield v. Heman Redfield*, Verdict, Box 68; all in Case Files in Suits against Collectors of Customs, 1833–1903, NARA-NY. Rao, *National Duties*.

3. For examples of depositions from England, see *Thomas Paton and David Stewart v. Jesse Hoyt*, Copy Notice of Issuing Commissions, Box 54; *Thomas Paton and David Stewart v. Jesse Hoyt*, Deposition, Box 54; *Thomas Paton and David Stewart v. Jesse Hoyt*, Depositions, Box 55; Case Files in Suits Against Collectors of Customs, 1833–1903, NARA-NY.

4. A survey of federal cases and state appellate cases from Connecticut, Massachusetts, New York, North Carolina, Ohio, South Carolina, and Virginia indicates that courts at these levels of the federal system regularly dealt with customary practices associated with textiles in a variety of commercial disputes and accorded them status as legal principles in ways that echoed Roger Taney's long underwear case. Federal case law affirmed Taney's reliance on the customary practices. For example, in *Bacon v. Bancroft*, 2 F. Cas. 325 (C.C.D. Mass. 1840), an action "to recover back the amount of duties, paid under protest, upon a quantity of gunny cloth . . . was submitted to the jury, under the instruction of the court, to find, whether the article in question was that known in commerce as cotton bagging, or was another and different article. It appeared by the testimony, that cotton bagging and gunny cloth were both well known in this country before the passing of the tariff, and that they were considered as different articles of commerce, and known by different names." For other examples where the nature of the goods, as defined by commercial custom, was crucial in customs matters, see *U.S. v. Breed*, 24 F. Cas. 1222, 1224 (C.C.D. Mass. 1832); *Adams v. Bancroft*, 1 F. Cas. 84, 84–85 (C.C.D. Mass. 1838); *Whiting v. Bancroft*, 29 F. Cas. 1055 (C.C.D. Mass. 1841); *Curtis v. Martin*, 44 U.S. 106, 11 L. Ed. 516 (1845).

5. For these points, see, in particular, Reva B. Siegel, "Home as Work: The First Woman's Rights Claims Concerning Wives' Household Labor, 1850–1880," *Yale Law Journal* 103 (1994): 1073–1217 and "The Rule of Love." Also see de la Fuente and Gross, *Becoming Free, Becoming Black*, and Edwards, *The People and Their Peace*.

6. Edwards, *The People and Their Peace*, esp. 64–132. Also see Gross, *Double Character*.
7. Edwards, *The People and Their Peace*, esp. 64–132. For the operation of local courts also see Cashwell, "To Restore Peace"; Gross, *Double Character*; Jones, *Birthright Citizens*; Kennington, *In the Shadow of Dred Scott*; Turner, "Rights and the Ambiguities of Law"; Turner, *Proving Pregnancy*; Twitty, *Before Dred Scott*; Steinberg, *The Transformation of Criminal Justice*; Welch, *Black Litigants*.
8. Steinberg, *The Transformation of Criminal Justice*. Rogers, *New York City-Hall Recorder*. For the difference between case records and accounts of those cases in the *New York City-Hall Recorder* see Cashwell, "To Restore Peace."
9. Rogers, *New York City-Hall Recorder*, vol. 1, preface (no page numbers). For background on Daniel Rogers, see Daniel Rogers Papers, NYHS. Also see Cashwell, "To Restore Peace."
10. Farah Peterson, "Interpretation as Statecraft." Also see McKinley, "Lobbying and the Petition Clause" and "Petitioning and the Making of the Administrative State." For the operation of state legislatures, see Cooper, "Cultures of Emotion"; Lamoreaux and Wallis, "Economic Crisis."
11. Wilson was a signatory of the Declaration of Independence and the US Constitution; Wythe signed the Declaration and left the Constitutional Convention to attend to his dying wife before he could sign that document; Reeve was an ardent supporter of the Revolution; Story was born too late to participate in the Revolution, but his father had been a member of the Sons of Liberty. For legal education, see James P. Ambuske and Randall Flaherty, "Reading Law in the Early Republic: Legal Education in the Age of Jefferson," in *The Founding of Thomas Jefferson's University*, ed. John A. Ragosta, Peter S. Onuf, and Andrew J. O'Shaughnessy (Charlottesville: University of Virginia Press, 2019), 224-57; Daniel R. Coquillette, *On the Battlefield of Merit: Harvard Law School, the First Century* (Cambridge, MA: Harvard University Press, 2015), 20–74; Michael Grossberg, "Institutionalizing Masculinity: The Bar as a Man's Profession," in *Meanings for Manhood: Masculinity in Victorian America*, ed. Mark C. Carnes and Clyde Griffen (Chicago: University of Chicago Press, 1990), 133–51; John H. Langbein, "Blackstone, Litchfield, and Yale: The Founding of the Yale Law School," in *History of the Yale Law School*, ed. Anthony Kronman (New Haven, CT: Yale University Press, 2004), 17–52; Hugh MacGill and R. Kent Newmyer, "Legal Education and Legal Thought, 1790–1920," in *The Cambridge History of Law in America*, ed. Michael Grossberg and Christopher Tomlins (Cambridge: Cambridge University Press, 2008), 2:36–67; Marian C. McKenna, *Tapping Reeve and the Litchfield Law School* (New York: Oceana, 1986); R. Kent Newmyer, "Harvard Law School, New England Legal Culture, and the Antebellum Origins of American Jurisprudence," *Journal of American History* 74, no. 3 (1987): 814–35; Andrew M. Siegel, "'To Learn and to Make Respectable Hereafter': The Litchfield Law School in Cultural Context," *New York Law Review* 73 (1998): 1978–2028.
12. For the dispersion of legal knowledge generally, see Bilder, *The Transatlantic Constitution*. For women in law, see Karen Berger Morello, *The Invisible Bar: The Woman Lawyer in America, 1638 to the Present* (New York: Random House, 1986), 3–38. Also suggestive, although from a later period, is Felice Batlan, *Women and Justice*

for the Poor: A History of Legal Aid, 1863–1945 (Cambridge: Cambridge University Press, 2015). The scholarship tends to stress women's exclusion from the practice of law, based on their exclusion from the legal profession, as it developed in the nineteenth century. See, for instance, Virginia G. Drachman, *Sisters in Law: Women Lawyers in Modern American History* (Cambridge, MA: Harvard University Press, 2001). But those professional barriers were less developed and rigid in the first half of the nineteenth century, when legal knowledge was more widely held and practiced. Women in the colonial period were savvy legal operators, when they had the means and access: Michael A. Blaakman, "Martha Bradstreet and the 'Epithet of Woman': A Story of Land, Libel, Litigation, and Legitimating 'Unwomanly' Behavior in the Early Republic," *Early American Studies: An Interdisciplinary Journal* 13, no. 3 (2015): 544–85; Sara T. Damiano, "'To Well and Truly Administer': Female Administrators and Estate Settlement in Newport, Rhode Island, 1730–1776," *New England Quarterly* 86 (March 2013): 89–124; Damiano, *To Her Credit*; and Cornelia Hughes Dayton, *Women before the Bar: Gender, Law, and Society in Connecticut, 1639–1789* (Chapel Hill: University of North Carolina Press, 1995). They continued to be so after the Revolution: Grossberg, *A Judgment for Solomon*; Hartog, *Man and Wife in America*.

13. Blackstone quoted in Langbein, "Blackstone, Litchfield, and Yale," 20; Story quote from 39n28. Kent, *Commentaries on American Law*; Reeve, *Law of Baron and Femme* (1816); Joseph Story, *Commentaries on the Constitution of the United States*, 3 vols. (Boston: 1833), and Story, *Commentaries on Equity Jurisprudence: As Administered in England and America*, 2 vols. (Boston: 1835–36). It took a while for Harvard Law School to get off the ground, and the school credits Story for its success. In 1828, there was only one faculty member who held an appointment and only one student was enrolled in 1828–29, although Story said there were none. Story, who had been a member of the US Supreme Court since 1812 and was responsible for circuit courts of appeal in the northeastern district, was appointed as the first Dane Professor of Law at Harvard in the fall of 1829. Soon other Dane professors were appointed in various fields of law. The first faculty member to hold the title of dean was Christopher C. Langdell, who served from 1870 to 1895. For the importance of legal texts and treatises in shaping the law, see Newmyer, "Harvard Law School." Also see Kellen Richard Funk, "The Lawyers' Code: The Transformation of American Legal Practice, 1828-1938," Ph.D. dissertation, Princeton University, 2018. Although his emphasis is on civil matters, the same currents were at work in criminal cases.

14. Aaron Burr Reeve and Tapping Reeve, "Notes of Lectures by Tapping Reeve at the Litchfield Law School, by A. B. Reeve," *Litchfield Law School Notebooks* (1802), 5 vols., https://digitalcommons.law.yale.edu/llsn/5. University of Virginia Law School, John W. Hartman Center for Sales, Advertising and Marketing History, DU, https://idn.duke.edu/ark:/87924/r4ns0np2p. Also see the 1828 Catalog Project of the first law library at the University of Virginia, http://archives.law.virginia.edu/catalogue/; Litchfield Law School Sources, Documents Collection Center, Yale Law School, https://documents.law.yale.edu/litchfield-law-school-sources. Also see Steven Sheppard, ed., *The History of Legal Education in the United States: Commentaries and Primary Sources* (Pasadena, CA: Salem, 1999). Scholars emphasize the difference

between the legal culture of the northern and southern states, but they were working from the same texts with it came to property, contracts, and commercial law.
15. *Canadian Law Times* 26 (1906): 304. John William Smith, *A Compendium of Mercantile Law* (London: 1834). Some of the books assigned by the University of Virginia Law School, for instance, did note the claims of wives and children to clothing, although references were uneven. Some made reference to practices associated with textiles that had legal implications, but none of them elaborated on the legal practices governing the trade in textiles as a systematic set of principles.
16. Blackstone, *Commentaries on the Laws of England*, 2:435–36; by contrast, see 1:421–33.
17. Blackstone, *Commentaries on the Laws of England*, vol. 4. See "Coincidence of Lectures in Litchfield Notebooks," Litchfield Law School Sources, https://documents.law.yale.edu/litchfield-law-school-sources/coincidence-lectures-litchfield-notebooks.
18. For graduates of Litchfield Law School, see Litchfield Historical Society, Litchfield Law School Students, https://web.archive.org/web/20090228171353/http://www.litchfieldhistoricalsociety.org/lawschool/students.html.
19. Rogers, *New York City-Hall Recorder*. Edwards, *The People and Their Peace*.
20. While federal and state courts regularly dealt with cases involving the principles attached to textiles, references to those principles made it clear that they existed in the realm of customary practice, not in written texts. In *Anderson v. Chick*, 8 S.C. Eq. 118, 126 (S.C. App. L. & Eq. 1830), one South Carolina jurist expressed frustration with the fact that rules regarding the exchange of cloth were not written down, like the rules regarding other, often less valuable forms of property: "Why all this legal form and parade as to land, when we know it often happens, that a bale of goods, sold by an auctioneer with little ceremony, and perhaps in ten minutes, is oftentimes of more value than half of the farms in the country. A bale of broad cloths, or a box of linens, will oftentimes sell for more money than would be sufficient to buy two thousand acres of good land." A survey of statute collections from Connecticut, Massachusetts, New York, North Carolina, Ohio, South Carolina, and Virginia indicates that textiles appear most prominently in the context of the state clothing the military, prisoners, state employees and paupers. In North Carolina, Virginia, and South Carolina, textiles appeared in relationship to laws regarding feeding and clothing enslaved people. The closest thing to the legal principles of textiles were in sections about debtors, which affirmed wives' claims to clothing. Massachusetts, for example, mandated that "the widow shall nevertheless be entitled to her apparel, and such other of the personal estate as the Judge of Probate shall determine necessary, according to her quality and degree; and such part of the personal estate, as the judge may allow the widow"; Asahel Stearns et al., *General Laws of Massachusetts* (Boston: 1823), 1:106.
21. *Laws of the State of New-York* (Albany, NY: 1802), 1:253–57. Amasa J. Parker, George Wolford, and Edward Wade, eds., *Revised Statutes of the State of New York* (Albany, NY: 1859), 3:947–82; for misdemeanors, see 971–82. Also see Funk, "The Lawyers' Code."
22. Moses King, comp., *King's Handbook of New York City: An Outline History and Description of the American Metropolis* (Boston: 1892), 25–26, 483–86; Jonathan

Rubinstein, "From the King's Peace to the Patrol Car: The Origins of the City Police," *New York Magazine*, May 1973, 44–48; Edward H. Savage, *A Chronological History of the Boston Watch and Police, from 1631 to 1865* (Boston: 1865). For Richmond, see Joshua D. Rothman, *Notorious in the Neighborhood: Sex and Families Across the Color Line in Virginia, 1787–1867* (Chapel Hill: University of North Carolina Press, 2003), 99–100. For the general patterns, see Steinberg, *The Transformation of Criminal Justice*.

23. *People v. John Ryan*, January 10, 1833, NYMA. For the presence of lawyers in other cases, see *People v. Michael Plunkett*, January 15, 1840; *People v. John Tinson*, August 8, 1845; *People v. John Moran*, October 14, 1845; *People v. William McCready*, February 23, 1850; *People v. Morris Hartz*, April 15, 1850; *People v. Herman Eicke*, April 15, 1850; *People v. Jonas Silver*, April 15, 1850; *People v. David Wild*, May 21, 1850; *People v. Daniel Goodmanson*, July 12, 1850; all in NYMA.

24. For examples of cases involving discussions of chisels, skeleton keys, and other means of breaking in, see *People v. William Hall and George Morton*, December 5, 1839; *People v. John Sullivan and Thomas Smith*, September 14, 1844; *People v. Mary Kinney and Bridget Scully*, August 9, 1845; *People v. John Jefferson*, April 11, 1850; *People v. John Jefferson*, April 11, 1850; *People v. James Meehan and Robert Florence*, June 7, 1850; *People v. William Megram*, July 8, 1850; *People v. Robert Adams and Robert Davis*, September 9, 1850. For examples of cases involving degrees of burglary from January 1856, see *People v. Thomas Williams and James de Caton*, January 14, 1856; *People v. John Brown*, January 14, 1856; *People v. Thomas Roach*, January 16, 1856; *People v. Richard Harris*, January 16, 1856; *People v. John Moore and George Mason*, January 16, 1856; *People v. Henry Brown*, January 16, 1856; *People v. John Wallace Campbell*, January 16, 1856; all in NYMA.

25. *People v. David Kipp et al.*, August 9, 1845; *People v. Mary Reed*, September 16, 1845; both in NYMA. Also see *People v. John Schroder*, September 5, 1845; *People v. Eliza Davis*, November 15, 1839; *People v. John Baker and Charles Hayden*, December 5, 1839; *People v. William Hall and George Morton*, December 5, 1839; *People v. Nathan Rhodes*, July 3, 1844 (two cases); *People v. John Sullivan and Thomas Smith*, September 14, 1844; *People v. Ann Herdman*, October 24, 1844; *People v. George Hoyt*, May 24, 1850; *People v. Charles Healy*, July 8, 1850; *People v. Joseph Van Voorhies and James McCauley*, August 9, 1850; *People v. Thomas Wilson*, August 9, 1850; all in NYMA.

26. See, for example, *State v. Cash* (a slave), 1830; *State v. Henry* (a slave), 1831; *State v. John* (a slave), 1831; *State v. Walt* (a slave), 1831; *State v. Edward Carter* (a free man of color), 1835; *State v. Matt* (a slave), 1838; *State v. Daniel* (a slave), 1840; *State v. Essex* (a slave), 1840; *State v. Jack* (a slave), 1843; *State v. Dorcas and Jack* (both slaves), 1844; all in Trial Papers, Court of Magistrates and Freeholders, Kershaw County, SCDAH. For the creeping effects of professionalization in rural areas, see Edwards, *The People and Their Peace*, particularly 205–85.

27. *People v. Catherine Brennan and Ann Allison*, May 15, 1844, NYMA. Figuring the exact number of women involved in textile cases is impossible because the court records contain only complaints that went to trial. But the numbers are suggestive. In 1800, in the fifty-four cases identified as involving disputed textiles, sixteen women

were actively involved in prosecutions in cases that involved property to which they had claims. By contrast, in the sixty-seven cases identified from February to September 1850, only seven women were actively involved in the prosecutions. Some of those cases, moreover, were either about wives acting as agents in a family business or seemed like efforts to hide property in wives' names.

28. *People v. Abraham Rias*, September 12, 1850; *People v. Hannah McGee*, April 10, 1844; both in NYMA. Also see *People v. Hannah McGee*, April 10, 1844; *People v. William Smith*, October 15, 1844; *People v. John Langan and Mary Thorne*, October 21, 1844; *People v. Christina Grossman*, May 13, 1850; *People v. William Smith*, January 14, 1856; *People v. Henry Brown*, January 16, 1856; all NYMA. Sometimes it was clear from the testimony that married women were operating a store, but even they obscured that fact in their testimony, keeping up the pretense that all property belonged to their husbands. For examples of married women shopkeepers whose status is unclear, see *People v. Catharine Ward*, January 12, 1826; *People v. Henry Verichen*, October 14, 1845; *People v. Morris Hartz*, April 15, 1850; all NYMA.

29. *Proceedings of the Woman's Rights Convention, Held at Akron, Ohio, May 28 and 29, 1851* (Cincinnati, OH: 1851), 11–14; quotes from 13. *The Proceedings of the Woman's Rights Convention, Held at Worcester, October 15th and 16th, 1851* (New York: 1852), 101. The proceedings at Seneca Falls also started out with Blackstone; see Proceedings of the Woman's Rights Conventions, Held at Seneca Falls & Rochester, N. Y., July & August, 1848 (New York: 1870), 4. Also see *Proceedings of the Ohio Women's Convention, Held at Salem . . . 1850* (Cleveland, OH: 1850), 8–9, 35–36; *Proceedings of the Woman's Rights Convention Held at the Broadway Tabernacle in the City of New York . . . 1853* (New York: 1853), 45, 51, 57–58; *Proceedings of the National Women's Rights Convention, Held at Cleveland, Ohio* (Cleveland, OH: 1854), 6; *Proceedings of the Ninth National Woman's Rights Convention Held in New York City . . . 1859* (Rochester, NY: 1859), 5, 13. Elizabeth Cady Stanton, Susan B. Anthony, and Matilda Joslyn Gage, eds., *History of Woman Suffrage*, 2nd ed. (New York: 1889), 1:173–74, 3:48–50. Dawn M. Winters, "'The Ladies are Coming!': A New History of Antebellum Temperance, Women's Rights, and Political Activism" (PhD diss., Carnegie Mellon University, 2018), particularly 84, 106, 256–57. For background on Nichols, see Marilyn S. Blackwell and Kristen T. Oertel, *Frontier Feminist: Clarina Howard Nichols and the Politics of Motherhood* (Lawrence: University Press of Kansas, 2010). Nichols and her new husband moved to Kansas in 1845 to work for abolition. After her husband's death, she continued to work for abolition, temperance, and women's rights, including married women's property ownership, mothers' right to custody of their children, and equal education, as well as suffrage.

30. *The Proceedings of the Woman's Rights Convention, Held at Worcester*, 97–111; quotes from 101–2. For a different version of this story, see *Proceedings of the Woman's Rights Convention Held at the Broadway Tabernacle in the City of New York . . . 1853*, 24–31, 45, 57. In "Home as Work," Siegel argues that the denial of rights became the means of expressing larger problems of women's inequality within the women's rights movement more generally in the nineteenth century. Also see Alison D. Morantz, "There's No Place Like Home: Homestead Exemption and

Judicial Constructions of Family in Nineteen-Century America," *Law and History Review* 24 (Summer 2006): 245-295.

31. For the woman fleeing her husband, see *The Proceedings of the Woman's Rights Convention, Held at Worcester*, 106-7, quotes from 107. For the rum-drinker, see *The Proceedings of the Woman's Rights Convention, Held at Syracuse, September 8th, 9th, and 10th, 1852* (Syracuse, NY: 1852), 23-24. For similar uses of husbands' seizure of clothing as a metaphor for the injustices of general laws, see *Proceedings of the Woman's Rights Convention Held at the Broadway Tabernacle in the City of New York . . . 1853*, 74; *Proceedings of the National Women's Rights Convention, Held at Cleveland, Ohio*, 5, 8-9; *Proceedings of the Ninth National Woman's Rights Convention Held in New York City . . . 1859*, 13; Stanton et al., *History of Woman Suffrage*, vol. 1, 173-74; for Jesse Daniel Ames, see Jacquelyn Dowd Hall, *Revolt against Chivalry: Jesse Daniel Ames and the Women's Campaign Against Lynching* (New York: Columbia University Press, 1979), 27; original quote from Jessie Daniel Ames Interview, n.d. [1965-66?], Southern Oral History Project Collection, SHC.

Chapter 12

1. Virginia, 2:140, R. G. Dun & Co., BL; there is also a reference to a Mrs. Harris in Scotsville in the same volume, 74. Josh Lauer, *Creditworthy: A History of Consumer Surveillance and Financial Identity in America* (New York: Columbia University Press, 2017), especially 26-50; James D. Norris, *R. G. Dun & Co., 1841-1900: The Development of Credit- Reporting in the Nineteenth Century* (Westport, CT: Greenwood, 1978); Rowena Olegario, *A Culture of Credit: Embedding Trust and Transparency in American Business* (Cambridge, MA: Harvard University Press, 2006), esp. 36-79; Olegario, *The Engine of Enterprise: Credit in America* (Cambridge, MA: Harvard University Press, 2016), 13-78. Also see Bertram Wyatt-Brown, *Lewis Tappan and the Evangelical War against Slavery* (Cleveland: Press of Case Western Reserve University, 1969).

2. Virginia, 2:140, R. G. Dun & Co., BL. R. G. Dun and Co. did not cover all states equally well in the 1840s and 1850s, when the firm was starting out. But Virginia was particularly well documented, in both rural and urban areas, probably because it was such a valuable market for New York suppliers. Married women in the textile business tended to cluster in commercial centers, as did other male merchants and tailors. For other examples of married women in Virginia, see for instance Virginia, Mrs. E. F. Marshall, 2:57; Mrs. M. E. Brockenbrough, 2:86; Mrs. F. E. Elliott, 2:92; Catherine P. Purvis, 2:94; Mrs. Ann Spicer, 2:135; Mrs. J. W. Winston, 2:152. Mrs. J. H. Padgett, 3:207; Harriett H. Jenkins, 3:250; Mrs. Lucy H. Ward, 5:361; J. R. Bryson, 5:379; Mrs. O. R. Hill, 6:478; Mrs. S. E. Hayth, 7:526H, 526K; Mrs. Lucy C. Young, 10:301; Mrs. M.A. Butterfield, 10:301; Mrs. A. W. Smith, 10:354(3); Mrs. E. Brannan, 43:53; Mrs. Bowles, 43:55; Mrs. Dederer, 43:61; Mrs. Everett, 43:63; Mrs. C. Vigiline, 43:82; Mrs. V. L. Blank, 43:87; Mrs. E. Lyon, 43:100; Mrs. B. Rosenfeld,

43:167; all in R. G. Dun & Co., BL. Some of these women may have been widowed, although agents generally indicated whether women's husbands were alive.

3. Sometimes agents made their doubts about single women clear. Virginia: Miss H. Ford, 3:206, Miss Eliza Berry, 3:206; Miss Jane Simpson, 9:55; Miss Issabella Hillman, 43:113. Ohio: Charles E. James, 78:12 (who is seen as a front for the women in his family); M. W. Baird, 78:75 and 195. For the general dismissal of women, see Virginia: Miss L. J. Lazenby, 6:434; Miss E. I. Garret, 8:236d; Miss Jane Simpson, 9:55. Ohio: Miss E. Lee, 78:53; Miss Martha Alcorn, 101:247. Connecticut: Miss Fanny Stanton, 45:A3. Massachusetts: Miss H. B. Cook and Lydia P. Francis, 13:45; Mrs. Swasey and Miss E. I. Swasey, 13:71; Miss Lizzie Saunders, 13:77; Miss Alice Birch, 13:90; Miss Roby M. Sherman, 13:93; Miss Susan Henry, 13:105. Reports on women in New Orleans tended to be more positive generally, perhaps because of the longstanding acceptance of married women's separate property in both French and Spanish law. Louisiana: Mrs. Jeffers, 10:310 and 531; Mrs. Blair, 10:327; Miss T. Deter and Mrs. G. Taber, 10:353; Miss E. W. Rogers, 10:410. Also see Geraldin and Ross., Missouri, 36:155. All in R.G. Dun & Co., BL.

4. Virginia, 2:140, R. G. Dun & Co., BL. The implications are evident in the economic decline of women's businesses in the textile trade. As Gamber argues in *The Female Economy*, women's millinery establishments declined in the second half of the nineteenth century because women could not access credit, like white men could. For a particularly insightful new study of efforts to eliminate racial restrictions and their connection to questions of mobility, particularly across state lines, see Masur, *Until Justice Be Done*.

5. Quotes from Virginia: L. Powell, 2:147; Lewis Cohen, 43:86; Moses Hecht and Bro., 43:214; R. G. Dun & Co., BL. For the elements of good credit, see Judy Hilkey, *Character Is Capital: Success Manuals and Manhood in Gilded Age America* (Chapel Hill: University of North Carolina Press, 1997); Olegario, *A Culture of Credit*, 80–118; Olegario, *The Engine of Enterprise*, 13–78. Also see Finn, *The Character of Credit*.

6. Quote from John Cochran and Co., Ohio, 78:74; for the unfortunate tailor, see L. Powell, Virginia, 2:147. For examples of men who merited caution, despite appearances, see W. N. Roach, Virginia, 2:77; G. W. Dillard, Virginia, 2:77; L. Powell, Virginia, 2:147; Rudolph Massey, Virginia, 3:203; all in R. G. Dun & Co., BL.

7. For family connections and personal ties, see for example Adams, *The Familial State*; Haggerty, *The British-Atlantic Trading Community*; Hamilton, *Social and Economic Networks*; Mann, *Neighbors and Strangers*; Muldrew, *The Economy of Obligation*; Pearsall, *Atlantic Families*; Romney, *New Netherland Connections*; Vicente, *Clothing the Spanish Empire*. The scholarship has tended to accept the overarching narrative of change from personal ties to impersonal assessments based on individual character. Recent scholarship, however, has emphasized the persistence of those networks: Mandy L. Cooper, "Too Big to Fail? Families, Internal Improvement, and State Government in Antebellum North Carolina, *Journal of the Early Republic* 41 (Fall 2021): 349-72; Cooper, "Cultures of Emotion"; Crowston, *Credit, Fashion, Sex*; Farber, "State-Building After War's End"; Hyde, *Empires, Nations, and Families*; Finn, *The Character of Credit*; Lamoreaux, *Insider Lending*. By contrast, scholars who do

not follow actual business practices on the ground tend to emphasize change; see for instance Lauer, *Creditworthy*; Olegario, *A Culture of Credit*; Olegario, *The Engine of Enterprise*.

8. For the importance of Quaker networks, see David Harris Sacks, *The Widening Gate: Bristol and the Atlantic Economy, 1450-1700* (Berkeley: University of California Press, 1991), particularly 304-29; Jordan Landes, *London Quakers in the Trans-Atlantic World: The Creation of an Early Modern Community* (New York: Palgrave, 2015). Olegario, *A Culture of Credit*, 119-38, argues that credit reporting firms, such R. G. Dun and Company, found Jewish businesses suspect because they operated through closed networks, which resembled those of Quakers, based in their own families and communities, which the agents saw as less transparent.

9. Haltunen, *Confidence Men and Painted Women*. Also see Mihm, *A Nation of Counterfeiters*. For emotions in business culture, see Cooper, "Cultures of Emotion"; John Corrigan, *Business of the Heart: Religion and Emotion in the Nineteenth Century* (Berkeley: University of California Press, 2002). Short stories and serialized novels ran regularly in the periodical literature, with these basic themes. They appeared not only in periodicals directed at women, such *Godey's Ladies Book*, but also in daily and weekly newspapers. These stock characters and issues also appeared in fiction. The novels of Charles Dickens provide excellent examples, as do those of Louisa May Alcott.

10. *Blythe v. Capus*, Richmond City, Hustings Court, Suit Papers, Ended Causes, folder May 1787 no. 3, box 8, May 1787; *MacRae v. Harris*, Richmond City, Hustings Court, Suit Papers, Ended Causes, folder April-June 1785, box 3, January to September 1785; *Crawford and Dunn v. Organ*, Richmond City, Hustings Court, Suit Papers, Ended Causes, folder August 1815, box 25; *John Henry v. Samuel Horner*, Richmond City, Hustings Court, Suit Papers, Ended Causes, folder July 1816 2, box 27; all in LV. The civil cases involving small debts also dominated the New London County Court; New London, County Court, Files, 1800-1850, CSL. While the ratio of civil to criminal cases varied in other places, most civil cases involved small debts: Criminal Docket, 1829-1831, Magistrates Court, Charleston County, SCDAH (these are actually civil cases); Dockets of the Magistrates Court, 1842-53, Spartanburg County, SCDAH; Philadelphia Court Records, box 1, Arbitrations Records and box 2, Miscellaneous Records, McAllister Collection, LCP; Thomas Cheyney Docketbooks, HSP; Derby, Justice Records, Justice Thomas Clark, 1777-1803, Justice Court Records, box 551, CSL; Lyme, Justice Records of David F. Sill, 1794-1812, Justice Court Records, box 554, CSL; Lyme, Justice Records of William Noyes, 1790-1806, Justice Court Records, box 554, CSL; Goshen Justice Court, 1797-1820, Justice Court Records, box 553, CSL.

11. For an overview of Colles's career, see the biographical note at the beginning of volume one of the three volumes of transcribed correspondence: Colles Family Papers, 1:1-3, NYPL; vols. 1-3 contain the letters that the biographical note summarizes. For wholesalers suing merchants, see note 15 to this chapter. For the role of wholesalers, see Olegario, *A Culture of Credit*, 13-35.

12. Quotes from Colles Family Papers, 1:2; W. I. Ingersoll to James Colles, vol. 1, February 10, 1816; W. I. Ingersoll to James Colles, vol. 1, December 29, 1816; W. I. Ingersoll to

James Colles, vol. 1, February 6, 1816. Also see W. I. Ingersoll to James Colles, vol. 1, December 29, 1816. All in Colles Family Papers, NYPL. For the 1819 Panic, see Nelson, *A Nation of Deadbeats*.
13. *Daniel Lord v. Simon Carew*, case #85, February 1833, New London County, County Court, Records of Trials, vol. 33, February 1833–November 1842, CSL. *Hamilton, King & Dow v. Chauncey I. Beach and George H. Beach*, case #133, folder 10, June 1842; *Hamilton, King & Dow v. John G. Latimer*, case #134, folder 10, June 1842; *Hamilton, King & Dow v. Chauncey I. Beach and George H. Beach*, case #138, folder 11, June 1842; all New London County, County Court, Files, box 403, June 1842 to November 1842, CSL. For the close relationships in the commercial community that once kept wholesalers from suing, see Michael Woods, "The Culture of Credit in Colonial Charleston," *South Carolina Historical Magazine* 99 (October 1998): 374–79.
14. *State v. John H. Piker*, October term 1844, vol. 32, part 4, Boston Municipal Court, 1929–1933, MSA. John H. Piker seems to have started his business in Dover at a moment of upheaval. Cocheco Print Works completed its new factory there in 1844, at the same time that it began replacing native-born workers, who had been organizing to protest declining working conditions, with Irish immigrants. Many smaller, less stable manufacturing enterprises like Piker's took advantage of the situation, setting up shop in old mills and employing those who were laid off from or quit the big textile firms. See Cathleen Beaudoin, "A Yarn to Follow: The Dover Cotton Factory 1812–1821," Dover Public Library website, https://www.dover.nh.gov/government/city-operations/library/history/a-yarn-to-follow-the-dover-cotton-factory-18121821.html.
15. *State v. John H. Piker*, October term 1844, vol. 32, part 4, Boston Municipal Court, 1929–1933, MSA.
16. *People v. Gustavus Thompson*, May 15, 1844, NYMA. There are actually two cases against him, by different firms, on the same date. For similar cases, see *People v. James Smith*, September 10, 1845; *People v. Absalom Bostick*, October 23, 1844; *People v. Jacob Platts*, October 10, 1845; *People v. Henry Verichen*, October 14, 1845; *People v. William Burtch* (2), October 20, 1845; *People v. Eugene Foliot*, November 12, 1845; *People v. Jacob Platts*, November 13, 1845; *People v. James Connell*, March 23, 1850; *People v. James F. Cross*, April 3, 1850; *People v. Luther Archer*, June 14, 1850; *People v. Charles Healy*, July 8, 1850; *People v. Joel W. Holcomb*, December 20, 1855; all in NYMA. Also see *State v. John H. Piker*, October term 1844, vol. 32, part 4, Boston Municipal Court, 1929–1933, MSA.
17. For examples of credit ratings within and among firms: Reference books (credit ratings), vols. 13 and 14, Fisher, Blashfield and Company Records, NYPL; New York Trade Agency, Reports, 1851, NYHS. Also see R. W. Hidy, "Credit Rating Before Dun and Bradstreet," *Bulletin of the Business Historical Society* 13 (1939): 81–88. For the problems of assessing credit at a distance, see Lewis E. Atherton, "The Problem of Credit Rating in the Antebellum South," *Journal of Southern History* 12 (November 1946): 534–56. For the development of Dun and its business model, see Lauer, *Creditworthy*, 26–50; Norris, *R. G. Dun & Co.*; Olegario, *A Culture of Credit*, 36–79; Olegario, *The Engine of Enterprise*, 13–78. Also see Wyatt-Brown, *Lewis Tappan*.

18. See the following for the general logic of this process: Bouk, *How Our Days Became Numbered*; Brown, "Blanks"; Sarah E. Igo, *The Averaged American: Surveys, Citizens, and the Making of a Mass Public* (Cambridge, MA.: Harvard University Press, 2007); Jonathan Levy, *Freaks of Fortune: The Emerging World of Capitalism and Risk in America* (Cambridge, MA: Harvard University Press, 2012).
19. Recent work emphasizes the importance of those family ties in enabling women's participation in trade and commerce, see Haggerty, *The British-Atlantic Trading Community*; Hartigan-O'Connor, *Ties that Buy*; Miles, *Dawn of Detroit*; Romney, *New Netherland Connections*; Sleeper-Smith, *Indigenous Prosperity*; Van Kirk, *Many Tender Ties*; Vicente, *Clothing the Spanish Empire*; Zabin, "Women's Trading Networks"; Zabin, *Dangerous Economies*. For the continued importance of those ties for women, see Cooper, "Cultures of Emotion."
20. Alexander Duval, Virginia, 7:558, R. G. Dun & Co., BL. The Lehman Brothers began as dry goods merchants in Montgomery, Alabama, in the 1840s, https://www.immigrantentrepreneurship.org/entry.php?rec=20. Marcus Goldman started as a peddler in Philadelphia, https://www.immigrantentrepreneurship.org/entry.php?rec=100#_edn14. Both from Immigrant Entrepreneurship: German-American Business Biographies, 1720 to the Present, German Historical Institute, Washington, DC.
21. The quote is from a report for a white man, not a woman or a man of color, indicating that some white men did not meet the necessary standard either. J. H. Simpson, Ohio, 101:211, R. G. Dun & Co., BL. Also see Mrs. E. M. Rich, Ohio, 101:101, 181, 296, 297; Mrs. A. D. Johnson, Ohio, 78:12; R. G. Dun & Co., BL.
22. James Chesnut to Richard Singleton, July 17, 1834, James Chesnut Papers, SCL; also in Edwards, *People and Their Peace*, 193–94. Another famous example is Harriet Jacobs's grandmother, who managed to carve out a space for herself in New Bern, North Carolina, but who would never have been able to translate those privileges to a place where no one knew her; Harriet Jacobs, *Incidents in the Life of a Slave Girl, Written by Herself*, edited by Jean Fagan Yellin (Cambridge, MA: Harvard University Press, 2000).
23. For recent work that explores efforts to dismantle racially discriminatory laws, see Bonner, *Remaking the Republic*; Gosse and Waldstreicher, *Revolutions and Reconstructions*; Gronningsater, *The Arc of Abolition*; Jones, *All Bound Up Together*; Jones, *Birthright Citizens*; Masur, *Until Justice Be Done*; Leslie A. Schwalm, *Emancipation's Diaspora: Race and Reconstruction in the Upper Midwest* (Chapel Hill: University of North Carolina Press, 2009).
24. For warning out, see Cornelia Hughes Dayton and Sharon V. Salinger, *Robert Love's Warnings: Searching for Strangers in Colonial Boston* (Philadelphia: University of Pennsylvania Press, 2014). For the link between poor laws and racial restrictions, see Masur, "State Sovereignty and Migration" and *Until Justice Be Done*. Also see Elizabeth Stordeur Pryor, *Colored Travelers: Mobility and the Fight for Citizenship before the Civil War* (Chapel Hill: University of North Carolina Press, 2016); Samantha Seeley, "Freedom and the Politics of Migration after the American Revolution," in *Revolutions and Reconstructions*, ed. Van E. Gosse and David Waldstreicher, 84–101. Historian Kunal Parker argues in *Making Foreigners: Immigration and Citizenship Law in*

America, 1600–2000 (New York: Cambridge University Press, 2015) that restrictions on the movement of free Blacks formed the basis for exclusionary immigration laws more generally. Hidetaka Hirota, *Expelling the Poor: Atlantic Seaboard States and the Nineteenth-Century Origins of American Immigration Policy* (New York: Oxford University Press, 2017), makes a similar argument about poor laws and immigration policies, although the focus is on the Irish.

25. Just as the presumption was that people of African descent were enslaved unless proved otherwise, so it was that marriage was the appropriate state for women. Telling in this regard is Sachs, *Home Rule*, 71–93, 120–43.
26. Mrs. Henry Lichton, Louisiana, 10:393; Miss E. W. Rogers, Louisiana, 10:410; Mrs. Jeffers, Louisiana, 10:310 and 531; all in R. G. Dun & Co., BL.
27. Mrs. S. E. Hayth, Virginia, 7:526 H, 526 I; Mrs. M. A. Butterfield, Virginia, 10:301, R. G. Dun & Co., BL. For the importance of married women's control of family property, see Cooper, "Cultures of Emotion"; Jones-Rogers, *They Were Her Property*. Although married women controlled family property through various legal mechanisms, they did not have the property rights necessary to own it in their own names, which placed limits on accessing the kind of commercial credit discussed here.
28. Mrs. Yatsapaugh, Virginia, 3:189; Mrs. J. H. Padgett, Virginia, 3:207; Mrs. Minken, Ohio, 78:84 and 192; all R. G. Dun & Co., BL.
29. Mrs. Everett, Virginia, 43:63; Mrs. M. A. Keblinger, Virginia, 2:135; R. G. Dun & Co., BL.
30. For an overview of the acts relating to married women's property, see Joan Hoff, *Law, Gender, and Injustice: A Legal History of U.S. Women* (New York: New York University Press, 1991), 377–82. Also see Norma Basch, *In the Eyes of the Law: Women, Marriage and Property in Nineteenth-Century New York* (Ithaca, NY: Cornell University Press, 1982); Richard H. Chused, "Married Women's Property Law: 1800–1850," *Georgetown Law Journal* 71 (June 1983): 1359–1424; Catherine B. Cleary, "Married Women's Property Rights in Wisconsin, 1846–1872," *Wisconsin Magazine of History* 78, no. 2 (Winter 1994–95): 113–26;; Bernie D. Jones, "Revisiting the Married Women's Property Acts: Recapturing Protection in the Face of Equity," *Journal of Gender, Social Policy and the Law* 22, no. 1 (2013): 91–147; Suzanne D. Lebsock, "Radical Reconstruction and the Property Rights of Southern Women," *Journal of Southern History* (May 1977): 195–216; Carole D. Shammas, "Re-Assessing the Married Women's Property Acts," *Journal of Women's History* 6, no. 1 (Spring 1994): 9–30. For a fascinating analysis that roots married women's property acts in women's claims on their husbands' labor and property for their support, see Winters, "The Ladies are Coming!" Also see Balleisen, *Navigating Failure*, for the general strategy of shifting assets to families to avoid financial failure. For the long view, which emphasizes the endurance of legal principles that treated land, in particular, as a family asset, see Claire Priest, "Creating an American Property Law: Alienability and Its Limits in American History," *Harvard Law Review* 120 (December 2006): 385–459; Priest, *Credit Nation*.
31. For the limitations of married women's property acts and the intransigence of coverture, see Norma Basch, "Invisible Women: The Legal Fiction of Marital Unity in Nineteenth-Century America," *Feminist Studies* 5 (Summer 1979): 346–66; Basch,

In the Eyes of the Law; Hoff, *Law, Gender, and Injustice*, particularly 117–50; Joan Hoff-Wilson, "The Unfinished Revolution: Changing Legal Status of U.S. Women," *Signs* 13 (Autumn 1987): 7–36; Kerber, "Why Diamonds"; Siegel, "Home as Work." For marriage settlements, see Salmon, *Women and the Law of Property*, 81–119; Salmon, "Women and Property in South Carolina." For particularly evocative studies highlighting the extent to which wealthy white women in the nineteenth century controlled property, including property in enslaved people, see Cooper, "Cultures of Emotion"; Jones-Rogers, *They Were Her Property*.

32. Theophilus Parsons, *Laws of Business for all the States and Territories of the Union and the Dominion of Canada* (Hartford: 1888); H. A. Gaston, *The Ready Lawyer; or, The Business Men's, Farmers', Mechanics', Miners' and Settlers' Legal Adviser* (New York: 1883); S. R. Kneeland, *The Commercial Law Register: A Manual of the International Merchants' Protective Law Association* (Albany: 1873). Mrs. A. D. Johnson, Ohio, 78:12. Also see Charles E. James, Ohio, 78:12. Both in R. G. Dun & Co., BL. Many thanks to Naomi Lamoreaux for drawing my attention to the commercial guides. For the legal problems of different property laws in different states, see Priest, "Creating an American Property Law."

33. Eliza Berry, Virginia, 3:206, R. G. Dun & Co., BL. For other examples, see note 3 to this chapter.

34. Kneeland, *The Commercial Law Register*, 3.

35. Wyatt-Brown, *Lewis Tappan*.

36. M. W. Baird, Ohio, 78:75 and 195, R. G. Dun & Co., BL.

Chapter 13

1. Jean H. Baker, *Mary Todd Lincoln: A Biography* (New York: W. W. Norton, 1987), 271–80; Keckley, *Behind the Scenes*, 87–140.

2. May 13, 1808, 3, *Reifs Philadelphia Gazette*; May 27, 1808, 2, *New-Bedford Mercury*; June 7, 1808, 1, *Concord Gazette*; all in NewsBank/Readex, Database: America's Historical Newspapers. For the global reach of the ready-made clothing trade, see Lemire, *Global Trade*, 114–35. For smallpox, see Elizabeth Fenn, *Pox Americana: The Great Smallpox Epidemic of 1775–82* (New York: Hill & Wang, 2001). For concerns about disease and clothing later, in the Civil War, see Weicksel, "The Dress of the Enemy."

3. One such story that appeared in the *New-Jersey Journal*, October 4, 1803, 2 was reprinted numerous times: *New Hampshire Gazette* (Portsmouth, NH), October 10, 1803, 2; *Philadelphia Repository and Weekly Register*, October 22, 1803, 342; *Eastern Argus* (Portland, ME), November 10, 1803, 4; *Pittsfield (MA) Sun*, December 5, 1803, 4; *Farmers' Cabinet* (Amherst, MA), December 6, 1803, 4; *Republican Spy* (Springfield, MA), December 6, 1803, 4; *The Reporter*, (Brattleboro, VT), December 19, 1803, 4; *American Commercial Daily Advertiser* (Baltimore, MD), October 8, 1809, 1; *Windham (CT) Herald*, September 28, 1809, 4; *Washington (PA) Reporter*,

November 13, 1809, 4,; *Reporter* (Lexington, KY), November 28, 1809, 4; *Fredonian* (Boston), February 20, 1810,; , *Palladium* (Frankfort, KY), November 14, 1811, 3. For examples of other, similarly anti-Semitic associations of Jews with old clothes, see *Centinel of Freedom* (Newark, NJ), January 25, 1803, 3; *Daily Advertiser* (New York City), December 27, 1802, 3; *Commercial Advertiser* (New York City), July 29, 1802, 3; *Daily Advertiser*, July 29, 1800, 3. All in NewsBank/Readex, Database: America's Historical Newspapers. Also see Woloson, *In Hock*, 21–53.

4. *Columbian Centinel*, October 9, 1811, 3; *Connecticut Herald*, July 30, 1811, 1; *Reifs Philadelphia Gazette*, December 8, 1807, 3; *Newburyport Herald*, February 28, 1806, 1; all in NewsBank/Readex, Database: America's Historical Newspapers.
5. Woloson, *In Hock*, 112–23. As Woloson argues, it was around the 1830s when portrayals of pawning soured.
6. Weicksel, "'Peeled' Bodies, Pillaged Homes," 117 and 118.
7. *Harper's Weekly*, April 1, 1865.
8. *Harper's Weekly*, April 1, 1865.
9. Civil Rights Act, 14 U.S. Statutes at Large 27 (1866).
10. Edwards, *People and Their Peace*, particularly 205–98; Welke, *Law and the Borders of Belonging*.
11. Heather Cox Richardson, *The Death of Reconstruction: Race, Labor, and Politics in the Post-Civil War North* (Cambridge, MA: Harvard University Press, 2001); Schwalm, *Emancipation's Diaspora*.
12. Pamela Brandwein, *Rethinking the Judicial Settlement of Reconstruction* (Cambridge: Cambridge University Press, 2011). Brandwein argues that the US Supreme Court did not change direction and abandon the principle of supporting African Americans' rights until the late 1880s, when Melville W. Fuller became chief justice. Also see G. Edward White, "The Origins of Civil Rights in America," *Case Western Reserve Law Review* 64 (Spring 2014): 755–816. For cases supporting African Americans' political rights, see for instance *Ex Parte Siebold*, 100 U.S. 371 (1879); *Neal v. Delaware*, 103 U.S. 370 (1880); and *Ex Parte Yarbrough*, 110 U.S. 651 (1884).
13. *Civil Rights Cases*, 109 U.S. 3 (1883); quote on 61. Penningroth, "Everyday Use," .
14. *Bradwell v. Illinois*, 83 U.S. 130 (1873).
15. Quotes in Keckley, *Behind the Scenes*, 115, 116; Baker, *Mary Todd Lincoln*, 272.
16. Keckley, *Behind the Scenes*, 115–140; quotes from 124. Where Keckley lays the blame on Brady and Keyes, Baker, *Mary Todd Lincoln*, 271–80, faults Lincoln and her chronic need for attention.
17. Keckley, *Behind the Scenes*, 142.
18. "Old Clothes," *Frank Leslie's Illustrated Newspaper*, October 26, 1867.
19. *New York World*, October 17, 1867.
20. *New York World*, October 17, 1867.
21. *Daily Eastern Argus*, October 17, 1867.
22. *Daily Eastern Argus*, October 17, 1867.
23. *New York World*, October 17, 1867; also see *Daily Eastern Argus*, October 19, 1867.
24. *New Orleans Times*, October 20, 1867.
25. *New York Herald*, October 19, 1867.

26. *Napa County Weekly Reporter*, October 26, 1867.
27. "Great Government Auction!" *Patriot* (Harrisburg, PA), October 29, 1867.
28. Baker, *Mary Todd Lincoln*, 272.
29. Cooper, "Cultures of Emotion." Also see Joanne B. Freeman, *Affairs of Honor: National Politics in the New Republic* (New Haven, CT: Yale University Press, 2001).
30. *New York Herald*, October 19, 1867.

Bibliography

Primary

Adams Papers Digital Edition. MSH, http://www.masshist.org/publications/adams-papers/.
Alger, Horatio. *Ragged Dick; or, Street Life in New York with the Boot Blacks*. New York: A. K. Loring, 1868.
The American Ladies Pocket Book for 1797. Philadelphia: 1796.
The American Ladies' Pocket-Book for the Year 1810. Philadelphia: 1809.
The American Ladies' Pocket-Book; or Useful Register of Business and Amusement for the Year 1803. Philadelphia: 1802.
Blackstone, William. *Commentaries on the Laws of England.* , 4 vols. 1765–69; repr., Chicago: University of Chicago Press, 1979.
Briggs, Mrs. D. B. *Madame Briggs' Improved Diagram for Cutting Ladies' & Children's Dresses, Basques, Boys' Coats, &c*. Albany, NY: s.n. [1857?].
Burn, Richard. *Burn's Abridgement, or The American Justice; Containing the Whole Practice, Authority and Duty of Justices of the Peace; with Correct Forms of Precedents Relating Thereto, and Adapted to the Present Situation of the United States*. Dover, NH: 1792.
Burn, Richard. *The Justice of the Peace and Parish Officer*. London: 1755.
Butterfield, L. H., Marc Friedlaender, and Mary-Jo Kline, eds. *The Book of Abigail and John: Selected Letters of the Adams family, 1762-1784*. Cambridge, MA: Harvard University Press, 1975.
Commerce and Navigation of the United States: Letter from the Secretary of the Treasury, Transmitting Statements Shewing the Commerce and Navigation of the United States, from the Year Ending the 30th September 1821. Washington, DC: Department of the Treasury, 1822.
Commerce and Navigation of the United States: Letter from the Secretary of the Treasury, Communicating the Annual Statement of the Commerce and Navigation of the United States for the Year Ending September 30, 1841. Washington, DC: Department of the Treasury, 1838–45.
Commissioners on Practice and Pleadings. *Code of Civil Procedure of the State of New-York*. Albany, NY: 1850.
Cooper, Thomas, and David James McCord. *The Statutes at Large of South Carolina*. 10 vols. Columbia, SC: 1836–41.
Coxe, Tench. *An Address to an Assembly of the Friends of American Manufacturers*. Philadelphia: 1787.
Craft, William, and Ellen Craft. *Running a Thousand Miles for Freedom; Or, The Escape of William and Ellen Craft from Slavery*. London: 1860.

Daboll, Nathan. *The New-England Almanac, and Gentlemen and Ladies' Diary, for the Year of our Lord Christ, 1797*. New London, CT: 1796.

Dalton, Michael. *The Countrey Justice*. London: 1619.

Dalton, Michael. *The Countrey Justice*. London: 1697.

Davies, Benjamin. *The Bank Torpedo; or, Bank Notes Proved to Be a Robbery on the Public, and the Real Cause of the Distresses of the Poor*. New York: 1810.

Davis, J. C. Bancroft. *The Massachusetts Justice: A Treatise upon the Powers and Duties of Justices of the Peace*. Worcester, MA: 1847.

Dickens, Charles. *Oliver Twist*. London: 1839.

Digest of Accounts of Manufacturing Establishments in the United States, and of Their Manufactures. Washington, DC: 1823.

A Digest of the Civil Laws Now in Force in the Territory of Orleans: With Alterations and Amendments Adapted to Its Present System of Government. New Orleans: 1803.

Documents Relative to the House of Refuge, Instituted by The Society for the Reformation of Juvenile Delinquency in the City of New-York in 1824. New York: 1832.

Dutton, Henry. *A Revision of Swift's Digest of the Laws of Connecticut: Assisted by N. A. Cowdrey*. Rev. ed. 2 vols. New Haven, CT: 1851–1862.

Freeman, Samuel. *The Massachusetts Justice: Being a Collection of the Laws of the Commonwealth of Massachusetts, Relative to the Power and Duty of Justices of the Peace*. 2nd ed. Boston: 1802.

Gaston, H. A. *The Ready Lawyer; or, The Business Men's, Farmers', Mechanics', Miners' and Settlers' Legal Adviser*. New York: 1883.

Greene, Asa. *The Perils of Pearl Street, Including a Taste of the Dangers of Wall Street*. New York: 1834.

Grenier, Meinrad. *Code of Practice of the State of Louisiana, Containing Rules of Procedure in Civil Actions*. New Orleans: 1844.

Hening, William Waller. *The New Virginia Justice, Comprising the Office and Authority of a Justice of the Peace, in the Commonwealth of Virginia*. Richmond, VA: 1795.

Hening, William Waller. *The New Virginia Justice, Comprising the Office and Authority of a Justice of the Peace in the Commonwealth of Virginia*. 2nd ed. Richmond, VA: 1819.

The History of a Little Frenchman and His Bank Notes: Rags, Rags, Rags. Philadelphia: 1815.

Houghton, Asa. *The Gentlemen's and Ladies' Diary: Or an Almanack for the Year of the Creation, According to Sacred Writ, 5759, and of the Christian Era, 1797*. Worcester, MA: 1796.

Jacobs, Harriet. *Incidents in the Life of a Slave Girl, Written by Herself*. Edited by Jean Fagan Yellin. Cambridge, MA: Harvard University Press, 2000.

Keckley, Elizabeth Hobbs. *Behind the Scenes: Or Thirty Years a Slave, and Four Years in the White House*. Hillsborough, NC: Eno, 2016.

Kent, James. *Commentaries on American Law*. 4 vols. New York: 1826–30.

King, Moses, comp. *King's Handbook of New York City: An Outline History and Description of the American Metropolis*. Boston: 1892.

Kirkland, Elithe Hamilton. *Love Is a Wild Assault*. Garden City, NY: Doubleday, 1959.

Kneeland, S. R. *The Commercial Law Register: A Manual of the International Merchants' Protective Law Association*. Albany, NY: 1873.

The Ladies' Self Instructor in Millinery and Mantua Making, Embroidery and Applique, Canvas-Work, Knitting, Netting, and Crochet-Work. Philadelphia: 1855.

Laws and Ordinances Made and Established by the Aldermen & Commonalty of the City of New York. New York: 1827.

Laws and Ordinances, Ordained and Established by the Mayor, Aldermen and Commonalty of the City of New-York. New York: 1812.
Laws and Ordinances Ordained and Established by the Mayor, Aldermen, and Commonalty of the City of New-York. New York: 1817.
Laws of the State of New-York. 2 vols. Albany, NY: 1802.
MacPherson, David. *Annals of Commerce, Manufactures, Fisheries, and Navigation*, vol. 3. London: 1805.
Madame Restell!: Her Secret Life-History from Her Birth to Her Suicide: Full Details: Showing How She Became Rich: Who Her Victims Were, and How She Held Them in Her Power: Her Tricks and Devices: What She Did and How She Did: All About Her: "The Most Terrible Being Ever Born." [New York?]: [1890?].
Martin, Francois Xavier. *The Office and Authority of a Justice of the Peace, and of Sheriffs, Coroners, &c: According to the Laws of the State of North-Carolina.* N.p.: 1791.
Munn, John. *Observations on British Wool and the Manufacturing of it in this Kingdom.* London: 1739.
North-American Calendar, or an Almanack for the Year of our Lord 1797. Providence, RI: 1796.
Oak Hall, or the Glory of Boston: A Poem. Boston: 1846.
O'Neall, John Belton. *The Negro Law of Slavery.* Columbia, SC: 1848.
Parker, Amasa J., George Wolford, and Edward Wade, eds. *Revised Statutes of the State of New York.* 4 vols. Albany, NY: 1859–63.
Parsons, Theophilus. *Laws of Business for all the States and Territories of the Union and the Dominion of Canada.* Hartford, CT: 1888.
Peddle, Mrs. M. *Rudiments of Taste, in a Series of Letters from a Mother to Her Daughters.* Philadelphia: 1795.
Philadelphia African-American Census. Friends Historical Library of Swarthmore College. Available online at https://repository.upenn.edu/mead/32/.
Potter, Henry. *The Office and Duty of a Justice of the Peace, A Guide to Sheriffs, Coroners, Clerks, Constables, and Other Civil Officers, According to the Laws of North Carolina.* Raleigh, NC: 1816.
Proceedings of the National Women's Rights Convention, Held at Cleveland, Ohio, on Wednesday, Thursday, and Friday, October 5th, 6th, and 7th, 1853. Cleveland, OH: 1854.
Proceedings of the Ninth National Woman's Rights Convention Held in New York City, Thursday May 12, 1859. Rochester, NY: 1859.
Proceedings of the Woman's Rights Convention, Held at Akron, Ohio, May 28 and 29, 1851. Cincinnati, OH: 1851.
Proceedings of the Woman's Rights Convention Held at the Broadway Tabernacle in the City of New York on Tuesday and Wednesday, Sept 6th and 7th, 1853. New York: 1853.
The Proceedings of the Woman's Rights Convention, Held at Syracuse, September 8th, 9th, and 10th, 1852. Syracuse, NY: 1852.
Proceedings of the Ohio Women's Convention, Held at Salem, April 19th and 20th, 1850; with an Address by J. Elizabeth Jones. Cleveland: 1850.
The Proceedings of the Woman's Rights Convention, Held at Worcester, October 15th and 16th, 1851. New York: 1852.
Proceedings of the Woman's Rights Conventions, Held at Seneca Falls & Rochester, N. Y., July & August, 1848. New York: 1870.
Reeve, Tapping. *Law of Baron and Femme; of Parent and Child; of Guardian and Ward; of Master and Servant; and of the Powers of Court of Chancery.* New Haven, CT: 1816.

Reeve, Tapping. *Law of Baron and Femme; of Parent and Child; of Guardian and Ward; of Master and Servant; and of the Powers of Court of Chancery*. Albany, NY: 1862.

Robinson, Conway. *Forms Adapted to the Practice in Virginia*. Vol. 1, *Containing Forms in the Courts of Law in Civil Cases*. Richmond: 1841.

Rogers, Daniel, ed. *The New-York City Hall Recorder*. 6 vols. New York: 1816–22.

Savage, Edward H. *A Chronological History of the Boston Watch and Police, from 1631 to 1865*. Boston: 1865.

Sheppard, Steven, ed. *The History of Legal Education in the United States: Commentaries and Primary Sources*. Pasadena, CA: Salem, 1999.

Smith, John William. *A Compendium of Mercantile Law*. London: 1834.

The South-Carolina Justice of Peace, Containing All the Duties, Powers and Authorities of that Office, as Regulated by the Laws Now of Force in this State, and Adapted to the Parish and County Magistrate. Philadelphia: 1788.

Stanton, Elizabeth Cady, Susan B. Anthony, and Matilda Joslyn Gage, eds. *History of Woman Suffrage*. 2nd ed. 3 vols. New York: 1889; e-text prepared by Richard J. Shiffer and the Project Gutenberg, 2009.

A Statistical Inquiry into the Condition of the People of Colour of the City and Districts of Philadelphia. Philadelphia: 1849.

Stearns, Asahel, Lemuel Shaw, and Theron Metcalf. *General Laws of Massachusetts*. 2 vols. Boston: 1823.

Story, Joseph. *Commentaries on Equity Jurisprudence: As Administered in England and America*. 2 vols. Boston: 1835–36.

Story, Joseph. *Commentaries on the Constitution of the United States*. 3 vols. Boston: 1833.

Styles, John. "The Spinning Project." http://spinning-wheel.org/.

Swaim, Benjamin. *The North Carolina Justice: Containing . . . Forms and Precedents Relating to the Office and Duty of a Justice of the Peace and Other Public Officers, According to Modern Practice*. 2nd ed. Raleigh, NC: 1846.

Swift, Zephaniah. *A Digest of the Law of Evidence, in Civil and Criminal Cases: and a Treatise on Bills of Exchange, and Promissory Notes*. Hartford, CT: 1810.

Swift, Zephaniah. *A System of Laws of the State of Connecticut*. 2 vols. Windham, CT: 1795–96.

Swift, Zephaniah. *A System of Laws of the State of Connecticut*. Rev. ed. New Haven, CT: 1822.

Town and Country Almanack for the Year of Our Lord, 1797. Norwich, CT 1796.

Trial of Madame Restell, Alias Ann Lohman: For Abortion and Causing the Death of Mrs. Purdy. New York: 1841.

Tryon, Rolla Milton. *Household Manufactures in the United States, 1640–1860: A Study in Industrial History*. Chicago: University of Chicago Press, 1917.

Tucker, St. George. *Blackstone's Commentaries*. 5 vols. Philadelphia: 1803.

Tupper, Frederick, and Helen Tyler Brown, eds. *Grandmother Tyler's Book: The Recollections of Mary Palmer Tyler (Mrs. Royall Tyler), 1775–1866*. New York: 1925.

US Treasury Department. *Alexander Hamilton's Report on the Subject of Manufactures, Made in His Capacity of Secretary of the Treasury, on the Fifth of December, 1791*. 6th ed. Philadelphia: 1827.

US Treasury Department. *Statement of the Arts and Manufactures of the United States of America for the Year 1810*. Philadelphia: 1814.

Waterman, Joshua. *Michigan Justice's Guide; Being a Treatise on the Civil and Criminal Jurisdiction of Justices of the Peace, Written Expressly for the State of Michigan*. N.p.: 1848.

Waterman, Joshua. *The Wisconsin and Iowa Justice: Being a Treatise on the Civil and Criminal Jurisdiction of Justices of the Peace, Written Expressly for the States of Wisconsin and Iowa, Containing Directions and Practical Forms for Every Case which Can Arise before a Justice.* New York: 1853.

Webb, Charles Henry. *The Wickedest Woman in New York.* New York: 1868.

Wilcox, P. B. *Practical Forms in Actions, Personal and Real, and in Chancery, Now in Common Use in the State of Ohio.* Columbus, OH: 1848.

Secondary

Abelson, Elaine S. *When Ladies Go A-Thieving: Middle-Class Shoplifters in the Victorian Department Store.* New York: Oxford University Press, 1990.

Ablavsky, Gregory. "Empire States: The Coming of Dual Federalism." *Yale Law Journal* 128 (May 2019): 1792–1869.

Ablavsky, Gregory. "Species of Sovereignty: Native Nationhood, the United States, and International Law, 1783–1795." *Journal of American History* 106 (December 2019): 591–613.

Adams, Julia. *The Familial State: Ruling Families and Merchant Capitalism in Early Modern Europe.* Ithaca, NY: Cornell University Press, 2005.

Adams, Willi Paul. *The First American Constitutions: Republican Ideology and the Making of the State Constitution in the Revolutionary Era.* Chapel Hill: University of North Carolina Press, 1980.

Ambuske, James P., and Randall Flaherty. "Reading Law in the Early Republic: Legal Education in the Age of Jefferson." In *The Founding of Thomas Jefferson's University*, edited by John A. Ragosta, Peter S. Onuf, and Andrew J. O'Shaughnessy, 224-57. Charlottesville: University of Virginia Press, 2019.

Amussen, Susan Dwyer. "'Being Stirred to Much Unquietness': Violence and Domestic Violence in Early Modern England." *Journal of Women's History* 6 (Summer 1994): 70–89.

Anderson, Dean L. "The Flow of European Trade Goods in the Western Great Lakes Region, 1715–1760." In *The Fur Trade Revisited: Selected Papers of the Sixth North American Fur Trade Conference, Mackinac Island, Michigan, 1991*, edited by Jennifer S. H. Brown, W. J. Eccles, and Donald P. Heldman, 93–117. East Lansing: Michigan State University Press, 1994.

Anderson, Margo J. *The American Census: A Social History.* New Haven, CT: Yale University Press, 1988.

Anishanslin, Zara. *Portrait of a Woman in Silk: Hidden Histories of the British Atlantic World.* New Haven, CT: Yale University Press, 2016.

Atherton, Lewis E. "The Problem of Credit Rating in the Antebellum South." *Journal of Southern History* 12 (November 1946): 534–56.

Auslander, Leora. "Beyond Words." *American Historical Review* 110 (October 2005): 1015–45.

Auslander, Leora. *Cultural Revolutions: The Politics of Everyday Life in Britain, North America and France.* New York: Berg, 2009.

Ayers, Edward L. *Vengeance and Justice: Crime and Punishment in the Nineteenth-Century American South.* New York: Oxford University Press, 1984.

Bagnall, William R. *The Textile Industries of the United States* Cambridge, MA: Riverside, 1893.
Bailyn, Bernard. *The New England Merchants in the Seventeenth Century*. Cambridge, MA: Harvard University Press, 1955.
Baker, Jean H. *Mary Todd Lincoln: A Biography*. New York: W. W. Norton, 1987.
Balleisen, Edward J. *Navigating Failure: Bankruptcy and Commercial Society in Antebellum America*. Chapel Hill: University of North Carolina Press, 2001.
Banner, Stuart. *How the Indians Lost Their Land: Law and Power on the Frontier*. Cambridge, MA: Harvard University Press, 2005.
Baptist, Edward. *The Half Has Never Been Told: Slavery and the Making of America Capitalism*. New York: Basic Books, 2014.
Bardaglio, Peter. *Reconstructing the Household: Families, Sex, and the Law in the Nineteenth-Century South*. Chapel Hill: University of North Carolina Press, 1995.
Barnet, Teresa. *Sacred Relics: Pieces of the Past in Nineteenth-Century America*. Chicago: University of Chicago Press, 2014.
Basch, Norma. *In the Eyes of the Law: Women, Marriage and Property in Nineteenth-Century New York*. Ithaca, NY: Cornell University Press, 1982.
Basch, Norma. "Invisible Women: The Legal Fiction of Marital Unity in Nineteenth-Century America." *Feminist Studies* 5 (Summer 1979): 346–66.
Batlan, Felice. *Women and Justice for the Poor: A History of Legal Aid, 1863–1945*. Cambridge: Cambridge University Press, 2015.
Baumgarten, Linda. "Plains, Plaid, and Cotton: Woolens for Slave Clothing." *Ars Textrina* 15 (1991): 203–22.
Baumgarten, Linda. *What Clothes Reveal: The Language of Clothing in Colonial and Federal America: The Williamsburg Collection*. Williamsburg, VA: Colonial Williamsburg Foundation, 2003.
Baumgarten, Linda, and Kimberly Smith Ivey. "Textiles: Trade and Fashions." *Magazine Antiques* 159 (January 2001): 226–33.
Bean, Susan S. *Yankee India: American Commercial and Cultural Encounters with India in the Age of Sail, 1784–1860*. Salem, MA: Peabody Essex Museum, 2001.
Beard, Mary Ritter. *Women as Force in History: A Study of Traditions and Realities*. New York: MacMillan, 1946.
Beckert, Sven. *Empire of Cotton: A Global History*. New York: Vintage, 2014.
Beckert, Sven, and Seth Rockman, eds. *Slavery's Capitalism: A New History of America's Economic Development*. Philadelphia: University of Pennsylvania Press, 2016.
Benton, Lauren. *A Search for Sovereignty: Law and Geography in European Empires, 1400–1900*. New York: Cambridge University Press, 2011.
Bercaw, Nancy D. *Gendered Freedoms: Race, Rights, and the Politics of Household in the Delta, 1861–1875*. Gainesville: University Press of Florida, 2003.
Bilder, Mary. *The Transatlantic Constitution: Colonial Legal Culture and the Empire*. Cambridge, MA: Harvard University Press, 2004.
Blaakman, Michael A. "The Marketplace of American Federalism: Land Speculation across State Lines in the Early Republic." *Journal of American History*, 107 (December 2020): 583–608.
Blaakman, Michael A. "Martha Bradstreet and the 'Epithet of Woman': A Story of Land, Libel, Litigation, and Legitimating "Unwomanly" Behavior in the Early Republic." *Early American Studies: An Interdisciplinary Journal* 13, no. 3 (2015): 544–85.

Blackhawk, Maggie. "Federal Indian Law as Paradigm within Public Law." *Harvard Law Review* 132 (May 2019): 1787–1877.
Blackwell, Marilyn S., and Kristen T. Oertel. *Frontier Feminist: Clarina Howard Nichols and the Politics of Motherhood*. Lawrence: University Press of Kansas, 2010.
Blaine, Marcia Schmidt. "Ordinary Women: Government and Custom in the Lives of New Hampshire Women, 1690–1770." PhD diss., University of New Hampshire, 1999.
Blaine, Marcia Schmidt. "The Power of Petitions: Women and the New Hampshire Provincial Government, 1695–1770." *International Review of Social History* 46 (December 2001): 57–77.
Blanck, Emily. "Seventeen Eighty-Three: The Turning Point in the Law of Slavery and Freedom in Massachusetts." *New England Quarterly* 75 (March 2002): 24–51.
Blewett, Mary H. "Manhood and the Market: The Politics of Gender and Class among the Textile Workers of Fall River, Massachusetts, 1870–1880." In *Work Engendered: Toward of New History of American Labor*, edited by Ava Baton, 92–113. Ithaca, NY: Cornell University Press, 1991.
Blewett, Mary H. *Men, Women, and Work: Class, Gender, and Protest in the New England Shoe Industry, 1780–1910*. Urbana: University of Illinois Press, 1988.
Blewett, Mary H. "Work, Gender, and the Artisan Tradition in New England Shoemaking, 1780–1860." *Journal of Social History* 17 (Winter 1983): 221–48.
Blewett, Mary H. *The Yankee Yorkshireman: Migration Lived and Imagined*. Urbana: University of Illinois Press, 2009.
Bloch, Ruth H. "American Female Ideals in Transition: The Rise of the Moral Mother." *Signs* 4 (Winter 1978): 237–52.
Bloch, Ruth H. *Gender and Morality in Anglo-American Culture, 1650–1800*. Berkeley: University of California Press, 2003.
Block, Sharon. *Rape and Sexual Power in Early America*. Chapel Hill: University of North Carolina Press, 2006.
Bonner, Christopher James. *Remaking the Republic: Black Politics and the Creation of American Citizenship*. Philadelphia: University of Pennsylvania Press, 2020.
Bouk, Dan. *How Our Days Became Numbered: Risk and the Rise of the Statistical Individual*. Chicago: University of Chicago Press, 2015.
Bouton, Terry. *Taming Democracy: "The People," the Founders, and the Troubled Ending of the American Revolution*. New York: Oxford University Press, 2007.
Boydston, Jeanne. *Home and Work: Housework, Wages, and the Ideology of Labor in the Early Republic*. New York: Oxford University Press, 1990.
Boydston, Jeanne. "'To Earn Her Daily Bread,'" *Radical History Review* 35 (1986): 6–25.
Boydston, Jeanne. "The Woman Who Wasn't There: Women's Market Labor and the Transition to Capitalism in the United States." *Journal of the Early Republic* 16 (Summer 1996): 183–206.
Brandwein, Pamela. *Rethinking the Judicial Settlement of Reconstruction*. Cambridge: Cambridge University Press, 2011.
Breen, Timothy H. "'Baubles of Britain': The American and Consumer Revolutions of the Eighteenth Century." *Past and Present* 119 (May 1988): 73–104.
Breen, Timothy H. "An Empire of Goods: The Anglicization of Colonial America, 1690–1776." *Journal of British Studies* 25 (October 1986): 467–99.
Breen, Timothy H. *The Marketplace of Revolution: How Consumer Politics Shaped American Independence*. New York: Oxford University Press, 2004.

Brewer, Holly. *By Birth or Consent: Children, Law, and the Anglo-American Revolution in Authority*. Chapel Hill: University of North Carolina Press, 2005.

Brewer, Holly. "Entailing Aristocracy in Colonial Virginia: 'Ancient Feudal Restraints' and Revolutionary Reforms." *William and Mary Quarterly* 54 (1997): 307–46.

Brewer, Holly. "The Transformation of Domestic Law." In *The Cambridge History of Law in American*, vol. 1, edited by Christopher L. Tomlins and Michael Grossberg, 288–323. New York: Cambridge University Press, 2008.

Brodie, Janet Farrell. *Contraception and Abortion in 19th Century America*. Ithaca, NY: Cornell University Press, 1994.

Brown, Jennifer S. J. *Strangers in Blood: Fur Trade Company Families in Indian Country*. Vancouver: University of British Columbia Press, 1980.

Brown, Kathleen M. *Foul Bodies: Cleanliness in Early America*. New Haven, CT: Yale University Press, 2009.

Brown, Matthew P. "Blanks: Data, Method, and the British American Print Shop." *American Literary History* 29 (Summer 2017): 228–47.

Buck, Anne. "Buying Clothes in Bedfordshire: Customers and Tradesmen, 1700–1800." *Textile History* 22 (January 1991): 211–37.

Bushman, Richard, L. *The Refinement of America: Persons, Houses, and Cities*. New York: Knopf, 1992.

Bushman, Richard, L. "Shopping and Advertising in Colonial America." In *Of Consuming Interests: The Style of Life in the Eighteenth Century*, edited by Cary Carson, Ronald Hoffman, and Peter J. Albert, 233–51. Charlottesville: University Press of Virginia, 1994.

Butterfield, Kevin. *The Making of Tocqueville's America: Law and Association in the Early Nineteenth Century United States*. Chicago: University of Chicago Press, 2015.

Bynum, Victoria E. *Unruly Women: The Politics of Social and Sexual Control in the Old South*. Chapel Hill: University of North Carolina Press, 1992.

Byrnes, Thomas. *1886 Professional Criminals of America*. New York: Chelsea House, 1969.

Calvert, Karin. "The Function of Fashion in Eighteenth-Century America." In *Of Consuming Interests: The Style of Life in the Eighteenth Century*, edited by. Cary Carson, Ronald Hoffman, and Peter J. Albert, 252–83. Charlottesville: University Press of Virginia, 1994.

Camp, Stephanie M. H. *Enslaved Women and the Geography of Everyday Resistance in the Plantation South, 1830–1865*. Chapel Hill: University of North Carolina Press, 2004.

Candee, Richard. "The 'Great Factory' at Dover, New Hampshire: The Dover Manufacturing Co. Print Works, 1825." *Old-Time New England* 66 (Summer-Fall 1975): 39–51.

Carlson, A. Cheree. *The Crimes of Womanhood: Defining Femininity in a Court of Law*. Urbana: University of Illinois Press, 2009.

Carpenter, Daniel. *Democracy by Petition: Popular Politics in Transformation, 1790-1870*. Cambridge: Harvard University Press, 2021.

Carpenter, Daniel. "Recruitment by Petition: American Antislavery, French Protestantism, English Suppression." *Perspectives on Politics* (September 2016): 700–723.

Carpenter, Daniel, and Benjamin Schneer. "Party Formation Through Petitions: The Whigs and the Bank War of 1832–1834." *Studies in American Political Development* (October 2015): 213–34.

Carpenter, Daniel, and Colin D. Moore. "When Canvassers Became Activists: Antislavery Petitioning and the Political Mobilization of American Women." *American Political Science Review* (August 2014): 479–98.

Carruthers, Bruce G., and Wendy Nelson Espeland. "Accounting for Rationality: Double-Entry Bookkeeping and the Rhetoric of Economic Rationality." *American Journal of Sociology* 97 (1991): 31–69.

Carson, Cary. "The Consumer Revolution in Colonial British America: Why Demand?" In *Of Consuming Interests: The Style of Life in the Eighteenth Century*, edited by Cary Carson, Ronald Hoffman, and Peter J. Albert, 483–697. Charlottesville: University Press of Virginia, 1994.

Carson, Cary, Ronald Hoffman, and Peter J. Albert, eds. *Of Consuming Interests: The Style of Life in the Eighteenth Century*. Charlottesville: University Press of Virginia, 1994.

Cashin, Joan, ed. *War Matters: Material Culture in the Civil War Era*. Chapel Hill: University of North Carolina Press, 2019.

Cashwell, Meggan. "'To Restore Peace and Tranquility to the Neighborhood': Violence, Legal Culture and Community in New York City, 1799–1827." PhD diss., Duke University, 2019.

Chassagne, Serge. "Calico Printing in Europe before 1780." In *The Cambridge History of Western Textiles*, edited by David Jenkins, 1:513–27. Cambridge: Cambridge University Press, 2003.

Chrisman-Campbell, Kimberly. *Fashion Victims: Dress at the Court of Louis XVI and Marie-Antoinette*. New Haven, CT: Yale University Press, 2015.

Chused, Richard H. "Married Women's Property Law: 1800–1850." *Georgetown Law Journal* 71 (June 1983): 1359–1424.

Clark, Christopher. *The Communitarian Moment: The Radical Challenge of the Northampton Association*. Ithaca, NY: Cornell University Press, 1995.

Clark, Christopher. *The Roots of Rural Capitalism: Western Massachusetts, 1780–1860*. Ithaca, NY: Cornell University Press, 1990.

Clarkson, Leslie. "The Linen Industry in Early Modern Europe." In *The Cambridge History of Western Textiles*, edited by David Jenkins, 1:473–92. Cambridge: Cambridge University Press, 2003.

Cleary, Catherine B. "Married Women's Property Rights in Wisconsin, 1846–1872." *Wisconsin Magazine of History* 78, no. 2 (Winter 1994–95): 113–26.

Cleary, Patricia. *Elizabeth Murray: A Woman's Pursuit of Independence in Eighteenth-Century America*. Amherst: University of Massachusetts Press, 2000.

Cleary, Patricia. "'She Will Be in the Shop': Women's Sphere of Trade in Eighteenth-Century Philadelphia and New York." *Pennsylvania Magazine of History and Biography* 119 (July 1995): 181–202.

Cohen, David Steven. *The Dutch-American Farm*. New York: New York University Press, 1992.

Cohen, Deborah. *Household Gods: The British and Their Possessions*. New Haven, CT: Yale University Press, 2006.

Cohen, Joanna. *Luxurious Citizens: The Politics of Consumption in Nineteenth-Century America*. Philadelphia: University of Pennsylvania Press, 2017.

Cohen, Patricia Cline. *A Calculating People: The Spread of Numeracy in Early America*. Chicago: University of Chicago Press, 1982.

Cole, Arthur Harrison. *The American Wool Manufacture*. Cambridge, MA: Harvard University Press, 1926.

Cook, Charles M. *The American Codification Movement: A Study of Antebellum Legal Reform*. Westport, CT: Greenwood, 1981.

Cooper, Mandy L. "Cultures of Emotion: Families, Friends, and the Making of the United States." PhD diss., Duke University, 2018.

Cooper, Mandy L. "Too Big to Fail? Families, Internal Improvement, and State Government in Antebellum North Carolina. *Journal of the Early Republic* 41 (Fall 2021): 349-72.

Coquillette, Daniel R. *On the Battlefield of Merit: Harvard Law School, the First Century.* Cambridge, MA: Harvard University Press, 2015.

Cornell, Saul. *The Other Founders: Anti-Federalism and the Dissenting Tradition in America, 1788–1828.* Chapel Hill: University of North Carolina Press, 1999.

Corrigan, John. *Business of the Heart: Religion and Emotion in the Nineteenth Century.* Berkeley: University of California Press, 2002.

Cott, Nancy F. *The Bonds of Womanhood: "Woman's Sphere" in New England, 1780–1835.* New Haven, CT: Yale University Press, 1977.

Crowston, Clare Haru. *Credit, Fashion, Sex: Economies of Regard in Old Regime France.* Durham, NC: Duke University Press, 2013.

Crowston, Clare Haru. *Fabricating Women: The Seamstresses of Old Regime France, 1675–1791.* Durham, NC: Duke University Press, 2001.

Crowston, Clare Haru. "Family Affairs, Wives, Credit, Consumption and the Law in Old Regime France." In *Family, Gender, and Law in Early Modern France*, edited by Suzanne Desan and Jeffrey Merrick, 62–100. University Park: Pennsylvania State University Press, 2009.

Curtis, Christopher Michael. *Jefferson's Freeholders and the Politics of Ownership in the Old Dominion.* New York: Cambridge University Press, 2012.

Damiano, Sara T. *To Her Credit: Women, Finance, and the Law in Eighteenth-Century New England Cities.* Baltimore: Johns Hopkins University Press, 2021.

Damiano, Sara T. "'To Well and Truly Administer': Female Administrators and Estate Settlement in Newport, Rhode Island, 1730–1776." *New England Quarterly* 86 (March 2013): 89–124.

David, Paul A., and Peter Solar. "A Bicentenary Contribution to the History of the Cost of Living in America." *Research in Economic History* 2 (1977): 1–80.

Dayton, Cornelia Hughes. *Women before the Bar: Gender, Law, and Society in Connecticut, 1639–1789.* Chapel Hill: University of North Carolina Press, 1995.

Dayton, Cornelia Hughes, and Sharon V. Sallinger. *Robert Love's Warnings: Searching for Strangers in Colonial Boston.* Philadelphia: University of Pennsylvania Press, 2014.

Desan, Christine. *Making Money: Coin, Currency, and the Coming of Capitalism.* Oxford: Oxford University Press, 2015.

Desan, Christine, and Sven Beckert, eds. *American Capitalism: New Histories.* New York: Columbia University Press, 2018.

Diefendorf, Barbara. "Women and Property in Ancien Régime France: Theory and Practice in Dauphiné and Paris." In *Early Modern Conceptions of Property*, edited by John Brewer and Susan Staves, 170–93. London: Routledge, 1995.

Diner, Hasia R. *Roads Taken: The Great Jewish Migration to the New World and the Peddlers Who Forged the Way.* New Haven, CT: Yale University Press, 2015.

Downs, Gregory P. *The Second American Revolution: The Civil War-Era Struggle over Cuba and the Rebirth of the American Republic.* Chapel Hill: University of North Carolina Press, 2019.

Drachman, Virginia G. *Sisters in Law: Women Lawyers in Modern American History.* Cambridge, MA: Harvard University Press, 2001.

Dubber, Markus Dirk. *Police Power: Patriarchy and the Foundations of American Government*. New York: Columbia University Press, 2005.

Dublin, Thomas. "Women and Outwork in a Nineteenth-Century New England Town: Fitzwilliam, New Hampshire, 1830–1860." In *The Countryside in the Age of Capitalist Transformation: Essays in the Social History of Rural America*, edited by Steven Hahn and Jonathan Prude, 51–70. Chapel Hill: University of North Carolina Press, 1985.

Dublin, Thomas. *Women at Work: The Transformation of Work and Community in Lowell, Massachusetts, 1826–1860*. New York: Columbia University Press, 1979.

DuBois, Carol Ellen. *Feminism and Suffrage: The Emergence of Independent Women's Movement in America, 1848–1869*. Ithaca, NY: Cornell University Press, 1978.

DuPlessis, Robert S. *The Material Atlantic: Clothing in the New World, 1650–1800*. Cambridge: Cambridge University Press, 2016.

Eaton, Linda. *Printed Textiles: British and American Cottons and Linens, 1700–1850*. New York: Monacelli, 2014.

Edwards, Laura F. *Gendered Strife and Confusion: The Political Culture of Reconstruction*. Urbana: University of Illinois Press, 1997.

Edwards, Laura F. "James and His Striped Velvet Pantaloons: Textiles, Commerce, and the Law in the New Republic." *Journal of American History* 107 (September 2020): 336–61.

Edwards, Laura F. *A Legal History of the Civil War and Reconstruction: A Nation of Rights*. New York: Cambridge University Press, 2015.

Edwards, Laura F. "The Legal World of Elizabeth Bagby's Commonplace Book: Federalism, Women, and Governance." *Journal of the Civil War Era* 9 (December 2019): 504–23.

Edwards, Laura F. "The Material Conditions of Dependency: The Hidden History of Free Women's Control of Property in the Early Nineteenth-Century South." In *Signposts: New Directions in Southern Legal History*, edited by Sally Hadden and Patricia Minter, 171–92. Athens, Georgia: University of Georgia Press, 2013.

Edwards, Laura F. *The People and Their Peace: Legal Culture and the Transformation of Inequality in the Post-Revolutionary South*. Chapel Hill: University of North Carolina Press, 2009.

Edwards, Laura F. "Sarah Allingham's Sheet and Other Lessons from Legal History." *Journal of the Early Republic* 38 (Spring 2018): 121–47.

Edwards, Laura F. "Textiles: Popular Culture and the Law." *Buffalo Law Review* 64 (January 2016): 193–214.

Enstad, Nan. *Ladies of Labor, Girls of Adventure: Working Women, Popular Culture, and Labor Politics at the Turn of the Twentieth Century*. New York: Columbia University Press, 1999.

Erickson, Amy Louise. *Women and Property: In Early Modern England*. New York: Routledge, 1993.

Fairchilds, Cissie. "The Production and Marketing of Populuxe Goods in Eighteenth-Century Paris." In *Consumption and the World of Goods*, edited by John Brewer and Roy Porter, 228–60. New York: Routledge, 1993.

Farber, Hannah. "Sailing on Paper: The Embellished Bill of Lading in the Material Atlantic, 1720–1864." *Early American Studies* 17 (Winter 2019): 37–83.

Farber, Hannah. "State-Building after War's End: A Government Financier Adjusts His Portfolio for Peace." *Journal of the Early Republic* 38 (Spring 2018): 67–76.

Farnie, Douglas. "Cotton, 1780–1914." In *The Cambridge History of Western Textiles*, edited by David Jenkins, 2:721–60. Cambridge: Cambridge University Press, 2003.

Fehrenbacher, Don E. *The Dred Scott Case: Its Significance in American Law and Politics.* New York: Oxford University Press, 1978.

Feldman, Egal. *Fit for Men.* Washington, DC: Public Affairs, 1960.

Fenn, Elizabeth. *Pox Americana: The Great Smallpox Epidemic of 1775–82.* New York: Hill & Wang, 2001.

Ferreira, Maria João Pacheco. "Chinese Textiles for Portuguese Tastes." In *Interwoven Globe: The Worldwide Textile Trade, 1500–1800,* edited by Amelia Peck, 44–55. New Haven, CT: Yale University Press for the Metropolitan Museum of Art, 2013.

Fields, Barbara Jeanne. *Slavery and Freedom on the Middle Ground: Maryland during the Nineteenth Century.* New Haven, CT: Yale University Press, 1985.

Finley, Alexandra J. "'Cash to Corinna': Domestic Labor and Sexual Economy in the 'Fancy Trade.'" *Journal of American History* 104 (September 2017): 410–30.

Finley, Alexandra J. *An Intimate Economy: Enslaved Women, Work, and America's Domestic Slave Trade.* Chapel Hill: University of North Carolina Press, 2020.

Finn, Margot. *The Character of Credit: Personal Debt in English Culture, 1740–1914.* New York: Cambridge University Press, 2003.

Finn, Margot. "Debt and Credit in Bath's Court of Requests, 1829–1839." *Urban History* 21 (1994): 211–36.

Finn, Margot. "Women, Consumption and Coverture in England, c. 1760–1860." *Historical Journal* 39 (September 1996): 703–22.

Folbre, Nancy. *The Invisible Heart: Economics and Family Values.* New York: New Press, 2001.

Folbre, Nancy. *Valuing Children: Rethinking the Economics of the Family.* Cambridge, MA: Harvard University Press, 2008.

Forbath, William E. "The Ambiguities of Free Labor: Labor and the Law in the Gilded Age." *Wisconsin Law Review* 4 (1985): 767–817.

Ford, Lisa. *Settler Sovereignty: Jurisdiction and Indigenous People in America and Australia, 1788–1836.* Cambridge, MA: Harvard, University Press, 2010.

Forsyth, Grant D. "Special Interest Protectionism and the Antebellum Woolen Textile Industry: A Contemporary Issue in Historical Context." *American Journal of Economics and Sociology* 65 (November 2006): 1025–58.

Foster, Helen Bradley. *"New Raiments of Self": African American Clothing in the Antebellum Period.* Oxford: Berg, 1997.

Fox-Genovese, Elizabeth. *Within the Plantation Household: Women in the Old South.* Chapel Hill: University of North Carolina Press, 1988.

Franklin, John Hope. *The Free Negro in North Carolina, 1790–1860.* 1943; repr., New York: Russell & Russell, 1969.

Frederickson, George M. *Black Image in the White Mind: The Debate on Afro-American Character and Destiny, 1817–1914.* New York: Harper, 1971.

Freeman, Joanne B. *Affairs of Honor: National Politics in the New Republic.* New Haven, CT: Yale University Press, 2001.

Fuente, Alejandro de la, and Ariela Gross. *Becoming Free, Becoming Black: Race, Freedom, and Law in Cuba, Virginia, and Louisiana.* Cambridge: Cambridge University Press, 2020.

Funk, Kellen Richard. "*The Lawyers' Code: The Transformation of American Legal Practice, 1828-1938.*" Ph.D. dissertation, Princeton University, 2018

Gamber, Wendy. *The Female Economy: The Millinery and Dressmaking Trades, 1860–1930.* Urbana: University of Illinois Press, 1997.

Gamber, Wendy. "A Gendered Enterprise: Placing Nineteenth-Century Businesswomen in History." *Business History Review* 72 (Summer 1998): 188–217.

Gamber, Wendy. "'Reduced to Science': Gender, Technology, and Power in the American Dressmaking Trade, 1860–1910." *Technology and Culture* 36, no. 3 (July 1995): 455–82.

Games, Alison. *The Web of Empire: English Cosmopolitans in an Age of Expansion, 1560–1660*. New York: Oxford University Press, 2008.

Gamble, Robert J. "The Promiscuous Economy: Cultural and Commercial Geographies of Secondhand in the Antebellum City." In *Capitalism by Gaslight: Illuminating the Economy of Nineteenth Century America*, edited by Brian P. Luskey and Wendy A. Woloson, 31–52. Philadelphia: University of Pennsylvania Press, 2015.

Genovese, Eugene D. *Roll, Jordan, Roll: The World the Slaves Made*. New York: Vintage, 1976.

Gilfoyle, Timothy J. *City of Eros: New York City, Prostitution, and the Commercialization of Sex, 1820–1920*. New York: Norton, 1992.

Glymph, Thavolia. *Out of the House of Bondage: The Transformation of the Plantation Household*. Cambridge: Cambridge University Press, 2008.

Goff, Lisa. *Shantytown, USA: Forgotten Landscapes of the Working Poor*. Cambridge, MA: Harvard University Press, 2016.

Goldin, Claudia. "The Economic Status of Women in the Early Republic: Quantitative Evidence." *Journal of Interdisciplinary History* 16 (1986): 375–404.

Gordon, Robert W. "Critical Legal Histories." *Stanford Law Review* 36 (January 1984): 56–107.

Gordon, Sarah Barringer. "The African Supplement: Religion, Race, and Corporate Law in Early National America." *William and Mary Quarterly* 72 (July 2015): 385–422.

Gordon, Sarah Barringer. "The First Disestablishment: Limits on Church Power and Property Before the Civil War." *University of Pennsylvania Law Review* 162 (January 2014): 307–72.

Gosse, Van E. *The First Reconstruction: Black Politics in America, From the Revolution to the Civil War*. Chapel Hill: University of North Carolina Press, 2020.

Gosse, Van E. "In the Woodpile: Negro Electors in the First Reconstruction." In *Revolutions and Reconstructions: Black Politics in the Long Nineteenth Century*, 66–83. Philadelphia: University of Pennsylvania Press, 2020.

Gosse, Van E., and David Waldstreicher, eds. *Revolutions and Reconstructions: Black Politics in the Long Nineteenth Century*. Philadelphia: University of Pennsylvania Press, 2020.

Gould, Eliga H. *Among the Powers of the Earth: The American Revolution and the Making of a New World Empire*. Cambridge, MA: Harvard University Press, 2012.

Gould, Eliga H. "Entangled Histories, Entangled Worlds: The English-Speaking Atlantic as a Spanish Periphery." *American Historical Review* 112 (June 2007): 764–68.

Gould, Eliga H. "Zones of Law, Zones of Violence: The Legal Geography of the British Atlantic, circa 1772." *William and Mary Quarterly* 60 (July 2003): 471–510.

Gowing, Laura. *Domestic Dangers: Women, Words, and Sex in Early Modern London*. Oxford: Clarendon, 1996.

Graber, Mark. *Dred Scott and the Problem of Constitutional Evil*. New York: Cambridge University Press, 2006.

Green, Fletcher. *Constitutional Development in the South Atlantic States, 1776–1860*. New York: W. W. Norton, 1966.

Green, Jack. *Negotiated Authorities: Essays in Colonial Political and Constitutional History*. Charlottesville: University of Virginia Press, 1994.

Greenberg, Joshua R. *Advocating the Man: Masculinity, Organized Labor, and the Household in New York, 1800–1840*. New York: Columbia University Press, 2008.

Gronningsater, Sarah L. H. *The Arc of Abolition: The Children of Gradual Emancipation and the Origins of National Freedom*. Philadelphia: University of Pennsylvania Press, forthcoming 2021.

Gronningsater, Sarah L. H. "'Expressly Recognized by Our Election Laws': Certificates of Freedom and the Multiple Fates of Black Citizenship in the Early Republic." *William and Mary Quarterly* 75 (July 2018): 465–506.

Gronningsater, Sarah L. H. "Practicing Formal Politics Without the Vote: Black New Yorkers in the Aftermath of 1821." In *Revolutions and Reconstructions: Black Politics in the Long Nineteenth Century*, edited by Van E. Gosse and David Waldstreicher, 116–38. Philadelphia: University of Pennsylvania Press, 2020.

Gross, Ariela J. *Double Character: Slavery and Mastery in the Antebellum Southern Courtroom*. Princeton, NJ: Princeton University Press, 2000.

Gross, Ariela J. *What Blood Won't Tell: A History of Race on Trial in America*. Cambridge, MA: Harvard University Press, 2008.

Grossberg, Michael. "Institutionalizing Masculinity: The Bar as a Man's Profession." In *Meanings for Manhood: Masculinity in Victorian America*, edited by Mark C. Carnes and Clyde Griffen, 133–51. Chicago: University of Chicago Press, 1990.

Grossberg, Michael. *A Judgment for Solomon: The d'Hauteville Case and Legal Experience in Antebellum America*. New York: Cambridge University Press, 1996.

Gullickson, Gay. *Spinners and Weavers of Auffay, Rural Industry and the Sexual Division of Labor in a French Village, 1750–1850*. New York: Cambridge University Press, 1986.

Gunderson, Joan R., and Gwen Victor Gampel. "Married Women's Legal Status in Eighteenth-Century New York and Virginia." *William and Mary Quarterly* 39 (January 1982): 114–34.

Gutman, Herbert G. *Work, Culture, and Society in Industrializing America: Essays in American Working-Class and Social History*. New York: Knopf, 1976.

Guy, John. "One Thing Leads to Another: Indian Textiles and the Early Globalization of Style." In *Interwoven Globe: The Worldwide Textile Trade, 1500–1800*, edited by Amelia Peck, 13–27. New Haven, CT: Yale University Press for the Metropolitan Museum of Art, 2013.

Haag, Pamela. "The 'Ill-Use of a Wife': Patterns of Working-Class Violence in Domestic and Public New York City, 1860–1880." *Journal of Social History* 25 (Spring 1992): 447–77.

Haggerty, Sheryllynne. *The British-Atlantic Trading Community 1760–1810: Men, Women, and the Distribution of Goods*. Leiden: Brill, 2006.

Hall, Jacquelyn Dowd. *Revolt against Chivalry: Jesse Daniel Ames and the Women's Campaign against Lynching*. New York: Columbia University Press, 1979.

Haltunnen, Karen. *Confidence Men and Painted Women: A Study of Middle-Class Culture in America, 1830–1870*. New Haven, CT: Yale University Press, 1986.

Hamilton, Marsha L. *Social and Economic Networks in Early Massachusetts: Atlantic Connections*. University Park: Pennsylvania State University Press, 2009.

Handley, Sasha. "Objects, Emotions and an Early Modern Bed-Sheet." *History Workshop Journal* 85 (April 2018): 169–94.

Harris, Leslie M. *In the Shadow of Slavery: African Americans in New York City, 1626–1863*. Chicago: University of Chicago Press, 2003.

Hartigan-O'Connor, Ellen. "Abigail's Accounts: Economy and Affection in the Early Republic." *Journal of Women's History* 17 (Fall 2005): 35–58.
Hartigan-O'Connor, Ellen. "Gender's Value in the History of Capitalism." *Journal of the Early Republic* 36 (Winter 2016): 613–53.
Hartigan-O'Connor, Ellen. "The Personal Is Political Economy." *Journal of the Early Republic* 36 (Summer 2016): 335–41.
Hartigan-O'Connor, Ellen. "Public Sales and Public Values in Eighteenth-Century North America." *Early American Studies* 13 (Fall 2015): 749–73.
Hartigan-O'Connor, Ellen. *The Ties That Buy: Women and Commerce in Revolutionary America*. Philadelphia: University of Pennsylvania Press, 2009.
Hartog, Hendrik. *Man and Wife in America: A History*. Cambridge, MA: Harvard University Press, 2000.
Hartog, Hendrik. "Pigs and Positivism." *Wisconsin Law Review* 4 (July 1985): 899–935.
Haulman, Kate. *The Politics of Fashion in Eighteenth Century America*. Chapel Hill: University of North Carolina Press, 2011.
Hedges, James B. *The Browns of Providence Plantations: Colonial Years*. Cambridge, MA: Harvard University Press, 1952.
Hedges, James B. *The Browns of Providence Plantation: The Nineteenth Century*. Providence, RI: Brown University Press, 1968.
Hedges, James B. "The Brown Papers: The Record of a Rhode Island Business Family." *Proceedings of the American Antiquarian Society* (April 1941): 21–36.
Heerman, Scott. *The Alchemy of Slavery: Human Bondage and Emancipation in the Illinois Country, 1730–1865*. Philadelphia: University of Pennsylvania Press, 2018.
Hemphill, Katie M. *Bawdy City: Commercial Sex and Regulation in Baltimore, 1790–1915*. New York: Cambridge University Press, 2020.
Hepburn, A. Barton. *A History of the Currency of the United States with a Brief Description of the Currency Systems of all Commercial Nations*. New York: Macmillan, 1915.
Herbert, Amanda E. *Female Alliances: Gender, Identity, and Friendship in Early Modern Britain*. New Haven, CT: Yale University Press, 2014.
Herrup, Cynthia B. *The Common Peace: Participation and the Criminal Law in Seventeenth-Century England*. New York: Cambridge University Press, 1987.
Heuvel, Danielle van den. "New Products, New Sellers? Changes in the Dutch Textile Trades, c. 1650–1750." In *Selling Textiles in the Long Eighteenth Century: Comparative Perspectives from Western Europe*, edited by Jon Stobart and Bruno Blondé, 118–37. New York: Palgrave Macmillan, 2014.
Hewitt, Nancy A. *Women's Activism and Social Change: Rochester, New York, 1822–1872*. Ithaca, NY: Cornell University Press, 1982.
Hidy, R. W. "Credit Rating before Dun and Bradstreet." *Bulletin of the Business Historical Society* 13 (1939): 81–88.
Higgs, Edward. "Women, Occupations, and Work in the Nineteenth Century Censuses." *History Workshop Journal* 23 (1987): 59–63.
Hilkey, Judy. *Character Is Capital: Success Manuals and Manhood in Gilded Age America*. Chapel Hill: University of North Carolina Press, 1997.
Hilliard, Kathleen. *Masters, Slaves, and Exchange: Power's Purchase in the Old South*. New York: Cambridge University Press, 2014.
Hinks, Peter P. *To Awaken My Afflicted Brethren: David Walker and the Problem of Antebellum Slave Resistance*. University Park: Pennsylvania State University Press, 1997.

Hirota, Hidetaka. *Expelling the Poor: Atlantic Seaboard States and the Nineteenth-Century Origins of American Immigration Policy.* New York: Oxford University Press, 2017.

Hoff, Joan. *Law, Gender, and Injustice: A Legal History of U.S. Women.* New York: Hew York University Press, 1991.

Hoff-Wilson, Joan. "The Unfinished Revolution: Changing Legal Status of U.S. Women." *Signs* 13 (Autumn 1987): 7–36.

Holton, Woody. *Forced Founders: Indians, Debtors, Slaves, and the Making of the American Revolution in Virginia.* Chapel Hill: University of North Carolina Press, 1999.

Holton, Woody. *Unruly Americans and the Origins of the Constitution.* New York: Hill & Wang, 2007.

Hood, Adrienne D. "Flax Seed, Fibre and Cloth: Pennsylvania's Domestic Linen Manufacture and Its Irish Connection, 1700–1830." In *The European Linen Industry in Historical Prespective,* edited by Brenda Collens and Philip Ollerenshaw, 13958. New York: Oxford University Press, 2003.

Hood, Adrienne D. "The Gender Division of Labor in the Production of Textiles in Eighteenth-Century, Rural Pennsylvania (Rethinking the New England Model)." *Journal of Social History* 27 (Spring 1994): 537–61.

Hood, Adrienne D. *The Weaver's Craft: Cloth, Commerce, and Industry in Early Pennsylvania.* Philadelphia: University of Pennsylvania Press, 2003.

Horwitz, Morton J. *The Transformation of American Law, 1780–1860.* Cambridge, MA: Harvard University Press, 1977.

Howard, Ronald W. "From Proprietary Colony to Royal Province." In *The Empire State: A History of New York,* edited by Milton N. Klein, 113–29. Ithaca, NY: Cornell University Press, 2005.

Howell, Martha. "Women's Work in the New and Light Draperies of the Low Countries." In *The New Draperies in the Low Countries and England, 1300–1800,* edited by N. B. Harte, 197–216. New York: Oxford University Press, 1997.

Hseuh, Vicki. *Hybrid Constitutions: Challenging Legacies of Law, Privilege, and Culture in Colonial America.* Durham, NC: Duke University Press, 2010.

Hufton, Olwen H. *The Poor of Eighteenth-Century France 1750–1789.* Oxford: Clarendon, 1974.

Hulsebosch, Daniel. *Constituting Empire: New York and the Transformation of Constitutionalism in the Atlantic World, 1664–1830.* Chapel Hill: University of North Carolina Press, 2005.

Hunter, Tera W. *To 'Joy My Freedom: Southern Black Women's Lives and Labors after the Civil War.* Cambridge, MA: Harvard University Press, 1997.

Hurst, James Willard. *Law and the Conditions of Freedom in the Nineteenth-Century United States.* Madison: University of Wisconsin Press, 1956.

Hyde, Anne F. *Empires, Nations, and Families: A New History of the North American West, 1800–1860.* Lincoln: University of Nebraska Press, 2011.

Igo, Sarah E. *The Averaged American: Surveys, Citizens, and the Making of a Mass Public.* Cambridge, MA: Harvard University Press, 2007.

Inikori, Joseph E. "Slavery the Revolution in Cotton Textile Production in England." *Social Science* History 13 (Winter 1989): 343–79.

Innes, Maurie D. *The Politics of Taste in Antebellum Charleston.* Chapel Hill: University of North Carolina Press, 2005.

Jackson-Houlston, C. M. "'The Burial-Place of the Fashions': The Representation of the Dress of the Poor in Illustrated Serial Prose by Dickens and Hardy." *Textile History* 33, no. 1 (2002): 98–111.

Jeffrey, Julie Roy. *The Great Silent Army of Abolitionism: Ordinary Women and the Antislavery Movement*. Chapel Hill: University of North Carolina Press, 1998.

Jenkins, David, ed. *The Cambridge History of Western Textiles*. 2 vols. Cambridge: Cambridge University Press, 2003.

Jenkins, David. "The Western Wool Textile Industry in the Nineteenth Century." In *The Cambridge History of Western Textiles*, edited by David Jenkins, vol. 2, 761–89. Cambridge: Cambridge University Press, 2003.

Johnson, Walter. *River of Dark Dreams: Slavery and Empire in the Cotton Kingdom*. Cambridge, MA: Harvard University Press, 2013.

Johnson, Wilbur S. *Weaving a Common Thread: A History of the Woolen Industry in the Top of the Shenandoah Valley*. Winchester, VA: Winchester-Frederick County Historical Society, 1990.

Jones, Ann, and Peter Stallybrass. *Renaissance Clothing and the Materials of Memory*. New York: Cambridge University Press, 2000.

Jones, Bernie D. "Revisiting the Married Women's Property Acts: Recapturing Protection in the Face of Equity." *Journal of Gender, Social Policy and the Law* 22, no. 1 (2013): 91–147.

Jones, Fred Mitchell. *Middlemen in the Domestic Trade of the United States, 1800–1860*. Urbana: University of Illinois Press, 1937.

Jones, Jennifer. *Sexing La Mode: Gender, Fashion and Commercial Culture in Old Regime France*. New York: Berg, 2004.

Jones, Martha. *All Bound Up Together: The Woman Question in African American Public Culture, 1830–1900*. Baltimore: Johns Hopkins University Press, 2007.

Jones, Martha. *Birthright Citizens: A History of Race and Rights in Antebellum America*. New York: Cambridge University Press, 2018.

Jones, Norman L., and Daniel Wolf. *Local Identities in Late Medieval and Early Modern England*. New York: Palgrave Macmillan, 2007.

Jones-Rogers, Stephanie. *They Were Her Property: White Women as Slave Owners in the American South*. New Haven, CT: Yale University Press, 2019.

Jordan, Brian Matthew. "Benjamin F. Butler, *Ex Parte Millligan*, and the Unending Civil War." In *Ex Parte Milligan Reconsidered: Race and Civil Liberties from the Lincoln Administration to the War on Terror*, edited by Stewart L. Winger and Jonathan W. White, 27–51. Lawrence: University Press of Kansas.

Jordan, Jean. "Women Merchants in Colonial New York." *New York History* 58 (1977): 412–39.

Jordan, Winthrop D. *White over Black: American Attitudes toward the Negro, 1550–1812*. Chapel Hill: University of North Carolina Press, 1968.

Kahn, Philip, Jr. *A Stitch in Time: The Four Seasons of Baltimore's Needle Trades*. Baltimore: Maryland Historical Society, 1989.

Kantrowitz, Stephen. *More than Freedom: Fighting for Black Citizenship in a White Republic, 1829–1889*. New York: Penguin, 2012.

Katz, Stanley N. "Explaining the Law in Early American History: Introduction." In "Forum Explaining the Law in Early American History—A Symposium," edited by Stanley N. Katz. Special issue, *William and Mary Quarterly* 50 (January 1993): 3–6.

Kennington, Kelly. *In the Shadow of Dred Scott: St. Louis Freedom Suits and the Legal Culture of Slavery in Antebellum America*. Athens, Georgia: University of Georgia Press, 2017.

Kerber, Linda K. *No Constitutional Right to Be Ladies: Women and the Obligations of Citizenship*. New York: Hill & Wang, 1998.

Kerber, Linda K. "Why Diamonds Really Are a Girl's Best Friend: Another American Narrative." *Daedalus* 141 (Winter 2012): 89–100.

Kerber, Linda K. *Women of the Republic: Intellect and Ideology in Revolutionary America*. Chapel Hill: University of North Carolina Press, 1980.

Kessler-Harris, Alice. *Out to Work: A History of Wage-Earning Women in the United States*. New York: Oxford University Press, 1982.

Kessler-Harris, Alice. *A Woman's Wage: Historical Meanings and Social Consequences*. Lexington: University of Kentucky Press, 1990.

Kidwell, Claudia B. *Cutting a Fashionable Fit: Dressmakers' Drafting Systems in the United States*. Washington DC: Smithsonian Institution Press, 1979.

King. Steven. "Reclothing the English Poor, 1750–1840." *Textile History* 33, no. 1 (2002): 37–47.

King, Steven, and Christiana Payne. "Introduction: The Dress of the Poor." *Textile History* 33 (2002): 1–8.

Klein, Rachel N. *Unification of a Slave State: The Rise of the Planter Class in the South Carolina Backcountry, 1760–1808*. Chapel Hill: University of North Carolina Press, 1990.

Konig, David Thomas "A Summary View of the Law of British America." In "Forum Explaining the Law in Early American History—A Symposium," edited by Stanley N. Katz. Special issue, *William and Mary Quarterly* 50 (January 1993): 42–50.

Kowaleski-Wallace, Elizabeth. *Consuming Subjects: Women, Shopping, and Business in the Eighteenth Century*. New York: Columbia University Press, 1997.

Kramer, Larry D. *The People Themselves: Popular Constitutionalism and Judicial Review*. New York: Oxford University Press, 2004.

Kulik, Gary. "Dams, Fish, and Farmers: Defense of Public Rights in Eighteenth-Century Rhode Island." In *The Countryside in the Age of Capitalist Transformation: Essays in the Social History of Rural America*, edited by Steven Hahn and Jonathan Prude, 25–50. Chapel Hill: University of North Carolina Press, 1985.

Kulik, Gary. "Factory Discipline in the New Nation: Almy, Brown & Slater and the First Cotton-Mill Workers, 1790–1808." *Massachusetts Review* 28 (Spring 1987): 164–84.

Kulik, Gary. "Pawtucket Village and the Strike of 1824: The Origins of Class Conflict in Rhode Island." *Radical History Review* 1 (May 1978): 5–38.

LaCroix, Alison. *The Ideological Origins of American Federalism*. Cambridge, MA: Harvard University Press, 2010.

Lamoreaux, Naomi. *Insider Lending: Banks, Personal Connections, and Economic Development in Industrial New England*. Cambridge: Cambridge University Press, 1994.

Lamoreaux, Naomi. "Rethinking the Transition to Capitalism in the Early American Northeast." *Journal of American History* 90 (September 2003): 437–61.

Lamoreaux, Naomi, and John Joseph Wallis. "Economic Crisis, General Laws, and the Mid-Nineteenth-Century Transformation of American Political Economy." *Journal of the Early Republic* 41 (Fall 2021): 403-33.

Landes, Jordan. *London Quakers in the Trans-Atlantic World: The Creation of an Early Modern Community*. New York: Palgrave, 2015.

Lane, Penelope. "Work on the Margins: Poor Women and the Informal Economy of Eighteenth- and Early Nineteenth-Century Leicestershire." *Midland History* 22 (1997): 85–99.

Langbein, John H. "Blackstone, Litchfield, and Yale: The Founding of the Yale Law School." In *History of the Yale Law School*, edited by Anthony Kronman, 17–52. New Haven, CT: Yale University Press, 2004.

Lauer, Josh. *Creditworthy: A History of Consumer Surveillance and Financial Identity in America*. New York: Columbia University Press, 2017.

Lebsock, Suzanne. *The Free Women of Petersburg: Status and Culture in a Southern Town, 1784-1860*. New York: Norton, 1984.

Lebsock, Suzanne D. "Radical Reconstruction and the Property Rights of Southern Women." *Journal of Southern History* (May 1977): 195-216.

Lemire, Beverly. "Consumerism in Preindustrial and Early Industrial England: The Trade in Secondhand Clothes." *Journal of British Studies* 27 (January 1988): 1–24.

Lemire, Beverly. *Dress, Culture, and Commerce: The English Clothing Trade before the Factory, 1660-1800*. London: Macmillan, 1997.

Lemire, Beverly. "Fashioning Cottons: Asian Trade, Domestic Industry and Consumer Demand, 1660-1780." In *The Cambridge History of Western Textiles*, edited by in David Jenkins, vol. 1, 493–512. Cambridge: Cambridge University Press, 2003.

Lemire, Beverly. *Fashion's Favourite: The Cotton Trade and the Consumer in Britain, 1660-1800*. New York: Oxford University Press, 1991.

Lemire, Beverly. *Global Trade and the Transformation of Consumer Cultures: The Material World Remade, c. 1500-1820*. New York: Cambridge University Press, 2018.

Lemire, Beverly. "'A Good Stock of Clothes': The Changing Market for Cotton Clothing in Britain, 1750-1800." *Textile History* 22 (January 1991): 311–28.

Lemire, Beverly. "Peddling Fashion: Salesmen, Pawnbrokers, Taylors, Thieves and the Second-Hand Clothes Trade in England c. 1700–1800." *Textile History* 22 (1991): 67–82.

Lemire, Beverly. "Second-hand Beaux and 'Red-armed Belles': Conflict and the Creation of Fashions in England, c. 1660–1800." *Continuity and Change* 15 (December 2000): 391–417.

Lemire, Beverly. "Shifting Currency: The Culture and Economy of the Second Hand Trade in England, c. 1600–1850." In *Old Clothes, New Looks*, edited by Alexandra Palmer and Hazel Clark, 29–48. New York: Bloomsbury Academic, 2005.

Lemire, Beverly. "The Theft of Clothes and Popular Consumerism in Early Modern England." *Journal of Social History* 24 (Winter 1990): 255–76.

Leonard, Gerald, and Saul Cornell. *The Partisan Republic: Democracy, Exclusion, and the Fall of the Founders' Constitution, 1780s–1830s*. Cambridge: Cambridge University Press, 2019.

Lepore, Jill. *Book of Ages: The Life and Opinions of Jane Franklin*. New York: Knopf, 2013.

Levy, Jonathan. *Freaks of Fortune: The Emerging World of Capitalism and Risk in America*. Cambridge, MA: Harvard University Press, 2012.

Luskey, Brian P. *On the Make: Clerks and the Quest for Capital in Nineteenth-Century America*. New York: New York University Press, 2016.

Luskey, Brian P., and Wendy A. Woloson, eds. *Capitalism by Gaslight: Illuminating the Economy of Nineteenth Century America*. Philadelphia: University of Pennsylvania Press, 2015.

MacGill, Hugh, and R. Kent Newmyer. "Legal Education and Legal Thought, 1790–1920." In *The Cambridge History of Law in America*. Vol. 2, *The Long Nineteenth*

Century, 1789–1920, edited by Michael Grossberg and Christopher Tomlins, 36–67. Cambridge: Cambridge University Press, 2008.

MacKay, Lynn. "Why They Stole: Women in the Old Bailey, 1779–1798." *Journal of Social History* 32 (Spring 1999): 623–39.

Malka, Adam. *The Men of Mobtown: Policing Baltimore in the Age of Slavery and Emancipation*. Chapel Hill: University of North Carolina Press, 2019.

Mann, Bruce H. *Neighbors and Strangers: Law and Community in Early Connecticut*. Chapel Hill: University of North Carolina Press, 1987.

Mann, Bruce H. *Republic of Debtors: Bankruptcy in the Age of American Independence*. Cambridge, MA: Harvard University Press, 2002.

Maris-Wolf, Ted. *Free Blacks and Re-Enslavement Law in Antebellum Virginia*. Chapel Hill: University of North Carolina Press, 2015.

Marsh, Ben. "The Republic's New Clothes: Making Silk in the Antebellum United States." *Agricultural History* 86 (Fall 2012): 206–34.

Martin, Ann Smart. *Buying Into the World of Goods: Early Consumers in Backcountry Virginia*. Baltimore: Johns Hopkins University Press, 2008.

Martin, Luc. "The Rise of the New Draperies in Norwich, 1550–1622." In *The New Draperies in the Low Countries and England, 1300–1800*, edited by N. B. Harte, 245–74. New York: Oxford University Press, 1997.

Masur, Kate. *An Example for All the Land: Emancipation and the Struggle over Equality in Washington, D.C.* Chapel Hill: University of North Carolina Press, 2010.

Masur, Kate. "State Sovereignty and Migration before Reconstruction." *Journal of the Civil War Era* 9 (December 2019): 588–611.

Masur, Kate. *Until Justice Be Done: America's First Civil Rights Movement, From the Revolution to Reconstruction*. New York: Norton, 2020.

Matson, Cathy D. *Merchants and Empire: Trading in Colonial New York*. Baltimore: Johns Hopkins University Press, 1998.

McCombs, Dorothy. "Spinning and Weaving in Montgomery County." *Journal of the Roanoke Valley Historical Society* 11, no. 1 (1980): 73–104.

McCurry, Stephanie. *Confederate Reckoning: Power and Politics in the Civil War South*. Cambridge, MA: Harvard University Press, 2010.

McCurry, Stephanie. *Masters of Small Worlds: Yeoman Households, Gender Relations, and the Political Culture of the Antebellum South Carolina Low Country*. New York: Oxford University Press, 1995.

McCusker, John J. *Money and Exchange in Europe and America, 1600–1775*. Chapel Hill: University of North Carolina Press, 1978.

McKenna, Marian C. *Tapping Reeve and the Litchfield Law School*. New York: Oceana, 1986.

McKinley, Maggie. "Lobbying and the Petition Clause." *Stanford Law Review* 68 (May 2016): 1165–1205.

McKinley, Maggie. "Petitioning and the Making of the Administrative State." *Yale Law Journal* 127 (April 2018): 1538–1637.

McMurry, Sally. *Families and Farmhouses in Nineteenth-Century America: Vernacular Design and Social Change*. New York: Oxford University Press, 1988.

Mendelsohn, Adam. *The Rag Race: How Jews Sewed Their Way to Success in America and the British Empire*. New York: New York University Press, 2014.

Mendelsohn, Adam. "The Rag Race: Jewish Secondhand Clothing Dealers in England and America." In *Capitalism by Gaslight: Illuminating the Economy of Nineteenth*

Century America, edited by Brian P. Luskey and Wendy A. Woloson, 76–92. Philadelphia: University of Pennsylvania Press, 2015.

Meranze, Michael. *Laboratories of Virtue: Punishment, Revolution, and Authority in Philadelphia, 1760–1835*. Chapel Hill: University of North Carolina Press, 1996.

Mihm, Stephen. *A Nation of Counterfeiters: Capitalists, Con Men, and the Making of the United States*. Cambridge, MA: Harvard University Press, 2009.

Miles, Tyia. *All That She Carried: The Journey of Ashley's Sack, a Black Family Keepsake*. New York: Random House, 2021.

Miles, Tiya. *The Dawn of Detroit: A Chronicle of Slavery and Freedom in the City of the Straits*. New York: New Press, 2017.

Miller, Marla R. *Betsy Ross and the Making of America*. New York: Henry Holt, 2010.

Miller, Marla R. "The Last Mantuamaker: Craft Tradition and Commercial Change in Boston, 1760–1840." *Early American Studies* 4 (Fall 2006): 372–424.

Miller, Marla R. *The Needle's Eye: Women and Work in the Age of Revolution*. Amherst: University of Massachusetts Press, 2006.

Miller, Perry. *The Life of the Mind in America: From the Revolution to the Civil War*. New York: Harcourt, Brace & World, 1965.

Mohanty, Gail Fowler. "Experimentation in Textile Technology, 1788–1790, and Its Impact on Handloom Weaving and Weavers in Rhode Island." *Techology and Culture* 29 (January 1988): 1–33.

Mohanty, Gail Fowler. "Handloom Outwork and Outwork Weaving in Rural Rhode Island, 1810–1821." *American Studies* 30 (Fall 1989): 41–68.

Mohanty, Gail Fowler. "Putting Up with Putting-Out: Power-Loom Diffusion and Outwork for Rhode Island Mills, 1821–1829." *Journal of the Early Republic* 9 (Summer 1989): 191–216.

Mohanty, Gail Fowler. *Textiles in America, 1650–1870*. New York: W. W. Norton, 1984.

Montgomery, Florence M. *Printed Textiles: English and American Cottons and Linens, 1700–1850*. New York: Viking, 1970.

Morantz, Alison D. "There's No Place Like Home: Homestead Exemption and Judicial Constructions of Family in Nineteen-Century America." *Law and History Review* 24 (Summer 2006): 245-295.

Morello, Karen Berger. *The Invisible Bar: The Woman Lawyer in America, 1638 to the Present*. New York: Random House, 1986.

Morgan, Edmund. *The Birth of the Republic, 1763–1789*. Rev. ed. Chicago: University of Chicago Press, 1977.

Muldrew, Craig. *The Economy of Obligation: The Culture of Credit and Social Relations in Early Modern England*. New York: St. Martin's, 1998.

Nash, Gary B. *The Forgotten Fifth: African Americans in the Age of Revolution*. Cambridge, MA: Harvard University Press, 2006.

Nash, Gary B. *The Urban Crucible: Social Change, Political Consciousness, and the Origins of the American Revolution*. Cambridge, MA: Harvard University Press, 1979.

Narrett, David E. "Dutch Customs of Inheritance, Women, and the Law in Colonial New York City." In *Authority and Resistance in Early New York*, edited by William Pencak and Conrad Wright, 27–55. New York: New York Historical Society, 1988.

Narrett, David E. "Men's Wills and Women's Property Rights in Colonial New York." In *Women in the Age of the American Revolution*, edited by Ronald Hoffman and Peter J. Albert, 91–133. Charlottesville: University of Virginia Press, 1989.

Nathans, Sydney. *To Free a Family: The Journey of Mary Walker*. Cambridge, MA: Harvard University Press, 2012.

Nelson, Scott Reynolds. *A Nation of Deadbeats: An Uncommon History of America's Financial Disasters*. New York: Alfred A. Knopf, 2012.

Nenadic, Stana. "The Social Shaping of Business Behaviour in the Nineteenth-Century Women's Garment Trades." *Journal of Social History* 31 (Spring 1998): 625–45.

Newman, Simon P. *Embodied History: The Lives of the Poor in Early Philadelphia*. Philadelphia: University of Pennsylvania Press, 2003.

Newmyer, R. Kent. "Harvard Law School, New England Legal Culture, and the Antebellum Origins of American Jurisprudence." *Journal of American History* 74, no. 3 (1987): 814–35.

Norris, James D. *R. G. Dun & Co., 1841–1900: The Development of Credit- Reporting in the Nineteenth Century*. Westport, CT: Greenwood, 1978.

Novak, William J. "The American Law of Association: The Legal-Political Construction of Civil Society." *Studies in American Political Development* 15 (Fall 2001): 163–88.

Novak, William J. "The Legal Transformation of Citizenship in Nineteenth-Century America." In *The Democratic Experiment: New Directions in American Political History*, edited by Meg Jacobs, William J. Novak, and Julian E. Zelizer, 85–119. Princeton, NJ: Princeton University Press, 2003.

Novak, William J. *The People's Welfare: Law and Regulation in Nineteenth-Century America*. Chapel Hill: University of North Carolina Press, 1996.

Nunley, Tamika Y. *At the Threshold of Liberty: Women, Slavery, and Shifting Identities in Washington, D.C.* Chapel Hill: University of North Carolina Press, 2021.

Ogilvie, Sheilagh. *A Bitter Living: Women, Markets, and Social Capital in Early Modern Germany*. Oxford: Oxford University Press, 2003.

Olegario, Rowena. *A Culture of Credit: Embedding Trust and Transparency in American Business*. Cambridge, MA: Harvard University Press, 2006.

Olegario, Rowena -. *The Engine of Enterprise: Credit in America*. Cambridge, MA: Harvard University Press, 2016.

Olwell, Robert. *Masters, Slaves, and Subjects: The Culture of Power in the South Carolina Low Country, 1740–1790*. Ithaca, NY: Cornell University Press, 1998.

Opal, J. M. *Avenging the People: Andrew Jackson, the Rule of Law, and the American Nation*. New York: Oxford University Press, 2017.

Osterud, Nancy Grey. *The Bonds of Community: The Lives of Farm Women in Nineteenth-Century New York*. Ithaca, NY: Cornell University Press, 1991.

Osterud, Nancy Grey. "The Valuation of Women's Work: Gender and the Market in Dairy Farming Community during the Late Nineteenth Century." *Frontiers* 10, no. 2 (1988): 18–24.

Ownby, Ted. *American Dreams in Mississippi: Consumers, Poverty, and Culture, 1830–1998*. Chapel Hill: University of North Carolina Press, 1999.

Ownby, Ted, and Becca Walton, eds. *Clothing and Fashion in Southern History*. Jacksonville: University Press of Mississippi, 2020.

Pargas, Damian Alan. *Slavery and Forced Migration in the Antebellum South*. New York: Cambridge University Press, 2015.

Parker, Kunal. *Making Foreigners: Immigration and Citizenship Law in America, 1600–2000*. New York: Cambridge University Press, 2015.

Pateman, Carole. *The Sexual Contract*. Stanford, CA: Stanford University Press, 1988.

Payne, Christiana. "'Murillo-like Rags or Clean Pinafores': Artistic and Social Preferences in the Representation of the Dress of the Rural Poor." *Textile History* 33, no. 1 (2002): 48–62.

Pearsall, Sarah M. S. *Atlantic Families: Lives and Letters in the Later Eighteenth Century*. New York: Oxford University Press, 2008.

Peck, Amelia. "'India Chints' and 'China Taffaty': East Indian Company Textiles for the North American Market." In *Interwoven Globe: The Worldwide Textile Trade, 1500–1800*, edited by Amelia Peck, 102–19. New Haven, CT: Yale University Press for the Metropolitan Museum of Art, 2013.

Peck, Amelia, ed. *Interwoven Globe: The Worldwide Textile Trade, 1500–1800*. New Haven, CT: Yale University Press for the Metropolitan Museum of Art, 2013.

Peiss, Kathy. *Cheap Amusements: Working Women and Leisure in Turn-of-the-Century New York*. Philadelphia: Temple University Press, 1985.

Penningroth, Dylan C. *The Claims of Kinfolk: African American Property and Community in the Nineteenth-Century South*. Chapel Hill: University of North Carolina Press, 2003.

Penningroth, Dylan C. "Everyday Use: A History of Civil Rights in Black Churches." *Journal of American History* 107 (March 2021): 871–98.

Peterson, Farah. "Constitutionalism in Unexpected Places." *Virginia Law Review* 106 (May 2020): 559–609.

Peterson, Farah. "Interpretation as Statecraft: Chancellor Kent and the Collaborative Era of American Statutory Interpretation." *Maryland Law Review* 77 (2018): 712–73.

Phillips, Ulrich Bonnell. *American Negro Slavery: A Survey of the Supply, Employment, and Control of Negro Labor as Determined by the Plantation Regime*. New York: D. Appleton, 1918.

Pitts, Yvonne. *Family, Law, and Inheritance in America: A Social and Legal History of Nineteenth-Century Kentucky*. Cambridge: Cambridge University Press, 2013.

Poovey, Mary. *History of the Modern Fact: Problems of Knowledge in the Sciences of Wealth and Society*. Chicago: University of Chicago Press, 1998.

Porter, Glenn, and Harold C. Livesay. *Merchants and Manufacturers: Studies in the Changing Structure of Nineteenth-Century Marketing*. Baltimore: Johns Hopkins University Press, 1971.

Postrel, Virginia. *The Fabric of Civilization: How Textiles Made the World*. New York: Basic Books, 2020.

Preston, Anne. "'To Learn Me the Whole of the Trade': Conflict between a Female Apprentice and a Merchant Tailor in Ante-Bellum New England." *Labor History* 24 (Spring 1983): 259–73.

Priest, Claire. "Creating an American Property Law: Alienability and Its Limits in American History." *Harvard Law Review* 120 (December 2006): 385–459.

Priest, Claire. *Credit Nation: Property Laws and Institutions in Early America*. Princeton, NJ: Princeton University Press, 2021.

Priest, Claire. "Currency Policies and Legal Development in Colonial New England." *Yale Law Journal* 110 (2001): 1303–1405.

Prude, Jonathan. *The Coming of the Industrial Order: Town and Factory Life in Rural Massachusetts, 1810–1860*. New York: Cambridge University Press, 1983.

Prude, Jonathan. "To Look Upon the 'Lower Sort': Runaway Ads and the Appearance of Unfree Laborers in America, 1750–1800." *Journal of American History* 78 (June 1991): 124–59.

Raffel, Marta Cotterell. *The Laces of Ipswich: The Art and Economics of an Early American Industry, 1750–1840*. Hanover, NH: University Press of New England, 2003.

Rao, Gautham. *National Duties: Custom Houses and the Making of the American State*. Chicago: University of Chicago Press, 2016.

Rasmussen, Margaret Byrd Adams. "Waging War with Wool: Thomas Jefferson's Campaign for American Commercial Independence from England." *Material Culture* 41 (Spring 2009): 17–37.

Ray, Arthur. "Indians as Consumers in the Eighteenth Century." In *Old Trails and New Directions: Papers of the Third North American Fur Trade Conference*, edited by Carol M. Judd and Arthur J. Ray, 255–71. Toronto: University of Toronto Press, 1980.

Reagan, Leslie J. *When Abortion Was a Crime: Women, Medicine, and the Law in the United States, 1867–1973*. Berkeley: University of California Press, 1997.

Reddy, William M. *The Rise of Market Culture: The Textile Trade and French Society, 1750–1900*. New York: Cambridge University Press, 1984.

Ribeiro, Aileen. *The Art of Dress: Fashion in England and France 1750 to 1820*. New Haven, CT: Yale University, 1995.

Richardson, Heather Cox. *The Death of Reconstruction: Race, Labor, and Politics in the Post-Civil War North*. Cambridge, MA: Harvard University Press, 2001.

Rink, Oliver. "Life in New Netherland." In *The Empire State: A History of New York*, edited by Milton N. Klein, 61–86. Ithaca, NY: Cornell University Press, 2005.

Roche, Daniel. *The Culture of Clothing: Dress and Fashion in the Ancien Regime*. Translated by Jean Birrell. Cambridge: Cambridge University Press, 1994.

Rockman, Seth. "Negro Cloth: Mastering the Market for Slave Clothing in Antebellum America." In *American Capitalism: New Histories*, edited by Christine Desan and Sven Beckert, 170–94. New York: Columbia University Press, 2018.

Rockman, Seth. "Plantation Goods and the National Economy of Slavery." Unpublished manuscript.

Rockman, Seth. *Scraping By: Wage Labor, Slavery, and Survival in Early Baltimore*. Baltimore: Johns Hopkins University Press, 2009.

Romney, Susanah Shaw. *New Netherland Connections: Intimate Networks and Atlantic Ties in Seventeenth-Century America*. Chapel Hill: University of North Carolina Press, 2014.

Rosen, Deborah A. *Border Law: The First Seminole War and American Nationhood*. Cambridge, MA: Harvard University Press, 2015.

Rosenthal, Caitlin. "Storybook-Keepers: Narratives and Numbers in Nineteenth Century America." *Common-place* 12 (2012), http://www.common-place.org/vol-12/no-03/rosenthal.

Rothman, Adam. *Slave Country: American Expansion and the Origins of the Deep South*. Cambridge, MA: Harvard University Press, 2005.

Rothman, Joshua D. *Notorious in the Neighborhood: Sex and Families Across the Color Line in Virginia, 1787–1867*. Chapel Hill: University of North Carolina Press, 2003.

Rothstein, Natalie. "Silk in the Early Modern Period, c. 1500–1780." In *The Cambridge History of Western Textiles*, edited by David Jenkins, 1:528–61. Cambridge: Cambridge University Press, 2003.

Rothstein, Natalie. "Silk: The Industrial Revolution and After." In *The Cambridge History of Western Textiles*, edited by David Jenkins, 2:790–808. Cambridge: Cambridge University Press, 2003.

Rubinstein, Jonathan. "From the King's Peace to the Patrol Car: The Origins of the City Police." *New York Magazine* 6 (May 1973): 44–48.

Rutz-Robbins, Kristi. "'Divers Debts': Women's Participation in the Local Economy, Albemarle, North Carolina, 1663–1729." *Early American Studies* 4 (Fall 2006): 425–41.

Ryan, Mary P. *Cradle of the Middle Class: The Family in Oneida County, New York, 1790–1865*. New York: Cambridge University Press, 1981.

Sachs, Honor. "'Freedom By A Judgment': The Legal History of an Afro-Indian Family." *Law and History Review* 30 (February 2012): 173–203.

Sachs, Honor. *Home Rule: Households, Manhood, and National Expansion on the Eighteenth-Century Kentucky Frontier*. New Haven, CT: Yale University Press, 2015.

Sacks, David Harris. *The Widening Gate: Bristol and the Atlantic Economy, 1450–1700*. Berkeley: University of California Press, 1991.

Sadosky, Leonard J. *Revolutionary Negotiations: Indians, Empires, and Diplomats in the Founding of America*. Charlottesville: University of Virginia Press, 2009.

Saler, Beth. *The Settlers' Empire: Colonialism and State Formation in America's Old Northwest*. Philadelphia: University of Pennsylvania Press, 2015.

Salmon, Marylynn. "Women and Property in South Carolina: The Evidence from Marriage Settlements, 1730–1830." *William and Mary Quarterly* 39 (October 1982): 655–85.

Salmon, Marylynn. *Women and the Law of Property in Early America*. Chapel Hill: University of North Carolina Press, 1986.

Sandage, Scott A. *Born Losers: A History of Failure in America*. Cambridge, MA: Harvard University Press, 2005.

Sanderson, Elizabeth. "The Edinburgh Milliners, 1720–1820." *Costume* 20 (1986): 18–28.

Saville, Julie. *The Work of Reconstruction: From Slave to Wage Laborer in South Carolina, 1860–1870*. New York: Cambridge University Press, 1994.

Schantz, Mark S. "The Janus-Faced Character of Martial Law in the American Civil War, or the Strange Case of Lieutenant Alanson L. Sanborn and Dr. David M. Wright." In *Ex Parte Milligan Reconsidered: Race and Civil Liberties from the Lincoln Administration to the War on Terror*, edited by Stewart L. Winger and Jonathan W. White, 72–101. Lawrence: University Press of Kansas.

Schwalm, Leslie A. *Emancipation's Diaspora: Race and Reconstruction in the Upper Midwest*. Chapel Hill: University of North Carolina Press, 2009.

Schwalm, Leslie A. *A Hard Fight for We: Women's Transition from Slavery to Freedom in South Carolina*. Urbana: University of Illinois Press, 1997.

Schweiger, Beth Barton. *A Literate South: Reading before Emancipation*. New Haven, CT: Yale University Press, 2019.

Scranton, Philip. *Proprietary Capitalism: The Textile Manufacture at Philadelphia, 1800–1885*. New York: Cambridge University Press, 1983.

Seeley, Samantha. "Freedom and the Politics of Migration After the American Revolution." In *Revolutions and Reconstructions: Black Politics in the Long Nineteenth Century*, edited by Van E. Gosse and David Waldstreicher, 84–101. Philadelphia: University of Pennsylvania Press, 2020.

Shaimon, S. Laurence. "The History of Imprisonment for Debt and Insolvency Laws in Pennsylvania as They Evolved from the Common Law." *American Journal of Legal History* 4 (July 1960): 205–25.

Shammas, Carole. "The Decline of Textile Prices in England and British America prior to Industrialization." *Economic History Review* 47 (August 1994): 483–507.

Shammas, Carole. "Re-Assessing the Married Women's Property Acts." *Journal of Women's History* 6, no. 1 (Spring, 1994): 9–30.

Shankman, Andrew. "Toward a Social History of Federalism: The State and Capitalism To and From the American Revolution." *Journal of the Early American Republic* 37 (Winter 2017): 615–653.

Shannon, Timothy J. "Dressing for Success on the Mohawk Frontier: Hendrick, William Johnson, and the Indian Frontier." *William and Mary Quarterly* 53 (January 1996): 13–42.

Shattuck, Martha Dickinson. "Women and Trade in New Netherlands." *Itinerario* 18, no. 2 (July 1994): 40–49.

Shelton, Cynthia J. *The Mills of Manayunk: Industrialization and Social Conflict in the Philadelphia Region, 1787–1837*. Baltimore: Johns Hopkins University Press, 1986.

Shelton, Cynthia J. "The Role of Labor in Early Industrialization: Philadelphia, 1787–1837." *Journal of the Early Republic* 4 (Winter 1984): 365–94.

Siegel, Andrew M. "'To Learn and to Make Respectable Hereafter': The Litchfield Law School in Cultural Context." *New York Law Review* 73 (1998): 1978–2028.

Siegel, Reva B. "Home as Work: The First Woman's Rights Claims Concerning Wives' Household Labor, 1850–1880." *Yale Law Journal* 103 (1994): 1073–1217.

Siegel, Reva B. "'The Rule of Love': Wife Beating as Prerogative and Privacy." *Yale Law Journal* 105 (June 1996): 2117–2206.

Siegenthaler, Hansjorg. "What Price Style? The Fabric-Advisory Function of the Drygoods Commission Merchant, 1850–1860." *Business History Review* 41, no. 1 (1967): 36–61.

Sievens, Mary Beth. "Female Consumerism and Household Authority in Early National New England." *Early American Studies* 4 (Fall 2006): 353–71.

Simler, Lucy. "She Came to Work: The Female Labor Force in Chester County, 1750–1820." *Early American Studies* 5 (Fall 2007): 427–53.

Simonton, Deborah, and Anne Montenach, eds. *Female Agency in the Urban Economy: Gender in European Towns, 1640–1830*. New York: Routledge, 2013.

Sinha, Manisha. *The Counter-Revolution of Slavery: Politics and Ideology in Antebellum South Carolina*. Chapel Hill: University of North Carolina Press, 2000.

Sleeper-Smith, Susan. "Encounter and Trade in the Early Atlantic World." In *Why You Can't Teach United States History without American Indians*, edited by Susan Sleeper-Smith, Juliana Barr, Jean M. O'Brien, Nancy Shoemaker, and Scott Many Stevens, 26–42. Chapel Hill: University of North Carolina Press, 2015.

Sleeper-Smith, Susan. *Indigenous Prosperity and American Conquest: Indian Women of the Ohio River Valley, 1690–1792*. Chapel Hill: University of North Carolina Press, 2018.

Sleeper-Smith, Susan, ed. *Rethinking the Fur Trade: Cultures of Exchange in an Atlantic World*. Lincoln: University of Nebraska Press, 2009.

Sleeper-Smith, Susan, Juliana Barr, Jean M. O'Brien, Nancy Shoemaker, and Scott Many Stevens. eds. *Why You Can't Teach United States History without American Indians*. Chapel Hill: University of North Carolina Press, 2015.

Smail, Daniel Lord. *Legal Plunder: Households and Debt Collection in Late Medieval Europe*. Cambridge, MA: Harvard University Press, 2016.

Smiles, Sam. "Defying Comprehension: Resistance to Uniform Appearance in Depicting the Poor, 1770s to 1830s." *Textile History* 33, no. 1 (2002): 23–36.

Smith, Rogers M. *Civic Ideals: Conflicting Visions of Citizenship in U.S. History*. New Haven, CT: Yale University Press, 1997.

Solar, Peter. "The Linen Industry in the Nineteenth Century." *The Cambridge History of Western Textiles*, edited by David Jenkins 2:809–23. Cambridge: Cambridge University Press, 2003.

Spufford, Margaret. *The Great Reclothing of Rural England: Petty Chapmen and Their Wares in the Seventeenth Century*. London: Hambledon, 1984.
Spufford, Margaret, and Susan Mee. *The Clothing of the Common Sort, 1570–1700*. New York: Oxford University Press, 2017.
Stanley, Amy Dru. "Beggars Can't Be Choosers: Compulsion and Contract in Postbellum America." *Journal of American History* 78 (March 1992): 1265–93.
Stanley, Amy Dru. *From Bondage to Contract: Wage Labor, Marriage, and the Market in the Age of Slave Emancipation*. New York: Cambridge University Press, 1998.
Stansell, Christine. *City of Women: Sex and Class in New York, 1789–1860*. Urbana: University of Illinois Press, 1987.
Stansell, Christine. "The Origins of the Sweatshop: Women and Early Industrialization in New York City." In *Working-Class America: Essays on Labor, Community, and American Society*, edited by Michael H. Frisch and Daniel J. Walkowitz, 78–103. Urbana: University of Illinois Press, 1983.
Starke, Barbara M., Lillian O. Holloman, and Barbara K. Nordquist. *African American Dress and Adornment: A Cultural Perspective*. Dubuque, IA: Kendall/Hunt, 1990.
Steinberg, Allen. *The Transformation of Criminal Justice: Philadelphia, 1800–1880*. Chapel Hill: University of North Carolina Press, 1989.
Steinfeld, Robert J. *Coercion, Contract, and Free Labor in the Nineteenth Century*. New York: Cambridge University Press, 2001.
Storey, Joyce. "Printed Cottons in Victorian America" *Textile History* 15 (Fall 1984): 246–48.
Stretton, Tim. *Women Waging Law in Elizabethan England*. New York: Cambridge University Press, 1998.
Sturtz, Linda L. *Within Her Power: Propertied Women in Colonial Virginia*. New York: Routledge, 2002.
Styles, John. "Clothing the North: The Supply of Non-Elite Clothing in the Eighteenth-Century North of England." *Textile History* 25 (January 1994): 139–66.
Styles, John. *The Dress of the People*. New Haven, CT: Yale University Press, 2007.
Styles, John. "Involuntary Consumers? Servants and Their Clothes in Eighteenth-Century England." *Textile History* 33, no. 1 (2002): 9–21.
Styles, John. *Threads of Feeling: The London Foundling Hospital's Textile Tokens, 1740–1770*. London: Foundling Hospital, 2013.
Tani, Karen M. *States of Dependency: Welfare, Rights, and American Governance, 1935–1972*. New York: Cambridge University Press, 2016.
Tani, Karen M., and Sarah Mayeux. "Federalism Anew." *American Journal of Legal History* 56 (2016): 128–38.
Tebbutt, Melanie. *Making Ends Meet: Pawnbroking and Working-Class Credit*. New York: St. Martin's, 1983.
Tetrault, Lisa. *The Myth of Seneca Falls: Memory and the Women's Suffrage Movement, 1848–1898*. Chapel Hill: University of North Carolina Press, 2014.
Thompson, E. P. *Customs in Common*. London: Merlin, 1991.
Thompson, E. P. *The Making of the English Working Class*. New York: Pantheon, 1964.
Thompson, E. P. *Whigs and Hunters: The Origin of the Black Act*. London: Allen Lane, 1975.
Thompson, Michael D. "'Some Rascally Business': Thieving Slaves, Unscrupulous Whites, and Charleston's Illicit Waterfront Trade." In *Capitalism by Gaslight: Illuminating the Economy of Nineteenth Century America*, edited by Brian P. Luskey and Wendy A. Woloson, 150–67. Philadelphia: University of Pennsylvania Press, 2015.

Thompson, Michael D. *Working on the Dock of the Bay: Labor and Enterprise in an Antebellum Southern Port*. Columbia: University of South Carolina Press, 2015.

Thornton, John K. *Africa and Africans in the Making of the Atlantic World*. 2nd ed. New York: Cambridge University Press, 1998.

Tomlins, Christopher L. *Freedom Bound: Law, Labor, and Civic Identity in Colonizing English America, 1580–1865*. New York: Cambridge University Press, 2010.

Tomlins, Christopher L. *Law, Labor, and Ideology in the Early American Republic*. New York: Cambridge University Press, 1993.

Tomlins, Christopher L., and Bruce H. Mann, eds. *The Many Legalities of Early America*. Chapel Hill: University of North Carolina Press, 2001.

Tucker, Barbara M. *Samuel Slater and the Origins of American Textile Industry*. Ithaca, NY: Cornell University Press, 1984.

Turner, Felicity. Proving Pregnancy: Gender, Law, and Medical Knowledge in Nineteenth-Century America. Chapel Hill: University of North Carolina Press, forthcoming 2022).

Turner, Felicity. "Rights and the Ambiguities of Law: Infanticide in the Nineteenth-Century U.S. South." *Journal of the Civil War Era* 4 (September 2014): 350–72.

Twitty, Anne. *Before* Dred Scott: *Slavery and Legal Culture in America's Confluence, 1787–1857*. New York: Cambridge University Press, 2016.

Ulrich, Laurel Thatcher. *The Age of Homespun: Objects and Stories in the Creation of an American Myth*. New York: Knopf, 2001.

Ulrich, Laurel Thatcher. "Hannah Barnard's Cupboard: Female Property and Identity in Eighteenth Century New England." In *Through a Glass Darkly: Reflections on Personal Identity in Early America*, edited by Ronald Hoffman, Mechal Sobel, and Federicka Teute, 238–73. Chapel Hill: University of North Carolina Press, 1997.

Ulrich, Laurel Thatcher. "Martha Ballard and Her Girls: Women's Work in Eighteenth-Century Maine." In *Work and Labor in Early America*, edited by Stephen Innes, 70–105. Chapel Hill: University of North Carolina Press, 1988.

Ulrich, Laurel Thatcher. *A Midwife's Tale: The Life of Martha Ballard, Based on Her Diary, 1785–1812*. New York: Knopf, 1980.

Ulrich, Laurel Thatcher. "Wheels, Looms, and the Gender Division of Labor in Eighteenth Century New England." *William and Mary Quarterly* 55 (January 1998): 3–38.

Van Kirk, Sylvia. *Many Tender Ties: Women in Fur-Trade Society, 1670–1870*. Norman: University of Oklahoma Press, 1983.

Vicente, Marta V. *Clothing the Spanish Empire: Families and the Calico Trade in the Early Modern Atlantic World*. New York: Palgrave MacMillan, 2006.

Vickery, Amanda. *Behind Closed Doors: At Home in Georgian England*. New Haven, CT: Yale University Press, 2009.

Vickery, Amanda. *The Gentleman's Daughter: Women's Lives in Georgian England*. New Haven, CT: Yale University Press, 1998.

Vickery, Amanda. "His and Hers: Gender, Consumption and Household Accounting in Eighteenth-Century England." *Past and Present* 1, supp. 1 (2006): 12–38.

Vlach, John Michael. *Back of the Big House: The Architecture of Plantation Slavery*. Chapel Hill: University of North Carolina Press, 1993.

Von Daacke, Kirt. *Freedom Has a Face: Race, Identity, and Community in Jefferson's Virginia*. Charlottesville: University Press of Virginia, 2012.

Vries, Jan de. "The Industrial Revolution and the Industrious Revolution." *Journal of Economic History* 54, no. 2 (June 1994): 249–70.

Waldstreicher, David. "Reading the Runaways: Self-Fashioning, Print Culture, and Confidence in Slavery in the Eighteenth-Century Mid-Atlantic." *William and Mary Quarterly* 56 (April 1999): 243–72.

Walker, Garthine. "Women, Theft and the World of Stolen Goods." In *Women, Crime, and the Courts in Early Modern England*, edited by Jennifer Kermode and Garthine Walker, 81–105. Chapel Hill: University of North Carolina Press, 1994.

Walker, Tamara. *Exquisite Slaves: Race, Clothing, and Status in Colonial Peru*. New York: Cambridge University Press, 2017.

Ware, Caroline F. *The Early New England Cotton Manufacture: A Study in Industrial Beginnings*. Boston: Houghton Mifflin, 1931.

Watt, Melinda. "'Whims and Fancies': Europeans Respond to Textiles from the East." In *Interwoven Globe: The Worldwide Textile Trade, 1500–1800*, edited by Amelia Peck, 82–103. New Haven, CT: Yale University Press for the Metropolitan Museum of Art, 2013.

Weatherill, Lorna. "Consumer Behaviour, Textiles and Dress in the Late Seventeenth and Early Eighteenth Century." *Textile History* 22 (January 1991): 297–310.

Weicksel, Sarah Jones. "The Dress of the Enemy: Clothing and Disease in the Civil War Era." *Civil War History* 63, no. 2 (June 2017): 133–50.

Weicksel, Sarah Jones. "'Peeled' Bodies, Pillaged Homes: Looting and Material Culture in the American Civil War Era." In *Objects of War: The Material Culture of Conflict and Displacement*, edited by Leora Auslander and Tara Zahra, 111–38. Ithaca, NY: Cornell University Press, 2018.

Welch, Kimberly. "Arteries of Capital: William Johnson and the Practice of Black Moneylending in the Antebellum U.S. South." *Slavery and Abolition* (June 2019): 1–23.

Welch, Kimberly. *Black Litigants in the Antebellum American South*. Chapel Hill: University of North Carolina Press, 2018.

Welch, Kimberly. "William Johnson's Hypothesis: A Free Black Man and the Problem of Legal Knowledge in the Antebellum United States South." *Law and History Review* 37 (February 2019): 89–124.

Welke, Barbara Y. *Law and the Borders of Belonging in the Long Nineteenth Century United States*. New York: Cambridge University Press, 2010.

Welke, Barbara Y. *Recasting American Liberty: Gender, Race, Law, and the Railroad Revolution, 1865–1920*. New York: Cambridge University Press, 2001.

Wenimont, Jacqueline. *Numbered Lives: Life and Death in Quantum Media*. Cambridge, MA: MIT Press, 2018.

White, G. Edward. "The Origins of Civil Rights in America." *Case Western Reserve Law Review* 64 (Spring 2014): 755–816.

White, Jonathan W. *Abraham Lincoln and Treason in the Civil War: The Trials of John Merryman*. Baton Rouge: Louisiana State University Press, 2011.

White, Jonathan W. "Martial Law and the Expansion of Civil Liberties during the Civil War." In Ex Parte Milligan *Reconsidered: Race and Civil Liberties from the Lincoln Administration to the War on Terror*, edited by Stewart L. Winger and Jonathan W. White, 52–72. Lawrence: University Press of Kansas.

White, Shane. *Somewhat More Independent: The End of Slavery in New York City, 1770–1810*. Athens, Georgia: University of Georgia Press, 1991.

White, Sophie. "This Gown Was Much Admired and Made Many Ladies Jealous: Fashion and the Forging of Elite Identities in French Colonial New Orleans." In *George Washington's South*, edited by in T. Harvey and G. O'Brien, 86–118. Gainesville: University of Florida Press, 2004.

White, Sophie. *Wild Frenchmen and Frenchified Indians: Material Culture and Race in Colonial Louisiana*. Philadelphia: University of Pennsylvania Press, 2012.

Whittenburg, James P. "Planters, Merchants, and Lawyers: Social Change and the Origins of the North Carolina Regulation." *William and Mary Quarterly* 34 (April 1977): 215–38.

Wilentz, Sean. *Chants Democratic: New York City and the Rise of the American Working Class, 1788–1850*. New York: Oxford University Press, 1984.

Wilf, Steven. *Law's Imagined Republic: Popular Politics and Criminal Justice in Revolutionary America*. New York: Cambridge University Press, 2010.

Winters, Dawn M. "'The Ladies Are Coming!': A New History of Antebellum Temperance, Women's Rights, and Political Activism." PhD diss., Carnegie Mellon University, 2018.

Witt, John Fabian. *Lincoln's Code: The Laws of War in American History*. New York: Free Press, 2012.

Woloson, Wendy A. *In Hock: Pawning in America from Independence through the Great Depression*. Chicago: University of Chicago Press, 2009.

Wood, Kirsten E. *Masterful Women: Slaveholding Widows from the American Revolution through the Civil War*. Chapel Hill: University of North Carolina Press, 2004.

Woods, Michael. "The Culture of Credit in Colonial Charleston." *South Carolina Historical Magazine* 99 (October 1998): 374–79.

Wright, Chester W. *Wool-Growing and the Tariff: A Study in the Economic History of the United States*. Boston: Houghton Mifflin, 1910.

Wrightson, Keith. "Two Concepts of Order: Justices, Constables, and Jurymen in Seventeenth-Century England." In *An Ungovernable People: The English and Their Law in the Seventeenth and Eighteenth Centuries*, edited by John Brewer and John Styles, 21–46. New Brunswick, NJ: Rutgers University Press, 1980.

Wulf, Karin. *Not All Wives: Women of Colonial Philadelphia*. Ithaca, NY: Cornell University Press, 2000.

Wyatt-Brown, Bertram. *Lewis Tappan and the Evangelical War against Slavery*. Cleveland: Press of Case Western Reserve University, 1969.

Young, Alfred F., ed. *The American Revolution*. DeKalb: Northern Illinois University Press, 1976.

Young, Alfred F. *The Shoemaker and the Tea Party: Memory and the American Revolution*. Boston: Beacon, 1999.

Young, Jeffrey Robert. *Domesticating Slavery: The Master Class in Georgia and South Carolina, 1670–1837*. Chapel Hill: University of North Carolina Press, 1999.

Zabin, Serena. *Dangerous Economies: Status and Commerce in Imperial New York*. Philadelphia: University of Pennsylvania Press, 2009.

Zabin, Serena. "Women's Trading Networks and Dangerous Economies in Eighteenth-Century New York City." *Early American Studies* 4 (Fall 2006): 291–321.

Zagarri, Rosemarie. *Revolutionary Backlash: Women and Politics in the Early American Republic*. Philadelphia: University of Pennsylvania Press, 2007.

Zakim, Michael. "Bookkeeping as Ideology: Capitalist Knowledge in Nineteenth-Century America." *Common-place* 6 (2006), http://www.common-place.org/vol-06/no-03/zakim.

Zakim, Michael. "Customizing the Industrial Revolution: The Reinvention of Tailoring in the Nineteenth Century." *Winterthur Portfolio* 33, no. 1 (Spring 1998): 41–58.

Zakim, Michael -. "A Ready-Made Business: The Birth of the Clothing Industry in America." *Business History Review* 73 (Spring 1999): 61–90.

Zakim, Michael. *Ready-Made Democracy: A History of Men's Dress in the American Republic, 1760–1860*. Chicago: University of Chicago Press, 2003.

Zakim, Michael. "Seamstresses and Whores: Working Women, Women's Work, and the Rise of the American Middle Class, 1820–1860." *Historia: Journal of the Historical Society of Israel* 15 (2005): 73–101.

Zelizer, Viviana A. *The Social Meaning of Money*. Princeton, NJ: Princeton University Press, 1997.

Index

For the benefit of digital users, indexed terms that span two pages (e.g., 52–53) may, on occasion, appear on only one of those pages.

abolition/abolitionists, 43–44, 173–74, 256. *See also* African Americans; Grimké, Angelina; Grimké, John Faucheraud; Grimké, Sarah; Reconstruction amendments; Tappan, Lewis; Walker, David
    advocacy for general rules to eliminate slavery, 269
    African Americans need for protection of federal authority, 286–87
    brief flirtation in southern states, 23
    Civil Rights Cases, 288
    limitations of, 286–87
    sheltering of George Kirk, 269*f*
    US Army policy toward African Americans, 285
accounting methods. *See* diaries; ledgers
Adams, Abigail, 137
Adams, John, 137
Africa
    trade with Portugal, 5
    trading patterns, 4–5
African Americans. *See also* abolition/abolitionists; enslaved people; Free Blacks; Gray, Rosenah; Munro, Susan
    attainment of men's civil/political rights, 11–12
    census (1847) data, 133–34
    depiction in *Harper's Weekly,* 283–85
    Dred Scott v. Sandford decision, 40, 247, 285–86
    extension of rights for, 15
    Fourteenth Amendment and, 252
    gradual emancipation of, 33–34
    laws relating to property rights, 22, 37, 60–61
    legal principles of textiles for, 250–51
    legal status determination in the Mayor's Court, 34–35
    legal status of free Blacks, 268–69
    need for protection of federal authority, 286–87
    Negro recruits at Charleston, 284*f*
    nominal freedom in the upper South, 34–35
    personal liberty cases involving, 247
    Reconstruction amendments and, 257, 285–86
    related legal restrictions in New York, 33–34
    related legal restrictions in Richmond, Virginia, 34–35
    representation in print culture, 116
    roles in the textile trade, 281
    Tappan's focus on extending rights of, 257–58
    wearing of United States Army uniforms, 284–85
Alexander, Mary
    business background, 25–26
    successful textile merchandising, 62, 66, 67*f,* 69–70
Allingham, Sarah, 53–54, 195–98, 200–1, 202, 206–7
Allison, Ann, 212–13
Allison, James, 125
Ames, Harriet Ann, 166–67, 175–76
Ames, Jesse Daniel, 254–55
anti-lynching activism, 254
anti-Semitism, 281
At the Spinning Wheel (Bacher), 87*f*
auction houses, 182–83, 226–27

Bacher, Otto Henry, 87f, 88f
Bagby, Elizabeth, 94–95, 103–5, 137–38, 166, 167
Ballard, Martha, 155–57
Bangs, Nabby, 162–63
Bangs, Nathaniel, 162–63
Bangs, Ruth, 162–63
beaver hats, 5
Billings, Elizabeth, 1–3, 7–9, 11
Blackstone, William
   Blackstone's Commentaries, 22–23, 243, 244
   on common law conflicts, 22–23
   on the rights of married women, 22–23, 25
Bliss, Sarah, 173, 175
Blythe v. Capus, 51f, 261
Boardman, Elijah, 248
Board of Trade and Plantations report (1732), 60, 85
The Bobbin Girl (Homer), 51f
Boggos, Enoch, 156f
bookkeeping. *See* ledgers
Boston, Massachusetts
   Boston Tea Party, 5–6, 22–23
   colonial merchants in, 62
   cultivation of markets, 71–74
   establishment of a police force, 249
   Oak Hall, men's wear emporium, 220–24, 222f, 230
   textile distribution, 100–1
   textile thefts, 198
Boston Manufacturing Company, 91–92
Boydston, Jeanne, 337n.8, 348n.7, 348n.12
Bradford, Charles Frederick, 73–74, 74f
Brennan, Catherine, 212–13
Brewer, Holly, 310n.4, 323n.6
British East India Company, 5–6
British North America
   common law, 25–26
   crosscutting legal principles/practices, 25–26
   double bind of weavers, 89
   limited supply of wool, 5–6
   married womens' relationship to law, 35
   merchants ties to England/Scotland, 62
   textile operations of married women, 25–26

Brooks Brothers (New York City), 220–21, 230, 267
Brown, Samuel, 73
Burnham, Augusta, 139–40
Burnham, Lucy Ann, 139–40
Burns, Richard, 28
Burr, Aaron, 245–46
Bush, Charles Breen, 178f

Calhoun, John C., 245–46
calicos (Indian cottons), 73
   calico craze, 115
   eighteenth-century wearing prohibition, 111–12
   global production sites, 20
   import restrictions, 6
   use as payment for captive forced labor, 5
Campbell, James, 156f, 197–98
Canadian Law Times, 245
capital
   amassing of, by Jewish men, 281
   creditworthiness and, 75–76
   family ties and, 266
   formation practices, 174–75
   married women's challenges in raising, 293–94
   Mary Todd Lincoln's efforts at raising, 289–90
   merchant capital, 267
   theft's undermining value, 213–14
   use as collateral in commercial credit, 256–57
   use of clothing as, 130–51
   use of textiles as, 3, 59, 151, 186–87, 213, 223–24, 232, 282
carding machines, 84–86, 91–92
Cate, Rebecca, 158–61
Cauchois, Eliza, 173, 175, 206
children
   Blackstone's commentary related to, 244
   extinguishing of rights for, 237–38
   labor provided by, 83–85, 91–92, 132–33
   laws relating to property rights, 22, 23
   men's responsibilities for debts of, 122
   prosecutions for violence against, 50–52
   ragged clothing/legal claims to, 114–15

INDEX 419

"threads of feeling" from mothers, 29
token left by a mother, 30*f*
China
   Bradford's trips to, 74*f*
   British trading policies with, 62–63
   role of commission merchants, 63–64
   silks and cottons from, 4–5
   trade with Portugal, 5
civil law suits, 8–9, 49, 121, 154, 196, 200, 210, 234, 239, 256, 263–64
Civil Rights Act (1875), 288
Civil Rights Cases, 288
Clay, Edward Williams, 116, 117*f*, 180–81, 181*f*
cloth. *See* calicos (Indian cottons); cotton/cotton cloth; silk/silk cloth; wool/wool fabric
clothing (wearing apparel)
   as connection of wearer and the world, 2–3
   dual value of wearing, 149–50
   efforts at retrieving stolen clothing, 110–11
   judgment of others via their clothing, 111–12, 113, 114–15
   legal connection to the wearer, 1–2
   long underwear, 39–41
   neatness obsession, 113–14
   personal connections with owners, 110–11
   "ragged"/"raggedy" clothing, 112, 113–15
   ridicule for excessiveness, 116–18
   as statement of the wearer's character, 112–13
   types of, 3–4
   valuation of articles of, 119–20
   visual culture/imagery of, 109–10, 113, 116
Cobb, J. J., 92–93
Cocheco Manufacturing, (Dover, New Hampshire), 64, 67–68, 70, 214–15
Coles, Rebecca
   attribution of business to her husband, 131–32
   family background, 78
   textile manufactory ownership, 20, 78–101, 131–33, 134–35, 137–38

Colles, James, 261–64
colonial America. *See* North American colonies
colors, 4–5
Commentaries on American Law (Kent), 27, 241, 242–43
Commentaries on Equity Jurisprudence (Story), 242–43
Commentaries on the Constitution of the United States (Story), 242–43
The Commercial Law Register (Kneeland), 275–76
commission merchants, 63–64, 68, 75, 136–37, 261–62
common law
   Blackstone on conflicts, 22–23
   British common law restrictions on married women, 25–26, 35
   vs. private (civll) vs. public (criminal), 67–68
Compendium of Mercantile Law (Smith), 243–44, 245
Cooley, Amanda, 96–98, 130, 133, 150–51, 158, 161, 191
Cooley, Jane, 130–51
   deaths of the Cooley daughters, 191–92
   family background, 130, 133, 134–35
   fictitious "domestic dependency" of, 134–35
   textile business ownership, 29–31, 130–31, 133, 134–36, 147, 168–69, 191
Cooley, Juliann, 133, 134–35, 161, 168–69, 191
Cooney, Margaret, 119–20
cotton/cotton cloth
   carding of, 86–88
   categories/types of, 62–63, 69
   cheap, machine-made, 214–15, 216*f*
   cotton stockings, 116–18
   durability vs. wool, 217–19
   family manufacturing of cotton cloth, 82–83
   global demand for, 23
   impact of 1828 tariff on growers, 215–16
   Indian cottons, 4–5, 6, 61, 67–68, 115
   influence on the demand for wool, 217–19

cotton/cotton cloth (*cont.*)
   inundation of the markets
      (1830s), 214–15
   linens vs., 94
   mass production of, 67–68, 90–91
   mechanization of production, 70, 80–
      81, 84–85, 91–92
   outer garments, 120–21
   production of cotton goods, 64
   raw cotton production, 18
   spinning/weaving of, 90–91
   use in outfitting slaves in the
      South, 217–19
   valuation vs. silk, 125–26
The Countrey Justice (Dalton), 28
country stores, 178, 179f
court cases. *See also* United States (U.S.)
      Supreme Court; US District Court of
      the Southern District of New York
   appellate cases, 41
   assault cases, 198
   Blythe v. Capus, 51f, 261
   Bradwell v. State of Illinois, 289
   circuit courts, 55
   civil cases, 8–9, 49, 121, 154, 196, 200,
      210, 230–31, 234, 239, 256, 263–64
   civil vs. criminal cases, 208, 230–31
   claims to textiles, 201, 210–11
   clothing/infanticide cases, 29
   criminal cases, 52, 54, 208, 231, 234,
      246, 264
   debt cases, 188
   district courts, 40
   divorce cases, 35–36
   Dred Scott v. Sanford, 40
   economics of, 224
   of enslaved people, in their own
      name, 49
   exchange complaints, 177
   federal customs cases, 236f
   long underwear case, 39–41
   of married women, in their husband's
      name, 49
   municipal/county courts, 10
   neighbor complaints, 195–96
   owners filing of behalf of people the
      enslaved, 31–32
   personal liberty cases, 247
   property rights, 7
   public law and, 54
   In re Merryman, 40
   slavery cases, 46
   South Carolina, 53
   State v. Brummer, 21, 52, 209–10
   State v. Cain, Meshack, and Charles, 53
   textile-related, 8–9
   textiles/legal restrictions of slavery, 34
   theft cases, 119, 126–28, 144, 165–66,
      185, 197–99, 200–1, 202–3, 204–5,
      206, 213, 227–28, 239, 249
   *Thomas Paton and David Stewart v. Jesse
      Hoyt,* 236f
   violence cases, 197–98, 239
coverture/coverture practices
   Bagby's experience with, 40, 41, 166
   Cooley's experience with, 130
   Cooney's experience with, 177
   defined, 103–4
   dual aspects of, 106
   Harris's experience with, 256–57
   legal qualities of textiles and, 38, 50
   limitations for women, 15
   Mrs. Capus's property and, 50
   St. George Tucker on, 27
   women's claim to textiles and, 22–23,
      53–54, 103–4, 270–71, 272, 273–75
Coxe, Tench
   downplaying the importance of
      household production, 83–84
   generous definition of
      mechanization, 84
   Report on Manufactures (with
      Hamilton), 82–85, 132–33
credit. *See also* R. G. Dun and Company
   accessibility/inaccessibility of, 98–
      99, 122
   banknotes/coins vs., 122–23
   book credit, 171–72
   capitalism and, 6–7
   as contribution to success, 98
   credit networks, 153–54
   credit reports, reporting agencies, 75–
      76, 122, 256
   creditworthiness of businesses, 75–
      76, 125–26
   difficulties for Blacks, 180–81

extending of, 155, 183
keeping track in ledgers, 153
ledger entries, 156f, 157, 166
legal underpinnings of, 122, 186–87
onset of credit reports, 75–76, 122
as payment, 26–27, 29–31, 50, 59, 152
price adjustments for, 188
Quakers and, 260
requirements for getting, 107
stay laws and, 28
use of clothing as collateral, 173
use of textiles as, 3, 121, 153–54, 213, 223–24, 232
credit reports, reporting agencies, 75–76, 122, 256
crime/criminality. *See also* theft/thievery
  accusations against Brennan and Allison, 212–13
  civil form adjudication, 231
  complains/complaint forms, 143–44, 146–47
  debtors vs. convicted criminals, 230–31
  details required to be a crime, 199
  fraud, 264
  petty crimes, 239
  proliferation of criminal codes, 250–51
  property crimes, 213–14, 244–45
  public law and, 8–9, 48–49, 239
  racism, nativism, and, 225–26
  trials for civil and criminal cases, 54
  volume of New York statutes (1802), 247
  wearing of wool/linen in England, Spain, France, 6
Crowston, Clare, 4–5, 302–3n.5, 303n.6, 304nn.9–10, 332n.15, 335–36n.5, 340–41n.31, 341nn.35–36
currency, 107–29. *See also* exchange
  counterfeit bills/thievery, 122–24, 126–27, 128
  parody of worthless banknotes ("shinplasters"), 126f
  use of clothing as, 119–20
  use of handkerchiefs for, 14, 198–99
  use of marks by enslaved people, 124
  use of textiles as, 3, 59, 80, 120–21

Dalton, Michael, 28
Davies, Benjamin, 88–89

Davis, Deborah, 142–43
debt collection, 274
Declaration of Independence, 78
DeForest and Company (New Orleans), 69
Desan, Christine, 303–4n.8, 305–6n.16, 336–37n.6, 342n.2
DeVries, Jan, 85
diaries. *See also* ledgers
  of Ballard, Martha, 155–57
  of Cate, Rebecca, 158–61
  of Cooley, Amanda, 191
  of Cooley, Elizabeth, 169
  of Eyck, Margaret Ten, 152, 163f
  of Wayland, Anne Kagey, 158
domestic dependents. *See also* children; enslaved people; married women; servants
  Cooley's fictitious domestic dependency, 134–35
  defined, 22
  family labor and, 132–33
  laws relating to property rights, 22, 23
  nonactionable debts of, 122
  rights to dominate domestic dependents, 11–12
  varied degrees of subordination of, 39–40
Downing, Annis, 224–25, 226–27
Dred Scott v. Sandford, Supreme Court decision, 40, 247, 285–86

Elton, John, 251–52
enforcement, 195–211
  Allingham's case against Friel, 195–98, 200–1, 202, 206–8
  challenges, conflicts, frustrations, 206–8
  challenges at far-flung ports, 47–48
  choosing the right form for the offense, 199–200
  civil vs. criminal action, 208
  claims to rights and property, 198
  evidence of possession, 204
  evidentiary dilemma of trunks, 204–5
  extreme punishments for African Americans, 210–11
  federalism and, 14
  forms of legal adjudication of conflicts, 199

422 INDEX

enforcement (*cont.*)
  forms of legal impersonation, 197
  importance of details, 199
  importance of evidence, 200–6
  lax enforcement of oversight of enslaved people, 34–35
  by local courts, 187
  need for institutional backing, 234–35
  oral testimony vs. receipts, 203–4
  outcome of Gray/Munro cases, 201–2
  petty theft cases, 197–99, 249–50
  problems of enforcement, 254–55
  property disputes, 209–10
  of the rules of exchange, 4
  strategy to acquire witnesses, 202–3
  of textile market-related principles, 18–19, 229
  of trade restrictions, 19
  uneven enforcement issues, 270, 275–76
  usage as evidence, 205–6
  violence cases, 196, 197–98, 199–200
Enforcement Acts (Congress), 287–88
England
  associated patchwork of jurisdictions, 41–42
  beaver hats, 5
  Board of Trade and Plantations report, 60, 85
  export to colonial British North America, 62
enslaved people (slavery)
  ability to make legal claims to textiles, 1–2, 21, 210
  dependence on relationships to establish textile claims, 170
  dressing in cotton fiber clothes, 217–19
  escapes from, 64–65
  expectations of keeping items procured, or made themselves, 31–32
  extinguishing of rights for, 237–38
  failed escape of Caty/Elizabeth Billings, 1–3, 7–9, 11
  Fugitive Slave Act (1850), 269
  inability to prosecute their own cases, 33–34
  increased worth of well-dressed slaves, 31–32
  infliction of horrific punishment on, 210–11
  lack of legal support for claims on personal property, 37
  laws related to claims to clothing, 28–29
  laws relating to property rights, 21–22, 23
  legal rights of, 5
  limited property rights of, 28–29
  political cultures of, 13
  possession of trunks by, 146–47
  public law and, 53
  role as merchants/manufacturers, 13–14
  role of textiles in slave trade, 5
  South Carolina, related legal matters, 250–51
  South Carolina upcountry cases (1830s-1850s), 250–51
  southern states' prohibitions, 23–24
  southern states' sales of clothing to, 31–33
  stealing of master's clothing, 2
  use of marks for payment, 124
  white men's responsibilities for debts of, 122
Europe
  calico craze, 115
  centralization of currency control, 107–8
  role of mechanization in expansion of production, 85
  textile monopolies, 5–6
  trading patterns, 4–5
exchange (exchanges), 173–89. *See also* currency
  auctions/auction houses, 182–83, 184, 226–27
  bargaining, 183
  between cities, 71–73
  commercial exchanges, 13–14, 131–32, 155
  at country stores, 178, 179f
  enslavement for freedom, 33–34
  exchange laws, rules, 15, 19–20, 22, 48–49, 50, 55–56, 155
  ledgers and, 153–54
  licensing/zoning efforts, 176
  loaning vs. pawning, 186

methods of leveraging textiles, 185
pawning/pawnshops, 175–76, 226–27
peddlers/peddling, 7, 119–20, 140–41, 161–62, 164–65, 176–77, 178f, 226–27
post-Revolution rules of, 4
potential for thievery, 123–24
property exchanges, 154
secondhand merchandise/stores, 7, 97, 173–74, 182, 183, 226–27, 280–82
street trade markets, 173–75, 213
textiles as medium of, 107, 108–9, 119–21, 128
value of textiles, 18–19
Eyck, Margaret Ten, 152–72, 163f

family labor, 26, 132–33
federalism
 appellate law and, 55
 challenges to the portability of credit, 267
 Constitutional Amendments and, 286
 description, 10, 257–58
 legal scope of, 45–46
 rights-based principles/rules, 80, 194, 245, 247–49, 250–51, 254–55, 298
 textile-related legal principles, 38, 60, 193–94, 257–58
 vacillating institutional balance of, 247
Fifteenth Amendment (US Constitution), 285–86, 287–88, 289
Fourteenth Amendment (US Constitution), 276, 285–86, 287–90
Foxwell, Margaret, 141
France
 rights granted to women, 25
 trade policies, 6
 wives' claims to paraphernalia, 28
Francisco, Sarah Ann, 224–25, 226–27
Franklin, Benjamin, 23
Free Blacks
 ability to prosecute cases in their own name, 11
 cartoon caricatures of, 116, 180–81
 clothing trade participation by, 173–74
 efforts at achieving equality, 24
 Quaker support for, 133–34
 restrictions placed on, 7–8, 10, 24
 slavery's impact on, 268–69
 varied priveleges and restrictions, 270
 white supremacy and, 131, 180–81
Friel, Judith, 195–98, 200–1, 202, 206–7
Frink, Martha, 158, 161–62
Fugitive Slave Act (1850), 269

Gaston, H. A., 274–75
Gillray, James, 116, 118f
global trade
 patterns of, 4–5
gowns, 1, 3–4
Gray, Hannah, 138–39
Gray, Rosenah, 33, 119–20, 140–41, 142–43, 164–65, 201–2
Great Britain
 role of mechanization in expansion of production, 85
 "street trade" markets, 173–74
 taxation policies, 1760s, 62–63
 U.S. separation from, 76
Green, Asa, 178–81
Grimké, Angelina, 43–44
Grimké, John Faucheraud, 43–44
Grimké, Sarah, 43–44
Gross, Ariela, 306–8nn.18–19, 309n.3, 310–11n.7, 322–23n.4, 326n.17
Guernsey Frocks. See long underwear, legal case

Halley, Timothy, 142–43
Hamilton, Alexander, 82–85, 132–33, 135–36
Hamilton, Duggy, 223f
handkerchiefs, 3–4
 payments for, 161–62
 production of, 60–61
 silk handkerchiefs, 110, 116–18, 161
 thefts involving, 144, 198–99, 212
 use as currency, 14, 198–99
 value of (1830s), 125–26
hand labor
 continued importance of, 90–91
 economic opportunities created by, 79
 mass production using, 6
 myth of homespun and, 82–83
 role of mechanization in replacing, 84, 90–91, 92

hand labor (*cont.*)
   scaling up of, 85
   in wool production, 93
"Hannah Barnard's Cupboard" article (Ulrich), 150–51
Harper's Weekly
   Mrs. Lincoln's Wardrobe on Exhibition in New York, 294*f*
   Peddler's wagon, Charles Breen Bush, 178*f*
Harris, M. B., 122
   credit acquired by, 272
   credit reports of R. G. Dun and Company and, 122, 256–58
   millinery shop ownershop by, 256
Harris, William, 261
Harris, Wyatt, 37–38
Hartigan-O'Connor, Ellen, 305–6n.16, 312–13n.3, 326–27n.20, 344n.17, 352n.4, 357n.5
Hartog, Hendrik, 306–7n.18, 322–23n.4, 371–72n.12
Harvard Law School, 241–43
Hazard, Amy, 33
Hening, William Waller, 28
Henry, Sarah Winston Syme, 149–50
Hilliard, Kathleen, 301–2n.4, 303n.7, 309n.2, 317–18n.15, 318n.16, 344n.13, 355–56n.2, 356n.3, 357n.5, 362n.4
The History of a Little Frenchman and His Bank Notes: Rags, Rags, Rags pamphlet, 124–25
Hogarth, William, 31, 32*f*
Homer, Winslow, 51*f*
homespun fabric, 19, 61
   description, 81–82
   myth of, 82–83
hosiery, 3–4, 39–40, 82–83, 235
household manufacturing
   Coxe/Hamilton, observation on, 82–84, 132–33, 135–36
   regular trades vs., 132
   of textiles, 83–84

India
   British trading policies with, 62–63
   nankeen, 4–5, 64–65, 119, 219
   role of commission merchants, 63–64
   silks and cottons, 4–5
   trade with Portugal, 5
Indians (Native Americans), 5
   loss of land/sovereignty of, 24
   restrictions placed upon, 10
Indonesia, trading patterns, 4–5
industrious revolution (of DeVries), 85, 332n.15
In re Merryman, Supreme Court decision, 40

Jackson, Andrew, 126*f*
Jackson, Samuel, 251–52
Jacquard loom, 92, 99
Jefferson, Thomas, 62–63, 241–42
Jewish merchants, 281
Jones, Ann, 302–3n.5, 358n.10
Jones, Martha, 307–8n.19, 309n.3
The Justice of the Peace and Parish Officer (Burns), 28

Katz, Stanley, 42
Keckly, Elizabeth, 169–71, 279, 289–91, 295, 296*f*
Kent, James, 27, 241, 242–43. *See also Commentaries on American Law*
Kipp, David, 250
Kirk, George, 269*f*
Kirkland, Elithe Hamilton, 166–67
Kneeland, S. F., 275–76

labor
   family labor, 26, 132–33
   skills required for turning raw fibers into textile, 86–88
   southern states slave labor, 22
   women's labor, 78–79, 82, 88*f*, 131–32
laborers/workers. *See also* hand labor; women's labor
   advice to temper desires for, 115–16
   agricultural workers, 18
   claim rights conflicts with employers, 8–9, 13
   immigrant male/female workers, 91–92
   impact of mechanization, 101
   impoverishment of, 104–5
   legal claim to textiles and, 80

INDEX   425

limitation on property rights for, 18
low-paid pieceworkers, 98–99, 100–1
unskilled women pieceworkers, 80–81
white males within artisanal
   families, 85–86
lace/lacemaking, 26–27, 132, 139f, 183
law, definition, 234
*Law of Baron and Femme; of Parent and
   Child; of Guardian and Ward; of
   Master and Servant; and of the Powers
   of Court of Chancery* (Reeve), 26–27,
   242–43, 244–45
Lawrence, Amos A., 92–93
*Laws of Business for All the States
   and Territories of the Union
   and the Dominion of Canada*
   (Parsons), 274–75
ledgers. *See also* diaries
   of Ballard/Bagby, 157
   description, 153–54, 157
   dowries and, 150
   keeping track of credit in, 153
   legal principles of, 154–58
   preprinted ledgers, 153
   running tallies vs., 152–53
legal authority. *See also* court cases
   of coats, dresses, socks,
      handkerchiefs, 246–47
   deterioration of textiles' legal
      powers, 214
   dispersal among institutional
      jurisdictions, 40–41
   law, definition, 234
   of ledgers, 154–55, 248
   local practices, 47–48
   post-Revolution delegation to local
      venues, 196–97
   pre-Civil War shifting of, 193
   public vs. private laws, 54
   rights-based principles/rules, 80, 194,
      245, 247–49, 250–51, 254–55, 298
   in rural areas, 250–51
   sharing by states/federal
      government, 43
   of silks, woolens, linens, printed
      cottons, 248
   slaves/slavery and, 53
legal education, 241–44, 245–46

legal principle of textiles. *See also*
   enforcement; Taney, Roger, long
   underwear legal case
   absence of, in Blackstone's volume of
      public wrongs, 49
   importance of, 80–81
   local vs. federal level differences, 237–38
   for merchants, 59
   need for judges to know about
      textiles, 237
   New York/reclamation of stolen sheet
      case, 53–54
   pre-Civil War enforcement
      barriers, 234
   pre-Civil War shift, 12
   pre-/post-Revolution operating
      principles, 239
   private law and, 8, 48–50, 51f, 52, 54
   property rights and, 52
   protections of public law, 52
   public law and, 8–9, 49, 50–54, 56–
      57, 238–39
   rights of women, 80
   scope of, 7
   South Carolina/stolen fabric case, 40, 43
   *Thomas Paton and David Stewart v. Jesse
      Hoyt*, 236f
   undermining the power of, 229–30
   wholesalers vs. local retailers
      lawsuits, 261–62
legal system
   development of state sovereignty, 41
   dispersal of legal authority, 40–41
   early modern period principles, 25
   impact of pre–Civil War changes, 14
   laws relating to property rights, 21, 22
   legal qualities of textile-producing
      tools, 36–37
   Magistrates and Freeholders Court, 21
   misrepresentations within, 9
   post-Revolution set up, 4
   post-Revolution textile associations, 10
   protections of clothing/textiles, 108–9
   role of restrictions on most
      Americans, 24
Lemire, Beverly, 3–4, 5–6, 95, 175,
   303–4nn.7–10, 304–5nn.13–15,
   309n.2, 311n.9, 329n.4, 331–32n.13,

Lemire, Beverly (*cont.*)
    335–36n.5, 340–41nn.31–32, 342–
    43n.3, 344n.14, 344n.19, 356n.3,
    357–58nn.5–7, 359–60n.17, 362n.4,
    367n.7, 367n.6
Life in Philadelphia cartoons (Clay), 116,
    117*f*, 181*f*
Lincoln, Abraham, 40
Lincoln, Mary Todd
    efforts at leveraging her clothes for
        money, 279–80, 295–97
    financial difficulties of, 171, 279
    Harper's Weekly depiction of her
        wardrobe, 294*f*
    Keckly on Lincoln's fashion
        preferences, 279
linens
    bed linens, 1–2, 17–18, 35–36, 89
    household linens, 8, 14, 23, 142–43, 149,
        173–74, 214–15, 252, 279
    resistance to mechanization, 94
    table linens, 3–4, 82–83, 89
Litchfield Law School, 241–42, 245–46
Livingston, Phillip, 66, 69–70
    background, 62
    textile business of, 25–26
Logan, Deborah, 92–93
Lohman, Ann (aka Madam Restell)
    involvement in progressive reforms, 233
    robbery of dresses belonging to, 233
    testimony in stolen dresses case, 233–34
Lohman, Charles
    identification as owner, complainant,
        prosecutor of stolen dresses, 233–34
    presentation of testimony, physical
        proof, 235
    robbery of dresses owned by wife,
        Ann, 233–35
London Foundling Hospital (England),
    29, 30*f*
long underwear, legal case, 39–41
Love Is a Wild Assault (Kirkland), 166–67
Lowell, Francis Cabot, 91–92

machine-made thread and cloth, 94–
    95, 214–15
made-to-order clothing, 220–21
Magistrates and Freeholders Court, 21

Mann, Bruce, 305–6n.16, 306–7n.18, 328–
    29n.31, 333–34n.34, 345n.23, 352–
    53n.5, 353n.7, 353–54n.19, 361n.22
manufactories
    of Coles, Rebecca, 94–95, 131–
        33, 134–35
    of Cooley, Jane, 29–31, 130–31, 133,
        134–36, 147
    defined, 26
    of Tyler, Mary Palmer, 93–95, 143–44
    of wool cloth, 93–94
manufacturers (manufacturing), 78–101
    in China and India, 63–64
    commercial vs. non-commercial, 13–14
    cotton production, 80–81
    cottons/Cocheco Manufacturing, 64, 70
    disputes among, 10
    downfalls of, 75
    1820s manufacturing census, C4.P15
    1820s/opening of new markets, C3.P37
    elite white men as, 78
    in European countries, 5–6
    global market for textiles, 78–79
    homespun fabric, 19, 61, 81–83
    legal principles/practices, 6–7, 21–22
    limited abilities in colonial New
        England, 60
    manufacturing, defined, 78–79
    onset of credit reports, 75–76
    Pennsylvania 1828 statute, 24
    Rebecca Cole's textile business,
        20, 78–101
    Report on Manufactures (Hamilton and
        Coxe), 82–85, 132
    Taney/long underwear case, 47–48
    trafficking by, 6
    use of new technologies, 78–79
    wholesale vs. retail goods, 64
    of wool cloth, 93–94
Marara, Rosanna, 195, 200–1, 202, 206–7
Marbury v. Madison, 241
markets
    ad hoc markets, 7
    commercial markets, 13–14, 80–81
    cottons/African markets, 3, 61, 67–68
    export markets, 22, 89
    global markets, 6, 19–20, 23, 59, 65,
        68, 78–79

INDEX   427

limited market for tools, 3
opening of new markets, 1820s, 76–77
regulated markets, 9
"southern market," 69–70
street trade markets, 173–75, 213
married women
  ability to make legal claims to textiles, 1–2, 21
  acts in favor of being allowed to control property, 274
  attribution of a business to a husband, 131–32
  Blackstone on the rights of, 22–23, 25
  British common law restrictions, 25–26
  challenges in raising capital, 293–94
  claims to paraphernalia, 26–27
  coverture/coverture practices and, 22–23, 53–54, 103–4, 270–71, 272, 273–75
  extinguishing of rights for, 237–38
  laws relating to property rights, 22–23, 28
  property rights of, 12, 53–54, 252–53
  rights to sue in civil courts, 49
  role as merchants/manufacturers, 13–14
  textile operations in British North America, 25–26
  white men's responsibilities for debts of, 122
Marshall, John, 241
Mason and Lawrence, commission firm, 64, 67–68, 70, 71, 72f, 100–1
mass production, 98–99
  association with machines, factories, 78–79
  Bacher's image related to, 87f
  hand labor vs., 6, 90–91, 93, 99–100
  impact of machines on, 90–91, 100–1
  impact on pieceworkers, 98–99
  impact on small businesses, 98–99
  pros and cons of, 99–100
  standardized sizes and, 65, 99
  types of garments initially targeted for, 95–96
Masur, Kate, 269, 307–8n.19, 309n.3, 310–11n.7, 322–23n.4, 324n.8, 326n.18, 377n.4, 380–81nn.23–24

Mayor's Court (New York City), 33, 34–35, 53–54, 116–18, 173, 176, 177–78, 192, 195–96, 197, 207–8, 212
McClure, Elizabeth Ann (née Cooley), 96–98, 134–35, 138–39, 139f, 150–51, 158, 161, 191
McManamy, Hugh, 182
mechanization
  carding machines, 84–86, 91–92
  of cotton processing, 70, 80–81, 84, 91–92
  Coxe's generous definition of, 84
  forms of, with silk, wool, and cotton, 92
  hand labor vs., 90–91
  linen's resistance to, 94
  power looms, 84–85, 92, 214–15
  replacement for handwoven fabrics, 80–81
  role in replacing hand labor, 84
  of silk processing, 92
  of silk weaving, 92
  of spinning, 84–86, 91
  transition from households to factories, 88f
  types of tools, 84–85
  varied initial successes, 70
  water-powered machines, 91–92
  of weaving, 91
  of wool cloth manufacturing, 84–85, 91, 92, 93–94
merchants
  blurred line with customers, 59
  British crackdown on, 62–63
  in colonial British North America, 62
  colonial resentment of British merchants, 19
  commission merchants, 63–64, 68, 75, 136–37, 261–62
  Cooley's negotiations with, 29–31
  customs disputes by, 47–48
  dealing with legal disputes of, 10
  exchanges by, 175–76
  experience of European merchants, 5–6
  families/family ties, 62–64
  Jewish merchants, 281
  of lace products, 26–27
  ledgers kept by, 153

merchants (*cont.*)
   married women as merchants, 25–26, 29–31, 62
   preferences for uniformity of laws, 275–76
   privileges of white male merchants, 5–6, 21–22
   role of commission merchants, 63–64, 68, 75, 136–37, 261–62
   sales specificaly to Africans in the Americas, 61
   Scottish/British strategies, 63–64
   Taney/long underwear case and, 39–40, 43, 47–48, 49
   women/enslaved people as, 13–14, 31–32
Mexican-American War, 74–75
Middle East
   silks and cottons, 4–5
   trade with Portugal, 5
Miles, Tiya, 330n.7, 348n.10
military law, 49
moldering of cloth, 70–71
moralists
   concerns about textile availability, 115
   warnings about too much interest in clothing, 115–16
Munro, Susan, 165, 167, 177–78, 186, 201–2
Murray, Elizabeth, 62

nankeen, 64–65, 119, 219
Napoleonic Wars, 62–63
nation-states
   associated patchwork of jurisdictions, 41–42
   European's centralized currency control, 107–8
   textiles movement across borders of, 22
Neale, Jeremiah, 149–50
Netherlands, rights granted to women, 25
New York City
   Bowery Boys, 33
   clothes as currency, 119–20
   establishment of a police force, 249
   favoring of certain patterns by women in, 68
   Gray's collection of cloth, 33
   legal principles of textiles/slavery, 34
   Mayor's Court, 33, 34–35, 53–54, 116–18, 173, 176, 177–78, 192, 195–96, 197, 207–8, 212
   printing of forms for larceny, based on property values, 73
   ready-made clothing industry, 96–97
   Taney/long underwear case and, 39
New York City-Hall Recorder, 239, 240–41, 242–43, 246–47, 249
Nichols, Clarina, 252–54
North American colonies. *See also* British North America
   functioning of legislatures, 55
   importation of textiles, 6, 17–18
   legal principles of textiles, 41
   mid-eighteenth century weaving by women, 18
   naming of fabrics, 17, 20

Oak Hall (Boston men's wear emporium), 220–24, 222*f*, 230
O'Brien, Daniel, 230

Panic of 1837, 126*f*
paraphernalia
   Blackstone on wives' claims to, 27
   description, 25
   manuals of magistrates on, 28
   Reeve's affirmation of wives' claims to, 25, 26–27, 28, 35–36
   states approving wives' claims to, 28
   treatise writers non-recognition of wives' claims to, 27
   Tucker's version of wives' claims to, 27
   wives' claims in Louisiana, 28
Parsons, Theophilus, 274–75
pawning/pawnshops, 175–76, 226–27, 281
peddlers/peddling, 7, 119–20, 140–41, 161–62, 164–65, 176–77, 178*f*, 226–27
Penningroth, Dylan, 307–8n.19, 315–16n.9, 317–18n.15, 320n.28, 345n.27, 349–50n.25, 354n.26, 362n.2, 365n.17
Pennsylvania Prison Society, clothing as currency issues, 107–9
   cloth-making by male/female inmates, 108

description of problem, 107, 108
state/federal textile-related
  policies, 107–8
value liquidity of textiles, 108–9
visual ads, including clothing, of
  escaped prisoners, 109–10, 118–19
people of color. *See* African Americans;
  Free Blacks
*The Perils of Pearl Street, Including a
  Taste of the Dangers of Wall Street*
  (Green), 178–80
Perry, Henrietta, 149–50
petticoats, 1
Pinckney, Eliza Lucas, 70–71
pins/pin money, 9, 135–36
police forces, establishment of, 249
Portugal, textile trading, 5
power looms, 84–85, 92, 214–15
Priest, Claire, 305–6n.16, 342n.2, 345n.23,
  381n.30, 382n.33
private law, 8, 48–50, 51*f*, 52, 54
production of textiles. *See* textile production
property rights
  authority of employers, 24
  of domestic dependents, 22
  of enslaved people, 28–29
  and legal principle of textiles, 52
  of married women, 12, 53–54
  nonrecognition of textiles, 1–2
  procedural rights and, 50
  public law and, 52
  role of the public interest, 21, 43, 53
public law, 8–9, 49, 50–54, 56–57, 238–39

Quakers
  Barclay family, England bankers, 62
  census of free Black residents, 133–34
  credit and, 260
  resources/sales networks, 58, 260

R. G. Dun and Company
  business description, 75–76, 257
  collection of proprietary
    information, 265–66
  credit reports of Mr. M. B. Harris,
    122, 256–57
  focus on rights of white men with
    property, 267

influence of being married on
  calculations, 275
influence of federalism, 257–58
mix of personal and professional in
  reports, 258–60
Tappan's founding of, 256
*The Ready Lawyer: or, The Business
  Men's Farmers', Mechanics',
  Mines', and Settlers' Legal. Adviser*
  (Gaston), 274–75
ready-to-wear clothing, 220–21
Reconstruction amendments, 257–58
  Fifteenth Amendment, 285–86, 287–
    88, 289
  Fourteenth Amendment, 276, 285–
    86, 287–90
  Thirteenth Amendment, 171,
    280, 285–86
record keeping. *See* ledgers
Reeve, Tapping, 26–27, 242–43
  affirmation of wives' claims to
    paraphernalia, 25, 26–27, 28, 35–36
  *Law of Baron and Femme: of Parent
    and Child: of Guardian and Ward:
    of Master and Servant: and of tghe
    Powers of the Court of Chancery*
    (Reeve), 242–43, 244–45
Report on Manufactures (Hamilton and
  Coxe), 82–85, 132–33, 135–37
R.G. Dunn and Company, credit
  reports, 122
Richmond Hustings Court, types of
  cases, 261
rights-based principles/rules, 80, 194, 245,
  247–49, 250–51, 254–55, 298
rights-based rules, 194, 245, 247
Riley, Sally, 195, 206–8
Rockman, Seth, 6–7, 175, 335n.3, 336–
  37n.6, 337n.15, 346n.29, 357nn.5–6,
  367n.5, 368n.13
Rogers, Daniel, 239, 240–43, 246, 249. *See
  also* New York City-Hall Recorder
Ryan, John, 249–50

secondhand merchandise/stores
  ability to pay with credit, 183
  accommodating shopping experience
    at, 182

secondhand merchandise/stores (*cont.*)
  negative connotations of used clothing, 280–82
  purchases by people of marginal means, 97
  sales at street markets, 173–74
  sales of stolen property to, 226–27
  types of merchandise, 281
Seeley, Robert, 224–25
servants
  extinguishing of rights for, 237–38
  laws relating to property rights, 22, 23
Seven Years War, 89–90
sewing, 50
  by the Cooley family, 97–98, 134–35, 150–51
  by Martha Fink, 158
  mechanization and, 92, 98–99
  for simple clothes, undergarments, 95
  use of pins, 135–36
sewing machines, 98–94
Siegel, Reva B., 310n.4, 370n.5, 371n.11, 375–76n.30, 381–82n.31
silk/silk cloth, 4–5
  challenges in producing, 92
  challenges in working with, 91
  English silk stockings, 73
  importation of, 4–5, 17, 58, 221–23
  Jacquard loom and, 92, 99
  making of, by hand, 80–81, 90–91
  mechanization and, 84–85, 90–91, 92
  presence in young women's trousseaus, 148
  production/raising of worms by women, 18, 92–93
  purchase from peddlers, 177
  raising of worms by women, 92–93
  theft and, 9
  theft of Jackson silk clothing, 251–52
  theft of Lohman's silk dresses, 233
  Tyler's production of, 94–95
  use as currency, 119–20
  valuation of
  for young women's trousseaus, 148, 149
slaves/slavery. *See* enslaved people
Smith, John William, 243–44, 245
socks, 53, 204–5, 235, 246–47

South Carolina
  actions on behalf of enslaved people, 40, 56–57
  colonial government in, 42
  legal principles of textiles, 43
  rights to sue in civil courts by married women, 49
  State v. Brummer, 21, 52, 209–10
  women's rights to trade in their own names, 28
  Wyatt Harris, free Black man, legal case, 37
Spain
  trade policies, 6
  wives' claims to paraphernalia, 28
spindles, 84–85
spinning/spinning machines, 88*f*
  Cole's business use of, 81
  Cooley's business use of, 29–31, 36–37
  as the domain of women, 81, 85–86
  mechanization of, 84–86
  use of by Dover Manufacturing, 64
  water-powered machines, 91–92
Stallybrass, Peter, 302–3n.5, 343n.4
Story, Joseph, 242–43
street trade markets, 173–75, 213
"street trade" markets, in Great Britain, 173–74
Styles, John, 3–4, 302–3n.5, 303n.7, 311n.9, 316n.10, 323n.6, 329n.4, 331–32n.13, 337n.7, 337–38n.16, 340–41n.31, 342n.1, 343n.10, 358n.7, 359–60n.17, 362n.4, 369n.21
supercargoes, 73–75, 74*f*
Swift, Zephaniah, 27
A System of Laws of the State of Connecticut (Swift), 27

Talcott and Bowers (New Orleans commission house), 75
Taney, Roger, long underwear legal case, 39–57, 235. *See also* United States (U.S.) Supreme Court
  customs duties conflicts, 235
  deference to local pratices, 47–48
  Dred Scott decision, 247, 285–86
  instructions to jurors, 39–40
  knowledge of textile-related legal principles, 40

INDEX 431

long underwear legal case, 39–40
   public law and, 56–57
Tappan, Arthur, 265–66
Tappan, Lewis. *See also* R. G. Dun and
   Company
   abolition of slavery work, 257–
      58, 275–76
   failed silk wholesaling firm, 265–66
   founding of R. G. Dun and
      Company, 256
Tayloe, John, 60, 89–90
Taylor, George, 88–89
textile production. *See also* mass
      production; mechanization
   attractions of, 135, 138
   barring of women from, 85–86
   British discouragement of production
      in the colonies, 60
   categorization as domestic
      labor, 297–98
   Cate's coordination of, 158–59
   Coles's coordination of, 78–79,
      81, 89–90
   commercial elements of production, 83,
      135, 158–59
   Coxe's thoughts/comments on, 83, 84–
      85, 132–33
   credit provided by, 153–54
   economic value of labor in, 79
   as fact of life for women, 137–38
   family production, 132–33
   hand production specialization,
      79, 94–95
   harsh/deteriorating conditions, 101
   household production, 9
   impact of demand for cheaper textiles, 22
   integration of all aspects of, 91–92
   keeping records of, 158, 162–63, 166
   late eighteenth century
      production, 36–37
   legal options provided by, 105
   mingling of domestic and
      commercial, 81
   names of imported cloth, 20, 21
   nineteenth century business model
      adaptations, 64, 65–66
   predominance of imported cloth in the
      colonies, 60, 62–63
   related dynamics of nation's
      leaders, 23
   role of white males, 13–14, 26–27
   silk production, 92–93, 94–95
   Tayloe's organization of, 89–90
   tools required for, 36–37
   wool cloth production, 93–94
textiles. *See also* legal principle of textiles;
      textile production
   deterioration of legal powers of, 214
   domestic vs. market-oriented
      production, 158–59
   global market for, 78–79
   global trade and, 4
   household commercial
      production, 83–84
   impact of pre–Civil War changes, 14
   importance as legal economic
      instruments, 3–4
   influence of federalism, 257–58
   legal importance of relationships
      and, 11–12
   liquidity vs. banknotes, 127
   as mediation between individuals and
      their world, 109
   as medium of exchange, 107, 108–9,
      119–21, 128
   for men, 3–4
   moldering issues, 70–71
   moralists' concerns about availability
      of, 115
   naming history, 24
   ownership issues, 142–43
   role in establishing mother-child legal
      relationship, 29, 30*f*
   trunk storage issues, 143–47
   use as currency, 3, 59, 80, 107–29
   valuation of, 79, 108–9, 119–21,
      125–26
   as worthwhile investment, 141–42
textile trade
   colonial merchant resent of British
      efforts to control, 19
   long underwear case and, 47–48
   by married women, 26–27, 28, 29–31
   property law and, 55–56, 59
   public law and, 52
   by white men, 19, 58–59

theft/thievery
   accusation against Brennan and Allison, 212–13, 228, 229
   accusation against Cauchois, Eliza, 173
   accusation against McPhee, Catharine, 143–44
   accusations against Amos, enslaved man, 187–89
   accusations against Armstrong, Sally, 183–84
   accusations against Daniel, 37–38, 184
   accusations against enslaved people, 31–32
   accusations against Gray, Rosenah, 33
   accusations against Harris, Wyatt, 37, 184
   accusations against Hazard, Amy, 33
   accusations against McManamy, Hugh, 182
   accusations against Polly, 43
   by Billings, Elizabeth, 1, 2, 110–11
   by Caty, 2
   flaunting of the laws in stealing textiles, 128
   of Francisco's entire wardrobe, 224–25
   hawking of goods by thieves, 226–27
   involving banknotes, 126–27
   by married women, 9
   off-loading of stolen goods, 226–27
   professional trappings of, 224–26
   public lawsuits, 8–9
   relationship to property civil law rules, 52
   by Toby, enslaved man, 114–15
   twisting of legal principles by thieves, 227–28
   undermining of textiles as currency from, 213–14
   urbanization and, 226
Thirteenth Amendment (US Constitution), 171, 280, 285–86
"threads of feeling," 29
tools to produce textiles, clothing
   inclusion in 1820 manufacturing census, 84–85
   inclusion in 18210 manufacturing census, 132–33
   legal claims to, 3, 56
   legal qualities of, 36–37

   married women's property acts and, 273–74
   necessity for economic support, 56
   Pennsylvania 1828 statute, 28
   pins as essential tools, 135–36
   possesion by married women, 37
Tucker, St. George, 27
Turner, Felicity, 307–8n.19, 316n.11, 327n.22, 371n.6
Tyler, Mary Palmer, 93–95, 143–44

Ulrich, Laurel Thatcher, 82, 150–51, 302–3n.5, 306n.17, 309n.2, 312–13n.3, 319–20n.26, 327n.21, 335–36n.5, 337n.7, 337n.15, 337–38n.16, 338n.18, 338–39n.20, 340n.28, 340n.29, 340n.30, 349n.18, 350n.26, 350n.33, 354–55n.31, 356–57n.4
United States (U.S.)
   clothing theft, 119
   exportation of cotton cloth, 62–63
   negative connotations of secondhand clothing, 280
   post-American Revolution business strategies, 63–64
   separation from Great Britain, 76
   signing of Declaration of Independence, 78
   street exchange/street vendor markets, 173–74
United States (U.S.) Army, 69, 74–75, 285
United States (U.S.) Constitution
   Fifteenth Amendment, 285–86, 287–88, 289
   Fourteenth Amendment, 276, 285–86, 287–90
   Thirteenth Amendment, 171, 280, 285–86
United States (U.S.) Supreme Court
   Bradwell v. State of Illinois, 289
   Dred Scott v. Sandford, 40, 247, 285–86
   Fourteenth Amendment/women's rights decision, 289
   In re Merryman, 40
   rights/citizenship cases, 40
University of Pennsylvania Law School, 241–42
University of Virginia Law School, 243

US District Court of the Southern District of New York, 44f, 235–37

Van Buren, Martin, 126f
Vickery, Thomas, 197–98

Walker, David, 173–74
Walker, Mary, 170–71
War of 1812, 89–90
Washington, Mary, 149–50
water-powered machines, 91–92
Wayland, Anne Kagey, 158
weavers/weaving
  double bind situation in colonial British North America, 89
  initial male domination, 88–89
  male silk weavers, 88–89
  mechanization of silk weaving, 92
  women's move into, 89–90
Weicksel, Sarah Jones, 282–83, 303n.6, 382n.2, 383n.6
The Wheel of Three Generations (Bacher), 88f
white men
  cartoon caricatures of, 180–81
  handling of civil suits by, 9
  as manufacturers, 78
  property rights of, 11–12, 14, 24
  restrictions on poor white men, 10
  shopping by elite white men for female relatives, 66–67
  sole rights as merchants, 58–59
  suffrage rights, 24
  textiles as leg up for, 23
white supremacy
  cotton production and, 23
  defined/promotion of, 131
  Free Blacks and, 131, 180–81
William and Mary Law School, 241–42
Wilson, James, 241–42
wives. *See* married women
women. *See also* married women
  advice to temper desires for, 115–16
  attainment of property rights, 11–12
  attempts at earning pin money, 9
  Lohman, Ann, involvement in progressive reforms, 233
  pre-Revolution move into weaving, 89–90
  rights granted by continental law, 25

rights in France/Netherlands, 25
suitable fabric for, 3–4
unskilled pieceworkers, 80–81
women's labor
  devaluation of, 79, 131–32
  homespun fabric and, 82
  idealized conceptions of, 88f
  ideology of separate spheres and, 131–32
  legal issues, 85–86
  men-women/division of labor, 85–86
  nineteenth-century characterization of, 79
  raising of worms for silk, 92–93
  in ready-made clothing industry in New York City, 96–97
  Revolutionary-era false portrayal of, 82
  spinning as the domain of women, 81
  unskilled pieceworkers, 80–81
women's rights activism, 43–44, 257, 273–74
women's rights conventions, x–xi, 252–53
wool/wool fabric, 2–3
  carding and, 91
  characteristics of, 4–5, 217–19
  demand for/versatility of, 215–16
  durability vs. cotton, 217–19
  hand labor of wool fabrics, 80–81, 90–91, 93
  importation/importation categories, 4–5, 6, 58, 62–63
  influence of cotton on the demand for, 217–19
  limited supply in the British colonies, 5–6
  local production of, 18, 22, 36–37, 60, 86–88, 89, 134–35
  mechanization and, 84–85, 91, 92, 93–94
  spinning wheel processing, 36–37
  Tayloe's orders for, 60
  types of woolen fabric, 65–66
  use in working men's wardrobes, 219
  valuation of, 63–64
workers. *See* hand labor; laborers/workers; women's labor

Yale Law School, 241–42

www.ingramcontent.com/pod-product-compliance
Lightning Source LLC
LaVergne TN
LVHW011009250326
834688LV00004B/149